Moral Issues in Business

BA 310

William H. Shaw | Vincent Barry

CENGAGE
Learning

Australia • Brazil • Japan • Korea • Mexico • Singapore • Spain • United Kingdom • United States

Moral Issues in Business: BA 310

Moral Issues in Business, Thirteenth Edition
Shaw | Barry
© 2016, 2013, 2010 Cengage Learning. All rights reserved.

Library of Congress Control Number: 2014945691

ALL RIGHTS RESERVED. No part of this work covered by the copyright herein may be reproduced, transmitted, stored or used in any form or by any means graphic, electronic, or mechanical, including but not limited to photocopying, recording, scanning, digitizing, taping, Web distribution, information networks, or information storage and retrieval systems, except as permitted under Section 107 or 108 of the 1976 United States Copyright Act, without the prior written permission of the publisher.

> For product information and technology assistance, contact us at
> **Cengage Learning Customer & Sales Support, 1-800-354-9706**
>
> For permission to use material from this text or product,
> submit all requests online at **cengage.com/permissions**
> Further permissions questions can be emailed to
> **permissionrequest@cengage.com**

This book contains select works from existing Cengage Learning resources and was produced by Cengage Learning Custom Solutions for collegiate use. As such, those adopting and/or contributing to this work are responsible for editorial content accuracy, continuity and completeness.

Compilation © 2015 Cengage Learning

ISBN: 978-1-305-74476-9

WCN: 01-100-101

Cengage Learning

20 Channel Center Street
Boston, MA 02210
USA

Cengage Learning is a leading provider of customized learning solutions with office locations around the globe, including Singapore, the United Kingdom, Australia, Mexico, Brazil, and Japan. Locate your local office at:
www.international.cengage.com/region.
Cengage Learning products are represented in Canada by Nelson Education, Ltd.

For your lifelong learning solutions, visit **www.cengage.com /custom.**

Visit our corporate website at **www.cengage.com.**

CONTENTS

PREFACE vii

PART ONE | MORAL PHILOSOPHY AND BUSINESS 1

CHAPTER 1   THE NATURE OF MORALITY 1

Ethics 3
Moral versus Nonmoral Standards 4
Religion and Morality 10
Ethical Relativism 12
Having Moral Principles 14
Morality and Personal Values 17
Individual Integrity and Responsibility 19
Moral Reasoning 23
Study Corner 29
Case 1.1: Made in the U.S.A.—Dumped in Brazil, Africa, Iraq . . . 30
Case 1.2: Just Drop off the Key, Lee 33
Case 1.3: The A7D Affair 35

CHAPTER 2   NORMATIVE THEORIES OF ETHICS 54

Consequentialist and Nonconsequentialist Theories 56
Egoism 57
Utilitarianism 60
Kant's Ethics 66
Other Nonconsequentialist Perspectives 72
Utilitarianism Once More 77
Moral Decision Making: A Practical Approach 79
Study Corner 82
Case 2.1: Hacking into Harvard 83
Case 2.2: The Ford Pinto 85
Case 2.3: Blood for Sale 88

CHAPTER 3   JUSTICE AND ECONOMIC DISTRIBUTION 105

The Nature of Justice 107
The Utilitarian View 110
The Libertarian Approach 114
Rawls's Theory of Justice 120

Study Corner 128
Case 3.1: Eminent Domain 129
Case 3.2: Battling over Bottled Water 131
Case 3.3: Poverty in America 133

PART TWO | AMERICAN BUSINESS AND ITS BASIS 150

CHAPTER 4   THE NATURE OF CAPITALISM   150

Capitalism 151
Key Features of Capitalism 154
Two Arguments for Capitalism 157
Criticisms of Capitalism 160
Today's Economic Challenges 168
Study Corner 173
Case 4.1: Catastrophe in Bangladesh 174
Case 4.2: Licensing and Laissez Faire 176
Case 4.3: One Nation under Walmart 179
Case 4.4: A New Work Ethic? 181
Case 4.5: Casino Gambling on Wall Street 182
Case 4.6: Paying College Athletes 184

CHAPTER 5   CORPORATIONS   202

The Limited-Liability Company 203
Corporate Moral Agency 206
Rival Views of Corporate Responsibility 209
Debating Corporate Responsibility 216
Institutionalizing Ethics within Corporations 221
Study Corner 227
Case 5.1: Yahoo in China 228
Case 5.2: Drug Dilemmas 230
Case 5.3: Free Speech or False Advertising? 232
Case 5.4: Corporations and Religious Faith 234
Case 5.5: Charity to Scouts? 235
Case 5.6: Corporate Taxation 237

PREFACE

It is difficult to imagine an area of study that has greater importance to society or greater relevance to students than business ethics. As *Moral Issues in Business* enters its thirteenth edition, business ethics has become a well-established academic subject. Most colleges and universities offer courses in it, and scholarly interest continues to grow.

Yet some people still scoff at the idea of business ethics, jesting that the very concept is an oxymoron. To be sure, recent years have seen the newspapers filled with lurid stories of corporate misconduct and felonious behavior by individual businesspeople, and many suspect that what the media report represents only the proverbial tip of the iceberg. However, these scandals should prompt a reflective person not to make fun of business ethics but rather to think more deeply about the nature and purpose of business in our society and about the ethical choices individuals must inevitably make in their business and professional lives.

Business ethics has an interdisciplinary character. Questions of economic policy and business practice intertwine with issues in politics, sociology, and organizational theory. Although business ethics remains anchored in philosophy, even here abstract questions in normative ethics and political philosophy mingle with analysis of practical problems and concrete moral dilemmas. Furthermore, business ethics is not just an academic study but also an invitation to reflect on our own values and on our own responses to the hard moral choices that the world of business can pose.

GOALS AND ORGANIZATION

The purpose of this text is fourfold: to expose students to the important moral issues that arise in various business contexts; to provide students with an understanding of the moral, social, and economic environments within which those problems occur; to introduce students to the ethical and other concepts that are relevant for resolving those problems; and to assist students in developing the necessary reasoning and analytical skills for doing so. Although the book's primary emphasis is on business, its scope extends to related moral issues in other organizational and professional contexts.

Moral Issues in Business has four parts. Part One, "Moral Philosophy and Business," discusses the nature of morality and presents the main theories of normative ethics and the leading approaches to questions of economic justice. Part Two, "American Business and Its Basis," examines the institutional foundations of business, focusing on capitalism as an economic system and the nature and role of corporations in our society. Part Three, "Business and Society," concerns moral problems involving business, consumers, and the natural environment. Part Four, "The Organization and the People in It," identifies a variety of ethical issues and moral challenges that arise out of the interplay of employers and employees within an organization, including the problem of discrimination.

TOOLS AND TOPICS

TOOLS

Case studies enhance the main text. These cases vary in kind and in length, but they are all designed to enable instructors and students to pursue further some of the issues discussed in the text and to analyze them in more specific contexts. The case studies should provide a lively springboard for classroom discussions and the application of ethical concepts.

In addition, the book includes supplemental readings by other authors addressing both theoretical topics and applied issues, such as drug testing, sexual harassment, animal rights, downsizing, advertising, discrimination, and more. These readings permit selected topics to be studied in more detail and expose students to alternative perspectives and analyses. In selecting and editing the readings, we have sought to provide philosophically interesting essays that will engage students and lend themselves well to class discussion.

TOPICS

Moral Issues in Business covers a wide range of topics relevant to today's world. Three of these are worth drawing particular attention to.

Business and Globalization

The moral challenges facing business in today's globalized world economy are well represented in the book and seamlessly integrated into the chapters. For example, Chapter 1 discusses ethical relativism, Chapter 4 outsourcing and globalization, and Chapter 8 overseas bribery and the Foreign Corrupt Practices Act; and there are international examples or comparisons throughout the book. Moreover, almost all the basic issues discussed in the book (such as corporate responsibility, the nature of moral reasoning, and the value of the natural world—to name just three) are as crucial to making moral decisions in an international business context as they are to making them at home. In addition, cases 1.1, 2.3, 4.1, 5.1, 5.2, 6.3, 7.2, 7.5, 9.5, and 10.4 deal explicitly with moral issues arising in today's global economic system, as do the essays by Green (on "everybody's doing it"), Daly (on globalization), De George (on ethical dilemmas facing multinational corporations), and Fadiman (on doing business overseas). Also relevant, of course, is Schumacher's essay on Buddhist economics.

The Environment

Because of its ongoing relevance and heightened importance in today's world, an entire chapter, Chapter 7, with five case studies and supplementary essays by Peter Singer and W. Michael Hoffman, is devoted to this topic. In particular, the chapter highlights recent environmental disasters, the environmental dilemmas and challenges we face, and their social and business costs, as well as the changing attitude of business toward the environment and ecology.

Health and Health Care

Far from being a narrow academic pursuit, the study of business ethics is relevant to a wide range of important social issues—for example, to health and health care, which is currently the subject of much discussion and debate in the United States. Aspects of this topic are addressed in the text and developed in the following cases: 2.3: Blood for Sale, 4.2: Licensing and Laissez Faire, 5.2: Drug Dilemmas, 6.1: Breast Implants, 8.1: AIDS in the Workplace, and 9.4: Protecting the Unborn at Work.

CHANGES IN THIS EDITION

YOUR TEXTBOOK

Instructors who have used the previous edition will find the organization, general content, and overall design of the book familiar. However, the text has been revised throughout, as examples and information have been updated, and the clarity of its discussions and the accuracy of its treatment of both philosophical and empirical issues have been improved. At all times the goal has been to provide a textbook that students will find clear, understandable, and engaging.

Fifty-one case studies—more than ever before—now supplement the main text. Four of them are brand new; a number of the others have been revised or updated. Of the cases that are new to this edition, Case 4.1, "Catastrophe in Bangladesh," concerns responsibility for a factory collapse that killed over a thousand workers making clothing for Western firms; Case 4.6, "Paying College Athletes," examines the move to give athletes a greater share of the revenues from college sports; Case 5.4, "Corporations and Religious Faith," deals with the claim that corporations have a right to do business in a way that reflects the religious beliefs of their owners; and Case 5.6, "Corporate Taxation," discusses tax avoidance by large corporations.

Of the thirty-two supplementary readings, two are brand new. In Chapter 5, "The Toxic Side Effects of Shareholder Primacy," Lynn A. Stout defends the view that managers have a responsibility to guide their companies in a way that serves the interests of a variety of stakeholders and benefits the larger society against the prevailing doctrine that the sole duty of management is to maximize shareholder wealth. In Chapter 7, "Does It Make Sense to Be a Loyal Employee?" Juan M. Elegido contends that young managers are wrong to dismiss loyalty to the company as of little or no importance. In a variety of ways, he argues, a loyal commitment to one's employer can make one's life significantly richer.

YOUR MEDIA TOOLS

The *Moral Issues in Business* **CourseMate** brings course concepts to life with interactive learning, study, and exam preparation tools. Used as a supplement to the book or as a substitute for it, **CourseMate** includes an integrated eBook as well as valuable teaching and learning aids, such as quizzes, flashcards, and videos. These tools are designed to reinforce theories and concepts and to help students to understand and better retain the book's content and to review and study for tests. **CourseMate** can be accessed by searching for this book on CengageBrain.com.

WAYS OF USING THE BOOK

A course in business ethics can be taught in a variety of ways. Instructors have different approaches to the subject, different intellectual and pedagogical goals, and different classroom styles. They emphasize different themes and start at different places. No textbook can be all things to all instructors. And were it to succeed in this goal, it would lose its individual voice. Nevertheless, teachers have great flexibility in how they use *Moral Issues in Business* and in how they organize their courses because of the range of topics we have covered, because of the three types of material in the book (text, cases, and readings), and because of the amount of material we have provided.

Naturally, the book can be taught from cover to cover exactly as it is, but in a semester course this strategy will require a brisk pace. Many instructors will wish to linger on certain topics, touch briefly on others, and skip some altogether. Assigning all the cases and extra readings as well as the text of a chapter obviously provides for the greatest depth of coverage, but the text can easily be taught with only some of the cases or readings or just by itself. The book readily permits topics to be dealt with briefly by assigning only selections from the case studies, the readings, or the text itself, instead of the chapter as a whole. Depending on the instructor's approach, it is even possible to focus the course on the case studies or on the readings, and to assign the text only as background.

The chapters are relatively self-contained, so they can be taught in various orders without loss of coherence. Instructors eager to get to the specific moral issues discussed in later chapters could skip Parts One and Two (perhaps assigning only Solomon's "It's Good Business") and begin with the topics that interest them. Other instructors may choose to start with the analysis of capitalism in Chapter 4 or with the discussion of corporate responsibility in Chapter 5, then spend the bulk of the term on the chapters devoted to particular moral topics in business, before returning to some of the issues of Part One. Still other teachers may wish to devote much of a semester to the foundational concerns of Parts One and Two and deal more briefly and selectively with later matters.

* * *

ACKNOWLEDGMENTS

We wish to acknowledge our great debt to the many people whose ideas and writings have influenced us over the years. Philosophy is widely recognized to involve a process of ongoing dialogue. This is nowhere more evident than in the writing of textbooks, whose authors can rarely claim that the ideas being synthesized, organized, and presented are theirs alone. Without our colleagues, without our students, and without a larger philosophical community concerned with business and ethics, this book would not have been possible. We would especially like to thank the reviewers of this and earlier editions of *Moral Issues in Business* for their thoughtful criticisms and helpful suggestions: Thomas Adajian, North Carolina State University; Joseph Adamo, Cazenovia College; Lon Addams, Weber State University; Joseph Allegretti, Siena College; Dr. Nancy Almann, Tompkis Cortland Community College; Kent Anderson, Clarke University; Mark Anderson, Athens State University; Chris Boorse, University of Delaware; Sam Bruton, University of Southern Mississippi; Scott Calef, Xavier University of Louisiana; Linda Canzanella, Normandale Community College; Herbert Cassel, University of Indianapolis; Michael Clifford, Mississippi State University; Shari Collins-Chobanian, Arizona State University; John Corvino, Wayne State University; Timothy Davis, Community College of Baltimore County; Daniel Dombrowski, Seattle University; Michael Donovan, Cedar Crest College; Sandra Dreisbach, San Jose State University; Julia Driver, Brooklyn College; Kevin Dunagan, College of Dupage; Kenneth Ferguson, East Carolina University; Marilyn Fleckenstein, Niagara University; Marcy Fusilier, Northwestern State University of Louisiana; Andrew Gustafson, Creighton University; Frank Hatstat, Bellevue College; Merle Heckman, Keller Graduate School of Management; Regina Hobaugh, Holy Family University; Bernard Jackson, Regis College; David Kaiser, Hamline University; Jeff Langenderfer, Berry College; Janice Loutzenhiser, California State University, San Bernardino; Wade Maki, University of North Carolina, Greensboro; Krishna Mallick, Bentley College; Gregory Mellema, Calvin College; Bob Mellert, Brookdale Community College; Mark Michael, Austin Peay State University; Glenn Moots, Northwood University; Stephen Mumford, Gwynedd-Mercy College; Thomas O'Brochta, Loyola University of Chicago; Cynthia Orms, Georgia College and State University; K. Praveen Parboteeah, University of Wisconsin, Whitewater; Keith Price, DePaul University; Brad Reid, Lipscomb University; Carlos A. Sanchez, San Jose State University; Dennis Slivinski, California State University, Channel Islands; Nancy Snow, Marquette University; Art Stawinski, Benedictine University; James Stieb, Drexel University; Robert T. Sweet, Clark State Community College; Mojgan Taheri, California State University, Northridge; Nicholas Tirone, New England College; Danny Ursery, St. Edwards University; Thomas Wier, Hardin-Simmons University; and Myrna Wulfson, SUNY Rockland.

PART ONE | MORAL PHILOSOPHY AND BUSINESS

CHAPTER 1

THE NATURE OF MORALITY

INTRODUCTION

SOMETIMES THE RICH AND MIGHTY FALL. Take Kenneth Lay, for example. Convicted by a jury of conspiracy and multiple counts of fraud, he had been chairman and CEO of Enron until that once mighty company took a nose dive and crashed. Founded in the 1980s, Enron soon became a dominant player in the field of energy trading, growing rapidly to become America's seventh biggest company. Wall Street loves growth, and Enron was its darling, admired as dynamic, innovative, and—of course—profitable. Enron stock exploded in value, increasing 40 percent in a single year. The next year it shot up 58 percent and the year after that an unbelievable 89 percent. The fact that nobody could quite understand exactly how the company made its money didn't seem to matter.

Fortune magazine voted Enron America's "Most Innovative Company" for six consecutive years, and Enron proudly took to calling itself not just "the world's leading energy company" but also "the world's leading company." But when Enron was later forced to declare bankruptcy—at the time the largest Chapter 11 filing in U.S. history—the world learned that its legendary financial prowess was illusory and the company's success built on the sands of hype. And the hype continued to the end. Even with the company's financial demise fast approaching, Kenneth Lay was still recommending the company's stock to its employees—at the same time that he and other executives were cashing in their shares and bailing out.

Enron's crash cost the retirement accounts of its employees more than a billion dollars as the company's stock fell from the stratosphere to only a few pennies a share. Outside investors lost even more. The reason Enron's collapse caught investors by surprise—the company's market value was $28 billion just two months before its bankruptcy—was that Enron had always made its financial records and accounts as opaque as possible. It did this by creating a Byzantine financial structure of off-balance-sheet special-purpose entities—reportedly as many as 9,000—that were supposed to be separate and independent from the main company. Enron's board of directors condoned these and other dubious accounting practices and voted twice to permit executives to pursue personal interests that ran contrary to those of the company. When Enron was obliged to redo its financial statements for one three-year period, its profits dropped $600 million and its debts increased $630 million.

> THE REASON ENRON'S collapse caught investors by surprise ... was that Enron had always made its financial records and accounts as opaque as possible.

Still, Enron's financial auditors should have spotted these and other problems. After all, the shell game Enron was playing is an old one, and months before the company ran aground, Enron Vice President Sherron Watkins had warned Lay that the company could soon "implode in a wave of accounting scandals." Yet both Arthur Andersen, Enron's longtime outside auditing firm, and Vinson & Elkins, the company's law firm, had routinely put together and signed off on various dubious financial deals, and in doing so made large profits for themselves. Arthur Andersen, in particular, was supposed to make sure that the company's public records reflected financial reality, but Andersen was more worried about its auditing and consulting fees than about its fiduciary responsibilities. Even worse, when the scandal began to break, a partner at Andersen organized the shredding of incriminating Enron documents before

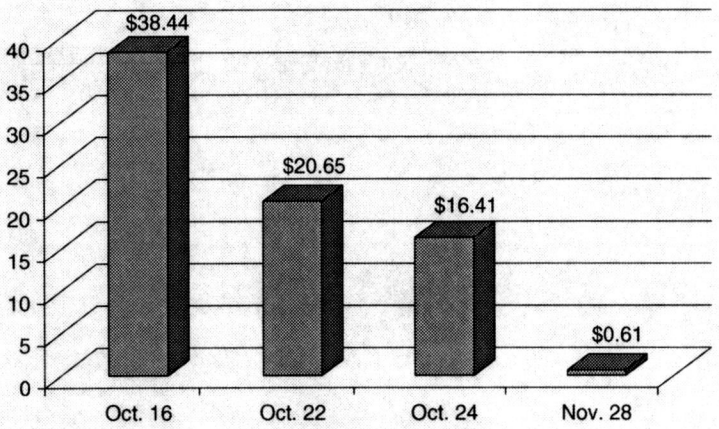

The collapse of Enron's stock price in late 2001

Stories of business corruption and of greed and wrongdoing in high places have always fascinated the popular press, and media interest in business ethics has never been higher. But one should not be misled by the headlines and news reports. Not all moral issues in business involve giant corporations and their well-heeled executives, and few cases of business ethics are widely publicized. The vast majority of them involve the mundane, uncelebrated moral challenges that working men and women meet daily.

Although the financial shenanigans at Enron were complicated, once their basic outline is sketched, the wrongdoing is pretty easy to see: deception, dishonesty, fraud, disregarding one's professional responsibilities, and unfairly injuring others for one's own gain. But many of the moral issues that arise in business are complex and difficult to answer. For example:

How far must manufacturers go to ensure product safety? Must they reveal everything about a product, including any possible defects or shortcomings? At what point does acceptable exaggeration become lying about a product or a service? When does aggressive marketing become consumer manipulation? Is advertising useful and important or deceptive, misleading, and socially detrimental? When are prices unfair or exploitative?

Are corporations obliged to help combat social problems? What are the environmental responsibilities of business, and is it living up to them? Are pollution permits a good idea? Is factory farming morally justifiable?

May employers screen potential employees on the basis of lifestyle, physical appearance, or personality tests? What rights do employees have on the job? Under what conditions may they be disciplined or fired? What, if anything, must business do to improve work conditions? When are wages fair? Do unions promote the interests of workers or infringe their rights? When, if ever, is an employee morally required to blow the whistle?

May employees ever use their positions inside an organization to advance their own interests? Is insider trading or the use of privileged information immoral? How much loyalty do workers owe their companies? What say should a business have over the off-the-job activities of its employees? Do drug tests violate their right to privacy?

What constitutes job discrimination, and how far must business go to ensure equality of opportunity? Is affirmative action a matter of justice, or a poor idea? How should organizations respond to the problem of sexual harassment?

investigators could lay their hands on them. As a result, the eighty-nine-year-old accounting firm was convicted of obstructing justice. The Supreme Court later overturned that verdict on a technicality, but by then Arthur Andersen had already been driven out of business. (The year before Enron went under, by the way, the Securities and Exchange Commission fined Andersen $7 million for approving misleading accounts at Waste Management, and it also had to pay $110 million to settle a lawsuit for auditing work it did for Sunbeam before it, too, filed for bankruptcy. And when massive accounting fraud was later uncovered at WorldCom, it came out that the company's auditor was—you guessed it—Arthur Andersen.)

Enron's fall also revealed the conflicts of interest that threaten the credibility of Wall Street's analysts—analysts who are compensated according to their ability to bring in and support investment banking deals. Enron was known in the industry as the "deal machine" because it generated so much investment banking business—limited partnerships, loans, and derivatives. That may explain why, only days before Enron filed bankruptcy, just two of the sixteen Wall Street analysts who covered the company recommended that clients sell the stock. The large banks that Enron did business with played a corrupt role, too, by helping manufacture its fraudulent financial statements. (Subsequent lawsuits have forced them to cough up some of their profits: Citibank, for example, had to pay Enron's victimized shareholders $2 billion.) But the rot didn't stop there. Enron and Andersen enjoyed extensive political connections, which had helped over the years to ensure the passage of a series of deregulatory measures favorable to the energy company. Of the 248 members of Congress sitting on the eleven House and Senate committees charged with investigating Enron's collapse, 212 had received money from Enron or its accounting firm.[1]

LEARNING OBJECTIVES

These questions typify business issues with moral significance. The answers we give to them are determined, in large part, by our moral standards—that is, by the moral principles and values we accept. What moral standards are, where they come from, and how they can be assessed are some of the concerns of this opening chapter. In particular, you will encounter the following topics:

1. The nature, scope, and purpose of business ethics
2. The distinguishing features of morality and how it differs from etiquette, law, and professional codes of conduct
3. The relationship between morality and religion
4. The doctrine of ethical relativism and its difficulties
5. What it means to have moral principles; the nature of conscience; and the relationship between morality and self-interest
6. The place of values and ideals in a person's life
7. The social and psychological factors that sometimes jeopardize an individual's integrity
8. The characteristics of sound moral reasoning

ETHICS

Ethics (or moral philosophy) is a broad field of inquiry that addresses a fundamental query that all of us, at least from time to time, inevitably think about—namely, How should I live my life? That question, of course, leads to others, such as: What sort of person should I strive to be? What values are important? What standards or principles should I live by? Exploring these issues immerses one in the study of right and wrong. Among other things, moral philosophers and others who think seriously about ethics want to understand the nature of morality, the meaning of its basic concepts, the characteristics of good moral reasoning, how moral judgments can be justified, and, of course, the principles or properties that distinguish right actions from wrong actions. Thus, ethics deals with individual character and with the moral rules that govern and limit our conduct. It investigates questions of right and wrong, fairness and unfairness, good and bad, duty and obligation, and justice and injustice, as well as moral responsibility and the values that should guide our actions.

You sometimes hear it said that there's a difference between a person's ethics and his or her morals. This can be confusing because what some people mean by saying that something is a matter of ethics (as opposed to morals) is often what other people mean by saying that it is a matter of morals (and not ethics). In fact, however, most people (and most philosophers) see no real distinction between a person's "morals" and a person's "ethics." And almost everyone uses "ethical" and "moral" interchangeably to describe people we consider good and actions we consider right, and "unethical" and "immoral" to designate bad people and wrong actions. This book follows that common usage.

BUSINESS AND ORGANIZATIONAL ETHICS

The primary focus of this book is ethics as it applies to business. **Business ethics** is the study of what constitutes right and wrong, or good and bad, human conduct in a business context. For example, would it be right for a store manager to break a promise to a customer and sell some hard-to-find merchandise to someone else, whose need for it is greater? What, if anything, should a moral employee do when his or her superiors refuse to look into apparent wrongdoing in a branch office? If you innocently came across secret information about a competitor, would it be permissible for you to use it for your own advantage?

> **SUMMARY**
> Ethics deals with individual character and the moral rules that govern and limit our conduct. It investigates questions of right and wrong, duty and obligation, and moral responsibility.

Recent business scandals have renewed the interest of business leaders, academics, and society at large in ethics. For example, the Association to Advance Collegiate Schools of Business, which comprises all the top business schools, has introduced new rules on including ethics in their curricula, and in recent years thousands of MBA students have signed the "MBA Oath," a voluntary pledge to "not advance my personal interests at the expense of my enterprise or society," to "refrain from corruption, unfair competition, or business practices harmful to society," and to "protect the human rights and dignity of all people affected by my enterprise."[2] But an appreciation of the importance of ethics for a healthy society and a concern, in particular, for what constitutes ethical conduct in business go back to ancient times. The Roman philosopher Cicero (106–43 BCE), for instance, discussed the example, much debated at the time, of an honest merchant from Alexandria who brings a large stock of wheat to Rhodes where there is a food shortage. On his way there, he learns that other traders are setting sail for Rhodes with substantial cargos of grain. Should he tell the people of Rhodes that more wheat is on the way, or say nothing and sell at the best price he can? Some ancient ethicists argued that although the merchant must declare defects in his wares as required by law, as a vendor he is free—provided he tells no untruths—to sell his goods as profitably as he can. Others, including Cicero, argued to the contrary that all the facts must be revealed and that buyers must be as fully informed as sellers.[3]

"Business" and "businessperson" are broad terms. A "business" could be a food truck or a multinational corporation that operates in several countries. "Businessperson" could refer to a street vendor or a company president responsible for thousands of workers and millions of shareholder dollars. Accordingly, the word **business** will be used here simply to mean any organization whose objective is to provide goods or services for profit. **Businesspeople** are those who participate in planning, organizing, or directing the work of business.

But this book takes a broader view as well because it is concerned with moral issues that arise wherever employers and employees come together. Thus, it addresses organizational ethics as well as business ethics. An *organization* is a group of people working together to achieve a common purpose. The purpose may be to offer a product or a service primarily for profit, as in business. But the purpose also could be health care, as in medical organizations; public safety and order, as in law enforcement organizations; education, as in academic organizations; and so on. The cases and illustrations presented in this book deal with moral issues and dilemmas in both business and nonbusiness organizational settings.

People occasionally poke fun at the idea of business ethics, declaring that the term is a contradiction or that business has no ethics. Such people take themselves to be worldly and realistic. They think they have a down-to-earth idea of how things really work. In fact, despite its pretense of sophistication, their attitude shows little grasp of the nature of ethics and only a superficial understanding of the real world of business. Reading this book should help you comprehend how inaccurate and mistaken their view is.

> **SUMMARY**
> Business ethics is the study of what constitutes right and wrong (or good and bad) human conduct in a business context. Closely related moral questions arise in other organizational contexts.

• • •

MORAL VERSUS NONMORAL STANDARDS

Moral questions differ from other kinds of questions. Whether the old computer in your office can copy a pirated DVD is a factual question. By contrast, whether you should copy the DVD is a moral question. When we answer a moral question or make a moral judgment, we appeal to moral standards. These standards differ from other kinds of standards.

Wearing shorts and a tank top to a formal dinner party is boorish behavior. Writing an essay that is filled with double negatives or lacks subject–verb agreement violates the basic conventions of proper language usage. Photographing someone at night without the flash turned on is poor photographic technique. In each case a standard is violated—fashion, grammatical, technical—but the violation does not pose a serious threat to human well-being.

Moral standards are different because they concern behavior that is of serious consequence to human welfare, that can profoundly injure or benefit people.[4] The conventional moral norms against lying, stealing, and killing deal with actions that can hurt people. And the moral principle that human beings should be treated with dignity and respect uplifts the human personality. Whether products are healthful or harmful, work conditions safe or dangerous, personnel procedures biased or fair, privacy respected or invaded—these are also matters that seriously affect human well-being. The standards that govern our conduct in these areas are moral standards.

> Moral standards concern behavior that seriously affects human well-being.

A second characteristic follows from the first. Moral standards take priority over other standards, including self-interest. Something that morality condemns—for instance, the burglary of your neighbor's home—cannot be justified on the nonmoral grounds that it would be a thrill to do it or that it would pay off handsomely. We take moral standards to be more important than other considerations in guiding our actions.

> Moral standards take priority over other standards.

A third characteristic of moral standards is that their soundness depends on the adequacy of the reasons that support or justify them. For the most part, fashion standards are set by clothing designers, merchandisers, and consumers; grammatical standards by grammarians and students of language; technical standards by practitioners and experts in the field. Legislators make laws, boards of directors make organizational policy, and licensing boards establish standards for professionals. In those cases, some authoritative body is the ultimate validating source of the standards and thus can change the standards if it wishes. Moral standards are not made by such bodies. Their validity depends not on official fiat but rather on the quality of the arguments or the reasoning that supports them. Exactly what constitutes adequate grounds or justification for a moral standard is a debated question, which, as we shall see in Chapter 2, underlies disagreement among philosophers over which specific moral principles are best.

> The soundness of moral standards depends on the adequacy of the reasons that support them.

Although these three characteristics set moral standards apart from other standards, it is useful to discuss more specifically how morality differs from three things with which it is sometimes confused: etiquette, law, and professional codes of ethics.

MORALITY AND ETIQUETTE

Etiquette refers to the norms of correct conduct in polite society or, more generally, to any special code of social behavior or courtesy. In our society, for example, it is considered bad etiquette to chew with your mouth open or to pick your nose when talking to someone; it is considered good etiquette to say "please" when requesting and "thank you" when receiving, and to hold a door open for someone entering immediately behind you. Good business etiquette typically calls for writing follow-up letters after meetings, returning phone calls, and dressing appropriately. It is commonplace to judge people's manners as "good" or "bad" and the conduct that reflects them as "right" or "wrong." "Good," "bad," "right," and "wrong" here simply mean socially appropriate or socially inappropriate. In these contexts, such words express judgments about manners, not about ethics.

The rules of etiquette are prescriptions for socially acceptable behavior. If you violate them, you're likely to be considered ill-mannered, impolite, or even uncivilized, but not necessarily immoral. If you want to fit in, get along with others, and be thought well

> ....
> SUMMARY
> We appeal to moral standards when we answer a moral question or make a moral judgment. Three characteristics of moral standards distinguish them from other kinds of standards.
> ....

of by them, you should observe the common rules of politeness or etiquette. However, what's considered correct or polite conduct—for example, when greeting an elderly person, when using your knife and fork, or when determining how close to stand to someone you're conversing with—can change over time and vary from society to society.

Although rules of etiquette are generally nonmoral in character, violations of those rules can have moral implications. For example, the male boss who refers to female subordinates as "honey" or "doll" shows bad manners. If such epithets diminish the worth of female employees or perpetuate sexism, then they also raise moral issues concerning equal treatment and denial of dignity to human beings. More generally, rude or impolite conduct can be offensive, and it may sometimes fail to show the respect for other persons that morality requires of us. For this reason, it is important to exercise care, in business situations and elsewhere, when dealing with unfamiliar customs or people from a different culture.

Scrupulous observance of rules of etiquette, however, does not make a person moral. In fact, it can sometimes camouflage ethical issues. In some parts of the United States sixty years ago, it was considered bad manners for blacks and whites to eat together. However, those who obeyed this convention were not acting in a morally desirable way. In the 1960s, black and white members of the civil rights movement sought to dramatize the injustice that lay behind this rule by sitting together in luncheonettes and restaurants. Although judged at the time to lack good manners, they thought that this was a small price to pay for exposing the unequal treatment and human degradation underlying this rule of etiquette.

MORALITY AND LAW

Before distinguishing between morality and law, let's examine the term *law*. Basically, there are four kinds of law: statutes, regulations, common law, and constitutional law.

Statutes are laws enacted by legislative bodies. For example, the law that defines and prohibits reckless driving on the highway is a statute. Congress and state legislatures enact statutes. (Laws enacted by local governing bodies such as city councils are usually termed *ordinances*.) Statutes make up a large part of the law and are what many of us mean when we speak of "laws."

Limited in their time and knowledge, legislatures often set up boards or agencies whose functions include issuing detailed regulations covering certain kinds of conduct—**administrative regulations**. For example, state legislatures establish licensing boards to formulate regulations for the licensing of physicians and nurses. As long as these regulations do not exceed the board's statutory powers and do not conflict with other kinds of law, they are legally binding.

Common law refers to the body of judge-made law that first developed in the English-speaking world centuries ago when there were few statutes. Courts frequently wrote opinions explaining the bases of their decisions in specific cases, including the legal principles those decisions rested on. Each of these opinions became a precedent for later decisions in similar cases. The massive body of precedents and legal principles that accumulated over the years is collectively referred to as "common law." Like administrative regulations, common law is valid if it harmonizes with statutory law and with still another kind: constitutional law.

Constitutional law refers to court rulings on the requirements of the Constitution and the constitutionality of legislation. The U.S. Constitution empowers the courts to decide whether laws are compatible with the Constitution. State courts may also rule on the constitutionality of state laws under state constitutions. Although the courts cannot make laws, they have far-reaching powers to rule on the constitutionality of laws and to declare them invalid if they conflict with the Constitution. In the United States, the Supreme Court has the greatest judiciary power and rules on an array of cases, some of which bear directly on the study of business ethics.

People sometimes confuse legality and morality, but they are different things. On one hand, breaking the law is not always or necessarily immoral. On the other hand, the legality of an action does not guarantee that it is morally right. Let's consider these points further.

> Legality should not be confused with morality. Breaking the law isn't always or necessarily immoral, and the legality of an action doesn't guarantee its morality.

1. **An action can be illegal but morally right.** For example, helping a Jewish family to hide from the Nazis was against German law in 1939, but it would have been a morally admirable thing to have done. Of course, the Nazi regime was vicious and evil. By contrast, in a democratic society with a basically just legal order, the fact that something is illegal provides a moral consideration against doing it. For example, one moral reason for not burning trash in your backyard is that it violates an ordinance that your community has voted in favor of. Some philosophers believe that sometimes the illegality of an action can make it morally wrong, even if the action would otherwise have been morally acceptable. But even if they are right about that, the fact that something is illegal does not trump all other moral considerations. Nonconformity to law is not always immoral, even in a democratic society. There can be circumstances where, all things considered, violating the law is morally permissible, perhaps even morally required.

   Probably no one in the modern era has expressed this point more eloquently than Dr. Martin Luther King, Jr. Confined in the Birmingham, Alabama, city jail on charges of parading without a permit, King penned his now famous "Letter from Birmingham Jail" to eight of his fellow clergymen who had published a statement attacking King's unauthorized protest of racial segregation as unwise and untimely. King wrote:

   > All segregation statutes are unjust because segregation distorts the soul and damages the personality. It gives the segregator a false sense of superiority and the segregated a false sense of inferiority. Segregation, to use the terminology of the Jewish philosopher Martin Buber, substitutes an "I-it" relationship for an "I-thou" relationship and ends up relegating persons to the status of things. Hence segregation is not only politically, economically, and sociologically unsound, it is morally wrong and sinful.... Thus it is that I can urge men to obey the 1954 decision of the Supreme Court,* for it is morally right; and I can urge them to disobey segregation ordinances, for they are morally wrong.[5]

2. **An action that is legal can be morally wrong.** For example, it may have been perfectly legal for the chairman of a profitable company to lay off 125 workers and use three-quarters of the money saved to boost his pay and that of the company's other top managers,[6] but the morality of his doing so is open to debate.

   Or, to take another example, suppose that you're driving to work one day and see an accident victim sitting on the side of the road, clearly in shock and needing medical assistance. Because you know first aid and are in no great hurry to get to your destination, you could easily stop and assist the person. Legally speaking, though, you are not obligated to stop and render aid. Under common law, the prudent thing would be to drive on, because by stopping you could thus incur legal liability

> **SUMMARY**
> Morality must be distinguished from etiquette (rules for well-mannered behavior), from law (statutes, regulations, common law, and constitutional law), and from professional codes of ethics (the special rules governing the members of a profession).

---

*In *Brown v. Board of Education of Topeka* (1954), the Supreme Court struck down the half-century-old "separate but equal doctrine," which permitted racially segregated schools as long as comparable quality was maintained.

You come upon this scene—the car is smoking, and it is clear that an accident just took place. In most states, you are not legally obligated to stop and offer help to the victims.

if you fail to exercise reasonable care and thereby injure the person. Many states have enacted so-called Good Samaritan laws to provide immunity from damages to those rendering aid (except for gross negligence or serious misconduct). But in most states, the law does not oblige people to give such aid or even to call an ambulance. Moral theorists would agree, however, that if you sped away without helping or even calling for help, your action might be perfectly legal but would be morally suspect. Regardless of the law, such conduct would almost certainly be wrong.

What then may we say about the relationship between law and morality? To a significant extent, law codifies a society's customs, ideals, norms, and moral values. Changes in law tend to reflect changes in what a society takes to be right and wrong, but sometimes changes in the law can alter people's ideas about the rightness or wrongness of conduct. However, even if a society's laws are sensible and morally sound, it is a mistake to see them as sufficient to establish the moral standards that should guide us. The law cannot cover all possible human conduct, and in many situations it is too blunt an instrument to provide adequate moral guidance. The law generally prohibits egregious affronts to a society's moral standards and in that sense is the "floor" of moral conduct, but breaches of moral conduct can slip through cracks in that floor.

PROFESSIONAL CODES

Somewhere between etiquette and law lie **professional codes of ethics**. These are the rules that are supposed to govern the conduct of members of a given profession. Adhering to these rules is a required part of membership in that profession. Violation of a professional code may result in the disapproval of one's professional peers and, in serious cases, loss of one's license to practice that profession. Sometimes these codes are unwritten and are part of the common understanding of members of a particular profession—for example, that professors should not date their students. In other instances, these codes or portions of them may be written down by an authoritative body so they may be better taught and more efficiently enforced.

These written rules are sometimes so vague and general as to be of little value, and often they amount to little more than self-promotion by the professional organization. The same is frequently true when industries or corporations publish statements of their ethical standards. In other cases—for example, with attorneys—professional codes can be very specific and detailed. It is difficult to generalize about the content of professional codes of ethics, however, because they frequently involve a mix of purely moral rules (for example, client confidentiality), of professional etiquette (for example, the billing of services to other professionals), and of restrictions intended to benefit the group's economic interests (for example, limitations on price competition).

Given their nature, professional codes of ethics are neither a complete nor a completely reliable guide to one's moral obligations. Not all the rules of a professional code are purely moral in character, and even when they are, the fact that a rule is officially enshrined as part of the code of a profession does not guarantee that it is a sound moral principle. As a professional, you must take seriously the injunctions of your profession, but you still have the responsibility to critically assess those rules for yourself.

> You should take seriously the code that governs your profession, but you still have a responsibility to assess its rules for yourself.

Regarding those parts of the code that concern etiquette or financial matters, bear in mind that by joining a profession you are probably agreeing, explicitly or implicitly, to abide by those standards. Assuming that those rules don't require morally impermissible conduct, then consenting to them gives you some moral obligation to follow them. In addition, for many, living up to the standards of one's chosen profession is an important source of personal satisfaction. Still, you must be alert to situations in which professional standards or customary professional practice conflicts with ordinary ethical requirements. Adherence to a professional code does not exempt your conduct from scrutiny from the broader perspective of morality.

WHERE DO MORAL STANDARDS COME FROM?

So far you have seen how moral standards are different from various nonmoral standards, but you probably wonder about the source of those moral standards. Most, if not all, people have certain moral principles or a moral code that they explicitly or implicitly accept. Because the moral principles of different people in the same society overlap, at least in part, we can also talk about the moral code of a society, meaning the moral standards shared by its members. How do we come to have certain moral principles and not others? Obviously, many things influence what moral principles we accept: our early upbringing, the behavior of those around us, the explicit and implicit standards of our culture, our own experiences, and our critical reflections on those experiences.

For philosophers, though, the central question is not how we came to have the particular principles we have. The philosophical issue is whether those principles can be justified. Do we simply take for granted the values of those around us? Or, like Martin Luther King, Jr., are we able to think independently about moral matters? By analogy, we pick up our nonmoral beliefs from all sorts of sources: books, conversations with friends, movies, various experiences we've had. What is important, however, is not how we acquired the beliefs we have, but whether or to what extent those beliefs—for example, that women are more emotional than men or that telekinesis is possible—can withstand critical scrutiny. Likewise, ethical theories attempt to justify moral standards and ethical beliefs. The next chapter examines some of the major theories of normative ethics. It looks at what some of the major thinkers in human history have argued are the best-justified standards of right and wrong.

> For philosophers, the important issue is not where our moral principles came from, but whether they can be justified.

But first we need to consider the relationship between morality and religion on the one hand and between morality and society on the other. Some people maintain that morality just boils down to religion. Others have argued for the doctrine of *ethical relativism*, which says that right and wrong are only a function of what a particular society takes to be right and wrong. Both those views are mistaken.

RELIGION AND MORALITY

Any religion provides its believers with a world view, part of which involves certain moral instructions, values, and commitments. The Jewish and Christian traditions, to name just two, offer a view of humans as unique products of a divine intervention that has endowed them with consciousness and an ability to love. Both these traditions posit creatures who stand midway between nature and spirit. On one hand, we are finite and bound to earth, not only capable of wrongdoing but also born morally flawed (original sin). On the other, we can transcend nature and realize infinite possibilities.

Primarily because of the influence of Western religion, many Americans and others view themselves as beings with a supernatural destiny, as possessing a life after death, as being immortal. One's purpose in life is found in serving and loving God. For the Christian, the way to serve and love God is by emulating the life of Jesus of Nazareth. In the life of Jesus, Christians find an expression of the highest virtue—love. They love when they perform selfless acts, develop a keen social conscience, and realize that human beings are creatures of God and therefore intrinsically worthwhile. For the Jew, one serves and loves God chiefly through expressions of justice and righteousness. Jews also develop a sense of honor derived from a commitment to truth, humility, fidelity, and kindness. This commitment hones their sense of responsibility to family and community.

Religion, then, involves not only a formal system of worship but also prescriptions for social relationships. One example is the mandate "Do unto others as you would have them do unto you." Termed the "Golden Rule," this injunction represents one of humankind's highest moral ideals and can be found in essence in all the great religions of the world:

> Good people proceed while considering that what is best for others is best for themselves. (*Hitopadesa*, Hinduism)
>
> Thou shalt love thy neighbor as thyself. (*Leviticus* 19:18, Judaism)
>
> Therefore all things whatsoever ye would that men should do to you, do ye even so to them. (*Matthew* 7:12, Christianity)
>
> Hurt not others with that which pains yourself. (*Udanavarga* 5:18, Buddhism)
>
> What you do not want done to yourself, do not do to others. (*Analects* 15:23, Confucianism)
>
> No one of you is a believer until he loves for his brother what he loves for himself. (*Traditions*, Islam)

Although inspiring, such religious ideals are very general and can be difficult to translate into precise policy injunctions. Religious bodies, nevertheless, occasionally articulate positions on more specific political, educational, economic, and medical issues, which help mold public opinion on matters as diverse as abortion, the environment, national defense, and the ethics of scientific research. Roman Catholicism, in particular, has a rich history of formally applying its core values to the moral aspects of industrial relations and economic life. Pope Francis's 2013 apostolic exhortation, "The Gospel of

Joy," stands in that tradition. There and elsewhere, the Pope has rejected an "economy of exclusion" and criticized blind faith in a free-market that perpetuates inequality—a message that politicians in Washington are starting to listen to.[7]

MORALITY NEEDN'T REST ON RELIGION

Many people believe that morality must be based on religion, either in the sense that without religion people would have no incentive to be moral or in the sense that only religion can provide moral guidance. Others contend that morality is based on the commands of God. None of these claims is convincing.

First, although a desire to avoid hell and to go to heaven may prompt some of us to act morally, this is not the only reason or even the most common reason that people behave morally. Often we act morally out of habit or just because that is the kind of person we are. It would simply not occur to most of us to swipe an elderly lady's purse, and if the idea did occur to us, we wouldn't do it because such an act simply doesn't fit with our personal standards or with our concept of ourselves. We are often motivated to do what is morally right out of concern for others or just because it is right. In addition, the approval of our peers, the need to appease our conscience, and the desire to avoid earthly punishment may all motivate us to act morally. Furthermore, atheists generally live lives as moral and upright as those of believers.

Second, the moral instructions of the world's great religions are general and imprecise: They do not relieve us of the necessity of engaging in moral reasoning ourselves. For example, the Bible says, "Thou shall not kill." Yet Christians disagree among themselves over the morality of fighting in wars, of capital punishment, of killing in self-defense, of slaughtering animals, of abortion and euthanasia, and of allowing foreigners to die from famine because we have not provided them with as much food as we might have. The Bible does not provide unambiguous solutions to these moral problems, so even believers must engage in moral philosophy if they are to have intelligent answers. On the other hand, there are lots of reasons for believing that, say, a cold-blooded murder motivated by greed is immoral. You don't have to believe in a religion to figure that out.

Third, although some theologians have advocated the **divine command theory**—that if something is wrong (like killing an innocent person for fun), then the only reason it is wrong is that God commands us not to do it—many theologians and certainly most philosophers would reject this view. They would contend that if God commands human beings not to do something, such as commit rape, it is because God sees that rape is wrong, but it is not God's forbidding rape that makes it wrong. The fact that rape is wrong is independent of God's decrees.

Most believers think not only that God gives us moral instructions or rules but also that God has moral reasons for giving them to us. According to the divine command theory, this would make no sense. In this view, there is no reason that something is right or wrong, other than the fact that it is God's will. All believers, of course, believe that God is good and that God commands us to do what is right and forbids us to do what is wrong. But this doesn't mean, say critics of the divine command theory, that it is God's saying so that makes a thing wrong, any more than it is your mother's telling you not to steal that makes it wrong to steal.

All this is simply to argue that morality is not necessarily based on religion in any of these three senses. That religion influences the moral standards and values of most of us is beyond doubt. But given that religions differ in their moral beliefs and that even members of the same faith often disagree on moral matters, you cannot justify a moral judgment simply by appealing to religion—for that will only persuade those who already agree with your particular interpretation of your particular religion. Besides, most

> The idea that morality must be based on religion can be interpreted in three different ways, none of which is very plausible.

> **SUMMARY**
> Morality is not necessarily based on religion. Although we draw our moral beliefs from many sources, for philosophers the issue is whether those beliefs can be justified.

religions hold that human reason is capable of understanding what is right and wrong, so it is human reason to which you will have to appeal in order to support your ethical principles and judgments.

ETHICAL RELATIVISM

Some people do not believe that morality boils down to religion but rather that it is merely a function of what a particular society happens to believe. This view is called **ethical relativism**, the theory that what is right is determined by what a culture or society says is right. What is right in one place may be wrong in another, because the only criterion for distinguishing right from wrong—and so the only ethical standard for judging an action—is the moral system of the society in which the act occurs.

Abortion, for example, is condemned as immoral in Catholic Ireland but is practiced as a morally neutral form of birth control in Japan. According to the ethical relativist, then, abortion is wrong in Ireland but morally permissible in Japan. The relativist is not saying merely that the Irish believe abortion is abominable and the Japanese do not; that is acknowledged by everyone. Rather, the ethical relativist contends that abortion is immoral in Ireland because the Irish believe it to be immoral and that it is morally permissible in Japan because the Japanese believe it to be so. Thus, for the ethical relativist there is no absolute ethical standard independent of cultural context, no criterion of right and wrong by which to judge other than that of particular societies. In short, what morality requires is relative to society.

Those who endorse ethical relativism point to the apparent diversity of human values and the multiformity of moral codes to support their case. From our own cultural perspective, some seemingly immoral moralities have been adopted. Polygamy, pedophilia, stealing, slavery, infanticide, and cannibalism have all been tolerated or even encouraged by the moral system of one society or another. In light of this fact, the ethical relativist believes that there can be no non-ethnocentric standard by which to judge actions.

Some thinkers believe that the moral differences between societies are smaller and less significant than they appear. They contend that variations in moral standards reflect differing factual beliefs and differing circumstances rather than fundamental differences in values. But suppose they are wrong about this matter. The relativist's conclusion still does not follow. A difference of opinion among societies about right and wrong no more proves that none of the conflicting beliefs is true or superior to the others than the diversity of viewpoints expressed in a college seminar establishes that there is no truth. In short, disagreement in ethical matters does not imply that all opinions are equally correct.

> Ethical disagreement does not imply that all opinions are equally correct.

Moreover, ethical relativism has some unsatisfactory implications. *First*, it undermines any moral criticism of the practices of other societies as long as their actions conform to their own standards. We cannot say that slavery in a slave society like that of the American South 175 years ago was immoral and unjust as long as that society held it to be morally permissible.

Second, and closely related, is the fact that for the relativist there is no such thing as ethical progress. Although moralities may change, they cannot get better or worse. Thus, we cannot say that moral standards today are more enlightened than were moral standards in the Middle Ages.

Third, from the relativist's point of view, it makes no sense for people to criticize principles or practices accepted by their own society. People can be censured for not living up to their society's moral code, but that is all. The moral code itself cannot be criticized because whatever a society takes to be right really is right for it. Reformers who identify injustices in their society and campaign against them are only encouraging people to be immoral—that is, to depart from the moral standards of their society—unless or until the majority of the society agrees with the reformers. The minority can never be right in moral matters; to be right it must become the majority.

The ethical relativist is correct to emphasize that in viewing other cultures we should keep an open mind and not simply dismiss alien social practices on the basis of our own cultural prejudices. But the relativist's theory of morality doesn't hold up. The more carefully we examine it, the less plausible it becomes. There is no good reason for saying that the majority view on moral issues is automatically right, and the belief that it is automatically right has unacceptable consequences.

RELATIVISM AND THE "GAME" OF BUSINESS

In his essay "Is Business Bluffing Ethical?" Albert Carr argues that business, as practiced by individuals as well as by corporations, has the impersonal character of a game—a game that demands both special strategy and an understanding of its special ethical standards.[8] Business has its own norms and rules that differ from those of the rest of society. Thus, according to Carr, a number of things that we normally think of as wrong are really permissible in a business context. His examples include conscious misstatement and concealment of pertinent facts in negotiation, lying about one's age on a résumé, deceptive packaging, automobile companies' neglect of car safety, and utility companies' manipulation of regulators and overcharging of electricity users. He draws an analogy with poker:

> Poker's own brand of ethics is different from the ethical ideals of civilized human relationships. The game calls for distrust of the other fellow. It ignores the claim of friendship. Cunning deception and concealment of one's strength and intentions, not kindness and openheartedness, are vital in poker. No one thinks any the worse of poker on that account. And no one should think any the worse of the game of business because its standards of right and wrong differ from the prevailing traditions of morality in our society.[9]

What Carr is defending here is a kind of ethical relativism: Business has its own moral standards, and business actions should be evaluated only by those standards.

One can argue whether Carr has accurately identified the implicit rules of the business world (for example, is misrepresentation on one's résumé really a permissible move in the business game?), but let's put that issue aside. The basic question is whether business is a separate world to which ordinary moral standards don't apply. Carr's thesis assumes that any special activity following its own rules is exempt from external moral evaluation, but as a general proposition this is unacceptable. The Mafia, for example, has an elaborate code of conduct, accepted by the members of the rival "families." For them, gunning down a competitor or terrorizing a local shopkeeper may be a strategic move in a competitive environment. Yet we rightly refuse to say that gangsters cannot be criticized for following their own standards. Normal business activity is a world away from gangsterism, but the point still holds. Any specialized activity or practice will have its own distinctive rules and procedures, but the morality of those rules and procedures can still be evaluated.

Moreover, Carr's poker analogy is itself weak. For one thing, business activity can affect others—such as consumers—who have not consciously and freely chosen to play

> **SUMMARY**
> Ethical relativism is the theory that right and wrong are determined by what one's society says is right and wrong. There are many problems with this theory. Also dubious is the notion that business has its own morality, divorced from ordinary ideas of right and wrong.

the "game." Business is indeed an activity involving distinctive rules and customary ways of doing things, but it is not really a game. It is the economic basis of our society, and we all have an interest in the goals of business (in productivity and consumer satisfaction, for instance) and in the rules business follows. Why should these be exempt from public evaluation and assessment? Later chapters return to the question of what these goals and rules should be. But to take one simple point, note that a business/economic system that permits, encourages, or tolerates deception will be less efficient (that is, work less well) than one in which the participants have fuller knowledge of the goods and services being exchanged.

By divorcing business from morality, Carr misrepresents both.

In sum, by divorcing business from morality, Carr misrepresents both. He incorrectly treats the standards and rules of everyday business activity as if they had nothing to do with the standards and rules of ordinary morality, and he treats morality as something that we give lip service to on Sundays but that otherwise has no influence on our lives.

* * *

HAVING MORAL PRINCIPLES

At some time in their lives most people pause to reflect on their own moral principles and on the practical implications of those principles, and they sometimes think about what principles people should have or which moral standards can be best justified. (Moral philosophers themselves have defended different moral standards; Chapter 2 discusses these various theories.) When a person accepts a moral principle, when that principle is part of his or her personal moral code, then naturally the person believes the principle is important and well justified. But there is more to moral principles than that, as the philosopher Richard Brandt emphasized. When a principle is part of a person's moral code, that person is strongly motivated to act as the principle requires and to avoid acting in ways that conflict with the principle. The person will tend to feel guilty when his or her own conduct violates that principle and to disapprove of others whose behavior conflicts with it. Likewise, the person will tend to hold in esteem those whose conduct shows an abundance of the motivation required by the principle.[10]

Accepting a moral principle is not a purely intellectual act like accepting a scientific hypothesis or a mathematical theorem.

Other philosophers have, in different ways, reinforced Brandt's point. To accept a moral principle is not a purely intellectual act like accepting a scientific hypothesis or a mathematical theorem. Rather, it also involves a desire to follow that principle for its own sake, the likelihood of feeling guilty about not doing so, and a tendency to evaluate the conduct of others according to the principle in question. We would find it very strange, for example, if Sally claimed to be morally opposed to cruelty to animals yet abused her own pets and felt no inclination to protest when some ruffians down the street set a cat on fire.

CONSCIENCE

People can, and unfortunately sometimes do, go against their moral principles, but we would doubt that they sincerely held the principle in question if violating it did not bother their conscience. We have all felt the pangs of conscience, but what exactly is **conscience** and how reliable a guide is it? Our conscience, of course, is not literally a little voice inside us. To oversimplify a complex piece of developmental psychology, our conscience evolved as we internalized the moral instructions of the parents or other authority figures who raised us as children.

When you were very young, you were probably told to tell the truth and to return something you filched to its proper owner. If you were caught lying or being dishonest, you were probably punished—scolded, spanked, sent to bed without dinner, or denied a privilege. In contrast, truth telling and kindness to your siblings were probably rewarded—with approval, praise, maybe even hugs or candy. Seeking reward and avoiding punishment motivate small children to do what is expected of them. Gradually, children come to internalize those parental commands. Thus, they feel vaguely that their parents know what they are doing even when the parents are not around. When children do something forbidden, they experience the same feelings as when scolded by their parents—the first stirrings of guilt. By the same token, even in the absence of explicit parental reward, children feel a sense of self-approval about having done what they were supposed to have done.

As we grow older, of course, our motivations are not so simple and our self-understanding is greater. We are able to reflect on and understand the moral lessons we were taught, as well as to refine and modify those principles. As adults we are morally independent agents. Yet however much our conscience has evolved and however much our adult moral code differs from the moral perspective of our childhood, those pangs of guilt we occasionally feel still stem from that early internalization of parental demands.

THE LIMITS OF CONSCIENCE

How reliable a guide is conscience? People often say, "Follow your conscience" or "You should never go against your conscience." Such advice is not very helpful, however. Indeed, it can sometimes be bad advice. *First*, when we are genuinely perplexed about what we ought to do, we are trying to figure out what our conscience ought to be saying to us. When it is not possible to do both, should we keep our promise to a colleague or come to the aid of an old friend? To be told that we should follow our conscience is no help at all.

Second, it may not always be good for us to follow our conscience. It all depends on what our conscience says. On the one hand, sometimes people's consciences do not bother them when they should—perhaps because they didn't think through the implications of what they were doing or perhaps because they failed to internalize strongly enough the appropriate moral principles. On the other hand, a person's conscience might disturb the person about something that is perfectly all right.

Consider an episode in Chapter 16 of Mark Twain's *The Adventures of Huckleberry Finn*. Huck has taken off down the Mississippi on a raft with his friend, the runaway slave Jim, but as they get nearer to the place where Jim will become legally free, Huck starts feeling guilty about helping him run away:

> It hadn't ever come home to me before, what this thing was that I was doing. But now it did; and it stayed with me, and scorched me more and more. I tried to make out to myself that I warn't to blame, because I didn't run Jim off from his rightful owner; but it warn't no use, conscience up and says, every time: "But you knowed he was running for his freedom, and you could a paddled ashore and told somebody." That was so—I couldn't get around that, no way. That was where it pinched. Conscience says to me: "What had poor Miss Watson done to you, that you could see her nigger go off right under your eyes and never say one single word? What did that poor old woman do to you, that you could treat her so mean? . . ." I got to feeling so mean and miserable I most wished I was dead.

Here Huck is feeling guilty about doing what we would all agree is the morally right thing to do. But Huck is only a boy, and his pangs of conscience reflect the principles that he has picked up uncritically from the slave-owning society around him. Unable to think independently about matters of right and wrong, Huck in the end decides to disregard his conscience. He follows his instincts and sticks by his friend Jim.

Telling someone to "follow your conscience" is not very helpful, and sometimes it can be bad advice.

....

SUMMARY
Accepting a moral principle involves a motivation to conform one's conduct to that principle. Violating the principle will bother one's conscience, but conscience is not a perfectly reliable guide to right and wrong.

....

The point here is not that you should ignore your conscience but that the voice of conscience is itself something that can be critically examined. A pang of conscience is like a warning. When you feel one, you should definitely stop and reflect on the rightness of what you are doing. But you cannot justify your actions simply by saying you were following your conscience. Terrible deeds have occasionally been committed in the name of conscience.

MORAL PRINCIPLES AND SELF-INTEREST

Sometimes doing what you believe would be morally right and doing what would best satisfy your own interests may be two different things. Imagine that you are in your car hurrying along a quiet road, trying hard to get to an important football game in time to see the kickoff. You pass an acquaintance who is having car trouble. He doesn't recognize you. As a dedicated fan, you would much prefer to keep on going than to stop and help him, thus missing at least part of the game. Although you might rationalize that someone else will eventually come along and help him out if you don't, deep down you know that you really ought to stop. **Self-interest**, however, seems to say, "Keep going."

Consider another example. You have applied for a new job, and if you land it, it will be an enormous break for you. It is exactly the kind of position you want and have been trying to get for some time. It pays well and will settle you into a desirable career for the rest of your life. The competition has come down to you and one other person, and you believe correctly that she has a slight edge on you. Now imagine that you could spread a nasty rumor about her that would guarantee that she wouldn't get the job, and that you could do this in a way that wouldn't come back to you. Presumably, circulating this lie would violate your moral code, but doing so would clearly benefit you.

Some people argue that moral action and self-interest can never really conflict. Although some philosophers have gone to great lengths to try to prove this, they are almost certainly mistaken. They maintain that if you do the wrong thing, then you will be caught, your conscience will bother you, or in some way "what goes around comes around," so that your misdeed will come back to haunt you. This is often correct. But unfortunate as it may be, sometimes—viewed just in terms of personal self-interest—it may pay off for you to do what you know to be wrong. People sometimes get away with their wrongdoings, and if their conscience bothers them at all, it may not bother them very much. To believe otherwise not only is wishful thinking but also shows a lack of understanding of morality.

> Morality restrains our self-interested desires. A society's moral standards allow conflicts to be resolved by an appeal to shared principles of justification.

Morality serves to restrain our purely self-interested desires so we can all live together. The moral standards of a society provide the basic guidelines for cooperative social existence and allow conflicts to be resolved by an appeal to shared principles of justification. If our interests never came into conflict—that is, if it were never advantageous for one person to deceive or cheat another—then there would be little need for morality. We would already be in heaven. Both a system of law that punishes people for hurting others and a system of morality that encourages people to refrain from pursuing their self-interest at great expense to others help make social existence possible.

Usually, following our moral principles is in our best interest. This idea is particularly worth noting in the business context. Recently, a number of business theorists have argued persuasively not only that moral behavior is consistent with profitability but also that the most morally responsible companies are among the most profitable.[11] Apparently, respecting the rights of employees, treating suppliers fairly, and being straightforward with customers pay off.

But notice one thing. If you do the right thing only because you think you will profit from it, you are not really motivated by moral concerns. Having a moral principle involves having a desire to follow the principle for its own sake—simply because it is the right thing to do. If you do the right thing only because you believe it will pay off, you might just as easily not do it if it looks as if it is not going to pay off.

In addition, there is no guarantee that moral behavior will always benefit a person in strictly selfish terms. As argued earlier, there will be exceptions. From the moral point of view, you ought to stop and help your acquaintance, and you shouldn't lie about competitors. From the selfish point of view, you should do exactly the opposite. Should you follow your self-interest or your moral principles? There's no final answer to this question. From the moral point of view, you should, of course, follow your moral principles. But from the selfish point of view, you should look out solely for "number one."

Which option you choose will depend on the strength of your self-interested or self-regarding desires in comparison with the strength of your other-regarding desires (that is, your moral motivations and your concern for others). In other words, your choice will depend on your character, on the kind of person you are, which depends in part on how you were raised. A person who is basically selfish will pass by the acquaintance in distress and will spread the rumor, whereas someone who has a stronger concern for others, or a stronger desire to do what is right just because it is right, will not.

Although it may be impossible to prove to selfish people that they should not do the thing that best advances their self-interest (because if they are selfish, then that is all they care about), there are considerations that suggest it is not in a one's overall self-interest to be a selfish person. People who are exclusively concerned with their own interests tend to have less happy and less satisfying lives than those whose desires extend beyond themselves. This is usually called the **paradox of hedonism**, but it might equally well be dubbed the "paradox of selfishness." Individuals who care only about their own happiness will generally be less happy than those who care about others. Moreover, people often find greater satisfaction in a life lived according to moral principle, and in being the kind of person that entails, than in a life devoted solely to self-gratification. Thus, or so many philosophers have argued, people have self-interested reasons not to be so self-interested. How do selfish people make themselves less so? Not overnight, obviously, but by involving themselves in the concerns and cares of others, they can in time come to care sincerely about those persons.

> When morality and self-interest conflict, what you choose to do will depend on the kind of person you are.

MORALITY AND PERSONAL VALUES

It is helpful to distinguish between morality in a narrow sense and morality in a broad sense. In a narrow sense, morality is the moral code of an individual or a society (insofar as the moral codes of the individuals making up that society overlap). Although the principles that constitute our code may not be explicitly formulated, as laws are, they do guide us in our conduct. They function as internal monitors of our own behavior and as a basis for assessing the actions of others. **Morality in the narrow sense** concerns the principles that do or should regulate people's conduct and relations with others. These principles can be debated, however. (Take, for example, John Stuart Mill's contention that society ought not to interfere with people's liberty when their actions affect only themselves.) And a large part of moral philosophy involves assessing rival moral principles. This discussion is part of the ongoing development in our moral culture. What is at stake are the basic standards that ought to govern our behavior—that is, the fundamental framework or ground rules that make coexistence possible. If there were not already fairly widespread agreement about these principles, our social order would not be sustainable.

> **SUMMARY**
> Part of the point of morality is to make social existence possible by restraining self-interested behavior. Sometimes doing what is morally right can conflict with one's personal interests. In general, though, following your moral principles will enable you to live a more satisfying life.

In addition we can talk about our **morality in the broad sense**, meaning not just the principles of conduct that we embrace but also the values, ideals, and aspirations that shape our lives. Many different ways of living our lives would meet our basic moral obligations. The type of life each of us seeks to live reflects our individual values—whether following a profession, devoting ourselves to community service, raising a family, seeking solitude, pursuing scientific truth, striving for athletic excellence, amassing political power, cultivating glamorous people as friends, or some combination of these and many other possible ways of living. The life that each of us forges and the way we understand that life are part of our morality in the broad sense of the term.

It is important to bear this in mind throughout your study of business ethics. Although this book's main concern is with the principles that ought to govern conduct in certain business-type situations—for example, whether a hiring officer may take an applicant's race into account, whether insider trading is wrong, or whether corporate bribery is permissible in countries where people turn a blind eye to it—your choices in the business world will also reflect your other values and ideals or, in other words, the kind of person you are striving to be. What sort of ideal do you have of yourself as a businessperson? How much weight do you put on profitability, for instance, as against the quality of your product or the socially beneficial character of your service?

The decisions you make in your career and much of the way you shape your working life will depend not only on your moral code but also on the understanding you have of yourself in certain roles and relationships. Your morality—in the sense of your ideals, values, and aspirations—involves, among other things, your understanding of human nature, tradition, and society; of one's proper relationship to the natural environment; and of an individual's place in the cosmos. Professionals in various fields, for example, will invariably be guided not just by rules but also by their understanding of what being a professional involves, and a businessperson's conception of the ideal or model relationship to have with clients will greatly influence his or her day-to-day conduct.

There is more to living a morally good life, of course, than being a good businessperson or being good at your job, as Aristotle (384–322 BCE) argued long ago. He underscored the necessity of our trying to achieve virtue or excellence, not just in some particular field of endeavor, but also as human beings. Aristotle thought that things have functions. The function of a piano, for instance, is to make certain sounds, and a piano that performs this function well is a good or excellent piano. Likewise, we have an idea of what it is for a person to be an excellent athlete, an excellent manager, or an excellent professor—it is to do well the types of things that athletes, managers, or professors are supposed to do.

But Aristotle also thought that, just as there is an ideal of excellence for any particular craft or occupation, similarly there must be an excellence that we can achieve simply as human beings. He believed that we can live our lives as a whole in such a way that they can be judged not just as excellent in this respect or in that occupation but as excellent, period. Aristotle thought that only when we develop our truly human capacities sufficiently to achieve this human excellence will we have lives blessed with happiness. Philosophers since Aristotle's time have been skeptical of his apparent belief that this human excellence would come in just one form, but many would underscore the importance of developing our various potential capacities and striving to achieve a kind of excellence in our lives. How we understand this excellence is a function of our values, ideals, and world view—our morality in a broad sense.

SUMMARY

Morality in the sense of the rules or principles that regulate one's conduct toward others can be distinguished from morality in the broader sense of the values, ideals, and aspirations that shape a person's life.

Aristotle also emphasized the importance of character and of being a person whose life displays the various virtues that human beings are capable of achieving. A virtue is a trait or settled disposition; for example, a courageous, generous, or kind person is one who habitually acts in ways that are courageous, generous, or kind. A generous person does not debate whether to act generously; for her or him acting generously is second nature. How we act, however, shapes the character we come to have; that is, we become a generous person by acting in generous ways whereas we come to be selfish or stingy by acting in stingy or selfish ways. For Aristotle, it was therefore important to model ourselves on those who are virtuous and to try to act as they act. As we shall see in the next section, though, different social environments can make it easier or harder to develop virtuous habits and to be the kind of person we want to be.

INDIVIDUAL INTEGRITY AND RESPONSIBILITY

Previous sections discussed what it is for a person to have a moral code, as well as the sometimes conflicting pulls of moral conscience and self-interest. In addition, we have seen that people have values and ideals above and beyond their moral principles, narrowly understood, that also influence the lives they lead. And we have seen the importance of reflecting critically on both moral principles and our ideals and values as we seek to live morally good and worthwhile lives. None of us, however, lives in a vacuum, and social pressures of various sorts always affect us. Sometimes these pressures make it difficult to stick with our principles and to be the kind of person we wish to be. Corporations are a particularly relevant example of an environment that can potentially damage individual integrity and responsibility.

ORGANIZATIONAL NORMS

One of the major characteristics of an organization—indeed, of any group—is the shared acceptance of **organizational norms** and rules by its members. Acceptance can take different forms; it can be conscious or unconscious, overt or implicit, but it is almost always present, because an organization can survive only if it holds its members together. Group cohesiveness requires that individual members "commit" themselves—that is, relinquish some of their personal freedom in order to further organizational goals. One's degree of commitment—the extent to which one accepts group norms and subordinates self to organizational goals—is a measure of one's loyalty to the "team."

The corporation's overarching goal is profit. To achieve this goal, top management sets specific targets for sales, market share, return on equity, and so forth. For the most part, the norms or rules that govern corporate existence are derived from these goals. But clearly there's nothing in either the norms or the goals that necessarily encourages moral behavior; indeed, they may discourage it.

According to a recent survey by the American Management Association, pressure to meet unrealistic business objectives and deadlines is the leading cause of unethical business conduct.[12] And mounting evidence suggests that most managers experience role conflicts between what is expected of them as efficient, profit-minded members of an organization, and what is expected of them as ethical persons. In a series of in-depth interviews with recent graduates of the Harvard MBA program, researchers Joseph L. Badaracco, Jr., and Allen P. Webb found that these young managers frequently received explicit instructions or felt strong organizational pressure to do things they believed to be sleazy, unethical, or even illegal.[13] Another survey found that a majority of managers at all levels experience "pressure from the top" to meet corporate goals and comply with corporate norms. Of the managers interviewed, 50 percent of top managers, 65 percent of middle managers, and 84 percent of lower managers agreed that they felt pressure to "compromise personal standards to achieve company goals."[14]

The young managers interviewed by Badaracco and Webb identified four powerful organizational "commandments" as responsible for the pressure they felt to compromise their integrity:

> First, performance is what really counts, so make your numbers. Second, be loyal and show us that you're a team player. Third, don't break the law. Fourth, don't overinvest in ethical behavior.[15]

Pressure to meet corporate objectives, to be a team player, and to conform to organizational norms can sometimes lead people to act unethically.

Although most corporate goals and norms are not objectionable when viewed by themselves, they frequently put the people who must implement them into a moral pressure cooker. In addition, people can overlook the ethical implications of their decisions just because they are busy working on organizational goals and not looking at things from a broader perspective. In these ways, the need to meet corporate objectives, to be a team player, and to conform to organizational norms can sometimes lead otherwise honorable individuals to engage in unethical conduct.

CONFORMITY

It is no secret that organizations exert pressure on their members to conform to norms and goals. What may not be so widely known is how easily individuals can be induced to behave as those around them do. A dramatic example is provided in the early conformity studies by social psychologist Solomon Asch.[16]

In a classic experiment, Asch asked groups of seven to nine college students to say which of three lines on a card matched the length of a single line on another card:

Only one of the subjects in each group was "naive," or unaware of the nature of the experiment. The others were shills or stooges of the experimenter, who had instructed them to make incorrect judgments in about two-thirds of the cases and in this way to pressure the naive subjects to alter their correct judgments.

The results were revealing. When the subjects were not exposed to pressure, they invariably judged correctly, but when the stooges all gave a false answer, the subjects changed their responses to conform with the unanimous majority judgments. When one shill differed from the majority and gave the correct answer, naive subjects maintained their position three-fourths of the time. However, when the honest shill switched to the majority view in later trials, the errors made by naive subjects rose to about the same level as that of subjects who stood alone against a unanimous majority.

Why did they yield? Some respondents said they didn't want to seem different, even though they continued to believe their judgments were correct. Others said that although their perceptions seemed correct, the majority couldn't be wrong. Still other subjects didn't even seem aware that they had caved in to group pressure. Even those who held their ground tended to be profoundly disturbed by being out of step with the majority and confessed to being sorely tempted to alter their judgments. Indeed, a subsequent study found that students who stood firm in their judgments suffered more anxiety than those who switched. One student with the strength of his correct convictions was literally dripping with perspiration by the end of the experiment.

In these experiments, which cumulatively included several hundred students, the subjects were not exposed to the authority symbols that people inside an organization face—bosses, boards of directors, professional peers—nor were they up against established policy and entrenched norms. Correct responses would not have had the serious career consequences that bucking the system can sometimes have for members of an organization: being transferred, dismissed, frozen in a position, or made an organizational pariah. And, of course, the students did not bring to these experiments the financial and personal investments that individuals bring to their jobs. Men and women within an organization are under greater pressure to conform than were the students in Asch's studies.

Groupthink

Almost all groups require some conformity from their members, but in extreme cases the demand for conformity can lead to what social psychologists call "groupthink." **Groupthink** happens when pressure for unanimity within a highly cohesive group overwhelms its members' desire or ability to appraise the situation realistically and consider alternative courses of action. The desire for the comfort and confidence that comes from mutual agreement and approval leads members of the group to close their eyes to negative information, to ignore warnings that the group may be mistaken, and to discount outside ideas that might contradict the thinking or the decisions of the group.

When under the sway of groupthink, group members may have the illusion that the group is invulnerable or that because the group is good or right, whatever it does is permissible. Individuals in the group tend to self-censor thoughts that go against the group's ideas and rationalize away conflicting evidence, and the group as a whole may implicitly or explicitly pressure potential dissenters to conform. Groupthink thus leads to irrational, sometimes disastrous decisions, and it has enormous potential for doing moral damage.

DIFFUSION OF RESPONSIBILITY

Pressure to conform to the group and to adhere to its norms and beliefs can lead to the surrender of individual moral autonomy. This tendency is enhanced by the fact that group actions frequently involve the participation of many people. As a result, responsibility for what an organization does can become fragmented or diffused throughout the group, with no single individual seeing himself or herself as responsible for what happens. Indeed, it may be difficult to say exactly who should be held accountable. This **diffusion of responsibility** inside an organization leads individuals to have a diluted or diminished sense of their own personal moral responsibilities. They tend to see themselves simply as small players in a process or as cogs in a machine over which they have no control and for which they are unaccountable. They rationalize to themselves contributing to actions, policies, or events that they would refuse to perform or to authorize if they thought the decision were entirely up to them. "It's not my fault," they think. "This would happen anyway, with or without me." Diffusion of responsibility encourages the moral myopia of thinking "I'm just doing my job," instead of taking a 20/20 look at the bigger picture.

> **SUMMARY**
> Several aspects of corporate structure and function work to undermine individual moral responsibility. Organizational norms, pressure to conform (sometimes leading to groupthink), and diffusion of responsibility inside large organizations can all make the exercise of individual integrity difficult.

> Diffusion of responsibility inside an organization can weaken people's sense of moral responsibility.

This sense of diminished individual moral responsibility for an outcome that many people bring about or allow to happen is something that social psychologists began studying more closely as a result of the sad case of Kitty Genovese, a young woman who was stabbed to death in the 1960s. Although the murder was not in itself so unusual, it made headlines and editorial pages across the nation because thirty-eight of her neighbors witnessed her brutal slaying. In answer to her pitiful screams of terror at 3 A.M., they came to their windows and remained there for the thirty or more minutes it took her assailant to brutalize her. (He evidently left for a while and then returned to finish her off.) Of the thirty-eight, not one attempted to intervene in any way; no one even phoned the police.

Why didn't Kitty Genovese's neighbors help her? Most social psychologists believe that an individual's sense of personal responsibility is inversely proportional to the number of people witnessing or involved in the episode. The more people who are observing an event, the less likely is any one of them to feel obliged to do something. In emergencies, we seem naturally to let the behavior of those around us dictate our response—a phenomenon often called **bystander apathy**. But the point is more general. In any large group or organization, diffusion of responsibility for its actions can lead individuals to feel anonymous and not accountable for what happens. Submerged in the group, the individual may not even question the morality of his or her actions.[17]

> Business corporations are no worse than other groups, but many of them do little to protect individual integrity and moral autonomy.

Pressure to conform to organizational norms and a diminished sense of personal responsibility for group behavior undermine individual integrity and moral autonomy. Business corporations are not necessarily worse than many other groups in this respect, but certainly the pressure in business to help the company make a profit or achieve its other goals, to do what is expected of you, and generally to be a loyal and cooperative team player can foster, or at least do nothing to inhibit, these group propensities. Beyond that, many corporations fail to institutionalize ethics. They don't articulate or communicate ethical standards to their members; they don't actively enforce them; and they retain structures and policies that thwart individual integrity. For example, when a Beech-Nut employee expressed concerns about the fact that the concentrate the company was producing for its "100% pure" apple juice contained nothing more than sugar, water, and chemicals, his annual performance review described his judgment as "colored by naïveté and impractical ideals."[18]

Employees frequently have to fight hard to maintain their moral integrity in a showdown with organizational priorities. Consider, for example, those Wall Street analysts pressured by their firms to recommend to clients stocks or bonds the analysts knew to be "junk" or "dogs."[19] More dramatically, on a June day in 2011, a US Airways captain with thirty years of experience stopped her flight from departing because she was worried that a backup power system was defective. The company pressured her to fly anyway, and when she refused to do so, security officials escorted her out of the airport and threatened to arrest her crew if they didn't cooperate. When other pilots backed her up and refused to fly the plane, US Airways finally had technicians service the plane. They confirmed that the component was faulty, and fixed it.[20]

Often, however, the problem facing people in business and other organization contexts is not that of doing what they believed to be right but rather of deciding what the right thing to do is. They can sometimes face difficult and puzzling moral questions, questions that need to be answered. How does one go about doing that? Is there some reliable procedure or method for answering moral questions? In science, the scientific method tells us what steps to take if we seek to answer a scientific question, but there is no comparable moral method for engaging ethical questions. There is, however, general agreement about what constitutes good moral reasoning.

MORAL REASONING

It is useful to view moral reasoning at first in the context of argument. An **argument** is a group of statements, one of which (called the **conclusion**) is claimed to follow from the others (called the **premises**). Here's an example of an argument:

ARGUMENT 1

If a person is a mother, the person is a female.

Fran is a mother.

Therefore, Fran is a female.

The first two statements (the premises) of this argument happen to entail the third (the conclusion), which means that if I accept the first two as true, then I must accept the third as also true. Not to accept the conclusion while accepting the premises would result in a contradiction—holding two beliefs that cannot both be true at the same time. In other words, if I believe that all mothers are females and that Fran is a mother (the premises), then I cannot deny that Fran is a female (the conclusion) without contradicting myself. An argument like this one, whose premises logically entail its conclusion, is a **valid argument**.

An **invalid argument** is one whose premises do not entail its conclusion. In an invalid argument, I can accept the premises as true and reject the conclusion without any contradiction. Thus:

ARGUMENT 2

If a person is a mother, the person is a female.

Fran is a female.

Therefore, Fran is a mother.

The conclusion of this argument does not necessarily follow from the true premises. I can believe that every mother is a female and that Fran is a female but deny that Fran is a mother without contradicting myself.

One way to show this is by means of a **counterexample**, an example that is consistent with the premises but is inconsistent with the conclusion. Let's suppose Fran is a two-year-old, a premise that is perfectly consistent with the two stated premises. If she is, she can't possibly be a mother. Or let's suppose Fran is an adult female who happens to be childless, another premise that is perfectly consistent with the stated premises but obviously at odds with the conclusion. If an argument is valid (such as Argument 1), then no counterexamples are possible.

A valid argument can have untrue premises, as in the following:

ARGUMENT 3

If a person is a female, she must be a mother.

Fran is a female.

Therefore, Fran must be a mother.

Like Argument 1, this argument is valid. If I accept its premises as true, I must accept its conclusion as true; otherwise I will contradict myself. However, although Argument 3 is valid, it is unsound because one of its premises is false—namely, "If a person is a female, she must be a mother." Realizing the patent absurdity of one of its premises, no sensible person would accept this argument's conclusion. But notice why the argument is unsound—not because the type of reasoning it involves is invalid but because one of the premises is false. **Sound arguments**, such as Argument 1, have true premises and valid reasoning. **Unsound arguments** have at least one false premise, as in Argument 3, or invalid reasoning, as in Argument 2, or both.

Now let's consider some **moral arguments**, which can be defined simply as arguments whose conclusions are moral judgments. Here are some examples that deal with affirmative action for women and minorities in the workplace:

ARGUMENT 4

If an action violates the law, it is morally wrong.

Affirmative action on behalf of women and minorities in personnel matters violates the law.

Therefore, affirmative action on behalf of women and minorities in personnel matters is morally wrong.

ARGUMENT 5

If an action violates the will of the majority, it is morally wrong.

Affirmative action on behalf of women and minorities in personnel matters violates the will of the majority.

Therefore, affirmative action on behalf of women and minorities in personnel matters is morally wrong.

ARGUMENT 6

If an action redresses past injuries that have disadvantaged a group, it is morally permissible.

Affirmative action on behalf of women and minorities in personnel matters redresses injuries that have disadvantaged these groups.

Therefore, affirmative action on behalf of women and minorities in personnel matters is morally permissible.

ARGUMENT 7

If an action is the only practical way to remedy a social problem, then it is morally permissible.

Affirmative action on behalf of women and minorities in personnel matters is the only practical way to remedy the social problem of unequal employment opportunity.

Therefore, affirmative action on behalf of women and minorities in personnel matters is morally permissible.

The first premise in each of these arguments is a moral standard, the second an alleged fact, and the conclusion a moral judgment. *Moral reasoning* or argument typically moves from a moral standard, through one or more factual judgments about some person, action, or policy related to that standard, to a moral judgment about that person, action, or policy. Good moral reasoning will frequently be more complicated than these examples. Often it will involve an appeal to more than one standard as well as to various appropriate factual claims, and its argumentative structure may be more elaborate. Still, these examples illustrate its most basic form.

DEFENSIBLE MORAL JUDGMENTS

If a moral judgment or conclusion is defensible, then it must be supportable by a defensible moral standard, together with relevant facts. A moral standard supports a moral judgment if the standard, taken together with the relevant facts, logically entails the moral judgment and if the moral standard itself is an acceptable standard. If someone argues that affirmative action for minorities and women is right (or wrong) but cannot produce a supporting principle when asked, then the person's position is considerably weakened. And if the person does not see any need to support the judgment by appealing to a moral standard, then he or she simply does not understand how moral concepts are used or is using moral words like "right" or "wrong" differently from the way they are commonly used.

Keeping this in mind—that moral judgments must be supportable by moral standards and facts—will aid your understanding of moral discourse, which can be highly complex and sophisticated. It will also sharpen your own critical faculties and improve your moral reasoning and ability to formulate relevant moral arguments.

> Moral judgments should be supported by moral standards and relevant facts.

PATTERNS OF DEFENSE AND CHALLENGE

In assessing arguments, one must be careful to clarify the meanings of their key terms and phrases. Often premises can be understood in more than one way, and this ambiguity may lead people to accept (or reject) arguments that they shouldn't. For example, "affirmative action" seems to mean different things to different people (see Chapter 11 on job discrimination). Before we can profitably assess Arguments 4 through 7, we have to agree on how we understand "affirmative action." Similarly, Argument 5 relies on the idea of "violating the will of the majority," but this notion has to be clarified before we can evaluate either the moral principle that it is wrong to violate the will of the majority or the factual claim that affirmative action does violate the majority's will.

Assuming that the arguments are logically valid in their form (as Arguments 4 through 7 are) and that their terms have been clarified and possible ambiguities eliminated, then we must turn our attention to assessing the premises of the arguments. Should we accept or reject their premises? Remember that if an argument is valid and you accept the premises, you must accept the conclusion.

Let's look at some further aspects of this assessment process:

1. **Evaluating the factual claims.** If the parties to an ethical discussion are willing to accept the moral standard (or standards) in question, then they can concentrate on the factual claims. Thus, for example, in Argument 4 they will focus on whether affirmative action on behalf of women and minorities is in fact illegal. In Argument 7 they will need to determine whether affirmative action is really the only practical way to remedy the social problem of unequal employment opportunity. Analogous questions can be asked about the factual claims of Arguments 5 and 6. Answering them in the affirmative would require considerable supporting data.

2. **Challenging the moral standard.** Moral disagreements do not always turn on factual issues. The moral standard on which a given moral argument relies may be controversial. One party might challenge the standard, contending that it is implausible or that we should not accept it. The critic might do this in several different ways—for example, by showing that there are exceptions to the standard, that the standard leads to unacceptable consequences, or that it is inconsistent with the arguer's other moral beliefs.

> **SUMMARY**
> Moral reasoning and argument typically appeal both to moral standards and to relevant facts. Moral judgments should be entailed by the relevant moral standards and the facts, and they should not contradict our other beliefs. Both standards and facts must be assessed when moral arguments are being evaluated.

In the following dialogue, for example, Lynn is attacking Sam's advocacy of the standard "If an action redresses past injuries that have disadvantaged a group, it is morally permissible":

Lynn: What would you think of affirmative action for Jews in the workplace?

Sam: I'd be against it.

Lynn: What about Catholics?

Sam: No.

Lynn: People of Irish extraction?

Sam: They should be treated the same as anybody else.

Lynn: But each of these groups and more I could mention were victimized in the past by unfair discrimination and probably in some cases continue to be.

Sam: So?

Lynn: So the standard you're defending leads to a judgment you reject: namely, that Jews, Catholics, and Irish should be compensated by affirmative action for having been disadvantaged. How do you account for this inconsistency?

At this point, Sam, or any rational person in a similar position, has three alternatives: abandon or modify the standard, alter his moral judgment, or show how women and minorities fit the original principle even though the other groups do not.

3. **Defending the moral standard.** When the standard is criticized, then its advocate must defend it. Often this requires invoking an even more general principle. A defender of Argument 6, for example, might uphold the redress principle by appealing to some more general conception of social justice. Or defenders might try to show how the standard in question entails other moral judgments that both the critic and the defender accept, thereby enhancing the plausibility of the standard.

In the following exchange, Tina is defending the standard of Argument 5: "If an action violates the will of the majority, it is morally wrong":

Tina: Okay, do you think the government should impose a national religion on all Americans?

Jake: Of course not.

Tina: What about requiring people to register their handguns?

Jake: I'm all for it.

Tina: And using kids in pornography?

Jake: There rightly are laws against it.

Tina: But the principle you're objecting to—that an action violating the will of the majority is wrong—supports your moral stance on all these issues.

Of course, Tina's argument is by no means a conclusive defense for her moral standard. Other moral standards could just as easily entail the judgments she cites, as Jake is quick to point out:

Jake: Now wait a minute. I oppose a state religion on constitutional grounds, not because it violates majority will. As for gun control, I'm for it because I think it will reduce violent crimes. And using kids in pornography is wrong because it exploits and endangers children.

Although Tina's strategy for defending the standard about majority rule proved inconclusive, it does illustrate a common and often persuasive way of arguing for a moral principle.

4. **Revising and modifying the argument.** Arguments 4 through 7 are only illustrations, and all the moral principles they mention are very simple—too simple to accept without qualification. (The principle that it is immoral to break the law in all circumstances, for example, is implausible. Nazi Germany furnishes an obvious counterexample to it.) But once the standard has been effectively challenged, the defender of the argument, rather than abandoning the argument altogether, might try to reformulate it. For instance, the defender might replace the original, contested premise with a better and more plausible one that still supports the conclusion. For example, Premise 1 of Argument 4 might be replaced by: "If an action violates a law that is democratically decided and that is not morally unjust, then the action is immoral." Or the defender might revise the conclusion of his or her argument, perhaps by restricting its scope. A more modest, less sweeping conclusion will often be easier to defend.

In this way, the discussion continues, the arguments on both sides of an issue improve, and we make progress in the analysis and resolution of ethical issues. In general, in philosophy we study logic and criticize arguments not to be able to score quick debating points but rather to be able to think more clearly and deeply about moral and other problems. Our goal as moral philosophers is not to "win" arguments but to arrive at the truth—or, put less grandly, to find the most reasonable answers to various ethical questions.

> **SUMMARY**
> Philosophical discussion generally involves the revision and modification of arguments; in this way progress is made in the analysis and resolution of moral and other issues.

REQUIREMENTS FOR MORAL JUDGMENTS

Moral discussion and the analysis of ethical issues can take different, often complicated, paths. Nevertheless, the preceding discussion implies that moral judgments should be (1) logical, (2) based on facts, and (3) based on sound or defensible moral principles. A moral judgment that is weak on any of these grounds is open to criticism.

Moral Judgments Should Be Logical

To say that moral judgments should be logical implies several things. *First*, as indicated in the discussion of moral reasoning, our moral judgments should follow logically from their premises. The connection between (1) the standard, (2) the conduct or policy, and (3) the moral judgment should be such that 1 and 2 logically entail 3. Our goal is to be able to support our moral judgments with reasons and evidence, rather than basing them solely on emotion, sentiment, or social or personal preference.

Second, our moral judgments should be logically compatible with our other moral and nonmoral beliefs. We must avoid inconsistency. Almost all philosophers agree that if we make a moral judgment—for example, that it was wrong of Smith to alter the figures she gave to the outside auditors—then we must be willing to make the same judgment in any similar set of circumstances—that is, if our friend Brown, our spouse, or our father had altered the figures. In particular, we cannot make an exception for ourselves, judging something permissible for us to do while condemning others for doing the very same thing.

> Our moral judgments should follow logically from their premises.

> Our moral judgments should be logically compatible with our other beliefs.

Moral Judgments Should Be Based on Facts

Adequate moral judgments cannot be made in a vacuum. We must gather as much relevant information as possible before making them. For example, an intelligent assessment of the morality of insider trading would require an understanding of, among other things, the different circumstances in which it can occur and the effects it has on the market and on other traders. The information supporting a moral judgment, the facts, should be relevant—that is, the information should actually relate to the judgment;

it should be complete or inclusive of all significant data; and it should, of course, be accurate or true.

Moral Judgments Should Be Based on Acceptable Moral Principles

We know that moral judgments are based on moral standards. At the highest level of moral reasoning, these standards embody and express very general moral principles. Reliable moral judgments must be based on sound moral principles—principles that are unambiguous and can withstand close scrutiny and rational criticism. What, precisely, makes a moral principle sound or acceptable is one of the most difficult questions that the study of ethics raises and is beyond the scope of this book. But one criterion is worth mentioning, namely, consistency with our **considered moral beliefs**.

These beliefs contrast with our gut responses, with beliefs based on ignorance or prejudice, and with beliefs we just happen to hold without having thought them through. As philosophy professor Tom Regan explains, our considered beliefs are those moral beliefs "we hold *after* we have made a conscientious effort . . . to think about our beliefs coolly, rationally, impartially, with conceptual clarity, and with as much relevant information as we can reasonably acquire."[21] We have grounds to doubt a moral principle when it clashes with such beliefs. Conversely, conformity with our considered moral beliefs is good reason for regarding it as provisionally established.

This does not imply that conformity with our considered beliefs is the sole or even basic test of a moral principle, any more than conformity with well-established beliefs is the exclusive or even fundamental test of a scientific hypothesis. (Copernicus's heliocentric hypothesis, for example, did not conform with what passed in the medieval world as a well-considered belief, the Ptolemaic view that the earth was the center of the universe.) But conformity with our considered beliefs seemingly must play some part in evaluating the many alternative moral principles that are explored in the next chapter.

> **SUMMARY**
> Moral judgments should be logical and based on facts and acceptable moral principles. Conformity with our considered moral beliefs is an important consideration in evaluating moral principles.

STUDY CORNER

KEY TERMS AND CONCEPTS

- administrative regulations
- argument
- business
- business ethics
- businesspeople
- bystander apathy
- common law
- conclusion
- conscience
- considered moral beliefs
- constitutional law
- counterexample
- diffusion of responsibility
- divine command theory
- ethical relativism
- ethics
- etiquette
- groupthink
- invalid argument
- moral arguments
- moral standards
- morality in the broad sense
- morality in the narrow sense
- organizational norms
- paradox of hedonism
- premises
- professional codes of ethics
- self-interest
- sound arguments
- statutes
- unsound arguments
- valid argument

POINTS TO REVIEW

- what happened at Enron (pp. 1–2)
- three characteristics of moral standards (p. 5)
- four types of law (p. 6)
- what King's violation of the law shows (p. 7)
- the point of the example of not stopping to help an accident victim (pp. 7–8)
- shortcomings of professional codes as an ethical guide (p. 9)
- where we get our moral standards (p. 9)
- three ways in which morality might be thought to be based on religion (p. 11)
- three unsatisfactory implications of ethical relativism (pp. 12–13)
- what's wrong with Carr's idea that business is a game with its own moral rules (pp. 13–14)
- what's involved in a person's accepting a moral principle (p. 14)
- why telling someone "Follow your conscience" isn't very helpful advice (p. 15)
- the point of the Huckleberry Finn example (pp. 15–16)
- what determines what a person will do when morality and self-interest collide (p. 17)
- morality in the broad sense vs. morality in the narrow sense (pp. 17–18)
- Aristotle and the ideal of achieving excellence (p. 18)
- what the experiments by Solomon Asch showed (pp. 20–21)
- dangers of groupthink (p. 21)
- diffusion of responsibility and the Kitty Genovese example (pp. 21–22)
- the difference between valid and invalid, sound and unsound, arguments (pp. 23–24)
- moral judgments as resting on moral standards and facts (p. 25)
- what it means to say moral judgments should be logical (p. 27)
- role of "considered moral beliefs" in the evaluation of moral principles (p. 28)

FOR FURTHER REFLECTION

1. To what extent do our moral ideas reflect the society around us, and to what extent are we free to think for ourselves about moral matters?
2. Describe a situation in which you felt pressured to act against your moral principles or where you felt torn between conflicting moral values, rules, or principles. What did you do?
3. How do you explain the fact that in the business world basically good people sometimes act immorally?

CASE 1.1

Made in the U.S.A.— Dumped in Brazil, Africa, Iraq . . .

WHEN IT COMES TO THE SAFETY OF YOUNG children, fire is a parent's nightmare. Just the thought of their young ones trapped in their cribs or beds by a raging nocturnal blaze is enough to make most mothers and fathers take every precaution to ensure their children's safety. Little wonder that when fire-retardant children's pajamas first hit the market, they proved an overnight success. Within a few short years more than 200 million pairs were sold, and the sales of millions more were all but guaranteed. For their manufacturers, the future could not have been brighter. Then, like a bolt from the blue, came word that the pajamas were killers. The U.S. Consumer Product Safety Commission (CPSC) moved quickly to ban their sale and recall millions of pairs. Reason: The pajamas contained the flame-retardant chemical Tris (2,3-dibromoprophyl), which had been found to cause kidney cancer in children.

Because of its toxicity, the sleepwear couldn't even be thrown away, let alone sold. Indeed, the CPSC left no doubt about how the pajamas were to be disposed of—buried or burned or used as industrial wiping cloths. Whereas just months earlier the manufacturers of the Tris-impregnated pajamas couldn't fill orders fast enough, suddenly they were worrying about how to get rid of the millions of pairs now sitting in warehouses.

Soon, however, ads began appearing in the classified pages of *Women's Wear Daily*. "Tris-Tris-Tris . . . We will buy any fabric containing Tris," read one. Another said, "Tris—we will purchase any large quantities of garments containing Tris." The ads had been placed by exporters, who began buying up the pajamas, usually at 10 to 30 percent of the normal wholesale price. Their intent was clear: to dump* the carcinogenic pajamas on overseas markets.[22]

Tris is not the only example of dumping. There were the 450,000 baby pacifiers, of the type known to have caused choking deaths, that were exported for sale overseas, and the 400 Iraqis who died and the 5,000 who were hospitalized after eating wheat and barley treated with a U.S.-banned organic mercury fungicide. Winstrol, a synthetic male hormone that had been found to stunt the growth of American children, was made available in Brazil as an appetite stimulant for children. DowElanco sold its weed killer Galant in Costa Rica, although the Environmental Protection Agency (EPA) forbade its sale to U.S. farmers because Galant may cause cancer. After the U.S. Food and Drug Administration (FDA) banned the painkiller dipyrone because it can cause a fatal blood disorder, Winthrop Products continued to sell dipyrone in Mexico City.

Manufacturers that dump products abroad clearly are motivated by profit, or at least by the hope of avoiding financial losses resulting from having to withdraw a product from the U.S. market. For government and health agencies that cooperate in the exporting of dangerous products, sometimes the motives are more complex.

For example, when researchers documented the dangers of the Dalkon Shield intrauterine device—among the adverse reactions were pelvic inflammation, blood poisoning, tubal pregnancies, and uterine perforations—its manufacturer, A. H.

Dumping is a term apparently coined by *Mother Jones* magazine to refer to the practice of exporting to other countries products that have been banned or declared hazardous in the United States.

Robins Co., began losing its domestic market. As a result, the company worked out a deal with the Office of Population within the U.S. Agency for International Development (AID), whereby AID bought thousands of the devices at a reduced price for use in population-control programs in forty-two countries.

The agencies involved say their motives are humanitarian. Because the death rate in childbirth is relatively high in third-world countries, almost any birth-control device is safer than pregnancy. Analogous arguments are used to defend the export of pesticides and other products judged too dangerous for use in the United States: Foreign countries should be free to decide for themselves whether the benefits of those products are worth their risks. In line with this, some third-world government officials insist that denying their countries access to these products is tantamount to violating their countries' national sovereignty.

This reasoning has found a sympathetic ear in Washington, for it turns up in the "notification" system that regulates the export of banned or dangerous products overseas. Based on the principles of national sovereignty, self-determination, and free trade, the notification system requires that foreign governments be notified whenever a product is banned, deregulated, suspended, or canceled by a U.S. regulatory agency. The State Department, which implements the system, has a policy statement on the subject that reads in part: "No country should establish itself as the arbiter of others' health and safety standards. Individual governments are generally in the best position to establish standards of public health and safety."

Critics of the system claim that notifying foreign health officials is virtually useless. For one thing, governments in poor countries can rarely establish health standards or even control imports into their countries. Indeed, most of the third-world countries where banned or dangerous products are dumped lack regulatory agencies, adequate testing facilities, and well-staffed customs departments.

Then there's the problem of getting the word out about hazardous products. In theory, when a government agency such as the EPA or the FDA finds a product hazardous, it is supposed to inform the State Department, which is to notify health officials

Another hazard dumped in third-world countries is what has become known as e-waste: toxic electronic products and parts.

in other nations. But agencies often fail to inform the State Department of the product they have banned or found harmful, and when it is notified, its communiqués typically go no further than U.S. embassies abroad. When foreign officials are notified by U.S. embassies, they sometimes find the communiqués vague or ambiguous or too technical to understand.

But even if communication procedures were improved or the export of dangerous products forbidden, there are ways that companies can circumvent these threats to their profits—for example, by simply changing the name of the product or by exporting the individual ingredients of a product to a plant in a foreign country. Once there, the ingredients can be reassembled and the product dumped. The United States does prohibit its pharmaceutical companies from exporting drugs banned in this country, but sidestepping the law is not difficult. "Unless the package bursts open on the dock," one drug company executive observes, "you have no chance of being caught."

Unfortunately for us, in the case of pesticides, the effects of overseas dumping are now coming home. In the United States, the EPA bans all crop uses of DDT and dieldrin, which kill fish, cause tumors in animals, and build up in the fatty tissue of humans. It also bans heptachlor, chlordane, leptophos, endrin, and many other pesticides, including 2,4,5-T (which contains the deadly poison dioxin, the active ingredient in Agent Orange, the notorious defoliant used in Vietnam) because they are dangerous to human beings. No law, however, prohibits the sale of DDT and these other U.S.-banned pesticides overseas, where thanks to corporate dumping they are routinely used in agriculture. In one three-month period, for example, U.S. chemical companies exported 3.9 million pounds of banned and withdrawn pesticides. The FDA now estimates, through spot checks, that 10 percent of our imported food is contaminated with residues of banned pesticides. And the FDA's most commonly used testing procedure does not even check for 70 percent of the pesticides known to cause cancer. With the doubling of exports of Mexican produce to the United States since the signing of the North American Free Trade Agreement (NAFTA), the problem of pesticide-laced food has only grown worse.[23]

Update

In 2013 researchers purchased 42 different types of foam furniture for children, including the popular Mickey Mouse couch, and found that all but four of them contained the toxic flame retardants that were banned years ago from children's pajamas—flame retardants that contain chemicals linked, not just to cancer, but also to diminished IQs and other problems. Although the chemical industry defends flame retardants as necessary to safeguard children, it turns out that they do not actually prevent fires. If you set a cushion on fire, it will burn right up.[24]

DISCUSSION QUESTIONS

1. Complete the following statements by filling in the blanks with either "moral" or "nonmoral" (e.g., factual, scientific, legal):
   a. Whether or not dumping should be permitted is a _____ question.
   b. "Are dangerous products of any use in the third world?" is a _____ question.
   c. "Is it proper for the U.S. government to sponsor the export of dangerous products overseas?" is a _____ question.
   d. Whether or not the notification system works as its supporters claim it works is a _____ question.
   e. "Is it legal to dump this product overseas?" is a _____ question.

2. Explain what dumping is, giving some examples. Does dumping raise any moral issues? What are they? What would an ethical relativist say about dumping?

3. Speculate on why dumpers dump. Do you think they believe that what they are doing is morally permissible? How would you look at the situation if you were one of the manufacturers of Tris-impregnated pajamas?

4. If no law is broken, is there anything wrong with dumping? If so, when is it wrong and why? Do any moral considerations support dumping products overseas when this violates U.S. law?

5. What moral difference, if any, does it make who is dumping, why they are doing it, where they are doing it, or what the product is?

6. Critically assess the present notification system. Is it the right approach, or is it fundamentally flawed?

7. Putting aside the question of legality, what moral arguments can be given *for* and *against* dumping? What is your position on dumping, and what principles and values do you base it on? Should we have laws prohibiting more types of dumping?

CASE 1.2

Just Drop off the Key, Lee

HINDSIGHT, THEY SAY, IS 20/20. So, in retrospect, it is not so surprising that the boom in real estate prices of just a few years ago was followed by a painful collapse. Encouraged by low interest rates and a willingness of banks to lend money to almost anybody, many people had jumped into the housing market, sometimes buying expensive homes with mortgages they could barely afford, based on the belief, celebrated in televisions shows like "Flip This House," that housing prices would continue to go up and up and up. But the law of gravity applies to housing prices, too, it seems. Inevitably, the housing market cooled down, and housing prices stopped rising; then they slowly reversed direction and began steadily declining. As a result, many people found themselves making mortgage payments on homes worth far less than what they had originally paid for them. Moreover, many of them had been talked into taking mortgages they didn't really understand, for example, mortgages with adjustable rates or with special "balloon" payments due after a few years, or that were too expensive for them to afford in the first place. The financial crisis of 2008 and the recession that followed only made things worse. Faced with monthly payments they could no longer sustain, these borrowers lost their homes through foreclosure. Widespread foreclosures, in turn, drove housing prices even lower, leaving more and more homeowners—by 2010 an estimated 5.4 million of them—"under water," that is, with mortgage balances at least 20 percent higher than the value of their homes.

Consider thirty-year-old software engineer, Derek Figg. He paid $340,000 for a home in the Phoenix suburbs. Two years later, its value had dropped to less than $230,000, but he still owed the bank $318,000. As a result, Figg decided to stop paying his mortgage, defaulted on his loan, and walked away from his home. Or consider Benjamin Koellmann. He paid $215,000 for an apartment in Miami Beach, which three years later was worth only $90,000. Although still paying his mortgage, he is thinking about following Figg's example.

What distinguishes Figg and Koellmann from many other homeowners whose homes are under water or who are in mortgage trouble is that both have good jobs and could afford to keep making their monthly payments—if they chose to. Moreover, they are smart guys and knew what they were doing, or thought they did, when they bought their homes. However, figuring that it would take years for their properties to regain their original value and that renting would be cheaper, they are among a growing number of homeowners who have either walked away from their mortgages or are considering it, not out of necessity, but because doing so is in their financial interest. Experts call this "strategic default." Or, in the words of an old Paul Simon song, "Just drop off the key, Lee, and get yourself free."

As any financial advisor will tell you, there are lots of good reasons not to default on a mortgage. A foreclosure ruins a consumer's credit record for seven years, and with a low credit score, one must pay a higher interest rate on auto and other loans. Moreover, some states allow lenders to seize bank deposits and other assets of people who default on mortgages. Benjamin Koellmann also worries that skipping out on his mortgage might hurt him with a future employer or diminish his chance of being admitted to graduate school. Still, there's no denying that for some borrowers simply mailing in the keys and walking away can make sense. But that leaves one question unanswered: Do they have a moral responsibility to meet their financial commitments?

The standard mortgage-loan document that a borrower signs says, "I promise to pay" the borrowed amount. A promise is a promise, many people believe; they think you should keep making your mortgage payments even if doing so is inconvenient. In fact, 81 percent of Americans agree that it is immoral not to pay your mortgage when you can. George Brenkert, professor of business ethics at Georgetown University, is one of them. He maintains that if you were not deceived by the lender about the nature of the loan, then you have a duty to keep paying. If everybody walked away from such commitments, he reasons, the result would be disastrous. As Paola Sapienza, a finance professor at Northwestern University, points out, each strategic default emboldens others to take the same step, which he describes as a "cascade effect" with potentially damaging consequences for the whole economy. Economist David Rosenburg adds that these borrowers were not victims. They "signed contracts, and as adults should be held accountable."

Others disagree. Brent White, a law professor at the University of Arizona, says that homeowners should base the decision whether to keep paying or walk away entirely on their own interests "unclouded by unnecessary guilt or shame." They should take their lead from the lenders, who, he says, "ruthlessly seek to maximize profits or minimize loss irrespective of concerns of morality or social responsibility." People who think like Professor White also argue that the banks fueled the housing boom in the first place by loaning money, based on unrealistic appraisals of home values, to people who were unlikely to be able to keep up their payments in order to resell those loans to other investors. Others suspect a double standard. Homeowners are criticized for defaulting but businesses often declare bankruptcy even when they have money in the bank and could keep paying their bills. In fact, doing so is often thought to be a smart move because it trims their debt load and allows them to break their union contracts.

Benjamin Koellmann, for his part, remains conflicted. "People like me are beginning to feel like suckers. Why not let it go in default and rent a better place for less? . . . There is no financial sense in staying." Still, he struggles with the ethical side of the question: "I took a loan on an asset that I didn't see as overvalued," he says. "As much as I would like my bank to pay for that mistake, why should it?" John Gourson, chief executive of the Mortgage Bankers Association, concurs with this. In addition, he says, defaulting on your mortgage and letting your home go into foreclosure hurts the whole neighborhood by lowering property values. He adds: "What about the message they still send to their family and their kids and their friends?"

For his part, Derek Figg admits that defaulting was the "toughest decision I ever made." Still, he faced a "claustrophobic situation," he says, because if ever he lost or quit his job, he would have been unable to sell his house and move somewhere else. Moreover, he says, lenders "manipulated" the housing market during the boom by accepting dubious appraisals. "When I weighed everything," he says, "I was able to sleep at night."[25]

....
DISCUSSION QUESTIONS
....

1. What would you do if you were in Figg's or Koellmann's situation? What factors would you consider?

2. Do people have a moral obligation to repay money that they borrow, as Professor Brenkert thinks, or is this simply a business decision based on self-interest alone, as Professor White thinks?

3. "It is morally permissible for homeowners whose homes are under water to default on their mortgages even if they could continue to pay them." What arguments do you see in favor of this proposition? What arguments do you see against it?

4. When it comes to paying your debts, does it matter whether you borrow money from a bank or from an individual person? Explain why or why not.

5. Suppose your moral principles imply that you should keep on paying your mortgage, but financial self-interest counsels you to walk away. How are you to decide what to do?

6. Repaying a loan is a legal obligation. Is it also a moral obligation? Explain why or why not.

7. Are the banks responsible for the housing boom that enticed people to buy homes at inflated prices? If so, does this affect whether you have an obligation to repay your loan? What about Professor White's contention that the banks themselves care only about maximizing profit?

Percentages	2005	2006	2007	2008	2009	2010	2011	2012	2013
Below 1%	X								
From 1% to 2%		X	X						
From 2% to 3%									X
From 3% to 4%				X			X	X	
From 4% to 5%					X	X			

U.S. foreclosure rates in recent years, in percentages

CASE 1.3

The A7D Affair

KERMIT VANDIVIER COULD NOT HAVE PREDICTED the impact on his life of purchase order P-237138, issued by LTV Aerospace Corporation.[26] The order was for 202 brake assemblies for a new Air Force light attack plane, the A7D, and news of the LTV contract was cause for uncorking the champagne at the B. F. Goodrich plant in Troy, Ohio, where Vandivier worked. Although the LTV order was a small one, it signaled that Goodrich was back in LTV's good graces after living under a cloud of disrepute. Ten years earlier, Goodrich had built a brake for LTV that, to put it kindly, hadn't met expectations. As a result, LTV had written off Goodrich as a reliable source of brakes.

LTV's unexpected change of heart after ten years was easily explained. Goodrich made LTV an offer it couldn't refuse—a ridiculously low bid for making the four-disk brakes. Had Goodrich taken leave of its financial senses? Hardly. Because aircraft brakes are custom-made for a particular aircraft, only the brakes' manufacturer has replacement parts. Thus, even if it took a loss on the job, Goodrich figured it could more than make up for it in the sale of replacement parts. Of course, if Goodrich bungled the job, there wouldn't be a third chance.

John Warren, a seven-year veteran and one of Goodrich's most capable engineers, was made project engineer and lost no time in working up a preliminary design for the brake. Perhaps because the design was faultless or perhaps because Warren was given to temper tantrums when criticized, co-workers accepted the engineer's plan without question. So there was no reason to suspect that young Searle Lawson, one year out of college and six months with Goodrich, would come to think Warren's design was fundamentally flawed.

Lawson was assigned by Warren to create the final production design. He had to determine the best materials for brake linings and identify any needed adjustments in the brake design. This process called for extensive testing to meet military specifications. If the brakes passed the grueling tests, they would then be flight-tested by the Air Force. Lawson lost no time in getting down to work. What he particularly wanted to learn was whether the brake could withstand the extreme internal temperatures, in excess of 1,000 degrees F, when the aircraft landed.

When the brake linings disintegrated in the first test, Lawson thought the problem might be defective parts or an unsuitable lining. But after two more consecutive failures, he decided the problem lay in the design: The four-disk design was simply too small to stop the aircraft without generating so much heat that the brake linings melted. In Lawson's view, a larger, five-disk brake was needed.

Lawson knew well the implications of his conclusion. The four-disk brake assemblies that were arriving at the plant would have to be junked, and more tests would have to be conducted. The accompanying delays would preclude on-time delivery of the production brakes to LTV.

Lawson reported his findings and recommendations to John Warren. Going to a five-disk design was impossible, Warren told him. Officials at Goodrich, he said, were already boasting to LTV about how well the tests were going. Besides, Warren was confident that the problem lay not in the four-disk design but in the brake linings themselves.

Unconvinced, Lawson went to Robert Sink, who supervised engineers on projects. Sink was in a tight spot. If he agreed with Lawson, he would be indicting his own professional judgment: He was the man who had assigned Warren to the job. What's more, he had accepted Warren's design without reservation and had assured LTV more than once that there was little left to do but ship them the brakes. To recant now would mean explaining the reversal not only to LTV but also to the Goodrich hierarchy. In the end, Sink, who was not an engineer, deferred to the seasoned judgment of Warren and instructed Lawson to continue the tests.

His own professional judgment overridden, Lawson could do little but carry on. He built a production model of the brake with new linings and subjected it to the rigorous qualification tests. Thirteen more tests were conducted, and thirteen more failures resulted. It was at this point that data analyst and technical writer Kermit Vandivier entered the picture.

Vandivier was looking over the data of the latest A7D test when he noticed an irregularity: The instrument recording some of the stops had been deliberately miscalibrated to indicate that less pressure was required to stop the aircraft than actually was the case. Vandivier immediately showed the test logs to test lab supervisor Ralph Gretzinger. He learned from the technician who miscalibrated the instrument that Lawson had requested the miscalibration. Lawson later said he was simply following the orders of Sink and the manager of the design engineering section, who were intent on qualifying the brakes at whatever cost. For his part, Gretzinger vowed he would never permit deliberately falsified data or reports to leave his lab.

A month later, the brake was again tested, and again it failed. Nevertheless, Lawson asked Vandivier to start preparing the various graph and chart displays for qualification. Vandivier refused and told Gretzinger what he'd been asked to do. Gretzinger was livid. He again vowed that his lab would not be part of a conspiracy to defraud. Then, bent on getting to the bottom of the matter, Gretzinger rushed off to see Russell Line, manager of the Goodrich Technical Services Section.

An hour later, Gretzinger returned to his desk looking like a beaten man. He knew he had only two choices: defy his superiors or do their bidding.

"You know," he said to Vandivier, "I've been an engineer for a long time, and I've always believed that ethics and integrity were every bit as important as theorems and formulas, and never once has anything happened to change my beliefs. Now this. . . . Hell, I've got two sons I've got to put through school and I just . . ." When his voice trailed off, it was clear that he would in fact knuckle under. He and Vandivier would prepare the qualifying data; then someone "upstairs" would actually write the report. Their part, Gretzinger rationalized, wasn't really so bad. "After all," he said, "we're just drawing some curves, and what happens to them after they leave here—well, we're not responsible for that." Vandivier knew Gretzinger didn't believe what he was saying about not being responsible. Both of them knew that they were about to become principal characters in a plot to defraud.

Unwilling to play his part, Vandivier decided that he, too, would confer with Line. Line was sympathetic; he said he understood what Vandivier was going through. But in the end he said he would not refer the matter to chief engineer H. C. "Bud" Sunderman, as Vandivier had suggested. Why not? Vandivier wanted to know.

"Because it's none of my business, and it's none of yours," Line told him. "I learned a long time ago not to worry about things over which I had no control. I have no control over this."

Vandivier pressed the point. What about the test pilots who might get injured because of the faulty brakes? Didn't their uncertain fate prick Line's conscience?

"Look," said Line, growing impatient with Vandivier's moral needling, "I just told you I have no control over this thing. Why should my conscience bother me?" Then he added, "You're just getting all upset over this thing for nothing. I just do as I'm told, and I'd advise you to do the same."

Vandivier made his decision that night. He knew, of course, he was on the horns of a dilemma. If he wrote the report, he would save his job at the expense of his conscience. If he refused, he would honor his moral code and, he was convinced, lose his job—an ugly prospect for anyone, let alone a forty-two-year-old man with a wife and several children. The next day, Vandivier phoned Lawson and told him he was ready to begin on the qualification report.

Lawson shot over to Vandivier's office with all the speed of one who knows that, swallowed fast, a bitter pill doesn't taste so bad. Before they started on the report, though, Vandivier, still uneasy with his decision, asked Lawson if he fully understood what they were about to do.

"Yeah," Lawson said acidly, "we're going to screw LTV. And speaking of screwing," he continued, "I know now how a whore feels, because that's exactly what I've become, an engineering whore. I've sold myself. It's all I can do to look at myself in the mirror when I shave. I make me sick."

For someone like Vandivier, who had written dozens of them, the qualification report was a snap. It took about a month, during which time the brake failed still another final qualification test, and the two men talked almost exclusively about the enormity of what they were doing. In the Nuremberg trials they found a historical analogy to their own complicity and culpability in the A7D affair. More than once, Lawson opined that the brakes were downright dangerous, that anything could happen during the flight tests. His opinion proved prophetic.

When the report was finished, copies were sent to the Air Force and LTV. Within a week test flights were begun at Edwards Air Force Base in California. Goodrich dispatched Lawson to Edwards as its representative, but he wasn't there long. Several "unusual incidents" brought the flight tests literally to a screeching halt. Lawson returned to the Troy plant, full of talk about several near crashes caused by brake trouble during landings. That was enough to send Vandivier to his attorney, to whom he told the whole sorry tale.

Although the attorney didn't think Vandivier was guilty of fraud, he was convinced that the analyst/writer was guilty of participating in a conspiracy to defraud. Vandivier's only hope, the attorney counseled, was to make a clean breast of the matter to the FBI. Vandivier did. At this point both he and Lawson decided to resign from Goodrich. In his letter of resignation, addressed to Russell Line, Vandivier cited the A7D report and stated: "As you are aware, this report contains numerous deliberate and willful misrepresentations which . . . expose both myself and others to criminal charges of conspiracy to defraud."

Vandivier was soon summoned to the office of Bud Sunderman, who berated him mercilessly. Among other things, Sunderman accused Vandivier of making irresponsible charges and of arch disloyalty. It would be best, said Sunderman, if Vandivier cleared out immediately. Within minutes, Vandivier had cleaned out his desk and left the plant.

Two days later Goodrich announced it was recalling the qualification report and replacing the old brake with a new five-disk brake at no cost to LTV.

Aftermath

- A year later, a congressional committee reviewed the A7D affair. Vandivier and Lawson testified as government witnesses, together with Air Force officers and a General Accounting Office team. All testified that the brake was dangerous.
- Robert Sink, representing the Troy plant, depicted Vandivier as a mere high school graduate with no technical training, who preferred to follow his own lights rather than organizational guidance. R. G. Jeter, vice president and general counsel of Goodrich, dismissed as ludicrous even the possibility that some thirty engineers at the Troy plant would stand idly by and see reports changed and falsified.
- The congressional committee adjourned after four hours with no real conclusion. The following day the Department of Defense, citing the A7D episode, made major changes in its inspection, testing, and reporting procedures.
- The A7D eventually went into service with the Goodrich-made five-disk brake.
- Searle Lawson went to work as an engineer for LTV assigned to the A7D project.
- Russell Line was promoted to production superintendent.
- Robert Sink moved up into Line's old job.
- Kermit Vandivier became a newspaper reporter for the *Daily News* in Troy, Ohio.

DISCUSSION QUESTIONS

1. Identify the main characters in this case, and explain what happened.
2. To what extent did Lawson, Vandivier, and Gretzinger consider the relevant moral issues before deciding to participate in the fraud? What was their reasoning? What would you have done if you were in their situation?
3. How did Sink and Line look at the matter? How would you evaluate their conduct?
4. Do you think Vandivier was wrong to work up the qualification report? Explain the moral principle or principles that underlie your judgment.
5. Was Vandivier right to "blow the whistle"? Was he morally required to so? Again, explain the moral principles on which your judgment is based.
6. Describe the different pressures to conform in this case and discuss the relevance of the concepts of groupthink and diffusion of responsibility. Do any of these factors excuse the conduct of particular individuals in this case? If so, who and why?
7. Should Goodrich be held morally responsible as a company for the A7D affair, or just the individuals involved?
8. What might Goodrich have done, and what steps should it take in the future, to ensure more moral behavior?

CHAPTER 2
NORMATIVE THEORIES OF ETHICS

INTRODUCTION

HEAD OF A PREMIER HEDGE FUND AND FORMER president of the NASDAQ stock exchange, Bernard Madoff was a respected financier with a sterling reputation. So, when he stated in a speech that "in today's regulatory environment, it's virtually impossible [for fund managers] to violate the rules," his listeners were unlikely to have doubted the truth of what he was saying. They were even less likely to have foreseen how eerily prophetic his words would turn out to be when the FBI arrested him a year later for perpetrating what may have been the greatest scam of all time.

Madoff's celebrated hedge fund, it turns out, was a total fraud—in essence, a gigantic Ponzi scheme. In a Ponzi scheme, a con artist takes in money from investors but keeps it for himself rather than investing it as promised. On paper, the profits of the investors continue to grow. If they want to redeem some of their fund shares for cash, the fraudster uses money from new investors to pay them. This keeps investors happy and content but clueless about what really happened to their money.

The fact that Madoff's phony hedge fund reported consistently strong returns in both good and bad markets, with never a down quarter, made a few financial analysts suspicious. However, the law doesn't require hedge funds to operate as transparently as it does mutual funds, and Madoff was notoriously secretive about his investment strategy. The Securities and Exchange Commission, which is charged with policing the financial marketplace, never noticed anything amiss, and most business observers and investment advisors simply thought that Madoff had the Midas touch. And so it seemed he did—until, that is, the financial crisis of 2008 when the meltdown on Wall Street led more and more of his investors to seek to redeem fund shares for cash. With new investors now few and far between, Madoff simply had no money to pay those investors who wanted to cash in some or all of their chips. Unable to keep the game up, he confessed to his sons that his fund was "one big lie." They promptly turned him in to the authorities.

> MADOFF'S celebrated hedge fund, it turns out, was a total fraud—in essence, a gigantic Ponzi scheme.

Madoff's victims included insurance companies, pension and investment funds, banks in Europe and Asia, and a number of prominent individuals, such as Hall of Fame baseball pitcher Sandy Koufax, filmmaker Steven Spielberg, and actors Kevin Bacon and John Malkovich. Many of these people were bilked for millions and millions of dollars, in some cases losing nearly all their savings. Likewise, some of the charities that had invested with Madoff were completely ruined. Having lost their assets, they were forced to shut down. A few investors, however, who had withdrawn money from their accounts on and off over the years, ended up in an ethical quandary. The money that they thought was in their Madoff accounts was, of course, gone, but over the years they had actually taken more money out of the fund, sometimes substantially more money, than they had initially put into it. But what they thought at the time to be legitimate profit was, they now realized, almost certainly money that Madoff had stolen from other clients. Should they keep quiet? Should they return the money to other investors, most of whom had ended up deep in the hole? Or should they insist that the money they received was legitimately theirs and push (along with all the other investors) to somehow get restitution of the balances that just a few weeks before they had assumed still remained in their Madoff accounts?

Under legal pressure, Boston philanthropist Carl Shapiro, an early investor with Madoff, agreed to hand over to other victims the $625 million he had received over the years from Madoff. Trustees representing Madoff's victims also sued Fred Wilpon and Saul Katz, the successful investors who own the New York Mets, on the grounds that they should have known that the $300 million they had earned from their Madoff accounts were "fictitious profits." The suit was settled in 2012 for about half that sum. As a general matter, though, the legal responsibilities of those Madoff investors who came out ahead are unclear; a number of legal battles are being waged, and some in Congress want to protect the profits of innocent Madoff investors. In addition, of course, it's unclear where any individual investor's money actually went. But it's not just factual or legal complexities that make the question difficult. There are competing moral considerations. If you yourself were scammed, it might seem that you have no moral obligation to help those whose losses were greater—after all, you were a victim, too. On the other hand, although Madoff was ostensibly paying you money that you were entitled to, you were, in fact, receiving embezzled funds. Do those later investors have a right to get their money back from you? Would you act wrongly in hanging on to what you were lucky enough to get from Madoff before his scheme crashed? Or are the Madoff investors morally required to pool their gains and try to equalize their losses?

You don't need to study moral philosophy to see that Madoff acted immorally. Only a complete scoundrel steals from charities, pension funds, and friends and acquaintances who have entrusted him with their life savings. In contrast, it is not easy to know what an investor should do, who got back from Madoff more than other investors did—perhaps even more than his or her initial investment. Even if the person wants to do the right thing, what exactly does morality require, and how are we to determine what that is? On what basis are we to judge what is right or wrong?

Chapter 1 explained that defensible moral judgments must be underwritten by sound moral principles. That is because when we judge something wrong, we are not judging simply that it is wrong but also that it is wrong for some reason or by virtue of some general characteristic.[1] Moral principles thus provide the basis for making moral judgments. The use of these principles, however, is not a mechanical process by which one cranks in data and out pops an automatic moral judgment. Rather, the principles provide a conceptual framework that guides us in making moral decisions. Careful thought and open-minded reflection are always necessary to work from one's moral principles to a considered moral judgment.

But what are the appropriate principles to rely on when making moral judgments? The truth is that there is no consensus among people who have studied ethics and reflected on these matters. Different theories exist as to the proper standard of right and wrong. As the British philosopher Bernard Williams put it, we are

In the 1920s, con artist Charles Ponzi told gullible investors that he could double their money in 90 days by buying postage reply coupons in other countries and redeeming them at the U.S. Post Office. In fact, he kept their money and paid early investors with money coming in from later investors.

heirs to a rich and complex ethical tradition, in which a variety of different moral principles and ethical considerations intertwine and sometimes compete.²

LEARNING OBJECTIVES

This chapter discusses the different normative perspectives and rival ethical principles that are our heritage. After distinguishing between what are called "consequentialist" and "nonconsequentialist" normative theories, it looks in detail at several ethical approaches, discussing their pros and cons and their relevance to moral decision making in an organizational context:

1. Egoism, both as an ethical theory and as a psychological theory
2. Utilitarianism, the theory that the morally right action is the one that achieves the most happiness for everyone concerned
3. Kant's ethics, with his categorical imperative and his emphasis on moral motivation and respect for persons
4. Other nonconsequentialist normative themes: duties, moral rights, and prima facie principles

The chapter concludes by suggesting a practical way of approaching moral decision making, which reflects the major concerns of the different normative theories that have been discussed.

CONSEQUENTIALIST AND NONCONSEQUENTIALIST THEORIES

In ethics, **normative theories** propose some principle or principles for distinguishing right actions from wrong actions. These theories can, for convenience, be divided into two kinds: consequentialist and nonconsequentialist.

According to **consequentialist theories**, the moral rightness of an action is determined solely by its results. If its consequences are good, then the act is right; if they are bad, the act is wrong. Consequentialists (moral theorists who adopt this approach) determine what is right by weighing the ratio of good to bad that an action will produce. The right act is the one that produces (or will probably produce) at least as great a ratio of good to evil as any other course of action open to the agent.

One question that arises here is: Consequences for whom? Should one consider the consequences only for oneself? Or the consequences for everyone affected? The two most important consequentialist theories, *egoism* and *utilitarianism*, are distinguished by their different answers to this question. Egoism advocates individual self-interest as its guiding principle. Utilitarianism holds that one must take into account everyone affected by the action. But both theories agree that rightness and wrongness are solely a function of an action's results.

By contrast, **nonconsequentialist** (or *deontological*) **theories** contend that right and wrong are determined by more than the likely consequences of an action. Nonconsequentialists do not necessarily deny that consequences are morally significant, but they believe that other factors are also relevant to the moral assessment of an action. For example, a nonconsequentialist would hold that for Kevin to break his promise to Cindy is wrong not simply because it has bad results (Cindy's hurt feelings, Kevin's damaged reputation, and so on) but because of the inherent character of the act itself. Even if more good than bad were to come from Kevin's breaking the promise, a nonconsequentialist might still view it as wrong. What matters is the nature of the act in question, not just its results. This idea will become clearer later in the chapter as we examine some specific nonconsequentialist principles and theories.

SUMMARY

Consequentialist moral theories see the moral rightness or wrongness of actions as a function of their results. If the consequences are good, the action is right; if they are bad, the action is wrong. Nonconsequentialist theories see other factors as also relevant to the determination of right and wrong.

EGOISM

A few years after Firestone first introduced its "500" steel-belted radial tires, it was discovered that their tread was prone to separate at high speeds, with a House subcommittee later concluding that the tires had led to thirty-four highway deaths. In response to the controversy, Firestone announced that it was discontinuing the "500." Newspapers at the time interpreted this to mean that Firestone would immediately remove the tires from the market. In fact, Firestone intended only a "rolling phaseout" and continued to manufacture the tire. When a Firestone spokesperson was later asked why the company had not corrected the media's misinterpretation of its intent, the spokesperson said that Firestone's policy was to ask for corrections only when it was beneficial to the company to do so—in other words, only when it was in the company's self-interest.

The view that equates morality with self-interest is referred to as **egoism**. According to it, an act is morally right if and only if it best promotes the agent's own interests. (Here an "agent" can be a single person or, as in the Firestone example, an organization.) Egoism makes personal advantage (both in the short term and the long run) the standard for measuring an action's rightness. If an action will produce more good for the agent than any alternative action would, then that action is the morally right one to perform.

Moral philosophers distinguish between two kinds of egoism: personal and impersonal. *Personal* egoists claim they should pursue their own best interests, but they do not say what others should do. *Impersonal* egoists claim that everyone should let self-interest guide his or her conduct.

MISCONCEPTIONS ABOUT EGOISM

Several misconceptions haunt both versions of egoism. One is that egoists do only what they like, that they believe in "eat, drink, and be merry." Not so. Undergoing unpleasant, even painful experience meshes with egoism, provided such temporary sacrifice is necessary for the advancement of one's long-term interests.

Another misconception is that all egoists endorse **hedonism**, the view that pleasure (or happiness) is the only thing that is good in itself, that it is the ultimate good, the one thing in life worth pursuing for its own sake. Although some egoists are hedonistic—as was the ancient Greek philosopher Epicurus (341–270 BCE)—other egoists have a broader view of what constitutes self-interest. Some of them identify a person's good with knowledge or power; others with what some modern psychologists call "self-actualization." Egoists may, in fact, hold any theory of what is good.

A final but very important misconception is that egoists cannot act honestly, be gracious and helpful, or otherwise promote other people's interests. Egoism, however, requires us to do whatever will best further our own interests, and doing this sometimes requires us to advance the interests of others. In particular, egoism tells us to benefit others when we expect that our doing so will be reciprocated or when the act will bring us pleasure or in some way promote our own good. For example, egoism might discourage a shopkeeper from trying to cheat customers because it is likely to hurt business in the long run. Or egoism might recommend to the chair of the board that she hire as a vice president her nephew, who is not the best candidate for the job but of whom she is very fond. Hiring the nephew might bring her more satisfaction than any other course of action, even if the nephew doesn't perform his job as well as someone else might.

PSYCHOLOGICAL EGOISM

According to egoism, we should assist others when doing so best promotes our own interests.

So egoism does not preach that we should never assist others but rather that we have no basic moral duty to do so. The only moral obligation we have is to ourselves. Although you and I are not required to act in the interests of others, we should if that is the best way to promote our own self-interest. In short: Always look out for "number one."

Proponents of the ethical theory of egoism generally attempt to derive their basic moral principle from the alleged fact that human beings are by nature selfish creatures. According to this doctrine, termed **psychological egoism**, people are, as a matter of fact, so constructed that they must behave selfishly. Psychological egoism asserts that all actions are selfishly motivated and that truly unselfish actions are therefore impossible. Even apparently self-sacrificial acts such as giving up one's own life to save the lives of one's children or blowing the whistle on organizational misdeeds at great personal expense are, according to psychological egoism, done to satisfy the person's own self-interested desires. For example, the parent may seek to perpetuate the family line or to avoid guilt, and the employee may be after fame or revenge.

PROBLEMS WITH EGOISM

There are strong objections to egoism as an ethical doctrine.

Although egoism as an ethical doctrine has always had its adherents, the theory is open to very strong objections. It is safe to say that few, if any, philosophers today would advocate it as either a personal or an organizational morality. Consider these objections:

1. **Psychological egoism is not a sound theory.** Self-interest motivates all of us to some extent, and we all know of situations in which someone pretended to be acting altruistically or morally but was really motivated only by self-interest. The theory of psychological egoism contends, however, that self-interest is the only thing that ever motivates anyone.

    This contention seems vulnerable to various counterexamples. Take the actual case of a man who, while driving a company truck, spotted smoke coming from inside a parked car and a child trying to escape from the vehicle. The man quickly made a U-turn, drove up to the burning vehicle, and found a little girl trapped in the back seat, restrained by a seat belt. Flames raged in the front seat as heavy smoke billowed from the car. Disregarding his own safety, the man entered the car and removed the child, who would otherwise have died from the flames and poisonous fumes. When the police and rescue workers arrived, he quietly slipped away.

    Or take a more mundane example. It's Saturday, and you feel like having a beer with a couple of pals and watching the ball game. On the other hand, you believe that you ought to take your two children to the zoo, as you earlier suggested to them you might. Going to the zoo would bring them a lot of pleasure—and besides, you haven't done much with them recently. Of course, you love your children, and it will bring you some pleasure to go to the zoo with them, but—let's face it—they've been rather whiny lately and you'd prefer to watch the ball game. Nonetheless, you feel an obligation and so you go to the zoo.

    These appear to be cases in which people are acting for reasons that are not self-interested. Of course, the reasons that lead you to take your children to the zoo—a sense of obligation, a desire to promote their happiness—are your reasons, but that by itself does not make them self-interested reasons. Still less does it show that you are selfish. Anything that you do is a result of your desires, but that fact doesn't establish what the believer in psychological egoism claims—namely, that the only desires you have, or the only desires that ultimately move you, are self-interested desires.

Proponents of the theory of psychological egoism will claim that deep down both the heroic man who saved the little girl and the unheroic parent who took the children to the zoo were really motivated by self-interest in some way or another. Maybe the hero was hoping to win praise or the parent to avoid criticism or outshine his or her spouse. Or maybe some other self-interested consideration motivated them. Adherents of psychological egoism can always claim that some yet-to-be-identified subconscious egoistic motivation is the main impulse behind any action.

At this point, though, psychological egoism sounds a little far-fetched, and we may suspect its advocates of trying to make their theory true by definition. Whatever example we come up with, they will simply claim that, contrary to appearances, somehow or other the person is really motivated only by self-interest. One may well wonder how scientific this theory is, or how much content it has, when the hero and the coward, the parent who goes to the zoo and the parent who stays home, are equally selfish in their motivations.

A defender of egoism as an ethical doctrine could concede that people are not fully egoistic by nature and yet continue to insist that morally people ought to pursue only their own interests. Yet without the doctrine of psychological egoism, the ethical thesis of egoism becomes less attractive. Other types of ethical principles are possible. We all care about ourselves, but how much sense does it make to see self-interest as the basis of right and wrong? Do we really want to say that someone acting altruistically is behaving immorally?

2. **Ethical egoism is not really a moral principle at all.** Many critics of egoism as an ethical standard contend that it misunderstands the nature and point of morality. As Chapter 1 explained, morality serves to restrain our purely self-interested desires so we can all live together. If our interests never came into conflict—that is, if it were never advantageous for one person to deceive or cheat another—then we would have no need for morality. The moral standards of a society provide the basic guidelines for cooperative social existence and allow us to resolve conflicts by appeal to shared principles of justification.

It is difficult to see how ethical egoism could perform this function. In a society of egoists, people might publicly agree to follow certain rules so their lives would run more smoothly. But it would be a very unstable world, because people would not hesitate to break the rules if they thought they could get away with it. Nor can egoism provide a means for settling conflicts and disputes, because it simply tells each party to do whatever is necessary to promote effectively his or her interests.

Many moral theorists maintain that moral principles apply equally to the conduct of all persons and that their application requires us to be objective and impartial. Moral agents are seen as those who, despite their own involvement in an issue, can be reasonably disinterested and objective—those who try to see all sides of an issue without being committed to the interests of a particular individual or group, including themselves. If we accept this attitude of detachment and impartiality as at least part of what it means to take a moral point of view, then we must look for it in any proposed moral principle.

Those who make egoism their moral standard are anything but objective, for they seek to guide themselves by their own best interests, regardless of the issue or circumstances. They do not even attempt to be impartial, except insofar as impartiality furthers their own interests. And, according to their theory, any third party offering advice should simply represent his or her own interest.

> **SUMMARY**
> Egoism is the consequentialist theory that an action is right if and only if it promotes the individual's best interests. Proponents of this theory base their view on the alleged fact that human beings are, by nature, selfish (the doctrine of psychological egoism). Critics of egoism argue that (1) psychological egoism is implausible, (2) egoism is not really a moral principle, and (3) egoism condones blatant wrongs.

3. **Ethical egoism condones blatant wrongs.** The most common objection to egoism as an ethical doctrine is that it sometimes condones actions that are blatantly immoral. Deception, theft, or even murder can be morally right according to the standard of egoism, if it advances the agent's self-interest (and the agent can get away with it).

   In response, the defender of egoism might argue that this objection begs the question by assuming that such acts are immoral and then repudiating egoism on this basis when, in fact, their morality is the very issue that moral principles such as egoism are meant to resolve. Still, egoism fails to do justice to some of our basic ideas about right and wrong. A moral principle that permits murder, if it successfully advances one's self-interest, clashes with our firmest moral convictions. If anything is wrong, that is wrong.

UTILITARIANISM

> Utilitarianism tells us to bring about the most happiness for everyone affected by our actions.
>
> Jeremy Bentham and John Stuart Mill were important early utilitarians.

Utilitarianism is the moral doctrine that we should always act to produce the greatest possible balance of good over bad for everyone affected by our actions. By "good," utilitarians understand happiness or pleasure. Thus, the greatest happiness of all constitutes the standard that determines whether an action is right or wrong. Although the basic theme of utilitarianism is present in the writings of many earlier thinkers, Jeremy Bentham (1748–1832) and John Stuart Mill (1806–1873) were the first to develop the theory explicitly and in detail. Both Bentham and Mill were philosophers with a strong interest in legal and social reform. They used the utilitarian standard to evaluate and criticize the social and political institutions of their day—for example, the prison system and the disenfranchisement of women. As a result, utilitarianism has long been associated with social improvement.

Bentham viewed a community as no more than the individual persons that it comprises. The interests of the community are simply the sum of the interests of its members. An action promotes the interests of an individual when it adds to the individual's pleasure or diminishes the person's pain. Correspondingly, an action augments the happiness of a community only insofar as it increases the total amount of individual happiness. This is what Bentham had in mind when he argued for the utilitarian principle that actions are right if they promote the greatest human welfare, wrong if they do not.

For Bentham, pleasure and pain are merely types of sensations. He offered a "hedonic calculus" of six criteria for evaluating pleasure and pain exclusively by their quantitative differences—in particular, by their intensity and duration. This calculus, he believed, makes possible an objective determination of the morality of anyone's conduct, individual or collective, on any occasion.

Bentham rejected any distinctions based on the type of pleasure except insofar as they might indicate differences in quantity. Thus, if equal amounts of pleasure are involved, throwing darts is as good as writing poetry and baking a cake as good as composing a symphony; watching Shakespeare's *Hamlet* has no more value than watching *Jersey Shore*. Although he himself was an intelligent, cultivated man, Bentham maintained that there is nothing intrinsically better about refined and intellectual pleasures than about crude or prosaic ones. The only issue is which yields the greater amount of enjoyment.

John Stuart Mill thought Bentham's concept of pleasure was too simple. He viewed human beings as having elevated faculties that allow them to pursue various higher kinds of pleasure. The pleasures of the intellect and imagination, in particular, have a higher value than those of mere physical sensation. Thus, for Mill the utility principle must take into consideration the relative quality of different pleasures and pains, not just their intensity and duration.

Although Bentham and Mill had different conceptions of pleasure, both men equated pleasure and happiness and considered pleasure the ultimate value. In this sense they are hedonists: Pleasure, in their view, is the one thing that is intrinsically good or worthwhile. Anything that is good is good only because it brings about pleasure (or happiness), directly or indirectly. Take education, for example. The learning process itself might be pleasurable to us; reflecting on or working with what we have learned might bring us satisfaction at some later time; or by making possible a career and life that we could not have had otherwise, education might bring us happiness indirectly. In contrast, critics of Bentham and Mill contend that things other than happiness are also inherently good—for example, knowledge, friendship, and aesthetic satisfaction. The implication is that these things are valuable even if they do not lead to happiness.

Bentham and Mill had different conceptions of pleasure, but they both equated it with happiness and believed that pleasure was the ultimate value.

Bentham and Mill cared about happiness because they implicitly identified it with well-being, that is, with what is good for people. In their view, our lives go well—we have well-being—just to the extent that our lives are pleasurable or happy. Some moral theorists have modified utilitarianism so that it aims at other consequences in addition to happiness. And some utilitarians, wary of trying to compare one person's happiness with another's, have interpreted their theory as requiring us not to maximize happiness but rather to maximize the satisfaction of people's desires or preferences. The focus here will be utilitarianism in its standard form, in which the good to be aimed at is human happiness or well-being, but what will be said about standard or classical utilitarianism applies, with the appropriate modifications, to other versions as well.

Although this chapter will later consider another form of utilitarianism, known as "rule utilitarianism," utilitarianism in its most basic version, often called **act utilitarianism**, states that we must ask ourselves what the consequences of a particular act in a particular situation will be for all those affected. If its consequences bring more net good than those of any alternative course of action, then this action is the right one and the one we should perform.

SIX POINTS ABOUT UTILITARIANISM

Before evaluating utilitarianism, one should understand some points that might lead to confusion and misapplication. *First*, when deciding which action will produce the greatest happiness, we must consider unhappiness or pain as well as happiness. Suppose, for example, that an action produces eight units of happiness and four units of unhappiness. Its net worth is four units of happiness. Suppose also that an opposed action produces ten units of happiness and seven units of unhappiness; its net worth is three units. In this case we should choose the first action over the second. In the event that both lead not to happiness but to unhappiness, and there is no third option, we should choose the one that brings fewer units of unhappiness.

Six important things to understand about utilitarianism.

Second, actions affect people to different degrees. Playing your radio loudly might enhance two persons' pleasure a little, cause significant discomfort to two others, and leave a fifth person indifferent. The utilitarian theory is not that each person votes on the basis of his or her pleasure or pain, with the majority ruling, but rather that we add up the various pleasures and pains, however large or small, and go with the action that brings about the greatest net amount of happiness.

Third, because utilitarians evaluate actions according to their consequences and because actions produce different results in different circumstances, almost anything

> **SUMMARY**
> Utilitarianism, another consequentialist theory, maintains that the morally right action is the one that provides the most happiness for all those affected. After assessing as best we can the likely results of each action, not just in the short term but in the long run as well, we are to choose the course of conduct that brings about the greatest net happiness.

might, in principle, be morally right in some particular situation. For example, whereas breaking a promise generally produces unhappiness, there can be circumstances in which, on balance, more happiness would be produced by breaking a promise than by keeping it. In those cases, utilitarianism would require us to break the promise.

Fourth, utilitarians wish to maximize happiness not simply immediately but in the long run as well. All the indirect ramifications of an act have to be taken into account. Lying might seem a good way out of a tough situation, but if and when the people we deceive find out, not only will they be unhappy, but also our reputations and our relationships with them will be damaged. This is a serious risk that a utilitarian cannot ignore.

Fifth, utilitarians acknowledge that we often do not know with certainty what the future consequences of our actions will be. Accordingly, we must act so that the expected or likely happiness is as great as possible. If I take my friend's money, unbeknownst to him, and buy lottery tickets with it, there is a chance that we will end up millionaires and that my action will have maximized happiness all around. But the odds are definitely against it; the most likely result is loss of money (and probably of a friendship, too). Therefore, no utilitarian could justify gambling with purloined funds on the grounds that it might maximize happiness.

Sometimes it is difficult to determine the likely results of alternative actions, and no modern utilitarian really believes that we can assign precise units of happiness and unhappiness to people. But as Mill reminds us, we actually do have quite a lot of experience as to what typically makes people happy or unhappy. In any case, as utilitarians our duty is to strive to maximize total happiness, even when it is difficult to know which action will produce the most good.

Finally, when choosing among possible actions, utilitarianism does not require us to disregard our own pleasure. Nor should we give it added weight. Rather, our own pleasure and pain enter into the calculus equally with the pleasures and pains of others. Even if we are sincere in our utilitarianism, we must guard against the possibility of being biased in our calculations when our own interests are at stake. For this reason, and because it would be time-consuming to do a utilitarian calculation before every action, utilitarians encourage us to rely on rules of thumb in ordinary moral circumstances. We can make it a rule of thumb, for example, to tell the truth and keep our promises, rather than to calculate possible pleasures and pains in every routine case, because we know that in general telling the truth and keeping promises result in more happiness than do lying and breaking promises.

UTILITARIANISM IN AN ORGANIZATIONAL CONTEXT

> Three features of utilitarianism make it appealing in an organizational context.

Several features about utilitarianism make it appealing as a standard for moral decisions in business and nonbusiness organizations.

First, utilitarianism provides a clear and straightforward basis for formulating and testing policies. By utilitarian standards, an organizational policy, decision, or action is good if it promotes the general welfare more than any other alternative. A policy is considered wrong (or in need of modification) if it does not promote total utility as well as some alternative would. Utilitarians do not ask us to accept rules, policies, or principles blindly. Rather, they require us to test their worth against the standard of utility.

Second, utilitarianism provides an objective and attractive way of resolving conflicts of self-interest. This feature of utilitarianism dramatically contrasts with egoism, which seems incapable of resolving such conflicts. By proposing a standard outside self-interest, utilitarianism greatly minimizes and may actually eliminate such disputes. Thus, individuals within organizations make moral decisions and evaluate their actions by appealing to a uniform standard: the general good.

Third, utilitarianism provides a flexible, result-oriented approach to moral decision making. By recognizing no actions of a general kind as inherently right or wrong, utilitarianism encourages organizations to focus on the results of their actions and policies, and it allows them to tailor their decisions to suit the complexities of their situations. This facet of utilitarianism enables organizations to make realistic and workable moral decisions.

CRITICAL INQUIRIES OF UTILITARIANISM

1. **Is utilitarianism really workable?** Utilitarianism instructs us to maximize happiness, but in difficult cases we may be very uncertain about the likely results of the alternative courses of action open to us. Furthermore, comparing your level of happiness or unhappiness with that of someone else is at best tricky, at worst impossible—and when many people are involved, the matter may get hopelessly complex. Even if we assume that it is possible to make comparisons and to identify the various possible results of each course of action that a person might take (and to determine the likelihood of each result), is it realistic to expect people to take the time to make those calculations and, if they do, to make them accurately? Some critics of act utilitarianism have contended that teaching people to follow the basic utilitarian principle would not in fact promote happiness because of the difficulties in applying utilitarianism accurately.

2. **Are some actions wrong, even if they produce good?** Like egoism, utilitarianism focuses on the results of an action, not on the character of the action itself. For utilitarians, no action is in itself objectionable. It is objectionable only when it results in less happiness than could otherwise have been brought about. Critics of utilitarianism, by contrast, contend that some actions can be immoral and thus things we must not do, even if doing them would maximize happiness.

    Suppose a dying woman has asked you to promise to send the $25,000 under her bed to her nephew in another part of the country. She dies without anyone else's knowing of the money or of the promise that you made. Now suppose, too, that you know the nephew is a spendthrift and a drunkard and, were the money delivered

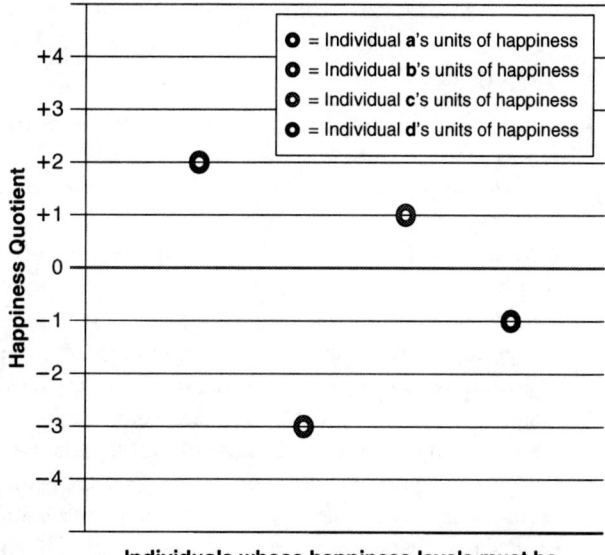

Individuals whose happiness levels must be measured and combined by the utilitarian.

Can we estimate the effects of our actions well enough for utilitarianism to work?

to him, it would be wasted in a week of outrageous partying. On the other hand, a very fine orphanage in your town needs such a sum to improve and expand its recreational facilities, something that would provide happiness to many children for years to come. It seems clear that on utilitarian grounds you should give the money to the orphanage, because this action would result in greater net happiness.

Many people would balk at this conclusion, contending that it would be wrong to break your promise, even if doing so would bring about more good than keeping it. Having made a promise, you have an obligation to keep it, and a deathbed promise is particularly serious. Furthermore, the deceased woman had a right to do with her money as she wished; it is not for you to decide how to spend it. Likewise, having been bequeathed the money, the nephew has a right to it regardless of how wisely or foolishly he might spend it. Defenders of utilitarianism, however, would insist that promoting happiness is all that really matters and warn you not to be blinded by moral prejudice.

Critics of utilitarianism respond that it is utilitarianism that is morally blind because it not only permits but sometimes even requires us to perform immoral actions. Philosopher Richard Brandt states the case against act utilitarianism this way:

> Act-utilitarianism . . . implies that if you have employed a boy to mow your lawn and he has finished the job and asks for his pay, you should pay him what you promised only if you cannot find a better use for your money. . . . It implies that if your father is ill and has no prospect of good in his life, and maintaining him is a drain on the energy and enjoyments of others, then, if you can end his life without provoking any public scandal or setting a bad example, it is your positive duty to take matters into your own hands and bring his life to a close.[3]

In the same vein, ethicist A. C. Ewing concludes that "[act] utilitarian principles, logically carried out, would result in far more cheating, lying and unfair action than any good man would tolerate."[4]

Defenders of act utilitarianism would reply that these charges are exaggerated. Although it is theoretically possible, for example, that not paying the boy for his work might maximize happiness, this is extremely unlikely. Utilitarians contend that only in very unusual circumstances will pursuit of the good conflict with our ordinary ideas of right and wrong, and in those cases—like the deathbed promise—we should put aside those ordinary ideas. The anti-utilitarian replies that the theoretical possibility that utilitarianism may require immoral conduct shows it to be an unsatisfactory moral theory.

3. **Is utilitarianism unjust?** Utilitarianism concerns itself with the sum total of happiness produced, not with how that happiness is distributed. If policy X brings two units of happiness to each of five people and policy Y brings nine units of happiness to one person, one unit each to two others, and none to the remaining two, then Y is to be preferred (eleven units of happiness versus ten), even though it distributes that happiness very unequally.

Worse still from the critic's point of view, utilitarianism may even require that some people's happiness be sacrificed in order to achieve the greatest overall amount of happiness. Sometimes the general utility may be served only at the expense of a single individual or group. For example, under the right of **eminent domain** (see Case 3.1), the government may appropriate private property for public use (after compensating the owner). Thus, the government may legally purchase your house from you to widen a highway—even if you don't want to sell the house or want more money than the government is willing to pay. The public interest is served at your private expense. Is this just?

SUMMARY

In an organizational context, utilitarianism provides an objective way to resolve conflicts of self-interest and encourages a realistic and result-oriented approach to moral decision making. But critics contend that (1) utilitarianism is not really workable, (2) some actions are wrong even if they produce good results, and (3) utilitarianism incorrectly overlooks considerations of justice and the distribution of happiness.

Or consider the Dan River experiment, part of the long-running controversy over the cause of brown lung disease. Claiming that the disease is caused by the inhalation of microscopic fibers in cotton dust, textile unions fought for years for tough regulations to protect their workers. The Occupational Safety and Health Administration (OSHA) responded by proposing cotton dust standards, which would require many firms to install expensive new equipment. A few months before the deadline for installing the equipment, officials at Dan River Mills, a textile manufacturer in Danville, Virginia, asked the government to waive the requirements for a time so that the company could conduct an experiment to determine the precise cause of brown lung disease. Both the state of Virginia and the U.S. Department of Labor allowed the extension. In response, the textile workers union contended, "It is simply unconscionable to allow hundreds of cotton mill workers to continue to face a high risk of developing brown lung disease."[5]

Suppose that the Dan River project did expose workers to what is considered a high risk of contracting lung disease. If so, then a small group of individuals—633 textile workers at ten locations in Danville, Virginia—were being compelled to carry the burden of isolating the cause of brown lung disease. Is that just?

Although their critics would say no, utilitarians would respond that it is, if the experiment maximizes the total good of society. Does it? In fact, the results of the experiment were inconclusive, but if the project had succeeded in identifying the exact cause of the disease, then thousands of textile workers across the country would have benefited. Researchers might also have discovered a more economical way to ensure worker safety than by installing expensive new equipment, which in turn would have profited both consumers and the textile industry. Certainly, utilitarians would consider the potentially negative impact on workers, but only as one factor among others. At the time of the decision, after the interests of all affected parties have been weighed, if extending the deadline is likely to yield the greatest net benefit or utility, then doing so is just—even though workers might be injured.

THE INTERPLAY BETWEEN SELF-INTEREST AND UTILITY

Both self-interest and utility play important roles in organizational decisions, and the views of many businesspeople blend these two theories. To the extent that each business pursues its own interests and each businessperson tries to maximize personal success, business practice can be called egoistic. But business practice is also utilitarian in that pursuing one's economic interests is thought to benefit society as a whole, and playing by the established rules of the competitive game is seen as advancing the social good. The classical capitalist economist Adam Smith (1723–1790) held such a view. He argued that leaving business and businesspeople free to pursue their self-interest will serve the good of society. Indeed, Smith believed that only through egoistic pursuits could the greatest economic benefit for the whole society be produced. The essence of Smith's position can be seen in the following passage from the *Wealth of Nations* (1776), in which Smith underscores the interplay between self-interest and the social good and between egoism and utilitarianism:

> Every individual is continually exerting himself to find out the most advantageous employment for whatever capital he can command. It is his own advantage, indeed, and not that of the society, which he has in view. But the study of his own advantage, naturally, or rather necessarily, leads him to prefer that employment which is most advantageous to the society....
>
> As every individual, therefore, endeavours as much as he can . . . to employ his capital . . . [so] that its produce may be of the greatest value, every individual necessarily

> Business practice is egoistic, but Adam Smith and others believe that it is also utilitarian because the pursuit of self-interest promotes the good of society.

labors to render the annual revenue of the society as great as he can. He generally, indeed, neither intends to promote the public interest, nor knows how much he is promoting it. . . . He intends only his own security; and by directing that industry in such a manner as its product may be of the greatest value, he intends only his own gain, and he is in this, as in many other cases, led by an invisible hand to promote an end which was no part of his intention. Nor is it always the worse for the society that it was no part of it. By pursuing his own interest he frequently promotes that of the society more effectually than when he really intends to promote it. I have never known much good done by those who affected to trade for the public good. It is an affectation, indeed, not very common among merchants, and very few words need be employed in dissuading them from it.[6]

Many today would agree with Smith* that the pursuit of self-interest is central to our economic system because it provides the motivating force that turns the wheels of commerce and industry. Although acknowledging that business is part of a social system and that certain ground rules are needed and should be followed, they would argue that society is best served by the active pursuit of self-interest within the established rules of business practice. Thus what we might call **business egoism**—the view that it is morally acceptable (or even morally required) for individuals to pursue their economic interests when engaged in business—is defended on utilitarian grounds.

* * *

KANT'S ETHICS

Most of us find the ideal of promoting human happiness and well-being an attractive one and, as a result, admire greatly people like Mother Teresa (1910–1997), who devoted her life to working with the poor. Despite the attractiveness of this ideal, many moral philosophers are critical of utilitarianism—particularly because, like egoism, it reduces all morality to a concern with consequences. Although nonconsequentialist normative theories vary significantly, adopting different approaches and stressing different themes, the writings of the preeminent German philosopher Immanuel Kant (1724–1804) provide an excellent example of a thoroughly nonconsequentialist approach to ethics. Perhaps few thinkers today would endorse Kant's theory on every point, but his work has greatly influenced subsequent philosophers and has helped shape our general moral culture.

Kant believed that moral reasoning is not based on factual knowledge and that the results of our actions do not determine whether they are right or wrong.

Kant sought moral principles that do not rest on contingencies and that define actions as inherently right or wrong apart from any particular circumstances. He believed that moral rules can, in principle, be known as a result of reason alone and are not based on observation (as are, for example, scientific judgments). In contrast to utilitarianism and other consequentialist doctrines, Kant's ethical theory holds that we do not have to know anything about the likely results of, say, my telling a lie to my boss in order to know that it is immoral. "The basis of obligation," Kant wrote, "must not be sought in human nature, [nor] in the circumstances of the world." Rather it is *a priori*, by which he meant that moral reasoning is not based on factual knowledge and that reason by itself can reveal the basic principles of morality.

GOOD WILL

Chapter 1 mentioned Good Samaritan laws, which shield from lawsuits those rendering emergency aid. Such laws, in effect, give legal protection to the humanitarian impulse behind emergency interventions. They formally recognize that the interventionist's heart

---

*Chapter 4 examines Smith's position in more detail.

was in the right place—that the person's intention was irreproachable. And because the person acted from right intention, he or she should not be held liable for any inadvertent harm except in cases of extreme negligence. The widely observable human tendency to introduce a person's intentions in assigning blame or praise is a good springboard for engaging Kant's ethics.

Nothing, said Kant, is good in itself except **good will**. This does not mean that intelligence, courage, self-control, health, happiness, and other things are not good and desirable. But Kant believed that their goodness depends on the will that makes use of them. Intelligence, for instance, is not good when exercised by an evil person.

By *will* Kant meant the uniquely human capacity to act from principle. Contained in the notion of good will is the concept of duty: Only when we act from a sense of duty does our action have **moral worth**. When we act only out of feeling, inclination, or self-interest, our actions—although they may be otherwise identical with ones that spring from the sense of duty—have no true moral worth.

Suppose that you're the owner of a small convenience store. Late one night a customer pays for his five-dollar purchase with a twenty-dollar bill, which you mistake for a ten. Only after the customer leaves do you realize you short-changed him. You race out the front door and find him lingering by a vending machine. You give him the ten dollars with your apologies, and he thanks you warmly.

Can we say that you acted from good will? Not necessarily. You may have acted from a desire to promote future business or to cultivate a reputation for honesty. If so, you would have acted in accordance with, but not from, duty. Your apparently virtuous gesture just happened to coincide with what duty requires. According to Kant, if you do not will the action from a sense of your duty to be fair and honest, your action lacks moral worth. Actions have true moral worth only when they spring from a recognition of duty and a choice to discharge it.

What determines our duty? How do we know what morality requires of us? Kant answered these questions by formulating what he called the "categorical imperative." This extraordinarily significant moral concept is the linchpin of Kant's ethics.

> **SUMMARY**
> Kant's theory is an important example of a purely nonconsequentialist approach to ethics. Kant held that only when we act from duty does our action have moral worth. Good will is the only thing that is good in itself.

THE CATEGORICAL IMPERATIVE

We have seen that egoists and utilitarians allow factual circumstances or empirical data to determine moral judgments. In contrast, Kant believed that reason alone can establish the moral law. We need not rely on empirical evidence relating to consequences and to similar situations. Just as we know, seemingly through reason alone, such abstract truths as "Every change must have a cause," so we can arrive at absolute moral truth through nonempirical reasoning and thereby discover our duty. For Kant, the moral law must hold in all circumstances, free from any internal contradiction. If we can formulate this law or rule, he thought, everyone would be obliged to follow it without exception.

Kant believed that there is just one command (imperative) that is categorical and thus necessarily binding on all rational agents, regardless of any other considerations. From this one categorical imperative (that is, from this universal command), we can derive all the specific commands of duty. Kant's **categorical imperative** says that we should always act in such a way that we can will the maxim of our action to be a universal law. So Kant's answer to the question "What determines whether an act is right?" is that an act is morally right if and only if we can will it as a universal law of conduct.

The obvious and crucial question that arises here is, "When are we justified in saying that the maxim of our action could become a universal law of conduct?"

By **maxim**, Kant meant the subjective principle of an action, the principle (or rule) that people in effect formulate in determining their conduct. For example, suppose building contractor Martin promises to install a sprinkler system in a project but is willing to break that promise to suit his purposes. His maxim can be expressed this way: "I'll make promises that I'll break whenever keeping them no longer suits my purposes." This is the subjective principle—the maxim—that directs his action.

Kant insisted that the morality of any maxim depends on whether we can logically will it to be a universal law governing everyone's conduct. Could Martin's maxim be universally acted on? That depends on whether the maxim as law would involve a contradiction. The maxim "I'll make promises that I'll break whenever keeping them no longer suits my purposes" could not be universally acted on because it involves a contradiction of will. On the one hand, Martin is willing that it be possible to make promises and have them honored. On the other, if everyone made promises without intending to keep them, then promises would not be honored in the first place, because it is in the nature of promises that they be believed. A law that allowed promise breaking would contradict the very nature of a promise. Similarly, a law that allowed lying would contradict the very nature of serious communication, for the activity of serious communication (as opposed to joking) requires that participants intend to speak the truth. I cannot, without contradiction, will both serious conversation and lying. By contrast, there is no problem, Kant thinks, in willing promise keeping or truth telling to be universal laws.

Consider, as another example, Kant's account of a man who, in despair after suffering a series of major setbacks, contemplates suicide. While still rational, the man asks whether it would be contrary to his duty to take his own life. Could the maxim of his action become a universal law of nature? Kant thinks not:

> His maxim is this: From self-love I make it my principle to shorten my life when its continued duration threatens more evil than it promises satisfaction. There only remains the question whether this principle of self-love can become a universal law of nature. One sees at once a contradiction in a system of nature whose law would destroy life by means of the very same feeling that acts so as to stimulate the furtherance of life. . . . Therefore, such a maxim cannot possibly hold as a universal law of nature and is, consequently, wholly inconsistent with the supreme principle of all duty.[7]

When Kant insists that a moral rule be consistently universalizable, he is saying that moral rules prescribe categorically, not hypothetically. A *hypothetical* prescription tells us what to do if we desire a particular outcome. Thus, "If I want people to like me, I should be nice to them" and "If you want to go to medical school, you must take biology" are **hypothetical imperatives**. They tell us what we must do on the assumption that we have some particular goal. If that is what we want, then this is what we must do; but if we don't want to go to medical school, then the command to take biology does not apply to us. In contrast, Kant's imperative is *categorical:* It commands unconditionally. It is necessarily binding on everyone, regardless of his or her specific goals or desires, regardless of consequences. A categorical imperative takes the form of "Do this" or "Don't do that"—no ifs, ands, or buts.

Universal Acceptability

There is another way of looking at the categorical imperative. Each person, through his or her own acts of will, legislates the moral law. The moral rules that we obey are not imposed on us from the outside. They are self-imposed and self-recognized, fully internalized principles. The sense of duty that we obey comes from within; it is an expression of our own higher selves.

Thus, moral beings give themselves the moral law and accept its demands on themselves. But that is not to say we can prescribe anything we want, for we are constrained by reason and its requirements. Because reason is the same for all rational beings, we all

---

*Sidebar (left margin):*

If you make a promise that you don't intend to keep, it is impossible to will the maxim governing your action as a universal law.

SUMMARY

Kant's categorical imperative states that an action is morally right if and only if we can will the maxim (or principle) represented by our action as a universal law. For example, a person making a promise with no intention of keeping it cannot universalize the maxim governing his action because if everyone followed this principle, promising would make no sense. Kant believed that the categorical imperative is binding on all rational creatures, regardless of their specific goals or desires and regardless of the consequences.

give ourselves the same moral law. In other words, when you answer the question "What should I do?" you must consider what all rational beings should do. You can embrace something as a moral law only if all other rational beings can also embrace it. It must have **universal acceptability**.

To see whether a rule or principle is a moral law, we can thus ask if what the rule commands would be acceptable to all rational beings. In considering lying, theft, or murder, for example, you must consider the act not only from your own viewpoint but also from the perspective of the person lied to, robbed, or murdered. Presumably, rational beings do not want to be lied to, robbed, or murdered. The test of the morality of a rule, then, is whether all rational beings looking at the matter objectively and impartially could accept the rule regardless of whether the action in question was performed by them or done to them. This is an important moral insight, and most philosophers see it as implicit in Kant's discussion of the categorical imperative, even though Kant (whose writings are difficult to understand) did not make the point in this form.

The principle of universal acceptability has important applications. Suppose a man advocates a hiring policy that discriminates against women. For this rule to be universally acceptable, the man would have to be willing to accept it if he were a woman, something he would presumably be unwilling to do. Or suppose the manufacturer of a product decides to market it even though the manufacturer knows that the product is unsafe when used in a certain common way and that consumers are ignorant of this fact. Applying the universal-acceptability principle, the company's decision makers would have to be willing to advocate marketing the product even if they were themselves in the position of uninformed consumers. Presumably they would be unwilling to do this. So the rule that would allow the product to be marketed would fail the test of universal acceptability.

Humanity as an End, Never as Merely a Means

In addition to the principle of universal acceptability, Kant explicitly offered another, very famous way of formulating the core idea of his categorical imperative. According to this formulation, as rational creatures we should always treat other rational creatures as ends in themselves and never as only means to our own ends. This formulation underscores Kant's belief that every human being has an inherent worth resulting from the sheer possession of rationality. We must always act in a way that respects this humanity in others and in ourselves. When brokers at the Dallas office of Prudential Securities encouraged unnecessary buying and selling of stocks by their clients in order to reap a commission (a practice called "churning"), they failed to do this. They were treating their clients simply as a means to their own ends and not respecting them as persons, as ends in themselves.[8]

As rational beings, humans would act inconsistently if they did not treat everyone else the way they themselves would want to be treated. Here we see shades of the Golden Rule. Indeed, Kant's moral philosophy can be viewed as a profound reconsideration of this basic nonconsequentialist principle. Because rational beings recognize their own inner worth, they would never wish to be used as if they were entities possessing value only as means to an end.

Kant maintained, as explained first, that an action is morally right if and only if we can will it to be a universal law of conduct. We now have two ways of reformulating his categorical imperative that may be easier to grasp and apply:

> *First reformulation*: An action is right if and only if its underlying principle is universally acceptable, that is, acceptable to all rational parties whether the action is done by them or to them.
>
> *Second reformulation*: One must always act so as to treat other people as ends in themselves.

Two alternative formulations of the categorical imperative.

KANT IN AN ORGANIZATIONAL CONTEXT

Like utilitarianism, Kant's moral theory has application for organizations.

First, the categorical imperative gives us firm rules to follow in moral decision making, rules that do not depend on circumstances or results and that do not permit individual exceptions. No matter what the consequences may be or who does it, some actions are always wrong. Lying is an example: No matter how much good might come from misrepresenting a product, such deliberate misrepresentation is always wrong. Similarly, it would be wrong to expose uninformed workers to some occupational health risk on the grounds that it advances medical knowledge.

Second, Kant introduces an important humanistic dimension into business decisions. One of the principal objections to egoism and utilitarianism is that they permit us to treat humans as means to ends. Kant's principles clearly forbid this. Many would say that respect for the inherent worth and dignity of human beings is much needed today in business, where encroaching technology and the pressure of globalization tend to dehumanize people under the guise of efficiency. Kant's theory puts the emphasis of organizational decision making where it belongs: on individuals. Organizations, after all, involve human beings working in concert to provide goods and services for other human beings. The primacy Kant gives the individual reflects this essential aspect of business.

Third, Kant stresses the importance of motivation and of acting on principle. According to Kant, it is not enough just to do the right thing; an action has moral worth only if it is done from a sense of duty—that is, from a desire to do the right thing for its own sake. The importance of this point is too often forgotten. Sometimes when individuals and organizations believe that an action promotes the interests of everyone, they are actually rationalizing—doing what is best for themselves and only imagining that somehow it will also benefit others. Worse still, they may defend their actions as morally praiseworthy when, in fact, they are only behaving egoistically. They wouldn't do the morally justifiable thing if they didn't think it would pay off for them. By stressing the importance of motivation, a Kantian approach serves as a corrective to this. Even an action that helps others has moral value for Kant only if the person doing it is morally motivated—that is, acting on principle or out of moral conviction.

> **SUMMARY**
> There are two alternative formulations of the categorical imperative. The first is that the action must be acceptable to all rational parties whether it is done by them or done to them. The second is that one must always treat other people as ends, never merely as means.

CRITICAL INQUIRIES OF KANT'S ETHICS

1. **What has moral worth?** According to Kant, the convenience store owner who returns the ten dollars to the customer is doing the right thing. But if his action is motivated by self-interest (perhaps he wants to get a reputation for honesty), then it does not have moral worth. That seems plausible. But Kant also held that if the owner does the right thing out of instinct, habit, or sympathy for the other person, then the act still does not have moral worth. Only if it is done out of a sense of duty does the action have moral value. Many moral theorists have felt that Kant was too severe on this point. Do we really want to say that giving money to famine relief has no moral worth if one is emotionally moved to do so by pictures of starving children rather than by a sense of duty? We might, to the contrary, find a person with strong human sympathies no less worthy or admirable than the person who gives solely out of an abstract sense of duty.

2. **Is the categorical imperative an adequate test of right?** Kant said that a moral rule must function without exception. Critics wonder why the prohibition against actions such as lying, promise breaking, and suicide must be exceptionless. They say that Kant failed to distinguish between saying that a person should not except himself or herself from a rule and that the rule itself cannot specify exceptions.

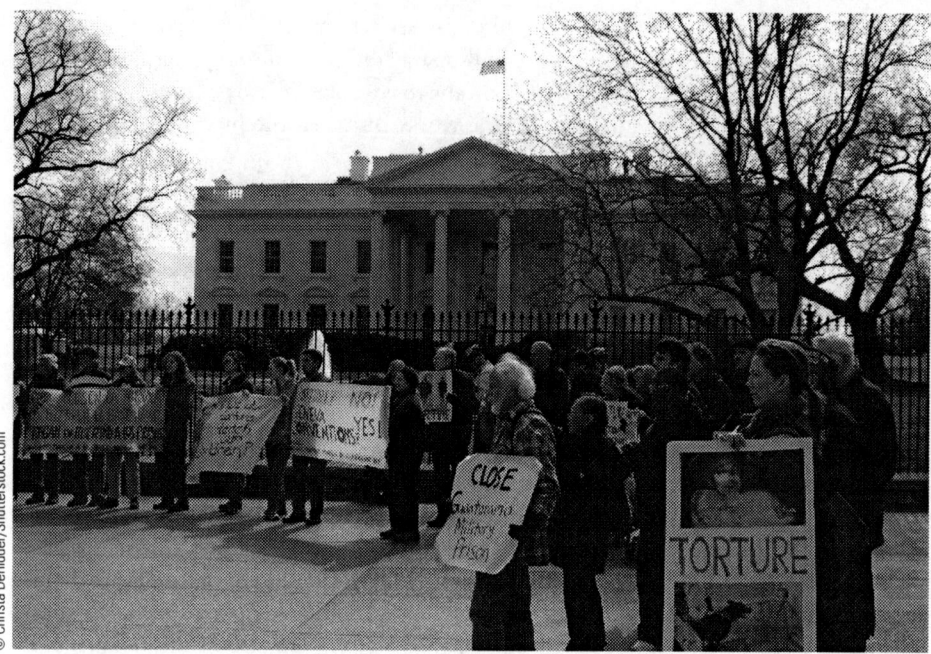

Is the categorical imperative an adequate test of right? A moral rule must function without exception, according to Kant. How applicable is that tenet to torture?

If stealing is wrong, it's wrong for me as well as for you. "Stealing is wrong, except if I do it" is not universalizable, for then stealing would be right for all to do, which contradicts the assertion that stealing is wrong. But just because no one may make of oneself an exception to a rule, it does not follow that the rule itself cannot specify exceptions.

Suppose, for example, that we decide that stealing is sometimes right, perhaps in the case of a person who is starving. Thus, the rule becomes "Never steal except when starving." This rule seems just as universalizable as "Never steal." The phrase "except. . . ." can be viewed not as justifying a violation of the rule but as building a qualification into it. Critics in effect are asking why a qualified rule is not just as good as an unqualified one. If it is, then we no longer need to state rules in the simple, direct, unqualified manner that Kant did.

In fairness to Kant, it could be argued that his universalization formula can be interpreted flexibly enough to meet commonsense objections. For example, perhaps we could universalize the principle that individuals should steal rather than starve to death or that it is permissible to take one's own life to extinguish unspeakable pain. Yet to qualify the rules against stealing, lying, and taking one's life seems to invite a non-Kantian analysis to justify the exceptions. One could, it seems, universalize more than one moral rule in a given situation: "Do not lie unless a life is at stake" versus "Lying is wrong unless necessary to avoid the suffering of innocent people." If so, then the categorical imperative would supply at best a necessary, but not a sufficient, test of right. But once we start choosing among various alternative rules, then we are adopting an approach to ethics that Kant would have rejected.

3. **What does it mean to treat people as means?** Kant's mandate that individuals must always be considered as ends in themselves and never merely as means expresses our sense of the intrinsic value of the human spirit and has profound moral appeal. Yet it is not always clear when people are being treated as ends and when merely as means. For example, Kant believed that prostitution is immoral because, by selling their sexual services, prostitutes allow themselves to be treated as means. Prostitutes,

SUMMARY
Kant's ethics gives us firm standards that do not depend on results; it injects a humanistic element into moral decision making and stresses the importance of acting on principle and from a sense of duty. Critics, however, worry that (1) Kant's view of moral worth is too restrictive, (2) the categorical imperative is not a sufficient test of right and wrong, and (3) distinguishing between treating people as means and respecting them as ends in themselves may be difficult in practice.

however, are not the only ones to sell their services. Anyone who works for a wage does so. Does that mean that we are all being treated immorally, because our employers are presumably hiring us as a means to advance their own ends? Presumably not, because we freely agreed to do the work. But then the prostitute might have freely chosen that line of work, too.

OTHER NONCONSEQUENTIALIST PERSPECTIVES

For Kant, the categorical imperative provided the basic test of right and wrong, and he was resolutely nonconsequentialist in his application of it. You know now what he would say about the case of the deathbed promise: The maxim permitting you to break your promise cannot be universalized, and hence it would be immoral of you to give the money to the orphanage, despite its bringing about more happiness. But nonconsequentialists are not necessarily Kantians, and several different nonutilitarian moral concerns emerged in the discussion of the deathbed promise example.

Critics of act utilitarianism believe that it is faulty for maintaining that we have one and only one moral duty. A utilitarian might follow various principles as rules of thumb, but they are only calculation substitutes. All that matters morally to utilitarians is the maximization of happiness. Yet this idea, many philosophers think, fails to do justice to the richness and complexity of our moral lives.

PRIMA FACIE OBLIGATIONS

One influential philosopher who argued this way was the British scholar W. D. Ross (1877–1971).[9] Ross rejected utilitarianism as too simple and as untrue to the way we ordinarily think about morality and about our moral obligations. We see ourselves, Ross and like-minded thinkers contend, as being under various moral duties that cannot be reduced to the single obligation to maximize happiness. Often these obligations grow out of special relationships into which we enter or out of determinate roles that we undertake. Our lives are intertwined with other people's in particular ways, and we have, as a result, certain specific moral obligations.

Ross believed that we have various moral duties that cannot be reduced to one single obligation to maximize happiness.

For example, as a professor, Rodriguez is obligated to assist her students in the learning process and to evaluate their work in a fair and educationally productive way—obligations to the specific people in her classroom that she does not have to other people. As a spouse, Rodriguez must maintain a certain emotional and sexual fidelity to her partner. As a parent, she must provide for the individual human beings who are her children. As a friend to Smith, she may have a moral responsibility to help him out in a time of crisis. Having borrowed money from Chang, Rodriguez is morally obligated to pay it back. Thus, different relationships and different circumstances generate a variety of specific moral obligations.

In addition, we have moral duties that do not arise from our unique interactions and relationships with other people. For example, we ought to treat all people fairly, do what we can to remedy injustices, and make an effort to promote human welfare generally. The latter obligation is important, but for a nonconsequentialist like Ross, it is only one among various obligations that people have.

At any given time, we are likely to be under more than one obligation, and sometimes these obligations can conflict—that is, we may have an obligation to do *A* and an obligation to do *B*, where it is not possible for us to do both *A* and *B*. For example, I promise to meet a friend on an urgent matter, and now, as I am hurrying there, I pass an injured person who is obviously in need of help. Stopping to aid the person will make it impossible for me to fulfill my promise. What should I do? For moral philosophers like Ross, there is no single answer for all cases. What I ought to do will depend on the circumstances and relative importance of the conflicting obligations. I have an obligation to keep my promise, and I have an obligation to assist someone in distress. What I must decide is which of these obligations is, in the given circumstance, the more important. I must weigh the moral significance of the promise against the comparative moral urgency of assisting the injured person.

Ross and many contemporary philosophers believe that all (or at least most) of our moral obligations are prima facie ones. A **prima facie obligation** is an obligation that can be overridden by a more important obligation. For instance, we take the keeping of promises seriously, but almost everyone would agree that in some circumstances—for example, when a life is at stake—it would be not only morally permissible, but morally required, to break a promise. Our obligation to keep a promise is a real one, and if there is no conflicting obligation, then we must keep the promise. But that obligation is not absolute or categorical; it could in principle be outweighed by a more stringent moral obligation. The idea that our obligations are prima facie is foreign to Kant's way of looking at things.

Consider an example that Kant himself discussed.[10] Imagine that a murderer comes to your door, wanting to know where your friend is so that he can kill her. Your friend is in fact hiding in your bedroom closet. Most people would agree that your obligation to your friend overrides your general obligation to tell the truth and that the right thing to do would be to lie to the murderer to throw him off your friend's trail. Although you have a genuine obligation to tell the truth, it is a prima facie obligation, one that other moral considerations can outweigh. Kant disagreed. He maintained that you must always tell the truth—that is, in all circumstances and without exception. For him, telling the truth is an absolute or categorical obligation, not a prima facie one.

Ross thought that our various prima facie obligations could be divided into seven basic types: duties of fidelity (that is, to respect explicit and implicit promises), duties of reparation (for previous wrongful acts), duties of gratitude, duties of justice, duties of beneficence (that is, to make the condition of others better), duties of self-improvement, and duties not to injure others.[11] Unlike utilitarianism, Ross's ethical perspective is pluralistic in recognizing a variety of genuine obligations. But contrary to Kant, Ross does not see these obligations as absolute and exceptionless. On both points, Ross contended that his view of morality more closely fits with our actual moral experience and the way we view our moral obligations.

Ross also saw himself as siding with commonsense morality in maintaining that our prima facie obligations are obvious. He believed that the basic principles of duty are as self-evident as the simplest rules of arithmetic and that any person who has reached the age of reason can discern that it is wrong to lie, to break promises, and to injure people needlessly. However, what we should do, all things considered, when two or more prima facie obligations conflict is often difficult to judge. In deciding what to do in any concrete situation, Ross thought, we are always "taking a moral risk."[12] Even after the fullest reflection, judgments about which of these self-evident rules should govern our conduct are only "more or less probable opinions which are not logically justified conclusions from the general principles that are recognised as self-evident."[13]

Ross's pluralistic ethical perspective differs from utilitarianism. Ross also rejected Kant's belief that our moral obligations are absolute and exceptionless.

ASSISTING OTHERS

Nonconsequentialists believe that utilitarianism presents too simple a picture of our moral world. In addition, they worry that utilitarianism risks making us all slaves to the maximization of total happiness. Stop and think about it: Isn't there something that you could be doing—for instance, volunteering at the local hospital or orphanage, collecting money for third-world development, helping the homeless—that would do more for the general good than what you are doing now or are planning to do tonight or tomorrow? Sure, working with the homeless might not bring you quite as much pleasure as what you would otherwise be doing, but if it would nonetheless maximize total happiness, then you are morally required to do it. However, by following this reasoning, you could end up working around the clock, sacrificing yourself for the greater good. This notion seems mistaken.

Most nonutilitarian philosophers, like Ross, believe that we have some obligation to promote the general welfare, but they typically view this obligation as less stringent than, for example, the obligation not to injure people. They see us as having a much stronger obligation to refrain from violating people's rights than to promote their happiness or well-being. From this perspective, a manufacturing company's obligation not to violate OSHA regulations and thereby endanger the safety of its employees is stronger than its obligation to open up day-care facilities for their children, even though the cost of the two is the same. The company, in other words, has a stronger duty to respect its legal and contractual employment-related obligations than to promote its employees' happiness in other ways. Likewise, for a company to violate people's rights by despoiling the environment through the discharge of pollutants would be morally worse than for it to decide not to expand a job training program in the inner city, even if expanding the program would bring about more total good.

Different nonutilitarian philosophers may weigh these particular obligations differently, depending on their particular moral theory. But they typically believe that we have a stronger duty not to violate people's rights or in some other way injure them than we do to assist people or otherwise promote their well-being. A utilitarian, concerned solely with what will maximize happiness, is less inclined to draw such a distinction.

Many moral philosophers draw a related distinction between actions that are morally required and charitable or **supererogatory actions**—that is, actions that would be good to do but not immoral not to do. Act utilitarianism does not make this distinction. Although we admire Mother Teresa and Albert Schweitzer for devoting their lives to doing good works among the poor, we see them as acting above and beyond the call of duty; we do not expect so much from ordinary people. Yet people who are not moral heroes or who fall short of sainthood may nonetheless be living morally satisfactory lives.

Nonutilitarian theorists see the distinction between morally obligatory actions and supererogatory actions not so much as a realistic concession to human weakness but as a necessary demarcation if we are to avoid becoming enslaved to the maximization of the general welfare. The idea here is that each of us should have a sphere in which we are free to pursue our own plans and goals, to carve out a distinctive life plan. These plans and goals are limited by various moral obligations, in particular by other people's rights, but the demands of morality are not all-encompassing.

MORAL RIGHTS

What, then, are rights, and what rights do people have? Broadly defined, a *right* is an entitlement to act or have others act in a certain way. The connection between rights and duties is that, generally speaking, if you have a right to do something, then someone else has a correlative duty to act in a certain way. For example, if you claim a "right" to drive, you mean that you are entitled to drive or that others should—that is, have a duty to—permit you to drive. Your right to drive under certain conditions is derived from our legal system and is thus considered a **legal right**.

In addition to rights that are derived from some specific legal system, we also have **moral rights**. Some of these moral rights derive from special relationships, roles, or circumstances in which we happen to be. For example, if Tom has an obligation to return Bob's car to him on Saturday morning, then Bob has a right to have Tom return his car. If I have agreed to water your plants while you are on vacation, you have a right to expect me to look after them in your absence. As a student, you have a right to be graded fairly, and so on.

Even more important are rights that do not rest on special relationships, roles, or situations. For example, the rights to life, free speech, and unhampered religious affiliation are widely accepted, not just as the entitlements of some specific political or legal system but as fundamental moral rights. More controversial, but often championed as moral rights, are the rights to medical care, decent housing, education, and work. Moral rights that are not the result of particular roles, special relationships, or specific circumstances are called **human rights**. They have several important characteristics.

First, human rights are universal. For instance, if the right to life is a human right, as most of us believe it is, then everyone, everywhere and at all times, has that right. By contrast, there is nothing universal about your right that I keep my promise to help you move or about my right to drive 65 miles per hour on certain roads.

Second, and closely related, human rights are equal rights. If the right to free speech is a human right, then everyone has this right equally. No one has a greater right to free speech than anyone else. In contrast, your daughter has a greater right than do the daughters of other people to your emotional and financial support.

Third, human rights are not transferable, nor can they be relinquished. If we have a fundamental human right, we cannot give, lend, or sell it to someone else. We cannot waive it, and no one can take it from us. That is what is meant in the Declaration of Independence when certain rights—namely, life, liberty, and the pursuit of happiness—are described as "unalienable." By comparison, legal rights can be renounced or transferred, as when one party sells another a house or a business.

Fourth, human rights are natural rights, not in the sense that they can be derived from a study of human nature, but in the sense that they do not depend on human institutions the way legal rights do. If people have human rights, they have these rights simply because they are human beings. They do not have them because they live under a certain legal system. Human rights rest on the assumption that people have certain basic moral entitlements merely because of their humanity. No authoritative body assigns them human rights. The law may attempt to protect human rights, to make them explicit and safe through codification, but the law is not their source.

Rights, and in particular human rights, can be divided into two broad categories: negative rights and positive rights. **Negative rights** reflect the vital interests that human beings have in being free from outside interference. The rights guaranteed in the Bill of Rights—freedom of speech, assembly, religion, and so on—fall within this category, as do the rights to freedom from injury and to privacy. Correlating with these are duties that we all have not to interfere with others' pursuit of these interests and activities. **Positive rights** reflect the vital interests that human beings have in receiving certain benefits. They are rights to have others provide us with certain goods, services, or opportunities. Today, positive rights often are taken to include the rights to education, medical care, equal job opportunity, comparable pay, and so on. Correlating with these are positive duties for appropriate parties to assist individuals in their pursuit of these interests.

Thus a child's right to education implies not only that no one should interfere with the child's education but also that the necessary resources for that education ought to be provided. In the case of some positive rights—for example, the right to a decent standard of living, as proclaimed by the United Nations' 1948 Human Rights Charter—who

> Human rights have four important characteristics.

> Philosophers distinguish negative rights from positive rights.

exactly has the duty to provide the goods and services required to fulfill those rights is unclear. Also, interpreting a right as negative or positive is sometimes controversial. For example, is my right to liberty simply the right not to be interfered with as I live my own life, or does it also imply a duty on the part of others to provide me with the means to make the exercise of that liberty meaningful?

The significance of positing moral rights is that they provide grounds for making moral judgments that differ radically from utilitarianism's grounds. Once moral rights are asserted, the locus of moral judgment becomes the individual, not society. For example, if workers have a moral right to be informed about potentially dangerous working conditions and to decide for themselves whether to undertake the work in question, then it would be wrong to violate this right—even if doing so would somehow promote the common good. Again, if employees have a right to compensation equal to what others receive for doing comparable work, then they cannot be paid less on the grounds that doing so would be economically efficient or in some other way result in greater overall utility.

Utilitarianism, in effect, treats all such entitlements as subordinate to the general welfare. Thus, individuals are entitled to act in a certain way and entitled to have others allow or aid them to so act only insofar as acknowledging this right or entitlement achieves the greatest good. The assertion of moral rights, therefore, decisively sets nonconsequentialists apart from utilitarians.

> **SUMMARY**
> Nonconsequentialists typically emphasize moral rights—entitlements to act in a certain way or to have others act in a certain way. These rights can rest on special relationships and roles, or they can be general human rights. Rights can be negative, protecting us from outside interference, or they can be positive, requiring others to provide us with certain benefits or opportunities.

NONCONSEQUENTIALISM IN AN ORGANIZATIONAL CONTEXT

We have already looked at Kant's ethics in an organizational context, but, as we have seen, many nonconsequentialists (like Ross) are not Kantians, and their ideas also have important implications for moral decision making in business and nonbusiness organizations.

First, in its non-Kantian forms nonconsequentialism stresses that moral decision making involves the weighing of different moral factors and considerations. Unlike utilitarianism, nonconsequentialism does not reduce morality solely to the calculation of consequences; rather, it recognizes that an organization must usually take into account other equally important moral concerns. Theorists like Ross emphasize that, contrary to what Kant believed, there can often be rival and even conflicting moral demands on an organization. For example, obligations to employees, stockholders, and consumers may pull a corporation in different directions, and determining the organization's proper moral course may not be easy.

Second, nonconsequentialism acknowledges that the organization has its own legitimate goals to pursue. There are limits to the demands of morality, and an organization that fulfills its moral obligations and respects the relevant rights of individuals is morally free to advance whatever (morally permissible) ends it has—public service, profit, government administration, and so on. Contrary to utilitarianism, organizations and the people in them need not see themselves as under an overarching obligation to seek continually to enhance the general welfare.

Third, nonconsequentialism stresses the importance of moral rights. Moral rights, and in particular human rights, are a crucial factor in most moral deliberations, including those of organizations. Before it acts, any morally responsible business or nonbusiness organization must consider carefully how its actions will impinge on the rights of individuals—not just the rights of its members, such as stockholders and employees, but also the rights of others, such as consumers. Moral rights place distinct and firm constraints on what sorts of things an organization can do to fulfill its own ends.

CRITICAL INQUIRIES OF NONCONSEQUENTIALISM

1. **How well justified are these nonconsequentialist principles and moral rights?**
    Ross maintained that we have immediate intuitive knowledge of the basic prima facie moral principles, and indeed it would seem absurd to try to deny that it is wrong to cause needless suffering or that making a promise imposes some obligation to keep it. Only someone the moral equivalent of colorblind could fail to see the truth of these statements; to reject them would seem as preposterous as denying some obvious fact of arithmetic—for example, that 12 + 4 = 16. Likewise, it appears obvious—indeed, as Thomas Jefferson wrote, "self-evident"—that human beings have certain basic and inalienable rights, unconditional rights that do not depend on the decrees of any particular government.

    Yet we must be careful. What seems obvious, even self-evident, to one culture or at one time in human history may turn out to be not only not self-evident but actually false. That the earth is flat and that heavier objects fall faster than lighter ones were two "truths" taken as obvious in former centuries. Likewise, the inferiority of women and of various nonwhite races was long taken for granted; this supposed fact was so obvious that it was hardly even commented on. The idea that people have a right to practice a religion that the majority "knows" to be false—or, indeed, to practice no religion whatsoever—would have seemed morally scandalous to many of our forebears and is still not embraced in all countries around the world. Today many vegetarians eschew meat eating on moral grounds and contend that future generations will consider our treatment of animals, factory farming in particular, to be as morally benighted as slavery. So what seems obvious, self-evident, or simple common sense may not be the most reliable guide to morally sound principles.

2. **Can nonconsequentialists satisfactorily handle conflicting rights and principles?**
    People today disagree among themselves about the correctness of certain moral principles. Claims of right, as we have seen, are often controversial. For example, do employees have a moral right to their jobs—an entitlement to be fired only with just cause? To some of us, it may seem obvious that they do; to others, perhaps not. And how are we to settle various conflicting claims of right? Jones, for instance, claims a right to her property, which she has acquired honestly through her labors—that is, she claims a right to do with it as she wishes. Smith is ill and claims adequate medical care as a human right. Because he cannot afford the care himself, acknowledging his right will probably involve taxing people like Jones and thus limiting their property rights.

To sum up these two points: *First*, even moral principles that seem obvious or a matter of common sense have to be examined critically; and *second*, nonconsequentialists should not rest content until they find a way of resolving disputes among conflicting prima facie principles or rights. This is not to suggest that nonconsequentialists cannot find deeper and theoretically more satisfactory ways of grounding moral claims and of handling disputes between them. The point to be underscored here is simply the necessity of doing so.

> **SUMMARY**
> In an organizational context, nonconsequentialism (in its non-Kantian forms) stresses the plurality of moral considerations to be weighed. While emphasizing the importance of respecting moral rights, it acknowledges that morality has limits and that organizations have legitimate goals to pursue. Critics question whether (1) nonconsequentialist principles are adequately justified and whether (2) nonconsequentialism can satisfactorily handle conflicting rights and principles.

• • •

UTILITARIANISM ONCE MORE

Until now, our discussion of utilitarianism has focused on the classic and most straightforward version of it, namely, act utilitarianism. According to act utilitarianism, we have one and only one moral obligation, the maximization of happiness for everyone concerned, and every action is to be judged by this standard. But a different utilitarian approach, called rule utilitarianism, is relevant to the discussion of the moral concerns characteristic of nonconsequentialism—in particular, relevant to the nonconsequentialist's criticisms of act utilitarianism. The rule utilitarian would, in fact, agree with many of these criticisms. (Rule utilitarianism has been formulated in different ways, but this discussion follows the version defended by Richard Brandt.)

Rule utilitarianism maintains that the utilitarian standard should be applied not to individual actions but to moral codes as a whole. The rule utilitarian asks what moral code (that is, what set of moral rules) a society should adopt to maximize happiness. The principles that make up that code would then be the basis for distinguishing right actions from wrong actions. As Brandt explains:

> A rule-utilitarian thinks that right actions are the kind permitted by the moral code optimal for the society of which the agent is a member. An optimal code is one designed to maximize welfare or what is good (thus, utility). This leaves open the possibility that a particular right act by itself may not maximize benefit. . . . On the rule-utilitarian view, then, to find what is morally right or wrong we need to find which actions would be permitted by a moral system that is "optimal" for the agent's society.[14]

The notion of an optimal moral code takes into account the difficulty of getting people to follow a given set of rules.

The "optimal" moral code does not refer to the set of rules that would do the most good if everyone conformed to them all the time. The meaning is more complex. The **optimal moral code** must take into account what rules can reasonably be taught and obeyed, as well as the costs of inculcating those rules in people. Recall from Chapter 1 that if a principle or rule is part of a person's moral code, then it will influence the person's behavior. The person will tend to follow that principle, to feel guilty when he or she does not live up to it, and to disapprove of others who fail to conform to it. Rule utilitarians must consider not just the benefits of having people motivated to act in certain ways but also the costs of instilling those motivations in them. As Brandt writes:

> The more intense and widespread an aversion to a certain sort of behavior, the less frequent the behavior is apt to be. But the more intense and widespread, the greater the cost of teaching the rule and keeping it alive, the greater the burden on the individual, and so on.[15]

Thus, the "optimality" of a moral code encompasses both the benefits of getting people to act in certain ways and the costs of bringing that about. Perfect compliance is not a realistic goal. "Like the law," Brandt continues, "the optimal moral code normally will not produce 100 percent compliance with all its rules; that would be too costly."[16]

Some utilitarian thinkers in earlier centuries adopted or came close to adopting rule utilitarianism (although they did not use that term). For example, the nineteenth-century legal theorist John Austin wrote: "Utility [should] be the test of our conduct, ultimately, but not immediately. . . . Our rules [should] be fashioned on utility; our conduct, on our rules."[17] This accords well with the rule-utilitarian idea that we should apply the utilitarian standard only to the assessment of alternative moral codes; we should not try to apply it to individual actions. We should seek to determine the specific set of principles that would in fact best promote total happiness for society. Those are the rules we should promulgate, instill in ourselves, and teach to the next generation.

WHAT WILL THE OPTIMAL CODE LOOK LIKE?

Rule utilitarians believe that the optimal moral code will not consist of just one rule—to maximize happiness.

Rule utilitarians such as Brandt argue strenuously that the ideal or optimal moral code for a society will not be the single act-utilitarian command to maximize happiness. They contend that teaching people that their only obligation is to maximize happiness would not in fact maximize happiness.

First, people will make mistakes if, before they act, they try to calculate the consequences of each and every thing they might possibly do. *Second*, if all of us were act utilitarians, practices such as keeping promises and telling the truth would be rather shaky, because we could expect others to keep promises or tell the truth only when they believed that doing so would maximize happiness. *Third*, the act-utilitarian principle is too demanding, because it seems to imply that each person should continually be striving to promote total well-being.

For these reasons, rule utilitarians believe that more happiness will come from instilling in people a pluralistic moral code, one with a number of different principles. By analogy, imagine a traffic system with just one rule: Drive your car in a way that maximizes happiness. Such a system would be counterproductive; we do much better in terms of total human well-being to have a variety of traffic regulations—for example, obey stop signs, yield to the right, and pass only on the left. In such a pluralistic system we cannot justify cruising through a red light with the argument that doing so maximizes total happiness by getting us home more quickly.

The principles of the optimal code would presumably be prima facie in Ross's sense—that is, capable of being overridden by other principles. Different principles would also have different moral weights. It would make sense, for example, to instill in people an aversion to killing that is stronger and deeper than the aversion to telling white lies. In addition, the ideal code would acknowledge moral rights. Teaching people to respect moral rights maximizes human welfare in the long run.

The rules of the optimal code provide the sole basis for determining right and wrong. An action is not necessarily wrong if it fails to maximize happiness; it is wrong only if it conflicts with the ideal moral code. Rule utilitarianism thus gets around many of the problems that plague act utilitarianism. At the same time, it provides a plausible basis for deciding which moral principles and rights we should acknowledge and how much weight we should attach to them. We try to determine those principles and rights that, generally adhered to, would best promote human happiness.

Still, rule utilitarianism has its critics. There are two common objections. *First*, act utilitarians maintain that a utilitarian who cares about happiness should be willing to violate rules in order to maximize happiness. Why make a fetish out of the rules?

Second, nonconsequentialists, while presumably viewing rule utilitarianism more favorably than act utilitarianism, still balk at seeing moral principles determined by their consequences. They contend, in particular, that rule utilitarians ultimately subordinate rights to utilitarian calculation and therefore fail to treat rights as fundamental and independent moral factors.

> **SUMMARY**
> Rule utilitarianism is a hybrid theory. It maintains that the correct principles of right and wrong are those that would maximize happiness if society adopted them. Rule utilitarianism applies the utilitarian standard not directly to individual actions but rather to the choice of the moral principles that are to guide individual action. Rule utilitarianism avoids many of the standard criticisms of act utilitarianism.

Critics of rule utilitarianism raise two objections.

MORAL DECISION MAKING: A PRACTICAL APPROACH

Theoretical controversies permeate the subject of ethics, and as we have seen, philosophers have proposed rival ways of understanding right and wrong. These philosophical differences of perspective, emphasis, and theory are significant and can have profound practical consequences. This chapter has surveyed some of these issues, but obviously it cannot settle all of the questions that divide moral philosophers. Fortunately, however, many problems of business and organizational ethics can be intelligently discussed and even resolved by people whose fundamental moral theories differ (or who have not yet worked out their own moral ideas in some systematic way). This section discusses some important points to keep in mind when analyzing and discussing business ethics and offers, as a kind of model, one possible procedure for making moral decisions.

In the abstract, it might seem impossible for people to reach agreement on controversial ethical issues, given that ethical theories differ so much and that people themselves place moral value on different things. Yet in practice moral problems are rarely so intractable that open-minded and thoughtful people cannot, by discussing matters calmly, rationally, and thoroughly, make significant progress toward resolving them. Chapter 1 stressed that moral judgments should be logical, should be based on facts, and should appeal to sound moral principles. Bearing this in mind can often help, especially when various people are discussing an issue and proposing rival answers.

> Recall that moral judgments should be logical and based on facts and sound moral principles.

First, in any moral discussion, make sure that the participants agree about the relevant facts. Often moral disputes hinge not on matters of moral principle but on differing assessments of what the facts of the situation are, what alternatives are open, or what the probable results of different courses of action will be. For instance, the directors of an international firm might acrimoniously dispute the moral permissibility of a new overseas investment. The conflict might appear to involve some fundamental clash of moral principles and perspectives when, in fact, it is the result of some underlying disagreement about the likely effects of the proposed investment on the lives of the local population. Until this factual disagreement is acknowledged and dealt with, little is apt to be resolved.

Second, once there is general agreement on factual matters, try to spell out the moral principles to which different people are, at least implicitly, appealing. Seeking to determine these principles will often help people clarify their own thinking enough to reach a solution. Sometimes they will agree on what moral principles are relevant and yet disagree over how to balance them. Identifying this discrepancy can be helpful. Bear in mind, too, that skepticism is in order when someone's moral stance on an issue appears to rest simply on a hunch or an intuition and cannot be related to some more general moral principle. As moral decision makers, we are seeking not only an answer to a moral issue but an answer that can be publicly defended, and the public defense of a moral judgment usually requires an appeal to general principle. By analogy, judges do not hand down judgments based simply on what strikes them as fair in a particular case. They must relate their decisions to general legal principles or statutes.

A reluctance to defend our moral decisions in public is almost always a warning sign. If we are unwilling to account for our actions publicly, chances are that we are doing something we cannot really justify morally. In addition, Kant's point that we must be willing to universalize our moral judgments is relevant here. We cannot sincerely endorse a principle if we are not willing to see it applied generally. Unfortunately, we occasionally do make judgments—for example, that Alfred's being late to work is a satisfactory reason for firing him—that rest on a principle we would be unwilling to apply to our own situations; hence the moral relevance of the familiar question: "How would you like it if . . . ?" Looking at an issue from the other person's point of view can cure moral myopia.

> SUMMARY
> Despite disagreements on controversial theoretical issues, people can make significant progress in resolving practical moral problems through open-minded and reflective discussion. One useful approach is to identify the (possibly conflicting) obligations, ideals, and effects in a given situation and then to determine where the emphasis should lie among these different considerations.

OBLIGATIONS, EFFECTS, IDEALS

As a practical basis for discussing moral issues in organizations, it is useful to try to approach those issues in a way that is acceptable to individuals with differing moral viewpoints. We want to avoid presupposing the truth of one particular theoretical perspective. By emphasizing factors that are relevant to various theories, both consequentialist and nonconsequentialist, we can find some common ground on which moral decision making can proceed. Moral dialogue can thus take place in an objective and analytical way, even if the participants do not fully agree on all philosophical issues.

What factors or considerations, then, seem important from most ethical perspectives? Following Professor V. R. Ruggiero, we can identify three shared concerns.[18] The first is with *obligations*, that is, with the specific duties or moral responsibilities that we have in a given situation. Every significant human action—personal and professional—arises in the context of human relationships. These relationships, the roles we have assumed, and the expectations created by our previous actions can be the source of particular duties and rights. In addition, we are obligated to respect people's human rights. Obligations bind us. In their presence, morality requires us, at least prima facie, to do certain things and to avoid doing others. Even utilitarians can agree with this.

A second concern common to most ethical systems is with the *effects* of our actions. When reflecting on a possible course of action, one needs to take into account its likely results. Although nonconsequentialists maintain that things other than consequences or results can affect the rightness or wrongness of actions, few if any of them would ignore consequences entirely. Almost all nonconsequentialist theories place some moral weight on the results of our actions. Practically speaking, this means that in making a moral decision, we must identify all the interested parties and how they would be affected by the different courses of action open to us.

The third consideration relevant to most ethical perspectives is the impact of our actions on important *ideals*. An **ideal** is some morally significant goal, virtue, or notion of excellence worth striving for. Clearly, different cultures impart different ideals and, equally important, different ways of pursuing them. Our culture respects virtues such as generosity, courage, compassion, and loyalty, as well as more abstract ideals such as peace, justice, and equality. In addition to these moral ideals, there are institutional or organizational ideals: efficiency, product quality, customer service, and so forth. Does a particular act serve or violate these ideals? Both consequentialists and nonconsequentialists can agree that this is an important consideration in determining the moral quality of actions.

In isolating these three concerns common to almost all ethical systems—obligations, effects, and ideals—Ruggiero provided a kind of practical synthesis of consequentialist and nonconsequentialist thought that seems appropriate for our purposes. A useful approach to moral questions in an organizational context will therefore reflect these considerations: the obligations that derive from organizational relationships or are affected by organizational conduct, the ideals at stake, and the effects or consequences of alternative courses of action. Any action that honors obligations while respecting ideals and benefiting people can be presumed to be moral. An action that does not pass scrutiny in these respects will be morally suspect.

This view leads to what is essentially a two-step procedure for evaluating actions and making moral choices. The *first step* is to identify the important considerations involved: obligations, effects, and ideals. Accordingly, we should ask if any basic obligations are involved. If so, what are they and who has them? Who is affected by the action and how? How do these effects compare with those of the alternatives open to us? What ideals does the action respect or promote? What ideals does it neglect or thwart? The *second step* is to decide which of these considerations deserves emphasis. Sometimes the issue may be largely a matter of obligations; other times, some ideal may predominate; still other times, consideration of effects may be the overriding concern.

If two or more obligations conflict, it is obvious that we should choose the stronger one, and when two or more ideals conflict, or when ideals conflict with obligations, we should obviously honor the more important one. Similarly, when rival actions have different results, we should prefer the action that produces the greater good or the lesser harm. But in real-world situations, deciding these matters is often difficult, and there is no easy way of balancing obligations, effects, and ideals when these considerations pull in different directions. The fact is that we have no sure procedure for making such comparative determinations, which involve assessing worth and assigning relative priorities to our assessments. In large part, the chapters that follow attempt to sort out the values

> A two-step approach to moral decision making is to identify the relevant obligations, ideals, and effects and then decide which consideration deserves the most emphasis.

and principles embedded in the tangled web of frequently subtle, ill-defined problems we meet in business and organizational life. It is hoped that examining these issues will help you (1) identify the obligations, effects, and ideals involved in specific moral issues and (2) decide where the emphasis should lie among the competing considerations.

STUDY CORNER

KEY TERMS AND CONCEPTS

- act utilitarianism
- business egoism
- categorical imperative
- consequentialist theories
- egoism
- eminent domain
- good will
- hedonism
- human rights
- hypothetical imperative
- ideal
- legal rights
- maxim
- moral rights
- moral worth
- negative rights
- nonconsequentialist theories
- normative theories
- optimal moral code
- positive rights
- prima facie obligations
- psychological egoism
- rule utilitarianism
- supererogatory actions
- universal acceptability
- utilitarianism

POINTS TO REVIEW

- consequentialist vs. nonconsequentialist normative theories (p. 56)
- personal vs. impersonal egoism (p. 57)
- the difference between egoism as an ethical theory and egoism as a psychological theory (p. 58)
- three problems with egoism (pp. 58–60)
- Bentham's and Mill's differing views of pleasure (pp. 60–61)
- six points about utilitarianism (pp. 61–62)
- three features of utilitarianism in an organizational context (pp. 62–63)
- three critical inquiries of utilitarianism (pp. 63–65)
- the deathbed-promise example (pp. 63–64)
- business as combining self-interest and social good (or egoism and utilitarianism) (pp. 65–66)
- the convenience store owner and acting from a sense of duty (p. 67)
- Martin's promise as an illustration of the categorical imperative (p. 68)
- hypothetical imperatives vs. the categorical imperative (p. 68)
- two alternative formulations of the categorical imperative (p. 69)
- three features of Kant's ethics in an organizational context (p. 70)
- three critical inquiries of Kant's ethics (pp. 70–72)
- how Ross's theory differs from utilitarianism and from Kant's categorical imperative (p. 73)
- four important characteristics of human rights (p. 75)
- the difference between negative and positive rights (p. 75)
- how rule utilitarianism differs from act utilitarianism (p. 78)
- the optimal moral code and the analogy with traffic rules (p. 79)
- two objections to rule utilitarianism (p. 79)
- two points drawn from Chapter 1 that can help moral discussions (p. 80)
- two-step procedure for morally evaluating actions and choices (p. 81)

FOR FURTHER REFLECTION

1. What value, if any, do you see in business students studying the basics of ethical theory?
2. Which normative theory or general approach to ethics do you find the most plausible or attractive, and why?
3. Can people who disagree about normative ethical theory still reach agreement on practical ethical questions in the business world? If so, how?

CASE 2.1

Hacking into Harvard

EVERYONE WHO HAS EVER APPLIED FOR admission to a selective college or who has been interviewed for a highly desired job knows the feeling of waiting impatiently to learn the result of one's application. So it's not hard to identify with those applicants to some of the nation's most prestigious MBA programs who thought they had a chance to get an early glimpse at whether their ambition was to be fulfilled. While visiting a *Businessweek Online* message board, they found instructions, posted by an anonymous hacker, explaining how to find out what admission decision the business schools had made in their case. Doing so wasn't hard. The universities in question—Harvard, Dartmouth, Duke, Carnegie Mellon, MIT, and Stanford—used the same application software from Apply Yourself, Inc. Essentially, all one had to do was change the very end of the applicant-specific URL to get to the supposedly restricted page containing the verdict on one's application. In the nine hours it took Apply Yourself programmers to patch the security flaw after it was posted, curiosity got the better of about 200 applicants, who couldn't resist the temptation to discover whether they had been admitted.[19]

Some of them got only blank screens. But others learned that they had been tentatively accepted or tentatively rejected. What they didn't count on, however, were two things: first, that it wouldn't take the business schools long to learn what had happened and who had done it and, second, that the schools in question were going to be very unhappy about it. Harvard was perhaps the most outspoken. Kim B. Clark, dean of the business school, said, "This behavior is unethical at best—a serious breach of trust that cannot be countered by rationalization." In a similar vein, Steve Nelson, the executive director of Harvard's MBA program, stated, "Hacking into a system in this manner is unethical and also contrary to the behavior we expect of leaders we aspire to develop."

It didn't take Harvard long to make up its mind what to do about it. It rejected all 119 applicants who had attempted to access the information. In an official statement, Dean Clark wrote that the mission of the Harvard Business School "is to educate principled leaders who make a difference in the world. To achieve that, a person must have many skills and qualities, including the highest standards of integrity, sound judgment and a strong moral compass—an intuitive sense of what is right and wrong. Those who have hacked into this web site have failed to pass that test." Carnegie Mellon and MIT quickly followed suit. By rejecting the ethically challenged, said Richard L. Schmalensee, dean of MIT's Sloan School of Management, the schools are trying to "send a message to society as a whole that we are attempting to produce people that when they go out into the world, they will behave ethically."

Duke and Dartmouth, where only a handful of students gained access to their files, said they would take a case-by-case approach and didn't publicly announce their individualized determinations. But, given the competition for places in their MBA programs, it's a safe bet that few, if any, offending applicants were sitting in classrooms the following semester. Forty-two applicants attempted to learn their results early at Stanford, which took a different tack. It invited the accused hackers to explain themselves in writing. "In the best case, what has been demonstrated here is a lack of judgment; in the worst case, a lack of integrity," said Derrick Bolton, Stanford's director of MBA admissions. "One of the things we try to teach at business schools is making good decisions and taking responsibility for your actions." Six weeks later, however, the dean of Stanford Business School, Robert Joss, reported, "None of those who gained unauthorized access was able to explain his or her actions to our satisfaction." He added that he hoped the applicants "might learn from their experience."

Given the public's concern over the wave of corporate scandals in recent years and its growing interest in corporate social responsibility, business writers and other media commentators warmly welcomed Harvard's decisive response. But soon there was some sniping at the decision by those claiming that Harvard and the other business schools had overreacted. Although 70 percent of Harvard's MBA students approved the decision, the undergraduate student newspaper, *The Crimson*, was skeptical. "HBS [Harvard Business School] has scored a media victory with its hard-line stance," it said in an editorial. "Americans have been looking for a sign from the business community, particularly its leading educational institutions, that business ethics are a priority. HBS's false bravado has given them one, leaving 119 victims in angry hands."

As some critics pointed out, Harvard's stance overlooked the possibility that the hacker might have been a spouse or a parent who had access to the applicant's password and personal identification number. In fact, one applicant said that this had happened to him. His wife found the instructions at *Businessweek Online* and tried to check on the success of his application. "I'm really distraught over this," he said. "My wife is tearing her hair out." To this, Harvard's Dean Clark responds, "We expect applicants to be personally responsible for the access to the website, and for the identification and passwords they receive."

Critics also reject the idea that the offending applicants were "hackers." After all, they used their own personal identification and passwords to log on legitimately; all they did was to modify the URL to go to a different page. They couldn't change anything in their files or view anyone else's information. In fact, some critics blamed the business schools and Apply Yourself more than they did the applicants. If those pages were supposed to be restricted, then it shouldn't have been so easy to find one's way to them.

In an interview, one of the Harvard applicants said that although he now sees that what he did was wrong, he wasn't thinking about that at the time—he just followed the hacker's posted instructions out of curiosity. He didn't consider what he did to be "hacking," because any novice could have done the same thing. "I'm not an IT person by any stretch of the imagination," he said. "I'm not even a great typist." He wrote the university a letter of apology. "I admitted that I got curious and had a lapse in judgment," he said. "I pointed out that I wasn't trying to harm anyone and wasn't trying to get an advantage over anyone." Another applicant said that he knew he had made a poor judgment but he was offended by having his ethics called into question. "I had no idea that they would have considered this a big deal." And some of those posting messages at *Businessweek Online* and other MBA-related sites believe the offending applicants should be applauded. "Exploiting weaknesses is what good business is all about. Why would they ding you?" wrote one anonymous poster.

Dean Schmalensee of MIT, however, defends Harvard and MIT's automatically rejecting everyone who peeked "because it wasn't an impulsive mistake." "The instructions are reasonably elaborate," he said. "You didn't need a degree in computer science, but this clearly involved effort. You couldn't do this casually without knowing that you were doing something wrong. We've always taken ethics seriously, and this is a serious matter." To those applicants who say that they didn't do any harm, Schmalensee replies, "Is there nothing wrong with going through files just because you can?"

To him and others, seeking unauthorized access to restricted pages is as wrong as snooping through your boss's desk to see whether you've been recommended for a raise. Some commentators, however, suggest there may be a generation gap here. Students who grew up with the Internet, they say, tend to see it as a wide-open territory and don't view this level of web snooping as indicating a character flaw.

DISCUSSION QUESTIONS

1. Suppose that you had been one of the MBA applicants who stumbled across an opportunity to learn your results early. What would you have done, and why? Would you have considered it a moral decision? If so, on what basis would you have made it?

2. Assess the morality of what the curious applicants did from the point of view of egoism, utilitarianism, Kant's ethics, Ross's pluralism, and rule utilitarianism.

3. In your view, was it wrong for the MBA applicants to take an unauthorized peek at their application files? Explain why you consider what they did morally permissible or impermissible. What obligations, ideals, and effects should the applicants have considered? Do you think, as some have suggested, that there is a generation gap on this issue?

4. Did Harvard and MIT overreact, or was it necessary for them to respond as they did in order to send a strong message about the importance of ethics? If you were a business-school admissions official, how would you have handled this situation?

5. Assess the argument that the applicants who snooped were just engaging in the type of bold and aggressive behavior that makes for business success. In your view, are these applicants likely to make good business leaders? What about the argument that it's really the fault of the universities for not having more secure procedures and not the fault of the applicants who took advantage of that fact?

6. One of the applicants admits that he used poor judgment but believes that his ethics should not be questioned. What do you think he means? If he exercised poor judgment on a question of right and wrong, isn't that a matter of his ethics? Stanford's Derrick Bolton distinguishes between a lapse of judgment and a lack of integrity. What do you see as the difference? Based on this episode, what, if anything, can we say about the ethics and the character of the curious applicants?

CASE 2.2

The Ford Pinto

THERE WAS A TIME WHEN THE "MADE IN JAPAN" label brought a predictable smirk of superiority to the face of most Americans. The quality of most Japanese products usually was as low as their price. In fact, few imports could match their domestic counterparts, the proud products of Yankee know-how. But by the late 1960s, an invasion of foreign-made goods chiseled a few worry lines into the countenance of U.S. industry. In Detroit, worry was fast fading to panic as the Japanese, not to mention the Germans, began to gobble up more and more of the subcompact auto market.

Never one to take a backseat to the competition, Ford Motor Company decided to meet the threat from abroad head-on. In 1968, Ford executives decided to produce the Pinto. Known inside the company as "Lee's car," after Ford president Lee Iacocca, the Pinto was to weigh no more than 2,000 pounds and cost no more than $2,000.[20]

Eager to have its subcompact ready for the 1971 model year, Ford decided to compress the normal drafting-board-to-showroom time of about three-and-a-half years into two. The compressed schedule meant that any design changes typically made before production-line tooling would have to be made during it.

Before producing the Pinto, Ford crash-tested various prototypes, in part to learn whether they met a safety standard proposed by the National Highway Traffic Safety Administration (NHTSA) to reduce fires from traffic collisions. This standard would have required that by 1972 all new autos be able to withstand a rear-end impact of 20 miles per hour without fuel loss and that by 1973 they be able to withstand an impact of 30 miles per hour. The prototypes all failed the 20-miles-per-hour test. In 1970, Ford crash-tested the Pinto itself, and the result was the same: ruptured gas tanks and dangerous leaks. The only Pintos to pass the test had been modified in some way—for example, with a rubber bladder in the gas tank or a piece of steel between the tank and the rear bumper.

Thus, Ford knew that the Pinto represented a serious fire hazard when struck from the rear, even in low-speed collisions. Ford officials faced a decision. Should they go ahead with the existing design, thereby meeting the production timetable but possibly jeopardizing consumer safety? Or should they delay production of the Pinto by redesigning the gas tank to make it safer and thus concede another year of subcompact dominance to foreign companies? Ford not only pushed ahead with the original design but also stuck to it for the next six years.

What explains Ford's decision? The evidence suggests that Ford relied, at least in part, on cost–benefit reasoning, which is an analysis in monetary terms of the expected costs and benefits of doing something. There were various ways of making the Pinto's gas tank safer. Although the estimated price of these safety improvements ranged from only $5 to $8 per vehicle, Ford evidently reasoned that the increased cost outweighed the benefits of a new tank design.

How exactly did Ford reach that conclusion? We don't know for sure, but an internal report, "Fatalities Associated with Crash-Induced Fuel Leakage and Fires," reveals the cost–benefit reasoning that the company used in cases like this. This report was not written with the Pinto in mind; rather, it concerns fuel leakage in rollover accidents (not rear-end collisions), and its computations applied to all Ford vehicles, not just the Pinto. Nevertheless, it illustrates the type of reasoning that was probably used in the Pinto case.

In the "Fatalities" report, Ford engineers estimated the cost of technical improvements that would prevent gas tanks from leaking in rollover accidents to be $11 per vehicle. The authors go on to discuss various estimates of the number of people killed by fires from car rollovers before settling on the relatively low figure of 180 deaths per year. But given that number, how can the value of those individuals' lives be gauged? Can a dollars-and-cents figure be assigned to a human being? NHTSA thought so. In 1972, it estimated that society loses $200,725 every time a person is killed in an auto accident (adjusted for inflation, today's figure would, of course, be considerably higher). It broke down the costs as follows:

Future productivity losses	
Direct	$132,000
Indirect	41,300
Medical costs	
Hospital	700
Other	425
Property damage	1,500
Insurance administration	4,700
Legal and court expenses	3,000
Employer losses	1,000
Victim's pain and suffering	10,000
Funeral	900
Assets (lost consumption)	5,000
Miscellaneous accident costs	200
Total per fatality	$200,725

Putting the NHTSA figures together with other statistical studies, the Ford report arrived at the following overall assessment of costs and benefits:

Benefits

Savings:	180 burn deaths, 180 serious burn injuries, 2,100 burned vehicles
Unit cost:	$200,000 per death, $67,000 per injury, $700 per vehicle
Total benefit:	(180 × $200,000) + (180 × $67,000) + (2,100 × $700) = $49.5 million

Costs

Sales:	11 million cars, 1.5 million light trucks
Unit cost:	$11 per car, $11 per truck
Total cost:	12.5 million × $11 = $137.5 million

Thus, the costs of the suggested safety improvements outweighed their benefits, and the "Fatalities" report accordingly recommended against any improvements—a recommendation that Ford followed.

Likewise in the Pinto case, Ford's management, whatever its exact reasoning, decided to stick with the original design and not upgrade the Pinto's fuel tank, despite the test results reported by its engineers. Here is the aftermath of Ford's decision:

- Between 1971 and 1978, the Pinto was responsible for a number of fire-related deaths. Ford puts the figure at 23; its critics say the figure is closer to 500. According to the sworn testimony of Ford engineers, 95 percent of the fatalities would have survived if Ford had located the fuel tank over the axle (as it had done on its Capri automobiles).

- NHTSA finally adopted a 30-miles-per-hour collision standard in 1976. The Pinto then acquired a rupture-proof fuel tank. In 1978, Ford was obliged to recall all 1971–1976 Pintos for fuel-tank modifications.

- Between 1971 and 1978, approximately fifty lawsuits were brought against Ford in connection with rear-end accidents in the Pinto. In the Richard Grimshaw case, in addition to awarding over $3 million in compensatory damages to the victims of a Pinto crash, the jury awarded a landmark $125 million in punitive damages against Ford (later reduced by the judge to $3.5 million).

- On August 10, 1978, the 1973 Ford Pinto that eighteen-year-old Judy Ulrich, her sixteen-year-old sister Lynn, and their eighteen-year-old cousin Donna were riding in was struck from the rear by a van near Elkhart, Indiana. The gas tank of the Pinto exploded on impact. In the fire that resulted, the three teenagers were burned to death. Ford was charged with criminal homicide. The judge in the case advised jurors that Ford should be convicted if it had clearly disregarded the harm that might result from its actions, and that disregard represented a substantial deviation from acceptable standards of conduct. On March 13, 1980, the jury found Ford not guilty of criminal homicide.

For its part, Ford has always denied that the Pinto is unsafe compared with other cars of its type and era. The company also points out that in every model year, the Pinto met or surpassed the government's own standards. But what the company doesn't say is that successful lobbying by it and its industry associates was responsible for delaying for seven years the adoption of any NHTSA crash standard. Furthermore, Ford's critics claim that there were more than forty European and Japanese models in the Pinto price and weight range with safer gas-tank position. "Ford made an extremely irresponsible decision," concludes auto safety expert Byron Bloch, "when they placed such a weak tank in such a ridiculous location in such a soft rear end."

Has the automobile industry learned a lesson from Ford's experience with the Pinto? Many people would probably answer, yes, carmakers are more concerned about safety these days. That's one reason it shocked the nation to learn in 2014 that General Motors had known for years that defective ignition switches on some of its models prevent their airbags from deploying in crashes. (The bags need to draw on the car's power system.) And yet—for reasons that are still unclear—the company did nothing about the problem, ignoring possible fixes proposed by its engineers and telling customers and accident victims that there was no evidence of a flaw. According to GM, the faulty switches have led to thirteen deaths, but an independent review of federal crash data puts the number of fatalities at 303.

Some consumers knew their Pintos were dangerous.

DISCUSSION QUESTIONS

1. What moral issues does the Pinto case raise?
2. Suppose Ford officials were asked to justify their decision. What moral principles do you think they would invoke? Assess Ford's handling of the Pinto from the perspective of each of the moral theories discussed in this chapter.
3. Utilitarians would say that jeopardizing motorists does not by itself make Ford's action morally objectionable. The only morally relevant matter is whether Ford gave equal consideration to the interests of each affected party. Do you think Ford did this?
4. Is cost–benefit analysis a legitimate tool? What role, if any, should it play in moral deliberation? Critically assess the example of cost–benefit analysis given in the case study. Is there anything unsatisfactory about it? Could it have been improved upon in some way?
5. Speculate about Kant's response to the idea of placing a monetary value on a human life. Is doing so ever morally legitimate?
6. What responsibilities to its customers do you think Ford had? What are the most important moral rights, if any, operating in the Pinto case?
7. Would it have made a moral difference if the savings resulting from not improving the Pinto gas tank had been passed on to Ford's customers? Could a rational customer have chosen to save a few dollars and risk having the more dangerous gas tank? What if Ford had told potential customers about its decision?
8. The maxim of Ford's action might be stated thus: "When the cost of a safety improvement would hurt the bottom line, it's all right not to make it." Can this maxim be universalized? Does it treat humans as ends in themselves? Would manufacturers be willing to abide by it if the positions were reversed and they were in the role of consumers?
9. Should Ford have been found guilty of criminal homicide in the Ulrich case?
10. Are carmakers these days concerned enough about safety? Why do you think GM failed to address the ignition switch problem?
11. Is it wrong for business to sell a product that is not as safe as it could be, given current technology? Is it wrong to sell a vehicle that is less safe than competing products on the market? Are there limits to how far automakers must go in the name of safety?

CASE 2.3

Blood for Sale

SOL LEVIN WAS A SUCCESSFUL STOCKBROKER in Tampa, Florida, when he recognized the potentially profitable market for safe and uncontaminated blood and, with some colleagues, founded Plasma International. Not everybody is willing to make money by selling his or her own blood, and in the beginning Plasma International bought blood from people addicted to drugs and alcohol. Although innovative marketing increased Plasma International's sales dramatically, several cases of hepatitis were reported in recipients. The company then began looking for new sources of blood.[21]

Plasma International searched worldwide and, with the advice of a qualified team of medical consultants, did extensive testing. Eventually they found that the blood profiles of several rural West African tribes made them ideal prospective donors. After negotiations with the local government, Plasma International signed an agreement with several tribal chieftains to purchase blood.

Business went smoothly and profitably for Plasma International until a Tampa paper charged that Plasma was purchasing blood for as little as fifteen cents a pint and then reselling it to hospitals in the United States and South America for $25 per pint. In one recent disaster, the newspaper alleged, Plasma International had sold 10,000 pints, netting nearly a quarter of a million dollars.

The newspaper story stirred up controversy in Tampa, but the existence of commercialized blood marketing systems in the United States is nothing new. Approximately half the blood and plasma obtained in the United States is bought and sold like any other commodity. By contrast, the National Health Service in Great Britain relies entirely on a voluntary system of blood donation. Blood is neither bought nor sold. It is available to anyone who needs it without charge or obligation, and donors gain no preference over nondonors.

In an important study, economist Richard Titmuss showed that the British system works better than the American one in terms of economic and administrative efficiency, price, and blood quality. The commercialized blood market, Titmuss argued, is wasteful of blood and plagued by shortages. In the United States, bureaucratization, paperwork, and administrative overhead result in a cost per unit of blood that is five to fifteen times higher than it is in Great Britain. Hemophiliacs, in particular, are disadvantaged by the U.S. system and have enormous bills to pay. In addition, commercial markets are much more likely to distribute contaminated blood.

Titmuss also argued that the existence of a commercialized system discourages voluntary donors. People are less apt to give blood if they know that others are selling it. Psychologists have found similar conflicts between financial incentives and moral or altruistic conduct in other areas.[22] Philosopher Peter Singer has elaborated on this point in the case of blood:

> If blood is a commodity with a price, to give blood means merely to save someone money. Blood has a cash value of a certain number of dollars, and the importance of the gift will vary with the wealth of the recipient. If blood cannot be bought, however, the gift's value depends upon the need of the recipient. Often, it will be worth life itself. Under these circumstances blood becomes a very special kind of gift, and giving it means providing for strangers, without hope of reward, something they cannot buy and without which they may die. The gift relates strangers in a manner that is not possible when blood is a commodity.
>
> This may sound like a philosopher's abstraction, far removed from the thoughts of ordinary people. On the contrary, it is an idea spontaneously expressed by British donors in response to Titmuss's questionnaire. As one woman, a machine operator, wrote in reply to the question why she first decided to become a blood donor: "You can't get blood from supermarkets and chain stores. People themselves must come forward; sick people can't get out of bed to ask you for a pint to save their life, so I came forward in hopes to help somebody who needs blood."

The implication of this answer, and others like it, is that even if the formal right to give blood can coexist with commercialized blood banks, the respondent's action would have lost much of its significance to her, and the blood would probably not have been given at all. When blood is a commodity, and can be purchased if it is not given, altruism becomes unnecessary, and so loosens the bonds that can otherwise exist between strangers in a community. The existence of a market in blood does not threaten the formal right to give blood, but it does away with the right to give blood which cannot be bought, has no cash value, and must be given freely if it is to be obtained at all. If there is such a right, it is incompatible with the right to sell blood, and we cannot avoid violating one of these rights when we grant the other.[23]

Both Titmuss and Singer believe that the weakening of the spirit of altruism in this sphere has important repercussions. It marks, they think, the increasing commercialization of our lives and makes similar changes in attitude, motive, and relationships more likely in other fields. And, indeed, the introduction of money often changes relationships. Day-care centers, for example, sometimes have a problem with parents showing up late to collect their children, forcing teachers to stay after closing time. To solve the problem, economists recommend charging parents a fee for being tardy. However, when this solution was tested at ten day-care centers in Israel, the result was that the number of late pick-ups doubled.[24] Whereas before the parents had viewed themselves as having a responsibility to the hard-working staff to pick up their children on time and felt guilty about failing to do so, now they saw the matter in purely commercial terms, a service to be purchased for a fee.

Update

Dr. Arthur Matas, a prominent kidney-transplant surgeon, is pushing for one change that it's doubtful either Titmuss or Singer would like. Lately, he's been traveling the United States making the case for lifting the legal ban on kidney sales. That ban was imposed in 1984 by an outraged Congress after a Virginia physician had proposed buying kidneys from poor people and selling them to the highest bidder. By contrast, Dr. Matas isn't trying to make money. He would like the government to handle kidney sales, and the kidneys to go to whoever is at the top of the current waiting list, whether the patient is rich or poor. And that list grows longer every year as the gap continues to widen—it's now nearly five to one—between patients in need and the number of kidneys available from either living or deceased donors.

With eligible patients often waiting for five or six years, more and more people are taking Dr. Matas seriously, but many experts still balk at the idea of organ sales. One of them is Dr. Francis Delmonico, a professor at Harvard University and president of the network that runs the nation's organ-distribution system. He worries that Dr. Matas' plan would exploit the poor and vulnerable, that it would cause altruistic kidney donations to wither, and that wealthy patients would manage to find a way around a regulated market to get a kidney faster.[25]

DISCUSSION QUESTIONS

1. Is Sol Levin running a business "just like any other business," or is his company open to moral criticism? Defend your answer by appeal to moral principle.

2. Did Plasma International strike a fair bargain with the West Africans who supplied their blood to the company? Or is Plasma guilty of exploiting them in some way? Explain your answer.

3. What are the contrasting ideals of the British and U.S. blood systems? Which system, in your opinion, better promotes human freedom and respect for people? Which system better promotes the supply of blood?

4. Examine the pros and cons of commercial transactions in blood from the egoistic, the utilitarian, and the Kantian perspectives.

5. Are Titmuss and Singer correct to suggest that the buying and selling of blood reduces altruism? Does knowing that you can sell your blood (and that others are selling theirs) make you less inclined to donate your blood?

6. Singer suggests that although the right to sell blood does not threaten the formal right to give blood, it is incompatible with "the right to give blood, which cannot be bought, which has no cash value, and must be given freely if it is to be obtained at all." Assess that idea. Is there such a right?

7. Many believe that commercialization is increasing in all areas of modern life. If so, is it something to be applauded or condemned? Is it wrong to treat certain things—such as human organs—as commodities?

8. Do you believe that we have a moral duty to donate blood? If so, why and under what circumstances? If not, why not?

CHAPTER 3
JUSTICE AND ECONOMIC DISTRIBUTION

INTRODUCTION

IT SEEMS STRANGE TO RECALL THAT UNTIL THE early years of the twentieth century, there was no federal tax on personal income. Only when the Sixteenth Amendment to the U.S. Constitution was adopted in 1913 did Congress gain the right to tax people's income. Since then, the income tax laws have grown enormously complex. At around 70,000 pages, the federal tax code is more than two and a half times longer than it was in 1985.[1] Lawyers study for years to master the intricacies of the system, and most people with middle incomes or better require professional assistance to file their annual tax forms.

Because the tax rules do so much to shape the character of our economy and the distribution of income and wealth across the country, their fairness is frequently a political issue—thus the controversy over Congress's 2013 decision to raise the top marginal tax rate from 35 to 39.6 percent. This made it what it had been back in 2000, but it now applies only to income over $400,000. Still, if you are wealthy, that tax rate might seem high to you. However, as Table 3.1 shows, until Ronald Reagan lowered it, the tax rate for the wealthiest individuals had been 63 percent and, until the early 1960s, it had been 91 percent.

When President Reagan reduced taxes on the wealthy, he also eliminated some important tax loopholes. But the most significant feature of his personal tax philosophy was its rejection of the principle of "progressivity"—namely, that the wealthy ought to pay taxes at a higher rate than the poor. Today's income tax system, with seven different tax brackets, remains progressive, but some complain that in reality those who are less well-to-do often end up paying more. One of the people making this charge is—surprisingly enough—Warren Buffett, the nation's second richest man. Recently, he says, he earned $46 million but paid only 18 percent of it in federal tax, whereas the average tax rate paid by his employees, whose salaries range from $60,000 to $750,000, was 33 percent. Buffett is convinced that this is no statistical fluke. In fact, he is willing to bet anyone $1 million (to be paid to a charity selected by the winner) that the average tax rate (income and payroll) paid by the 400 wealthiest people in the country is lower than that paid by their secretaries and receptionists.[2]

> THE RICHEST 1 PERCENT receives nearly $1 out of every $4.

Still, it remains true that America's wealthier citizens pay the bulk of the nation's income tax—for the simple reason that most of the nation's income goes to them. The richest 1 percent of the population receives nearly $1 out of every $4 generated by the U.S. economy.[3] The 1 percent's average after-tax income is $1.3 million, whereas the bottom 20 percent averages less than $18,000 a year.[4] This is part of a trend over the past thirty years toward an increasingly unequal distribution of national income in the United States, with those who are already well off now getting a larger share of the pie than ever before. Today the after-tax income of the richest 20 percent of income earners is greater than that of the bottom 80 percent combined.[5] The income of the top 0.1 percent is even more dazzling. They receive in a day and a half about what the bottom 90 percent earn in a year.[6]

From World War II through 1980, the inflation-adjusted income of the median family more than doubled, but since then it has been relatively flat despite the fact that more wives have entered the workforce.[7] In fact, adjusted for inflation, wages for men remain

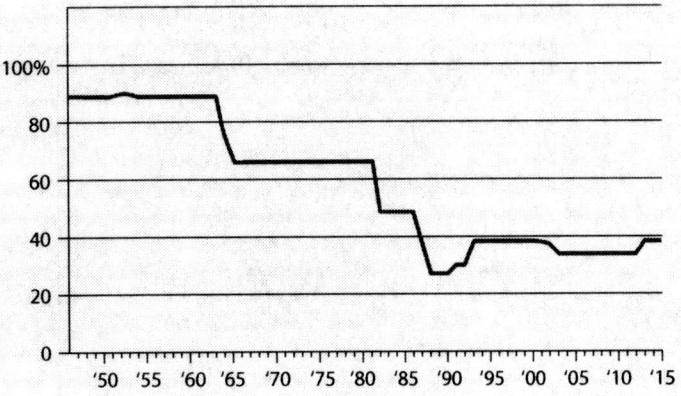

Table 3.1 Top Marginal Income Tax Rate

below their 1973 peak.[8] This is despite the fact that per capita economic production in the United States has expanded by 93 percent.[9] In contrast, middle-level managers have fared much better, and top executives have done spectacularly well. *Forbes* magazine calculates average annual CEO pay (salary, bonuses, and long-term compensation) at the 500 largest American companies to be $10.5 million.[10] This dwarfs what CEOs receive in other countries, such as Japan.[11]

Since 1980 the compensation of the top American CEOs has grown from 42 times to more than 300 times greater than that of the average person working under them.[12] The median weekly salary of full-time workers is $776.[13] If the average CEO works 60 hours a week and 52 weeks a year, then he or she earns that much every fourteen minutes. Since 1990 CEO pay has gone up by 571 percent. In comparison, corporate profits have grown by a relatively modest 114 percent, and the average worker's pay, adjusted for inflation, has barely budged.[14] A schoolteacher who made $31,000 in 1990 would now make $177,000 if teachers' salaries had grown at the same rate as CEO pay.

While those on top do better than ever, life continues to be a struggle for people in the middle and lower echelons. Indeed, according to some economists, the lack of middle-class income growth is "the defining issue of our time."[15] Although our economy has created millions of new jobs in the last two decades, most of them pay relatively low wages.[16] That's one reason the middle class has shrunk.[17] Productivity gains have gone predominantly to investors, not to wage earners, with capitalists grabbing a larger share of the national income at the expense of workers.[18] Whereas output per hour and real hourly compensation rose hand in hand from 1950 to 1980, U.S. Department of Labor statistics indicate that since then compensation has lagged behind.[19] Although the average American family works hard—twelve weeks more each year than thirty years ago[20]—many families have trouble coping. Most American jobs do not pay enough to support a full household or to provide what most people feel are necessities,[21] and the number of people who define themselves as "have-nots" has increased.[22] For a variety of reasons, moreover, people's incomes are more volatile, and their lives less economically secure, these days. For example, the chance that a person or family will experience a year-to-year drop in income of more than 50 percent has almost doubled since the 1970s (from one in twenty to about one in eleven).[23]

These trends are even more alarming when set against the background of the extremely unequal distribution of wealth in this country. The top 1 percent (about one-and-a-half million families) not only receives a disproportionate share of the national income but also owns nearly 40 percent of the nation's total net worth. That's double the share of total national wealth owned by the top 1 percent in 1976 and is more than that owned by the entire bottom 90 percent of U.S. households. This economic elite owns half of all stocks, mutual funds, financial securities, and trusts; two-thirds of all business equity; and 36 percent of nonresidential real estate.[24] In contrast, the bottom 60 percent of Americans owns only 5 percent of the nation's wealth, and the lowest 40 percent less than 1 percent.[25] Moreover, the richest of the rich have pulled even farther away from everyone else. The top 0.01 percent (about 16,000 families) possesses $6 trillion in assets; that's equal to the combined wealth of the bottom two-thirds of the country.[26]

Although the United States has always prided itself on being a land of opportunity, it has less upward mobility than do most English-speaking or Western European nations.[27] In particular, Americans on the bottom rung are more likely to be stuck there, with less chance of getting ahead than their counterparts in other advanced nations.[28] "You can't take solace anymore in the American dream of working hard and migrating up through society," says William J. McDonough, president of the Federal Reserve Bank of New York.[29] Or as one Federal Reserve Bank economist puts it, "The apple falls even closer to the tree than we thought."[30]

One reason, of course, is that parents work very hard to transmit their advantages to their children, especially with respect to education, a crucial determinant of future income. These days, social class increasingly determines access to college.

Three-quarters of the students at the nation's top 146 universities hail from the richest fourth of the nation. Only 3 percent of them come from the bottom income quartile and only 10 percent from the bottom half of the income scale. This means that at an elite university you are twenty-five times more likely to run into a rich student than a poor one.[31] Even at the better state universities, the number of students from families making more than $100,000 has increased to 40 percent. In general, qualified high school graduates from low-income families are only one-third as likely to complete a bachelor's degree as are students from families earning $75,000 or more.[32]

There is nothing inevitable about declining social mobility or about large inequalities in income and wealth. They are not brute facts of nature, even in market-oriented societies. For example, the distribution of income in Germany and Japan is far more equal than that in the United States, even though both are just as thoroughly capitalist, and an American is three times more likely to be poor than is someone in Italy.[33] Rather, political choices determine how income and wealth are distributed and what sort of assistance is given to those who are struggling to get by. The United States simply chooses to spend a smaller percentage of its GDP than European countries do in combating inequality and pursuing policies intended to assist the bottom half of society to advance.[34] That's why, for example, 17 percent of America's children live in poverty but only 3 percent of Norway's do.[35] More generally, it is the reason that income inequality, according to CIA figures, is greater in the United States than it is in Europe or Russia or even countries such as Tunisia or Egypt that recently rebelled against their oligarchs.[36] How much inequality and what sort of socioeconomic disparities a society is willing to accept reflect both its moral values and the relative strength of its contending social and political forces.

This chapter focuses on the subject of economic justice, which concerns the constellation of moral issues raised by a society's distribution of wealth, income, status, and power. Ethical questions arise daily about these matters. Is it just, for example, that CEOs pull in astronomical salaries and help themselves to enormous benefits when this reduces the profits of stockholders, who own the company? Or, to take another issue, thanks to modern technology, today's hospitals are able to perform life-prolonging feats of medicine that were undreamed of only a couple of decades ago, but these services are often extraordinarily costly. Who, then, should have access to them? Those who can afford them? Any who need them? Those who are most likely to benefit?

LEARNING OBJECTIVES

Chapter 2 discussed several basic moral theories and the general principles of right and wrong associated with them. This chapter focuses on the more specific topic of justice and economic distribution—that is, on the principles that are relevant to the moral assessment of society's distribution of economic goods and services. Although the topic is an abstract one, it is particularly relevant to the study of business ethics, because it concerns the moral standards to be used in evaluating the socioeconomic framework within which both business and nonbusiness organizations operate. Specifically, this chapter will examine these topics:

1. The concept of justice, its relation to fairness, equality, rights, and what people deserve, and some rival principles of economic distribution
2. The utilitarian approach to justice in general and economic justice in particular
3. The libertarian theory, which places a moral priority on liberty and free exchange
4. The egalitarian social-contract theory of John Rawls

THE NATURE OF JUSTICE

Justice is an old concept with a rich history, a concept that is fundamental to any discussion of how society ought to be organized. Philosophical concern with justice goes back at least to ancient Greece. For Plato and some of his contemporaries, justice seems to have been the paramount virtue or, more precisely, the sum of virtue with regard to our relations with others. Philosophers today, however, generally distinguish justice from the whole of morality. The complaint that something is unjust is more specific than that it is bad or immoral. What, then, makes an act, policy, or institution unjust? Unfortunately,

> Questions of justice typically focus on fairness, equality, desert, or rights.

the terms *just* and *unjust* are vague, and different people use them in different ways. Still, talk of justice or injustice typically focuses on at least one of several related ideas: fairness, equality, desert, and rights.

First, **justice** is often used to mean *fairness*. Justice frequently concerns the fair treatment of members of groups of people or else looks backward to the fair compensation of prior injuries. Exactly what fairness requires is difficult to say, and different standards may be pertinent in different cases. If corporate manager Smith commits bribery, he is justly punished under our laws. If other managers commit equally serious crimes but are allowed to escape punishment, then Smith suffers a comparative injustice because he was unfairly singled out. But Smith and other white-collar criminals are treated unfairly and thus unjustly, although this time for the opposite reason, if stiffer sentences are meted out to common criminals for less grave offenses.

One way unfairness creates injustice occurs when like cases are not treated in the same fashion. Following Aristotle, most philosophers believe that we are required, as a formal principle of justice, to treat similar cases alike except where there is some relevant difference. This principle emphasizes the role of impartiality and consistency in justice, but it is a purely formal principle because it is silent about which differences are relevant and which are not. Furthermore, satisfying this formal requirement does not guarantee that justice is done. For example, a judge who treats similar cases alike can succeed in administering fairly and nonarbitrarily a law that is itself unjust (like a statute requiring racial segregation).

Related to Aristotle's fairness requirement is a second idea commonly bound up with the concept of justice: *equality*. Justice is frequently held to require that our treatment of people reflect their fundamental moral equality. While Aristotle's formal principle of justice does not say whether we are to assume equality of treatment until some difference between cases is shown or to assume the opposite until some relevant similarities are demonstrated, a claim of injustice based on equality is meant to place the burden of proof on those who would endorse unequal treatment. Still, the premise that all persons are equal does not establish a direct relationship between justice and economic distribution. We all believe that some differences in the treatment of persons are consistent with equality (punishment, for example), and neither respect for equality nor a commitment to equal treatment necessarily implies an equal distribution of economic goods.

Despite equality, then, individual circumstances—in particular, what a person has done—make a difference. We think it is unjust, for example, when a guilty person goes free or an innocent person hangs, regardless of how others have been treated. This suggests that in addition to equal or impartial treatment, justice has a third aspect, the idea of *desert*. Justice requires that people get what they deserve or, as a number of ancient moralists put it, that each receive his or her due.

This is closely related to a fourth and final idea—namely, that one is treated unjustly when one's moral *rights* are violated. John Stuart Mill, in fact, made this the defining characteristic of injustice. In his view, what distinguishes injustice from other types of wrongful behavior is that it involves a violation of the rights of some identifiable person:

> Whether the injustice consists in depriving a person of a possession, or in breaking faith with him, or in treating him worse than he deserves, or worse than other people who have no greater claims—in each case the supposition implies two things: a wrong done, and some assignable person who is wronged. . . . It seems to me that this feature in the case—a right in some person, correlative to the moral obligation—constitutes the specific difference between justice and generosity or beneficence. Justice implies something which it is not only right to do, and wrong not to do, but which some individual person can claim from us as a moral right.[37]

> **SUMMARY**
> Justice is one important aspect of morality. Talk of justice and injustice generally involves appeals to the related notions of fairness, equality, desert, and rights. Economic or distributive justice concerns the principles appropriate for assessing society's distribution of social benefits and burdens, particularly wealth, income, status, and power.

The Alderson Federal Prison Camp in West Virginia housed domestic guru Martha Stewart. Similar to this detention center, Butner Federal Correctional Institution, where convicted Ponzi-schemer Bernie Madoff is serving his sentence, is the type of institution that has come to be known as a "country-club prison." How is this sort of description likely to affect some people's notion of just desert and equality of justice?

RIVAL PRINCIPLES OF DISTRIBUTION

Justice, then, is an important subclass of morality in general, a subclass that generally involves appeals to the overlapping notions of fairness, equality, desert, and rights. Turning to the topic of **distributive justice**—that is, to the proper distribution of social benefits and burdens (in particular, economic benefits and burdens)—we see that a number of rival principles have been proposed. Among the principles most frequently recommended as a basis of distribution are these: to each an equal share, to each according to individual need, to each according to personal effort, to each according to social contribution, and to each according to merit. Each one of these principles has its advocates, and each seems plausible in some circumstances, but only in some. There are problems with each. For example, if equality of income was guaranteed, then the lazy would receive as much as the industrious; however, effort is hard to measure and compare, and what one is able to contribute to society may depend on one's luck in being at the right place at the right time. And so on. No single principle seems to work in enough circumstances to be defended successfully as the sole principle of justice in distribution.

It often seems that we simply employ different principles of distributive justice in different circumstances. For example, corporations in certain industries may be granted tax breaks because of their social contribution whereas welfare payments generally rest on need, and business firms typically base promotions on meritorious performance. Moreover, multiple principles may often be relevant to a single situation. Sometimes they may pull in the same direction, as when wealthy professionals such as doctors defend their high incomes simultaneously on grounds of superior effort, merit, social contribution, and even (because of the high cost of malpractice insurance) need. Or the principles may pull in different directions, as when a teacher must balance effort against performance in assigning grades to pupils. Some philosophers are content to leave the situation here. As they see it, there are various equally valid, prima facie principles of just distribution—equality, need, effort, and so on—and one must try to find the principle

Some philosophers believe that there are a number of equally valid principles of just distribution. We must determine which one best applies in a given situation.

that best applies in the given circumstances. If several principles seem to apply, then one must simply weigh them the best one can.

In his book *Spheres of Justice*, Michael Walzer pursues a more sophisticated version of this pluralistic approach.[38] Skeptical of the assumption that justice requires us to implement (in different contexts) some basic principle or set of principles, Walzer argues

> that different goods ought to be distributed for different reasons, in accordance with different procedures, by different agents; and that all these differences derive from different understandings of the social goods themselves—the inevitable product of historical and cultural particularism.[39]

Different norms and principles govern different distributive spheres, and these norms and principles are shaped by the implicit social meanings of the goods in question. He continues:

> Every social good or set of goods constitutes, as it were, a distributive sphere within which only certain criteria and arrangements are appropriate. [For example], money is inappropriate in the sphere of ecclesiastical office. . . . There is no single standard [against which all distributions are to be measured]. But there are standards (roughly knowable even when they are also controversial) for every social good and every distributive sphere in every particular society.[40]

As Walzer sees it, distributive criteria are determined by the particular historically shaped social meanings of the goods in question. The philosophical task is to tease out the inner logic of each type of good, thus revealing the tacit, socially shared values that govern (or should govern) its distribution.

Walzer's historically informed discussion of topics such as medical care or dirty and degrading work are rich and intriguing, but his view implies that when it comes to issues of distributive justice, the best philosophers can do is to try to unravel the implicit, socially specific norms that govern the distribution of different goods in a particular society. Many contemporary philosophers disagree. They believe that we should step farther back than Walzer does from existing norms and social arrangements and seek some general theory of justice in economic distribution, on the basis of which we can assess current social practices. Three such theories are the utilitarian, the libertarian, and the Rawlsian (egalitarian).

> **SUMMARY**
> Economic distribution might be based on pure equality, need, effort, social contribution, or merit. Each of these principles is plausible in some circumstances but not in others. In some situations, the principles pull us in different directions. Dissatisfied with a pluralistic approach, moral philosophers have sometimes sought to develop more general theories of justice.
>
> Other philosophers seek a general theory of economic justice. The utilitarian, libertarian, and Rawlsian theories are important examples.

THE UTILITARIAN VIEW

For utilitarians, as Chapter 2 explained, happiness is the overarching value. Whether one assesses the rightness and wrongness of actions in terms of how much happiness they produce, as an act utilitarian does, or uses happiness as the standard for deciding what moral principles a society should accept as the basis for determining right and wrong, as a rule utilitarian does, happiness is the only thing that is good in and of itself. On that utilitarians are agreed.

Earlier we considered John Stuart Mill's idea that injustice involves the violation of the rights of some identifiable person. This is what distinguishes it from other types of immoral behavior. But if injustice involves the violation of moral rights, how does a utilitarian like Mill understand talk of rights? According to Mill, to have a right to something is to have a valid claim on society to protect me in the possession of that thing, either by the force of law or through education and opinion. And I have that valid claim in the first place because society's protection of my possession of that thing is warranted on utilitarian grounds. "To have a right, then, is . . . to have something which society ought to defend me in the possession of. If the objector goes on to ask why it ought, I can give him no other reason than general utility."⁴¹ What utilitarianism identifies as rights are certain moral rules, the observance of which is of the utmost importance for the long-run, overall maximization of happiness.

Accordingly, Mill summed up his view of justice as follows:

> Justice is a name for certain classes of moral rules which concern the essentials of human well-being more nearly, and are therefore of more absolute obligation, than any other rules for the guidance of life; and the notion which we have found to be of the essence of the idea of justice—that of a right residing in an individual—implies and testifies to this more binding obligation.
>
> The moral rules which forbid mankind to hurt one another (in which we must never forget to include wrongful interference with each other's freedom) are more vital to human well-being than any maxims, however important, which only point out the best mode of managing some department of human affairs.⁴²

Although justice for Mill was ultimately a matter of promoting social well-being, not every issue of social utility was a matter of justice. The concept of justice identifies certain important social utilities—that is, certain rules or rights, the upholding of which is crucial for social well-being.

For utilitarians, then, justice is not an independent moral standard distinct from their general principle. Rather, the maximization of happiness ultimately determines what is just and unjust. Critics of utilitarianism contend that knowing what will promote happiness is always difficult. People are bound to estimate consequences differently, thus making the standard of utility an inexact and unreliable principle for determining what is just. Mill, however, did not see much merit in this criticism. For one thing, it presupposes that we all agree about what the principles of justice are and how to apply them. This is far from the case, Mill argued. Indeed, without utilitarianism to provide a determinate standard of justice, one is always left with a plethora of competing principles, all of which seem to have some plausibility but are mutually incompatible.

As an example, Mill pointed to the conflict between two principles of justice that occurs in the realm of economic distribution. Is it just or not, he asked, that more talented workers should receive a greater remuneration? There are two possible answers to this question:

> On the negative side of the question it is argued that whoever does the best he can deserves equally well, and ought not in justice to be put in a position of inferiority for no fault of his own; that superior abilities have already advantages more than enough . . . without adding to these a superior share of the world's goods; and that society is bound in justice rather to make compensation to the less favoured for this unmerited inequality of advantages than to aggravate it.⁴³

This argument sounds plausible, but then so does the alternative answer:

> On the contrary side it is contended that society receives more from the more efficient labourer; that, his services being more useful, society owes him a larger return for them; that a greater share of the joint result is actually his work, and not to allow his claim to it is a kind of robbery; that, if he is only to receive as much as others, he can only be justly required to produce as much.⁴⁴

Here we have two conflicting principles of justice. How are we to decide between them? The problem, Mill said, is that both principles seem plausible:

> Justice has in this case two sides to it, which it is impossible to bring into harmony, and the two disputants have chosen opposite sides; the one looks to what it is just that the individual should receive, the other to what it is just that the community should give.⁴⁵

Mill believed that justice concerns certain rules or rights that are vitally important for human well-being.

SUMMARY

Utilitarianism holds that the maximization of happiness ultimately determines what is just and unjust. Mill contended, more specifically, that the concept of justice identifies certain rules or rights—the upholding of which is crucial for promoting well-being—and that injustice always involves violating the rights of some identifiable individual.

Each disputant is, from his or her own point of view, unanswerable. "Any choice between them, on grounds of justice," Mill continued, "must be perfectly arbitrary." What, then, is the solution? For Mill, the utilitarian, it was straightforward: "Social utility alone can decide the preference."[46] The utilitarian standard must be the ultimate court of appeal in such cases. Only the utilitarian standard can provide an intelligent and satisfactory way of handling controversial questions of justice and of resolving conflicts between competing principles of justice.

UTILITARIANISM AND ECONOMIC DISTRIBUTION

The utilitarian theory of justice ties the question of economic distribution to the promotion of social well-being or happiness. Utilitarians favor whichever economic system will bring the most good for society as a whole. But what system is that? Utilitarianism itself, as a normative theory, provides no answer. The answer depends on the relevant social, economic, and political facts. A utilitarian must understand the various possibilities, determine their consequences, and assess the available options. Obviously, this is not a simple task. Deciding what sort of economic arrangements would best promote human happiness requires the utilitarian to consider many things, including (1) the type of economic ownership (private, public, or mixed); (2) the way of organizing production and distribution in general (pure laissez faire, markets with government planning and regulation, or fully centralized planning); (3) the type of authority arrangements within the units of production (worker control versus managerial prerogative); (4) the range and character of material incentives; and (5) the nature and extent of social security and welfare provisions.

Utilitarianism doesn't tell us which economic system will produce the most happiness. That question hangs on the social, economic, and political facts.

As a matter of historical fact, utilitarians in the early nineteenth century tended to favor free trade and the laissez-faire view of Adam Smith that unregulated market relations and free competition best promote the total social good.[47] Today it is probably fair to say that few, if any, utilitarians believe happiness would be maximized by a pure nineteenth-century-style capitalism, without any welfare arrangements. However, they are not in agreement on the question of what economic arrangements would in fact maximize happiness. Nonetheless, many utilitarians would favorably view increased **worker participation** in industrial life and more equal distribution of income.

Worker Participation

In his *Principles of Political Economy*, originally published in 1848, Mill argued for the desirability of breaking down the sharp and hostile division between the producers, or workers, on the one hand, and the capitalists, or owners, on the other. Not only would this be a good thing, it was also, he thought, something that the advance of civilization was tending naturally to bring about: "The relation of masters and workpeople will be gradually superseded by partnership, in one or two forms: in some cases, association of the labourers with the capitalist; in others, and perhaps finally in all, association of labourers among themselves."[48] These developments would not only enhance productivity but also—and more important—promote the fuller development and well-being of the people involved. The aim, Mill thought, should be to enable people "to work with or for one another in relations not involving dependence."[49]

By the association of labor and capital, Mill had in mind different schemes of profit sharing. For example, "in the American ships trading to China, it has long been the custom for every sailor to have an interest in the profits of the voyage; and to this has been ascribed the general good conduct of those seamen." This sort of association, however, would eventually give way to a more complete system of worker cooperatives:

> The form of association, however, which if mankind continue to improve, must be expected in the end to predominate, is not that which can exist between a capitalist as chief, and workpeople without a voice in the management, but the association of the labourers themselves on terms of equality, collectively owning the capital with which they carry on their operations, and working under managers elected and removable by themselves.[50]

In *Principles*, Mill discussed several examples of successful cooperative associations and viewed optimistically the future of the cooperative movement:

> Eventually, and in perhaps a less remote future than may be supposed, we may, through the cooperative principle, see our way to a change in society, which would combine the freedom and independence of the individual, with the moral, intellectual, and economical advantages of aggregate production; and which . . . would realize, at least in the industrial department, the best aspirations of the democratic spirit.[51]

What that transformation implied for Mill was nothing less than "the nearest approach to social justice, and the most beneficial ordering of industrial affairs for the universal good, which it is possible at present to foresee."[52]

Greater Equality of Income

Utilitarians are likely to be sympathetic to the argument that steps should be taken to reduce the great disparities in income that characterize our society today. They are likely to believe that making the distribution of income more equal is a good strategy for maximizing happiness. One reason is that inequality appears to be correlated with various social ills. More equal societies, such as Sweden and Finland, with a relatively narrow gap separating their richest and poorest citizens score higher on various indices of social well-being. In terms of infant mortality, life expectancy, malnutrition, obesity, teenage pregnancy, economic insecurity, personal anxiety, and other measures, they fare better than do societies like the United States that have greater inequality.[53] There is also evidence that equality promotes economic growth.[54]

Another reason utilitarians tend to favor greater inequality of income goes back to what economists would call the **declining marginal utility of money**. This phrase simply means that successive additions to one's income produce, on average, less happiness or welfare than did earlier additions.

The declining utility of money follows from the fact, as Professor Richard Brandt explains it, that the outcomes we want are preferentially ordered, some being more strongly wanted than others:

> So a person, when deciding how to spend his resources, picks a basket of groceries which is at least as appealing as any other he can purchase with the money he has. The things he does not buy are omitted because other things are wanted more. If we double a person's income, he will spend the extra money on items he wants less (some special cases aside), and which will give less enjoyment than will the original income. The more one's income, the fewer preferred items one buys and the more preferred items one already has. On the whole, then, when the necessities of life have been purchased and the individual is spending on luxury items, he is buying items which will give less enjoyment. . . . This conclusion corresponds well with commonsense reflection and practice.[55]

The obvious implication is that a more egalitarian allocation of income—that is, an allocation that increases the income of those who now earn less—would boost total happiness. Brandt, for one, therefore defends equality of after-tax income on utilitarian grounds, subject to the following exceptions: supplements to meet special needs,

SUMMARY
Utilitarians must examine various factual issues to determine which economic system and principles will best promote social well-being or happiness. Many utilitarians favor increased worker participation and a more equal distribution of income.

supplements necessary for incentives or to allocate resources efficiently, and variations to achieve other socially desirable ends, such as population control.[56] Brandt states that this guiding principle of distribution is of only prima facie force and may have to be balanced against other principles and considerations. Still, it illustrates the point that utilitarians today are likely to advocate increased economic equality.

THE LIBERTARIAN APPROACH

Whereas utilitarians associate justice with social utility, philosophers who endorse what is called **libertarianism** identify justice with an ideal of liberty. For them, liberty is the prime value, and justice consists in permitting each person to live as he or she pleases, free from the interference of others. Accordingly, one libertarian asserts: "We are concerned with the condition of men in which coercion of some by others is reduced as much as possible in society."[57] Another maintains that libertarianism is "a philosophy of personal liberty—the liberty of each person to live according to his own choices, provided he does not attempt to coerce others and thus prevent them from living according to their choices."[58] Such views show clearly the libertarian's association of justice with liberty and of liberty itself with the absence of interference by other persons.

> Libertarians refuse to restrict individual liberty even if doing so would increase overall happiness.

Libertarians firmly reject utilitarianism's concern for total social well-being. Utilitarians are willing to restrict the liberty of some, to interfere with their choices, if doing so will promote greater net happiness than not doing so. Libertarians cannot stomach that approach. As long as you are not doing something that interferes with anyone else's liberty, then no person, group, or government should disturb you in living the life you choose—not even if its doing so would maximize social happiness.

Although individual liberty is something that all of us value, it may not be the only thing we value. For the libertarian, however, liberty takes priority over other moral concerns. In particular, justice consists solely of respect for individual liberty. A libertarian world, with a complete commitment to individual liberty, would be a very different world from the one we now live in. Consider the following: The government registers young men for military service and can, if it chooses, draft them; laws prevent adults from viewing certain kinds of pornography and from ingesting substances that the legislature deems harmful or immoral (such as marijuana and cocaine); and the state imposes taxes on our income to—among many other things—support needy citizens, provide loans to college students, and fund various projects for the common good. From a libertarian perspective, none of these policies is just.

Given the assumption that *liberty* means "noninterference," libertarians generally agree that liberty allows only a minimal or "night-watchman" state. Such a state is limited to the narrow functions of protecting its citizens against force, theft, and fraud; enforcing contracts; and performing other such basic maintenance functions. In this view, a more extensive state—in particular, one that taxes its better-off citizens to support the less fortunate ones—violates the liberty of individuals by forcing them to support projects, policies, or persons they have not freely chosen to support.

> **SUMMARY**
> The libertarian theory identifies justice with liberty, which libertarians understand as living according to our own choices, free from the interference of others. They reject utilitarianism's concern for total social well-being.

NOZICK'S THEORY OF JUSTICE

Although libertarians differ in how they formulate their theory, the late Harvard professor Robert Nozick's *Anarchy, State, and Utopia* is a very influential statement of the libertarian case.[59] Nozick's challenging and powerful advocacy of libertarianism has stimulated much debate, obliging philosophers of all political persuasions to take the libertarian theory seriously. His views are thus worth presenting in detail.

Nozick begins from the premise that people have certain basic moral rights, which he calls **Lockean rights**. By alluding to the political philosophy of John Locke (1632–1704), Nozick wishes to underscore that these rights are both negative and natural. They are negative because they require only that people forbear from acting in certain ways—in particular, that we refrain from interfering with others. Beyond this, we are not obliged to do anything positive for anyone else, nor is anyone required to do anything positive for us. We have no right, for example, to be provided with satisfying work or with any material goods that we might need. These negative rights, according to Nozick, are natural in the sense that we possess them independently of any social or political institutions.

These individual rights impose firm, nearly absolute restrictions (or, in Nozick's phrase, "side constraints") on how we may act. We cannot morally infringe on someone's rights for any purpose. Not only are we forbidden to interfere with a person's liberty in order to promote the general good, we are prohibited from doing so even if violating that individual's rights would somehow prevent other individuals' rights from being violated. Each individual is autonomous and responsible and should be left to fashion his or her own life free from the interference of others—as long as doing so is compatible with the rights of others to do the same. Only an acknowledgment of this almost absolute right to be free from coercion, Nozick argues, fully respects the distinctiveness of individuals, each with a unique life to lead.

A belief in these rights shapes Nozick's theory of economic justice, which he calls the **entitlement theory**. Essentially, Nozick maintains that people are entitled to their holdings (that is, goods, money, and property) as long as they have acquired them fairly. Stated another way, if you have obtained your possessions without violating other people's Lockean rights, then you are entitled to them and may dispose of them as you choose. No one else has a legitimate claim on them. If you have secured a vast fortune without injuring other people, defrauding them, or otherwise violating their rights, then you are morally permitted to do with your fortune whatever you wish—bequeath it to a relative, endow a university, or squander it in riotous living. Even though other people may be going hungry, justice imposes no obligation on you to help them.

> According to Nozick's theory, you are entitled to your holdings if you have acquired them without violating other people's rights.

The *first principle of Nozick's entitlement theory* concerns the original acquisition of holdings—that is, the appropriation of unheld goods or the creation of new goods. If a person acquires a holding in accordance with this principle, then he or she is entitled to it. If, for example, you discover and remove minerals from the wilderness or make something out of materials you already legitimately possess, then you have justly acquired this new holding. Nozick does not spell out this principle or specify fully what constitutes a just original acquisition, but the basic idea is clear and reflects the thinking of John Locke.

Property is a moral right, said Locke, because individuals are morally entitled to the products of their labor. When they mix their labor with the natural world, they are entitled to the resulting product. Thus, if a man works the land, then he is entitled to the land and its products because through his labor he has put something of himself into them. This investment of self through labor is the moral basis of ownership, Locke wrote, but he acknowledged limits to this right:

> In the beginning . . . men had a right to appropriate, by their labour, each one of himself, as much of the things of nature, as he could use. . . . Whatsoever he tilled and reaped, laid up and made use of, before it spoiled, that was his peculiar right; whatsoever he enclosed, and could feed, and make use of, the cattle and product was also his. But if either the grass of his inclosure rotted on the ground, or the fruit of his planting perished without gathering, and laying up, this part of the earth . . . was still to be looked on as waste, and might be the possession of any other.[60]

In this early **state of nature** (the phrase is Locke's) prior to the formation of government, property rights were limited not only by the requirement that one not waste what one claimed, but also by the restriction that "enough and as good" be left for others—that is, that one's appropriation not make others worse off. Later, however, with the introduction of money, Locke thought that both these restrictions were overcome. You can pile up money beyond your needs without its spoiling; and if your property is used productively and the proceeds are offered for sale, then your appropriation leaves others no worse off than before.

Nozick's second principle concerns transfers of already-owned goods from one person to another: how people may legitimately transfer holdings to others and how they may legitimately get holdings from others. If a person possesses a holding because of a legitimate transfer, then he or she is entitled to it. Again, Nozick does not work out the details, but it is clear that acquiring something by purchase, as a gift, or through exchange would constitute a legitimate acquisition. Gaining something through theft, force, or fraud would violate the principle of justice in transfer.

Nozick's third and final principle states that one can justly acquire a holding only in accord with the two principles previously discussed. If you come by a holding in some other way, you are not entitled to it.

Nozick sums up his theory this way:

1. A person who acquires a holding in accordance with the principle of justice in acquisition is entitled to that holding.

2. A person who acquires a holding in accordance with the principle of justice in transfer, from someone else entitled to the holding, is entitled to the holding.

3. No one is entitled to a holding except by (repeated) applications of principles 1 and 2.

In short, the distribution of goods in a society is just if and only if all are entitled to the holdings they possess. Nozick calls his entitlement theory "historical" because what matters is how people come to have what they have. If people are entitled to their possessions, then the distribution of economic holdings is just, regardless of what the actual distribution happens to look like (for instance, how far people are above or below the average income) or what its consequences are.

NOZICK'S WILT CHAMBERLAIN EXAMPLE

Nozick argues that respect for liberty inescapably leads one to repudiate other conceptions of economic justice in favor of his entitlement approach. One of his most ingenious examples features Wilt Chamberlain, the late basketball star.

Suppose, Nozick says, that things are distributed according to your favorite non-entitlement theory, whatever it is. (He calls this distribution D_1.) Now imagine that Wilt Chamberlain signs a contract with a team that guarantees him $5 from the price of each ticket. Whenever people buy a ticket to a game, they drop $5 into a special box with Chamberlain's name on it. To them, seeing him play is worth $5. Imagine then that in the course of a season, 1 million people attend his games, and Chamberlain ends up with far more than the average income—far more, indeed, than anyone else in the society earns. This result (D_2) upsets the initial distributional pattern (D_1). Can the proponent of D_1 complain? Nozick thinks not:

> Is [Chamberlain] entitled to this income? Is this new distribution, D_2, unjust? If so, why? There is *no* question about whether each of the people was entitled to the control over the resources they held in D_1; because that was the distribution (your favorite) that (for the purposes of the argument) we assumed was acceptable. Each of these persons *chose* to give [$5] of their money to Chamberlain. . . . If D_1 was a just distribution, and people voluntarily moved from it to D_2, transferring parts of their

---

SUMMARY

The libertarian philosopher Robert Nozick defends the entitlement theory. This theory holds that the distribution of goods, money, and property is just if people are entitled to what they have—that is, if they have acquired their possessions without violating the rights of anyone else.

All that matters for Nozick is how people came to have what they have, not the pattern or results of the distribution of goods.

shares they were given under D_1 . . . isn't D_2 also just? If the people were entitled to dispose of the resources to which they were entitled (under D_1), didn't this include their being entitled to give it to, or exchange it with, Wilt Chamberlain? Can anyone else complain on grounds of justice?[61]

Having defended the legitimacy of Chamberlain's new wealth, Nozick pushes his case further, arguing that any effort to maintain some initial distributional arrangement like D_1 will interfere with people's liberty to use their resources as they wish. To preserve this original distribution, he writes, society would have to "forbid capitalist acts between consenting adults":

> The general point illustrated by the Wilt Chamberlain example . . . is that no [non-entitlement] principle of justice can be continuously realized without continuous interference with people's lives. Any favored pattern would be transformed into one unfavored by the principle, by people choosing to act in various ways; for example, by people exchanging goods and services with other people, or giving things to other people. . . . To maintain a pattern one must either continually interfere to stop people from transferring resources as they wish to, or continually (or periodically) interfere to take from some persons resources that others for some reason chose to transfer to them.[62]

THE LIBERTARIAN VIEW OF LIBERTY

Libertarianism clearly involves a commitment to leaving market relations—buying, selling, and other exchanges—totally unrestricted.* Force and fraud are forbidden, of course, but there should be no meddling with the uncoerced exchanges of consenting individuals. Not only is the market morally legitimate, but any attempt to interfere with voluntary and nonfraudulent transactions between adults will be unacceptable, even unjust. Thus, libertarians are for economic laissez faire and against any governmental economic activity that interferes with the marketplace, even if the point of the interference is to enhance the performance of the economy.

It is important to emphasize that libertarianism's enthusiasm for the market rests on this commitment to liberty. By contrast, utilitarians who defend an unregulated market do so on the ground that it works better than either a planned, socialist economy or the sort of regulated capitalism with some welfare benefits that we in fact have in the United States. If a utilitarian defends laissez faire, he or she does so because of its consequences. If we convinced a utilitarian that some other form of economic organization would better promote human well-being, the utilitarian would advocate that instead. With libertarians this is definitely not the case. As a matter of fact, libertarians typically agree with Adam Smith that unregulated capitalist behavior best promotes everyone's interests. But even if, hypothetically, someone like Nozick were convinced that some sort of socialism or welfare capitalism would outperform laissez-faire capitalism economically—leading, say, to greater productivity, a shorter workday, and a higher standard of living—he or she would still reject this alternative as morally unacceptable. To tinker with the market, however beneficial it might be, would involve violating someone's liberty.

Libertarians say that their commitment to an unrestricted **free market** reflects the priority of liberty over other values. However, libertarians do not value liberty in the mundane sense of people's freedom to do what they want to do. Rather, libertarians understand freedom in terms of their theory of rights, thus building a commitment to private property into their concept of liberty. According to them, being able to do what you want does not automatically represent an increase in your liberty. It does so only if you remain within the boundaries set by the Lockean rights of others. Likewise, one is unfree or coerced only when one's rights are infringed.

> **SUMMARY**
> In the Wilt Chamberlain example, Nozick argues that other theories of economic justice inevitably fail to respect people's liberty.

> Libertarians build a commitment to private property into their concept of liberty.

---

*Chapter 4 examines the nature of market economies in general and capitalism in particular.

Imagine, for example, that having purchased the forest in which I occasionally stroll, the new owner bars my access to it. It would seem that my freedom has been reduced because I can no longer ramble where I wish. But libertarians deny that this is a restriction of my liberty. My liberty is restricted if and only if someone violates my Lockean rights, which no one has done. Suppose that I go for a hike in the forest anyway. If the sheriff's deputies arrest me, they prevent me from doing what I want to do. But according to libertarianism, they do not restrict my liberty, nor do they coerce me. Why not? Because my hiking in the forest violates the landowner's rights.

Here libertarians seem driven to an unusual use of familiar terminology, but they have no choice. They cannot admit that abridging the landowner's freedom to do as he wants with his property would expand my freedom. If they did, then their theory would be in jeopardy. They would have to acknowledge that restricting the liberty or property rights of some could enhance the liberty of others. In other words, if their theory committed them simply to promoting as much as possible the goal of people doing what they want to do, then libertarians would be in the position of balancing the freedom of some against the freedom of others. But this sort of balancing and trading off is exactly what libertarians dislike about utilitarianism.

If liberty means being free to do what you want, it's not true that libertarians value it above everything else. What they value are Lockean property rights, which then set the parameters of liberty. Libertarians frequently contend that (1) private property is necessary for freedom and (2) any society that doesn't respect private property rights is coercive. But libertarianism makes 1 true by definition, and 2 is incorrect. Any system of property (whether Lockean, socialist, or something in between) necessarily puts restrictions on people's conduct; its rules are coercive. What one system of property permits, another forbids. Society X prevents me from hiking in your woods, whereas society Y prevents you from stopping me. Both systems of rules are coercive. Both grant some freedoms and withhold others.

MARKETS AND FREE EXCHANGE

> Libertarians don't contend that people morally deserve what they get in a free market, but only that they are entitled to it.

Libertarians defend market relations, then, as necessary to respect human liberty (as their theory understands liberty). However, in doing so, libertarians do not assert that, morally speaking, people *deserve* what they receive from others through gift or exchange, only that they are *entitled* to whatever they receive. The market tends generally, libertarians believe, to reward people for skill, diligence, and successful performance. Yet luck plays a role, too. Jack makes a fortune from having been in the right place at the right time with jeggings, while Jill loses her investment because the market for bottled water collapses. The libertarian position is not that Jack deserves to be wealthy and Jill does not; rather, it is that Jack is entitled to his holdings if he has acquired them in accordance with the principles of justice.

The same point comes up with regard to gifts and inheritance. Inheritance strikes many people as patently unfair. How can it be just, they ask, that one child inherits a vast fortune, the best schooling, and social, political, and business connections that will ensure his or her future, while another child inherits indigence, inferior schooling, and connections with crime? At birth neither youngster deserves anything—a fact suggesting, perhaps, that an equal division of holdings and opportunities would be the only fair allocation. For his part, Nozick contends that deserving has no bearing on the justice of inherited wealth; people are simply entitled to it as long as it is not ill-gotten. Or looking at it the other way, if one is entitled to one's holdings, then one has a right to do with them as one wishes, including using them to benefit one's children.

According to libertarians, a totally free market is necessary for people to exercise their fundamental rights. Sometimes, however, unregulated market transactions can lead to disastrous results. Unfortunately, this is more than just a theoretical possibility. Amartya Sen, the Nobel Prize-winning economist, has shown how in certain circumstances changing market entitlements have led to mass starvation. Although the average person thinks of famine as caused simply by a shortage of food, Sen and other experts have established that famines are frequently accompanied by no shortfall of food in absolute terms. Indeed, even more food may be available during a famine than in nonfamine years—if one has the money to buy it. Famine occurs because large numbers of people lack the financial wherewithal to obtain the necessary food.[63]

For example, drought may cause food output in one area to decline and the peasants in that area to starve because they lack the means to buy food from elsewhere, even though there is no dearth of food in the country as a whole (Ethiopia in 1973). Or famine may result when the purchasing power of one occupational group shoots up, ruining the chances of other groups, whose nominal incomes have not changed, to buy food (Bengal in 1943). A reduction of food output because of potato blight triggered the great Irish famine of the 1840s, which killed a higher proportion of the population than any other famine in recorded history. But if one looks at the United Kingdom as a whole, there was no shortage of food. Food could certainly have moved from Britain to Ireland if the Irish could have afforded to purchase it. As it was, at the height of the famine, food was exported from Ireland to England because the prosperous English could pay a higher price for it.[64]

Libertarians would find it immoral and unjust to force people to aid the starving or to tax the affluent in order to set up programs to relieve hunger or prevent famines in the first place. Nor does justice require that a wealthy merchant assist the hungry children in his community to stay alive. And it would certainly violate the merchant's property rights for the children to help themselves to his excess food. Nevertheless, although justice does not require that one assist those in need, libertarians would generally acknowledge that we have some humanitarian obligations toward others. Accordingly, they would not only permit but also presumably encourage people to voluntarily assist others. Justice does not require the merchant to donate, and it forbids us from forcing him to do so, but charity on his part would be a good thing. This reflects the libertarian's firm commitment to **property rights**: What you have legitimately acquired is yours to do with as you will.

Unregulated market transactions can sometimes lead to disastrous results, as Amartya Sen has shown.

SUMMARY
Libertarians operate with a distinctive concept of liberty, defend free exchange and laissez-faire markets without regard to results, put a priority on freedom over all other values, and see property rights as existing prior to any social arrangements. Critics contest each of these features of libertarianism.

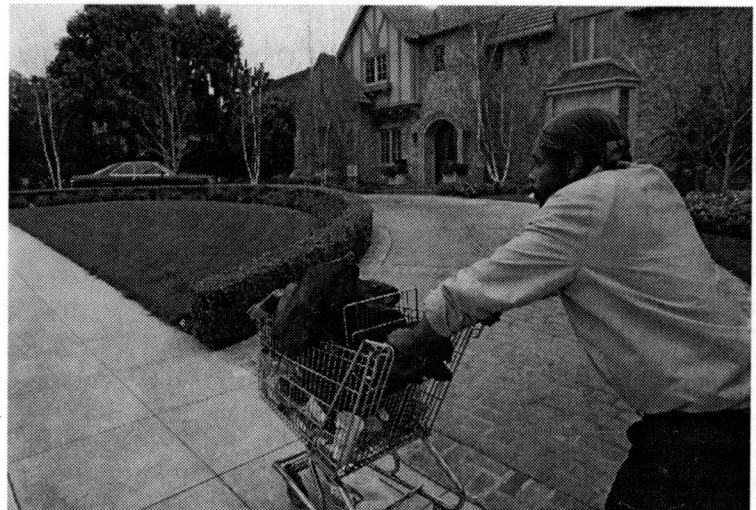

According to the libertarian theory of justice, the people who own the house in the background have no obligation to assist the homeless. The wealth that they have acquired is theirs to dispose of entirely as they wish.

PROPERTY RIGHTS

Nozick's theory makes property rights nearly sacrosanct. From the perspective of libertarianism, property rights grow out of one's basic moral rights, reflecting one's initial creation or appropriation of the product, some sort of exchange or transfer between consenting persons, or a combination of these. Property rights exist prior to any social arrangements and are morally antecedent to any legislative decisions that a society might make. However, Nozick's critics argue that it is a mistake to think of property as a simple, pre-social relation between a person and a physical thing.

First, property is not restricted to material objects like cars, watches, or houses. In developed societies, it may include abstract goods, interests, and claims. For instance, property may include the right to pay debts with the balance in a bank account, the right to dividends from a corporate investment, and the right to collect from a pension plan one has joined. In fact, the courts have counted as property a wide range of items such as new life forms, an original idea, pension payments, the news, or a place on the welfare rolls.[65]

Second, property ownership involves a bundle of different rights governing one's ability to possess, use, manage, dispose of, or restrict others' access to something in certain specified ways. The nature of this bundle differs among societies, as do the types of things that can be owned. In any society, property ownership is structured by the various implicit or explicit rules and regulations governing the legitimate acquisition and transfer of various types of goods, interests, and claims. Not only do property rights differ between societies, but the nature of ownership can also change over time in any given society. As a general trend, the social restrictions on property ownership in the United States have increased dramatically during our history (much to the displeasure of libertarians).

For these reasons, most nonlibertarian social and political theorists view property rights as a function of the particular institutions of a given society. This is not to say that a society's property arrangements cannot be criticized. On the contrary, their morality can be assessed just as the morality of any other institution can.

RAWLS'S THEORY OF JUSTICE

A Theory of Justice by John Rawls (1921–2002) is generally thought to be the most influential work of the post–World War II period in social and political philosophy, at least in the English language.[66] Not only has Rawls's elegant theory touched a responsive chord in many readers, but also his book helped rejuvenate serious work in normative theory. Even those who are not persuaded by Rawls find themselves obliged to come to terms with his thinking. Although Rawls's basic approach is not difficult to explain (and Rawls himself had sketched out his key concepts in earlier articles), *A Theory of Justice* elaborates his ideas with such painstaking care and philosophical thoroughness that even vigorous critics of the book (such as his colleague Robert Nozick) pay sincere tribute to its many virtues.

By his own account, Rawls presents his theory as a modern alternative to utilitarianism, one that he hopes will be compatible with the belief that justice must be associated with fairness and the moral equality of persons. Rawls firmly wishes to avoid reducing justice to a matter of society utility. At the same time, his approach differs fundamentally from Nozick's. Rawls conceives of society as a cooperative venture among its members, and he elaborates a conception of justice that is thoroughly social. He does not base his theory, as Nozick does, on the postulate that individuals possess certain natural rights prior to any political or social organization.

Two features of Rawls's theory are particularly important: his hypothetical contract approach and the principles of justice that he derives with it. Rawls's strategy is to ask what we would choose as the fundamental principles to govern society if, hypothetically, we were to meet for this purpose in what he calls the **original position**. He then elaborates the nature of this original position, the constraints on the choice facing us, and the reasoning that he thinks people in the original position would follow. In this way, Rawls offers a modern variant of social contract theory, in the tradition of Hobbes, Locke, Rousseau, and other earlier philosophers. Rawls argues that people in the original position would agree on two principles as the basic governing principles of their society and that these principles are, accordingly, the principles of justice. The first is a guarantee of certain familiar and fundamental liberties to each person. The second—more controversial—holds in part that social and economic inequalities are justified only if those inequalities benefit the least advantaged members of society. These principles are examined at some length later in this chapter.

> Rawls's strategy is to ask what principles people would choose to govern their society if they were in the "original position."

THE ORIGINAL POSITION

Various principles of economic justice have been proposed, but an important question for philosophers is whether, and how, any such principles can be justified. Thinking of possible principles of economic distribution is not very difficult, but proving the soundness of such a principle, or at least showing it to be more plausible than its rivals, is a challenging task. After all, people seem to differ in their intuitions about what is just and unjust, and their sentiments are bound to be influenced by their social position. Nozick's entitlement theory, for example, with its priority on property rights, is bound to seem more plausible to a corporate executive than to a migrant farmworker. The justice of a world in which some children are born into wealth while other children struggle to get by on welfare is unlikely to seem as obvious to the poor as it may to the well-to-do.

The strategy Rawls employs to identify and justify the basic principles of justice is to imagine that people come together for the purpose of deciding on the ground rules for their society, in particular on the rules governing economic distribution. Although in the past groups of people have written down constitutions and similar political documents, never have the members of a society decided from scratch on the basic principles of justice that should govern them. Nor is it even remotely likely that people will do this in the future. What Rawls imagines is a thought experiment. The question is hypothetical: What principles would people choose in this sort of original position? If we can identify these principles, Rawls contends, then we will have identified the principles of justice precisely because they are the principles that we would all have agreed to.

The Nature of the Choice

On what basis are we to choose these principles? The most obvious answer is that we should select principles that strike us as just. But this won't work. Even if we all agreed about what is just and unjust, we would be relying on our already existing ideas about justice as a basis for choosing the principles to govern our society. Philosophically, this approach doesn't accomplish anything. We would simply be going in a circle, using our existing conception of justice to prove the principles of justice.

Rawls suggests instead that we imagine people in the original position choosing solely on the basis of self-interest: Each individual chooses the set of principles for governing society that will be best for himself or herself (and loved ones). We don't have to imagine that people are antagonistic or that outside of the original position they are selfish; we simply imagine that they hope to get the group to choose those principles that will, more than any other possible principles, benefit them. If people in the original position can agree on some governing principles on the basis of mutual self-interest, then these principles will be, Rawls thinks, the principles of justice. Why? Because the principles are agreed to under conditions of equality and free choice. By analogy, if we make up a game and all agree ahead of time, freely and equally, on how the game is to be played, nobody can later complain that the rules are unfair.

The Veil of Ignorance

If people in the original position are supposed to choose principles on the basis of self-interest, agreement seems unlikely. If Carolyn has vast real estate holdings, she will certainly want rules that guarantee her extensive property rights, whereas her tenants are likely to support rules that permit rent control. Likewise, the wealthy will tend to advocate rules rather like Nozick's entitlement theory, whereas the poor will, on the basis of their self-interest, desire a redistribution of property. Conflicts of self-interest seem bound to create totally irreconcilable demands. For instance, artists may contend that they should be rewarded more than professional people, men that they should earn more than women, and laborers that they merit more than people with desk jobs.

Given that some rules would benefit one group while other rules would benefit another, it seems improbable that people in the original position would concur. As a way around this problem, Rawls asks us to imagine that people in the original position do not know what social position or status they hold in society. They do not know whether they are rich or poor, nor do they know their personal talents and characteristics—whether, for example, they are athletic or sedentary, artistic or tone deaf, intelligent or not very bright, or physically sound or handicapped in some way. They do not know their race or even their gender. Behind what Rawls calls the **veil of ignorance**, people in the original position know nothing about themselves personally or about what their individual situation will be once the rules are chosen and the veil is lifted. They do, however, have a general knowledge of history, sociology, and psychology—although no specific information about the society they will be in once the veil is lifted.

Under the veil of ignorance, the people in Rawls's original position have no knowledge about themselves or their situation that would lead them to argue from a partial or biased point of view. No individual is likely to argue that some particular group—such as white men, property owners, star athletes, or philosophers—should receive special social and economic privileges when, for all that individual knows, he or she will be nonwhite, propertyless, unathletic, and bored by philosophy when the veil is lifted. Because individuals in the original position are all equally ignorant of their personal predicaments and they are all trying to advance their self-interest, agreement is possible. The reasoning of any one person will be the same as the reasoning of each of the others, for each is in identical circumstances and each has the same motivation. As a result, no actual group has to perform Rawls's thought experiment. People who read Rawls's book can imagine that they are in the original position and then decide whether they would choose the principles Rawls thinks they would.

The veil of ignorance eliminates bias and makes the original position a fair way of choosing principles.

The veil of ignorance, in effect, forces people in the original position to be objective and impartial and makes agreement possible. Also, according to Rawls, the fact that people have no special knowledge that would allow them to argue in a biased way accords with our sense of fairness. The circumstances of the original position are genuinely equal and fair, and because of this, the principles agreed to under these conditions have a good claim to be considered the principles of justice.

CHOOSING THE PRINCIPLES

Although people in the original position are ignorant of their individual circumstances, they know that whatever their particular goals, interests, and talents turn out to be, they will want more, rather than less, of what Rawls calls **primary social goods**. These include not only income and wealth but also rights, liberties, opportunities, status, and self-respect. Of course, once the veil of ignorance is lifted, people will have more specific ideas about what is good for them. For example, they may choose a life built around religion, one spent in commerce and industry, or one devoted to academic study. But whatever these particular individual goals, interests, and plans turn out to be, they will almost certainly be furthered, and definitely never limited, by the fact that people in the original position secured for themselves more rather than less in the way of primary goods.

How, then, will people in the original position choose their principles? *A Theory of Justice* explores in depth the reasoning that Rawls thinks would guide their choice. At the heart of Rawls's argument is the contention that people in the original position will be conservative, in the sense that they will not wish to gamble with their futures. In setting up the ground rules for their society, they are determining their own fates and those of their children. This exercise is not something to be taken lightly, a game to be played and replayed. Rather, with so much at stake, people will reason cautiously.

Consider, for example, the possibility that people in the original position will set up a feudal society: 10 percent of the population will be nobles, living a life of incredible wealth, privilege, and leisure; the other 90 percent will be serfs, toiling away long hours to support the extravagant lifestyles of the aristocracy. Perhaps some people would consider the joy of being a pampered noble so great that they would vote for such an arrangement behind the veil of ignorance, but they would be banking on a long shot. When the veil of ignorance is lifted, the odds are nine to one that they will be poor and miserable serfs, not lords. Rawls thinks that people in the original position will not, in fact, gamble with their futures. They will not agree to rules that make it overwhelmingly likely that they will have to face a grim life of hardship.

Rawls argues that for similar reasons, people in the original position will not adopt the utilitarian standard to govern their society, because the utilitarian principle might sacrifice the well-being of some to enhance society's total happiness. People in the original position, Rawls argues, will not be willing to risk sacrificing their own happiness, once the veil of ignorance is lifted, for the greater good.

What people in the original position would actually do, Rawls believes, is follow what game strategists call the **maximin rule** for making decisions. According to this rule, you should select the alternative under which the worst that could happen to you is better than the worst that could happen to you under any other alternative—that is, you should try to *maxi*mize the *min*imum that you will receive. This rule makes sense when you care much more about avoiding an unacceptable or disastrous result (such as being a serf) than about getting the best possible result (being a noble) and when you have no real idea what odds you are facing. It is a conservative decision principle, but Rawls thinks that people in the original position will find it a rational and appropriate guideline for their deliberations.

RAWLS'S TWO PRINCIPLES

Rawls argues that after considering various alternatives, people in the original position will eventually endorse the following two principles as the fundamental governing principles of their society:

1. Each person is to have an equal right to the most extensive total system of equal basic liberties compatible with a similar system of liberty for all.[67]

2. Social and economic inequalities are to satisfy two conditions: First, they are to be attached to positions and offices open to all under conditions of fair equality of opportunity; and second, they are to be to the greatest expected benefit of the least-advantaged members of society.[68]

> **SUMMARY**
> John Rawls's theory of justice lies within the social-contract tradition. He asks us to imagine people meeting in the original position to choose the basic principles that are to govern their society. Although in this original position people choose on the basis of self-interest, we are to imagine that they are behind a veil of ignorance, with no personal information about themselves. Rawls contends that any principles agreed to under these circumstances have a strong claim to be considered the principles of justice.

Rawls believes that people in the original position would endorse his two principles.

> These are the principles of justice because they would be agreed to in an initial situation of equality and fairness.

These principles, because they are agreed to in an initial situation of equality and fairness, will be the principles of justice. Once these two principles of justice have been endorsed, people in the original position can gradually be given more information about their specific society. They can then go on to design their basic social and political institutions in more detail.

According to Rawls, the first principle takes priority over the second, at least for societies that have attained a moderate level of affluence. The liberties Rawls has in mind are the traditional democratic ones of freedom of thought, conscience, and religious worship, as well as freedom of the person and political liberty. Explicitly absent are "the right to own certain kinds of property (e.g., means of production), and freedom of contract as understood by the doctrine of laissez-faire." The first principle guarantees not only equal liberty to individuals but also as much liberty to individuals as possible, compatible with others having the same amount of liberty. There is no reason why people in the original position would settle for anything less.

All regulations could be seen as infringing on personal liberty, because they limit what a person may do. The law that requires you to drive on the right-hand side of the road denies you the freedom to drive on either side whenever you wish. Some would argue that justice requires only an equal liberty. For example, as long as every motorist is required to drive on the right-hand side of the road, justice is being served; or if everyone in a dictatorial society is forbidden to criticize the leader's decisions, then all are equal in their liberty. But Rawls argues that if more extensive liberty is possible, without inhibiting the liberty of others, then it would be irrational to settle for a lesser degree of liberty. In the case of driving, permitting me to drive on either side of the road would only interfere with the liberty of others to drive efficiently to their various destinations, but introducing right-turn-on-red laws enhances everyone's liberty. In the dictatorship example, free speech could be more extensive without limiting anyone's liberty.

The second principle concerns social and economic inequalities. Regarding inequalities, Rawls writes:

> It is best to understand not *any* differences between offices and positions, but differences in the benefits and burdens attached to them either directly or indirectly, such as prestige and wealth, or liability to taxation and compulsory services. Players in a game do not protest against there being different positions, such as batter, pitcher, catcher, and the like, nor to there being various privileges and powers as specified by the rules; nor do the citizens of a country object to there being the different offices of government such as president, senator, governor, judge, and so on, each with their special rights and duties.[69]

Rather, at issue are differences in wealth and power, honors and rewards, and privileges and salaries that attach to different roles in society.

Rawls's second principle states that insofar as inequalities are permitted—that is, insofar as it is compatible with justice for some jobs or positions to bring greater rewards than others—these positions must be open to all. In other words, there must be meaningful equality of opportunity in the competition among individuals for those positions in society that bring greater economic and social rewards. This, of course, is a familiar ideal, but what exactly a society must do to achieve not just legal but full and fair equality of opportunity will be a matter of debate.

The other part of the second principle is less familiar and more controversial. Called the **difference principle**, it is the distinctive core of Rawls's theory. It states that inequalities are justified only if they work to the benefit of the least-advantaged members of society. By "least-advantaged," Rawls simply means those who are least well-off. But what does it mean to require that inequalities work to the benefit of this group?

Imagine that we are back in the original position. We wish to make sure that under the principles we choose, the worst that can happen to us once the veil of ignorance is lifted is still better than the worst that might have happened under some other arrangement. We might, therefore, choose strict social and economic equality. With an equal division of goods, there's no risk of doing worse than anyone else and no danger of being sacrificed to increase the total happiness of society. In the case of liberty, people in the original position do insist on full equality, but with social and economic inequality, the matter is a little different.

Suppose, for instance, that as a result of dividing things up equally, people lack an incentive to undertake some of the more difficult work that society needs done. It might then be the case that allowing certain inequalities—for example, paying people more for being particularly productive or for undertaking the necessary training to perform some socially useful task—would work to everyone's benefit, including those who would be earning less. If so, then why not permit those inequalities?

Compare these two diagrams:

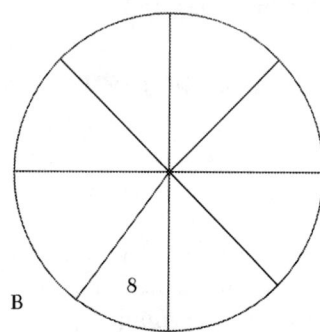

Each pie represents a possible social and economic distribution among eight basic groups in society (the number eight is arbitrary). In Figure A, things are divided equally; in Figure B, unequally. Suppose, then, that because a society permits inequalities as an incentive to get people to work harder or to do work that they otherwise would not have wanted to do, the overall amount to be distributed among society's members increases—that is, the economic pie grows in size from A to B, and the people with the thinnest slice of B are better-off than they would have been with an equal slice of A.

Which society will people in the original position prefer? Obviously the one represented by Figure B, because the least they could receive in B (the slice labeled 8) is bigger than any of the eight equal slices in A. People in the original position do not care about equality of distribution as a value in and of itself; they want the social and economic arrangement that will provide them with the highest minimum.

Rawls is not trying to prove that the benefits received by the better-off will always, or even usually, trickle down to the least advantaged (although, of course, some people believe that). Rather, his point is simply that people in the original position would not insist on social and economic equality at all costs. If permitting some people to be better-off than the average resulted in the least-well-off segment of society being better-off than it would have been under a strictly equal division, then this is what people in the original position will want. Rawls's difference principle is intended to capture this idea. Rawls's principles permit economic inequalities only if they do in fact benefit the least advantaged.

Consider the recurrent proposal to lower further the income tax on capital gains (that is, on personal income from the sale of assets like stocks, bonds, and real estate). Proponents claim that reducing the tax will spur trading in financial assets, which in turn will lead to growth in tax revenues, and that the cut will trigger more long-term

> **SUMMARY**
> Rawls argues that people in the original position would follow the maximin rule for making decisions. They would choose principles guaranteeing that the worst that could happen to them is better than the worst that could happen to them under any rival principles. Rawls argues that they would agree on two principles: (1) Each person has a right to the most extensive scheme of liberties compatible with others having the same amount of liberty. (2) To be justified, any inequalities must be to the greatest expected benefit of the least advantaged and open to all under conditions of fair equality of opportunity.

> People in the original position do not want equality at all costs. They will permit inequality if it improves the lot of the least advantaged.

investment, helping revitalize the economy. Critics of the proposal contest both claims. Still, everyone agrees that the tax break would certainly increase the income of those who are already very rich because the wealthiest 0.1 percent of the nation receives half of all capital-gains income.[70] Will lowering taxes on the rich benefit the least-advantaged members of society more in the long run than any alternative tax policy?

This question illustrates the application of Rawls's difference principle in a practical context, but we must remember that Rawls intends his principles to be used not as a direct guide to day-to-day policy decisions but rather as the basis for determining what form society's primary social, political, and economic institutions should take in the first place. What will these institutions look like? More specifically, what sort of economic system will best satisfy Rawls's difference principle? Rawls does not answer this question. He sees it as primarily a question for economists and other social scientists, whereas the task of philosophers like himself is the preliminary one of working out a satisfactory conception of justice. Rawls does appear to believe, however, that a liberal form of capitalism, with sufficient welfare provisions, would satisfy his principles, but he does not rule out the possibility that a democratic socialist system could do so as well.

FAIRNESS AND THE BASIC STRUCTURE

Rawls rejects utilitarianism because it could permit an unfair distribution of benefits and burdens.

Rawls intends his theory as a fundamental alternative to utilitarianism, which he rejects on the grounds that maximizing the total well-being of society could permit an unfair distribution of burdens and benefits. Utilitarianism, in Rawls's view, treats people's pleasures and pains as completely interchangeable: A decrease of happiness here is justified by greater happiness there. Within a person's own life, such trade-offs are sensible. An increase of pain now (as the dentist fills a cavity in my tooth) is justified in terms of greater happiness later (no painful, rotted tooth). But between individuals, as when Jack's happiness is decreased to provide Jill with a more-than-compensating gain, such trade-offs are morally problematic.

Thus Rawls stresses that, in his view,

> each person possesses an inviolability founded on justice that even the welfare of society as a whole cannot override. . . . Therefore . . . the rights secured by justice are not subject to political bargaining or to the calculus of social interests.[71]

And he emphasizes that the difference principle

> excludes, therefore, the justification of inequalities on the grounds that the disadvantages of those in one position are outweighed by the greater advantages of those in another position. This rather simple restriction is the main modification I wish to make in the utilitarian principle as usually understood.[72]

Contrary to Nozick, Rawls believes that social justice concerns the basic structure of society, not transactions between individuals.

Rawls, however, is equally unsympathetic to the libertarian approach adopted by Nozick. Contrary to the entitlement theory, he argues that the primary subject of justice is not, in the first instance, transactions between individuals but rather "the **basic structure**, the fundamental social institutions and their arrangement into one scheme." Why? As Rawls explains:

> Suppose we begin with the initially attractive idea that the social circumstances and people's relationships to one another should develop over time in accordance with free agreements fairly arrived at and fully honored. Straightaway we need an account of when agreements are free and the social circumstances under which they are reached are fair. In addition, while these conditions may be fair at an earlier time, the accumulated results of many separate and ostensibly fair agreements . . . are likely in the course of time to alter citizens' relationships and opportunities so that the conditions for free and fair agreements no longer hold. The role of the institutions that belong to the basic structure is to secure just background conditions against which the actions

of the individuals and associations take place. Unless this structure is appropriately regulated and adjusted, an initially just social process will eventually cease to be just, however free and fair particular transactions may look when viewed by themselves.[73]

Additional considerations support taking the basic structure of society as the primary subject of justice—in particular, the fact that the basic structure shapes the wants, desires, hopes, and ambitions of individuals. Thus, Rawls continues:

> Everyone recognizes that the institutional form of society affects its members and determines in large part the kind of person they want to be as well as the kind of person they are. The social structure also limits people's ambitions and hopes in different ways.... So an economic regime, say, is not only an institutional scheme for satisfying existing wants but a way of fashioning desires and aspirations in the future.[74]

Rawls stresses that because the basic structure is the proper focus of a theory of justice, we cannot expect the principles that apply to it to be simply an extension of the principles that govern everyday individual transactions:

> The justice of the basic structure is, then, of predominant importance. The first problem of justice is to determine the principles to regulate inequalities and to adjust the profound and long-lasting effects of social, natural, and historical contingencies, particularly since these contingencies combined with inequalities generate tendencies that, when left to themselves, are sharply at odds with the freedom and equality appropriate for a well-ordered society. In view of the special role of the basic structure, we cannot assume that the principles suitable to it are natural applications, or even extensions, of the familiar principles governing the actions of individuals and associations in everyday life which take place within its framework. Most likely we shall have to loosen ourselves from our ordinary perspective and take a more comprehensive viewpoint.[75]

BENEFITS AND BURDENS

The passages quoted here touch on a theme that is central to Rawls's theory. Inevitably, there will be natural differences among human beings—in physical prowess, mental agility, and so on—but there is nothing natural or inevitable about the weight attached by society to those differences. For Rawls, a desirable feature of any account of justice is that it strives to minimize the social consequences of purely arbitrary, natural differences. He stresses that no one deserves his or her particular natural characteristics. We cannot say that Angelina Jolie deserves to be beautiful or that Albert Einstein deserved to be blessed with an excellent mind any more than we can say that Fred merits his shortness or Pamela her nearsightedness. Their attributes are simply the result of a genetic lottery. But Rawls goes beyond this to argue that even personal characteristics like diligence and perseverance reflect the environment in which one was raised:

> We do not deserve our place in the distribution of native endowments, any more than we deserve our initial starting place in society. That we deserve the superior character that enables us to make the effort to cultivate our abilities is also problematic; for such character depends in good part upon fortunate family and social circumstances in early life for which we can claim no credit. The notion of desert does not apply here.[76]

Accordingly, Rawls thinks we cannot really claim moral credit for our special talents or even our virtuous character. In Rawls's view, then, if our personal characteristics are not something that we deserve, we have no strong claim to the economic rewards they might bring. On the contrary, justice requires that the social and economic consequences of these arbitrarily distributed assets be minimized:

> The difference principle represents, in effect, an agreement to regard the distribution of natural talents as in some respects a common asset and to share in the greater social

> **SUMMARY**
> Rawls rejects utilitarianism because it might permit an unfair distribution of burdens and benefits. Contrary to the entitlement theory, he argues that the primary focus of justice should be the basic social structure, not transactions between individuals. He contends that society is a cooperative project for mutual benefit and that justice requires us to reduce the social and economic consequences of arbitrary natural differences among people.

> Rawls believes that justice tries to minimize the social consequences of purely arbitrary, natural differences. People do not deserve the attributes they were born with or that reflect their environment and upbringing.

and economic benefits made possible by the complementarities of this distribution. Those who have been favored by nature, whoever they are, may gain from their good fortune only on terms that improve the situation of those who have lost out. The naturally advantaged are not to gain merely because they are more gifted, but only to cover the costs of training and education and for using their endowments in ways that help the less fortunate as well. No one deserves his greater natural capacity nor merits a more favorable starting place in society. But, of course, this is no reason to ignore, much less to eliminate these distinctions. Instead, the basic structure can be arranged so that these contingencies work for the good of the least fortunate. Thus we are led to the difference principle if we wish to set up the social system so that no one gains or loses from his arbitrary place in the distribution of natural assets or his initial position in society without giving or receiving compensating advantages in return.[77]

This important passage from *A Theory of Justice* reflects well Rawls's vision of society as a cooperative project for mutual benefit.

STUDY CORNER

KEY TERMS AND CONCEPTS

basic structure
declining marginal utility of money
difference principle
distributive justice
entitlement theory

free market
justice
libertarianism
Lockean rights
maximin rule
original position

primary social goods
property rights
state of nature
veil of ignorance
worker participation

POINTS TO REVIEW

- distribution of income and wealth in the United States (pp. 105–106)
- four related ideas bound up with the concept of justice (p. 108)
- Aristotle's formal principle of justice (p. 108)
- John Stuart Mill's definition of injustice (p. 108)
- some different principles often used as a basis of distribution (p. 109)
- Walzer's pluralistic approach to distributive justice (p. 110)
- how a utilitarian like Mill looks at justice (p. 111)
- Mill's discussion of whether more talented workers should receive greater pay (pp. 111–112)
- Mill's view of worker participation (pp. 112–113)
- utilitarianism and the declining marginal utility of money (p. 113)
- Locke's account of property rights (pp. 115–116)
- three principles of Nozick's entitlement theory (pp. 115–116)
- the point of the Wilt Chamberlain example (p. 117)
- how libertarians understand freedom in terms of rights (pp. 117–118)
- Amartya Sen's analysis of famines (p. 119)
- how libertarians and nonlibertarians differ in their view of property rights (p. 120)
- the nature of the choice and the reasoning people would use in the original position (pp. 121–123)
- Rawls's two principles of justice (pp. 123–124)
- the point illustrated by the diagram on p. 125
- how Rawls's theory differs from utilitarianism and libertarianism (pp. 126–127)
- why Rawls thinks we should minimize the social consequences of natural differences (p. 127)

FOR FURTHER REFLECTION

1. What does the concept of justice mean to you?
2. Which theory of distributive justice do you find most convincing?
3. Is the United States an economically just society?

CASE 3.1

Eminent Domain

SUSETTE KELO'S NONDESCRIPT, PINK CLAPBOARD house sits above the Thames River in the Fort Trumbull area of New London, Connecticut. It's surrounded by vacant lots, where neighbors once lived. One by one, these neighbors have left, and their homes have been razed. Their property has been taken over by the City of New London, which has used its power of eminent domain to clear the land where dozens of homes once stood in order to prepare the way for new development.[78]

Eminent domain is the ancient right of government to take property from an individual without consent for the common good—for example, to build a highway, an airport, a dam, or a hospital. The U.S. Constitution recognizes that right, permitting private property to be taken for "public use" as long as "just compensation" is paid. In this case, however, New London is taking land from one private party and giving it to another. By tearing down Susette Kelo's old neighborhood, the city hopes to attract new development, which in turn will help revitalize the community and bring in more tax revenue. "This isn't for the public good," says Kelo, a nurse who works three jobs. "The public good is a firehouse or a school, not a hotel and a sports club."

Connecticut officially designates New London a blighted area. When the Navy moved its Undersea Warfare Center away from New London, taking 1,400 jobs with it, the city's already high rate of unemployment only got worse. Much of its housing stock is old and second-rate. The Fort Trumbull area, in particular, is—or was, anyway—a rather gritty neighborhood, where earlier generations of immigrants struggled to get a start. But New London saw a chance to turn things around when the pharmaceutical company Pfizer built a $350 million research center along the river below historic Fort Trumbull. Since then, city and state governments have created a park around the fort, cleaned up the Navy's old asbestos-laden site, and opened the riverfront to public access. Now the city wants to build a hotel, office buildings, and new homes to fill the riverfront blocks around Fort Trumbull. And it's not talking about new homes for people like Susette Kelo.

"We need to get housing at the upper end, for people like the Pfizer employees," says Ed O'Connell, the lawyer for the New London Development Corporation, which is in charge of the city's redevelopment efforts. "They are the professionals, they are the ones with the expertise and the leadership qualities to remake the city—the young urban professionals who will invest in New London, put their kids in school, and think of this as a place to stay for 20 or 30 years." And housing developers want open space to work with; they don't want to build around a few old properties like Ms. Kelo's and that of her neighbors, Wilhelmina and Charles Dery.

Age 87 and 85, respectively, they live in the house Wilhelmina was born in. The city is willing to pay a fair price for their home, but it's not an issue of money. "We get this all the time," says their son Matt. "'How much did they offer? What will it take?' My parents don't want to wake up rich tomorrow. They just want to wake up in their own home."

Unfortunately for the Derys, in 2005 the U.S. Supreme Court upheld the city's condemnation rights. In a close, 5-to-4 decision, it ruled that compulsory purchase to foster economic development falls under "public use" and is thus constitutionally permissible. "Promoting economic development is a traditional and long accepted function of government," Justice John Paul Stevens wrote for the majority. Intended to increase jobs and tax revenues, New London's plan "unquestionably serves a public purpose." In her dissenting opinion, however, Justice Sandra Day O'Connor objected: "Under the banner of economic development, all private property is now vulnerable to being taken and transferred to another private owner, so long as it might be upgraded. . . . Nothing is to prevent the state from replacing any Motel 6 with a Ritz-Carlton, any home with a shopping mall, or any farm with a factory."

The Supreme Court's decision pushes the debate over eminent domain back to the states and local communities. Although many cities have successfully used eminent domain to rebuild decayed urban areas or spark economic growth,[79] resistance to it has intensified, with political and legal battles being fought far beyond Susette Kelo's home in New London. For example, in Highland Park, New Jersey, the owners of a photography studio worry that a plan to redevelop their street will force them out of the location they've occupied for twenty-five years. In Port Chester, New York, a state development agency wants the site of a small furniture plant for a parking lot for Home Depot, and its owners are resisting. And in Salina, New York, twenty-nine little businesses—with names like Butch's Automotive and Transmission, Syracuse Crank and Machine, Gianelli's Sausage, and Petersen Plumbing—are battling local government's use of eminent domain to pave the way for DestiNY's proposed 325-acre, $2.67 billion research-and-development park.

Like New London, Salina desperately needs big ideas and big development, and it may not get another chance soon. But is tearing down these businesses fair? "We're here," says Philip Jakes-Johnson, who owns Solvents & Petroleum Service, one of the twenty-nine businesses in question. "We pay our taxes. We build companies and run them without tax breaks." Brian Osborne, another owner, adds: "Everything I and my family have worked for over the past 25 years is at stake because of the way eminent domain is being used in this state and across the country."

Update

In 2009, Pfizer announced that, as a cost-cutting measure, it was closing its New London facility and transferring its 1,400 employees to a campus the company owns in Groton, Connecticut.

Addendum

Richmond, California, a city of 100,000 people, has been hit hard by the recession and the real-estate meltdown. Sixteen percent of its homeowners have lost their homes in foreclosure, leaving many neighborhoods blighted with vacant and abandoned properties. With real estate worth half of what it was in 2006, 28 percent of Richmond's homeowners are "underwater," meaning that they owe more on their mortgages than their homes are worth—on average, about 45 percent more. Neither the government nor the investors who own the mortgage loans have been able to solve the problem, largely because the mortgages were bundled into pools and resold to thousands of investors around the world, and the rules governing many of those pools forbid mortgages from being modified unless they are already in default, even if it might be in the investors' interest to do so. Now the mayor of Richmond, Gayle McLaughlin, wants to use the city's power of eminent domain to buy properties with shaky mortgages and restructure the loans, thus restoring equity to homeowners and keeping them from defaulting. She argues that preventing foreclosures and the blight of vacant

Susette Kelo challenged the city of New London's use of eminent domain.

properties is a legitimate public purpose. Some scholars agree with this, contending that the city's novel use of eminent domain would enable the trustees who control the mortgage pools to get rid of bad loans. But Wall Street and various real-estate interests disagree and are lobbying vigorously against the plan. They don't like the precedent it sets, even if the plan would be good for Richmond and possibly for investors, too.[80]

DISCUSSION QUESTIONS

1. Did New London treat Susette Kelo and her neighbors fairly? Assuming that the proposed development would help to revitalize New London, is it just for the city to appropriate private property around Fort Trumbull?

2. Are towns such as New London and Salina pursuing wise, beneficial, and progressive social policies, or are their actions socially harmful and biased against ordinary working people and small-business owners?

3. Do you believe that eminent domain is a morally legitimate right of government? Explain why or why not.

4. "If 'just compensation' is paid, then by definition those who lose their property cannot claim that they have been treated unjustly." Assess this argument. Can compensation be just even if one of the parties is unwilling to accept it?

5. Is it fair to the community if an individual refuses payment and blocks a socially useful project? Putting legal issues aside, are there situations in which it would be morally permissible for government to seize private property for the public good with less than full compensation or even with no compensation at all?

6. Assess the concept of eminent domain, in general, and the plight of Susette Kelo and her neighbors, in particular, from the point of view of the different theories of justice discussed in this chapter. Is it possible to square the government's exercise of eminent domain with a libertarian approach to justice?

CASE 3.2

Battling over Bottled Water

WATER IS THE LIFEBLOOD OF THE EARTH, but by 2025, according to the United Nations, two-thirds of the world's population could face chronic shortages of water. In fact, some countries are already importing huge supertankers of freshwater from other countries. But one place that's definitely not short of water is the state of Michigan, which has 11,000 lakes and is surrounded by Lakes Michigan, Huron, Superior, and Erie. So it came as a surprise to some that the Nestlé company's new Ice Mountain bottled-water plant in Mecosta County, Michigan, dredged up so much controversy when it began pumping water from a local spring.[81]

Nestlé's willingness to invest $100 million to build a new 410,000-square-foot bottling plant in Mecosta reflects the fact that bottled water is big business, with annual sales of $6 billion (up 35 percent since 1997). Many county residents, in fact, are thrilled about Nestlé's being there. The Ice Mountain plant employs about a hundred people at $12 to $23 per hour, significantly more than many local jobs pay. And the company shells out hundreds of thousands of dollars in local taxes. Township supervisor Maxine McClellan says, "This is probably the best project we've ever brought into Mecosta County." She adds that she wants "a diversified economy where our kids don't have to move away to find jobs."

The problem, as some local residents see it, is that Nestlé has also built a 12-mile stainless steel pipeline from the plant to Sanctuary Spring, which sits on an 850-acre private deer-hunting ranch and is part of the headwaters of the Little Muskegon River, which flows into the Muskegon and then into Lake Michigan. The company started pumping 130 gallons of water every minute from the spring, with plans to increase that to 400 gallons per minute, or about 262 million gallons a year. But whose water is Nestlé pumping? That's the question being asked by Michigan Citizens for Water Conservation (MCWC), a local Mecosta group that has filed suit contesting Nestlé's right to the spring's waters. Although the company has a ninety-nine-year lease on the land, MCWC contends that the water itself is a public resource. As Jim Olson, MCWC's lawyer, explains it, under the doctrine of "reasonable use" the owners of a stream can use its water for drinking, boating, swimming, or anything else "as long as it's in connection with their land." But, he argues, "this does not include the right to transport water to some distant land for [some other] use. We're arguing that the same is true with groundwater—you can't sever it from the estate."

Michigan State Senator Ken Sikkema, who chaired a task force on Michigan water issues, rejects that argument: "A farmer pumps water out of the ground, waters potatoes, and sends the potatoes to Illinois—there's no real difference. The water in those potatoes is gone." This reasoning hasn't assuaged the fears of three American Indian tribes who have joined the fray. Citing an 1836 treaty that protects their fishing and hunting rights in the Great Lakes region, they have brought a federal lawsuit against Nestlé and the state of Michigan to stop what they see as a massive water grab. "Our fear," says a spokesperson for the Little Traverse Bay Bands of Odawa Indians, "is that the export could significantly and permanently damage the fishery."

However, David K. Ladd, head of the Office of Great Lakes, argues that bottled water is a special case. Legally, he contends, it's a "food," regulated by the Food and Drug Administration. "There's no difference between Perrier bottling water, Gerber making baby food, or Miller brewing beer. When you incorporate water from the basin into a product, it's no longer water per se." And Brendan O'Rourke, an Ice Mountain plant manager, adds that the 262 million gallons it wants to pump are less than 1 percent of the annual recharge rate of the local watershed, equivalent to just 14 minutes of evaporation from the surface of Lake Michigan.

For their part, scientists opposed to the project argue that Nestlé's pumping has already lowered the local water table and that northern pike are having trouble spawning in a stream fed by Sanctuary Spring. Jim Olson argues that the Ice Mountain plant should reduce its water consumption to 100 gallons per minute or less, not increase it to 400 gallons. "Every gallon removed is needed for the stream to sustain itself," he states. "The right to withdraw groundwater does not include the right to diminish . . . existing or future uses."

To the surprise of many, Michigan state court judge Lawrence Root bought that argument and upheld the MCWC's lawsuit. Ruling that the environment is at risk no matter how much water Nestlé draws out, he ordered the pumps turned off. Two years later, an appellate court reversed Judge Root's decision, and MCWC and Nestlé subsequently entered an agreement limiting Nestlé's withdrawals from Sanctuary Spring to 250 gallons per minute—although there has been some legal skirmishing between the two antagonists since then. In the meantime, however, the political tide has turned against Nestlé. Small towns in Maine and California have opposed its building new bottled water plants in their jurisdictions; Congress has held hearings into the diversion of groundwater by bottled water companies and other businesses; and Michigan has passed legislation that, among other things, makes it virtually impossible for operations such as the Ice Mountain plant to remove more than 100,000 gallons of groundwater per day.

DISCUSSION QUESTIONS

1. Should people in Michigan be concerned about how, and by whom, the state's ground water is used? In your view, what issues of justice does this case raise?

2. Would Nestlé's pumping 262 million gallons of water per year from Sanctuary Spring constitute "reasonable use"? Is the company treating either local residents or the Native American tribes unfairly, or would it be unfair to restrict Nestlé's use of water from the spring?

3. Is groundwater a public resource, the use of which is appropriate for society to regulate? Or is it the property of those who own the land to use as they see fit? Who has the strongest claim on groundwater—the owners of the land from which it is pumped, the original inhabitants of the area (that is, the local Indian tribes), local residents, citizens of the whole Great Lakes region, or all Americans?

4. Assess this case from the perspective of the utilitarian, libertarian, and Rawlsian theories of justice. How would each address the case? Which theory's approach do you find the most helpful or illuminating?

CASE 3.3

Poverty in America

AS A RESULT OF THE ECONOMIC CRISIS and recession of 2008–09—the most serious economic meltdown since the Great Depression of the 1930s—an additional 4 million Americans have fallen into poverty. Altogether, around 50 million adults now live below the poverty line, officially defined as an income below $11,490 for a single adult or less than $23,550 for a family of four.[82] Nearly fifty years after President Lyndon Johnson declared "war on poverty," 16 percent of our fellow citizens, many of them children, continue to live in penury. That's about one out of every six people. Even before the current economic collapse, the average American adult had a 60 percent chance of living at least one year below the poverty line and a 33 percent chance of experiencing dire poverty.[83]

Poverty is particularly hard on children. Among other things, it mars their brain development. This is not just a result of poor nutrition or exposure to environmental toxins, as one might expect. Rather, researchers have found that children growing up in very poor families experience unhealthy levels of stress hormones that impair memory and language acquisition.[84] Still, many people think that those described as "poor" in the United States are pretty well-off by world standards. The truth is, in life expectancy, twenty-year-old U.S. males rank thirty-sixth among the world's nations, and twenty-year-old U.S. females rank twenty-first. Our infant mortality rate is worse than that in twenty-one other Western nations. Beijing's infant mortality rate, for instance, is lower than New York City's. In fact, if our infant mortality rate were as good as Cuba's, we would save an additional 2,212 babies each year. If it were as good as Singapore's, we'd save 18,900 babies.[85]

Furthermore, millions of Americans endure hunger. According to the U.S. Department of Agriculture, 14.5 percent of U.S. households lack "food security," and in 7 million American households one or more persons go hungry during the year.[86] In addition, one out of every four Americans lives in substandard housing, and in most cities a visitor is likely to see people roaming the streets in tattered clothing, picking their food out of garbage cans and sleeping in doorways or in makeshift shacks and abandoned cars. Contrary to the popular perception that the homeless consist mostly of young men with drug, alcohol, or mental-health problems, the majority are simply jobless individuals or families who cannot afford housing. Reliable figures are hard to come by, but over 600,000 Americans are probably homeless on any given night, and between 2.3 and 3.5 million people are homeless sometime during the year.[87]

People in different walks of life and in different circumstances experience poverty. Many others live on the edge of poverty and are in continual danger of falling into it through illness, job loss, or other misfortune. In the United States today, the "working poor"—members of the labor force who do not earn enough to pull themselves and their families out of poverty—number 10.4 million.[88] They represent a higher percentage of the workforce than in the 1970s as well-paid unionized manufacturing jobs have been replaced by nonunion service jobs.[89] At $7.25 per hour, the minimum wage is less in real terms than it was in the 1960s and 1970s. Someone working 40 hours a week, every week, for that wage cannot raise his or her family out of poverty. In fact, according to an advocacy group, a minimum-wage earner can afford to pay rent and utilities on a one-bedroom apartment in only four counties in the whole country.[90]

Many poor people are unable to work and depend on outside assistance, but living decently on welfare has always been difficult, if not impossible. The old system of AFDC (Aid to Families with Dependent Children) was popular when it was created in 1935 and most AFDC recipients were widows. But by the 1990s, fewer than 2 percent of recipients were widows, and most had never been married to their child's other parent.[91] Public support for the program ebbed as many Americans came to believe that AFDC discouraged its recipients from marrying and from working. As a result, benefits grew even stingier. By the time AFDC came to an end in 1996, welfare benefits had fallen, in real terms, to 51 percent of what they had been in 1971.[92] With annual cash allowances for a family on AFDC ranging from $1,416 in Mississippi to $6,780 in New York, even in the most generous states stipends were never enough to allow a family to escape from poverty.[93]

In 1996, Congress replaced AFDC with TANF (Temporary Assistance to Needy Families). Under the new system, the entitlement of poor people to support has been replaced by block grants to the states to run their own welfare programs. The grants are limited to a certain amount of money; if they run out, the states are not required to make additional expenditures. Welfare recipients are required to work for pay or to enroll in training programs, and financial support is limited to a lifetime maximum of five years. This shift in policy has been controversial. Since the TANF system began, the number of people receiving welfare benefits has declined, but experts disagree about the reasons: Is it a growing economy offering more opportunities, the success of the new approach in encouraging welfare recipients to make themselves employable, or simply people who are not able to take care of themselves being denied support?[94] Even now, with soaring unemployment and the worst economic crisis in decades, the number of people receiving assistance remains near a forty-year low.[95]

One thing that is clear is the large number of women living in poverty. This includes women with inadequate income following divorce, widowhood, or retirement, as well as women raising children alone. Wage discrimination against women is one factor. Women who work full-time, year-round earn only about two-thirds of what men earn. And millions of women hold full-time jobs that pay wages near or below the poverty line.

Women's responsibilities for child rearing are another important factor. Despite many changes in recent years, women continue to have primary responsibility in this area. When marriages break up, mothers typically take custody and bear the major financial burden. Fewer than half the women raising children alone are awarded child support, and fewer than half of those entitled to it receive the full amount. Of family households headed by women, 38.4 percent have incomes below $25,000 and 21 percent have incomes below $15,000.[96] Not only do households headed by women earn only half the median income of all households, but also their overall net worth is two-thirds less.[97]

Most poor people in our nation—about two-thirds of them—are white, but blacks are about two and a half times more likely to be poor. Whereas one out of every ten white Americans is poor, one of every four African Americans and one out of every five Hispanics live below the poverty line. Many members of these minority communities have succeeded in moving up the economic ladder, but the overall picture is disheartening. African American family income, to pick just one statistic, is only 62.8 percent that of white family income.[98]

Although it is doubtful that there is more social mobility in the United States than in Europe, what is certainly clear is that Americans believe that they have plenty of it. In line with that belief, 71 percent of them, but only 40 percent of Europeans, think that the poor have a good chance to escape their plight.[99] Americans figure that the poor can push their way out of poverty on their own because they typically assume that one's success or failure is largely determined by factors within one's own control.[100] Americans, even poor Americans, favor individualistic explanations of poverty (such as lack of effort or ability, deficient morals, and poor work habits) over structural explanations (such as inadequate schooling, low wages, and lack of jobs), whereas Europeans favor structural explanations of poverty over individualistic explanations.[101] They tend to see the poor as unfortunate rather than as personally responsible for their condition.

Seventy percent of Germans, for example, express the belief that people are poor because of imperfections in society, not their own laziness, whereas 70 percent of Americans hold the opposite view.[102] Because of that belief and because the majority of Americans believe that redistribution favors racial minorities (an idea they tend to dislike), they support the present political system, which assists those at the socioeconomic bottom far less than European governments do. Indeed, cash assistance for poor families in the United States amounts to only one-tenth of 1 percent of the nation's economic output; the average for O.E.C.D. countries is 11 times greater.[103] That's one reason you are twice as likely to be poor if you live in the United States than if you live in Western Europe.[104]

DISCUSSION QUESTIONS

1. Does the existence of poverty imply that our socioeconomic system is unjust? Does the concentration of poverty in certain groups make it more unjust than it would be otherwise?

2. What are the causes of poverty? Are they structural or individual? How is one's answer to this question likely to affect one's view of the justice or injustice of poverty?

3. What moral obligation, if any, do we have individually and as a society to reduce poverty? What steps could be taken? What role should business play?

4. How would a utilitarian view the facts about poverty? What are the implications for our society of the concept of the declining utility of money?

5. How would a libertarian like Nozick view poverty in the United States? How plausible do you find the libertarian's preference for private charity over public assistance?

6. How would our economy be assessed from the point of view of Rawls's difference principle? Can it be plausibly maintained that, despite poverty, our system works to "the greatest expected benefit of the least advantaged"? Is this an appropriate standard?

PART TWO | AMERICAN BUSINESS AND ITS BASIS

CHAPTER 4

THE NATURE OF CAPITALISM

INTRODUCTION

OCTOBER IS OFTEN SAID TO BE A BAD MONTH FOR stocks. This was certainly true in 2008. On Friday, October 10, 2008, the Dow Jones Industrial Average capped the worst week in its 112-year history with its most volatile day ever as the index swung 1,019 points in one trading session. In the weeks that followed, the gyrating stock market calmed down. As the dust settled, however, stockholders and mutual fund investors—many of them employees diligently saving for retirement—were forced to come to terms with the cold reality that their portfolios were worth only about half of what they had been a year before. And what was true of Wall Street was also true of Hong Kong, Mumbai, Tokyo, Johannesburg, Frankfurt, and London as stock markets around the world bottomed out. Capitalism is a worldwide system, and what happens on Wall Street reverberates around the globe, and vice versa, because the economies of all capitalist nations are intricately interconnected and their markets tightly intertwined.

In this case, it was the United States that pushed the world economic system into crisis. The collapse of the U.S. subprime mortgage market, following the bursting of the real estate bubble, had been causing financial jitters since early in 2008. But only that autumn did it become clear that a number of once rich and haughty U.S. financial institutions were floating perilously on an ocean of debt. In an effort to maximize profit, they had underwritten loans that left them with potential liabilities thirty to forty times greater than their underlying assets. With that kind of exposure, it doesn't take much to bring the whole house of cards down. And that's what began happening.

> THE COLLAPSE OF THE U.S. subprime mortgage market, following the bursting of the real estate bubble, had been causing financial jitters since early in 2008.

When AIG, the world's biggest insurer, began tottering, the U.S. government rushed to its assistance, fearing that its collapse would wreak havoc throughout the financial system. The government had already facilitated the sale, first of Bear Stearns, the investment bank and brokerage firm, and then of Washington Mutual Bank to JPMorgan Chase because both institutions were about to go under, and it had also effectively nationalized the mortgage giants Fannie Mae and Freddie Mac in order to keep them afloat. Now, after rescuing AIG, the U.S. Treasury Department and Federal Reserve Board were worried that they were sending the wrong message to the business world, namely, that they were prepared to rescue any financial firm that needed help. So, a few days after bailing out AIG, they decided to let Lehman Brothers, a global financial services firm that was in deep trouble, go bust. The rapid demise of Lehman Brothers and the government's willingness to let it happen, however, immediately caused credit markets to panic, the movement of capital to freeze, investors to flee, the stock market to plunge—and the world economy to begin sliding inexorably into recession.

Governments around the world moved quickly to try to stabilize financial markets and free up credit by lowering interest rates and propping up their banks and other financial institutions. The United States pumped money into its financial system on an unprecedented scale—taking over bad assets, guaranteeing debts, and pouring new capital into private capitalist firms. Anyone predicting even a few months earlier that liberals and conservatives in Congress would rapidly unite to approve a bank bailout of over

CHAPTER FOUR THE NATURE OF CAPITALISM **151**

$700 billion—that's more than $2,000 for every man, woman, and child in the country—would have been dismissed as a lunatic. But that's what happened. Moreover, a few months later the government bailed out General Motors and Chrysler, which were floundering, and oversaw their restructuring.

Although these emergency operations could not stave off the worst economic slump that most Americans had ever seen, they probably prevented the financial meltdown of 2008 from turning into a 1930s-style depression. After the crisis, as most of the loans it had made were repaid with interest and the assets it had acquired were sold, the government eventually recovered 97 percent of the money it had dispensed. But its unprecedented economic intervention may have changed the face of capitalism forever.

But what exactly is the nature of the economic system called capitalism? What are its underlying values, principles, and economic philosophy? What has it accomplished, and what are its prospects for the future? This chapter examines these and related questions.

Looking back in history, one must credit capitalism with helping break the constraints of medieval feudalism, which had severely limited individual possibilities for improvement. In place of a stifling economic system, capitalism offered opportunities for those blessed with imagination, an ability to plan, and a willingness to work. Capitalism must also be credited with enhancing the abundance and diversity of consumer goods beyond Adam Smith's wildest dreams. It has increased material wealth and the standard of living and has converted cities from modest bazaars into treasure troves of dazzling merchandise. In light of such accomplishments and the acculturation process that tends to glorify them, it is all too easy to overlook capitalism's theoretical and operational problems.

LEARNING OBJECTIVES

This chapter attempts to identify some of these problems and their moral ramifications. It provides some basic historical and conceptual categories for understanding the socioeconomic framework within which business transactions occur and moral issues arise. In particular, the following topics are addressed:

1. The definition of capitalism and its major historical stages
2. Four of the key features of capitalism: companies, profit motive, competition, and private property
3. Two classical moral justifications of capitalism—one based on the right to property and the other on Adam Smith's concept of the invisible hand
4. Fundamental criticisms of capitalism—in particular, the persistence of inequality and poverty, capitalism's implicit view of human nature, the rise of economic oligarchies, the shortcomings of competition, and employees' experience of alienation and exploitation on the job
5. The problems facing capitalism in the United States today—in particular, the decline of manufacturing, along with job outsourcing and the trade deficit; an excessive focus on the short term; and changing attitudes toward work

TARP Outflows (in Billions of Dollars)

- Banks & other Financial Institutions — 187
- Fannie & Freddie — 80
- Auto Companies — 68
- AIG — 245
- Toxic Assets Purchased — 18.6
- Other — 10

President George W. Bush signed into law the Troubled Asset Relief Program, or TARP, to address the financial meltdown resulting, primarily, from the subprime mortgage crisis. Under his administration and that of President Obama, TARP funds were used to bail out a number of American banks and other companies, thus helping to stabilize the economy.

SOURCE: http://www.propublica.org/ion/bailout

CAPITALISM

Capitalism can be defined as an economic system that operates on the basis of profit and market exchange and in which the major means of production and distribution are in private hands. The United States, which has the world's largest national economy, is a capitalist country. All manufacturing firms are privately owned, including those that produce military hardware for the government. Almost all other businesses—small, medium, and large—are also privately owned, including banks, insurance firms, power companies, and transportation companies. Although the government itself expends money on many things, no central governing body dictates to these private owners what or how much of anything will be produced. For example, officials at Apple, Caterpillar, or Ford Motor Company design their products and set their own production goals in anticipation of consumer demand.

The private ownership and market aspects of capitalism contrast with its polar opposite, socialism. **Socialism** is an economic system characterized by public ownership of property and a planned economy. Under socialism, a society's productive equipment is owned not by individuals (capitalists) but by public bodies. Socialism depends primarily on centralized planning rather than on a market system for both its overall allocation of resources and its distribution of income; crucial economic decisions are made not by individuals but by government. In the former Soviet Union, for example, government agencies decided the number of automobiles—including models, styles, and colors—to be produced each year. Top levels of the Soviet government formulated production and cost objectives, which were then converted to specific production quotas and budgets that individual plant managers had to follow.

A hybrid economic system advocated by some socialists (and once approximated by the former Yugoslavia) is **worker control socialism**. Individual firms respond to a market when deciding what to produce and acquiring the necessary factors of production. However, the workforce of each enterprise controls the enterprise (although it may elect or hire managers to oversee day-to-day operations), and profits accrue to the workers as a group to divide in whatever manner they agree on. Although the workers manage their factories, the capital assets of each enterprise are owned by society as a whole and not by private individuals.

> **SUMMARY**
> Capitalism is an economic system in which production and distribution are in private hands, operating on the basis of profit and market exchange. Socialism is an economic system characterized by public ownership of property and a planned economy. Worker control socialism is a hybrid, market-oriented form of socialism.

HISTORICAL BACKGROUND OF CAPITALISM

What we know as "capitalism" did not fully emerge until the Renaissance in Europe during the fifteenth and sixteenth centuries. Before the Renaissance, business exchanges in medieval Europe were organized through guilds, which were associations of individuals involved in the same trade.

Today if you want a pair of shoes, you head for a shoe store, where you find an array of shoes. If nothing strikes your fancy, you set out for another shop, and perhaps another, until at last you find what you want. Or, if still disappointed, you might ask the store clerk to order a pair in your size from the manufacturer or its distributor. You certainly wouldn't ask the clerk to have someone make you a pair of shoes. Under the guild organization, shoemakers were also shoe sellers and made shoes only to fill orders. If they had no orders, they made no shoes. The shoemaker's sole economic function was to make shoes for people when they wanted them. His labor allowed him to maintain himself, not advance his station in life. When the shoemaker died, his business went with him—unless he had a son to inherit and carry on the enterprise. As for shoe quality and cost, the medieval shopper could generally count on getting a good pair of shoes at a fair price because the cobblers' guild strictly controlled quality and price.

Weaving was another big medieval trade. In fact, in the fourteenth century, weaving was the leading industry in the German town of Augsburg. Little wonder, then, that an enterprising young man named Hans Fugger became a weaver when he settled there in 1357. But young Hans had ambitions that stretched far beyond the limits of the weaving trade and the handicraft guild system. And they were grandly realized, for within three short generations a family of simple weavers was transformed into a great German banking dynasty.[1]

Not content with being a weaver, Hans Fugger began collecting and selling the products of other weavers. Soon he was directly employing the other weavers, paying them for their labor, and selling their products as his own. His sons continued the business and expanded it in new directions, as did his grandsons, especially Jacob Fugger, the foremost capitalist of the Renaissance. Among other things, Jacob Fugger lent large sums of money to the Hapsburg emperors to finance their wars. In return, he obtained monopoly rights on silver and copper ores, which he then traded. When Fugger bought the mines themselves, he acquired all the components necessary to erect an extraordinary financial dynasty and to make himself one of the richest people of all time.

Like latter-day titans of American industry, Fugger employed thousands of workers and paid them wages, controlled all his products from raw material to final market, set his own quality standards, and charged whatever the traffic would bear. In one brief century, what was once a handicraft inseparable from the craftsperson had become a company that existed outside any family members. What had once motivated Hans Fugger—namely, maintenance of his station in life—had given way to gain for gain's sake, the so-called profit motive. Under Jacob Fugger, the company amassed profits—a novel concept—that well exceeded the needs of the Fugger family. And the profits were measured not in goods or land but in money.

Capitalism has undergone changes since then. The kind of capitalism that emerged in the Fuggers' time is often termed **mercantile capitalism**, which is capitalism that is based on mutual dependence between state and commercial interests. Central to mercantile capitalism is the belief that the economic health of a nation is determined by the bullion (precious metals, gold, and silver) it possesses and that therefore government should regulate production and trade with the goal of encouraging exports while keeping out imports, thus building up the nation's bullion reserves. A prudent nation should strive to be economically self-sufficient while using sea power, if it can, to control foreign markets and establish colonies for the benefit of the mother country.

During the eighteenth and nineteenth centuries, however, new economic ideas spread. These emphasized the importance of competition and open markets and of freeing trade and production from government oversight. Trade between nations was now seen as mutually beneficial, and national wealth and prosperity were no longer identified with bullion. With the Industrial Revolution, industrialists replaced merchants as the dominant power in a capitalist economy, and the period of **industrial capitalism** emerged, which is associated with large-scale industry. In the United States, the confluence of many factors after the Civil War—including a sound financial base, the technology for mass production, expanding markets for cheaply manufactured goods, and a large and willing labor force—produced industrial expansion. Exploiting these fortuitous conditions was a group of hard-driving, visionary entrepreneurs called "robber barons" by their critics and "captains of industry" by their supporters: Cornelius Vanderbilt, Cyrus McCormick, Andrew Carnegie, John D. Rockefeller, Jay Gould, and others.

As industrialization increased, so did the size and power of business. The private fortunes of a few individuals could no longer underwrite the accelerated growth of business activity. The large sums of capital necessary could be raised only through a corporate form of business, in which risk and potential profit were distributed among numerous investors. The success—indeed, survival—of a business enterprise came to depend on its having the financial wherewithal to reduce prices while expanding production and either eliminating or absorbing competition. As various industries strove to strengthen their financing and shore up their assets, what is called **financial capitalism** emerged, characterized by pools, trusts, holding companies, and the interpenetration of banking, insurance, and industrial interests. Hand in hand with this development, the trend continued toward larger and larger corporations, controlling more and more of the country's economic capacity.

The economic and political challenges of the Great Depression of the 1930s helped usher in still another phase of capitalism, often called **state welfare capitalism**, in which government plays an active role in the economy, attempting to smooth out the boom-and-bust pattern of the business cycle through its fiscal and monetary policies. In addition, government programs like Social Security and unemployment insurance seek to enhance the welfare of the workforce, and legislation legitimizes the existence of trade unions. Conservative politicians sometimes advocate less government control of business, but in reality the governments of all capitalist countries are deeply involved in the management of their economies.

These days, the increasingly worldwide scale of capitalism leads many contemporary commentators to see **globalized capitalism** as a new stage or level of capitalist development. Capitalism has always involved international trade, but today—thanks to the computer, the Internet, satellites, cell phones, and other technological advances—the economies of most countries are becoming more and more integrated, a process labeled *globalization*. Although the world is still far from constituting a single global economy, investment capital is more mobile than ever, and the currencies, stock exchanges, and economic fortunes of all capitalist countries are bound together in a single financial system. The business operations of a growing number of companies take place on a world stage. Capitalist enterprises are more likely than ever before to utilize foreign components and draw on foreign labor or services, to export products or provide services abroad, and to acquire or start foreign subsidiaries or engage in joint ventures with overseas companies. Many apparently national companies produce one component in one country and another component in a different country, assemble them in a third country, and market them throughout the world.

Although the study of capitalism's evolution is best left to economic historians, it is important to keep in mind capitalism's dynamic nature. There is nothing fixed and immutable about this or any other economic system; it is as susceptible to the forces of change as any other institution. Nevertheless, the capitalism we know today does have some prominent features that were evident in the earliest capitalistic businesses.

.....

> **SUMMARY**
> Capitalism has gone through several stages: mercantile, industrial, financial, and state welfare. Many believe we are now at a new stage, globalized capitalism.

> Although capitalism will continue to evolve, it has four characteristic features.

KEY FEATURES OF CAPITALISM

Complete coverage of capitalism's central features and defining characteristics has filled many a book. Four features of particular significance—the existence of companies, profit motive, competition, and private property—will be discussed here.

COMPANIES

Chapter 2 mentioned the Firestone case, in which a media misrepresentation was left uncorrected. When asked why Firestone officials had not corrected the error, a Firestone spokesperson said that Firestone's policy was to ask for corrections only when it was beneficial to the company to do so. Expressions like "Firestone's policy" and "beneficial to the company" reflect one key feature of capitalism: the existence of companies or business firms separate from the human beings who work for and within them.

"It's not in the company's interests," "The company thinks that," "From the company's viewpoint," "As far as the company is concerned"—all of us have heard, perhaps even used, expressions like these that treat a business organization like a person or at least like a separate and distinct entity. This way of speaking reflects a basic characteristic of capitalism: Capitalism permits the creation of companies or business organizations that exist separately from the people associated with them. We take the existence of companies for granted, but some experts believe that it is not church or state but the company that is "the most important organization in the world."[2]

Today the big companies we're familiar with—General Electric, Microsoft, Verizon, Procter & Gamble—are, in fact, incorporated businesses, or corporations. Chapter 5 discusses the nature of the modern corporation, including its historical evolution and its social responsibilities. Here it's enough to observe that, in the nineteenth century, Chief Justice John Marshall defined a *corporation* as "an artificial being, invisible, intangible, and existing only in the contemplation of law." Although a corporation is not something that can be seen or touched, it does have prescribed rights and legal obligations within the community. Like you or me, a corporation may enter into contracts and may sue or be sued in courts of law. It may even do things that the corporation's members disapprove of. The corporations that loom large on our economic landscape hark back to a feature of capitalism evident as early as the Fugger dynasty: the existence of the company.

PROFIT MOTIVE

A second characteristic of capitalism lies in the motive of the company: to make profit. As dollar-directed and gain-motivated as our society is, most of us take for granted that the human being is by nature an acquisitive creature who, left to his or her own devices, will pursue profit with all the instinctual vigor of a cat chasing a mouse. However, as economist Robert Heilbroner points out, the "profit motive, as we understand it, is a very recent phenomenon. It was foreign to the lower and middle classes of Egyptian, Greek, Roman, and medieval cultures, only scattered throughout the Renaissance times, and largely absent in most Eastern civilizations." The medieval church taught that no Christian ought to be a merchant. "Even to our Pilgrim forefathers," Heilbroner writes, "the idea that gain ought to be a tolerable—even a useful—goal in life would have appeared as nothing short of a doctrine of the devil."[3]

Profit in the form of money is the lifeblood of the capitalist system. Companies and capitalists alike are motivated by a robust appetite for monetary gain. Indeed, the **profit motive** implies and reflects a critical assumption about human nature: that human beings are basically economic creatures, who recognize and are motivated by their own economic interests.

> The profit motive is central to capitalism. It assumes that economic self-interest motivates human beings.

COMPETITION

If self-interest and an appetite for profit drive individuals and companies, then what stops them from bleeding society dry? What stops capitalists from ripping off the rest of society?

Adam Smith provided an answer in his famous treatise on political economy, *An Inquiry into the Nature and Causes of the Wealth of Nations* (1776). Free **competition**, said Smith, is the regulator that keeps a community activated only by self-interest from degenerating into a mob of ruthless profiteers. When traditional restraints are removed from the sale of goods and from wages and when all individuals have equal access to raw materials and markets (the doctrine of **laissez faire**, from the French meaning "to let [people] do [as they choose]"), we are all free to pursue our own interests. In pursuing our own interests, however, we come smack up against others similarly motivated. If any of us allow blind self-interest to dictate our actions—for example, by price gouging or employee exploitation—we will quickly find ourselves beaten out by competitors who charge less or pay better wages. Competition thus regulates individual economic activity.

To sample the flavor of Smith's argument, imagine an acquisitive young woman in a faraway place who wants to pile up as much wealth as possible. She looks about her and sees that people need and want strong twilled cotton trousers, so she takes her investment capital and sets up a jeans factory. She charges $45 for a pair of jeans and soon realizes handsome profits. The woman's success is not lost on other business minds, especially manufacturers of formal slacks and dresses, who observe a sharp decline in those markets. Wanting a piece of the jeans action, numerous enterprises start up jeans factories. Many of these start selling jeans for $40 a pair. No longer alone in the market, our hypothetical businesswoman must check her appetite for profit by lowering her price or risk folding. As the number of jeans on the market increases, their supply eventually overtakes demand, and the price of jeans declines further and further. Inefficient manufacturers start dropping like flies. As the competition thins out, the demand for jeans slowly balances with the supply, and the price regulates itself. Ultimately, an equilibrium is reached between supply and demand, and the price of jeans stabilizes, yielding a normal profit to the efficient producer.

> Competition makes individual pursuit of self-interest socially beneficial.

In much this way, Adam Smith tried to explain how economic competition steers the individual pursuit of self-interest in a socially beneficial direction. By appealing to their self-interest, society can induce producers to provide it with what it wants—just as manufacturers of formal slacks and dresses were enticed into jeans production. But competition keeps prices for desired goods from escalating; high prices are self-correcting because they call forth an increased supply.

PRIVATE PROPERTY

In its discussion of the libertarian theory of justice, Chapter 3 emphasized that property should not be identified only with physical objects like houses, bicycles, and smartphones because one can own things, such as stock options, that are not physical things at all. Nor should ownership be thought of as a simple relationship between the owner and the thing owned. Rather, property ownership involves a complex bundle of rights and rules governing how, under what circumstances, and in what ways both the owner and others can use, possess, dispose of, and have access to the thing in question.

> Capitalism requires private ownership of the means of production.

Private property is central to capitalism. To put it another way, capitalism as a socioeconomic system is a specific form of private property. What matters for capitalism is not private property simply in the sense of personal possessions, because a socialist society can permit people to own cars, television sets, and jogging shoes. Rather, capitalism requires private ownership of the major *means of production* and distribution. The means of production and distribution include factories, warehouses, offices, machines, computer systems, trucking fleets, agricultural land, and whatever else makes up the economic resources of a nation. Under capitalism, private hands control these basic economic assets and productive resources. Thus, the major economic decisions are made by individuals or groups acting on their own in pursuit of profit. These decisions are not directly coordinated with those of other producers, nor are they the result of some overall plan. Any profits (or losses) that result from these decisions about production are those of the owners.

> ....
> SUMMARY
> Four key features of capitalism are the existence of companies, profit motive, competition, and private property.
> ....

Capital, as an economic concept, is closely related to private property. Putting it simply, capital is money that is invested for the purpose of making more money. Individuals or corporations purchase various means of production or other related assets and use them to produce goods or provide services, which are then sold. They do this not for the purpose of being nice or of helping people out but rather to make money—more money, they hope, than they spent to make the goods or provide the services in the first place. Using money to make money is at the heart of the definition of capitalism.

TWO ARGUMENTS FOR CAPITALISM

People tend to take for granted the desirability and moral legitimacy of the political and economic system they live in. Americans are no exception. We are raised in a society that encourages individual competition, praises capitalism, promotes the acquisition of material goods, and worships economic wealth. Newspapers, television, movies, and other forms of popular culture celebrate these values, and rarely are we presented with fundamental criticisms of or possible alternatives to our socioeconomic order. It is not surprising, then, that most of us blithely assume, without ever bothering to question, that our capitalist economic system is a morally justifiable one.

Yet as thinking people and moral agents, we need to reflect on the nature and justifiability of our social institutions. The proposition that capitalism is a morally acceptable system is open to debate. Whether we decide that capitalism is morally justified will depend, at least in part, on which general theory of justice turns out to be the soundest. Chapter 3 explored in detail the utilitarian approach, the libertarian alternative, and the theory of John Rawls. Now, against that background, this chapter looks at two basic ways defenders of capitalism have sought to justify their system: (1) the argument that the moral right to property guarantees the legitimacy of capitalism and (2) the utilitarian-based economic argument of Adam Smith. The chapter then considers some criticisms of capitalism.

THE NATURAL RIGHT TO PROPERTY

As Americans, we live in a socioeconomic system that guarantees us certain property rights. Although we are no longer permitted to own other people, we are certainly free to own a variety of other things, from livestock to stock certificates and from our own homes to whole blocks of apartment buildings. A common defense of capitalism is the argument that people have a fundamental, **natural right to property** and that our capitalist system is simply the outcome of this right.

| One argument for capitalism is that it reflects people's natural right to property.

In Chapter 3, we saw how Locke attempted to base the right to property in human labor. According to Locke, when individuals mix their labor with the natural world, they are entitled to the results. This idea seems plausible in many cases. For example, if Carl diligently harvests coconuts on the island he shares with Adam, while Adam himself idles away his days, then most of us would agree that Carl has an entitlement to those coconuts that Adam lacks. But property ownership as it actually exists in the real world today is a complex, socially shaped phenomenon. This is especially true in the case of sophisticated forms of corporate and financial property—for example, bonds and stock options.

One could, of course, reject the whole idea of a natural right to property as a fiction, as, for example, utilitarians do. In their view, although various property systems are possible, there is no natural right that things be owned privately, or collectively, or in any particular way whatsoever. The moral task, according to utilitarians, is to determine which property system, which way of organizing production and distribution, has the greatest utility.

Even if one believes that there is a natural right to property at least under some circumstances, one need not believe that this right leads to capitalism or that there is a right to have a system of property rules and regulations exactly like the one we now have in the

> **SUMMARY**
> One basic defense of capitalism rests on a supposed natural moral right to property. Utilitarians deny the existence of such rights; other critics doubt that this right entitles one to have a system of property rules and regulations identical to the one we now have in the United States.

United States. In other words, even if Carl has a natural right to his coconuts, there may still be moral limits on how many coconuts he can rightfully amass and what he can use them for. When he takes his coconuts to the coconut bank and receives more coconuts as interest, his newly acquired coconuts are not the result of any new labor on his part. When we look at capitalistic property—that is, at socioeconomic environments in which people profit from ownership alone—then we have left Locke's world far behind.

A defender of capitalism may reply, "Certainly, there's nothing unfair about Carl's accruing these extra coconuts through his investment; after all, he could have eaten his original coconuts instead." And, indeed, within our system this reasoning seems perfectly correct. It is the way things work in our society. But this fact doesn't prove that Carl has some natural right to use his coconuts to earn more coconuts—that is, that it would be unfair or unjust to set up a different economic system (for example, one in which he had a right to consume coconuts but no right to use them to accrue more coconuts). The argument here is simply that the issue is not an all-or-nothing one. We may have a fundamental right to property, without that right being unlimited or guaranteeing capitalism as we know it.

ADAM SMITH'S CONCEPT OF THE INVISIBLE HAND

Relying on the idea of a natural right to property is not the only way and probably not the best way to defend capitalism. Another, very important argument defends capitalism in terms of the many economic benefits the system brings, claiming that the free and unrestrained market system that exists under capitalism is more efficient and more productive than any other possible system and is thus to be preferred on moral grounds. Essentially, this is a utilitarian argument, but one doesn't have to be a utilitarian to take it seriously. As mentioned in Chapter 2, almost every normative theory puts some moral weight on the consequences of actions. Thus if capitalism does indeed work better than other ways of organizing economic life, then this outcome will be a relevant moral fact—one that will be important, for instance, for Rawlsians.

> A second argument for capitalism is that it is the most efficient and productive economic system. This is basically a utilitarian consideration.

This section sketches Adam Smith's economic case for capitalism, as presented in *The Wealth of Nations*. Smith argues that when people are left to pursue their own interests, they will, without intending it, produce the greatest good for all. Each person's individual and private pursuit of wealth results—as if guided (in Smith's famous words) by an **invisible hand**—in the most beneficial overall organization and distribution of economic resources. Although the academic study of economics has developed greatly since Smith's times, his classic arguments remain extraordinarily influential.

Smith took it for granted that human beings are, by nature, acquisitive. Self-interest and personal advantage, specifically in an economic sense, may not be all that motivate people, but they do seem to motivate most people much of the time. At any rate, they are powerful enough forces that any successful economic system must strive to harness them. We are, Smith thought, strongly inclined to act so as to acquire more and more wealth.

In addition, humans have a natural propensity for trading—"to truck, barter, and exchange." Unlike other species, we have an almost constant need for the assistance of others. Yet because people are creatures of self-interest, it is folly for us to expect others to act altruistically toward us. We can secure what we need from others only by offering them something they need from us:

> Whoever offers to another a bargain of any kind, proposes to do this. Give me that which I want, and you shall have this which you want, is the meaning of every such offer; and it is in this manner that we obtain from one another the far greater part of those good offices which we stand in need of. It is not from the benevolence of the butcher, the brewer, or the baker that we expect our dinner, but from their regard to their own interest. We address ourselves, not to their humanity but to their self love, and never talk to them of our own necessities but of their advantages.[4]

This disposition to trade, said Smith, leads to the division of labor—dividing the labor and production process into areas of specialization, which is the prime means of increasing economic productivity.

Thus, Smith reasoned that the greatest utility will result from unfettered pursuit of self-interest. Individuals should be allowed unrestricted access to raw materials, markets, and labor. Government interference in private enterprise should be eliminated, free competition encouraged, and economic self-interest made the rule of the day. Because human beings are materialistic, acquisitive creatures, we will, if left free, engage in labor and exchange goods in a way that results in the greatest benefit to society. In our efforts to advance our own economic interests, we inevitably act to promote the economic well-being of society generally:

> Every individual is continually exerting himself to find the most advantageous employment for whatever capital he can command. It is his own advantage, indeed, and not that of the society, which he has in view. . . . [But] by directing that industry in such a manner as its produce may be of the greatest value, he [is] . . . led by an invisible hand to promote an end that was no part of his intention. . . . By pursuing his own interest he frequently promotes that of society more effectually than when he really intends to promote it.[5]

To explain why pursuit of self-interest necessarily leads to the greatest social benefit, Smith invoked the law of supply and demand, which was alluded to in our discussion of competition. The law of supply and demand tempers the pursuit of self-interest exactly as competition keeps the enterprising capitalist from becoming a ruthless profiteer. The law of supply and demand similarly solves the problems of adequate goods and fair prices.

Some think the law of supply and demand even solves the problem of fair wages, for labor is another commodity up for sale like shoes or jeans. Just as the price of a new product at first is high, like the jeans in our earlier hypothetical example, so, too, are the wages of labor in a new field. But as labor becomes more plentiful, wages decline. Eventually they fall to a point at which inefficient laborers are eliminated and forced to seek other work, just as the inefficient manufacturers of jeans were forced out of that business and into others. And like the price of jeans, the price of labor then stabilizes at a fair level. As for the inefficient laborers, they find work and a living wage elsewhere. In seeking new fields of labor, they help maximize the majority's opportunities to enjoy the necessities, conveniences, and trifles of human life.

SUMMARY
Utilitarian defense of capitalism is associated with the classical economic arguments of Adam Smith. Smith believed that human beings are acquisitive and that they have a natural propensity for trading, and he insisted that when people are left free to pursue their own economic interests, they will, without intending it, produce the greatest good for all.

A traditional supply–demand curve. The point at which supply and demand meet is called the "equilibrium" and determines the price.

Some modern defenders of capitalism claim that it operates as Smith envisioned and can be justified on the same utilitarian grounds. But not everyone agrees.

CRITICISMS OF CAPITALISM

These two arguments for capitalism have not persuaded everyone that it is a morally justifiable system, and there are both theoretical and operational objections to it that need to be considered. *Theoretical* criticisms challenge capitalism's fundamental values, basic assumptions, or inherent economic tendencies. *Operational* criticisms focus more on capitalism's alleged deficiencies in actual practice (as opposed to theory)—in particular, on its failure to live up to its own economic ideals.

The following criticisms are a mix of both theoretical and operational concerns. They raise political, economic, and philosophical issues that cannot be fully assessed here. The debate over capitalism is a large and important one; the presentation that follows should be viewed as a stimulus to further discussion and not as the last word on the pros and cons of capitalism.

INEQUALITY

Chapter 3 and Case 3.3 documented the profound economic inequality that exists in our capitalist society. The disparity in personal incomes is enormous; a tiny minority of the population owns the vast majority of the country's productive assets; and our society continues to be marred by poverty and homelessness. With divisions of social and economic class comes inequality of opportunity. A child born to a working-class family, let alone to an unwed teenager in an inner-city ghetto, has life prospects and possibilities that pale beside those of children born to wealthy, stock-owning parents. This reality challenges capitalism's claim of fairness, and the persistence of poverty and economic misfortune provides the basis for a utilitarian objection to it.

Critics argue that poverty and inequality challenge the fairness of capitalism and its claim to advance the interests of all. Defenders of capitalism respond to this in different ways.

Few doubt that poverty and inequality are bad things, but defenders of capitalism make several responses to those who criticize it on these grounds:

1. A few extreme supporters of capitalism simply deny that it is responsible for poverty and inequality. Rather, they say, government interference with the market causes these problems. Left to itself, the market would eliminate unemployment and poverty while ultimately lessening inequality. But neither theoretical economics nor the study of history supports this reply. Most economists and social theorists would agree that in the past eighty years or so activist government policies have done much, in all the Western capitalist countries, to reduce poverty and (to a lesser extent) inequality.

2. More moderate defenders of capitalism concede that in its pure laissez-faire form, capitalism does nothing to prevent and may even foster inequality and poverty. However, they argue that the system can be modified or its inherent tendencies corrected by political action, so that inequality and poverty are reduced or even eliminated. Critics of capitalism reply that the policies necessary to seriously reduce inequality and poverty are either impossible within a basically capitalist economic framework or unlikely to be carried out in any political system based on capitalism.

3. Finally, defenders of capitalism argue that the benefits of the system outweigh this weak point. Inequality is not so important if living standards are rising and if even

the poor have better lives than they did in previous times. This contention rests on an implicit comparison with what things would be like if society were organized differently and is, accordingly, difficult to assess. Naturally, it seems more plausible to those who are relatively favored by, and content with, the present economic system than it does to those who feel disadvantaged by it.

Some critics of capitalism go on to maintain that, aside from inequalities of income and ownership, the inequality inherent in the worker–capitalist relationship is itself morally undesirable. John Stuart Mill found capitalism inferior in this respect to more cooperative and egalitarian economic arrangements. "To work at the bidding and for the profit of another," he wrote, "is not . . . a satisfactory state to human beings of educated intelligence, who have ceased to think themselves inferior to those whom they serve."[6] The ideal of escaping from a system of "superiors" and "subordinates" was well expressed by the great German playwright and poet Bertolt Brecht when he wrote that "He wants no servants under him / And no boss over his head."[7]

HUMAN NATURE AND CAPITALISM

The theory of capitalism rests on a view of human beings as rational economic creatures, individuals who recognize and are motivated largely by their own economic self-interest. Adam Smith's defense of capitalism, for instance, assumes that consumers have full knowledge of the diverse choices available to them in the marketplace. They are supposed to know the price structures of similar products, to be fully aware of product differences, and to be able to make the optimal choice regarding price and quality.

But the key choices facing today's consumers are rarely simple. From foods to drugs, automobiles to appliances, fertilizers to computers, the modern marketplace is a cornucopia of products whose nature and nuances require a high level of consumer literacy. Even with government agencies and public interest groups to aid them, today's consumers are rarely an equal match for powerful industries that can influence prices, control product quality, and create and shape markets. The effectiveness of advertising, in particular, is difficult to reconcile with the picture of consumers as the autonomous, rational, and perfectly informed economic maximizers that economics textbooks presuppose when they attempt to demonstrate the benefits of capitalism. Consumers frequently fall short of perfect rationality and often seem under the sway of social and psychological forces they are unaware of.

According to some critics of capitalism, however, what is objectionable about capitalism's view of human beings as essentially economic creatures is not this gap between theory and reality but rather the fact that it presents little in the way of an ideal to which either individuals or societies may aspire. As George Soros puts it, "Humans are capable of transcending the pursuit of narrow self-interest. Indeed, they cannot live without some sense of morality. It is market fundamentalism, which holds that the social good is best served by allowing people to pursue their self-interest without any thought for the social good . . . that is a perversion of human nature."[8] Not only does capitalism rest on the premise that people are basically acquisitive, individualistic, and materialistic, but in practice capitalism strongly reinforces those human tendencies. Capitalism, its critics charge, presents no higher sense of human mission or purpose, whereas other views of society and human nature do.

Christianity, for example, has long aspired to the ideal of a truly religious community united in *agape*, selfless love. And socialism, because it views human nature as malleable, hopes to see people transformed from the "competitive, acquisitive beings that they are (and that they are *encouraged* to be) under all property-dominated, market-oriented systems." In the more "benign environment of a propertyless, nonmarket social system,"

SUMMARY
Critics question the basic assumptions of capitalism (theoretical challenges) and whether it has delivered on its promises (operational challenges). One criticism is that capitalism produces severe inequality and is unable to eliminate poverty. Another is that capitalism wrongly assumes that human beings are rational economic maximizers and that well-being comes from ever greater material consumption. It is also alleged that capitalism offers us no higher sense of human purpose.

Critics charge that capitalism reinforces materialism and offers no higher sense of human purpose.

socialists believe that more cooperative and less selfish human beings will emerge.⁹ Such positive ideals and aspirations are lacking in capitalism—or so its critics charge.

Finally, an implicit assumption of capitalism is that human beings find increased well-being through ever greater material consumption. That's why the avid pursuit of economic gain, as mediated through the invisible hand of the market, is supposed to make us all better off. Moreover, contemporary capitalism needs people to keep on buying and consuming goods for the system to continue running. Consumer demand makes the economic wheels turn. And that, in turn, requires people in general to choose working more so they can consume more rather than working less, having more leisure, and buying fewer things. However, this bias in favor of material consumption runs up against the fact, according to social psychologists, that people today—in America, Europe, and Japan—are no more pleased with their lives than people were in the 1950s, despite the very substantial increase in standard of living that all these societies have enjoyed.¹⁰

> *Capitalism operates on the debatable assumption that human beings find increased well-being through ever greater material consumption.*

COMPETITION ISN'T WHAT IT'S CRACKED UP TO BE

As we have seen, one of the key features of capitalism is competition. Unfettered competition supposedly serves the collective interest while offering rich opportunities for the individual. But competition is one of the targets of capitalism's critics. They contend that capitalism breeds oligopolies that eliminate competition and concentrate economic power, that a system of corporate welfare protects many businesses from true marketplace competition, and finally that competition is neither generally beneficial nor desirable in itself.

> *Critics contend that capitalism's supposed commitment to competition is belied by oligopoly and corporate welfare. Some also challenge the belief that competition is desirable and beneficial.*

Capitalism Breeds Oligopolies

As early as the middle of the nineteenth century, the German philosopher and political economist Karl Marx (1818–1883) argued that capitalism leads to **oligopolies**—a concentration of property and resources, and thus economic power, in the hands of a few. High costs, complex and expensive machinery, intense competition, and the advantages of large-scale production all work against the survival of small firms, said Marx. Many see proof of Marx's argument in today's economy.

Before the Industrial Revolution, capitalism was characterized by comparatively free and open competition among a large number of small firms. As late as 1832, for instance, hardly any private firms in the United States had ten or more employees.¹¹ Since then, the economy has come to be dominated by a relatively small number of enormous companies that, to a distressing extent, can conspire to set prices, eliminate competition, and monopolize an industry. For example, the five biggest oil refiners in the United States control 56 percent of the market (up from 35 percent in 1993).¹² Four airlines control 69 percent of domestic air travel, and two brewing companies sell 65 percent of the nation's beer.¹³ Or take the banking sector. Although there are more than 8,000 banks in the United States, the four top lenders control more than 35 percent of all deposits (up from 5 percent in 1998), and the top ten financial institutions control 54 percent of all financial assets.¹⁴

Today, the 500 largest U.S. firms constitute at least three-quarters of the American economy. They frequently have revenues that exceed the revenues of state governments and the gross domestic product (GDP) of many countries: The annual revenue of General Motors, for instance, is greater than the GDP of more than 148 countries, and that of Walmart outweighs the combined GDP of all of sub-Saharan Africa.¹⁵ Increasingly multinational in character, these giant corporations do business around the globe, disavowing allegiance to any particular nation. In fact, more than a quarter of the world's economic activity comes from the two hundred largest corporations. Since the 1980s, wave after wave of corporate takeovers and mergers has further accelerated the trend toward oligopoly and ever greater economic concentration. The latest wave crested in 2007 with a record-setting $4.74 trillion worth of merger and acquisition deals worldwide, since then receding to an annual rate of about half that.

True, antitrust laws have sometimes fostered competition by breaking up monopolies, as happened with Standard Oil and AT&T. More recently, the government went after Microsoft for "exclusionary and predatory" businesses practices. On the whole, however, such actions have proved ineffectual in halting the concentration of economic power. And despite calls to break up or restrict the operations of those banks and other financial institutions that are so large that the government cannot allow them to fail without endangering the whole economy (as happened in 2008), financial reform legislation passed by Congress in 2010 and intended to prevent future crises did not address this problem at all.

Because of their sway over the market and their political clout, the gigantic corporations that we know today have so altered the face of capitalism that Adam Smith would have trouble recognizing it. As a result, in terms of competition, our present-day economic system differs significantly from the textbook model of capitalism. One expert puts it this way:

> In surveying the American business system it is obvious that competition still exists; however, it is not a perfect competition. Often it is not price competition at all. With the possible exception of some farm markets where there are still large numbers of producers of similar and undifferentiated products (wheat, for instance), virtually every producer of goods and services has some control over price. The degree of control varies from industry to industry and between firms within an industry. Nevertheless, it does exist and it amounts to an important modification in our model of a free-enterprise economy.[16]

These days, in fact, some of the most vigorous corporate competition occurs not in the marketplace but in Washington, D.C., where companies jockey for competitive advantage by getting Congress to pass laws that help them and hold back their rivals.[17] More than 500 American companies now maintain permanent offices there, employing 61,000 lobbyists.[18] And that doesn't include corporate-sponsored foundations, centers, and institutes that also try to steer public policy in profitable, industry-friendly directions. Altogether, U.S. companies spend well over $3 billion a year lobbying Washington, with the pharmaceutical industry leading the pack. In a recent six-year period, it spent $759 million to influence 1,400 congressional bills.[19]

Corporate Welfare Programs Protect Businesses

When the United States slapped tariffs ranging from 8 to 30 percent on imported steel in 2001, it was continuing a thirty-year tradition of cosseting the steel industry with various subsidies and protections that have cost the country a small fortune. Moreover, what's good for one industry can be bad for the rest of the country. Businesses that use steel, for example, employ roughly forty times more people than do steel producers. According to the Institute for International Economics, until a ruling by the World Trade Organization led to the steel tariffs being canceled, between 45,000 and 75,000 jobs were lost because higher steel prices made U.S. steel-using industries less competitive.[20] Similarly, U.S. quotas on sugar imports in recent years have resulted in the domestic price of sugar being three and a half times the world market price. As a result, to survive, American candy makers have been forced to move production to countries where sugar is cheaper at the cost of thousands of U.S. jobs.[21]

From 1995 to 2012, U.S. taxpayers spent more than $256 billion on subsidies to farmers, with the fattest subsidies going to the richest farmers.[22] In fact, 10 percent of the recipients received 65 percent of the loot.[23] When it comes to cotton, the disparity is even greater. Of the $19.1 billion that cotton growers received in a recent ten-year period, more than 80 percent went to only 10 percent of the recipients.[24] Meanwhile, more than 200 different kinds of subsidies support America's ethanol program. The oil industry itself receives a 51-cent federal subsidy for each gallon of ethanol it mixes with gasoline, and there is a 54-cent per gallon tariff on imported ethanol.[25] Subsidies for farmers and tariffs on steel, sugar, and ethanol are only the most blatant examples of the way **corporate welfare** assists business and protects it from competition. Thanks to duties, fees, and restrictions on imported products, American consumers pay far more for goods than they otherwise would. And that, of course, is in addition to what corporate subsidies cost consumers as taxpayers.

Not content with handcuffing their foreign competition, some American companies seek to benefit even more directly from tariffs and other trade restrictions. For instance, in recent years, the Commerce Department has imposed anti-dumping duties on Chinese manufacturers of wooden furniture who are believed to sell their products at "less than fair value." U.S. law allows companies hurt by competition they believe to be unfair to submit to the department every year a list of exporters that should be reviewed. The department then has eighteen months to determine whether to subject those foreign companies to tougher duties. Fearing the uncertainty of the review process and a possible increase in duties, many Chinese companies pay cash to the American furniture makers in return for being removed from the review list. Although this appears to be legal, "everyone in the industry in the United States and China understands that these payments are clever shakedowns," says William Silverman, a lawyer representing U.S. furniture retailers who import Chinese products.[26]

Every year the federal government doles out billions of dollars to private business in direct subsidy programs.[27] For example, the U.S. Agriculture Department's Market Access Program spends millions funding both generic and brand-name advertising abroad for American agricultural products, and the U.S. Forest Service builds roads and subsidizes logging in national forests for the benefit of private timber companies. The Foreign Military Financing Program assists foreign countries to purchase U.S. military products—to the tune of around $4.5 billion a year. Other government-sponsored corporate welfare programs include the Export Enhancement Program, the Export-Import Bank, and the Overseas Private Investment Corporation. The latter two agencies provide loans and financial guarantees for corporate energy projects. Among the beneficiaries are Unocal, which was loaned $350 million to develop an oil and gas field in Indonesia, and ExxonMobil, which received $500 million in financing to build a pipeline in Cameroon.[28]

Precise figures are impossible to come by, but the federal government clearly spends more on corporate welfare than it does on either homeland security or on social welfare programs for the poor.[29] In addition, there are the tax breaks that corporations receive. A recent U.S. government report revealed that during a seven-year period of soaring profits, 55 percent of large U.S. corporations had at least one year of paying no tax at all.[30] It's not surprising, then, that some American companies pay more in taxes to foreign governments than they do to their own government—in ExxonMobil's case five times as much.[31]

State governments also pamper business with subsidies and protectionist restrictions on competition. It's impossible to put a price tag on these, but looking at the Internet alone, experts calculate that state impediments to buying and selling cost consumers $15 billion a year. For example, Georgia forbids the online sale of contact lenses, and

SUMMARY

Critics of capitalism also charge that competition is not what it's cracked up to be because (1) capitalism breeds oligopolies, (2) corporate welfare often shelters business from competition, and (3) competition is not a good thing.

Oklahoma the online sale of caskets. And all fifty states shield their car dealers from competition by prohibiting manufacturers from selling directly to consumers over the Internet.[32] In addition, cities and states frequently provide tax breaks to corporations to lure them to, or prevent them from leaving, the local area. These subsidies cost taxpayers $50 billion a year, but for many reasons, they rarely pay off in jobs or higher overall tax revenues.[33] State and local governments also allow private companies to fund projects with tax-exempt bonds.[34]

As staggering as corporate welfare already is, it was taken to a whole new level in 2008 by the federal government's $700 billion Troubled Assets Relief Program (TARP). Put together in response to the financial meltdown, TARP enabled the government to purchase non-liquid, difficult-to-value assets from banks and other financial institutions, in particular so-called collateralized debt obligations, which had been hit hard by foreclosures caused by the real estate slump. The theory was that by authorizing the Treasury Department to buy these "troubled assets"—assets, that is, that the banks couldn't sell on the open market for the simple reason that no one was willing to buy them—TARP would increase the banks' liquidity and improve their balance sheets, thus stabilizing the financial system. In addition to "cash for trash," TARP provided funds for the government to purchase loans from and make direct equity investments in the banks themselves, and the Treasury Department was creative in finding ways to assist the banks outside the TARP framework at a potential cost to tax payers that was greater than TARP itself. Given the crisis that the nation was facing, few doubt the necessity of something like TARP or of the Treasury Department's taking bold measures. And in the end almost all the TARP funds were repaid. Nevertheless, with few strings attached, and with most banks choosing to shore up their bottom line by sitting on the money (or using it for executive bonuses) rather than to help stimulate the economy by lending it out, the bailout represents an unprecedented commitment of taxpayer money to save what had been some of the largest and wealthiest firms in the country, and their well-heeled managers, from the consequences of their own greed, recklessness, and mismanagement.

Competition Is Not a Good

Because the profit motive governs capitalism, it should not be surprising that even those companies that preach the doctrine of free competition are willing to shelve it when collusion with other firms, or government tariffs and subsidies, make higher profits possible. How else to explain the fact that the United States forbids foreign companies from owning airlines in America and prevents foreign airlines from flying routes that pick up passengers at more than one American city? In these ways, capitalism fails to live up to its own ideal. This was something that worried Adam Smith, who once wrote, "People of the same trade seldom meet together, even for merriment or diversion, but the conversation ends in a conspiracy against the public, or in some contrivance to raise prices."[35]

Unlike Adam Smith, however, some critics of capitalism repudiate competition as an ideal, arguing that it is neither beneficial in general nor desirable in itself. They point to empirical studies establishing that in business there is frequently a negative correlation between performance and individual competitiveness.[36] In other words, it is often cooperation, rather than competitiveness, that best enhances both individual and group achievement. According to Alfie Kohn, the reason is simple: "Trying to do well and trying to beat others are two different things."[37] Competition is an extrinsic motivator; not only does it not produce the kinds of results that flow from enjoying the activity itself, but also the use of extrinsic motivators can undermine intrinsic motivation and thus

> Critics of competition contend that cooperation leads to better individual and group performance.

adversely affect performance in the long run. The unpleasantness of competition can also diminish people's performance.

Critics also contend that cooperation is more efficient than competition.

The critics also contend that competition often precludes the more efficient use of resources that cooperation allows. When people work together, coordination of effort and an efficient division of labor are possible. By contrast, competition can inhibit economic coordination, cause needless duplication of services, retard the exchange of information, foster copious litigation, and lead to socially detrimental or counterproductive results such as business failures, mediocre products, unsafe working conditions, and environmental neglect. When presented with examples of the beneficial results of competition, the critics argue that on closer inspection the supposed advantages turn out to be short-lived, illusory, or isolated instances.

EXPLOITATION AND ALIENATION

Karl Marx argued that as the means of production become concentrated in the hands of the few, the balance of power between capitalists (bourgeoisie) and laborers (proletariat) tips further in favor of the bourgeoisie. Because workers have nothing to sell but their labor, said Marx, the bourgeoisie is able to exploit them by paying them less than the true value created by their labor. In fact, Marx thought, it is only through such **exploitation** that capitalists are able to make a profit and increase their capital. And the more capital they accumulate, the more they can exploit workers. Marx predicted that eventually workers would revolt. Unwilling to be exploited further, they would rise and overthrow their oppressors and set up an economic system that would truly benefit all.

The development of capitalist systems since Marx's time belies his forecast. Legal, political, and economic changes have tempered many of the greedy, exploitative dispositions of early capitalism. The twentieth century witnessed legislation curbing egregious worker abuse, guaranteeing a minimum wage, and ensuring a safer and more healthful work environment. The emergence of labor unions and their subsequent victories significantly enlarged the worker's share of the economic pie. Indeed, many of the specific measures proposed by Marx and his collaborator Friedrich Engels in the *Communist Manifesto* (1848) have been implemented in capitalist countries: a program of graduated income tax, free education for all children in public schools, investiture of significant economic control in the state, and so on.

Still, many would say that although democratic institutions may have curbed the excesses of capitalism, they can do nothing to prevent the alienation of workers that results from having to do unfulfilling work. Again, because of the unequal positions of capitalist and worker, laborers must work for someone else—they must do work imposed on them as a means of satisfying the needs of others. As a result, they inevitably come to feel exploited and debased. And this is true, critics of capitalism claim, not just of manual laborers but also of white-collar workers, many of whom identify with the cubicle dwellers of the cartoon strip *Dilbert*.

Marx argued that under capitalism workers are alienated in several different ways.

But what about workers who are paid handsomely for their efforts? They, too, said Marx, remain alienated, for as the fruits of their labor are enjoyed by someone else, their work ultimately proves meaningless to them. The following selection from Marx's "Economic and Philosophic Manuscripts" (1844) summarizes his notion of **alienation** as the separation of individuals from the objects they create, which in turn results in one's separation from other people, from oneself, and ultimately from one's human nature:

> The worker is related to the *product of his labor* as to an *alien* object. For it is clear . . . that the more the worker expends himself in work the more powerful becomes the world of objects which he creates in face of himself, the poorer he

becomes in his inner life, and the less he belongs to himself.... The worker puts his life into the object, and his life then belongs no longer to himself but to the object.... What is embodied in the product of his labor is no longer his own. The greater this product is, therefore, the more he is diminished. The *alienation* of the worker in his product means not only that his labor becomes an object, assumes an *external* existence, but that it exists independently, *outside himself*, and alien to him, and that it stands opposed to him as an autonomous power....

What constitutes the alienation of labor? First, that the work is *external* to the worker, that it is not part of his nature; and that, consequently, he does not fulfill himself in his work but denies himself.... His work is not voluntary but imposed, *forced labor*. It is not the satisfaction of a need, but only a *means* for satisfying other needs. Its alien character is clearly shown by the fact that as soon as there is no physical or other compulsion it is avoided like the plague. External labor, labor in which man alienates himself, is a labor of self-sacrifice.... Finally, the external character of work for the worker is shown by the fact that it is not his own work but work for someone else, that in work he does not belong to himself but to another person....

We have now considered the act of alienation of practical human activity, labor, from two aspects: (1) the relationship of the worker to the *product of labor* as an alien object which dominates him... [and] (2) the relationship of labor to the *act of production within labor*. This is the relationship of the worker to his own activity as something alien and not belonging to him.... This is *self-alienation* as against the above-mentioned alienation of the *thing*.[38]

In Marx's view, when workers are alienated they cannot be truly free. They may have the political and social freedoms of speech, religion, and governance, but even with these rights, individuals still are not fully free. Freedom from government interference and persecution does not necessarily guarantee freedom from economic exploitation and alienation, and it is for this kind of freedom that Marx and Engels felt such passion.

Some would say that one need not wade through Marxist philosophy to get a feel for what Marx and others mean by worker alienation. Just talk to workers themselves, as writer Studs Terkel did. In different ways the hundreds of workers from diverse occupations whom Terkel interviewed speak of the same thing: dehumanization.

> Mike Fitzgerald ... is a laborer in a steel mill. "I feel like the guys who built the pyramids. Somebody built 'em. Somebody built the Empire State Building, too. There's hard work behind it. I would like to see a building, say the Empire State, with a foot-wide strip from top to bottom and the name of every bricklayer on it, the name of every electrician. So when a guy walked by, he could take his son and say, 'See, that's me over there on the 45th floor. I put that steel beam in.' ... Everybody should have something to point to."
>
> Sharon Atkins is 24 years old. She's been to college and acidly observes, "The first myth that blew up in my face is that a college education will get you a worthwhile job." For the last two years she's been a receptionist at an advertising agency. "I didn't look at myself as 'just a dumb broad' at the front desk, who took phone calls and messages. I thought I was something else. The office taught me differently."
>
> ... Harry Stallings, 27, is a spot welder on the assembly line at an auto plant. "They'll give better care to that machine than they will to you. If it breaks down, there's somebody out there to fix it right away. If I break down, I'm just pushed over to the other side till another man takes my place. The only thing the company has in mind is to keep that machine running. A man would be more eager to do a better job if he were given proper respect and the time to do it."[39]

SUMMARY

Karl Marx was an important nineteenth-century critic of capitalism. He argued that workers are exploited by capitalism and inevitably experience alienation.

TODAY'S ECONOMIC CHALLENGES

Capitalism faces a number of important critical questions, both theoretical and operational. These criticisms are a powerful challenge, especially to capitalism in its pure laissez-faire form. But, as we have seen, today's capitalism is a long way from the laissez-faire model. Corporate behemoths able to control markets and sway governments have replaced the small-scale entrepreneurs and free-wheeling competition of an earlier day. And governments in all capitalist countries actively intervene in the economic realm; they endeavor to assist or modify the so-called invisible hand; and over the years they have reformed or supplemented capitalism with programs intended to enhance the security of the workforce and increase the welfare of their citizens.

This reality complicates the debate over capitalism. Its defenders may be advocating either the pure laissez-faire ideal or the modified state welfare capitalism that we in fact have. Likewise, those who attack the laissez-faire ideal may do so on behalf of a modified, welfarist capitalism, or they may criticize both forms of capitalism and defend some kind of socialism, in which private property and the pursuit of profit are no longer governing economic principles. We thus have a three-way debate over the respective strengths and weaknesses of laissez-faire capitalism, state welfare capitalism, and socialism.

The rest of this chapter leaves this fundamental debate behind. Instead of looking at criticisms of capitalism in general and at issues relevant to any capitalist society, it examines some of the more specific socioeconomic challenges facing the United States today. These include (1) the decline of American manufacturing and the related problems posed by the outsourcing of jobs and the growing U.S. trade deficit; (2) business's obsession with short-term results; (3) and changing attitudes toward work.

THE DECLINE OF AMERICAN MANUFACTURING

Historically, capitalists have made money by producing goods. Manufacturing was the backbone of the American economy and the basis of our prosperity. In industry after industry, however, U.S. companies have conceded manufacturing dominance to foreign competitors. Today, for example, one can't buy a television made in the United States, Walmart employs more people than the Big Three automakers do, and more Americans work in government than in manufacturing. Whereas manufacturing accounted for 27 percent of GDP in the mid-1960s, since then it has fallen to half that,[40] and for the

Manufacturing has declined in the United States as American companies have conceded manufacturing dominance to foreign competitors.

As a percentage of gross domestic product, manufacturing in the United States has declined by more than 50 percent since the 1960s.

Manufacturing (bottom portion in red) as percentage of GDP in the mid-60s

Manufacturing (bottom portion in red) as percentage of GDP today first time since the Industrial Revolution, manufacturing employs less than 10 percent of the American workforce.[41]

Since the 1980s, many U.S. manufacturers have been closing up shop or curtailing their operations and becoming marketing organizations for other producers, usually foreign. The result is the evolution of a new kind of company: manufacturers that do little or no manufacturing. They may perform a host of profit-making functions—from design to distribution—but they lack their own production base. Instead, they **outsource**, buying parts or whole products from other producers, both at home and abroad. The traditional vertical structure of manufacturing, in which the manufacturer makes nearly all crucial parts, is thereby replaced by a network of small operators. Companies that in years past were identified with making goods of all sorts now are likely to produce only the package and the label. In contrast to traditional manufacturers, they have become, in current business jargon, **hollow corporations**.

Proponents of the new system describe it as flexible and efficient, a logical outcome of the drive to lower the costs of doing business. But critics worry whether the United States can prosper without a strong manufacturing base. As Tsutomu Ohshima, a senior manufacturing director of Toyota Motor Corporation, puts it: "You can't survive with just a service industry."[42] In wages, productivity, and innovation, the service sector fails to compare with basic industry. Manufacturing jobs generate significantly more goods and services from other industries than do service jobs and three times as many additional employment opportunities.[43] Because the rate of technical change is higher in manufacturing than in other sectors, it's hard to imagine the United States sustaining its technological leadership with a withered manufacturing sector.[44]

Outsourcing Jobs

As America's manufacturing base dwindles and U.S. firms outsource more and more of their operations, millions of jobs have moved abroad. That's not surprising when a Barbie doll that retails in America for $9.99 costs only 35 cents for a Chinese factory to make, including the price of labor.[45] But it's no longer just blue-collar jobs that are disappearing. Many upscale, nonmanufacturing jobs also are migrating overseas. Engineers, financial analysts, computer technicians, and other white-collar workers living in countries such as Russia, India, and the Philippines now handle airline reservations, design chips, edit books, draw architectural blueprints, provide accounting services, process loans and insurance claims, and engage in research and development for American corporations.[46] Because skilled, highly educated foreigners work for far less than do their American counterparts, outsourcing these jobs overseas makes U.S. firms leaner and more profitable. But can America lose these jobs and still prosper, especially if outsourcing also exerts downward pressure on the salaries of the jobs that remain? That's the question that is worrying more and more people.

Most mainstream economists are upbeat. They believe that outsourcing jobs increases shareholder wealth and benefits consumers by keeping prices down and that as old jobs move overseas, the economy will create new ones at home—higher-level jobs that add greater product value than the lost jobs did. Although they can't predict the new industries and occupations that will emerge to replace the old ones, these economists are confident that it will happen. Even in this optimistic scenario, however, there are genuine human costs. Sometimes economists refer to this downside as "short-term friction," but of course that's not how it feels to those workers whose relatively high-paying jobs are outsourced. They still have bills and mortgages to pay. And there's no reason to suppose that they will be the ones who eventually fill the "replacement" positions that the economy will supposedly create. Moreover, if they remain unemployed, settle for lower-paid

SUMMARY
Our capitalist socioeconomic system is facing a number of challenges. These include the decline of American manufacturing and the related problems of job outsourcing and a growing trade deficit. Economists disagree about whether outsourcing benefits America overall and about the risks posed by our foreign indebtedness.

work, or retire early, their lowered incomes affect their families, communities, and local businesses. In this way, then, the welfare of some is being sacrificed for the greater good of society.

A minority of economists, however, are challenging the rosy assumption that, despite the costs, outsourcing benefits America overall.[47] Going back to the nineteenth-century economist David Ricardo, conventional economic theory has taught that a country should focus on producing for the world market those goods in which it has a **comparative advantage**—the goods that it can produce at a lower opportunity cost than other countries can (that is, that it can produce more cheaply relative to other goods than is the case in other countries).* If countries sell what they are comparatively better at producing and buy from other countries what those countries are comparatively better at producing, then free trade benefits everyone. But the situation changes, or so some economists are now arguing, if a country's competitive edge comes solely from cheaper labor, especially in a world in which advanced telecommunication makes it possible for brainpower to zip around the world. In this case, there's no identifiable point at which the outsourcing process should stop: Even the so-called replacement jobs will move overseas. In theory, of course, wages in countries such as China and India should eventually rise to the point where outsourcing provides no benefit to American firms. But it will be decades and decades before that happens, if it ever does, and in the meantime white-collar wages in the United States have a long way to fall. In addition, if cheaper white-collar labor slashes the prices of those exports in which the United States has a comparative advantage, that could hurt the economy overall. For these reasons, even Paul Samuelson, the dean of American economists, has acknowledged that "comparative advantage cannot be counted on to create . . . net gains greater than net losses from trade."[48]

The U.S. Trade Deficit

As the United States continues to run an enormous trade deficit, its foreign borrowing keeps increasing—with risky consequences, according to some economists.

For forty years, the United States has been steadily losing its share of both foreign and domestic markets. The nation's huge balance-of-trade deficit is the most visible sign of this. After decades and decades of trade surpluses, the United States has posted a trade deficit every year since 1975. America currently imports twice as much merchandise as it exports. Before the recent recession slowed its growth, our trade deficit had burgeoned to over $700 billion annually, equivalent to almost 6 percent of our GDP. With the country's continuing trade deficits, its reliance on foreign borrowing has increased, and foreign creditors now provide two-thirds of America's net domestic investment. Today we owe the rest of the world around $3 trillion (one-third of it to the Chinese)—twice what we owed in 2000.[49]

Some economists believe that it is irrelevant that the United States buys more than it sells. Although we are now the world's largest debtor nation, they reason, we are still the world's largest and most important economy, so foreigners don't mind lending us money. Other economists, however, are worried by the country's consumption-happy ways. They fear that the United States is creating unsustainable global imbalances—imbalances that they see as the root cause of the global economic crisis.[50] In their view, unless both domestic savings and the production of tradable goods increase dramatically, these imbalances will go on causing economic pain at home and serious dislocations abroad.[51] Many economists also worry that its growing trade deficit makes the United States vulnerable to economic extortion. What happens, they ask, if foreigners choose

---

Comparative advantage does not mean *absolute* advantage. What Ricardo showed was that two countries can benefit from trade even if one is better (or more efficient) than the other at producing everything.

to stop financing our debt? Finally, the trade deficit and our growing international debt have meant an enormous transfer of American assets into foreign hands. The rest of the world now owns significantly more of the United States than it owns of other countries—equivalent to more than 10 percent of the total combined value of the stock market and all residential real estate in the United States. And this gap expands every year as assets, dividends, and interest flow to foreign owners.[52]

EXCLUSIVE FOCUS ON THE SHORT TERM

Observers of the business scene have long charged that U.S. companies are preoccupied with short-term performance at the expense of long-term strategies. According to the critics, this **short-term focus** tends to make U.S. corporations unimaginative, inflexible, and ultimately uncompetitive. These business strategists urge U.S. companies to become more visionary—to define long-term goals and to be willing to stick to them even at the expense of short-term profit. Some businesspeople have accepted that advice, as evidenced by the willingness of Amazon and other dot-com companies to lose money for years as they attempt to build market share. Yet many American companies appear less willing than foreign rivals to gamble on long-term research and development or to sacrifice current profits for benefits ten or fifteen years into the future. By comparison with countries such as Germany and Japan, established U.S. corporations continue to be obsessed with their stock market performance and to govern themselves far more by short-term indicators such as share value and quarterly profits. As a result, they often sacrifice capital improvements or fail to make strategic investments.[53] Some worry that America may lose its technological edge because of this.[54]

> Many observers believe that American corporations are too focused on short-term performance.

An exclusive focus on the short term can also encourage dubious business practices. As management consultants Adrian Slywotsky and Richard Wise write, "Many [American] companies with apparently strong growth records in recent years have achieved them through relatively short-term, unsustainable tactics—acquisitions, international expansion, price increases, or accounting gimmicks."[55] Indeed, many theorists blame the financial meltdown of 2008–09 on a short-term focus on profits that ignored long-term risks.[56]

Moreover, there's no question that corporate America's obsession with short-term performance—when coupled with what former Federal Reserve chairman Alan Greenspan famously called "infectious greed"[57]—has created a high-pressure economic environment conducive to fraudulent behavior. Since the exposure of criminal conduct at Enron in late 2001, a long list of companies—including Adelphia Communications, Computer Associates, Dynegy, Global Crossing, Qwest, Rite Aid, Tyco International, WorldCom, Xerox, and Fannie Mae, to name the best-known cases—have been found to have manipulated financial data or committed outright fraud so as to appear to meet their short-term financial goals. These and other revelations of unethical conduct, in turn, have weakened the trust necessary for the efficient functioning of our economic system. That is why President George W. Bush once stated that "America's greatest economic need is higher ethical standards." Although it's true, as he also said, that "in the long run, there's no capitalism without conscience; there is no wealth without character," Bush may have neglected the extent to which a relentless emphasis on short-term results pressures some of the nation's most prominent business leaders to do things they normally wouldn't do.[58] As one business ethicist writes:

> An obsession with short-term performance can lead to fraudulent behavior.

> Managing a corporation with the single measure of share price is like flying a 747 for maximum speed. You can shake the thing apart in the process. It's like a farmer forcing more and more of a crop to grow, until the soil is depleted and nothing will

grow. Or like an athlete using steroids to develop muscle mass, until the body's health is damaged.

Enron's problem was not a lack of focus on shareholder value. The problem was a lack of accountability to anything except share value. This contributed to a mania, a detachment from reality. And it led to a culture of getting the numbers by any means necessary.[59]

CHANGING ATTITUDES TOWARD WORK

Some commentators believe that the socioeconomic problems facing us today include not only a shrunken manufacturing sector, outsourced jobs, a trade deficit, and a short-term performance mentality but also the challenge of coming to grips with people's changing attitudes toward government, social institutions, business, and work. And with regard to work in particular, there's little question that, in recent decades, people's ideas about its value and the role it should play in their lives have been evolving. The fabled American work ethic seems to be fading away. Or is it?

At first glance the answer would seem to be no. After all, Americans work a lot, more than workers in any other highly industrialized country. To take the most extreme contrast, the average American worker puts in nearly 400 hours more per year than his or her German counterpart.[60] But appearances can be deceptive.

The so-called **work ethic** values work for its own sake, seeing it as something necessary for every person. It also emphasizes the belief that hard work pays off in the end and is thus part and parcel of the American Dream. "If you work hard enough," the expression goes, "you'll make it." Today, however, fewer people believe this than before. Two-thirds of Americans worry about having enough to meet basic family expenses, and nearly 60 percent of them believe they are paid less than they deserve. Fear of being thrown out of work is greater than at any time since the 1970s, and a majority doubts that the next generation will enjoy a higher standard of living.[61] Some experts believe that as people become less optimistic about the future and begin to doubt that their efforts will pay off, they become less interested in work than in looking out for themselves. Paul Kostek, a career development expert, contends that "people more so than ever are looking out for themselves and focus on what they want out of their career as the old social contract is broken." "I see more of a 'me-first' attitude," adds management professor Abigail Hubbard.[62]

In addition, with increased education, people are rearranging their ideas about what's important and about what they want from life. The evidence can be seen in the workplace itself. For example, it is not uncommon for operative workers to balk at doing the monotonous tasks their ancestors once accepted, albeit grudgingly. Loyalty to employers seems on the decline, and loyalty to fellow workers seems on the rise. Turnover rates in many industries are enough to make discontinuity an expensive problem. Organizational plans, schedules, and demands no longer carry the authoritative clout they once did; workers today often subordinate them to personal needs. Moreover, employee sabotage and violence, once unheard-of, occur frequently enough today to worry management.

According to an international survey about what matters to people in different cultures, Americans place work eighth in importance behind values such as their children's education and a satisfactory love life. (In Japan, by contrast, work ranks second only to good health.)[63] Another survey reveals that more and more Americans—both men and women—are shelving job success to be with their families.[64] Although generalizing about people's attitudes toward work is difficult, basically employees today seem willing to work hard at tasks they find interesting and rewarding as long as they have the freedom to influence the nature of their jobs and pursue their own lifestyles. They have a growing expectation that work should provide self-respect, nonmaterial rewards, and

---

People's attitudes about work are changing, and some worry that the famous American work ethic is disappearing.

SUMMARY

An exclusive focus on short-term performance can prevent business from pursuing long-term goals and strategies, and it can encourage dubious, even fraudulent, business practices. People's changing attitudes toward work represent another challenge facing our socioeconomic system, according to some experts.

substantial opportunities for personal growth. And they have a growing willingness to demand individual rights, justice, and equality on the job.

If industry is to improve productive capacity and be competitive, it must seriously confront these changing social attitudes. As Paul Bernstein argues, it is counterproductive to compare today's worker with an idealized worker of yesteryear. Rather, we must acknowledge that we have a new work ethic, which in Bernstein's words

> is part and parcel of the individual desire for meaningful and challenging labor in which some autonomy is an integral feature. An increasingly professionalized work force will not accept a golden embrace unless it is accompanied by fulfilling jobs that have been designed for a labor force that sees work in relation to family, friends, leisure and self-development. Work, for most of us, continues as an important part of our lives, but only in relation to our total experience.[65]

STUDY CORNER

KEY TERMS AND CONCEPTS

alienation	globalized capitalism	outsource
capital	hollow corporations	profit motive
capitalism	industrial capitalism	short-term focus
comparative advantage	invisible hand	socialism
competition	laissez faire	state welfare capitalism
corporate welfare	mercantile capitalism	work ethic
exploitation	natural right to property	worker control socialism
financial capitalism	oligopolies	

POINTS TO REVIEW

- how capitalism, socialism, and worker control socialism differ (p. 152)
- the story of the Fugger dynasty (pp. 152–153)
- five historical stages of capitalism and their characteristics (pp. 153–154)
- four key features of capitalism (pp. 154–156)
- criticisms of the natural-right-to-property argument for capitalism (pp. 157–158)
- how the invisible hand guides self-interest in a socially beneficial direction (pp. 158–159)
- responses to criticisms of capitalism because of inequality and poverty (pp. 160–161)
- capitalism's questionable assumptions about human nature (pp. 161–162)
- oligopolies and corporate welfare under capitalism (pp. 162–165)
- why some critics reject competition as an ideal (pp. 165–166)
- different ways workers are alienated, according to Marx (pp. 166–167)
- the decline of American manufacturing, its manifestations and implications (pp. 168–169)
- conflicting views of outsourcing (pp. 169–170)
- why the trade deficit causes some economists to worry (pp. 170–171)
- negative consequences of an exclusive focus on the short term (p. 171)
- changes in the work ethic (pp. 172–173)

FOR FURTHER REFLECTION

1. What do you see as the strongest moral consideration in favor of capitalism? What do you see as the strongest objection to it?
2. How capitalist is our economic system today?
3. What do you see as the major economic challenges facing our society today and, in particular, your generation?

CASE 4.1

Catastrophe in Bangladesh

RANA PLAZA WAS A NONDESCRIPT EIGHT-STORY building in a modest suburb of Dhaka, Bangladesh. Owned by Sohel Rana, a politically well-connected figure, it housed a bank and a few shops on its lower floors, but most of Rana Plaza was given over to five garment factories. They employed around 5,000 people making clothes for companies in North America and Europe. In April 2013, cracks appeared in the building's structure. Building inspectors ordered Rana Plaza to be evacuated, after which the bank and the shops immediately closed—but not the garment factories. They ordered their employees to return to work the following day. On that fateful day—April 24, 2013—at around 9:00 a.m., Rana Plaza collapsed. 1,129 garment workers were killed, and around 2,500 were injured. It was the deadliest garment factory disaster ever, and probably the most lethal accidental collapse of a building in modern history.[66]

In the aftermath, Sohel Rana and the owners of the five garment factories were arrested along with an engineer who was accused of having helped Rana to add three illegal stories to the building. The Bangladesh High Court ordered the property seized and the assets of the factory owners frozen to ensure that the workers' salaries were paid. The Bangladesh government suspended the local mayor and several inspectors who were accused of negligence in renewing the licenses of the garment factories. Families of the victims received some short-term assistance from the government, but workers who are too seriously injured to work are desperate, and in many families, children have had to go to work because their mothers are dead.

Since the disaster, there has been some soul searching in the West. Documents and remnants of apparel link the Rana Plaza factories to twenty-five European and American clothing brands or clothing retailers, including Walmart. That's not too surprising. Almost all the clothing that Americans and Europeans wear is manufactured in poor countries like Bangladesh. And no wonder. Although the minimum wage for garment workers in Bangladesh was recently doubled, it is still only $38 per month. As a result, since 1998 clothing costs for American consumers have dropped 7 to 8 percent, and corporate profits have been high. In this world of globalized capitalism, many people are asking, what are the responsibilities of companies and consumers to workers in faraway countries?

One monitoring group estimates that Bangladesh's 5,000 factories could be elevated to Western safety standards for, on average, $600,000. That would add up to $3 billion. However, if that were spread over five years, it would add only about 10 cents to the factory price of each of the 7 billion garments that Bangladesh sells every year to Western brands. Meanwhile, several prominent retailers and labor groups have joined forces to create an estimated $40 million compensation fund to aid the victims of the Rana Plaza collapse. Among the retailers who have contributed to the fund are Bon Marché, El Corte Inglés, Primark, and Loblaw, a Canadian company. "Following the collapse," says Robert Chant, a senior vice president at Loblaw, "we came very quickly to the conclusion that compensation was not only a necessity for the survivors, but a responsibility for the many retailers sourcing from Rana Plaza."

No American companies, however, have agreed to join the compensation efforts. Walmart, for example, denies that it has any responsibility, saying that the garments it sold were produced there without its knowledge by a Canadian contractor. And it is true that Western companies do not own third-world garment factories like those in Rana Plaza, and they do not directly employ the workers who make the apparel they sell. Those workers work for companies that work for other companies that provide the garments to Western clothing companies and retailers.

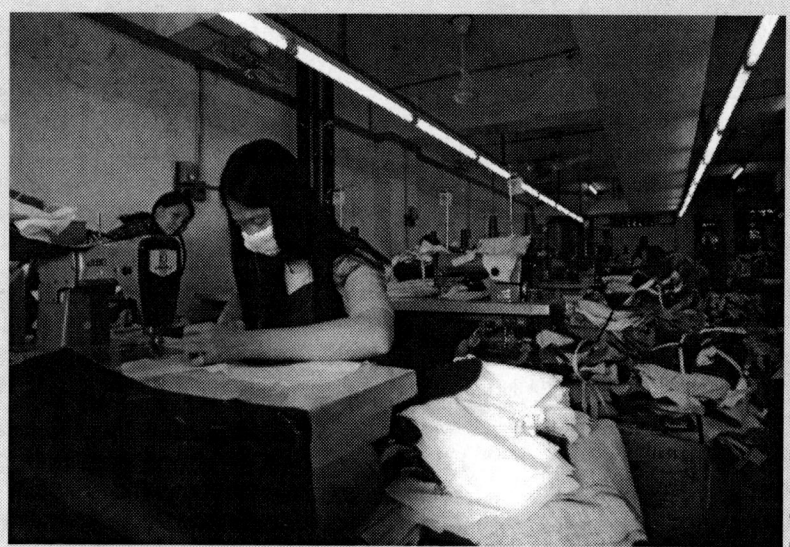

The word "sweatshop" conjures up visions of women and children toiling in cramped and dingy workplaces for paltry wages. But if you lived in a third-world country and had no other opportunity but a low-wage sweatshop job, you might well be happy to take it. Critics contend that such "opportunities" still amount to exploitation.

Some experts believe that American companies are worried about possible legal liability or are afraid that they will appear hypocritical after denying that they were knowingly involved with the factories at Rana Plaza. Dan Rees of the International Labor Organization believes that contributing to the fund would not lead to liability. "At the moment, this effort needs support," he says. "It needs the backing of companies that were in Rana Plaza when it collapsed, that were there in the recent past before it collapsed, and that weren't there at all and want to show solidarity with the industry."

While they may be dragging their feet on compensation, Western retailers have reacted to public outrage over Rana Plaza by launching a major push to improve safety at the Bangladeshi factories they do business with. Instead of joining forces, though, they have divided into two, sometimes feuding camps. The largest—the Bangladesh Accord for Fire and Building Safety—has more than 150 members. The Accord includes 14 American companies, but most of its members are European. The other organization—the Alliance for Bangladesh Worker Safety—comprises 26 companies, all of them American or Canadian. Both organizations are off to a good start, hiring inspectors and investigating factories in Bangladesh, but they argue about who is doing a better job. Fifteen American universities have sided with the Accord, telling the licensees who produce the sweatshirts and other clothing bearing their logos to join it rather than the Alliance. Some observers are bothered by the division of safety efforts, but Professor Dara O'Rouke, an expert on workplace monitoring at the University of California, Berkeley, believes that the Accord-Alliance competition has an upside. "It's pushing both sides to raise the bar on what they are doing to improve safety," she says.

DISCUSSION QUESTIONS

1. Are workers in overseas garment factories exploited? What are the moral pros and cons of outsourcing garment manufacturing to countries where workers are paid so little?

2. Is outsourcing an inevitable feature of globalized capitalism? Are sweatshops? Do Americans gain more from sweatshops (in terms of cheaper products) than they lose (in terms of jobs)?

3. American Apparel is a clothing manufacturer, distributor, and retailer that does not outsource. It pays its workers, on average, over $12 an hour. Could other U.S. clothing companies do the same thing?

4. Do companies have a responsibility to monitor the conduct of the companies that they do business with either directly (suppliers, contractors) or indirectly (subcontractors)? Do clothing companies have a responsibility to see that the people who ultimately make their clothes do so in safe working conditions? Do they have a responsibility to see that those people are paid a decent wage?

5. Do companies whose clothing was being made in Rana Plaza have an obligation to help the victims or their families? What about companies who have had clothing made there in the past, but not at the time of the collapse? Dan Rees suggests that even garment companies with no association with Rana Plaza should contribute out of solidarity with the industry. Explain why you agree or disagree with this.

6. In your view, are Western companies sincere about trying to improve factory safety, or is it just a public-relations effort?

7. Do American consumers who wear clothing produced in countries like Bangladesh bear some responsibility for the wages and conditions of workers there? Do they bear some responsibility for the Rana Plaza collapse? Many consumers know or at least suspect that the clothes they wear are made in third-world sweatshops. Does this affect their moral responsibilities?

8. Many American consumers say that they don't like having their clothes made by poor and exploited foreign workers. Would you pay more for clothing that is made in factories that meet American safety standards? If so, how much more?

9. What, if anything, should consumers do to make foreign factories safer? Can consumer pressure get American companies to improve the pay and working conditions of foreign factory workers?

CASE 4.2

Licensing and Laissez Faire

THE UNITED STATES IS A CAPITALIST COUNTRY, and our system of medical care is, to a significant extent, organized for profit. True, many hospitals are nonprofit, but the same cannot be said of doctors, who, judged as a whole, form an extremely affluent and privileged occupational group.

Sometimes physicians themselves seem a little uncomfortable about the business aspect of their professional lives or worry that outsiders will misinterpret their attention to economic matters. For example, the professional journal *Medical Economics*, which discusses pocketbook issues such as malpractice insurance, taxes, fees, and money management ("Are You Overpaying Your Staff?" is a typical cover story), works hard at not being available to the general public. When a subscriber left his copy on a commercial airliner, another reader found it and sent the mailing label to the magazine; the magazine's editor sent a cautionary note to the subscriber. The editor advises readers to "do your part by restricting access to your personal copies of the magazine. Don't put them in the waiting room, don't leave them lying about in the examination rooms, and don't abandon them in public places."[67]

Medical Economics probably suspects that even in our capitalist society many people, including probably most doctors, would not like to think of physicians simply as medical entrepreneurs who are in it for the money. And, indeed, many people here and many more in other countries criticize our medical system for being profit oriented. They think medical care should be based on need and that ability to pay should not affect the quality of medical treatment one receives. Interestingly, though, some people criticize medical practice in the United States as being insufficiently market oriented; prominent among them was the late Milton Friedman, a Nobel Prize-winning economist at the University of Chicago.

Friedman was a long-standing critic of occupational licensure in all fields. His reasoning is straightforward: Licensure—the requirement that one obtain a license from a recognized authority in order to engage in an occupation—restricts entry into the field. Licensure thus permits the occupational or professional group to enjoy a monopoly in the provision of services. In Friedman's view, this contravenes the principles of a free market to the disadvantage of us all.

Friedman had no objection to certification—that is, to public or private agencies certifying that an individual has certain skills. But he rejected the policy of preventing people who do not have such a certificate from practicing the occupation of their choice. Such a policy restricts freedom and keeps the price of the services in question artificially high. When one reads the long lists of occupations for which some states require a license—librarians, tree surgeons, pest controllers, well diggers, barbers, carpet installers, movie projectionists, florists, upholsterers, makeup artists, even potato growers, among many others[68]—Friedman's case gains plausibility. But Friedman pushed his argument to include all occupations and professions.

Does this mean we should let incompetent physicians practice? Friedman would say yes.[69] In his view, the American Medical Association (AMA) is simply a trade union, though probably the strongest one in the United States. It keeps the wages of its members high by restricting the number of those who can practice medicine.

The AMA does this not only through licensure but also, even more effectively, through controlling the number of medical schools and the number of students admitted to them. Today, for instance, over 42,000 applicants vie every year for roughly 18,000 medical school vacancies. The medical profession, Friedman charged, limits entry into the field both by turning down applicants to medical school and by making standards for admission and licensure so difficult as to discourage many young people from ever trying to gain admission. And, in fact, fewer students apply to medical school these days than in the 1990s.

Viewed as a trade union, the AMA has been singularly effective. As recently as the 1920s, physicians were far down the list of professionals in terms of income; the average doctor made less than the average accountant. Today physicians constitute the profession that arguably has the highest status and the best pay in the country. The median income for primary-care physicians is $157,000. For general surgeons it is $265,000. And in certain specialties, it is a great deal higher. Cardiologists, pain specialists, radiologists, hand surgeons, and others often earn over half a million dollars a year.[70] American doctors earn far more than their foreign counterparts do, even in countries where average wages are similar to those in the United States. Still, the medical establishment remains worried. It believes that there are too many doctors in the United States, and that "this surplus breeds inefficiency and drives up costs."[71]

The economic logic behind this proposition is murky. An increase in the supply of barbers, plumbers, or taxi drivers does not drive up the cost of getting a haircut, having your pipes fixed, or taking a cab. Why should it be different with doctors? Critics of the medical profession believe that its real worry is the prospect of stabilizing or even declining incomes. In any case, the doctors have written two prescriptions.

The first is to reduce the number of medical students by closing some medical schools; the second is to make it more difficult for foreign doctors to practice in the United States. Although the medical establishment has often expressed concern about the quality of foreign medical training, today the worry is strictly a matter of quantity. "We've got to stop the pipeline of foreign medical graduates," says Dr. Ed O'Neil of the Center for the Health Professions at the University of California, San Francisco. "They are a big chunk of physician oversupply. . . . We're just trying to be rational."[72] As for homegrown doctors, Congress followed medical advice. To stem the supposed glut, it decided a few years ago to pay hospitals around the country hundreds of millions of dollars to decrease the number of physicians they train. It now turns out, however, that the United States (which already has fewer doctors per 1,000 people than do almost all European countries[73]) is predicted to have a physician shortage of at least 125,000 by 2025.[74]

Medical licensure restricts the freedom of people to practice medicine and prevents the public from buying the medical care it wants. Nonetheless, most people would probably defend the principle of licensure on the grounds that it raises the standards of competence and the quality of care. Friedman would contest this. By reducing the amount of care available, he contended, licensure also reduces the average quality of care people receive. (By analogy, suppose that automobile manufacturers were forbidden to sell any car that did not have the quality of a Mercedes-Benz. As a result, people who owned cars would have cars of higher average quality than they do now. But because fewer people could afford cars and more of them would, therefore, have to walk or ride bicycles, such a regulation would not raise the quality of transportation enjoyed by the average person.) Friedman charged, furthermore, that the monopoly created by the licensing of physicians has reduced the incentive for research, development, and experimentation, both in medicine and in the organization and provision of services.

Since Friedman initially presented his argument, some of the alternatives to traditional practice that he proposed have come to pass; prepaid services have emerged, and group- and clinic-based practices are on the increase. But what about his main contention that instead of licensure we should allow the marketplace to sort out the competent from the incompetent providers of medical services?

Friedman's critics contend that even if the licensing of professionals "involves violating a moral rule" against restricting individuals' "freedom of opportunity," it is still immoral to allow an unqualified person to engage in potentially harmful activities without having subjected the person to adequate tests of competence.[75] Despite the appeal of Friedman's arguments on behalf of free choice, the danger still remains, they say, that people will be victimized by the incompetent.

Consider, for example, the dietary supplements and bogus medications—things like "healing gels" or "iconic silver"—offered as preventions or cures for the H1N1 (swine flu) virus.[76] Or the quack remedies and treatments peddled to AIDS patients here and abroad. Bottles of processed pond scum and concoctions of herbs, injections of hydrogen peroxide or of cells from the glands of unborn calves, the eating of bee pollen and garlic, $800 pills containing substances from mice inoculated with the AIDS virus, and even whacking the thymus gland of patients to stimulate the body's immune system—all these are among the treatments that have been offered to desperate people by the unscrupulous and eccentric. Deregulation of the medical field seems most unlikely to diminish such exploitation.

DISCUSSION QUESTIONS

1. What explains the fact that licenses are required for so many occupations? What do you see as the pros and cons of occupational licensure in general? Does it have benefits that Friedman overlooked?

2. Do you believe that licensure in medicine or any other field is desirable? If so, in which fields and under what circumstances? What guidelines would you use to determine where licensure is needed?

3. Is occupational licensure consistent with the basic principles and values of capitalism? Is it a violation of the free-market ideal? How would you respond to the argument that licensure illegitimately restricts individual freedom to pursue a career or a trade?

4. Does licensure make the market work more or less effectively? Would you agree that as long as consumers are provided with accurate information, they should be permitted to make their own choices with regard to the services and products they purchase—even when it comes to medical care? Or is licensing necessary to protect them from making incorrect choices?

5. Friedman and others view the AMA as a trade union, and they believe that the high incomes of doctors are due more to artificial restrictions on the free market than to the inherent value of their services. Is this an accurate or fair picture of the medical profession?

6. Is licensing an all-or-nothing issue? Or is it possible that although only licensed professionals should be permitted to perform certain services, paraprofessionals and laypersons could perform less expensively but equally competently other services now monopolized by licensed professionals?

CASE 4.3

One Nation under Walmart

THE HUGE CORPORATIONS THAT PRODUCE our cars, appliances, computers, and other products—many of them household names like Nike, Coca-Cola, and Johnson & Johnson—are a familiar feature of contemporary capitalism.

But Walmart represents something new on the economic landscape. Now the world's largest company, Walmart has achieved its corporate preeminence not in production but in retail. No other retailer, at any time or in any place, has ever come close to being as large and influential as Walmart has become. After years of nonstop growth, there are now more than 8,400 Walmart stores worldwide, and 140 million shoppers visit its U.S. stores each week. And the company is opening more stores all the time as it moves beyond its stronghold in the rural South and Midwest and into urban America. In fact, 82 percent of American households purchase at least one item from Walmart every year. As a result, the company's marketplace clout is enormous: It controls about 30 percent of the market in household staples; it sells 15 percent of all magazines and 15–20 percent of all CDs, videos, and DVDs; and it is expected to control soon over 35 percent of U.S. food sales. For most companies selling consumer products, sales from Walmart represent a big chunk of their total business: 28 percent for Dial, 24 percent for Del Monte, and 23 percent for Revlon. Walmart is also responsible for 10 percent of all goods imported to the United States from China.[77]

The good news for consumers is that Walmart has risen to retail supremacy through the bargain prices it offers them. The retail giant can afford its low prices because of the cost efficiencies it has achieved and the pressure it puts on suppliers to lower their prices. And the larger the store gets, the more market clout it has and the further it can push down prices for its customers.

Everyone, of course, loves low prices, but not everyone, it seems, loves Walmart. Why not? Here are some of the charges that critics level against the retail behemoth:

- Walmart's buying power and cost-saving efficiencies force local rivals out of business, thus costing jobs, disrupting local communities, and injuring established business districts. One Walmart worker replaces approximately 1.4 other local retail workers, and typically within five years after a Walmart supercenter opens, two other supermarkets close. Further, Walmart often insists on tax breaks when it moves into a community, so its presence does little or nothing to increase local tax revenues.

- Walmart is staunchly anti-union and pays low wages. Its labor costs are 20 percent lower than those of unionized supermarkets; its average sales clerk earns only $8.23 an hour, and most of its employees must survive without company health insurance. Small wonder that employee turnover is 44 percent per year. Moreover, because of its size, Walmart exerts a downward pressure on retail wages and benefits throughout the country. Critics also charge that Walmart's hard line on costs has forced many factories to move overseas, which sacrifices American jobs and holds wages down.

- Government welfare programs subsidize Walmart's poverty-level wages. According to one congressional report, a 200-employee store costs the government $42,000 a year in housing assistance, $108,000 in children's health care, and $125,000 in tax credits and deductions for low-income families. And internal Walmart documents, leaked to the press, confirm that 46 percent of the children of Walmart's 1.33 million workers are uninsured or on Medicaid. The document also discusses strategies for holding down spending on health care and other benefits—for example, by hiring more part-time workers and discouraging unhealthy people from working at the store by requiring all jobs to include some physical labor.

First Lady Michelle Obama teamed up with Walmart on an initiative that will result in the company offering a larger selection of healthy foods at more affordable prices. What does such an alliance suggest about the relationship between business and society and between business and politics?

- As Walmart grows and grows, and as its competitors fall by the wayside, consumer choices narrow, and the retail giant exerts ever greater power as a cultural censor. Walmart, for example, won't carry music or computer games with mature ratings. As a result, the big music companies now supply the chain with sanitized versions of the explicit CDs that they provide to radio stations and that are sold elsewhere. The retailer has removed racy magazines such as *Maxim* and *FHM* from its racks, and it obscures the covers of *Glamour*, *Redbook*, and *Cosmopolitan* with binders. Although many locations offer inexpensive firearms, Walmart won't sell Preven, a morning-after pill—the only one of the top ten drug chains to decline to do so.

For these reasons, Walmart's expansion is frequently meeting determined local resistance, as concerned residents try to preserve their communities and their local stores and downtown shopping areas from disruption by Walmart through petitions, political pressure, and zoning restrictions. As one economist remarks, for Walmart "the biggest barrier to growth" is not competition from rivals such as Target or Winn-Dixie stores but "opposition at the local level." As a result, Walmart has begun responding to the criticism that it is a poor corporate citizen and miserly employer by improving employee health insurance coverage and adopting greener business practices. And even its usual critics applauded when the company responded rapidly to Hurricane Katrina, sending truckloads of water and food, much of it reaching residents before federal supplies did.

When it comes to Walmart, Professor John E. Hoopes of Babson College encourages people to take a long-term view: "The history of the last 150 years in retailing would say that if you don't like Walmart, be patient. There will be new models eventually that will do Walmart in, and Walmart won't see it coming." And, indeed, in recent years the company's sales growth has slipped as the Internet has changed people's shopping habits and as other discounters have done a better job of attracting affluent consumers and providing higher quality and better service.

In the meantime, where you stand on Walmart probably depends on where you sit, as Jeffrey Useem writes in *Fortune* magazine: "If you're a consumer, Walmart is good for you. If you're a wage-earner, there's a good chance it's bad for you. If you're a Walmart shareholder, you want the company to grow. If you're a citizen, you probably don't want it growing in your backyard. So, which one are you?"

DISCUSSION QUESTIONS

1. Do you like Walmart? Do you shop there? If so, how frequently? If not, why not?

2. Is there a Walmart store in your area? If so, has it had any impact on your community or on the behavior of local consumers? If there's no store in your area, would you be in favor of Walmart opening one? Explain why or why not.

3. Is Walmart's rapid rise to retail dominance a positive or a negative development for our society? What does it tell us about capitalism, globalization, and the plight of workers?

4. Can a retailer ever become too large and too powerful?

5. Is opposition to Walmart's expansion a legitimate part of the political process or is it unfair interference with our market system and a violation of the company's rights? Do opponents of Walmart have any valid concerns?

CASE 4.4

A New Work Ethic?

YOU WOULD THINK THAT EMPLOYEES WOULD do something if they discovered that a customer had died on the premises.

But that's not necessarily so, according to the Associated Press, which reported that police discovered the body of a trucker in a tractor trailer rig that had sat—with its engine running—in the parking lot of a fast-food restaurant for nine days. Employees swept the parking lot around the truck but ignored the situation for over a week until the stench got so bad that someone finally called the police.

That lack of response doesn't surprise James Sheehy, a human resources manager in Houston, who spent his summer vacation working undercover at a fast-food restaurant owned by a relative.[78] Introduced to coworkers as a management trainee from another franchise location who was being brought in to learn the ropes, Sheehy was initially viewed with some suspicion, but by the third day the group had accepted him as just another employee. Sheehy started out as a maintenance person and gradually rotated through various cooking and cleaning assignments before ending up as a cashier behind the front counter.

Most of Sheehy's fellow employees were teenagers and college students who were home for the summer and earning additional spending money. Almost half came from upper-income families and the rest from middle-income neighborhoods. More than half were women, and a third were minorities. What Sheehy reports is a whole generation of workers with a frightening new work ethic: contempt for customers, indifference to quality and service, unrealistic expectations about the world of work, and a get-away-with-what-you-can attitude.

Surveys show that employee theft is on the rise throughout the business world.[79] Sheehy's experience was in line with this. He writes that the basic work ethic at his place of employment was a type of gamesmanship that focused on milking the place dry. Theft was rampant, and younger employees were subject to peer pressure to steal as a way of becoming part of the group. "It don't mean nothing," he says, was the basic rationale for dishonesty. "Getting on with getting mine" was another common phrase, as coworkers carefully avoided hard work or dragged out tasks like sweeping to avoid additional assignments.

All that customer service meant was getting rid of people as fast as possible and with the least possible effort. Sometimes, however, service was deliberately slowed or drive-through orders intentionally switched in order to cause customers to demand to see a manager. This was called "baiting the man," or purposely trying to provoke a response from management. In fact, the general attitude toward managers was one of disdain and contempt. In the eyes of the employees, supervisors were only paper-pushing functionaries who got in the way.

Sheehy's coworkers rejected the very idea of hard work and long hours. "Scamming" was their ideal. Treated as a kind of art form and as an accepted way of doing business, scamming meant taking shortcuts or getting something done without much effort, usually by having someone else do it. "You only put in the time and effort for the big score" is how one fellow worker characterized the work ethic he shared with his peers. "You got to just cruise through the job stuff and wait to make the big score," said another. "Then you can hustle. The office stuff is for buying time or paying for the groceries."

By contrast, they looked forward to working "at a real job where you don't have to put up with hassles." "Get out of school and you can leave this to the real dummies." "Get an office and a computer and a secretary and you can scam your way through anything." On the other hand, these young employees believed that most jobs were like the fast-food industry: automated, boring, undemanding and unsatisfying, and dominated by difficult people. Still, they dreamed of an action-packed business world, an image shaped by a culture of video games and action movies. The college students in particular, reports Sheehy, believed that a no-holds-barred, trample-over-anybody, get-what-you-want approach is the necessary and glamorous road to success.

DISCUSSION QUESTIONS

1. How typical are the attitudes that Sheehy reports? Does his description of a new work ethic tally with your own experiences?

2. What are the implications for the future of American business of the work ethic Sheehy describes?

3. Some might discount Sheehy's experiences either as being the product of one particular industry or as simply reflecting the immaturity of young employees. Would you agree?

4. Is it reasonable to expect workers, especially in a capitalist society, to be more devoted to their jobs, more concerned with quality and customer service, than Sheehy's coworkers were? What explains employee theft?

5. In what ways does the culture of our capitalist society encourage attitudes like those Sheehy describes?

CASE 4.5

Casino Gambling on Wall Street

CDO STANDS FOR "COLLATERALIZED DEBT obligation," and before the financial meltdown of 2008, hardly any nonspecialists were familiar with this arcane acronym. A CDO is a collection of individual debts (for example, home mortgages) that are bundled together in one investment pool. That pool can then be divided into different sections (or "tranches"), representing different degrees of risk, and sold to investors. An individual lender, such as a credit card company, may put together a CDO, or an investment firm may create a CDO from a package of loans from different lenders. Although abused during the housing bubble, CDOs perform a useful economic function. They allow lenders to focus on loan origination and investors to buy interest-earning securities.[80]

What serves no obvious economic function, however, are so-called synthetic CDOs, which represent a bet on the performance of a package of loans owned by others. For example, Goldman Sachs brokered a synthetic CDO, known as Abacus-2007 AC1, based on the performance of a group of subprime loans. But unlike a normal CDO, a synthetic like Abacus contains no actual bonds or mortgage loans; it merely references assets owned by other people. As with other synthetic CDOs, one side of the option was betting that the value of a bundle of assets (owned by other people) would rise; the other side of the option was betting that it would fall. In principle, it's no different from wagering on the Yankees against the Dodgers or on a cricket fight. "With a synthetic CDO, it's a pure bet," says Erik F. Gering, a former securities lawyer and now a law professor at the University of New Mexico. "It is hard to see what the social value is."

In the two years before the financial meltdown of 2008, over $100 billion in synthetic CDOs were issued, and everyone agrees that, by increasing the instability of the system, they were an important factor in that crisis. Moreover, their use represents a shift in the culture of investment banks from a focus on finding the most productive allocation of savings to an emphasis on maximizing profit through proprietary trading and arranging casino-like wagers for market participants. For these reasons, many business writers and financial experts are critical of synthetic CDOs and other purely speculative derivatives, believing that they should be severely limited or even prohibited. However, companies such as Goldman Sachs and others make $20 billion a year putting them together, and these firms lobbied strongly and successfully to see that the financial reform bill of 2010 didn't significantly restrict them. In their defense, one industry insider says, "I believe that synthetic CDOs have a very useful purpose in facilitating the management of risk. . . . Such instruments facilitate the flow of capital."

But it is difficult for even the heartiest champion of synthetic CDOs to defend the Abacus-2007 AC1 deal with a straight face. Goldman Sachs put it together for hedge fund tycoon John Paulson based on a group of lousy mortgage loans that he had selected for the sole purpose of betting that their value would go down. As with any synthetic CDO, of course, Goldman Sachs needed to find investors who would take the opposite position, which it did—the two largest being ABN Amro and IKB Deutsche Industriebank—and it was paid $15 million for closing the deal. Those companies, however, were not told that Paulson was betting against them nor that he had selected the underlying subprime mortgages only because he believed they were sure to lose value. And, sure enough, Abacus-2007 AC1 soon produced a $1.5 billion loss for ABN and an $840 million loss for IKB—but a $1 billion gain for Paulson.

Goldman Sachs's defenders say that ABN and IKB were sophisticated investors who should have known what they were doing and that who is on the other side of a CDO is not something that is routinely disclosed. So perhaps ABN and IKB deserved what they got—after all, one might argue, they had no real business undertaking a synthetic CDO as opposed to underwriting or insuring actual subprime loans. But, still, it's hard to square Goldman Sachs's treatment of them with the principle displayed on the company's website: "Our client's interests always come first."

Goldman Sachs, of course, is not the only financial institution to manipulate its customers. The Securities and Exchange Commission has accused Citigroup, for example, of putting together a package of mortgage-backed securities without telling investors that it was betting against them—that the fund was designed to fail. When it did, Citi earned $160 million while its investors lost $700 million. On the other hand, spread across the country are thousands of small community banks and not-for-profit credit unions. Believing that their job is to serve the community, they often take a personal interest in their customers, making loans to local businesses, lending small sums to individuals who have fallen into financial trouble, or bending over backwards to help those who can't keep up their mortgage payments. "They support you personally," says one customer. "Customers . . . can walk in and talk to the president," adds another, "and know he isn't sucking in their money and betting against them on proprietary securities."[81]

DISCUSSION QUESTIONS

1. Are synthetic CDOs a legitimate business investment, or are they pure gambling? If the former, what are their benefits? If the latter, should banks and other companies be allowed to wager on whatever they want if they like the odds and think they can make money that way?

2. In your view, what does the rise of synthetic CDOs tell us about contemporary capitalism?

3. Should synthetic CDOs be regulated in some way or even banned altogether?

4. Should Goldman Sachs have disclosed Paulson's role to IKB and ABN? In not doing so, did it act immorally? What obligations, effects, and ideals are relevant to answering these questions?

5. Did John Paulson do anything wrong? Explain why or why not.

6. As the top banks continue to get larger and larger, can small, community-oriented banks survive? Contrast the models of capitalism represented by the two types of banks. Where do you bank?

CASE 4.6

Paying College Athletes

CAM NEWTON IS THE STAR QUARTERBACK of the Carolina Panthers. In his last year at Auburn University, he won the Heisman trophy, led his team to a national championship, and was the highest NFL draft pick. Although that degree of success couldn't have been predicted when Newton graduated from high school, that he had enormous talent and potential was obvious to college coaches around the country. Allegedly, his father offered to have Newton sign with Mississippi State University for a $180,000 under-the-table payment, a charge he denies. But what would be wrong with a system, some people are now asking, which permitted universities to bid for the services of players like Newton and to do so above board?[82]

College football is big business. With the introduction of a playoff system for the national championship, the television and other revenues that go to college football programs and to the NCAA promise to double or even triple. Right now that money subsidizes the escalating salaries of coaches and athletic directors, who at the top football schools often make millions of dollars a year, as well as underwriting the construction of new and better football facilities. None of it goes to the players who make the system possible. That strikes some people as unfair. After all, for players at Division 1 schools, football is a full-time, year-round job. Shouldn't they be compensated for doing it? Why should coaches get big salaries and players nothing?

Flush with money from television rights and maybe feeling a little guilty about sharing none of it with college athletes, the five largest football conferences—the SEC, ACC, Pac-12, Big 12, Big Ten—agree. They are pushing the NCAA to allow colleges to pay players a modest stipend, perhaps a few thousand dollars a year, and to permit college athletes to sign advertising endorsements. Various salary cap plans are also being tossed around that would limit the total amount that any college can spend on players. Critics of these ideas argue that players are already compensated. They receive tuition, room and board, and an education as well as a package of professional coaching and strength and fitness training that would, if purchased on the open market, be very expensive. In addition, they get exposure to scouts from the NFL. Critics also point to the fact that the vast majority of football programs—maybe nine out of ten—make no money. Some of them would be hard pressed to pay their players much money.

On the other hand, there are those who think that set stipends and salary caps are, at best, a halfway measure. They want a completely free market, in which colleges would bid for the services of high school recruits and those recruits would be free to negotiate contracts with the universities who want them. On this scenario, in the future a football powerhouse might pay $180,000 for a player with Cam Newton's potential. But then player salaries might not go that high if it turns out that very few universities could afford to offer anywhere near that much. Still, the biggest and richest athletic departments would almost certainly buy up the best college athletes, disrupting any semblance of competitive balance. Free-market advocates see no problem with this. They contend, in response, that the wealthiest programs—those with the big-name coaches, top-of-the-line athletic facilities, and super-duper dormitories for athletes—already get the lion's share of the top college players.

Still, this free-market, capitalistic approach runs up against the older ideal of college athletes as student amateurs. The National Labor Relations Board, however, has decisively rejected that ideal as a kind of myth. In March 2014, it ruled that football players on scholarship at Northwestern University have a right to form a union and bargain collectively over such things as how much time they devote to football, the control exerted by coaches, and the scholarships they receive, which the Board deemed a contract for compensation. The NLRB notes that Northwestern recruited players for their athletic skill, not their academic ability, and that it reported $235 million in revenue from football between 2003 and 2012. It also noted that players spend "many more hours" on football than on their studies—50 to 60 hours per week during a one-month training camp and 40 to 50 hours per week during the football season. The NLRB ruling sets a precedent that would clearly extend to other private universities. (State law regulates collective bargaining at public universities.)

For its part, the NCAA rejects the notion that student-athletes are employees. After all, if college football players are no longer amateurs, then why insist that they be students and go to classes? Players would still represent the college they worked for on the football field, but they would be university employees, not students. That would make college football, in the most competitive conferences, a minor league of the NFL, but it would at least have the advantage of ending the recurrent scandals associated with efforts to keep athletes academic eligible.

DISCUSSION QUESTIONS

1. What would be the likely results of letting universities bid financially for college athletes? Would allowing college players to negotiate the best contract they can be good or bad for college athletics? Would such a system be fair to schools that have less money to spend on athletes?

2. Is playing Division 1 college football a job? Should it bring monetary compensation? Are college athletes exploited workers? Are they being treated unfairly by not being allowed to share directly in the revenue that college football generates?

3. Should college players have the right to unionize? Is it a matter of fairness? How would unionization affect college athletics?

4. Is the ideal of the amateur student athlete representing his or her university already obsolete, or is it worth striving to preserve?

5. If college athletics becomes completely professional, is there any reason to continue to require that athletes also be students?

6. Assuming college athletes should have a greater share of athletic revenues, what sort of compensation system would you design?

CHAPTER 5

CORPORATIONS

INTRODUCTION

SIXTY YEARS AGO THE VICE PRESIDENT OF FORD Motor Company described the modern business corporation as the dominant institution of American society. Today, few observers would disagree. As one of them puts it, "The modern corporation is *the* central institution of contemporary society."[1] As an aggregate, corporations wield awesome economic clout, and the 500 largest U.S. companies constitute at least three-quarters of the American economy. But the dominant role of corporations in our society extends well beyond that. Not only do corporations produce almost all the goods and services we buy, but also they and their ethos permeate everything from politics and communications to athletics and religion. And their influence is growing relentlessly around the world.

By any measure, the biggest corporations are colossi that dominate the earth. Many of them employ tens of thousands of people, and the largest have hundreds of thousands in their ranks. PepsiCo, for example, has about 278,000 employees worldwide, General Electric approximately 305,000, and IBM 435,000—not to mention the 2.1 million people who work for Walmart, the world's largest private-sector employer. And their revenues are dazzling. For example, Dell Computer takes in more than $57 billion a year, Procter & Gamble $84 billion, IBM $104 billion, AT&T $127 billion, and Ford $134 billion. Recently, Royal Dutch Shell topped the list with an annual revenue of $481.7 billion. ExxonMobil came in third at $449.9 billion but earned $44.9 billion in profit—just $300 million short of the world record, which it had set a couple of years before. By comparison, Austria's GDP is approximately $359 billion, Chile's $341 billion, and New Zealand's $122 billion. The state of California, which has far and away the largest annual revenue of any U.S. state, makes less than half of what General Motors does. Kansas takes in only about $4.5 billion, and Vermont about a fifth of that.

> BY ANY MEASURE, the biggest corporations are colossi that dominate the earth.

And many corporations are growing larger and wealthier every year. For example, Time Inc. merged with Warner Communications to form Time Warner. Seven years later Time Warner combined with Turner Broadcasting. Then in January 2001, in a move that shook up Wall Street, Time Warner and America Online merged. At a stroke, the new company they created, initially called AOL Time Warner, then simply Time Warner, was valued at $350 billion. What does $350 billion mean? At the time it was equivalent to the GDP of Saudi Arabia and greater than the combined GDPs of Hungary, the Czech Republic, Bulgaria, Serbia, Bolivia, and Kenya. It was also more than the industrial output of the United Kingdom or the manufacturing output of China.

But nothing stays the same forever. In 2013 Time Warner shed Time, Inc., its magazine division. Following its divesture of AOL, Time Warner Cable, the Warner Music Group, and the Time Warner Book Group, this move completed the company's devolution from a corporate colossus to a pure television and movie production company. Still, Time Warner is no mom-and-pop operation; it remains the 105th largest company in the United States.

Like any other modern corporation, in principle Time Warner is a three-part organization, made up of (1) **stockholders**, who provide the capital, own the corporation, and enjoy liability

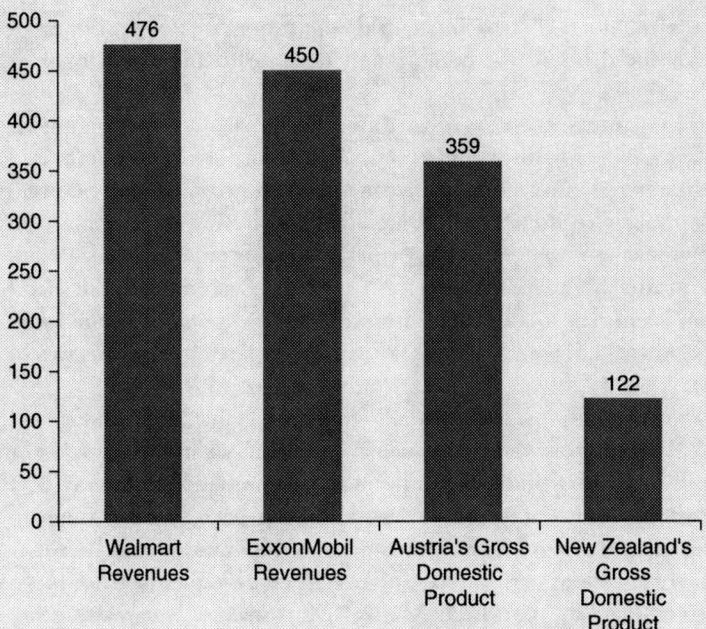

Comparison of the two top American corporations' revenues with the gross domestic product of two nations. Values are in billions of dollars.

It provides the corporation's overall framework, the formal chain of command, which ensures that the company's profit objectives are pursued.

The emergence of corporate behemoths like Chevron or Bank of America is one of the more intriguing chapters in the evolution of capitalism. Certainly neither John Locke nor Adam Smith ever imagined the huge capitalist enterprises that emerged in the nineteenth century—in their day hardly any private firms had more than a handful of employees—and that today dominate America's and, indeed, the world's economic, political, and social life. This book isn't the place to analyze why a people committed to an individualistic social philosophy and a free-competition market economy allowed vast oligopolistic economic entities to develop. Rather, the concern here is with the problem of applying moral standards to corporate organizations and with understanding their social responsibilities.

limited to the amount of their investments; (2) managers, who run the business operations; and (3) employees, who produce the goods and services. However, many corporate giants such as ExxonMobil or Citigroup are, to quote business analyst Anthony J. Parisi, less like a single company and more like "a fabulously wealthy investment club with a limited portfolio." Such companies invest in subsidiaries, whose heads "oversee their territories like provincial governors, sovereigns in their own lands but with an authority stemming from the power center. . . . The management committee exacts its tribute (the affiliate's profits from current operations) and issues doles (the money needed to sustain and expand those operations)."[2] In the best-run organizations the management system is highly structured and impersonal.

....
LEARNING OBJECTIVES
....

More specifically, after reviewing the history of the corporation, this chapter examines the following topics:

1. The debate over whether corporations are moral agents and can be meaningfully said to have moral responsibilities

2. The controversy between the narrow view and the broader view of corporate responsibility

3. Three key arguments in this debate: the invisible-hand argument, the let-government-do-it argument, and the business-can't-handle-it argument

4. The importance of institutionalizing ethics within corporations and how this may be done

⋯

THE LIMITED-LIABILITY COMPANY

If you ask a lawyer for a definition of **corporation**, you will probably hear something like the following: A corporation is a thing that can endure beyond the natural lives of its members and that has incorporators who may sue and be sued as a unit and who are able to consign part of their property to the corporation for ventures of limited liability. **Limited liability** is a key feature of the modern corporation. The members of the corporation—unlike the members of a partnership or the proprietors of a business—are financially liable for the debts of the organization only up to the extent of their investments.

Limited-liability companies—corporations—differ from partnerships and other forms of business association in two other ways as well. *First*, a corporation is not formed simply by an agreement entered into among its first members. An organization becomes incorporated by being publicly registered or in some other way having its existence officially acknowledged by the law. *Second*, unlike a partner, who is automatically entitled to his or her share of the profits of a partnership as soon as they are ascertained, the shareholder in a corporation is entitled to a dividend from the company's profits only when it has been "declared." Under U.S. law, dividends are usually declared by the directors of a corporation.

When we think of corporations, we naturally think of giants such as General Motors, ExxonMobil, Microsoft, or Walmart, which exert enormous influence over our economy and society. But the local independently owned convenience store may be a corporation, and historically the concept of a corporation has been broad enough to encompass churches, trade guilds, and local governments. Corporations may be either *for-profit* or *nonprofit* organizations. Princeton University, for example, is a nonprofit corporation. By contrast, Safeway, Lockheed Martin, McDonald's, and many other familiar companies aim to make money for shareholders. Corporations may be privately owned or owned (wholly or in part) by the government. Almost all U.S. corporations are privately owned; but Renault of France, for example, was once a publicly owned, for-profit corporation. A small group of investors may own all the outstanding shares of a privately owned, profit-making corporation (a **privately held company**). Mars, Bechtel, Chrysler, and Enterprise Rent-A-Car are examples. Or stock may be traded among the general public (a **publicly held company**). All companies whose stocks are listed on the New York and other stock exchanges are publicly held corporations.

In 1911 Nicholas Murray Butler, president of Columbia University, declared that "the limited liability corporation is the single greatest discovery of modern times. . . . Even steam and electricity are far less important . . . and . . . would be reduced to comparative impotence without it."[3] Many business theorists and historians still agree with that assessment. But several stages mark the evolution of the corporation. The corporate form itself developed during the early Middle Ages, and the first corporations were towns, universities, and ecclesiastical orders. They were chartered by government and regulated by public statute. As corporate bodies, they existed independently of the particular individuals who constituted their membership at any given time. By the fifteenth century, the courts of England had evolved the principle of limited liability—thus setting limits, for example, on how much an alderman of the Liverpool Corporation might be required to pay if the city went bankrupt. During the medieval period, however, the law did not grant corporate status to purely profit-making associations. In those days, something besides economic self-interest had to be seen as uniting the members of the corporation: religion, a trade, shared political responsibilities.

This state of affairs changed during the Elizabethan era, as the incorporation of business enterprises began. European entrepreneurs were busy organizing trading voyages to the East and to North America. The East India Company, which epitomizes the great trading companies of this period, was formed in 1600, when Queen Elizabeth I granted to a group of merchants the right to be "one body corporate" and bestowed on it a trading monopoly to the East Indies. In the following decades, numerous other incorporated

---

In addition to the limited liability of their members, corporations differ from partnerships in two ways.

SUMMARY

Corporations are legal entities, with legal rights and responsibilities similar but not identical to those enjoyed by individuals. Business corporations are limited-liability companies—that is, their owners or stockholders are liable for corporate debts only up to the extent of their investments.

firms were granted trading monopolies and colonial charters. Much of North America's settlement, in fact, was initially underwritten as a business venture.

Although the earliest corporations typically held special trading rights from the government, their members did not pool capital. Rather, they individually financed voyages using the corporate name and absorbed the loss individually if a vessel sank or was robbed by pirates. But as ships became larger and more expensive, no single buyer could afford to purchase and outfit one, and the loss of a ship would have been ruinous to any one individual. The solution was to pool capital and share liability. Thus emerged the prototype of today's corporations.[4]

The first instance of the corporate organization of a manufacturing enterprise in the United States occurred in 1813, but only after the Civil War did the movement toward the corporate organization of business gain steam.[5] The loosening of government restrictions on corporate chartering procedures in the nineteenth century marks this final stage of corporate evolution. Until the mid-1800s, prospective corporations had to apply for charters—in England to the Crown, and in the United States to state government. Charters were custom-crafted; each one was an individual act of legislation. Charters were often burdened with precise terms or limited to specific business objectives, all in the name of promoting the public good. (For example, a corporation might be chartered for the sole purpose of shipping freight between two cities, or a charter might designate where the new corporation could begin and end its proposed railroad line.) Critics of the incorporation system charged that it fostered favoritism, corruption, and unfair monopolies. Gradually, the old system of incorporation was replaced by the system we know today, in which corporate status is granted essentially to any organization that fills out the forms and pays the fees.

| In the nineteenth century, government loosened restrictions on corporate charters.

Lurking behind this change were two important theoretical shifts. *First*, underlying the old system was the mercantilist idea that a corporation's activities should advance some specific public purpose. But Adam Smith and, following him, Alexander Hamilton, the first U.S. secretary of the treasury, challenged the desirability of a direct tie between business enterprise and public policy. They believed that businesspeople should be encouraged to explore their own avenues of enterprise and that the "invisible hand" of the market would direct their activities in a socially beneficial direction more effectively than any public official could.

| Two ideas were behind this change

Second, when nineteenth-century reformers argued for changes in incorporation procedures, they talked not only about government favoritism and the advantages of a laissez-faire approach but also about the principle of a corporation's right to exist.[6] Any petitioning body with the minimal qualifications, they asserted, has the right to receive a corporate charter. By contrast, the early Crown-chartered corporations were clearly creations of the state, in accordance with the legal-political doctrine that corporate status was a privilege bestowed by the government as it saw fit. The reformers, however, argued that incorporation is a by-product of the people's right of association, not a gift from the state.

Even though the right of association supports relaxed incorporation procedures, the state must still incorporate companies and guarantee their legal status. Corporations must be recognized by the law as a single agent in order to enjoy their rights and privileges. To a large extent, then, the corporation remains, as Chief Justice John Marshall put it in 1819, "an artificial being, invisible, intangible, and existing only in the contemplation of the law."[7]

SUMMARY
What we know as the modern business corporation has evolved over several centuries, and incorporation is no longer the special privilege it once was.

Corporations are clearly legal agents. They can enter into contracts, own property, and sue and be sued. But are they also moral agents? Corporations have definite legal responsibilities, but what, if any, social and moral responsibilities do they have?

CORPORATE MORAL AGENCY

In 2010, the Supreme Court dropped a political bombshell. In reviewing a case that most observers thought would revolve on the technicalities of campaign finance law, the Court, in a broad and unexpected ruling in *Citizens United v. Federal Election Commission*, struck down those provisions of the McCain-Feingold Act that had prohibited corporations from making "electioneering communications" before a presidential primary or a general election. In a split 5-to-4 decision, it held that corporations have a basic First Amendment right to participate in the political process and that the government may not prevent them from spending money to support the candidates they favor. Writing for the majority, Justice Anthony M. Kennedy argued that the Constitution prohibits "restrictions distinguishing among different speakers, allowing speech by some but not others." Although McCain-Feingold had allowed corporations to set up political action committees to advocate for their causes, this exception was not enough, Kennedy wrote, because it still "does not allow corporations to speak."

In a long and vigorous dissent, Justice John Paul Stevens criticized the decision for the damage it would do to our democracy and for "the conceit that corporations must be treated identically to natural persons in the political sphere." But *Citizens United* was not entirely without precedent. Over the years the Court has granted corporations certain First Amendment protections and extended them other constitutional rights as well—for example, to due process (Fourteenth Amendment), against unreasonable searches and seizures (Fourth Amendment), to a jury trial (Seventh Amendment), to freedom from double jeopardy (Fifth Amendment), and to compensation for government takings (Fifth Amendment). Still, in holding that the First Amendment gives corporations basically the same political rights as individual citizens, the Court further blurred the distinction between real persons and artificial or legal persons. However, in doing so, it has provided a basis for claiming that if corporations enjoy the same moral and political rights as citizens, then they bear the same responsibilities that individual human beings do. In other words, if corporations have the same rights that moral agents have, then, like individuals, they can and should be held morally responsible for their actions.

Cases like Citizens United *have blurred the distinction between individuals and corporations.*

The problem, of course, is that they are not human beings. Or, to quote Lord Thurlow, an eighteenth-century lawyer, how can you "expect a corporation to have a conscience, when it has no soul to be damned and no body to be kicked?"[8] But although corporations are not people, they are collective entities that in some sense really exist, and they have an identity above and beyond the people whom they comprise at any given time. And the law recognizes them as "persons." Do they have moral obligations just as individual human beings do? Can they be held morally responsible, not just legally liable, for the things they do? The answer to these questions hangs on another question, namely: Does it make sense to view corporations as moral agents—that is, as entities capable of making moral decisions? If so, then corporations can be held morally responsible for their actions. They—and not just the individual human beings who make them up—can be seen as having moral obligations and as being blameworthy for failing to meet those obligations. They can, accordingly, be praised or blamed, even punished, for the decisions they make and the actions and policies they undertake.

If corporations are moral agents, then they can be seen as having obligations and as being morally responsible for their actions, just as individuals are.

The task of determining whether corporations can make moral decisions is anything but simple. Immediately, we must ponder whether it makes sense to say that any entity other than an individual person can make decisions in the first place, moral or otherwise.

CAN CORPORATIONS MAKE MORAL DECISIONS?

Corporate internal decision (CID) structures amount to established procedures for accomplishing specific goals. For example, consider ExxonMobil's system, as depicted by Anthony J. Parisi:

> All through the Exxon system, checks and balances are built in. Each fall, the presidents of the 13 affiliates take their plan for the coming year and beyond to New York for review at a meeting with the management committee and the staff vice presidents. The goal is to get a perfect corporate fit. Some imaginary examples: The committee might decide that Exxon is becoming too concentrated in Australia and recommend that Esso Eastern move more slowly on that continent. Or it might conclude that if the affiliates were to build all the refineries they are proposing, they would create more capacity than the company could profitably use. One of the affiliates would be asked to hold off, even though, from its particular point of view, a new refinery was needed to serve its market.[9]

The implication here is that any decisions coming out of ExxonMobil's annual sessions are formed and shaped to effect corporate goals, "to get a perfect corporate fit." Metaphorically, all data pass through the filter of established corporate procedures, objectives, and decision-making guidelines. The remaining distillation constitutes the decision. Certainly, the participants actively engage in decision making. But in addition to individual persons, the other major component of corporate decision making consists of the framework in which policies and activities are determined.

The CID structure lays out lines of authority and stipulates under what conditions personal actions become official corporate actions. Some philosophers have compared the corporation to a machine or have argued that because of its structure it is bound to pursue its profit goals single-mindedly. As a result, they claim, it is a mistake to see a corporation as being morally responsible or to expect it to display such moral characteristics as honesty, considerateness, and sympathy. Only the individuals within a corporation can act morally or immorally; only they can be held responsible for what it does.

Others have argued in support of **corporate moral agency**. The CID structure, like an individual person, collects data about the impact of its actions. It monitors work conditions, employee efficiency and productivity, and environmental impacts. Professors Kenneth E. Goodpaster and John B. Matthews argue that as a result, there is no reason a corporation cannot show the same kind of rationality and respect for persons that individual human beings can. By analogy, they contend, it makes just as much sense to speak of corporate moral responsibility as it does to speak of individual moral responsibility.[10] Thomas Donaldson agrees. He argues that a corporation can be a moral agent if moral reasons enter into its decision making and if its decision-making process controls not only the company's actions but also its structure of policies and rules.[11]

Philosopher Peter French arrives at the same conclusion in a slightly different way.[12] The CID structure, says French, in effect absorbs the intentions and acts of individual persons into a "corporate decision." Perhaps no corporate official intended the course or objective charted by the CID structure, but, French contends, the corporation did. And he believes that these corporate intentions are enough to make corporate acts "intentional" and thus make corporations "morally responsible." Professor of philosophy Manuel Velasquez demurs. An act is intentional, says Velasquez, only if the entity that formed the intention brings about the act through its bodily movements. But it is only the people who make up the corporation who carry out the acts attributed to it. Velasquez concludes that only corporate members, not the corporation itself, can be held morally responsible.[13]

....
SUMMARY
The question of corporate moral agency is whether a corporation is the kind of entity that can make moral decisions and bear moral responsibility for its actions. Philosophers disagree about whether CID structures make it reasonable to see corporations as morally responsible agents.
....

Corporate Punishment

The debate over corporate moral agency bears on the question of **corporate punishment**. Whether or not corporations are moral actors, the law can fine them, monitor and regulate their activities, and require the people who run them to do one thing or another. But one can talk in a literal sense about "punishing" corporations only if they are entities or "persons" capable of making moral decisions. And even if they are, not all the usual goals and methods of punishment make sense when applied to corporations. If corporations are moral agents, then the law can deter them with the threat of punishment, and it can force them to make restitution. Punishment can, perhaps, even rehabilitate a corporation, viewed as a moral agent. Retribution, as a goal of punishment, however, seems to have little application to corporations. And obviously corporations cannot be jailed for breaking the law. Even imposing fines on them can be problematic. Financial penalties stiff enough to have an impact can easily injure innocent parties, for example, if they lead to layoffs, plant closures, or higher prices for consumers.

For this reason, economics professor Edwin T. Burton opposes prosecuting corporations. "A company can't commit a crime," he says. Referring to the criminal charges brought against SAC Capital, which in 2013 was fined $1.2 billion for insider trading, he says, "They should only go after the people doing the things wrong. There are innocent bystanders, a lot of them, who get hurt [by prosecuting the company]." The Justice Department's Preet Bharara disagrees, arguing that there are lots of different ways to punish wrongdoing and deter criminal behavior. Sometimes you charge individuals and send them to jail, and "sometimes you try to make the world understand that an entire institution deserves to be held blameworthy." Law professor Lawrence M. Friedman concurs. He points to the "expressive value" of punishing corporations. Treating what the corporation did as a criminal matter, he says, "makes an important statement about the seriousness of the wrongness."[14]

VANISHING INDIVIDUAL RESPONSIBILITY

Some might argue that regardless of whether corporations as artificial entities can properly be held morally responsible, the nature and structure of a modern corporate organization allows nearly everyone in it to share moral accountability for what it does. In practice, however, this **diffusion of responsibility** can mean that no particular person or persons are held morally responsible. For example, does responsibility for an injury caused by a defective product fall on the shoulders of the worker who last handled the product, the foreman overseeing the running of the assembly line, the factory supervisor, the quality control team, the engineers who designed and tested the equipment, the regional managers who decided to produce the item, or the company's CEO, whose office is in another city? Indeed, each of these individuals may have been only following established procedures and decision-making guidelines. Inside a corporation it may often be difficult, even impossible, to assign responsibility for a particular outcome to any single individual because so many different people, acting within a given CID framework, contributed to it in small ways.

Assigning individual responsibility for corporate outcomes is difficult.

This masking of moral accountability may not seem so surprising. After all, in situations that don't involve corporations, praising and blaming can also be problematic. But it raises the troubling possibility that the size and impersonal bureaucratic structure of the corporation may so envelop its members that it becomes vacuous to speak of individual moral agency. This, in turn, raises the specter of actions without actors in any moral sense—of defective products, broken laws, or flouted contracts, without any morally responsible parties.

There are two ways to escape this uncomfortable conclusion. *One* is to attribute moral agency to corporations just as we do to individual persons. *The other*, not necessarily incompatible with the first, is to realize that these days too many people are willing, even eager, to duck personal responsibility—"it's not my job," "there's nothing I can do about it," "I was just following procedure"—by submerging it in the CID structures of the modern corporation. Perhaps until CID structures are reconstituted to deal explicitly with noneconomic matters, we can expect more of the same evasion of personal responsibility.

The issue of corporate moral agency undoubtedly will continue to exercise scholars. Meanwhile, the inescapable fact is that corporations are increasingly being accorded the status of biological persons, with all the rights and responsibilities implied by that status. Before it was gobbled up by another corporation, Continental Oil Company expressed in an in-house booklet the public perception and its implications as follows:

> No one can deny that in the public's mind a corporation can break the law and be guilty of unethical and amoral conduct. Events . . . such as corporate violation of federal laws and failure of full disclosure [have] confirmed that both our government and our citizenry expect *corporations* to act lawfully, ethically, and responsibly.
>
> Perhaps it is then appropriate in today's context to think of Conoco as a living corporation; a sentient being whose conduct and personality are the collective effort and responsibility of its employees, officers, directors, and shareholders.[15]

Today many companies and many of the people inside them accept without hesitation the idea that corporations are moral agents with genuinely moral, not just legal, responsibilities.

This point was illustrated when Colonial Pipeline of Atlanta published full-page advertisements in several newspapers headlined "We Apologize." The company used the ads to take responsibility for having spilled oil into the Reedy River of South Carolina three years before. True, the ads were part of a plea agreement with the U.S. Justice Department for having violated the Clean Water Act (the company also agreed to pay a $7 million fine). Yet the company's words had ethical overtones. As Laura Nash of Harvard Divinity School comments, they put "moral emotion into what is essentially a legal statement" because "the word 'apologize' . . . admits a sense of shame and humility."[16] Shame and humility were evident, too, when a few years later the world saw photographs of Charles Prince, the chief executive of Citigroup, and Douglas Petersen, Citibank Japan CEO, bowing their heads at a press conference in Tokyo in a public act of remorse for Citigroup's illegal actions in Japan.

If, then, it makes sense to talk about the social and moral responsibilities of corporations, either in a literal sense or as a shorthand way of referring to the obligations of the individuals that make up the corporation, what are these responsibilities?

• • •

RIVAL VIEWS OF CORPORATE RESPONSIBILITY

In 1963 Tennessee Iron & Steel, a subsidiary of United States Steel, was by far the largest employer, purchaser, and taxpayer in Birmingham, Alabama. In the same city at the same time, racial tensions exploded in the bombing of an African-American church, killing four black children. The ugly incident led some to blame U.S. Steel for not doing

---

This raises the possibility of actions for which no one is responsible. There are two ways to escape this conclusion.

SUMMARY

Individual responsibility can tend to vanish inside large, impersonal corporations. One response is to attribute moral agency to the corporation itself. Another is to refuse to let individuals duck their personal responsibility.

Assuming it makes sense to talk of the moral responsibilities of corporations, what are they?

more to improve race relations, but Roger Blough, chairman of U.S. Steel, defended his company:

> I do not either believe that it would be a wise thing for United States Steel to be other than a good citizen in a community, or to attempt to have its ideas of what is right for the community enforced upon the community by some sort of economic means....
>
> When we as individuals are citizens in a community we can exercise what small influence we may have as citizens, but for a corporation to attempt to exert any kind of economic compulsion to achieve a particular end in the racial area seems to me quite beyond what a corporation can do.[17]

Not long afterward, Sol M. Linowitz, chairman of the board of Xerox Corporation, declared in an address to the National Industrial Conference Board: "To realize its full promise in the world of tomorrow, American business and industry—or, at least, the vast portion of it—will have to make social goals as central to its decisions as economic goals; and leadership in our corporations will increasingly recognize this responsibility and accept it."[18] Thus, the issue of business's corporate responsibility was joined. Just what responsibilities does a corporation have? Is its responsibility to be construed narrowly as merely profit making? Or more broadly to include refraining from harming society and even contributing actively and directly to the public good?

THE NARROW VIEW: PROFIT MAXIMIZATION

As it happened, the year preceding the Birmingham incident had seen the publication of *Capitalism and Freedom*, in which economist Milton Friedman (1912–2006) forcefully advocated the **narrow view of corporate responsibility**, that business has no social responsibilities other than to maximize profits:

> The view has been gaining widespread acceptance that corporate officials . . . have a social responsibility that goes beyond serving the interest of their stockholders. . . . This view shows a fundamental misconception of the character and nature of a free economy. In such an economy, there is one and only one social responsibility of business—to use its resources and engage in activities designed to increase its profits so long as it stays within the rules of the game, which is to say, engages in open and free competition, without deception or fraud. . . . Few trends could so thoroughly undermine the very foundations of our free society as the acceptance by corporate officials of a social responsibility other than to make as much money for their stockholders as possible.[19]

Although from Friedman's perspective the only responsibility of business is to make money for its owners, obviously a business may not do literally anything whatsoever to increase its profits. Gangsters pursue profit maximization when they ruthlessly rub out their rivals, but such activity falls outside what Friedman referred to as "the rules of the game." Harvard professor Theodore Levitt echoed this point when he wrote, "In the end business has only two responsibilities—to obey the elementary canons of face-to-face civility (honesty, good faith, and so on) and to seek material gain."[20]

What, then, are the rules of the game? Obviously, elementary morality rules out deception, force, and fraud, and the rules of the game are intended to promote open and free competition. The system of rules in which business is to pursue profit is, in Friedman's view, one that is conducive to the laissez-faire operation of Adam Smith's "invisible hand" (discussed in Chapter 4). Friedman, a conservative economist, believed that if the market is allowed to operate with only the minimal restrictions necessary to

---

SUMMARY

Despite continuing controversy over the concept of corporate moral agency, the courts, the general public, and many companies find the notion of corporate responsibility useful and intelligible—either in a literal sense or as shorthand for the moral obligations of individuals in the corporation.

SUMMARY

The debate over corporate responsibility is whether it should be construed narrowly to cover only profit maximization or more broadly to include acting morally, refraining from socially undesirable behavior, and contributing actively and directly to the public good.

prevent fraud and force, society will maximize its overall economic well-being. Pursuit of profit, he insisted, is what makes our system go. Anything that dampens this incentive or inhibits its operation will weaken the ability of the "invisible hand" to deliver the economic goods. As one recent writers puts it, "Corporations that simply do everything they can to boost profits will end up increasing social welfare."[21]

Because the function of a business organization is to make money, the owners of corporations employ executives to accomplish that goal, thereby obligating these managers always to act in the interests of the owners. According to Friedman, to say that executives have *social* responsibilities beyond the pursuit of profit means that they must sometimes subordinate owner interests to some social objective, such as controlling pollution or fighting inflation. They are then spending stockholder money for general social interests—in effect, taxing the owners and spending those taxes on social causes. But taxation is a function of government, not private enterprise; executives are not public employees but employees of private enterprise. The doctrine that corporations have social responsibilities beyond profit making thus transforms executives into civil servants and business corporations into government agencies, thereby diverting business from its proper function in the social system.

Friedman was critical of those who would impose on business any duty other than that of making money, and he was particularly harsh with business leaders who take a broader view of their social responsibilities: They may believe that they are defending the free-enterprise system when they give speeches proclaiming that profit isn't the only goal of business or affirming that business has a social conscience and takes seriously its responsibility to provide employment, refrain from polluting, eliminate discrimination, and so on. But these business leaders are shortsighted; they are helping to undermine capitalism by implicitly reinforcing the view that the pursuit of profit is wicked and must be regulated by external forces.[22]

Friedman acknowledged that corporate activities are often described as an exercise of "social responsibility" when, in fact, they are intended simply to advance the company's self-interest. For example, it might be in the long-term self-interest of a corporation that is a major employer in a small town to spend money to enhance the local community by helping to improve its schools, parks, roads, or social services, thereby attracting good employees to the area, reducing the company's wage bill, or improving worker morale and productivity. By portraying its actions as dictated by a sense of social responsibility, the corporation can generate goodwill as a by-product of expenditures that are entirely justified by self-interest. Friedman had no problem with a company pursuing its self-interest by these means, but he rued the fact that "the attitudes of the public make it in the self-interest [of corporations] to cloak their actions in this way."[23] Friedman's bottom line was that the bottom line is all that counts, and he firmly rejected any notion of corporate *social* responsibility that would hinder a corporation's profit maximization.

THE BROADER VIEW: CORPORATE SOCIAL RESPONSIBILITY

The rival position to that of Friedman and Levitt is simply that business has obligations in addition to pursuing profits. The phrase "in addition to" is important. Advocates of the **broader view of corporate responsibility** do not believe there is anything wrong with corporate profit. They maintain, rather, that corporations have other responsibilities as well—to consumers, to employees, to suppliers and contractors, to the surrounding community, and to society at large. They see the modern corporation as a social institution that should consider the interests of all the groups it has an impact on.

> **SUMMARY**
> Proponents of the narrow view, such as Milton Friedman, contend that diverting corporations from the pursuit of profit makes our economic system less efficient. Business's only social responsibility is to make money within the rules of the game. Private enterprise should not take on social goals or public responsibilities; these should be left to government.

Critics of the narrow view believe that businesses have other obligations besides making a profit.

Sometimes called the **social entity model** or the **stakeholder model**, this broader view maintains that a corporation has obligations not only to its stockholders but also to other constituencies that affect or are affected by its behavior—that is, to all parties that have a legitimate interest (a "stake") in what the corporation does or doesn't do. Years ago, the chairman of Standard Oil of New Jersey expressed the basic idea this way: "The job of management is to maintain an equitable and working balance among the claims of the various directly affected interest groups . . . stockholders, employees, customers, and the public at large."[24]

If the adherents of the broader view share one belief, it is that corporations have responsibilities beyond simply enhancing their profits because, as a matter of fact, they wield such great social and economic power in our society and with that power must come social responsibility. As professor of business administration Keith Davis put it:

> One basic proposition is that *social responsibility arises from social power*. Modern business has immense social power in such areas as minority employment and environmental pollution. If business has the power, then a just relationship demands that business also bear responsibility for its actions in these areas. Social responsibility arises from concern about the consequences of business's acts as they affect the interests of others. Business decisions do have social consequences. Businessmen cannot make decisions that are solely economic decisions, because they are interrelated with the whole social system. This situation requires that businessmen's thinking be broadened beyond the company gate to the whole social system. Systems thinking is required.
>
> Social responsibility implies that a business decision maker in the process of serving his own business interests is obliged to take actions that also protect and enhance society's interests. The net effect is to improve the quality of life in the broadest possible way, however quality of life is defined by society. In this manner, harmony is achieved between business's actions and the larger social system. The businessman becomes concerned with social as well as economic outputs and with the total effect of his institutional actions on society.[25]

Proponents of the broader view, such as Davis, stress that modern business is intimately integrated with the rest of society. Business is not some self-enclosed world, like a private poker party. Rather, business activities have profound ramifications throughout society, and their influence on our lives is hard to escape. Business writer John Kay makes this point with reference to General Electric: "The company's activities are so extensive that you necessarily encounter them daily, often without knowing you are doing so. GE's business is our business even if we do not want it to be."[26]

As a result, although society permits and expects corporations to pursue their economic interests, they have other responsibilities as well. Thus, for example, it is wrong for corporations to raid the pension funds of their employees, as many have done,[27] or to evade taxes through creative accounting or by re-incorporating in tax havens such as Bermuda,[28] even if doing so is legal and enhances the bottom line. "We reasonably expect that GE should care that its engines are safe," writes John Kay, "not just that they comply with FAA procedures; that if there is a problem with its medical equipment the company will try to put it right, not cover it up; that GE financial statements are true and fair and not just compliant with accounting standards."[29]

Melvin Anshen has cast the case for the broader view of corporate responsibility in a historical perspective.[30] He maintains that there is always a kind of "social contract" between business and society. This contract is, of course, only implicit, but it represents a tacit understanding within society about the proper goals and responsibilities of business. In effect, in Anshen's view, society always structures the guidelines within which business is permitted to operate in order to derive certain benefits from business activity. For instance, in the nineteenth century, society's prime interest was rapid economic growth, which was viewed as the source of all progress, and the engine of economic growth was identified as the drive for profits by unfettered, competitive, private enterprise. That attitude was reflected in the then-existing social contract. Today, however, society has concerns and interests other than rapid economic growth—in particular, a concern for the quality of life and for the preservation of the environment. Accordingly, the social contract is in the process of being modified. In particular, Anshen writes, "it will no longer be acceptable for corporations to manage their affairs solely in terms of the traditional internal costs of doing business, while thrusting external costs on the public."[31]

In recent years we have grown more aware of the possible deleterious side effects of business activity, or what economists call **externalities**: the unintended negative (or in some cases positive) consequences that an economic transaction between two parties can have on some third party. Industrial pollution provides the clearest illustration. Suppose a factory makes widgets and sells them to your firm. A by-product of this economic transaction is the waste that the rains wash from the factory yard into the local river, waste that damages recreational and commercial fishing interests downstream. This damage to third parties is an unintended side effect of the economic transaction between the seller and the buyer of widgets.

Defenders of the new social contract, like Anshen, maintain that externalities should no longer be overlooked. In the jargon of economists, externalities must be "internalized"—that is, the factory should be made to absorb the cost of its pollution, either by disposing of its waste in an environmentally safe (and presumably more expensive) way or by paying for the damage the waste does downstream. On the one hand, basic fairness requires that the factory's waste no longer be dumped onto third parties. On the other hand, from the economic point of view, requiring the factory to internalize the externalities makes sense, for only when it does so will the price of the widgets it sells reflect their true social cost. The real production cost of the widgets includes not only labor, raw materials, machinery, and so on but also the damage done to the fisheries downstream. Unless the price of widgets is raised sufficiently to reimburse the fisheries for their losses or to dispose of the waste in some other way, the buyer of widgets is paying less than their true cost. Part of the cost is being paid by the fishing interests downstream.

Advocates of the broader view go beyond requiring business to internalize its externalities in a narrow economic sense. Keith Davis, for example, maintains that in addition to considering potential profitability, a business must weigh the long-range social costs of its activities as well. Only if the overall benefit to society is positive should business act:

> The expectation of the social responsibility model is that a detailed cost/benefit analysis will be made prior to determining whether to proceed with an activity and that social costs will be given significant weight in the decision-making process. Almost any business action will entail some social costs. The basic question is whether the benefits outweigh the costs so that there is a net social benefit. Many questions of judgment arise, and there are no precise mathematical measures in the social field, but rational and wise judgments can be made if the issues are first thoroughly explored.[32]

SUMMARY

Defenders of the broader view maintain that corporations have responsibilities that go beyond making money because of their great social and economic power. Business is governed by an implicit social contract that requires it to operate in ways that benefit society. In particular, corporations must take responsibility for the unintended side effects of their business transactions (externalities) and weigh the full social costs of their activities.

Advocates of the broader view believe that business must internalize its externalities and consider the social costs of its activities.

STOCKHOLDERS AND THE CORPORATION

When asked, most Americans say that a corporation's top obligation is to its employees; others say it is to the community or the nation, but only 17 percent think stockholders deserve the highest priority.[33] In fact, even a majority of managers reject a profit-only philosophy of corporate management.[34] Advocates of the narrow view, however, believe that those attitudes reflect a misunderstanding of the proper relationship between management and stockholders. Stockholders own the company. They entrust management with their funds, and in return management undertakes to make as much money for them as it can. As a result, according to proponents of the narrow view, management has a fiduciary duty to maximize shareholder wealth, a duty that is inconsistent with any social responsibility other than the relentless pursuit of profit.

The narrow view holds that management's responsibility to maximize shareholder wealth outweighs any other obligations.

The managers of a corporation do indeed have a **fiduciary responsibility** to look after the interests of shareholders, a duty that is clearly violated by corporate executives who take advantage of their position to enrich themselves at company expense with extravagant bonuses, stock options, and retirement packages or to waste corporate money on jets, apartments, private parties, and various personal services that lack any plausible business rationale. But it doesn't follow from this, as proponents of the narrow view maintain, that the corporation should be run entirely for the benefit of stockholders, that their interests always take priority over the interests of everyone else. To the contrary, argue critics of the narrow view, management has fiduciary responsibilities to other constituencies as well—for example, to employees, bondholders, and consumers. The duty to make money for shareholders is real, but it doesn't trump all of a company's other responsibilities. Indeed, it's debatable whether most shareholders believe that it does. Many of them may want the company they "own" to act in a morally responsible manner—say, by reducing its carbon footprint or by treating employees with respect—even if that means less profit.

Against that point of view, however, Milton Friedman argued, "The whole justification for permitting the corporate executives to be selected by the shareholders is that the executive is an agent serving the interests of his principal."[35] This justification disappears, he believed, when executives expend corporate resources in ways that don't necessarily enhance the bottom line. They are then acting more like public servants than like employees of a private enterprise. But even if one agrees with Friedman that stockholders select corporate managers to act as their agents and advance their interests, this doesn't prove that those executives are bound to act solely to increase shareholder wealth, ignoring all other moral considerations. Undertaking to look after other people's interests or promising to try to make money for them creates a genuine obligation, but that obligation is not absolute. It doesn't eliminate all other moral responsibilities. By analogy, promising to meet someone at a certain time and place for lunch creates an obligation, but that obligation doesn't override one's duty to assist someone having a heart attack. And something that it would be immoral for you to do (such as making a dangerous product) doesn't become right just because you're acting on behalf of someone else or promised him that you would do it.

SUMMARY

Advocates of the narrow view stress that management's fiduciary duty to the owners (stockholders) of a corporation takes priority over any other responsibilities and obligates management to focus on profit maximization alone. Critics challenge this argument. They also point out that the assumption that stockholders own or control the corporation is dubious.

Friedman believed that if executives "impose taxes on stockholders and spend the proceeds for 'social' purposes, they become 'civil servants,' and thus should be selected through a political process."[36] He considered such a proposal absurd or, at best, socialistic. Yet others contend that corporations are too focused on profits, and they fear the damage to society when firms are willing to sacrifice all other values on the altar of the bottom line. They don't think it absurd at all that corporations should take a broader view of their social role and responsibilities. They see nothing in the management–stockholder relationship that would morally forbid corporations from doing so.

Who Controls the Corporation?

According to the narrow view of corporate responsibility, stockholders own the corporation and select managers to run it for them. That model may make sense for some small firms or when venture capitalists invest in a start-up company, but it doesn't accurately reflect modern corporate reality. To begin with, most stockholders purchase shares in a company from current stockholders, who acquired their shares the same way. Very few investors put their money directly into a corporation; rather, they buy secondhand shares that were initially issued years before. They pick companies that look profitable or seem likely to grow or whose products or policies appeal to them, or they may simply be following the advice of their broker. And they are generally prepared to resell their shares, perhaps even the same day they bought them, if it is profitable to do so. Stockholders have no legal obligation to the company. They are a far-flung, diverse, and ever-changing group. They come and go, and rarely, if ever, have direct contact with the managers of the company or even know or care who they are.

For those reasons, then, it's implausible to see stockholders in, say, Home Depot or Procter & Gamble as being genuine owners or proprietors of the company. "A share of stock," write two legal experts, "does not confer ownership of the underlying assets owned by the corporation. Instead, it provides the holder with a right to share in the financial returns produced by the corporations' business." A share of stock is a financial instrument, more akin to a bond than to a car or building.[37]

Few economists or business theorists believe that stockholders are really in charge of the companies whose shares they hold or that they select the managers who run them. As long ago as 1932, Adolf Berle and Gardiner Means showed that because stock ownership in large corporations is so dispersed, actual control of the corporation has passed to management.[38] Today, as most business observers acknowledge, management handpicks the board of directors, thus controlling the body that is supposed to police it. "The CEO puts up the candidates; no one runs against them, and management counts the votes," says Nell Minow of Corporate Library, a corporate watchdog website. "We wouldn't deign to call this an election in a third-world country."[39] Even in those rare cases when shareholders put up their own candidates, such proxy fights are expensive and the incumbent management has the corporate coffers at its disposal to fight them.

> Stockholders do not really own or control the companies whose shares they hold.

As a result, the board of directors typically rubber-stamps the policies and recommendations of management. That's why it's not too surprising that the directors of Enron ignored shareholder interests and approved paying out $750 million in executive compensation—$140 million of it to its chairman—in a year when the company's entire net income was only $975 million. The Enron example is extreme, but since the 1990s the share of corporate net income going to top management has doubled; that's money that otherwise would have ended up in shareholders' pockets.[40] And how else to explain the fat payouts to CEOs when their companies do poorly or are acquired by other corporations[41] or the lavish retirement packages that boards bestow on former CEOs? These often include a million-dollar annual pension, an expensive apartment, a car and driver, and free use of the company aircraft.[42] True, in the past couple of decades, institutional investors like pension funds and large mutual funds have endeavored to increase their sway over corporate policies, and in 2011 the Securities and Exchange Commission (SEC) gave shareholders the right to a nonbinding vote on corporate compensation plans once every three years. But it's still exceedingly difficult for shareholders to change policies they don't like, because the voting rules are rigged in management's favor.[43] The upshot is simple, according to Michael Jensen, professor emeritus at Harvard Business School: "The CEO has no boss." That, he says, is "the major thing wrong with large public corporations in the United States."[44]

DEBATING CORPORATE RESPONSIBILITY

We can pursue the debate over corporate responsibility further by examining three arguments in support of the narrow view: the invisible-hand argument, the let-government-do-it argument, and the business-can't-handle-it argument. Advocates of the broader view of corporate responsibility reject all three.

THE INVISIBLE-HAND ARGUMENT

Adam Smith claimed that when each of us acts in a free-market environment to promote our own economic interests we are led by an invisible hand to promote the general good. Like-minded contemporary thinkers such as Friedman advance the same **invisible-hand argument**. They point out that corporations, in fact, were chartered by states precisely with utility in mind. If businesses are permitted to seek self-interest, their activities will inevitably yield the greatest good for society as a whole. To invite corporations to base their policies and activities on anything other than profit making is to politicize business's unique economic function and to hamper its ability to satisfy our material needs. As Roberto C. Goizueta, former CEO of Coca-Cola, argues, "businesses are created to meet economic needs." When they "try to become all things to all people, they fail. . . . We have one job: to generate a fair return for our owners."[45] Accordingly, corporations should not be invited to fight against prejudice, to combat global warming, to contribute to the local community, or to improve working conditions or enhance the lives of employees, except insofar as these activities increase profits.

Yet this argument allows that corporations may still be held accountable for their actions. To the degree that they fulfill or fail to fulfill their economic role, they can be praised or blamed. And they can rightly be criticized for breaking the law or violating the rules of the game—for example, by shady accounting practices that mislead investors about company assets. But corporations should not be held morally responsible for noneconomic matters; to do so would distort the economic mission of business in society and undermine the foundations of the free-enterprise system.

The invisible-hand argument, however, runs up against the fact that modern corporations bear about as much resemblance to Smith's self-sufficient farmers and craftspeople as today's military bears to the Continental militia. Given the sway they have over our economy and society and the enormous impact they have on our lives, our communities, and our environment, today's gigantic corporations are more like public enterprises than private ones. They constitute powerful economic fiefdoms, far removed from the small, competitive producers of classical economics. Perhaps within a restricted area of economic activity, when the parties to the exchange are roughly equal, then each pursuing self-interest can result in the greatest net good. But in the real world of large corporations, the concept of an invisible hand orchestrating the common good often stretches credulity. For example, California deregulated its electricity market to promote competition and give the invisible hand room to operate. But the result was a disaster. Instead of cheaper energy, the state got power blackouts and soaring prices as energy companies adroitly and greedily manipulated the market. Each time the state tried to make the market work better, energy sellers devised new ways to exploit the system. The state government only stanched the crisis by a costly intervention that has basically put it in the power business.[46]

The invisible-hand argument in favor of the narrow view of corporate responsibility is thus open to criticism as theoretically unsound and economically unrealistic.

Moreover, in practice the argument is complicated by the fact that corporations today find themselves in a social and political environment in which they are pressured by public opinion, politicians, the media, and various activist groups to act—or at least be perceived to be acting—as responsible corporate citizens, as socially conscious enterprises that acknowledge other values besides profit and that seek to make a positive contribution to our society. Few if any corporations can afford to be seen as exploiters of foreign labor, as polluters of the environment, or as indifferent to consumer welfare or the prosperity of our communities. Companies today religiously guard their name and their brands against the slander that they care only about profits. And the larger the corporation, the more susceptible it is to the demand that it behave with a developed sense of moral responsibility, and the more it needs to guard its image and to take steps to assure the public that it is striving to make the world a better place.

This explains why for several months in 2010–11 Chevron ran a campaign of dramatic full-page advertisements in the *Wall Street Journal*, *New York Times*, and other newspapers, each ad featuring a slogan, such as, "Oil companies should support the communities they're part of," "Oil companies should put their profits to good use," "It's time for oil companies to get behind renewable energy," or "Big Oil should support small business." Stamped in red after each statement were the words, "We agree." The company also ran a series of television ads in the same vein. Likewise, Rio-Tinto Alcan, the world's largest aluminum company, proclaims that it is committed to "maximizing value for all our stakeholders, especially by making a significant contribution . . . to the economic, social and environmental well-being of the communities in which we operate."[47] And Hewlett-Packard states that "a company has a responsibility beyond making a profit for its investors, including a commitment to enrich the business, lives and communities of its customers, partners and employees."[48]

Admittedly, some of this is merely public-relations posturing, but it's also true that business success in today's world requires companies to respond to society's demand that they act as morally responsible agents. For purely self-interested reasons, even corporations that take a very narrow view of their responsibilities may have to behave as if they held a broader view. For example, in a world in which 88 percent of young people believe that companies have a responsibility to support social causes and 86 percent of them say that they switch brands based on social issues, a world in which 72 percent of job seekers prefer to work for a company that supports social causes,[49] corporate philanthropy promotes the bottom line. Moreover, almost all studies indicate that socially responsible corporate behavior is positively correlated with financial success and that the most profitable companies treat their consumers, employees, and business partners ethically.[50] Ironically, then, this gives companies a self-interested reason not merely to pretend to have a broad sense of social responsibility but, rather, to become the kind of company that really does want to make a positive mark in the world. Of course, whether we are talking about individuals or about corporations, there's no guarantee that acting morally will always pay off, and indeed if that is one's only motivation for doing the right thing, then one can hardly be said to be acting morally. Even so, there's little reason for either individuals or companies to believe that acting selfishly or sacrificing moral values to profits will pay off for them in the long run.

The invisible-hand argument seems economically unrealistic. In addition, corporations today find it in their interest to acknowledge values other than profit.

THE LET-GOVERNMENT-DO-IT ARGUMENT

According to the narrow view of corporate responsibility, business's role is purely economic, and corporations should not be considered moral agents. Some adherents of this view, however, such as economist and social critic John Kenneth Galbraith

(1908–2006), reject the assumption that Smith's invisible hand will solve all social and economic problems or that market forces will moralize corporate activities. Left to their own self-serving devices, Galbraith and others warn, modern corporations will enrich themselves while impoverishing society. If they can get away with it, they will pollute, exploit workers, deceive customers, and strive to eliminate competition and keep prices high through oligopolistic practices. They will do those things, the argument continues, because as economic institutions they are naturally and quite properly profit motivated.

What is profitable for corporations, however, is not necessarily useful or desirable for society. How is the corporation's natural and insatiable appetite for profit to be controlled? Through government regulation, answer proponents of the **let-government-do-it argument**. They believe that the strong hand of government, through a system of laws and incentives, can and should bring corporations to heel. "I believe in corporations," Teddy Roosevelt once proclaimed. "They are indispensable instruments of our modern civilization; but I believe that they should be so supervised and so regulated that they shall act for the interests of the community as a whole."[51]

"Do not blame corporations and their top executives" for things like layoffs or urge them to acknowledge obligations beyond the bottom line, writes the economist Robert Reich, secretary of labor under President Clinton. "They are behaving exactly as they are organized to behave." He pooh-poohs moral appeals and rejects the idea that CEOs should seek to balance the interests of shareholders against those of employees and their communities. Rather, Reich says, "if we want corporations to take more responsibility" for the economic well-being of Americans, then government "will have to provide the proper incentives."[52]

> The let-government-do-it argument rejects broadening corporate responsibility just as much as the invisible-hand argument does.

This advice sounds realistic and is intended to be practical, but the let-government-do-it argument rejects the notion of broadening corporate responsibility just as firmly as the invisible-hand argument does. The latter puts the focus on the market. Galbraith's and Reich's argument puts it on the *visible* hand of government. The two positions agree, however, in thinking that it is misguided to expect or demand that business firms do anything other than pursue profit.

Critics of the let-government-do-it argument contend that it is a blueprint for big, intrusive government. Moreover, they doubt that government can control any but the most egregious corporate immorality. They fear that many questionable activities will be overlooked, safely hidden within the labyrinth of the corporate structure. Lacking intimate knowledge of the goals and sub-goals of specific corporations, as well as of their daily operations, government simply can't anticipate a specific corporation's moral challenges. Rather, it can prescribe behavior only for broad, cross-sectional issues, such as bribery, price fixing, and unfair competition.

Legislation can certainly address egregious corporate wrongdoing, but it cannot provide corporations with much specific guidance about how to act in socially beneficial ways. Consider, for example, PepsiCo's decision to buy directly from small corn farmers in Mexico (rather than through middle men) and to guarantee, before they plant their crops, the price it will pay them. This program has changed the farmers' lives (they no longer have to trek to the United States to work odd jobs to make ends meet), increased their incomes, and strengthened their communities.[53] No government legislation could have brought this about.

Finally, is government a credible custodian of morality? If recent experience has taught anything, it is that government officials are not always paragons of virtue. Looked at simply as another organization, government manifests many of the same structural characteristics that test moral behavior inside the corporation. Furthermore, given the awesome clout of corporate lobbyists, one wonders whether, as moral police, government officials will do anything more than impose the values and interests of their most generous financiers. Can we seriously expect politicians to bite the hand that feeds them?

THE BUSINESS-CAN'T-HANDLE-IT ARGUMENT

In support of the narrow view of corporate responsibility, some maintain that it is misguided to encourage corporations to address nonbusiness matters. According to the **business-can't-handle-it argument**, corporations are the wrong group to be entrusted with broad responsibility for promoting the well-being of society. They are not up to the job for two reasons: (1) they lack the necessary expertise and (2) in addressing noneconomic matters, they inevitably impose their own materialistic values on the rest of society.

Some argue that business is the wrong group on which to place broad social responsibilities for two reasons.

Corporations Lack the Expertise

Those who develop the first point contend that business can't handle the job—that it is the wrong group to rely on to promote the well-being of society—because corporate executives lack the moral and social expertise to make other-than-economic decisions. To assign them noneconomic responsibilities would be to put social welfare in the hands of inept custodians. For example, Robert Reich argues that corporate executives lack the moral authority to "balance profits against the public good" or "undertake any ethical balancing." They have no "expertise in making such moral calculations."[54] In his view, corporate leaders lack the moral insight or social know-how that a broader view of corporate responsibility would seem to require of them.

Against that, however, one can argue that we don't normally restrict the moral responsibilities of individuals, professional bodies, or other organizations to matters that fall within the narrow confines of their business or other expertise. We see nothing wrong, for example, with physicians advocating AIDS awareness or trying to promote the use of seat belts in automobiles, or with a teachers' union involving itself in a campaign to combat the use of illegal drugs. And ordinary citizens may sometimes have a duty to educate themselves about, and do what they can to address, social issues that fall outside their usual sphere of knowledge and activity. What, if anything, asks the critic, makes the social role of the corporation unique, so that its responsibilities and those of its employees should be confined solely to profit making?

The argument that corporations aren't up to addressing social issues because they lack the necessary expertise runs up against the fact that, often, it is only business that has the know-how, talent, experience, and organizational resources to tackle certain problems. If society, for example, wants to eradicate malaria in Africa or increase longevity at home, to reduce diesel engine emissions or retard global warming, to improve agricultural productivity while lowering the risks from pesticides, or to see that inner-city youth learn entrepreneurship or that community groups have the business skills necessary for success, then society will need the assistance of business. To take a specific illustration, Citibank supports microfinance programs in Mexico and India intended to give poor rural women the tiny loans they need, say, to buy a sewing machine and start their own business. True, as a Citigroup executive says, "there is not going to be a huge short-term profit" for the company.[55] But who is better able to help these women than a company like Citigroup?

Corporations Will Impose Their Values on Us

Others argue that corporations are the wrong group to address social issues, that business can't handle the assignment, for a different reason. They fear that if permitted to stray from strictly economic matters, corporate officials will impose their materialistic values on all of society. Broadening corporate responsibility will thus "materialize" society instead of "moralizing" corporate activity. More than fifty years ago, Harvard professor Theodore Levitt expressed this concern:

> The danger is that all these things [resulting from having business pursue social goals other than profit making] will turn the corporation into a twentieth-century equivalent of the medieval church.... For while the corporation also transforms itself in the process, at bottom its outlook will always remain materialistic. What we have then is the frightening spectacle of a powerful economic functional group whose future and perception are shaped in a tight materialistic context of money and things but which imposes its narrow ideas about a broad spectrum of unrelated noneconomic subjects on the mass of man and society. Even if its outlook were the purest kind of good will, that would not recommend the corporation as an arbiter of our lives.[56]

> **SUMMARY**
> Three arguments in favor of the narrow view are the invisible-hand argument, the let-government-do-it argument, and the business-can't-handle-it argument. Finding flaws in each of these arguments, critics maintain there is no solid basis for restricting corporate responsibility to profit making.

This argument seems to assume that corporations do not already exercise enormous discretionary power over us. But as Keith Davis points out, business already has immense social power. "Society has entrusted to business large amounts of society's resources," says Davis, "and business is expected to manage these resources as a wise trustee for society. In addition to the traditional role of economic entrepreneurship, business now has a new social role of trusteeship. As trustee for society's resources, it serves the interests of all claimants on the organization, rather than only those of owners, or consumers, or labor."[57]

As Paul Camenisch notes, business is already using its privileged position to propagate, consciously or unconsciously, a view of humanity and the good life.[58] Implicit in the barrage of advertisements to which we are subjected daily are assumptions about happiness, success, and human fulfillment. In addition, corporations or industry groups sometimes speak out in unvarnished terms about social and economic issues. For example, ExxonMobil disputes the notion that fossil fuels are the main cause of global warming and lobbies against capping global-warming emissions, while drug companies such as Eli Lilly, Procter & Gamble, and Bristol-Myers Squibb contribute to conservative think tanks that seek to reduce the regulatory powers of the U.S. Food and Drug Administration.

The point here is that business already promotes consumerism and materialistic values. It doesn't hesitate to use its resources to express its views and influence our political system on issues that affect its economic interests. If corporations take a broader view of their responsibilities, are they really likely to have a more materialistic effect on society, as Levitt suggests, than they do now? It's hard to believe they could. Levitt's view implies that there is some threat to society's values when corporations engage in philanthropy or use their economic and political muscle for other than purely self-interested ends. But society's values are not endangered when Sara Lee donates 2 percent of its pretax profits to charitable causes, mostly cultural institutions and organizations serving disadvantaged people,[59] or when General Mills gives away 3 percent of its domestic pretax earnings to community organizations, donates food to people in need, and helps inner-city companies to get up and running.[60] And where is the "materialization of society" if, instead of advertising on a silly situation comedy that reaches a large audience, a corporation spends the same amount underwriting a science program with fewer viewers solely out of a sense of social responsibility?

INSTITUTIONALIZING ETHICS WITHIN CORPORATIONS

The criticisms of these three arguments in support of the narrow view of corporate responsibility have led many people inside and outside business to adopt the broader view—that the obligations of the modern business corporation extend beyond simply making money for itself. Society grants corporations the right to exist and gives them legal status as separate entities. It does this not to indulge the profit appetites of owners and managers but, as Camenisch says, as a way of securing the necessary "goods and services to sustain and enhance human existence."[61] In return for its sufferance of corporations, society has the right to expect corporations not to cause harm, to take into account the external effects of their activities, and whenever possible to act for the betterment of society.

> Society permits corporations to exist and, in turn, expects them to act in a socially responsible way.

The list of corporate responsibilities goes beyond such negative injunctions as "Don't pollute," "Don't misrepresent products," and "Don't bribe." Included also are affirmative duties such as "See that your product or service makes a positive contribution to society," "Improve the skills of your employees," "Seek to hire the disabled or other disadvantaged persons," "Contribute to the betterment of your community," "Be as green as possible," and "Enrich working conditions." The responsibilities of corporations are not necessarily limited to activities that are intrinsically related to their business operations but may reflect social responsibilities that each of us, whether individuals or institutions, has simply by virtue of our being members of society. Precisely how far each of us must go to meet these responsibilities depends largely on our capacity to fulfill them, which, of course, varies from person to person, institution to institution. But given their considerable power and resources, large corporations seem better able to promote the common good than most individuals or small businesses.

How corporations are to promote the common good cannot be answered very specifically; this will depend on the type of firm and its particular circumstances. Proponents of broadening corporate responsibility would agree, though, that the first step is for corporations to expand their moral horizons and make ethical conduct a priority. How to do this? At least four actions seem called for. Corporations should:

> To make ethics a priority, corporations should do four things.

1. Acknowledge the importance, even necessity, of conducting business morally. Their commitment to ethical behavior should be unequivocal and highly visible, from top management down.

2. Make a real effort to encourage their members to take moral responsibilities seriously. This commitment would mean ending all forms of retaliation against those who buck the system and rewarding employees for evaluating corporate decisions in their broader social and moral contexts.

3. End their defensiveness in the face of public discussion and criticism. Instead, they should actively solicit the views of stockholders, managers, employees, suppliers, customers, local communities, and even society as a whole. Corporations should invite outside opinions and conduct a candid ethical audit of their organizational policies, priorities, and practices.

4. Recognize the pluralistic nature of the social system of which they are a part. Society consists of diverse, interlinked individuals and groups, all vying to maintain their autonomy and advance their interests. The actions of any one group invariably affect the interests of others. As part of society, corporations affect many groups, and these groups and the individuals they comprise affect corporations. Failing to realize this, corporations can lose sight of the social framework that governs their relationship with the external environment.

SUMMARY

To become more socially responsible, companies need to expand their moral horizons and make ethical conduct a priority. Doing so will require them to acknowledge the critical importance of ethics, to encourage morally responsible conduct by their employees, to recognize the pluralistic nature of our social system, and to be open to public discussion and review.

Undoubtedly, other general directives could be added to this list. Still, if corporate responsibility is to be expanded, then something like the preceding approach seems basic.

LIMITS TO WHAT THE LAW CAN DO

Critics of the let-government-do-it argument question Galbraith's and Reich's view that society should not expect business to behave morally but rather should simply use government to direct business's pursuit of profit in socially acceptable directions. This issue is worth returning to in the present context. All defenders of the broader view of corporate responsibility believe that more than laissez faire is necessary to ensure that business behavior is socially and morally acceptable. Yet there is a tendency to believe that law is a fully adequate vehicle for this purpose.

Stone gives three reasons why there are limits to what we can achieve through law.

Law professor Christopher Stone has argued, however, that there are limits on what the law can be expected to achieve.[62] Three of his points are particularly important. *First*, many laws, such as controls on the disposal of toxic waste, are passed only after there is general awareness of the problem; in the meantime, damage has already been done. The proverbial barn door has been shut only after the horse has left.

Second, formulating appropriate laws and designing effective regulations are difficult. It is hard to achieve consensus on the relevant facts, to determine what remedies will work, and to decide how to weigh conflicting values. In addition, our political system gives corporations and their lobbyists significant input into the writing of laws. Not only that, but the specific working regulations and day-to-day interpretation of the law require the continual input of industry experts. This is not a conspiracy but a fact of life. Government bureaus generally have limited time, staffing, and expertise, so they must rely on the cooperation and assistance of those they regulate.

Third, enforcing the law is often cumbersome. Legal actions against corporations are expensive and can drag on for years,* and the judicial process is often too blunt an instrument to use as a way of managing complex social and business issues. In fact, recourse to the courts can be counterproductive, and Stone argues that sometimes the benefits of doing so may not be worth the costs. Legal action may simply make corporations more furtive, breeding distrust, destruction of documents, and an attitude that "I won't do anything more than I am absolutely required to do."

People in business need to acknowledge that obeying the law is not their only obligation because the law alone cannot guarantee responsible business behavior.

What conclusion should be drawn? Stone is not arguing that regulation of business is hopeless. Rather, what he wants to stress is that the law cannot do it alone. We do not want a system in which businesspeople believe that their only obligation is to obey the law and that it is morally permissible for them to do anything not (yet) illegal. With that attitude, disaster is just around the corner. More socially responsible business behavior requires, instead, that corporations and the people within them not simply respond to the requirements of the law but also hold high moral standards—and that they themselves monitor their own behavior.

ETHICAL CODES AND ECONOMIC EFFICIENCY

It is, therefore, important that corporations examine their own implicit and explicit codes of conduct and the moral standards that are being propagated to their employees. As mentioned earlier in this chapter and in Chapter 1, there is no necessary trade-off

---

*For example, in 2013 a group of workers won a lawsuit for back pay, which they had filed against Penn Central railway forty-four years earlier.[63]

between profitability and ethical corporate behavior. Indeed, the contrary appears to be true: The most morally responsible companies are consistently among the most profitable companies. Yet ethical behavior in the business world is often assumed to come at the expense of economic efficiency. Defenders of the broader view, such as Anshen, as well as defenders of the narrow view, such as Friedman, seem to make this assumption. Anshen believes that other values should take priority over economic efficiency, whereas Friedman contends business should concern itself only with profit and, in this way, maximize economic well-being. In his important essay "Social Responsibility and Economic Efficiency," Nobel Prize-winning economist Kenneth Arrow has challenged this assumption.[64]

To begin with, says Arrow, any kind of settled economic life requires a certain degree of ethical behavior, some element of trust and confidence. Much business, for instance, is conducted on the basis of oral agreements. In addition, Arrow points out, "there are two types of situation in which the simple rule of maximizing profits is socially inefficient: the case in which costs are not paid for, as in pollution, and the case in which the seller has considerably more knowledge about his product than the buyer."

The first type of situation relates to the demand that corporations "internalize their externalities," discussed earlier in this chapter. In the second situation, in which the buyer lacks the expertise and knowledge of the seller, an effective moral code, either requiring full disclosure or setting minimal standards of performance (for example, the braking ability of a new automobile), enhances rather than diminishes economic efficiency. Without such a code, buyers may purchase products or services they don't need. Or because they don't trust the seller, they may refrain from purchasing products and services they do need. Either way, from the economist's point of view the situation is inefficient.

An effective professional or business moral code—as well as the public's awareness of this code—is good for business. Most of us, for example, have little medical knowledge and are thus at the mercy of doctors. Over hundreds of years, however, a firm code of ethical conduct has developed in the medical profession. As a result, people generally take for granted that their physician will perform with their welfare in mind. They rarely worry that their doctor might be taking advantage of them or exploiting them with unnecessary treatment. By contrast, used-car dealers have historically suffered from a lack of public trust.

For a code to be effective it must be realistic, Arrow argues, in the sense of connecting with the collective self-interest of business. And it must become part of the corporate culture, "accepted by the significant operating institutions and transmitted from one generation of executives to the next through standard operating procedures [and] through education in business schools."

For both Arrow and Stone, then, the development of feasible and effective business and professional codes of ethics must be a central focus of any effort to enhance or expand corporate responsibility. The question is how to create a corporate atmosphere conducive to moral decision making.

CORPORATE MORAL CODES

What can be done to improve organizational climate so that individuals can reasonably be expected to act ethically? If those inside the corporation are to behave morally, they need clearly stated and communicated ethical standards that are equitable and enforced. This development seems possible only if the standards of expected behavior are institutionalized—that is, only if they become a fixture in the corporate organization.

> **SUMMARY**
> Corporations and the people who make them up must have high moral standards and monitor their own conduct because there are limits to what the law can do to ensure that business behavior is socially and morally acceptable.

Ethics and efficiency aren't necessarily in opposition. Normal business activity requires some degree of ethics, and focusing only on profit maximization is socially inefficient in two situations.

> **SUMMARY**
> All settled economic life requires trust and confidence. The adoption of realistic and workable codes of ethics in the business world can actually enhance business efficiency. This is particularly true when there is an imbalance of knowledge between the buyer and the seller.

> There are several steps companies should take to institutionalize ethics.

To institutionalize ethics within corporations, Professor Milton Snoeyenbos suggests that top management should (1) articulate the firm's values and goals, (2) adopt a moral code applicable to all members of the company, (3) set up a high-ranking ethics committee to oversee, develop, and enforce the code, and (4) incorporate ethics training into all employee-development programs.[65]

The company's code of ethics should not be window dressing or so general as to be useless. A **corporate moral code** should set reasonable goals and subgoals, with an eye on blunting unethical pressures on subordinates. In formulating the code, the top-level ethics committee should solicit the views of corporate members at all levels regarding goals and subgoals, so that the final product articulates "a fine-grained ethical code that addresses ethical issues likely to arise at the level of subgoals."[66] Moreover, the committee should have full authority and responsibility to communicate the code and decisions based on it to all corporate members, clarify and interpret the code when the need arises, facilitate the code's use, investigate grievances and violations of the code, discipline violators and reward compliance, and review, update, and upgrade the code.

To help employees in ethically difficult situations, a good corporate ethics program must be user friendly. It should provide a support system with a variety of entry points, one that employees feel confident about using.[67] In addition, part of all employee-training programs should be devoted to ethics. At a minimum, this should include study of the code, review of the company's procedures for handling ethical problems, and discussion of employer and employee responsibilities and expectations. Snoeyenbos and others believe that institutionalizing ethics within the corporation in these ways, when supplemented by the development of industry-wide codes of ethics to address issues beyond a particular firm, will go far toward establishing a corporate climate conducive to individual moral decision making.

> **SUMMARY**
> To improve organizational climate so that we can reasonably expect individuals to act morally, corporations need to institutionalize ethics. Among other things, this involves articulating their values and goals, adopting a moral code, setting up an ethics committee, and including ethics training in their employee-development programs. Attention to corporate culture is also crucial to the successful institutionalization of ethics inside an organization.

CORPORATE CULTURE

During the past two decades, organizational theorists and writers on business management have increasingly emphasized "corporate culture" as the factor that makes one company succeed while another languishes. Although intangible in comparison with things like sales revenue and profit margin, corporate culture is often the key to a firm's success. According to one study, 30 percent of the difference in performance between companies can be attributed to differences in culture, but only 5 percent to differences in strategy.[68]

What is **corporate culture**? One writer puts it this way: "Culture is the pattern of shared values and beliefs that gives members of an institution meaning and provides them with rules for behavior in their organization."[69] A fuller definition is given by another writer, who describes corporate culture as "a general constellation of beliefs, mores, customs, value systems and behavioral norms, and ways of doing business that are unique to each corporation, that set a pattern for corporate activities and actions, and that describe the implicit and emergent patterns of behavior and emotions characterizing life in the organization."[70] Corporate culture may be both overt and implicit. The formal culture of a corporation, as expressed in idealized statements of principles and values, should also be distinguished from the informal culture that shapes the beliefs and behavior of individuals in the organization. In addition, there may be multiple and overlapping cultures within an organization because employees have different backgrounds, work in different divisions of the organization and even in different countries, and may be subject to different systems of rewards and sanctions.

Organizational theorists emphasize the importance of monitoring and managing corporate culture—beginning with an attempt to understand each corporation's distinctive culture—to prevent dysfunctional behavior and processes. As one consultant puts it, "A corporation's culture is what determines how people behave when they are not being watched."[71] If management does not make explicit the values and behavior it desires, the culture will typically develop its own norms, usually based on the types of behavior that lead to success within the organization. Thus, the desired values must be communicated and transmitted throughout the organization. Conduct congruent with them must be rewarded and conduct inconsistent with them sanctioned. Overlooking behavior that contradicts the desired norms can have the effect of encouraging and even rewarding it.

> Management must pay attention to the values and behavior reinforced by its corporate culture.

William Donaldson, former chairman of the U.S. Securities and Exchange Commission, emphasizes the importance of ethical leadership, of the example set by upper management. "The tone is set at the top," he says. "You must have an internal code that goes beyond the letter of the law to encompass the spirit of the company. Does that concept exist in all companies? No. All you have to do is look at executive compensation to recognize that we still have a long way to go."[72]

These points are crucial when it comes to corporate social responsibility. Management needs to understand the real dynamics of its own organization. At Sears, for example, new minimum work quotas and productivity incentives at its auto centers created a high-pressure environment that led employees to mislead customers and sell them unnecessary parts and services, from brake jobs to front-end alignments.[73] At Fannie Mae, an "earnings-at-any-cost culture" led to accounting fraud.[74] Goldman Sachs's formal culture proclaims that customers come first, but in fact, says one insider, employees refer to them as "Muppets."[75] Thus, it is necessary for socially responsible executives to ask: How do people get ahead in the company? What conduct is actually rewarded, what values are really being instilled in employees? Andrew C. Sigler, chairman of Champion International, stresses this point: "Sitting up here in Stamford, there's no way I can affect what an employee is doing today in Texas, Montana, or Maine. Making speeches and sending letters just doesn't do it. You need a culture and peer pressure that spells out what is acceptable and isn't and why. It involves training, education, and follow-up."[76]

Internal or external corporate responsibility audits can help close the gap between stated values, goals, and mission, on the one hand, and reality on the other.[77] Another aspect of follow-up is strict enforcement. For example, Chemical Bank terminates employees for violating the company's code of ethics even if they do nothing illegal, and Xerox dismisses people for minor manipulation of records and the padding of expense accounts. (By contrast, some of the nation's most prestigious stock brokerage firms have employed salespeople with long records of violating securities laws.[78]) In a recent but typical year, General Electric investigated 1,338 cases in which concerns had been raised internally about employee integrity. It dismissed 125 employees and took disciplinary action against 243 others for legal or ethical violations.[79] Executives at both Xerox and General Mills also emphasize that civic involvement is a crucial part of corporate ethics. As one General Mills executive puts it: "It's hard to imagine that a person who reads to the blind at night would cheat. . . ."[80]

Johnson & Johnson is widely seen as a model of corporate responsibility, especially because of its decisive handling of the Tylenol crisis of 1982, when seven people in the Chicago area died from cyanide-laced Extra-Strength Tylenol capsules. The company immediately recalled 31 million bottles of Tylenol from store shelves across the nation and notified 500,000 doctors and hospitals about the contaminated capsules. A toll-free consumer hotline was set up the first week of the crisis, and consumers were offered the opportunity to replace Tylenol capsules with a free bottle of Tylenol tablets. Johnson & Johnson was also open with the public instead of being defensive about the deaths.

Maurice Hank Greenberg was the CEO of American International Group (AIG), a long-prosperous and respected insurance company, when it suddenly collapsed. AIG was said to have fostered a corporate culture that accepted excessive risk. But is corporate culture alone capable of bringing down a company like AIG?

Accurate information was promptly released, and domestic employees and retirees were kept updated on developments. The chairman of the company appeared on the talk show *Donahue* and on *60 Minutes* to answer questions about the crisis, and other executives were interviewed by *Fortune* and the *Wall Street Journal*.

Despite the setback—the recall alone cost Johnson & Johnson $50 million after taxes—Tylenol rebounded within a year, in large part because the public never lost faith in Johnson & Johnson. Despite this happy ending, many companies fail to emulate Johnson & Johnson's example. A case in point is the RC2 Corporation, which makes Thomas the Tank Engine and other toy trains. In 2007, the public learned that many of the company's trains were made with lead paint, which can cause brain damage if a child ingests it. RC2, however, declined to issue refunds to unhappy parents but asked them to return the affected toys—at their own expense—in order to receive replacement trains and a free bonus gift. Unbelievable as it may seem, one of the toy trains that RC2 mailed out as a gift (a gray boxcar called Toad) was also made with lead paint. Even worse, RC2 executives hid from public view throughout this whole sorry episode, never explaining why their safety checks had failed or why they deserved to be trusted in the future.[81]

In the case of Johnson & Johnson, the company credits its seventy-year-old, one-page statement of values, known as the Credo, with enabling it to build the employee trust necessary for maintaining a firm corporate value system. The Credo acknowledges the company's need to make a sound profit while addressing its obligations to provide a quality product, to treat its employees fairly and with respect, and to be a good corporate citizen, supporting the community of which it is a member. The Credo is "the most important thing we have in this company," says chairman Ralph Larsen.

Creating and maintaining a morally sound corporate culture is an ongoing task, and even Johnson & Johnson hasn't always been able to live up to its own values. For instance, the company had to pay $7.5 million in fines and costs after admitting that wayward employees had shredded papers to hinder a federal probe into the marketing of an acne cream. "There was no excuse," admits Larsen. "But it is a huge undertaking to spread our values around the world."[82]

STUDY CORNER

KEY TERMS AND CONCEPTS

- broader view of corporate responsibility
- business-can't-handle-it argument
- CID structures
- corporate culture
- corporate moral agency
- corporate moral code
- corporate punishment
- corporation
- diffusion of responsibility
- externalities
- fiduciary responsibility
- invisible-hand argument
- let-government-do-it argument
- limited liability
- narrow view of corporate responsibility
- privately held company
- publicly held company
- social entity (stakeholder) model
- stockholders

POINTS TO REVIEW

- three ways corporations differ from partnerships (pp. 203–204)
- privately held versus publicly held companies (p. 204)
- historical evolution of the corporation (pp. 204–205)
- two theoretical shifts that led to the relaxing of incorporation procedures (p. 205)
- significance of the Supreme Court's *Citizens United* decision (p. 206)
- whether the CID structure is compatible with, or rules out, corporate moral responsibility (p. 207)
- the concept of corporate punishment (p. 208)
- problem of vanishing individual responsibility and two responses to it (pp. 208–209)
- Milton Friedman's view of corporate responsibility (pp. 210–211)
- Melvin Anshen's idea of a social contract between business and society (pp. 212–213)
- how both fairness and economics support the internalizing of externalities (p. 213)
- whether shareholders control the corporation (p. 215)
- criticisms of the invisible-hand argument (pp. 216–217)
- difference between the let-government-do-it and the invisible-hand arguments (pp. 217–219)
- two versions of the business-can't-handle-it argument (pp. 219–220)
- four things companies can do to become more socially responsible (p. 221)
- three limits to what we can expect the law to do (p. 222)
- two situations in which the rule of maximizing profits is socially inefficient (p. 223)
- what top management should do to institutionalize ethics inside the company (p. 223–224)
- the importance of creating a morally oriented corporate culture (pp. 224–226)

FOR FURTHER REFLECTION

1. Are corporations moral agents? Do they have moral responsibilities? Or, in your view, do only human beings have moral agency and moral obligations?
2. Which view of corporate social responsibility—the narrow or the broad—do you favor, and why?
3. What do you think companies should do to make themselves more moral organizations? How can they promote a healthy moral climate inside the company?

CASE 5.1

Yahoo in China

SHI TAO IS A THIRTY-SEVEN-YEAR-OLD CHINESE journalist and democracy advocate. Arrested for leaking state secrets in 2005, he was sentenced to ten years in prison. His crime? Mr. Shi had disclosed that the Communist Party's propaganda department had ordered tight controls for handling the anniversary of the infamous June 4, 1989, crackdown on demonstrators in Beijing's Tiananmen Square. A sad story, for sure, but it's an all too familiar one, given China's notoriously poor record on human rights. What makes Mr. Shi's case stand out, however, is the fact that he was arrested and convicted only because the American company Yahoo revealed his identity to Chinese authorities.[83]

You see, Mr. Shi had posted his information anonymously on a Chinese-language website called Democracy Forum, which is based in New York. Chinese journalists say that Shi's information, which revealed only routine instructions on how officials were to dampen possible protests, was already widely circulated. Still, the Chinese government's elite State Security Bureau wanted to put its hands on the culprit behind the anonymous posting. And for that it needed Yahoo's help in tracking down the Internet address from which huoyan1989@yahoo.com.cn had accessed his e-mail. This turned out to be a computer in Mr. Shi's workplace, Contemporary Business News in Changsha, China.

A few months after Shi's conviction, the watchdog group Reporters Without Borders revealed the story of Yahoo's involvement and embroiled the company in a squall of controversy. After initially declining to comment on the allegation, Yahoo eventually admitted that it had helped Chinese authorities catch Mr. Shi and that it had supplied information on other customers as well. But the company claimed that it had no choice, that the information was provided as part of a "legal process," and that the company is obliged to obey the laws of any country in which it operates. Yahoo co-founder, Jerry Yang, said: "I do not like the outcome of what happens with these things . . . but we have to comply with the law. That's what you need to do in business."

Some critics immediately spied a technical flaw in that argument: The information on Mr. Shi was provided by Yahoo's subsidiary in Hong Kong, which has an independent judiciary and a legal process separate from that of mainland China. Hong Kong legislation does not spell out what e-mail service providers must do when presented with a court order by mainland authorities. Commentators pointed out, however, that even if Yahoo was legally obliged to reveal the information, there was a deeper question of principle involved. As the *Financial Times* put it in an editorial: "As a general principle, companies choosing to operate in a country should be prepared to obey its laws. When those laws are so reprehensible that conforming to them would be unethical, they should be ready to withdraw from that market." Congressional representative Christopher H. Smith, a New Jersey Republican and chair of a House subcommittee on human rights, was even blunter: "This is about accommodating a dictatorship. It's outrageous to be complicit in cracking down on dissenters." And in an open letter to Jerry Yang, the Chinese dissident Liu Xiabo, who has himself suffered censorship, imprisonment, and other indignities, wrote: "I must tell you that my indignation at and contempt for you and your company are not a bit less than my indignation and contempt for the Communist regime. . . . Profit makes you dull in morality. Did it ever occur to you that it is a shame for you to be considered a traitor to your customer Shi Tao?"

Whether profit is dulling their morality is an issue that must be confronted not just by Yahoo but also by other Internet-related companies doing business in China. Microsoft, for example, recently shut down the MSN Spaces website of a popular Beijing blogger whose postings had run afoul of censors. Google agreed to apply the Chinese censors' blacklist to its new Chinese search engine. And a congressional investigative committee has accused Google, Yahoo, and Cisco of helping to maintain in China "the most sophisticated Internet control system in the world." In their defense, the companies ask what good it would do for them to pull out of the Chinese market. They contend that if they resist the Chinese government and their operations are closed down or if they choose to leave the country for moral reasons, they would only deny to ordinary Chinese whatever fresh air the Internet, even filtered and censored, can provide in a closed society. It's more important for them to stay there, play ball with the government, and do what they can to push for Internet freedom. As Yahoo chairman Terry S. Semel puts it: "Part of our role in any form of media is to get whatever we can into those countries and to show and to enable people, slowly, to see the Western way and what our culture is like, and to learn." But critics wonder what these companies, when they are complicit in political repression, are teaching the Chinese about American values.

Some tech companies are turning to the U.S. government for help. Bill Gates, for example, thinks that legislation making it illegal for American companies to assist in the violation of human rights overseas would help. A carefully crafted American anti-repression law would give Yahoo an answer the next time Chinese officials demand evidence against cyber-dissidents. We want to obey your laws, Yahoo officials could say, but our hands are tied; we can't break American law. The assumption is that China would have no choice but to accept this because it does not want to forgo the advantages of having U.S. tech companies operating there.

Still, this doesn't answer the underlying moral questions. At a November 2007 congressional hearing, however, a number of lawmakers made their own moral views perfectly clear. They lambasted Yahoo, describing the company as "spineless and irresponsible" and "moral pygmies." In response, Jerry Yang apologized to the mother of Shi Tao, who attended the hearing. Still, Yahoo has its defenders. Robert Reich, for instance, argues that "Yahoo! is not a moral entity" and "its executives have only one responsibility . . . to make money for their shareholders and, along the way, satisfy their consumers." And in this case, he thinks, the key "consumer" is the Chinese government.

Update

How to deal with China continues to confound American Internet companies. In 2010, upset by the hacking of its servers by the Chinese government, which was trying to gain information about dissidents, and uneasy about continuing its complicity in Internet censorship, Google closed its mainland-based search engine, automatically redirecting searches to its Hong Kong affiliate. Hong Kong has an independent legal system, and mainland Chinese censorship laws do not apply there. After further pressure from the Chinese government, Google replaced its automatic redirect from Google China to Google Hong Kong with a link to the latter. However, the connection breaks if users search for terms that the Chinese government considers politically sensitive—including such seemingly innocuous phrases as *ying di*, the Chinese word for "best actor," which might be used to refer to the Chinese premier, Li Keqiang. When Google tried to fight this by introducing a feature that warned users that their search term could break their connection to Google, Chinese authorities disabled the feature. After a long cat-and-mouse struggle in which Google kept modifying the feature and the authorities kept cutting off Chinese users, Google finally threw in the towel at the end of 2012 and gave up trying to warn its Chinese users about sensitive search terms.

DISCUSSION QUESTIONS

1. What moral issues does this controversy raise? What obligations should Yahoo have weighed in this situation? Was the company a "traitor" to its customer, as Liu Xiabo says?

2. In your view, was Yahoo right or wrong to assist Chinese authorities? What would you have done if you were in charge of Yahoo?

3. Is Jerry Yang correct that the company had "no choice"? Assuming that Yahoo was legally required to do what it did, does that justify its conduct morally?

4. Assess the actions of Yahoo and of Microsoft, Google, and Cisco from the point of view of both the narrow and the broader views of corporate responsibility. What view of corporate responsibility do you think these companies hold? Do you think they see themselves as acting in a morally legitimate and socially responsible way?

5. In light of this case, do you think it makes sense to talk of a corporation like Yahoo as a moral agent, or is it only the people in it who can be properly described as having moral responsibility?

6. Would American companies do more good by refusing to cooperate with Chinese authorities (and risk not being able to do business in China) or by cooperating and working gradually to spread Internet freedom? In general, under what circumstances is it permissible for a company to operate in a repressive country or do business with a dictatorial regime?

7. Assess the pros and cons of a law forbidding American high-tech companies from assisting repressive foreign governments.

CASE 5.2

Drug Dilemmas

EVERYONE KNOWS HOW HIGH THE COST of prescription medicines is these days, and many Americans dislike having to pay significantly more than Canadians or Europeans do for the very same drugs. Many of them also resent the huge profit margins that drug companies enjoy in comparison with other U.S. corporations. Year after year, for over two decades the drug industry has been far and away the most profitable sector of our economy. However, many people are also inclined to accept high prices as the cost we must bear for drug research and the development of new medicines. But, in fact, the prices drug companies charge bear little relationship to the cost of making or developing them, and those prices could be cut dramatically without coming close to threatening their R&D budgets. Less than 15 percent of the sales revenue of the large pharmaceutical companies goes into R&D, half what they spend on "marketing and administration."[84]

Moreover, the pharmaceutical industry is nowhere near as innovative as most people think. According to Marcia Angell, former editor in chief of the *New England Journal of Medicine*, only a handful of important drugs have been brought to the market in recent years, and they were based mostly on taxpayer-funded research. She writes, "The great majority of 'new drugs' are not new at all but merely variations on older drugs already on the market. These are called 'me-too' drugs. The idea is to grab a share of an established, lucrative market by producing something very similar to a top-selling drug." This is made possible by the fact that the FDA will generally approve a drug if it is better than a placebo. "It needn't be better than an older drug," Angell says. "In fact it may be worse. There is no way of knowing, since companies do not test their drugs against older ones for the same conditions at equivalent doses." Of the seventy-eight drugs approved by the FDA in a recent year, only seventeen contained new active ingredients, and the FDA classified only seven of those as improvements over older drugs. And none of those seven came from a major U.S. drug company.

When it comes to research and innovation, the record of the big, profitable pharmaceutical corporations contrasts poorly with that of the small biotechnology companies that are responsible for most of today's medical advances. CV Therapeutics of Palo Alto, California, is one such company. Founded by cardiologist Louis G. Lange, it has developed a new drug, ranolazine, which promises to be the first new treatment for angina in over twenty-five years. The *Journal of the American Medical Association* has praised ranolazine as helping patients for whom standard therapies have failed. But this medical breakthrough has brought an ethical dilemma with it. Patients in Russia and Eastern Europe constituted 60 percent of the 1,000 or so test subjects involved in the studies that enabled CV Therapeutics to develop the drug. Now that the drug is ready, does the company have a moral obligation to make its drug available to them?

Other drug companies today are struggling with the same dilemma. They frequently test experimental drugs overseas, where there is less red tape and both doctors and patients are keen to participate in the tests. In Russia, for example, doctors are eager for the money they can get as study monitors, traveling to medical offices to make sure protocols are being followed. They also receive medical equipment such as treadmills for exercise testing. For their part, patients see it as a chance to get medications that they cannot afford to buy and that their government doesn't pay for. Moreover, says Richard Leach, the American business manager of a company called Russian Clinical Trials, "Eastern European and Russian people tend to be very compliant. . . . They will follow the trial and they will do whatever is asked. If they have to keep a diary, they do it. If they have to make office visits, they do it."

With at least 40 percent of drug testing now done offshore, critics worry that drug companies are exploiting their human subjects. In the United States and other well-to-do countries, experimental subjects must be given full information about the nature of the research, and they have a right to refuse to participate without penalty or consequence for their usual health care. Not so in Africa and many poor regions, where doctors profit from enrolling their patients, and local officials sometimes encourage whole villages or provinces to enroll in research programs. Conducting research overseas not only saves drug companies money, but it also circumvents FDA restrictions, which require companies to gain its approval before human testing in the United States can begin. The FDA obliges companies to describe their proposed research in detail and to file plans for guaranteeing informed consent and for monitoring the progress of the study. They must set up a review board to monitor each clinical trial and to ensure that risks to human subjects are "reasonable in relation to anticipated benefits, if any, to subjects, and the importance of the knowledge that may reasonably be expected to result." In addition, all risk must be "minimized."

Requirements for foreign research are much looser, and there is very little oversight. "Companies can conduct preliminary studies of drugs in poorer countries before formal testing even begins," writes Marcia Angell. "Quite literally, the participants are used as guinea pigs, subjects of research that really should be done on experimental animals." And when it comes to formal testing, the FDA may not learn about it until the company applies for final approval of its new drug.

These moral issues, however, are not the concern of companies like Russian Clinical Trials. Nor do they see it as their business to ask what happens when the studies end. Dr. Alan Wood, general manager of Covance, another American firm that conducts medical trials in Eastern Europe, says quite plainly, "What our clients do is not our affair."

But what about the drug companies themselves? What, if anything, do they owe overseas test subjects when their new drugs pan out? Some companies never even sell their drugs in the poor countries where they were developed. Others do, but often there are few patients who can afford them. "This is something that the biotech industry, as it develops more and more drugs, will have to come to grips with," says Carl B. Feldbaum, president of the Biotechnology Industry Organization. "It's not that we are lacking compassion, but the economics are tough."

"Do we have an obligation to everyone in the trial or to everyone in the community, the province, the nation, the region, or the world?" asks Dr. Ruth Faden, director of the Berman Bioethics Institute at Johns Hopkins University. "We really haven't figured this out." She acknowledges, though, that "many physician investigators feel uncomfortable with the idea of using patients in studies and then not being able to continue to help them when the trial ends." We seem "to have hit a wall of moral unease," she says. "I'm not sure exactly where we ought to end up."

Dr. Lawrence O. Goskin, director of the Center for Law and the Public's Health at Georgetown and Johns Hopkins Universities, is also troubled. Drug companies, he says, should not be seen as "the deep pocket that helps everyone," yet there is something disturbing about "parachute research," in which a company drops into a country, conducts its drug research, and then leaves. "It raises the question of what ethical obligation, if any, there might be to give back and make sure there is access to the drug after the trials are over."

Drug companies are businesses, of course, and they have to decide whether they can earn enough money in a foreign country to justify applying for approval to market a new drug there, then setting up a business office, and hiring a sales force. Even if they decide to provide the drug to patients free of charge—so-called compassionate use—things are not so simple. They still have to set up a distribution system, train doctors to administer the drug, and monitor the patients who take it. In the case of life-saving drugs, such as those for combating AIDS, many companies do, in fact, provide them for free or at low cost in poor countries, especially to patients who were involved in their development. But with a drug like ranolazine it's more complicated. Angina can cause terrible, crushing chest pains, and it can make the lives of chronic sufferers miserable. Ranolazine can cut in half the number of angina attacks a patient suffers, but it's not a life-saving drug. It improves the quality of patients' lives, but it doesn't extend them.

Dr. Lange, meanwhile, is torn. His company is not a charity, and because CV Therapeutics is small, it can't afford to market ranolazine in countries where few people have enough money to buy it or to set up the distribution systems necessary to give it away. "We're not Merck," he says. "But we're concerned."

DISCUSSION QUESTIONS

1. What explains the high price of prescription medicines in the United States? What if anything should be done about it? Do you believe that in the United States drug prices reflect the operation of a fair and competitive market?

2. Given the nature of their product, do pharmaceutical companies have ethical responsibilities that other

corporations don't have? In your view, are the large U.S. drug companies good corporate citizens?
3. Are the large drug companies guilty of price gouging or of charging an unfair or exploitative price for their products? Should Americans be permitted to import drugs from Canada or other countries?
4. Assess the motivations of drug companies that do their testing overseas. Do you think test subjects are being exploited or taken advantage of? Under what circumstances, if any, are companies morally justified in testing overseas?
5. Do drug companies have an obligation to make new drugs available to patients who were involved in their development, either here or overseas? Does the size of the company make a difference? What would you do if you were Dr. Lange? What obligations, ideals, and consequences should he take into account?
6. Is it ethical for companies to decline to sell a useful drug like ranolazine in a poor country because they can make more money marketing it elsewhere?
7. When it comes to life-saving drugs, do pharmaceutical companies have a moral obligation to make them available in poor countries at little or no cost? Explain why or why not. What about effective but non-life-saving drugs like ranolazine?

CASE 5.3

Free Speech or False Advertising?

WITH ANNUAL SALES OF OVER $19 BILLION and annual profits of around $1.9 billion, Nike is one of the giants in the sports apparel business, and its trademark "Swoosh" logo is recognized around the world. However, for a company of its size, Nike directly employs surprisingly few workers—only about 22,000. That is because overseas contractors manufacture all Nike's products. These independent contractors employ approximately 600,000 workers at 910 factories, mostly in China, Indonesia, Vietnam, and Thailand.

Like many other firms, Nike outsources its manufacturing to take advantage of cheap overseas labor. But the price of doing so began getting higher for Nike in the late 1990s, when anti-sweatshop activists started campaigning against the company, charging that the third-world workers making its products were exploited and abused. Activists on many college campuses, for instance, encouraged their peers to boycott Nike shoes and clothing and tried to pressure their universities' athletic departments not to sign deals with Nike for team sports apparel.

Instead of ducking the issue, as other companies might have, Nike responded vigorously to the criticisms. At the University of North Carolina, for example, Nike ran full-page ads in the student newspaper, asserting that it was a good corporate citizen and upheld humane labor standards. It sent representatives to meet with student activists, and company CEO Philip Knight took the unusual step of showing up at an undergraduate seminar on corporate globalization to defend his company. Nike issued press releases and sent letters to many college presidents and athletic departments, asserting, among other things, that Nike paid "on average, double the minimum wage as defined in countries where its products are produced" and that its workers "are protected from physical and sexual abuse."

Enter Marc Kasky, a fifty-nine-year-old San Francisco activist. He thought Nike's campaign was misleading the public about working conditions inside its factories, so he sued the company for false advertising under California's consumer protection law. In Kasky's view, the case was simply a matter of protecting consumers from corporate deceit. In response, Nike argued that the statements in question were protected by the First Amendment because they were made in news releases, letters to the editor, and op-ed essays and because they related to the company's labor practices—which are a matter of public concern—and not the products it sold. Two lower courts agreed with Nike, but then the California Supreme Court overturned their verdict, ruling in a 4–3 decision that the company's campaign was essentially commercial speech (which generally receives less First Amendment protection than political or personal speech) even though Nike was not specifically talking about shoes. In the court's view, Nike's speech was directed at customers and dealt with its business operations; the form in which the information was released was irrelevant. The judges, however, didn't determine whether Nike really did abuse workers or mislead consumers; it left those factual questions for a trial court to decide.

Nike then appealed the case to the U.S. Supreme Court. California Attorney General Bill Lockyer filed a brief in support of Kasky, which seventeen other states joined. The brief contended that the case was not about free speech but rather about "Nike's ability to exploit false facts to promote commercial ends." Harvard law professor Laurence Tribe, however, defended the company, arguing that treating Nike's letters and press releases as equivalent to advertising would undercut the ability of companies to speak out on political issues. He urged that the California decision would have a "chilling effect on freedom of speech." To this, however, the chief author of the California brief, deputy attorney general Roland Reiter, responded: "I believe the concerns expressed are really overblown. We have a company talking about itself. It's difficult to see why holding them to the truth would cause any kind of calamity." USC law professor Erwin Chemerinsky agreed. He argued that it didn't matter whether Nike issued the information in the form of a press release: "If a company makes false statements about its product or practices with the intent of increasing profits, that's commercial speech."

After having heard the case, however, the Supreme Court declined to decide the substantive legal issues at stake. Instead, it dismissed the case on a technicality and sent it back to California for trial. Before the trial began, however, Nike settled out of court with Kasky. As part of the deal, Nike agreed to donate $1.5 million to the Fair Labor Association, a sweatshop-monitoring group, and in a joint statement, Kasky and Nike "mutually agreed that investments designed to strengthen workplace monitoring and factory worker programs are more desirable than prolonged litigation." A happy ending? Not in everyone's eyes. Friends of Nike argued that because the Supreme Court did not act forthrightly to protect corporate speech, companies will be reluctant to discuss public issues involving their products. Those on the other side, however, responded that when disclosing information about wages and working conditions, companies should be held to the same standards of truth and accuracy as when they disclose financial data.[85]

DISCUSSION QUESTIONS

1. In this case, was Nike engaged in commercial speech, or were its statements political or social speech? What determines whether speech is commercial or not?

2. Was the out-of-court settlement a reasonable resolution of this case? What would have been the good or bad consequences of the Supreme Court's deciding in Nike's favor? Of its deciding in Kasky's favor?

3. Should commercial speech receive less First Amendment protection than other types of speech, or does this violate the rights of corporations? Explain your answer.

4. Do corporations have the same moral rights as individual human beings? Should they have the same political rights? Is it morally permissible to limit the speech of corporations in ways that would be wrong if applied to the speech of individual citizens? If it is permissible, is it good public policy?

5. Does Nike have a social responsibility to address matters of public concern such as the working conditions in its overseas operations? If it chooses to do so, does it have an obligation to make its statements as truthful and accurate as it can? Under what circumstances should corporations be held liable for the truth of their public statements?

CASE 5.4

Corporations and Religious Faith

IN 2012 THE SUPREME COURT UPHELD MOST of the Affordable Care Act, President Obama's signature healthcare reform law. That law requires that employer-sponsored health care policies include contraceptive coverage. This is in line with a 2002 EEOC ruling that companies that provide prescription benefits to their employees but not birth control violate Title VII of the 1964 Civil Rights Act, which forbids discrimination on grounds of sex. Although the Obama administration has exempted religiously affiliated nonprofit employers, such as Catholic charities, from financing contraceptive coverage, for-profit companies remain bound by the requirement.

Two for-profit companies, however, are challenging the rule—Hobby Lobby Stores, an arts-and-crafts chain, and Conestoga Wood Specialities, which makes kitchen cabinet doors. Based on their Christian religious beliefs, the owners of the companies oppose forms of contraception that prevent the implantation of a fertilized egg, such as the morning-after pill and various intrauterine devices. They believe that life begins when the sperm fertilizes the egg and that these forms of contraception are equivalent to abortion, violating the right to life of the fertilized egg by preventing it from attaching to the lining of the uterus. (Even without such forms of contraception, in the natural course of things fertilized eggs often fail to implant, so that pregnancy never occurs.)

In June 2013, the U.S. Court of Appeals, Tenth Circuit, upheld Hobby Lobby's position. It ruled that a corporation, as a form of association, has a right to espouse its religious beliefs regardless of its profit-seeking status. The Green family, who own the company, formed it with the "intent to provide goods and services while adhering to Christian standards as they see them, and they have made business decisions according to those standards." The Court continued:

> Would an incorporated kosher butcher really have no claim to challenge a regulation mandating non-kosher butchering practices? . . . A religious individual may enter the for-profit realm intending to demonstrate to the marketplace that a corporation can succeed financially while adhering to religious values. As a court, we do not see how we can distinguish this form of evangelism from any other.

As the Court sees it, the owners of a company do not lose their right to follow their religious beliefs by incorporating, and it rejects the "notion that Free Exercise rights turn on Congress's definition of 'non-profit.'"

A month later, however, a different appellate court—the Third Circuit of the U.S. Court of Appeals—ruled against the Hahn family, who own Conestoga Wood Specialities, holding that "secular, for-profit corporations cannot engage in religious exercise." Although the owners may have a sincere religious objection to contraceptives that act on the fertilized egg, the Court reasoned, the owners are not identical with the corporation; it is a distinct legal entity. The Affordable Care Act does not require the Hahns to do anything. The responsibility for complying with the act falls on the corporation.

> "The fact that one person owns all of the stock does not make him and the corporation one and the same person, nor does he thereby become the owner of all the property of the corporation." . . . The Hahn family chose to incorporate and conduct business through Conestoga, thereby obtaining both the advantages and disadvantages of the corporate form. . . . The free exercise claims of a company's owners cannot "pass through" to the corporation.

The Court also rejected the contention that the Supreme Court's 2010 ruling in *Citizens United* extended not just political rights but also religious rights to corporations.

In both cases, the courts were concerned not only with the First Amendment but also with the federal Religious Freedom Restoration Act (RFRA) of 1993. That law sought to nullify a high court ruling that the state of Oregon could deny unemployment benefits to people for using illegal drugs even if the drug in question (peyote) was being used as part of a Native American religious ceremony. The RFRA provides, as a general rule, that "Government shall not substantially burden a person's exercise of religion." It can restrict a person's exercise of religion only if it has a compelling interest in doing so and if there is no less restrictive means of furthering that interest.

One key question, of course, is whether the law's reference to "persons" encompasses for-profit companies. On that point, which clearly has implications for the rights of corporations that go beyond the Affordable Care Act, the two appellate courts differ. Now the Supreme Court must weigh in and decide for or against the two faith-based companies.[86]

DISCUSSION QUESTIONS

1. Although corporations are not human beings, they have a number of legal and political rights. Do they also have a First Amendment right that "Congress shall make no law . . . prohibiting the free exercise" of their religion? If so, was that right violated in this case?

2. Is it possible for corporations to have religious beliefs, or can only human beings have such beliefs? If corporations can be said to have religious beliefs, are those beliefs the same as the beliefs of the owners? What if there is not a single owner, but a number of different stockholders? What about the religious beliefs of the managers or employees—are they relevant to determining what the corporation believes?

3. The Hahns have a right to exercise their religion. Does this right transfer to any corporations they own?

4. Are corporations "persons" within the meaning of the RFRA? Do you think that Congress intended that law to apply to corporations?

5. Assuming that the RFRA applies to Hobby Lobby and Conestoga Wood Specialities, does the requirement that their health-care policies include contraception impose a "substantial burden" on their exercise of religion? Explain why or why not.

6. Both companies are privately held, meaning that their shares do not trade on the stock market. Does this fact affect the issue? If so, how?

CASE 5.5

Charity to Scouts?

"I DON'T CARE WHAT BANK OF AMERICA DOES," fumed Lynn Martin at a meeting of the board of directors of Baytown Company, a San Francisco Bay Area firm that runs four different family-oriented restaurants and owns a string of six popular fast-food take-out establishments (called "Tip-Top"). "We took a principled stand at the time," she continued, "and I don't think there's enough evidence to justify changing our minds now."

Like a lot of local companies, Baytown supports various charitable causes in the Bay Area. The company has always figured that it had an obligation to give back more to the community than good food; besides, people in the Bay Area expect local companies to display a sense of social responsibility. Among the groups that Baytown has always helped support is the regional Boy Scouts district. Not only did Baytown think the Scouts worthy of its corporate help, but giving to the organization seemed to fit well with Tip-Top's all-American theme and with the family character of Baytown's other restaurants.

A simple thing suddenly got complicated, however, when the San Francisco Bay Area United Way decided to pull $1 million in annual funding for the Scouts because of the group's refusal to admit gays. Soon after that, Bank of America, Wells Fargo Bank, and Levi Strauss & Co. also decided to stop funding the Boy Scouts. A month later, Baytown's directors resolved to follow suit.

"We were pretty clear at the time," continued Martin, "that we didn't have any business supporting an organization that was perceived as discriminatory."

"Not me," said Tom Boyd. "I always thought that since the Boy Scouts are a private group, they can do whatever they want."

"Well, maybe they have a right to discriminate if they want, but that's not the point," said Ed Framers. "The rest of us agreed with Lynn that as a company we shouldn't be helping a group that discriminates. Of course, that was before everybody around the country started making such a fuss about companies' stopping their funding of the Scouts. We all know about those anti-gay groups demonstrating against the United Way and threatening to boycott the bank."

"Those groups hardly represent thinking in the Bay Area," Lynn Martin shot back.

"That's true," agreed Scott Arming, "but still we run a family-oriented business."

"What's that supposed to mean? Do you think gays and lesbians don't come to our restaurants? Do you think they don't have families? Do you think—"

"O.K., O.K.," Arming interjected.

"Lynn's right about that," Ed Framers said. "In fact, as far as I know, our customers never said much about it, one way or the other."

Executive Director Susan Lee then spoke up: "Well, I got a few phone calls about it, but there weren't really complaints. It was more people wanting to get more information about the situation. Of course, you always get a few cranks. . . ."

"Ain't that the truth," murmured Boyd to Framers.

"Anyway," Lee continued, "things are different now. Bank of America has reversed its decision and is resuming funding to the Boy Scouts because the Scouts have lifted their ban on gays."

"That's what the bank says," said Lynn Martin. "But the whole thing is pretty murky if you ask me. Here, look at the newspaper story. The article reports company spokesman Peter Magnani as explaining that

> the bank had first interpreted the Scouts membership policy as banning gay members. But after consulting with Boy Scouts national President John Clendenin, the organization clarified its policy and 'made it clear' that membership is open to all boys who subscribe to Scouting oaths and laws. 'We take that to mean all boys, regardless of their sexual orientation,' said Magnani.[87]

"But then," Martin continued, "the newspaper goes on to quote a spokesperson for the Boy Scouts of America as saying that there has been 'absolutely no change in our policy. We do not believe that homosexuals provide positive role models.' What are we supposed to make of that? It looks as if the bank is trying to wriggle out of a stand that turned out not to be as popular as it thought it would be."

"That sounds pretty cynical," Ed Framers said. "The bank says here that its decision 'was based solely on the Scouts' clarification of its policy,' and the Scouts' national president is quoted as saying that the organization is 'open to all boys as long as they subscribe to the Boy Scouts Oath and Law.' You weren't a Scout, Lynn, but I was, and the oath and law are only basic stuff about trustworthiness and honesty; there's nothing about sexuality. Besides we're talking about boys, not adults. I think the whole thing has been blown out of proportion."

Martin quickly responded, "Don't you think boys have sexual feelings? Come on, Ed, give me a break. And besides, if there is nothing in the Scout oath or whatever it is about sexuality, why does the organization have to take a stand one way or the other?"

"Maybe the Scouts shouldn't have taken a stand," Susan Lee inserted, "but at this point it looks as if we have to. When we stopped giving to the Scouts, that sent one message; if we reverse our decision now, that sends another. Frankly, I don't like being in the position of having to impose our values, one way or the other."

"Yes, but you yourself said that there's no way to avoid it," Lynn Martin shot back. "So we should at least stand behind the right values."

"And what are those?" asked Lee.

"I don't have the slightest idea myself," Tom Boyd whispered to Scott Arming.

Arming ignored him as he turned to the group: "You know, I think we are and should continue to be a socially responsible company. But maybe we should reconsider whether being socially responsible means giving to charitable causes in the first place. Is that something we are truly obligated to do, or are we just following a fad? I mean, I hate to bring up the bottom line, but every dollar we give to the Boy Scouts or anybody else is one less dollar for the company and its stockholders."

"Come on, Scott, you know it's not as simple as that," responded Susan Lee. "Charitable contributions bring us good will, and it's the kind of thing the community expects an enlightened company to do."

"You may not be persuaded, Scott," Ed Framers added, "but I think what Susan says is right. In any case, we don't need a debate about general principles. We need to figure out what we are going to do about the Boy Scouts."

The meeting continued . . .

DISCUSSION QUESTIONS

1. What do you think Baytown should do? Explain your reasoning. What business factors are relevant to your decision? What moral factors?
2. Are Baytown's directors operating with a broad or a narrow conception of corporate responsibility?
3. Were Baytown and the other companies right to have withdrawn their support from the Boy Scouts? Is there anything wrong with companies' attempting to influence the policies of an organization like the Scouts?
4. What do you think explains Bank of America's policy reversal? Is Lynn Martin's cynicism warranted?
5. Scott Arming doubts that businesses have an obligation to support charitable organizations. Do they?

CASE 5.6

Corporate Taxation

IN THE UNITED STATES, THE RATE AT WHICH corporations are taxed ranges from 15 to 35 percent, depending on the size of their income. That's a higher top marginal tax rate than in any other developed country. But 35 percent is only the nominal rate; few if any corporations actually pay that much. Over a recent five-year period, for example, General Electric paid 17.9 percent of its income in corporate taxes, and that includes not just federal tax but state, local, and foreign taxes as well. FedEx paid 20.1 percent in federal tax, Amazon 6.6 percent, and Ford Motor Company 4.2 percent. The reason for this is that the tax code provides corporations with plenty of exemptions. In fact, a study by the Government Accountability Office estimates that 80 or so business exemptions cut in half the revenue coming from corporate taxation. Two of the biggest corporate tax breaks are accelerated depreciation of machinery and equipment and deferral of income from foreign sources.[88]

That's one of the main reasons why these days corporations pay a smaller share of the nation's taxes than they used to. In the 1950s, the revenue from corporate taxation amounted to about a third of total federal tax revenue or about 6 percent of the nation's income. Today it amounts to less than a tenth—that is, to about $1 out of every $10 collected in federal tax—or about 2 percent of national income. Personal income taxes and payroll taxes (which support Social Security and Medicare) provide about 80 percent of the federal government's annual revenue.

For many companies, tax avoidance is a sophisticated game—almost an art form. In 2013 it came out that Apple, the nation's most profitable technology company, was also one of its most successful tax avoiders, thanks to a complex web of international subsidiaries the company has created. Many of those subsidiaries are incorporated in Ireland, where Apple negotiated a special tax rate of only 2 percent, although in fact they are run from Cupertino, California. Furthermore, even though they are incorporated in Ireland, some of these offshore entities have no stated country of tax residence and thus pay no taxes at all, even though they hold tens of billions of dollars.

Other companies, such as Microsoft and Google, engage in "transfer pricing." This shifts profits generated in the United States to offshore tax havens where the IRS can't get at them. Companies accomplish this trick by transferring intellectual property rights to specially created foreign subsidiaries, which then charge the parent company stiff licensing fees for using its own intellectual property. But even low-tech companies can be good at shell games like this. Caterpillar cut its tax bill by $300 million a year simply by putting the name of a Swiss subsidiary on the invoices for parts it sent from the United States to customers around the world. Even Starbucks figured out how to play the game. It told shareholders that it was making large profits in Britain but filed U.K. tax forms showing losses, resulting in its paying no British taxes at all for three years in a row, despite billions of dollars in sales there.

With the possible exception of Caterpillar, these companies have done nothing illegal. There is a difference between tax evasion, which is illegal, and tax avoidance, which is not. Emphasizing this distinction, Judge Learned Hand famously wrote:

> Anyone may arrange his affairs so that his taxes shall be as low as possible; he is not bound to choose that pattern which best pays the treasury. There is . . . nothing sinister in so arranging affairs as to keep taxes as low as possible. Everyone does it, rich and poor alike and all do right, for nobody owes any public duty to pay more than the law demands.

Still, it strikes many people as unfair when corporations seem to be dodging their fair share of the country's tax burden. That's probably why, when news of Starbucks's tax avoidance broke, the company voluntarily agreed to pay about $16 million in British taxes. "We believe that acting responsibly makes good business sense," says Corey duBrowa, senior vice president for global communications, "and payment of corporate tax in the U.K. is a good example of this ethos in action." Some business commentators applaud Starbucks. "Just because tax avoidance is legal," writes John Cassidy, "doesn't mean that it is right."

Allan Sloan agrees; although lower taxes mean higher profits, "going to extraordinary lengths to avoid taxes helps undermine companies' long term-interest by hurting society and by giving average people yet another reason to detest Big Business."

The world's richest economies are now cooperating in an effort to curb the tax avoidance strategies used by multinational corporations. It's worth noting, though, that some economists oppose corporate taxation in principle. They think only persons should be taxed. In their view, corporate taxation involves a kind of double taxation. Corporations pay tax on their income, which is then taxed again when it gets passed on to individuals in the form of dividends. Although the tax revenue that would be lost by abolishing the corporate income tax would have to be offset by higher taxation on individuals, doing so would, these economists believe, promote economic efficiency since companies would no longer spend so much time, energy, and money trying to avoid or reduce their taxes.

DISCUSSION QUESTIONS

1. In your opinion, do corporations now pay their fair share of taxes? Explain why or why not. If not, what should be done about it?

2. Do corporations have a social responsibility not to exploit loopholes in the tax system or use accounting tricks to dodge taxes? Explain why or why not.

3. If a company like Apple is not acting illegally, is there anything wrong with its tax avoidance gimmicks? In general, is there anything wrong with either individuals or corporations arranging their affairs so as to minimize their taxes? Is that all that Apple was doing?

4. Why do you think Starbucks decided to pay voluntarily taxes it was not legally required to pay? Was this the right decision from the moral point of view? From the business point of view? Should Apple do something similar?

5. Should corporate taxation be abolished? Explain why or why not.

6. Individual income from dividends and capital gains is now taxed at a lower rate than individual income from wages. Is this fair?

7. In order to avoid U.S. taxes, some long-standing American companies have reincorporated overseas, which they can do if, after a merger or acquisition, foreign shareholders own more than 20 percent of the company. Should companies be permitted to relocate for tax purposes? Is their doing so morally acceptable? Is it unpatriotic?

PART FOUR | THE ORGANIZATION AND THE PEOPLE IN IT

CHAPTER 8

THE WORKPLACE (1): BASIC ISSUES

INTRODUCTION

A MANUFACTURER OF VINYL REPLACEMENT windows, Republic Windows and Doors had been in business in Chicago for more than forty years. On December 2, 2008, however, it abruptly announced that it was bankrupt. The following day the company told its 260 employees that it would permanently cease operations two days later, at which point their health coverage would end. The company also told the workers that they would not be receiving any severance pay or even their accrued vacation or sick pay.

Republic's workforce is represented by a labor union, the United Electrical, Radio and Machine Workers of America, which immediately filed a complaint charging that the company had violated federal law by failing to give sixty days' notice of a plant closure and that it owed the workers $1.5 million in severance and vacation pay and an extension of their medical benefits. Not content with this, however, Republic's workers quickly took more drastic measures. In a move reminiscent of the famous Flint Sit-Down Strike of 1936–37 that led to the unionization of the U.S. auto industry, they voted to take over the company's plant and sit-in until their grievances were met. The country hadn't seen anything like it for decades, and there was an outpouring of support for the workers. People came by the occupied factory to offer food and donations, the Chicago police declined to intervene, and president-elect Barack Obama publicly sided with the workers.[1]

Why the popular support for the workers, who after all were seizing private property? One reason is that Bank of America had halted Republic's line of credit because of a downturn in sales and the harsh economic climate, thus making it impossible for the company to stay in business. This infuriated people across the nation because Bank of America had recently received $25 billion from the federal government precisely in order to provide it with the funds to continue making loans to businesses and thus help keep the country out of recession. And yet here was a real American company, one that still made things, and the bank was forcing it to go under. The sit-in became a rallying point for all those who resented the government's bailing out Wall Street and the big banks while ordinary employees were left to fend for themselves. Then the public learned that Republic's owners were not quite the innocent victims they claimed to be. Before declaring bankruptcy, they had begun surreptitiously removing machinery from the factory and shipping it to a plant in Iowa belonging to a company that they had just purchased. Stopping the owners from gutting the factory was what really motivated Republic's workers to take it over.

> THEN THE PUBLIC LEARNED that Republic's owners were not quite the innocent victims they claimed to be.

Widespread media attention, demonstrations in Chicago and other cities, and political pressure resulted in the sit-in at Republic ending after just six days, when Bank of America and JP Morgan Chase agreed to loan Republic sufficient money to cover the workers' severance pay, earned vacation pay, and an extension of their health benefits. Moreover, shortly after reading about the settlement, Kevin Surace, president and CEO of Serious Materials, a Sunnyvale, California, company that specializes in eco-friendly drywall and windows, decided to buy the plant. By March 2009 he had closed the deal and rehired all of Republic's workers.[2]

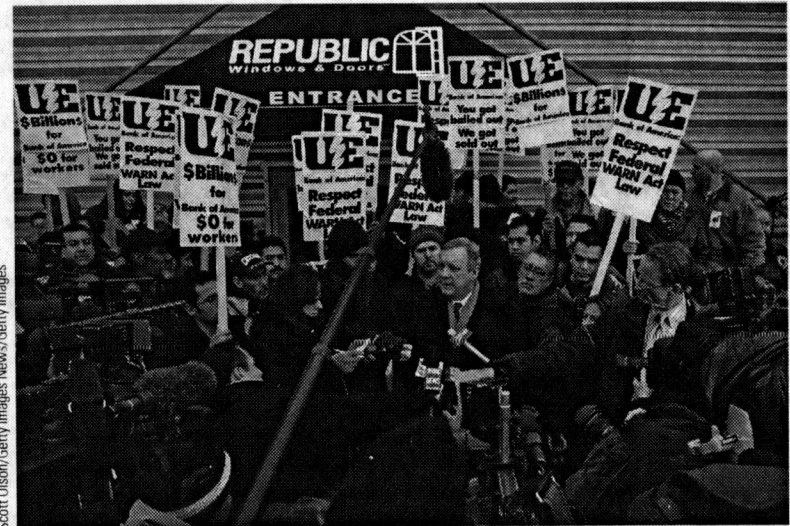

When Republic Windows and Doors announced bankruptcy and abruptly ceased operations, its workers occupied the plant. The discovery that Bank of America, the recent recipient of a federal government bailout, had closed the company's line of credit, making it impossible for it to continue operations, outraged many—as did the subsequent revelation that the company's owners had planned to strip the factory and move its machinery to another plant.

LEARNING OBJECTIVES

This story has a happy ending. But employees do not always succeed in having their rights respected, and they are not always treated fairly by their employers. The moral issues are rarely as black-and-white, though, as they were at Republic Windows. Many of the moral dilemmas that arise in the workplace, especially those concerning the civil liberties of employees and the personnel policies and procedures that govern hiring, firing, paying, and promoting them, are complicated and elude easy answer. This chapter looks at some of these issues, in particular:

1. The state of civil liberties in the workplace
2. The efforts of some successful companies to respect the rights and moral dignity of their employees
3. The moral issues that some key personnel matters—hiring, promotions, discipline and discharge, and wages—give rise to
4. The role and history of unions in our economic system, their ideals and achievements, and the moral issues they raise

CIVIL LIBERTIES IN THE WORKPLACE

Employees have all sorts of job-related concerns. Generally speaking, they want to do well at their assignments, to get along with their colleagues, and to have their contributions to the organization recognized. Their job tasks, working conditions, wages and benefits, and the possibility of promotion are among the many things that occupy their day-to-day thoughts. Aside from the actual work that they are expected to perform, employees, being human, are naturally concerned about the way their organizations treat them. Frequently they find that treatment to be morally deficient and complain that the organizations for which they work violate their moral rights and civil liberties.

Consider Lynne Gobbell, a machine operator who was fired for displaying a Democratic bumper sticker on her car, or John Stone, a car salesman who was fired by his Chicago-Bears-loving boss for wearing a Green Bay Packers tie to work, or Gonzalo Cotto, who lost his job as an aircraft factory worker for refusing to display an American flag at his workstation during a celebration of the Gulf War. Then there's

Louis MacIntire. A chemical engineer at DuPont for sixteen years, he was canned for writing a novel. Several characters in the book inveigh against various management abuses at the novel's fictional Logan Chemical Company and argue for a union for technical employees. Logan Chemical superficially resembles DuPont, and some of MacIntire's supervisors thought his veiled criticisms struck too close to home. Cotto and MacIntire tried suing their employers for violating their constitutional right of free speech, but the courts rejected their claims.[3]

The issue of free speech extends online, where companies have disciplined or discharged employees for the contents of their personal blogs or for comments on password-protected MySpace.com discussion boards. Dan Leone, a stadium worker, was fired by the Philadelphia Eagles for posting a Facebook note ("Dam[n] Eagles R Retarded") after the team traded a particular player. And Delta Air Lines sacked Ellen Simonetti for including mildly provocative photos of herself in a flight attendant's uniform on her blog, even though she wrote under a pseudonym and concealed the identity of her employer. In her blog, Rachel Mosteller, a North Carolina reporter, wrote:

> I really hate my place of employment. Seriously. Okay, first off. They have these stupid little awards that are supposed to boost company morale. So you go and do something "spectacular" (most likely, you're doing your JOB) and then somebody says "Why golly, that was spectacular." Then they sign your name on some paper, they bring you chocolate and some balloons. Okay two people in the newsroom just got it. FOR DOING THEIR JOB.

The next day she was fired—even though in her blog she never identifies herself, her employer, her coworkers, or her location.[4]

Cases like these illustrate what many see as the widespread absence of civil liberties in the workplace. "You should take your passport with you to work because all your rights as an American citizen disappear the second you walk through the office door," contends Lewis Maltby, president of the National Workrights Institute. Employees "think they have the protection of the Bill of Rights; they think they have a right to free speech; they think they have a right to privacy; and they think they have a right to be free of arbitrary punishment," he says. "And they're right—except when they go to work."[5]

David W. Ewing, former editor of *Harvard Business Review*, agrees. He sees the corporate invasion of employees' civil liberties as rampant and attacks it in scathing terms:

> In most . . . [corporate] organizations, during working hours, civil liberties are a will-o'-the-wisp. The Constitutional rights that employees have grown accustomed to in family, school, and church life generally must be left outdoors, like cars in the parking lot. As in totalitarian countries, from time to time a benevolent chief executive or department head may encourage speech, conscience, and privacy, but these scarcely can be called rights, for management can take them away at will. . . . It is fair to say that an enormous corporate archipelago has grown which, in terms of civil liberties, is as different from the rest of America as day is from night. In this archipelago . . . the system comes first, the individual second.[6]

Two historical factors, in Ewing's view, lie behind the absence of civil liberties and the prevalence of authoritarianism in the workplace. One of these factors is the rise of professional management and personnel engineering at the turn of the twentieth century, following the emergence of large corporations. This shaped the attitudes of companies toward their employees in a way hardly conducive to respecting their rights. As Frederick Winslow Taylor, generally identified as the founder of "scientific management," bluntly put it, "In the past, the man has been first. In the future, the system must be first."

The emergence of professional management and personnel engineering promoted workplace authoritarianism.

> So did the employer's traditional legal right to fire employees for no cause.

The other historical factor is that the law has traditionally given the employer a free hand in hiring and firing employees. In the nineteenth century, a Tennessee court expressed this doctrine in memorable form. Employers, the court held, "may dismiss their employees at will . . . for good cause, for no cause, or even for cause morally wrong, without thereby being guilty of legal wrong." Similarly, a California court upheld this traditional rule shortly before World War I, observing that the "arbitrary right of the employer to employ or discharge labor, with or without regard to actuating motives" is a proposition "settled beyond peradventure." The U.S. Supreme Court ratified this common-law principle in 1915, ruling that "an employer may discharge his employee for any reason, or for no reason." This "is an essential element of liberty."[7]

In addition, common law requires that an employee be loyal to an employer, acting solely for the employer's benefit in matters connected to work. The employee is duty-bound not to act or speak disloyally, except when in pursuit of his or her own interests outside work. It's no wonder, then, that traditional employer–employee law has hardly been supportive of the idea of freedom of speech and expression for employees. Against that background, the treatment of employees like Gonzalo Cotto, Louis MacIntire, or Rachel Mosteller and the refusal of the courts to see a First Amendment issue in cases like theirs are not surprising.

According to common law, then, unless there is an explicit contractual provision to the contrary—and only around 10 percent of American workers have such contracts[8]—every employment is **employment at will**, and either side is free to terminate it at any time without advance notice or reason. The common law, however, has been modified in important ways by congressional and state statutory provisions. The *Wagner Act* of 1935 (discussed later in this chapter) was, in this respect, a watershed. It prohibited firing workers because of union membership or union activities. The *Civil Rights Act of 1964* and subsequent legislation prohibit discrimination on the basis of race, religion, national origin, sex, or age. Equally important, employees in the public sector—that is, in federal, state, and local government—enjoy certain constitutional protections on the job and can be fired only "for cause." And many workers are protected by their union contracts from unjust dismissals.

> SUMMARY
> Writers such as David Ewing believe that too many corporations routinely violate the civil liberties of their employees. Historically, this authoritarianism stems from (1) the rise of professional management and personnel engineering and (2) the common-law doctrine that employees can be discharged without cause ("employment at will").

Thus, today working people have protection against some forms of unjust termination, and many of them enjoy the assurance that they can expect due process and that at least some of their civil liberties and other moral rights will be respected on the job. "But," writes Clyde Summers in *Harvard Business Review*, "random individuals who are unjustly terminated are isolated and without organizational or political voice. For them the harsh common law rule remains."[9] As a result, every year an estimated 200,000 employees are dismissed without cause.[10] Granted, that represents only a small fraction of the total number of discharged employees, but it still means that arbitrary actions by employers seriously disrupt many people's lives and that fear of dismissal is likely to have discouraged or intimidated even more employees from engaging in legitimate conduct or exercising their rights.

CURRENT TRENDS

The law is not static, however, and some courts have been willing in specific cases to break with tradition to protect employees' rights of speech, privacy, and conscience. The U.S. Supreme Court, for instance, has ruled that a state cannot deny unemployment benefits to employees who are fired because they refuse to work on their Sabbath day, even if they aren't members of an organized religion.[11] And in 1987, Montana became the first and so far the only state in the nation to enact legislation saying that workers cannot be fired without "good cause." Even without explicit legislation, wrongfully dismissed employees frequently have legal recourse. Thus, for example, a federal jury held that Mobil Chemical Company had wrongfully dismissed one of its top environmental officials after he refused to perform acts that would have violated federal and state environmental laws. The jury ordered Mobil to pay $375,000 in compensatory damages and $1 million in punitive damages.

But when Daniel Foley, district manager for Interactive Data Corporation, accurately reported to his employer that his new boss was under investigation by the FBI for embezzling funds on a former job, he was dismissed for "inadequate performance" three months later, despite a seven-year record of positive work reviews and a recent $6,700 bonus. Foley sued Interactive Data for wrongful termination, but the California Supreme Court decided that his dismissal did not violate the "public interest" and rejected his suit. And in 2006 the U.S. Supreme Court ruled that the Constitution does not protect public employees from retaliation by their supervisors for things they say in the performance of their work duties. Deputy District Attorney Richard Ceballos had urged his superiors to dismiss a pending criminal case because a police officer had allegedly lied to obtain a search warrant. His advice was rejected, and he was denied a promotion and transferred to a lesser position farther from his home. Writing for the majority in a 5-to-4 decision, Justice Anthony M. Kennedy distinguished between statements public employees make "pursuant to their official duties" and those they make as citizens contributing to the "civic discourse." The First Amendment may sometimes protect the second category but not the first.[12] (This decision concerns only public employees. For other employees, there is no general First Amendment protection at all.)

Thus, although the law seems to be gradually changing, leaving the common-law heritage of employer–employee doctrine behind, recent legal developments are complicated and not entirely consistent. The results not only depend on the details of each case but also vary from jurisdiction to jurisdiction and from court to court. As argued in Chapter 1, however, our moral obligations extend beyond merely keeping within the law.

True, some businesspeople not only support employment at will as a desirable legal policy but also embrace it as a moral doctrine. They reject the normative principle—accepted by most ordinary people—that employees should be fired only for just cause, and they deny that employers have any obligations to their employees beyond those specified by law or by explicit legal contract. Their actions, if not their words, suggest that they view the people who work for them as lacking any meaningful moral rights, seeing them as fungible assets—as means rather than ends in themselves—to be used in whatever way is profitable. But nowadays that is a minority perspective. More and more corporations are coming to acknowledge, and to design institutional procedures that respect, the rights and moral dignity of their employees. Moreover, the firms taking the lead in this regard are often among the most successful companies in the country.

This fact cuts against the old argument that corporate efficiency requires employees to sacrifice their civil liberties and other rights between 9 and 5. Without strict discipline and the firm maintenance of management prerogatives, it has been claimed, our economic system would come apart at the seams. An increasing body of evidence, however, suggests just the opposite. As Ewing writes:

> Civil liberties are far less of a threat to the requirements of effective management than are collective bargaining, labor-management committees, job enrichment, work participation, and a number of other schemes that industry takes for granted. Moreover, the companies that lead in encouraging rights—organizations such as . . . IBM . . . and Delta Air Lines—have healthier-looking bottom lines than the average corporation does.[13]

The law seems to be gradually moving away from employment at will, but our moral obligations are not limited to merely obeying the law.

COMPANIES THAT LOOK BEYOND THE BOTTOM LINE

Although under no legal compulsion to do so, a small but growing number of companies encourage employee questions and criticisms about company policies affecting the welfare of employees and the community. Some companies foster open communication through regular, informal exchanges between management and other employees. Others, such as Delta Air Lines, have top officials answer questions submitted anonymously by employees—in the absence of supervisors. Still others, such as General Electric, have a hotline for questions, worries, and reports of wrongdoing. Finally, some, like Dow Chemical, open the pages of company publications to employee questions and criticisms.

Union contracts frequently require companies to set up grievance procedures and otherwise attempt to see that their members are guaranteed due process on the job. Some enlightened nonunionized companies do the same. Some companies—including Johnson Wax, Procter & Gamble, and Aetna Life and Casualty—go further. These companies have long followed no-layoff policies. So do Lincoln Electric and Russell Corporation, the sweatshirt and athletic-wear manufacturer. Another example is Hewlett-Packard. A recession once reduced orders so much that HP management was considering a 10 percent cut in the workforce. Because laying off people was anathema, HP went a different route. It set up a working schedule of nine days out of ten for everybody in the company, from the CEO on down. The program stayed in place for six months, when orders picked up and the full ten-day schedule returned. "The net result of this program," said William Hewlett, "was that effectively all shared the burden of the recession, good people were not turned out on a very tough job market, and, I might observe, the company benefited by having in place a highly qualified work force when business returned."[14]

> Companies that respect employee rights and ensure a fair workplace tend to outperform other companies.

Not only, then, is it a moral duty of companies to respect the rights and dignity of their employees, in particular by acknowledging their civil liberties and guaranteeing them due process, but doing so can also work to the company's benefit by enhancing employee morale and, thus, the company's competitive performance. Summarizing volumes of research on human resources management and organizational behavior, Professor Bruce Barry writes that "employees who perceive that workplace procedures are fair are more likely to be satisfied with their jobs, to be committed to the organization, and to make extra contributions over and above job requirements. Evidence also links these justice perceptions with better work performance and with reduced levels of negative behaviors, such as workplace theft."[15] Hence, there is little basis for the widespread belief that efficient management is incompatible with a fair workplace environment. In fact, the publicly traded firms on *Fortune's* list of the 100 best companies to work for not only outperform the S&P 500, they "wallop it."[16]

"What I absolutely believe is that honoring the people who do the work can produce stunning results for the company," says Sidney Harmon, CEO of Harmon International Industries. "If the people in the factory believe there's a real effort to help improve their skills, provide opportunities for advancement and job security, they can do things that will blow your mind."[17] Some business writers push this point even further. For example, Robert Levering and Milton Moskowitz argue that

> The authoritarian work style—long the standard operating procedure in business—has failed. That failure is at the root of the poor performance of U.S. companies and massive layoffs in the [past]. When management is disconnected from the people who work in the company, it becomes easy to fire those people. And when workers are disconnected from what they do, it becomes easy not to care about the product or service.[18]

Of course, a company that does not sincerely consider employee rights to be of inherent moral importance is not likely to reap the benefits of enhanced business performance. Trust, as more and more management theorists are saying, is the key here, and employees can tell the difference between a company that has a genuine regard for their welfare and a company that only pretends to have moral concern.[19]

As mentioned in Chapter 1 and elsewhere, whether we are speaking of companies or of individuals, acting morally is generally in one's long-term interest: The lives of moral people tend to be more satisfying, and good companies tend to prosper. There is, however, no guarantee that one will always benefit by doing the right thing. But people or organizations that worry about whether doing the right thing will profit them or who act fairly and treat people decently only because they believe that doing so will advance their self-interest are unlikely to enjoy the benefits that accrue to those whose lives are genuinely governed by moral principle. Moreover, people or businesses who act ethically only because they believe it will pay off are likely to act unethically when they think that that will pay off.

So far, this chapter has affirmed that the workplace should provide an environment in which employees are treated fairly and their inherent dignity is respected, and it has argued that doing so can be perfectly compatible with a firm's business goals. Though important, those points are generalities. They do not provide much guidance for dealing with the specific moral issues and dilemmas that arise day in and day out on the job. The remainder of this chapter and the next take a closer look at some of these issues.

> **SUMMARY**
> Some very successful companies have taken the lead in respecting employees' rights and human dignity. Corporate profits and efficient management are compatible with a fair workplace environment.

HIRING

People make up organizations, and how an organization impinges on the lives of its members is a morally important matter. One obvious and very important way organizational conduct affects the welfare and rights of employees and potential employees is through personnel policies and procedures—that is, how the organization handles the hiring, firing, paying, and promoting of the people who work for it. These human resources procedures and policies structure an organization's basic relationship with its employees. This section on hiring and the next three sections—on promotions, discipline and discharge, and wages—look at some of the specific, morally relevant concerns to which any organization must be sensitive. Speaking generally, though, if a company's personnel decisions are to be fair, they must reflect policies and procedures that are based on criteria that are job related, clear and accessible, and applied equally.

A necessary task for almost any business is hiring. Employers strive to hire people who will enable the organization to produce the products or services it seeks to provide or to promote its other goals. Furthermore, the courts have used the principle of negligent hiring to broaden the liability of an employer for damage or injury caused by its employees—even after regular hours and away from the job site. For instance, Avis Rent-A-Car was required to pay $800,000 after a male employee raped a female employee; the jury found that the company had been negligent in hiring the man without thoroughly investigating his background.[20]

In making hiring decisions, employers must be careful to treat job applicants fairly. Determining what this involves is not always easy, but companies that put applicants on a "do not hire" list based on unverified secondhand reports or the impressions of people outside the company who have met the applicant are probably acting unjustly.[21] On the

> Fair personnel policies and decisions must be based on criteria that are clear, job related, and applied equally.

other hand, is it unfair when an applicant gets a leg up because he was referred by a current employee or a friend of the hiring manager?[22]

To bring out some of the moral issues in hiring, let's examine the principal steps it involves: screening, testing, and interviewing.

SCREENING

When firms recruit employees, they attempt to screen them—that is, to attract qualified applicants who have a good chance of succeeding at the job and to weed out applicants or potential applicants who are unlikely to work out. When done properly, **job screening** ensures a pool of competent candidates and guarantees that everyone has been dealt with fairly; when done improperly, it undermines effective recruitment and invites injustices into the hiring process.

Screening begins with a job description and a job specification. A **job description** lists all pertinent details about the content of a job, including its duties, responsibilities, working conditions, and physical requirements. A **job specification** describes the qualifications an employee needs, such as the pertinent skills, background, education, or work experience. Job descriptions and specifications must be complete and accurate. Otherwise, job candidates lack the necessary information for making informed decisions and can waste time and money pursuing jobs they are not suited for. In addition, disappointment and unfairness can result if a position is inaccurately described or wrongly classified.

That sounds simple enough. But in an effort to attract strong job candidates, hiring officers can easily, perhaps even unintentionally, begin to exaggerate what the job offers in regard to opportunities, travel, the ability to work from home, the budget one will control, and so on. And exaggeration can grow into blatant distortion. One recruiter offers this sample lexicon: "Character building" means that the job stinks, "mentoring" translates into babysitting your staff, and "work team environment" denotes noisy cubicles.[23] Exaggerations such as these may start innocently, but some businesses clearly and intentionally cross the line—for example, by deliberately misclassifying hourly workers as salaried employees to avoid paying them overtime.[24]

Wrongful Discrimination

One of the main moral concerns in screening is to avoid wrongful discrimination. For several decades, the law has forbidden discrimination against individuals on the basis of age, race, national origin, religion, or sex, and these factors should never be alluded to in job specifications or recruitment advertisements. Chapter 11 discusses the moral issues surrounding job discrimination, but it's clear that basing employment decisions on such factors almost always excludes potential employees on non-job-related grounds. Firms must therefore be careful to avoid job specifications that discriminate subtly ("excellent opportunity for college student") or employ gender-linked job terminology (e.g., "salesman" rather than "salesperson" or "waiter" rather than "server") that may discourage qualified candidates from applying.

Bona fide occupational qualifications (BFOQs) are job specifications to which the civil rights law does not apply. But BFOQs are very limited in scope. There are no BFOQs for race or color, and in the case of sex, BFOQs exist only to allow for authenticity (a male model) and modesty (a woman for a women's locker room attendant). In line with this, the Equal Employment Opportunity Commission (EEOC) filed a sex discrimination lawsuit against the restaurant chain Hooters, well known for its buxom "Hooter Girl" waitresses, for hiring only women as servers. Hooters resisted the decision,

> **SUMMARY**
> Fairness in personnel matters requires that policies, standards, and decisions affecting workers be directly job related, based on clear and available criteria, and applied equally.

claiming that the job position is legitimately defined as one that makes sex relevant. After some unfavorable publicity (for one thing, no men had complained of discrimination), the EEOC quietly dropped the suit.

In validating job specifications, firms are not permitted to rely on the preferences of their customers as a reason for discriminatory employment practices. For example, the fact that for decades airline passengers were accustomed to being attended to by young female flight attendants and may even have preferred them could not legally justify excluding men from this occupation. Similarly, a court has ruled that the fact that 20 percent of Domino's customers have a negative reaction to pizza deliverymen with beards does not constitute a substantial business justification for the company's no-beards rule. The EEOC holds that such rules discriminate against black men, who sometimes suffer from a genetic skin disorder that makes shaving difficult and painful.

Since Congress passed the **Americans with Disabilities Act (ADA)**, which became effective for all firms with fifteen or more employees in 1994, employers must be careful not to screen out disabled applicants who have the capacity to carry out the job. The ADA is intended, among other things, to protect the rights of people with disabilities to obtain gainful employment, and it forbids employers from discriminating against employees or job applicants with disabilities when making employment decisions. Employers must also make "reasonable accommodations" for an employee or a job applicant with a disability as long as doing so doesn't inflict "undue hardship" on the business.

Although the general moral imperative here is clear, in practice applying these concepts and making the appropriate determinations can be difficult. Respect for the rights of people with disabilities may sometimes have to be balanced against expense to the company or inconvenience to other employees, but the expense or inconvenience has to be very great indeed if it is to outweigh the moral injury and financial loss being borne by the person who is denied a job opportunity because of disability. There are other gray areas, too. For example, the ADA doesn't protect employees or job applicants who are addicted to drugs, but is it wrongful discrimination for a company to refuse to hire someone it had forced to resign two years earlier because of substance abuse but who is now rehabilitated?[25]

When screening potential employees, companies must also be careful to avoid unfairly excluding applicants on the basis of language, physical appearance, or lifestyle. And they should not automatically screen out potential employees because they lack qualifications that aren't really necessary or, contrariwise, are "overqualified" or because they have a gap in their employment history.

> When screening job applicants, employers should avoid excluding applicants for reasons that may be unfair or ill considered.

Language

Bilingual ability (English–Spanish, English–Vietnamese) may be a justifiable job specification in some areas of the United States, where such skills can be essential for successful job performance. But employers need to be aware of the danger of creating unnecessary specifications for a position, especially if they risk discriminating on the basis of national origin. Although the ability to communicate effectively in English is a common workplace requirement, it can impede the employment prospects of some workers. The EEOC has ruled in several cases that disqualifying a job applicant because the applicant has a pronounced foreign accent is unlawful national-origin bias unless it can be proved that the accent would hinder the job seeker's ability to perform the job. In line with this principle, the U.S. Court of Appeals in San Francisco determined that a heavy Filipino accent was a legitimate basis for rejecting an applicant for a job at a state department of motor vehicles office that required dealing with the public, even though the plaintiff had scored higher than all other candidates on a written examination.[26]

Physical Appearance

After one day, a Georgia employer changed its mind about a new employee because she "was overweight and had large breasts" and hired a smaller woman with less experience instead.[27] Though perfectly legal, the employer's conduct was morally questionable; at the very least, it was offensive and humiliating. In a handful of American cities, however, local ordinances prohibit discrimination against those who are short or overweight. On that basis, Jennifer Portnick brought a case against a San Francisco franchise of Jazzercise, a dance-fitness company. Portnick, who is 5 feet 8 inches tall and weighs 240 pounds, had applied for a job as an aerobics instructor, but Jazzercise rejected her application because it required instructors to have a "fit appearance." After the city of San Francisco sided with Portnick, Jazzercise revised its job criteria and now agrees that "it may be possible for people of varying weights to be fit."[28]

Lifestyle

Some employers wade into morally troubling waters by screening job applicants on the basis of lifestyle. For example, Multi-Developers Inc., a Georgia-based real-estate company, won't hire anyone who engages in recreational activities that are "high risk"— like motorcycling, skydiving, motor racing, mountain climbing, or flying one's own plane. In Indianapolis, Best Lock Corporation won't employ anyone who admits to taking even an occasional alcoholic drink. Other companies, such as Turner Broadcasting System, flatly refuse to hire smokers.[29] More and more companies are following suit.[30] They usually claim that doing so saves them money because employees who smoke have more health problems than nonsmokers. But many smokers resent being discriminated against as individuals on general statistical grounds. They suspect that what really underlies such policies is a holier-than-thou disapproval of smoking.

Educational Requirements

Ill-considered educational requirements are also potentially objectionable. Requiring more formal education than is truly needed for a job is unfair to less-educated candidates who, as a result, aren't even considered for the position. One of them might, in fact, turn out to be the best person for the job, which means that the firm also stands to lose.

The other side of the coin is to deny an applicant consideration because he or she seems "overqualified" in education or experience. "I'd never feel comfortable putting a really high-level candidate into a lower-level position," says one information technology recruiter. "We don't want to take you on if we think you might jump ship."[31] To avoid getting flagged as overqualified, however, some job seekers now play down their credentials by omitting advanced degrees from their résumés, changing lofty job titles, shortening descriptions of work experience, or omitting awards or other significant achievements. After sending out 100 copies of her résumé in search of receptionist work and receiving no responses, Kristin Konopka dropped her master's degree and teaching experience from her résumé. The slimmed-down version quickly brought her three callbacks and two interviews. On the other hand, recruiters and hiring officers are worried about people dumbing down their résumés. "How do I know I can trust them later down the road if there's something on their résumé they decided to take off so they could have a better chance of getting a job?" asks one.[32]

To avoid hiring someone who may become bored or frustrated by the job or who is likely to depart for greener pastures at the first opportunity, firms are justified in raising the issue. But they shouldn't proceed on the basis of assumptions that may be unwarranted. The employment ranks are filled with people successfully doing jobs for which they are technically overqualified.

> **SUMMARY**
> Misleading job descriptions and inaccurate job specifications deny applicants the information they need to make informed occupational decisions. Ordinarily, sex, age, race, national origin, and religion should not enter into personnel decisions. Discrimination against the disabled is now expressly forbidden by law. Screening on the basis of language, physical appearance, lifestyle, ill-considered educational requirements, or gaps in employment history may also be unfair.

Gap in Employment History

As traditional gender roles change, more and more men are leaving the work world for personal reasons, such as to help raise children while their wives complete professional training. These men often face obstacles when they return to work. Employers assume that a man who quit work once for personal reasons may do so again. Moreover, "there's still a stigma associated with men who put parenting on an equal footing with their jobs," says sociologist Scott Coltrane.[33] Thus, discontinuity of employment cuts some men off from job consideration, as it has so often done to women.

"The hurdles men face returning to the job market are about three times greater" than those faced by women, says Charles Arons, president and chief executive officer for Casco Industries, a Los Angeles-based employment and recruiting firm. "There isn't a male I know of in an executive position who would accept raising kids as a legitimate excuse for not working for three years." Thomas Schumann, director of selection and placement for Dayton-based Mead Corporation, agrees. "If other qualified candidates are available," he says, "my guess is that a personnel manager would go with somebody who doesn't raise that question."[34]

Certainly, employers in highly technical or rapidly changing fields are warranted in suspecting that an individual's career interruption may have left him (or her) out of touch. But to automatically disqualify a candidate because of that seems arbitrary and unfair.

TESTING

Testing is an integral part of the hiring process, especially in large firms. Tests are generally designed to measure the applicant's verbal, quantitative, and logical skills. Aptitude tests help determine an applicant's suitability for a job; skill tests measure the applicant's proficiency in specific areas, such as writing ability, data entry, or arithmetic; personality tests help determine the applicant's maturity and sociability. In addition, some firms engaged in the design and assembly of precision equipment administer dexterity tests to determine how nimbly applicants can use their hands and fingers.

To be successful, a test must be valid. **Test validity** refers to whether test scores correlate with performance in some other activity—that is, whether the test measures the skill or ability it is intended to measure. Just as important, tests must be reliable. **Test reliability** refers to whether test results are replicable—that is, whether a subject's scores will remain relatively consistent from test to test (so that a test taker won't score high one day and low the next). Clearly, not all tests are both valid and reliable. Many are not able to measure desired qualities, and others exhibit a woefully low level of forecast accuracy. Some companies use tests that haven't been designed for their particular situation. Legitimizing tests can be an expensive and time-consuming project, but if tests are used, the companies using them are obliged to ensure their validity and reliability.

Even when tests are valid and reliable, they can be unfair—for example, if the tests are culturally biased or if the skills they measure are irrelevant to job performance. The U.S. Supreme Court took a stand on this issue in 1971 in the case of *Griggs v. Duke Power Company*.[35] The case involved thirteen African-American laborers who were denied promotions because they scored low on a company-sponsored intelligence test involving verbal and mathematical puzzles. In its decision, the Court ruled that the Civil Rights Act prohibits employers from requiring a high school education or the passing of a general intelligence test as a prerequisite for employment or promotion without demonstrating that the associated skills relate directly to job performance. The *Griggs* decision makes it clear that if an employment practice such as testing has an adverse impact (or unequal effect) on minority groups, then the burden of proof is on the employer to

> Even tests that are valid and reliable can be unfair if culturally biased or irrelevant to job performance.

show the job-relatedness or business necessity of the test or other procedure. Duke Power Company couldn't do that.

In the aftermath of *Griggs* and other cases, many U.S. firms retreated from administering pre-employment tests because of doubts about their legal validity. In recent years, though, testing has made a comeback in both the public and the private sectors. Today, millions of job applicants are putting pencil to paper, or sitting down in front of a computer screen, to take skills tests, leadership tests, personality tests, loyalty tests, and tests to determine accident proneness—even tests to predict what an applicant's coworkers will think of him or her after a year on the job.[36] Management, of course, is seeking through testing to gain a potentially more productive group of workers whose skills, aptitudes, and attitudes match more closely the requirements of the job. The supposed objectivity of tests is often illusory, however. Chapter 9 will have more to say about testing when it discusses privacy, but clearly putting too much faith in tests can lead to arbitrary employment decisions, decisions that are unfair to candidates and not in the best interests of the company. Test results should therefore be treated as, at most, only one measure in an overall evaluative process. Indeed, many experts believe that even the best tests cannot substitute for face-to-face interviews.

INTERVIEWING

When moral issues arise in interviewing, they almost always relate to the manner in which the interview was conducted. Human resources experts rightly caution against rudeness, coarseness, hostility, and condescension in interviewing job applicants. In guarding against these qualities, personnel managers would do well to focus on the humanity of the individuals who sit across the desk from them, mindful of the very human need that has brought those people into the office. This is especially true when the interviewer might not otherwise identify closely with the person being interviewed because of cultural or other differences. Interviewers must exercise care to avoid thoughtless comments that may hurt or insult the person being interviewed—such as a passing remark about a candidate's physical disability or personal situation (a single parent, for instance). A comment that an unthinking interviewer might consider innocent or even friendly could be experienced as distressing or intrusive by the person across the table. For example, it can be very uncomfortable for candidates when interviewers ask, as a surprising number of them do, about their political affiliation or how they intend to vote.[37]

Roland Wall, a job placement counselor for individuals with disabilities, describes taking a developmentally disabled client, with an IQ of about 70, for a job interview. The personnel manager emerged from the room in which Wall's client was taking an initial test along with several other job applicants. The personnel manager asked Wall where his client was and was amazed to learn that she had gone in along with the others for testing. "Really?" he said. "I didn't see one in there." This personnel manager is probably more sensitive about people with disabilities than many employers, given his willingness to interview Wall's client, yet he assumed that because she was mentally retarded, the applicant would look a certain way—would look like "one."[38]

Even though everyone suffers from conscious and unconscious biases and stereotypes, interviewers should strive to free themselves as much as possible from these "idols of the mind," as the English philosopher Francis Bacon (1561–1626) called them. As Bacon put it: "The human understanding is like a false mirror, which, receiving rays irregularly, distorts and discolors the nature of things by mingling its own nature with it."[39] In short, we view things, people included, through the lens of our own

> **SUMMARY**
> A test is valid if it measures what it is meant to measure and reliable when it provides reasonably consistent results. Tests that lack validity or reliability are unfair. Tests may also be unfair if they are culturally biased or if the skills they measure do not relate directly to job performance.

> Interviewers should try to free themselves from unconscious biases, stereotypes, and preconceptions.

preconceptions. Interviewers need to keep this fact in mind. Panel interviews with a uniform list of questions for all applicants can also help increase objectivity.

That technique, however, wouldn't have helped the exceptionally well-qualified applicant who was turned down for a vice-presidential position at a West Coast sports company because he wore a dark, three-piece suit to the interview. His casually dressed interviewers simply took it for granted that he wouldn't fit into their laid-back operation.[40] This example connects to the more general problem that interviewers gravitate toward interviewees with a personality "similar to mine."[41] Indeed, research reveals that at law firms, consultancies, and investment banks the most important factor driving hiring recommendations was "shared leisure interests." Lacking "reliable predictors of future performance," writes Lauren Rivera, a sociologist at Northwestern University, assessors use "their own experiences as models of merit."[42]

Proponents of the new but increasingly popular **situational interview** claim that it predicts future job performance better than a standard interview does and also more accurately than résumé analysis, personality assessments, or pen-and-paper tests.[43] In situational interviews, job candidates have to engage in role playing in a mock office scenario. For example, they might have to face a company manager pretending to be a disgruntled customer. The company's interviewers watch and assess the candidates' performance: how they process the information given by "the customer," how they decide to handle the situation, the words they choose, and even their body language. Proponents of the technique believe that job candidates have a harder time putting on a false front during a situational interview than in a standard interview, but there's no escaping the fact that biases and preconceptions can affect the interviewers' assessment of the likely job performance of different candidates based on their role-playing skills.

> **SUMMARY**
> Most moral concerns in interviewing relate to how the interview is conducted. Interviewers should focus on the humanity of the candidate and avoid allowing their personal biases to color their evaluations.

PROMOTIONS

It's no secret that factors besides job qualifications often determine promotions. How long you've been with a firm, how well you're liked, whom you know, even when you were last promoted—all these influence promotions in the real business world. As with hiring, the key moral ideal here is fairness. Nobody would seriously argue that promoting the unqualified is fair or justifiable. It's a breach of duty to owners, other employees, and ultimately the general public. But many reasonable people debate whether promoting by job qualification alone is the fairest thing to do. Are other criteria admissible? If so, when, and how much weight should those criteria carry? These are tough questions with no easy answers. To highlight the problem, we consider seniority, inbreeding, and nepotism, three factors that sometimes serve as bases for promotions.

> Are seniority, inbreeding, and nepotism fair and reasonable bases for promotion?

SENIORITY

Seniority refers to longevity on a job or with a firm. Frequently job transfers or promotions are made strictly on the basis of seniority, but this policy can be problematic. Imagine that personnel manager Manuel Rodriguez needs to fill the job of quality-control supervisor. Carol Balke seems slightly better qualified for the job than Jim Turner, except in one respect: Turner has been on the job for three years longer than Balke. Whom should Rodriguez promote to quality-control supervisor?

The answer isn't easy. Those who would argue for Carol Balke—opponents of seniority—would undoubtedly claim that the firm has an obligation to fill the job with the most-qualified person. In this way, the firm is best served and the most qualified are rewarded. Those advancing Turner's promotion—proponents of seniority—would contend that the company should be loyal to its senior employees, that it should reward them for faithful service. In this way, employees have an incentive to work hard and to remain with the firm.

When company policies indicate what part seniority should play in promotions and job transfers, the problem abates but does not vanish. We can still wonder about the morality of the policy itself. In cases in which no clear policy exists, the problem begs for an answer.

The difficulty of the question is compounded by the fact that seniority in itself does not necessarily indicate competence or loyalty. Just because Jim Turner has been on the job three years longer than Carol Balke does not prove that he is more capable or dedicated to the company. Of course, in some instances seniority may be a real indicator of job qualifications. A pilot who has logged hundreds of hours of flying time with an airline is more qualified for captaincy than one who hasn't.

Then there's the question of employee expectations. If employees expect seniority to count substantially, management can injure morale and productivity by overlooking it. True, worker morale might suffer equally should seniority alone determine promotions. Ambitious and competent workers might see little point in refining skills and developing talents when positions are doled out strictly on the basis of longevity.

Because work situations vary, specifying what part, if any, seniority ought to play in promotions seems impossible—all the more reason, therefore, for management to consider carefully its seniority policies. Of paramount importance is that management recognize that it must seek both to promote those who are capable and qualified and who will perform well and to honor employees who have made prolonged and constructive contributions to the organization. A policy that provides for promotions strictly on the basis of qualifications seems heartless, whereas one that promotes by seniority alone seems mindless. The challenge for management is how to blend these dual responsibilities in a way that is beneficial to the firm and fair to all concerned.

INBREEDING

All the cautions about seniority apply with equal force to **inbreeding**, the practice of promoting exclusively from within the firm. In theory, whenever managers must fill positions, they should look to competence—that is, the ability to perform the job in question, regardless of whether the candidate is inside or outside the firm. In this way management best fulfills its responsibilities to the organization.

In practice, however, managers must seriously consider the impact of outside recruitment on in-house morale as well as their obligations to current employees. Although outsiders can bring a fresh perspective and even shake up a stagnant company culture, insiders can resent being passed over for advancement. This is natural. Years of loyal service, often involving personal sacrifice, create a unique relationship between employer and employee and, with it, obligations of gratitude and respect. The eighteen years that Christina Zhuy has worked for National Textile establish a relationship between her and the firm that does not exist between the company and an outsider it may be considering for the job Zhuy seeks. Some would argue that when determining promotions management has a moral obligation to remember this loyalty as well as the possible negative effects on company morale of ignoring it, especially when outside recruitment departs from established policy.

NEPOTISM

Nepotism (from the Latin word for nephew) is the practice of showing favoritism to relatives and close friends. Suppose a manager promotes a relative, her niece, say, strictly because of the relationship between them. Such an action would raise a number of moral concerns, chief among them disregard of managerial responsibilities to the organization and of fairness to other employees.

Not all instances of nepotism raise serious moral concerns. For example, when a firm is strictly a family operation and has as its purpose providing work for family members, nepotistic practices are generally justified. Moreover, many people believe that it is unfair to exclude a person from consideration for a job or for a promotion just because he or she is a relative or friend of someone in the company. In fact, Advest Group, a brokerage firm, traditionally brings sons and daughters into the organization. "Good work ethics seem to run throughout families," says senior vice president Robert Rulevich.[44] But that is probably a minority view. Today, it is more common for companies to prohibit the employment of relatives or, at least, to restrict such employment to avoid situations in which one relative is supervising another.

When it comes to senior executives, however, the matter may be different, because there's a long list of well-known, publicly traded companies that employ in lucrative positions the wives, children, and in-laws of their top managers or board members.[45] The companies in question contend that they hire and promote only on the basis of merit, but it's difficult to disagree with Charles Elson of the Center for Corporate Governance, who says, "It just doesn't look right." "It creates the appearance of a conflict of interest," adds Nell Minnow of the Corporate Library, a research firm focusing on corporate governance issues. "The burden of proof is on the company to prove it's an arms-length transaction, and that's hard to do."[46]

Even when a friend, a relative, or a spouse of a manager or some other high-ranking employee is qualified for a position or deserving of promotion, the decision can hurt company morale, breed resentment and jealousy, and create problems with regard to future placement, scheduling, or dismissal of the person. It can make him or her an object of distrust and hostility within the organization and even discourage qualified outsiders from seeking employment with the firm.

> **SUMMARY**
> Seniority, or longevity on the job, is not necessarily a measure of either ability or loyalty. The challenge for management is to promote the most competent while also recognizing long-term contributions to the company. Inbreeding, or promoting exclusively from within, presents similar challenges. Nepotism—showing favoritism to relatives or close friends—is not always objectionable, but it may slight managerial responsibilities to the organization and result in unfair treatment of other employees.

DISCIPLINE AND DISCHARGE

For an organization to function in an orderly, efficient, and productive way, managers and personnel departments establish guidelines for employee conduct based on performance factors such as punctuality, dependability, efficiency, cooperativeness, and adherence to the dress code and to other rules. This is not the place to examine the morality of specific rules and regulations; the organization's treatment of employees when infractions occur is our focus here. For example, it's one thing to speak with a person privately about some infraction and quite another to chastise or punish the person publicly. Also, trying to correct someone's behavior on a graduated basis, from oral warning to written reprimand to suspension or other punishment prior to dismissal, is different from firing someone for a first mistake. The point is that although discipline and discharge are inevitable and, indeed, necessary aspects of organizational life, they raise concerns about fairness, noninjury, and respect for persons in the way they're administered.

TWO BASIC PRINCIPLES

Just cause and due process are essential to the fair handling of disciplinary issues.

To create an atmosphere of fairness, one in which rules and standards are equally applied, the principles of "just cause" and "due process" must operate. **Just cause** requires that reasons for discipline or discharge deal directly with job performance. For example, Best Buy was probably justified in firing two Denver employees for tackling a shoplifter outside the store (who subsequently brandished a knife and escaped), even though they were celebrated as heroes in the local press.[47] It might not have been good public relations, but like most big retailers, the company has strict rules about approaching suspected shoplifters in order to minimize the risk of violence. On the other hand, AIC Securities lacked just cause for terminating with one day's notice an experienced employee with a good record because he had been diagnosed as having brain cancer.[48] And it's difficult to see why smoking in your car on company property is just cause for dismissal, even though you can be fired for it at two Motorola plants in Illinois.[49] Of course, distinguishing between a job-related and a non-job-related issue is not always easy and can be controversial.

In addition, how a person behaves outside work is often incompatible with the image a company wishes to project. Does the organization have a right to discipline its employees for off-the-job conduct—for example, the doctor who was fired by his HMO for criticizing it on a talk show and at an industry conference?[50] The answer depends largely on the legitimate extent of organizational influence over individual lives—that is, on where precisely the company's legitimate interests stop and one's private life begins. Such concerns raise complex questions about privacy that are explored further in Chapter 9.

The second principle related to fair worker discipline and discharge is **due process**, which refers to the fairness of the procedures an organization uses to impose sanctions on employees. Of particular importance is that the rules be clear and specific, that they be administered consistently and without discrimination or favoritism, and that workers who have violated them be given a fair and impartial hearing. Due process requires both the hearing of grievances and the setting up of a step-by-step procedure by which an employee can appeal a managerial decision.

DISMISSING EMPLOYEES

It is useful to distinguish among four types of discharge. **Firing** is for-cause dismissal—the result of employee theft, gross insubordination, release of proprietary information, and so on. **Termination** results from an employee's poor performance—that is, from his or her failure to fulfill expectations. **Layoff** usually refers to the temporary unemployment experienced by hourly employees and implies that they are "subject to recall." **Position elimination** designates the permanent elimination of a job as a result of workforce reduction, plant closing, or departmental consolidation.

Before dismissing an employee, management should follow a rational and unbiased decision-making process and analyze carefully the reasons leading to that decision. The organization must ask itself whether its treatment of the employee follows the appropriate procedures for that type of discharge, as those procedures are outlined in the employee handbook, in a collective bargaining agreement, or in a corporate policy statement. In addition, the company must guard against preferential treatment. Have there been employees who behaved in the same way but were not let go?

Even even-handedness and strict compliance with established procedures may not ensure fairness. For example, unless it is stated otherwise in a contract or employees have union representation, a company may not (depending on the type of case and where it occurs) be legally obligated to give reasons for firing an employee or to give advance notice. Employers who terminate someone without notice or cause may have been strictly faithful to contractual agreement or to established practice. But have they been just? Have they acted morally?

In answering those questions, it's helpful to distinguish between two employer responsibilities. Employers bear the responsibility of terminating the employment of workers who fail to fulfill their contractual obligations, but they also are obliged to terminate these workers as painlessly as possible. In other words, although employers have the right to fire, this does not mean they have the right to fire an employee in whatever way they choose. Because firing can be psychologically as well as financially devastating to employees, management should take steps to ease its effects. Moreover, crass firings hurt a company's reputation and impair its ability to attract top-notch employees.[51]

> Employers have the right to discharge employees who perform inadequately, but they should try to do so as painlessly as possible.

The literature on personnel management provides many suggestions for handling the discharge of employees compassionately and humanely, ranging from the recommendation not to notify employees of termination on Fridays, birthdays, wedding anniversaries, or the day before a holiday, to various steps to respect the terminated employee's privacy and dignity.[52] A company should not notify employees of their dismissal by e-mail,[53] nor should it give a longtime employee a pink slip, as General Dynamics did, on the day he returned to work after burying his six-year-old son.[54] And, certainly, no employer should do what John Patterson, former head of NCR, a computer company, once did. He fired an underperforming executive by taking his desk and chair outside, dousing it with kerosene, and setting it on fire in front of the poor man.[55] As a matter of policy, some companies routinely have security personnel immediately escort terminated employees out of the building to avoid their causing trouble, but this is demeaning and should be avoided except in unusual circumstances. Even when an employee is fired for misconduct, the company must be careful not to defame the person.

These days, many companies allow or even encourage employees to use their own smart phones and tablets for work-related activities. When they separate from the company, former employees are often surprised to find their phones or other devices wiped cleaned, their contents having been remotely erased by their former employer in an effort to secure company data. One ex-employee says that his iPhone looked "like it came straight from the factory." His apps, contacts, e-mail programs, family photos, and downloaded music had all vanished.[56]

The 2009 movie *Up in the Air* relates the story of a corporate downsizer. What ethical obligations do you believe companies have to employees they terminate?

One obvious thing employers can do to ease the trauma of firing is to provide sufficient notice. Although federal law requires companies to give sixty days' advance notice of plant closings, many companies ignore this legal obligation. Whenever employers have reason to suspect that employees will react to notice of their terminations in a hostile, destructive way, sufficient notice might merely take the form of severance pay. Morally speaking, what constitutes sufficient notice of termination depends primarily on the nature of the job, the availability of similar jobs, and the employee's length of service—not to mention the type of discharge and the reasons for it. Ideally, the length of notice should be spelled out in the work contract, as should the firm's policy with regard to severance pay and the maintenance of health insurance and other benefits after the end of employment.

For most people who have to do it, firing a worker is painfully difficult. To help managers with this unpleasant task, some large companies have counselors to help discharged employees deal with their emotions. Other companies seek the services of a displacement firm. For a fee, the firm sends in a specialist to work with the discharged employee to assess personal strengths and weaknesses, analyze the causes of the dismissal, and start planning a job search. Some companies grant laid-off staff continued access to employee-assistance programs that provide hotlines or counseling to deal with stress, depression, marital discord, and money problems.[57] They also try to include former employees in alumni networks, which can help them make new contacts and find jobs.

Companies that provide displacement and other services to discharged employees believe that doing so reduces resentment and possible litigation. Aiding terminated employees can prevent them from damaging a company's reputation with clients or potential future employees, and it can enhance the productivity and morale of employees who remain. Self-serving interests aside, however, companies that assist discharged employees and treat them with dignity deserve recognition for their attempt to ease the anguish of those who must fire and to help those who are terminated salvage both their interrupted careers and their self-respect.

Today, with downsizing, outsourcing, and economic recession combining to eliminate jobs, moral management requires careful study of responsibilities to workers. It's debatable whether Valiant Networks, a consulting company, did that. After laying off nearly one hundred workers, it asked them to return half of the bonuses they'd received six months earlier. Those bonuses were contingent on the employees staying with the company for a year—which the axed employees hadn't done.[58] When weighing their responsibilities to discharge employees, companies need to remember that termination of employment affects not only workers but their families and the larger community as well. It is impossible here to specify further what measures can or should be taken to ease the effects of displacement. Different circumstances suggest different approaches. Whatever the specific situation, though, firms have a moral obligation to terminate workers only for just cause and as a last resort, to follow due process and fair organizational procedures, and to treat dismissed employees as humanely as possible.

> **SUMMARY**
> Most moral issues in employee discipline and discharge concern how management carries out these unpleasant tasks. Just cause and due process are necessary for fair treatment. To ease the trauma associated with discharge, employers should provide sufficient warning, severance pay, and perhaps displacement counseling.

* * *

WAGES

Every employer faces the problem of setting wage rates and establishing salaries. From the moral point of view, it is obvious that firms should pay a fair or just wage, but what constitutes such a wage? Too many variables are involved to say with mathematical precision what a person should be paid for a particular job. The contribution to the firm, the market for labor and products, the competitive position of the company, the bargaining power of the firm and unions, seasonal labor fluctuations, and individual needs all conspire to make a simple answer impossible. The issue is further complicated by the fact that remuneration can also include health care, retirement benefits, perquisites like tips or a company car, and bonuses, commissions, and other incentive awards.

Although some writers believe that a fair wage is whatever an employee is willing to accept,[59] the moral issues are more complex than that. In an ethical organization the basis of remuneration should be distributive justice, with a wage and salary system that centers on the employee's value to the business—his or her contribution to the organization—and not on extrinsic, non-job-related considerations such as being a single parent or a relative of the CEO.[60] In addition, salary judgments should be made on criteria that are clear and publicly available and that are impersonally or objectively applied. Consideration of the following seven factors can provide the well-intentioned business manager with some ethical guidelines and help minimize the chances of setting unfair wages and salaries:

> Salaries should center on an employee's value to the business and be based on clear, publicly available criteria that are applied objectively. The following seven considerations are important.

1. **What is the law?** Federal law requires that businesses pay at least the minimum wage, but many of the nation's garment-sewing shops fail to do so. Since 1938, the federal Fair Labor Standards Act has required employers to pay overtime for every hour worked beyond forty in a week—a law that is violated when companies force employees to work off the clock or skip meal breaks.[61] The Fair Labor Standards Act doesn't apply to executives, professionals, and other white-collar workers, but as more and more office tasks become standardized, the old blue-collar/white-collar divide is blurring and a person's job title may not reveal what he or she really does. As a result some companies violate the law by failing to pay required overtime to certain office workers, technical and support personnel, accountants, mortgage brokers, store managers, and even stockbrokers.[62] Other companies violate wage laws when they misclassify workers as independent contractors, deny employees legally mandated benefits, or fail to distribute tips or other gratuities to them.[63]

2. **What is the prevailing wage in the industry?** The salaries given for similar positions in the industry can provide some direction for arriving at a fair wage, but this factor is not a moral barometer, and relying on it can be problematic. For example, when the Jackson, Mississippi, police department raised the pay of junior officers to stop their being poached by better-paying municipalities, the older and more senior officers, whose salaries were higher, charged age discrimination because they were left out.[64] Were they justified in doing so?

3. **What is the community wage level?** Some communities have a higher cost of living than others. For example, it is more expensive to live in New York City than in Little Rock. This is one reason many cities or counties and about a dozen states have enacted "living-wage" ordinances that raise the federal minimum wage by up to several dollars an hour. These days the concept of a community wage level includes not only basic maintenance but also medical coverage. In line with this, some states have begun publishing the names of companies with the most employees eligible for public health care programs in an attempt to shame them into improving health benefits.[65]

4. **What is the nature of the job itself?** Some jobs require more training, experience, and education than others. Some are stressful or very demanding, physically or emotionally. Some jobs are downright dangerous; others are viewed as demeaning or intrinsically undesirable. Risky, disagreeable, or unskilled jobs often attract the least-educated applicants and the most desperate for work, thus leading to possible worker exploitation. Although it is impossible to draw a precise correlation between the nature of the job and what someone should be paid, a relationship exists that must be taken into account.

5. **Is the job secure? What are its prospects?** Employment that promises little or no security fails to fulfill a basic need of employees. In such cases employers should seek to compensate workers through higher pay, better fringe benefits, or both. A secure job with a guarantee of regular work and excellent retirement benefits (such as a civil service position) may justify a more moderate wage. In addition, a relatively low salary may be acceptable for a job that is understood to be a stepping-stone to better positions inside the organization.

6. **What are the employer's financial capabilities?** What can the organization afford to pay? A start-up company with minimal cash flow and a narrow profit margin may be unable to pay more than a minimum wage. A mature company with a secure market position might easily afford to pay better wages.

7. **What are other employees inside the organization earning for comparable work?** To avoid discrimination and unfairness in setting wage rates, it is important to look at what the organization is already paying its present employees for work of a similar nature. Gross salary disparities that are not warranted by the nature of the work, the experience required, or other objective considerations can also hurt employee morale.

Companies should also think about how they pay their employees. Dozens of well-known businesses now pay hourly employees with prepaid cards, which they can use like a debit card to withdraw their wages. Switching from paychecks or direct deposit can save the company money. It sounds convenient for employees, too, but the fees can add up: $1.75 to make a withdrawal, $2.95 for a paper statement, $6 for a replacement card, and a $7 inactivity fee for not using the card. That can be a lot for a low-wage worker. Donald Yates, who works at a drive-through station at a McDonald's in Milwaukee, says that he spends $40 to $50 a month on fees associated with his JP Morgan Chase payroll card.[66]

Guidelines 6 and 7 have recently come to the fore as both employees and stockholders have begun scrutinizing the benefits and perks paid to top management. Studies have found that huge salary imbalances between those at the top and their employees create resentment: The greater the differential grows, the more employee loyalty declines and the more turnover increases.[67] That information will come as no surprise to employees of ITT, who saw the company lavish $10.4 million on Chairman Rand Araskog and $5.3 million on President Bob Rowman the very same year that it fired 125 of the 200 workers at company headquarters in order to save $20 million.[68] Nor will it surprise Caterpillar's employees. Their wages were frozen during a period when the company was recording record profits, amounting to $45,000 per year per employee, and the compensation of CEO Douglas Oberhelman jumped over 80 percent. The freeze was necessary to keep wages competitive with rival companies, Oberhelman says: "We can never make enough profit."[69] At the same time, many stockholders are getting tired of seeing company profits go to executives and not to them. Indeed, when one considers the astronomical salaries and bonuses that executives on Wall Street and at the big banks awarded themselves in 2008 after they had run their companies into the ground and left shareholders and taxpayers holding the bag, then their "executive compensation" begins to look like little more than looting.

Two other factors are equally important.

Two final factors are of equal importance with Guidelines 1 through 7. The *first* is job performance. Some people work harder or are more talented and thus accomplish more for the organization. Most businesses rightly seek to recognize and award achievement. Like an employee's base salary, however, bonuses and other awards must relate to business performance and be a function of criteria that are measurable and objectively applied. The *second* factor is how the wage agreement was arrived at. A fair wage presupposes a fair work contract, and the fairness of a work contract requires free negotiation and the informed and mutual consent of both employer and employee. When there's a surplus of workers eager and able to perform a given job, the employer enjoys a strong bargaining advantage. In situations where that advantage is great and workers are truly desperate for employment, the fairness of the work contract may be called into question.

Employees are motivated by many things. One of them is the desire to be fairly treated. Feeling that they have been reasonably rewarded for their efforts is crucial to people's self-esteem. Besides helping management discharge one of its prime moral responsibilities, establishing fair wages can enhance the work environment and remove a potential source of job dissatisfaction. This fact may help explain why economists have found that, year in and year out, firms paying the highest wages are the most profitable.[70] Costco, for example, which pays significantly better wages and provides more generous benefits than does Walmart, is also more profitable, and its employees are more loyal and productive.[71] Likewise, business is booming at the clothing company American Apparel, which, in an industry characterized by sweatshops, pays its workers $13 an hour along with overtime, health insurance, and subsidized lunches. (It even pays its mostly Latino workers while they take English classes on the premises.)[72] But nobody surpasses Semco, the Brazilian company, which lets workers set their own hours and pay. Its revenue increased from $35 million to $212 million in just six years.[73]

A LIVING WAGE

As mentioned earlier, many cities or counties and a handful of states have passed "living-wage" laws that raise the legally mandated minimum wage above federal requirements, sometimes by several dollars an hour. Often these laws apply only to businesses with city contracts, but some cities have extended them to cover all businesses above a certain size in the city's jurisdiction. In this context, a **living wage** is the amount of money a full-time employee needs to afford the necessities of life, support a family, and live above the poverty line.

Although there are different ways to determine what constitutes a living wage, the concept connects to Guideline 3 above because the amount of money in question will vary from community to community. Still, almost everywhere in the country it is impossible for a person who works full time but earns only the federally required minimum to pull himself or herself out of poverty, let alone support a family. This fact galvanizes the living-wage movement. Its supporters argue that employers have a moral obligation to pay a living wage, and they ground their case on the utilitarian injunction to promote human welfare, on the Kantian principle of respect for human dignity, or on the commonsense idea that some wages are so low as to be inherently exploitative.

Opponents of a mandated living wage argue that it is bad policy, favoring instead either eliminating or at least reducing the minimum wage.[74] They contend that living-wage laws are hard on local companies because they raise the cost of doing business. Such laws can also cost taxpayers money because local government must pay more for the goods and services it uses. Moreover, raising the price of anything inevitably lowers the demand for it. Hence, opponents argue, living-wage laws only serve to reduce the number of jobs. They also contend that living-wage advocates exaggerate the number of employees trying to support families on the minimum wage. Many low-wage workers are teenagers, living at home. Raising their wages won't help to reduce poverty. Moreover, they argue, if poverty is the issue, then this problem should be addressed by government programs, not by interfering in the marketplace and setting wages by fiat.

SUMMARY

The factors that bear on the fairness of wages include the law, the prevailing wage in the industry, the community wage level, the nature of the job, the security of the job, the company's financial capabilities, and the wages the company is paying other employees for comparable work. Also important are job performance and the manner in which the wage is established. Fairness requires a legitimate work contract, one arrived at through free negotiation and informed and mutual consent.

Various moral considerations support the idea that businesses should pay a living wage.

Critics of living-wage laws believe they cost jobs.

Standard economic theory affirms the principle that raising the minimum wage will, other things being equal, lower the demand for minimum-wage labor, thus putting some people at the bottom end of the scale out of work. These people also may be hurt if higher wages attract more skilled people to compete for those jobs. The real world, however, is complicated, and empirical evidence suggests that, in practice, increasing the minimum wage does not necessarily cost jobs or hurt the poor more than it helps them.[75] Living-wage advocates also insist that even if those laws do lead to some job loss, it is still wrong to offer people employment that does not meet this standard. It is worth it for a community to have better-paying jobs even if there are fewer jobs as a result. Moreover, advocates of living-wage laws contend that business really can afford to pay better wages and that in this day of growing economic inequality it is important to pressure them to do so.

LABOR UNIONS

This chapter and Chapter 9 are concerned with a number of moral issues that arise in the workplace between employer and employees, but no discussion of the workplace should overlook one institution that has done much to shape employer–employee relations in modern economies, influencing the terms and conditions of employment and shaping the environment in which people work—namely, labor unions. Accordingly, this section briefly examines the history and economic role of unions, the ideals that motivate them, and some of the moral dilemmas they raise.

HISTORY OF THE UNION MOVEMENT

Unions have increased the security and standard of living of working people and contributed to social stability and economic growth.

Yet employers have resisted unions at every step.

In a famous remark, Franklin D. Roosevelt said that free and independent labor unions are characteristic of a free and democratic modern nation. Many economists and students of the union movement go on to give it primary credit for raising the standard of living and increasing the security of working people in the United States. They argue that almost all the benefits enjoyed by employees today, whether they happen to be in unions or not, can be traced to union victories or to union-backed legislation. At the same time, the higher wages, paid vacations, health benefits, retirement programs, and increased job security that unions have brought have, in turn, contributed to social stability in the country and, through enhanced demand, to economic growth itself. Yet as the history of the labor movement reveals, employers have opposed unionization and union demands at almost every step of the way—often with violence.

Just as the roots of capitalism can be traced to the handicraft guilds, so the earliest efforts of American unionism can be found in the craft unions of the eighteenth century. At that time, groups of skilled artisans—carpenters, shoemakers, tailors, and the like—formed secret societies for two basic reasons: to equalize their relationship with their employers and to professionalize their crafts. They agreed on acceptable wages and working hours and pledged not to work for any employer who didn't provide them, and they set minimal admission standards for their crafts. They also agreed to keep their allegiance secret—and for good reason. Until the second half of the nineteenth century, the courts frequently convicted workers of criminal conspiracy merely for joining together, even if no strike or other illegal activity took place.

Labor historians generally consider the Knights of Labor, established in 1869, to be the first truly national trade union. The Knights endeavored to call together all workers, skilled and unskilled, black and white, male and female, into one mighty association. The Knights were followed by the American Federation of Labor (AFL). Founded in 1886, the AFL united the great national craft unions, such as iron- and steelworkers, boilermakers, tailors, coal miners, and printers, in a closely knit organizational alliance. Appealing to better-paid skilled workers, the AFL soon surpassed the Knights, and the latter eventually faded away. Under the temperate leadership of Samuel Gompers, the AFL's membership reached 500,000 within seven years, growing to around 2 million by 1917.

During this period, companies routinely used the 1890 Sherman Act, which outlawed business monopolies, to obtain anti-strike injunctions from the courts on the grounds that strikes illegally restrained trade. Usually it was sufficient merely for a company to allege that a strike might cause harm, and it was rewarded with an injunction, which made union organizing exceedingly difficult. However, with the stock-market crash of 1929 and the Great Depression that followed, public sympathy shifted toward workers. In 1932, Congress passed the *Norris–LaGuardia Act*, which prohibited federal injunctions in nonviolent labor disputes. Then in 1935 it enacted the **National Labor Relations Act** (also called the **Wagner Act**). The most important of all our labor laws, it guarantees employees the right to organize and join unions and to bargain collectively through representatives of their own choosing. It prohibits employers from interfering with employees trying to organize unions, from attempting to gain control over labor unions, from treating union workers differently from nonunion workers, and from refusing to bargain with union representatives. The act helped increase union membership to almost 12 million by the end of World War II in 1945. Most of these members belonged to the Congress of Industrial Organizations (CIO), an offshoot of the AFL that brought together various workers—auto, sheet metal, steel, and so on—into industry-wide unions. The distinct advantage of the CIO over the AFL was that CIO unions could call a firm's entire workforce out on strike rather than just its skilled workers.

Increasing union strength raised public suspicions and fears of union power. Many businesspeople and political critics encouraged these worries and quickly pointed to the wave of strikes after World War II as evidence of union abuse of power. In 1947 a newly elected Republican Congress passed the **Taft–Hartley Act**, which amended the National Labor Relations Act. Taft–Hartley outlaws *closed shops* (which hire only union members) and permits individual states to ban *union shops* (which require employees to join the union within a specified time after being hired). Today, twenty-four states, mostly in the South and West, are so-called **right-to-work states**, with **open-shop laws** on their books. These laws prohibit union contracts requiring all employees on a job site to either join the union or pay the equivalent of union dues once hired. Taft–Hartley also prohibits various labor practices designated as unfair, such as sympathetic strikes and secondary boycotts (discussed later in this chapter).

THE PLIGHT OF UNIONS TODAY

In 1955, the AFL and the CIO merged to form the **AFL-CIO**. Since then, unions have attempted to increase membership by recruiting outside basic industry—for example, in education, government, white-collar professions, and service jobs. But they have been only moderately successful. For the past twenty years, union membership has been falling, both absolutely and as a percentage of the workforce. Whereas unions represented 36 percent of the private-sector workforce in the 1950s and 20 percent in the early 1980s, today union members constitute only 6.7 percent (or approximately 7.3 million workers plus an additional 7.2 million government workers). Union membership as a percentage of the workforce is at its lowest level in the United States since 1916, substantially below what it is in Japan and most Western nations—for instance, Australia, Belgium, France, Germany, the Netherlands, and the United Kingdom. This fact may explain why hourly compensation for production workers in manufacturing is less in the United States than in those countries; in fact, on average American workers make only 85 percent of what European workers earn and only 72 percent of what their German counterparts make.[76]

In recent years, unions have been more and more on the defensive, as the industries in which they have traditionally been based have declined. The number of days lost to strikes, for instance, has been at a record low, and many unions have been forced to go along with decreases in wages and benefits. Meanwhile, the general political climate has been unfavorable to labor for the past three decades. President Reagan set the anti-union tone back in the 1980s when he fired nearly 12,000 striking air traffic controllers and broke their union. The union had been considered powerful, but it was soundly defeated. Pushed by business interests, in recent years the federal government has moved to tighten its regulation of unions and to restrict their ability to organize.[77] And several states that had been considered pro-labor, such as Wisconsin, Indiana, and Michigan, have recently passed anti-union legislation.

On the legal front, labor unions suffered a major setback when the U.S. Supreme Court ruled that private employers could "replace permanently" striking workers, even though the 1935 Wagner Act makes it illegal for employers to retaliate against workers who go on strike by "firing" them. Whatever the terminology, if workers risk losing their jobs because of a strike, then the balance of power in collective bargaining is dramatically altered. Instead of negotiating in good faith, a company can now provoke a strike, hire new workers to replace the pickets, and cut costs. And management has done exactly that in a number of cases, as many corporations have grown increasingly and aggressively anti-union.

Employers hire anti-union management consultants, hold mandatory anti-union meetings, show anti-union videos at work, have supervisors meet individually with employees to disparage unions, and distribute anti-union leaflets at work or mail them to employees' homes.[78] They try to break existing unions or prevent their formation by harassing and even firing pro-union workers and by waging vigorous, often illegal anti-union campaigns. For example, if a Walmart store thinks its employees may be planning to organize a union, corporate headquarters dispatches a union-busting team by corporate jet to deal with the problem. When, after somehow dodging the corporate police, the meat-cutting department of a Texas Walmart voted to join the Union of Food and Commercial Workers, the company responded a week later by closing the department and firing the offending employees. And it shuttered a whole store in Quebec a few months after it became the only unionized Walmart in North America.[79] It's not surprising, then, that although nearly half of the country's 84 million nonunion workers say they would vote for a union at their company, many are too intimidated to take a pro-union stance.[80]

Sometimes, even when an individual company is not anti-union, outside forces step in to fight the unions. In 2011, for instance, Volkswagen opened an assembly plant in Chattanooga, Tennessee. Surprisingly, the company was receptive to efforts by the United Auto Workers to unionize the plant. That's because unionization would have enabled it to establish a German-style works council in the plant. (U.S. labor law makes it illegal for a company to set up a works council unless the workers are represented by an outside union.) Such councils seek to foster collaboration among management and representatives of both white- and blue-collar workers as they forge policies on plant rules, working hours, vacation, and other matters. Volkswagen feels that this gives the company a competitive advantage. "They have this standardized across the world," says one employee. "We feel we are not as competitive if we don't have this collaboration." However, the governor of Tennessee and one of its senators opposed unionization of the plant, and various business-related groups organized against it with advertisements,

> In recent years, unions have been on the defensive.

SUMMARY

Working people struggled for decades to form unions and win their legal recognition. Although unions are responsible, directly or indirectly, for many of the benefits employees today enjoy, a changing economy, hostile political environment, and aggressive anti-union policies have weakened them.

pressure groups, and legal challenges. Regardless of what Volkswagen wants, they think any sort of unionization is a bad thing.[81] Their campaign succeeded, too. In February 2014, workers at the plant voted against unionizing.

Some years ago Richard Edwards and Michael Podgursky summarized labor's situation in words that still hold true today:

> Bargaining structures built up over many years are crumbling and collapsing.... Rising product market competition, deregulation, and technological changes; adverse labor force dynamics; worsening public policy; and the legacy of the long stagnation have thrust the labor movement into a qualitatively new stage. This new period is characterized ... by: (a) greater corporate mobility, power, and militancy; (b) ineffective labor law and a growing indifference, and in some cases, outright opposition of the government towards organized labor and collective bargaining; and (c) a waning belief in unions as the agents of working class interests. In these hostile circumstances, American unions face a difficult and troubling future.[82]

However, periods of economic crisis and dislocation, when accompanied by high corporate profits and a public perception of greed and unfairness, sometimes lead to increased unionization and stronger labor organizations. Some think that may begin to happen now. Moreover, many economists believe that the lack of bargaining power of ordinary American workers has made the current economic recession worse.[83] For this reason among others, President Obama has spoken of the "need to level the playing field for workers and the unions that represent their interests."[84] One way unions would like to do this is through "card check." At the same time, various other groups are stepping forward to defend the interests of nonunion workers.

Card Check

Under the National Labor Relations Act, there are two main ways for workers to form a union. One is for a majority of the workers at a company to demonstrate their desire for a union by signing up to join it (**card check**). Alternatively, if 30 percent or more of the workers sign a petition requesting union representation, then an election is organized and employees vote by secret ballot whether to have a union. However, employers can refuse to recognize a union chosen by majority signup and can demand an election instead. Recently, Congress has considered legislation that would force employers to recognize unions formed by card check. Proponents of the measure see it as a necessary response to employers' aggressive anti-union campaigns, which too often lead to union-certification elections being a mockery of democracy. They think card check gives workers a fairer chance to unionize by making it possible for them to do so before the company can begin retaliating against them. Election campaigns are also difficult for unions these days because plants are smaller and companies more decentralized. Among corporate and business leaders, however, there is fervent opposition to the measure, which they describe as an attack on the secret ballot. They contend that with card check individual workers can be pressured to sign up. To this, organized labor's supporters respond that it is companies that do the intimidating, not unions. They argue that what really concerns business, and why it is spending millions of dollars to combat the measure, is not a love of elections but rather the prospect of increased unionization. Some business leaders admit this. "We like driving the car," says Walmart CEO Lee Scott, "and we're not going to give the steering wheel to anybody but us." Bernie Marcus, cofounder and former CEO of Home Depot, agrees: "This is the demise of a civilization." Business leaders who are not actively fighting card check, he says, "should be shot; should be thrown out of their goddamn jobs."[85]

Worker Advocacy Groups

With unions as weak as they are these days, various worker advocacy groups have begun sprouting up around the country, agitating for the rights of low-wage workers in non-unionized sectors. One group marched 200 miles to the headquarters of Publix supermarkets to urge it to pay more for its tomatoes so farmworkers would earn more. Other groups have organized strikes by fast-food workers; backed Black Friday protests at Walmart; protested low wages, unpaid overtime, and misappropriated tips at various restaurants; and demonstrated against giving Apple tax breaks. The AFL-CIO, traditionally touchy about working with outside groups, is deepening its ties with them. One official spoke of creating a "labor movement that speaks for all workers, whether or not you have a [union] card in your pocket." Business groups, however, are upset. They think such groups should be subject to the same restrictions that labor unions face, such as financial disclosure, regular elections of leadership, and bans on certain sorts of picketing.[86]

UNION IDEALS

From the beginning, unions have fought to protect workers from abuses of power at the hands of employers. Employers have tremendous power over individual workers. They can hire and fire, relocate and reassign, set work hours and wages, and create rules and control working conditions. Acting individually, a worker rarely is an employer's equal in negotiating any of these items. The position of most workers acting independently is further weakened by their lack of capital, occupational limitations, and personal and family needs. Furthermore, whereas employers obviously need workers, they rarely need any particular worker. They can, generally speaking, select whomever they want, for whatever reasons they choose.

Interestingly, Adam Smith himself recognized this fundamental imbalance in his classic *The Wealth of Nations*. Regarding the respective bargaining power of workers and their "masters," or employers, he wrote that "upon all ordinary occasions" employers "have the advantage in the dispute, and force the other into a compliance with their terms."

> The masters, being fewer in number, can combine much more easily.... We have no acts of parliament against combining to lower the price of work; but many against combining to raise it. In all such disputes the masters can hold out much longer.... Though they did not employ a single workman, [employers] could generally live a year or two upon the stocks which they have already acquired. Many workmen could not subsist a week, few could subsist a month, and scarce any a year without employment. In the long run the workman may be as necessary to his master as his master is to him, but the necessity is not so immediate.[87]

In an attempt, then, to redress the balance of power in their dealings with employers, workers band together. In acting as a single body, a union, workers in effect make employers dependent on them in a way that no individual worker can. The result is a rough equality or mutual dependence, which serves as the basis for *collective bargaining*—negotiations between the representatives of organized workers and their employers over things such as wages, hours, rules, work conditions, and, increasingly, participation in decisions affecting the workplace. As the World Bank and others have recognized, by giving workers a collective voice, unions do not just push up wages. They also can improve productivity and efficiency, promote stability in the workforce, and make government less likely to meddle in the labor market.

Certainly no one can object to unionism's initial and overriding impulse: to protect workers from abuse and give them a voice in matters that affect their lives. Indeed, those two goals reflect two lofty moral ideals: noninjury and autonomy. Ironically, it is out of respect for these ideals that some individuals criticize modern unions.

The critics argue that union shops infringe on the autonomy and right of association of individual workers. Even if workers are not required to join the union but only to pay union dues or its equivalent, the critics contend, this still infringes on their freedom. In addition, evidence suggests that unionized companies sometimes treat nonunion personnel less favorably than they treat union members. Some workers have gone to court to argue that favoritism to union members is discriminatory and unlawful. Whether it is or not, it certainly raises a moral question about the right to determine for oneself organizational membership and participation.

Taking the union's viewpoint reveals competing ideals and other consequences that must be considered. *First,* there is organized labor's ideal of solidarity, which is vital to collective bargaining and to winning worker equality. Union proponents point to the fact that workers in unionized workplaces earn more than nonunionized workers and that per capita personal income is higher in states with free collective bargaining than in right-to-work states. For instance, of the twenty-four right-to-work states, only five have personal incomes above the national average. Practically speaking, if workers receive union benefits without having to pay dues, then they lack an incentive to join the union, which greatly weakens the union's ability to improve wages and strengthen workers' rights.

Second, there is a question of fairness. Is it fair for a nonunion worker to enjoy the benefits won by union members—often at great personal and organizational expense? This question arises most clearly when employees don't have to join the union but must nevertheless pay the equivalent of union dues. This policy is designed to eliminate free riders while respecting the individual worker's freedom of choice. Opponents claim that it does not so much eliminate free riders as create forced passengers.

> Unions seek to protect workers and give them a voice. Some people, however, base their criticism of unions on these same ideals.

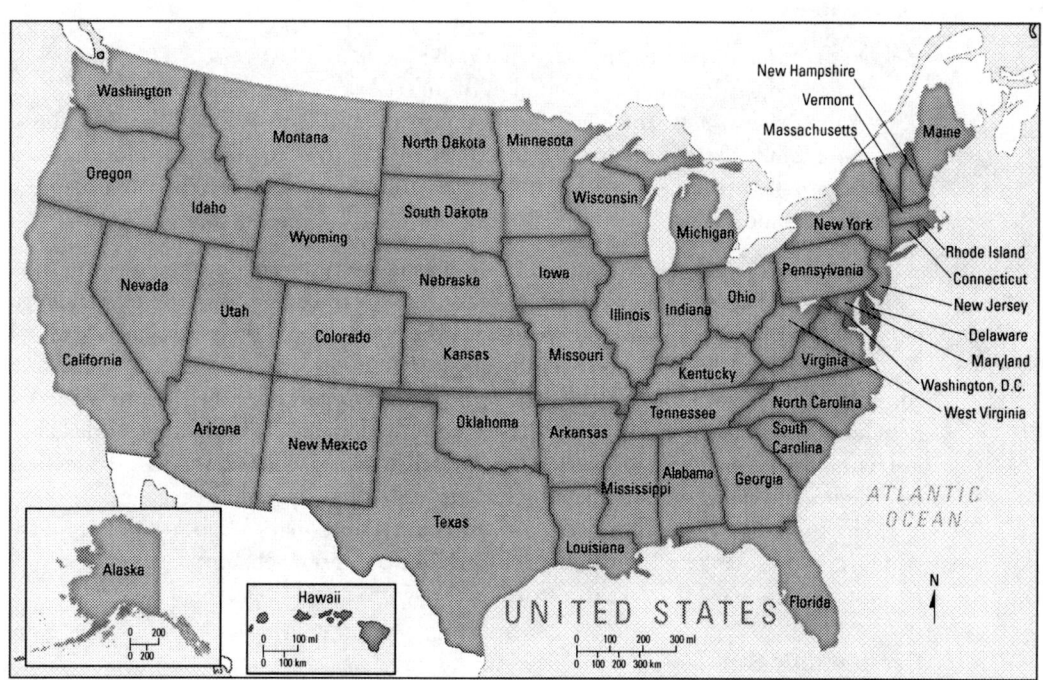

This map shows the states (in green) where employees at unionized workplaces can be required to be members of the union (or to pay dues or fees to the union) as a condition of employment and the states where the law forbids this.

UNION TACTICS

The tactics unions use to try to get management to accept their demands also raise moral issues.

Direct Strikes

By withholding their labor in a strike, workers try to compel an employer to meet their demands.

The legal right to strike is labor's most potent tool in labor–management negotiations. A strike occurs when an organized body of workers withholds its labor in an effort to pressure the employer to comply with its demands. On libertarian principles, it is clear that employees have a right to agree among themselves to stop working for an employer. However, because strikes can cause financial injuries to both employer and employee, inconvenience and perhaps worse to consumers, and economic dislocations in society, they raise serious moral questions. On the other hand, sometimes workers cannot obtain justice and fair play in the workplace in any other way. Austin Fagothey and Milton A. Gonsalves suggest the following conditions of a justified strike:[88]

1. **Just cause.** Strikes are justified only if the reasons for them are serious and job related. Certainly, inadequate pay, excessive hours, and dangerous and unhealthful working conditions are legitimate worker grievances and provide just cause for a strike. Minor workplace irritants, political ambition, and petty jealousies or personal likes and dislikes do not constitute just cause and thus cannot justify a strike.

2. **Proper authorization.** For a strike to be legitimate, it must be duly authorized. This means, first, that workers themselves must freely reach the decision without coercion and intimidation. Second, if the workers are organized, then the proposed strike must receive union backing (although this condition becomes difficult to apply when the local union chapter and the national organization don't see eye-to-eye).

3. **Last resort.** To be justified, a strike must come as a last resort. This condition acknowledges the serious potential harm of strikes. A basic moral principle is that we should always use the least injurious means available to accomplish the good we desire. Since there is an array of less drastic collective-bargaining tactics that can and usually do achieve worker objectives, all these should be exhausted before a strike is called.

Even when a strike is warranted, however, not every means of implementing it is morally justified. In general, non-violent picketing and an attempt by striking workers to publicize their cause and peacefully persuade others not to cross the picket line are moral means of striking. Physical violence, threats, intimidation, and sabotage are not. More controversially, Fagothey and Gonsalves argue that if workers have the right to withhold their labor and strike, then employers have a right to fill their jobs with other workers but not with professional strikebreakers, whose presence incites violence and whose function extends beyond doing work to denying strikers justice and the right to organize.

The preceding discussion deals with **direct strikes**—that is, cessation of work by employees with the same industrial grievance. There is, however, another kind of strike, far more controversial than the direct strike: the sympathetic strike.

Sympathetic Strikes

A **sympathetic strike** occurs when workers who have no particular grievance of their own decide to strike in support of others. Sympathetic strikes can even take on global proportions, as when American dockside workers refused to unload freighters from the

---

SUMMARY

Unions attempt to protect workers from abuse and give them a voice in matters that affect their lives. Critics charge that forcing workers to join unions infringes on autonomy and the right of association. They allege that union workers receive discriminatory and unlawful favoritism. In response, union sympathizers stress fairness and the importance of solidarity.

Soviet Union to show support of the Solidarity movement in Poland. Frequently, the sympathetic strike involves several groups of workers belonging to different unions but employed by the same company. Acting on a grievance, one group strikes. But because it is so small, it enlists the aid of the other groups; it asks them to engage in a sympathetic strike. In circumstances like this, a sympathetic strike does not seem to differ in any morally significant way from a direct strike. Indeed, it could be argued that the affiliated groups have obligations of loyalty and beneficence to join the strike. It is true, of course, that the sympathetic strikers do not have personal grievances, but they do have the same unjust employer, and they are in a position to help remedy that injustice by withholding their labor.[89]

On the other hand, however, sometimes sympathetic strikes involve employees who work for a different employer striking in support of other workers. Such strikes differ significantly from direct strikes or sympathetic strikes against the same employer. For one thing, the employers being struck out of sympathy may be perfectly innocent victims whose treatment of workers is beyond reproach. They may have lived up to their end of the work contract, only to have their workers break it.

Sympathetic strikes can be very effective, however. J. P. Stevens & Co., once the second-largest company in the U.S. textile industry, fought unionization for decades. The company engaged in a variety of flagrantly unfair labor practices and refused to recognize or bargain collectively with the union despite various court orders to do so.[90] During a boycott of J. P. Stevens products, United Auto Workers members at a General Motors plant in Canada refused to install J. P. Stevens carpeting in the cars they were producing, thus shutting down the assembly line. In less than half a day, J. P. Stevens carpeting was gone from the plant. Had U.S. workers done something similar, both they and the textile workers union would have been subject to legal action, but J. P. Stevens would not have been able to refuse to bargain as long as it did.

Boycotts and Corporate Campaigns

Besides strikes, unions also use boycotts to support their demands. A **primary boycott** occurs when union members and their supporters refuse to buy products from a company being struck. A **secondary boycott** occurs when people refuse to patronize companies that handle products of struck companies. The Taft–Hartley Act prohibits unions from organizing secondary boycotts. However, because agricultural laborers are not covered by the Wagner Act, Taft–Hartley doesn't apply to them, so the United Farm Workers union was legally able to use this tactic successfully in the 1960s and 1970s.

The express purpose of any boycott is the same as that of a strike: to hurt the employer or company financially and thus strengthen the union's bargaining position. In general, a boycott is justifiable when it meets the same conditions as a strike. In the case of the secondary boycott, which is like a sympathetic strike, the damage is extended to those whose only offense may be that they are handling the products of the unjust employer—and perhaps they are handling them out of financial necessity. In such cases, Fagothey and Gonsalves reject secondary boycotts. But this assessment seems too automatic and doesn't allow us to weigh the likely harms and benefits in particular cases.[91]

A relatively new pressure tactic by organized labor is the so-called **corporate campaign**, in which unions enlist the cooperation of a company's creditors to pressure the company to allow its employees to unionize or to comply with other union demands. For example, several unions united to mount a corporate campaign to force Washington Gas Company to settle a dispute with the International Union of Gasworkers. The Teamsters, the Service Employees International Union, the Laborers' International

---

SUMMARY
Direct strikes may be justified when there is just cause and proper authorization and when they are called as a last resort. Because they involve the cessation of work in support of other workers with a grievance, sympathetic strikes raise distinct moral concerns. Primary boycotts seem morally comparable to direct strikes, and secondary boycotts analogous to sympathetic strikes. In corporate campaigns, unions enlist the cooperation of a company's creditors to pressure the company to permit unionization or agree to union demands.

Like a strike, a boycott tries to strengthen the union's bargaining position. A secondary boycott is analogous to a sympathetic strike.

Union, and the Communications Workers of America joined forces with several local unions to pressure Crestar Bank—where Washington Gas had a line of credit—to intervene on the union side. To lean on Crestar, the unions had at their disposal pension funds, payroll accounts, normal operating capital for their organizations, and even the mortgages on their buildings. Crestar complained that it was only caught in the middle. "We are not a party to the dispute," said spokesman Barry Koling. "We are neutral with respect to the issues between them." But union spokesman Jorge Rivera responded, "We judge our business partners by their actions concerning workers."[92]

At the heart of the corporate campaign is the issue of corporate governance. In pressuring financial institutions with mass withdrawals and cancellations of policies, unions and administrators of public employee pension funds are trying to influence those institutions' policies and business relationships. And when the financial institutions accede to union demands, they in turn pressure the recalcitrant company to change its business policies. The harshest critics of the corporate campaign call it corporate blackmail. Its champions view it as an effective way to get financial institutions and companies to become good corporate citizens. Such tactics, they say, are necessary at a time when wages are stagnating, economic inequality is increasing, and management has been so successful at exploiting labor laws and regulations to undermine unions and thwart their recruitment efforts.

STUDY CORNER

KEY TERMS AND CONCEPTS

- AFL-CIO
- Americans with Disabilities Act (ADA)
- bona fide occupational qualifications (BFOQs)
- card check
- corporate campaign
- direct strike
- due process
- employment at will
- firing
- inbreeding
- job description
- job screening
- job specification
- just cause
- layoff
- living wage
- National Labor Relations Act
- nepotism
- open-shop laws
- position elimination
- primary boycott
- right-to-work state
- secondary boycott
- seniority
- situational interview
- sympathetic strike
- Taft–Hartley Act
- termination
- test reliability
- test validity
- Wagner Act

POINTS TO REVIEW

- two historical factors behind workplace authoritarianism (pp. 381–382)
- why efficiency doesn't require sacrificing employees' civil liberties and rights (pp. 383–384)
- importance of job descriptions and job specifications (p. 386)
- potentially unfair bases of screening (pp. 387–389)
- requirements of the ADA (p. 387)
- ways in which employment tests can be unfair (p. 389)
- Supreme Court's decision in *Griggs v. Duke Power Company* (pp. 389–390)
- what we can learn from Francis Bacon (pp. 390–391)
- pros and cons of nepotism, inbreeding, and promotion on the basis of seniority (pp. 391–393)
- two key principles related to discipline and discharge (p. 394)
- four types of discharge (p. 394)
- seven guidelines to bear in mind when assessing the fairness of wages (pp. 397–398)
- two other important factors that bear on the fairness of wages (pp. 398–399)

- considerations for and against living-wage laws (pp. 399–400)
- historical development of unions (pp. 400–401)
- situation of unions today (pp. 401–403)
- the pros and cons of card check (p. 403)
- what Adam Smith had to say about workers and masters (p. 404)
- the goals and ideals of unions (pp. 404–405)
- what the critics of unions say (p. 405)
- different types of strikes and boycotts (pp. 406–408)

FOR FURTHER REFLECTION

1. Give examples, if possible from your own employment experiences, of companies' respecting the rights of employees and of companies' failing to do so.
2. When it comes to a company's personnel policies and procedures—that is, how it handles the hiring, firing, promoting, and paying of the people who work for it—what do you see as the most important moral principles for it to bear in mind?
3. Explain why you either support or disapprove of unions.

CASE 8.1

AIDS in the Workplace

CARLA LOMBARD ALWAYS WORKED WELL WITH people. So when she opened her Better Bagels bagel shop seven years ago, she anticipated that managing her employees would be the easy part. She had worked for enough different bosses that she thought she knew what it took to be a good employer. Whether she was up to the financial side of running a business was her worry. As it turned out, however, Better Bagels flourished. Not only did Carla go on to open three smaller branches of Better Bagels, but her bakery also made daily wholesale deliveries to dozens of coffee shops and restaurants around the city. No, the business was prospering. It was just that the personnel issues turned out to be more difficult than she had ever expected. Take this week, for example.

On Tuesday, Carla was in the main bagel shop when around noon Tom Walters's ex-wife, Frances, came in. Tom oversaw a lot of the early-morning baking at that shop and like most of Carla's employees put in his share of time working the sales counter. He was a good worker, and Carla had been considering promoting him next month to manager of one of the branch shops. After ordering a bagel, Frances took Carla aside. She beat around the bush for a few minutes before she got to her point, because she was there to tell Carla that Tom had AIDS. Frances said she was telling Carla because she "always liked her and thought she was entitled to know because she was Tom's employer." Carla barely knew Frances, and she was so taken aback that she was at a loss for words. She was shocked and embarrassed and didn't know whether she should even discuss Tom with Frances. While Carla was still trying to recover herself, Frances took her bagel and left.

Carla was still concerned and upset when she saw Tom the next day. Perhaps he had been thinner and looked tired more often the last few months, Carla thought to herself. But she couldn't be sure, and Tom seemed to be his usual upbeat self. Carla wanted to discuss Frances's visit with Tom, but she couldn't bring herself to mention it. She had always liked Tom, but—face it, she thought—he's my employee, not my friend.

And it's his business. If I were an employee, I wouldn't want my boss asking me about my health.

Later, however, she began to wonder if it wasn't her business after all. She overheard some customers saying that people were staying away from the local Denny's franchise because one of its cooks was reported to have AIDS. The rumor was that some of his fellow employees had even circulated a petition saying that the cook should go, but a local AIDS support group had intervened, threatening legal action. So the cook was staying, but the customers weren't. Carla knew something about AIDS and thought some of what her customers were saying was bigoted and ill informed. She was pretty sure that you couldn't transmit HIV through food—including bagel—preparation, but she thought that maybe she should double-check her information. But what was really beginning to worry her were the business implications. She didn't want a Denny's-like situation at Better Bagels, but in her customers' comments she could see the possibility of something like that happening once the word got out about Tom, especially if she made him a manager. Carla was running a business, and even if her customers' fears might be irrational or exaggerated, she couldn't force them to visit her shops or eat her bagels.

Carla knew it was illegal to fire Tom for having AIDS, and in any case that's not the kind of person she was. But she couldn't afford to skirt the whole problem, she realized, as some large companies do, by simply sending the employee home at full pay. Doing that deprives the employee of meaningful work, to be sure, but it removes any difficulties in the workplace, and the employee has no legal grounds for complaint if he or she is left on the payroll. And then, of course, there was always the question of Tom's future work performance. Putting the question of promotion aside, if he really was ill, as Frances had said, his work performance would probably decline, she thought. Shouldn't she begin developing some plan for dealing with that?

Update

Frances was misinformed. Tom didn't have AIDS. He had developed multiple sclerosis, a degenerative disease of the central nervous system. It's not fatal, but the course of the disease is unpredictable. Attacks can occur at any time and then fade away. A person can feel fine one day, only to have an attack the next day that causes blurred vision, slurred speech, numbness, or even blindness and paralysis. Tom was never worried about losing his job, and he was pretty sure he could continue to perform well at it, maybe even move higher in the business either with Carla or with another employer. But he kept his condition to himself, hiding his symptoms and covering up occasional absences and trips to the doctor, because he was worried that customers and colleagues would perceive him differently. He didn't want looks of pity if he stumbled or constant questions about how he was feeling.

DISCUSSION QUESTIONS

1. What are the moral issues in this case? What ideals, obligations, and consequences must Carla Lombard consider? What rights, if any, are at stake? Will it make a difference whether Carla adopts a Kantian approach or a utilitarian approach to this situation?

2. Would it be wrong of Carla to ask Tom Walters about his health? Why or why not? Defend your answer by appeal to moral principle.

3. Suppose Tom had AIDS. What should Carla do? Is an employee's HIV status a job-related issue? In particular, is it a factor Carla should consider in deciding whether to promote Tom? What part, if any, should the attitudes of Tom's coworkers play in Carla's decision?

4. How should companies address the problem of public fear and prejudice when employees with AIDS have direct contact with customers?

5. Should companies develop programs or policies that deal specifically with AIDS? If so, what characteristics should they have? Or should they deal with the problem only on a case-by-case basis? Should large corporations develop AIDS-awareness programs? Or should AIDS be treated no differently than any other disease?

6. Does Tom have a moral obligation to disclose his medical condition to Carla—and, if so, at what point? Suppose a job applicant has a chronic, potentially debilitating medical condition. Should he or she reveal that fact before being hired? Would it be wrong not to mention the disease if the interviewer inquires about the applicant's health?

CASE 8.2

Web Porn at Work

AL SMETANA IS THE FOUNDING PRESIDENT OF a medium-size, midwestern manufacturing firm, Rayburn Unlimited. He's proud of the way his company has grown, and done so on the basis of an organizational culture committed to honesty, integrity, and the intrinsic value of each individual. But now those values are being put to the test.

It began when Al learned that an employee had tapped into the company's computer system and figured out how to read people's e-mail and to learn what websites they visited. Determining who the culprit was wasn't difficult. When confronted about it, the employee admitted what he had done. Al immediately terminated his employment. But as he left, the employee said angrily, "Just ask Lindley about his computer usage," referring to Craig Lindley, associate vice president for human resources and an old friend of Al's. Although Al didn't trust the discharged employee, he was disturbed by his comment and reluctant to let it go. So he called Craig Lindley into his office and asked him about it.

After a few minutes of gentle questioning, Craig started weeping. When he recovered himself, he explained that for the past year or so he had been hooked on pornography on the web and at the office sometimes spent an hour or so a day looking at it. Al asked him whether his wife knew. Craig said she didn't. He was too ashamed of his habit to talk to her or anybody else about it. Al then told him to take the rest of the day off, to think the matter over, and to return to Al's office the next morning. When Craig left, Al stood and looked out the window, silently asking himself what he should do.[93]

DISCUSSION QUESTIONS

1. Is Craig Lindley's behavior a sign of some psychological problem that Rayburn Unlimited should help him overcome, perhaps with personal counseling? Or is dismissal called for? Should Al Smetana fire Craig to send a message to other employees not to misuse company time and resources?

2. Does Al have just cause for dismissing Craig? Does it matter whether or not Rayburn Unlimited has an explicit policy regarding computer use? Suppose it has such a policy and Craig violated it. Does that settle the matter? Would it affect your judgment of the case if Craig had helped draw up that policy?

3. Does the fact that Craig is a valued member of the company with a long record of service make a difference? Or that he is a personal friend of Al's?

4. Was it right for Al to have asked Craig about his computer usage in the first place? Did he violate Craig's privacy or civil liberties?

5. Because Al fired the employee who violated the company's computer system, would it be inconsistent or unfair of him to treat Craig any differently?

6. Al Smetana and Rayburn Unlimited are committed to honesty and integrity (the upholding of which seems to support dismissal) and the intrinsic worth of each individual (which might argue for more lenient treatment). Are these values in conflict? What would you do if you were Al?

CASE 8.3

Speaking Out about Malt

WHEN MARY DAVIS, ASSOCIATE VICE PRESIDENT for plant management at Whitewater Brewing Company, wrote an article for a large metropolitan newspaper in her state, she hadn't realized where it would lead. At first she was thrilled to see her words published. Then she was just worried about keeping her job.

It all started when her husband, Bob, who was working on his MBA, talked her into taking an evening class with him. She did and, to her surprise, really got into the course, spending most of her weekends that semester working on her term project—a study of wine and beer marketing. Among other things her essay discussed those respectable wine companies like E. & J. Gallo (the nation's largest) that market cheap, fortified wines such as Thunderbird and Night Train Express. With an alcohol content 50 percent greater and a price far less than regular wine, these screw-top wines are seldom advertised and rarely seen outside poor neighborhoods, but they represent a multimillion dollar industry. Skid-row winos are their major consumers, a fact that evidently embarrasses Gallo, because it doesn't even put its company name on the label.

Mary's essay went on to raise some moral questions about the marketing of malt liquor, a beer brewed with sugar for an extra punch of alcohol. It has been around for about forty years; what is relatively new is the larger size of the container. A few years ago, the industry introduced malt liquor in 40-ounce bottles that sell for about three dollars. Packing an alcohol content roughly equivalent to six 12-ounce beers or five cocktails, 40s quickly became the favorite high of many inner-city teenagers. Ads for competing brands stress potency—"It's got more" or "The Real Power"—and often use gang slang. Get "your girl in the mood quicker and get your jimmy thicker," raps Ice Cube in a commercial for St. Ides malt liquor. Like baggy pants and baseball caps turned backward, 40s soon moved from the inner city to the suburbs. Teenage drinkers like the quick drunk, and this worries drug counselors. They call 40s "liquid crack" and "date rape brew."

Mary's instructor liked her article and encouraged her to rewrite it for the newspaper. The problem was that Whitewater also brews a malt liquor, called Rafter, which it had recently started offering in a 40-ounce bottle. True, Mary's article mentioned Whitewater's brand only in passing, but top management was distressed by her criticisms of the whole industry, which, they thought, damaged its image and increased the likelihood of further state and federal regulation. The board of directors thought Mary had acted irresponsibly, and Ralph Jenkins, the CEO, had written her a memo on the board's behalf instructing her not to comment publicly about malt liquor without first clearing her remarks with him. Mary was hurt and angry.

"I admit that the way the newspaper edited my essay and played up the malt liquor aspect made it more sensationalistic," Mary explained to her colleague Susan Montoya, "but everything I said was true."

"I'm sure it was factual," replied Susan, "but the company thought the slant was negative. I mean, lots of ordinary people drink Rafter."

"I know that. Bob even drinks it sometimes. I don't know why they are so upset about my article. I barely mentioned Rafter. Anyway, it's not like Rafter is a big moneymaker. Most of our other beers outsell it."

"Well," continued Susan, "the company is really touchy about the whole issue. They think the product is under political attack these days and that you were disloyal."

"That's not true," Mary replied. "I'm no troublemaker, and I have always worked hard for Whitewater. But I do think they and the other companies are wrong to market malt liquor the way they do. It only makes a bad situation worse."

The next day Mary met with Ralph Jenkins and told him that she felt Whitewater was "invading," as she put it, her rights as a citizen. In fact, she had been invited to speak about wine and beer marketing at a local high school as part of its antidrug campaign. She intended to keep her speaking engagement and would not subject her remarks to company censorship.

Jenkins listened but didn't say much, simply repeating what he had already written in his memo. But two days later Mary received what was, in effect, an ultimatum. She must either conform with his original order or submit her resignation.

DISCUSSION QUESTIONS

1. Do you think Mary Davis acted irresponsibly or disloyally? Does Whitewater have a legitimate concern about her speaking out on this issue? Does the company have a right to abridge her freedom of expression?
2. Is your answer to question 1 affected by whether you agree or disagree with the views Mary Davis expressed?
3. Should there be any limits on an employee's freedom of expression? If not, why not? If so, under what circumstances is a company justified in restricting an employee's right to speak out?
4. The case presentation doesn't specify whether the newspaper article identified Mary Davis as an employee of Whitewater. Is that a relevant issue? Does it matter what position in the company Mary Davis holds?
5. What do you think Mary Davis ought to do? What moral considerations should she weigh? Does she have conflicting obligations? If so, what are they?
6. Is the company right to be worried about what Mary Davis writes or says, or is the board of directors exaggerating the potential harm to Whitewater of her discussing these issues?
7. Assume a CEO like Ralph Jenkins is legitimately worried that an employee is making damaging statements about the company. How should the CEO handle the situation? Is discharge or some sort of discipline called for? Should the company adopt a formal policy regarding employee speech? If so, what policy would you recommend?

CASE 8.4

Have Gun, Will Travel . . . to Work

ORGANIZATIONAL THEORISTS AND EMPLOYEE advocates frequently emphasize the importance, from both a moral and a practical point of view, of companies' respecting the rights of their employees. Many employees spend long hours at work and remain tethered to the job by phone or computer even when they are off-site; not just their careers but also their friendships, social identity, and emotional lives are tied up with their work. All the more reason, it seems, that companies should recognize and respect their moral, political, and legal rights. But enshrined in our Constitution is one right that frequently gets overlooked in discussions of the workplace: the right to bear arms.[94]

In 2002 Weyerhaeuser, the Seattle-based timber-products company, fired several employees at an Oklahoma plant who were discovered to have violated company policy by keeping guns in their vehicles. Their dismissal provoked a response from the National Rifle Association (NRA) and other gun-rights advocates, which since then have been lobbying for legislation that would make it illegal for companies to bar employees from leaving guns in their cars in company parking lots. Although no state requires companies to allow workers to carry weapons into the workplace, four states have passed laws guaranteeing them the right to keep guns in their cars, and several other states are weighing whether to follow suit. Gun advocates argue that licensed gun owners should have access to their weapons in case they need them on the trek to and from work. If an employer can ban guns from workers' cars, "it would be a wrecking ball to the Second Amendment" of the U.S. Constitution, says Wayne LaPierre, executive vice president of the NRA.

Brian Siebel, a senior attorney at the Brady Center to Prevent Gun Violence, thinks otherwise. He sees these laws as "a systematic attempt to force guns into every nook and cranny in society and prohibit anyone, whether it's private employers or college campuses . . . from barring guns from their premises." But that's not how UCLA law professor Eugene Volokh looks at it. "It's part of the general movement," he says, "to allow people to have guns for self-defense not only at home, but in public places where they're most likely needed." For his part, LaPierre of the NRA contends that the legal right of people to have guns for personal protection is largely nullified if employers can ban guns from the parking lot. "Saying you can protect yourself with a firearm when you get off work late at night," he argues, "is meaningless if you can't keep it in the trunk of your car when you're at work."

Interpreting the somewhat ambiguous language of the Second Amendment is not easy. It only says, "A well-regulated Militia, being necessary to the security of a free State, the right of the people to keep and bear Arms, shall not be infringed." All jurists agree, however, that the Second Amendment does not make all forms of gun control unconstitutional and that, like the rest of the Bill of Rights, it places restrictions only on what government, not private parties, may do.

In particular, the Second Amendment does not give gun owners a constitutionally protected right to carry their weapons onto somebody else's private property against the wishes of the owner. "If I said to somebody, 'You can't bring your gun into my house,' that person's rights would not be violated," explains Mark Tushnet, a Harvard law professor. For this reason, the American Bar Association sides with business owners and endorses "the traditional property rights of private employers and other private property owners to exclude" people with firearms. Steve Halverson, president of a Jacksonville, Florida, construction company agrees that business owners should be allowed to decide whether to allow weapons in their parking lots. "The larger issue is property rights," he says, "and whether you as a homeowner and I as a business owner ought to have the right to say what comes onto our property." However, Tennessee state senator Paul Stanley, a Republican sponsor of legislation requiring that guns be allowed in company parking lots, begs to differ. "I respect property and business rights," he says. "But I also think that some issues need to overshadow this. . . . We have a right to keep and bear arms." Other gun advocates think that the property-rights argument is a red herring. Corporations are not individuals, they argue, but artificial legal entities, whose "rights" are entirely at the discretion of the state. What's really going on, they think, is that some companies have an anti-gun political agenda.

Property rights, however, aren't the only thing that companies are concerned about. Business and other organizations have a widely acknowledged duty to keep their workplaces—and their employees—as safe as possible, and that means, many of them believe, keeping their campuses free of weapons. There are more than 500 workplace homicides per year; in addition, 1.5 million employees are assaulted at work, many of them by coworkers or former employees. Having guns anywhere in the vicinity, many employers worry, can only make volatile situations more deadly. "There's no need to allow guns [into] parking lots," says the Brady Center's Siebel. "The increased risks are obvious." Steve Halveson drives that point home, too. "I object to anyone telling me that we can't . . . take steps necessary to protect our employees." For him it's no different from banning guns from his construction sites or requiring workers to wear hard hats. "The context is worker safety, and that's why it's important."

DISCUSSION QUESTIONS

1. Do you have not only a legal right but also a moral right to own a gun? Assume that either the Second Amendment or state law gives you a legal right to keep a gun in your car when you drive. Do you also have a moral right to do this? Do you have either a moral or a legal right to park a car with a loaded gun in a privately owned public parking lot regardless of what the lot's owner wants?

2. In your view, do employees have either a moral or a legal right to park cars with guns in them in the company parking lot? If so, what about the property rights and safety

concerns of employers? If employees don't have this right, would it be good policy for companies to allow them to stow guns in their cars anyway? Do companies have good grounds for being concerned about weapons in their parking lots?

3. Do you agree with the NRA that if companies ban guns from their parking lots, this restriction would take "a wrecking ball to the Second Amendment" or nullify the right of people to have weapons for self-defense? Explain why or why not. In your view, have gun advocates been guilty of politicizing this issue? Do you think state legislatures are right to get involved, or should the matter be left to companies and employees to settle?

4. Because the workplace is the company's private property, the company could choose, if it wished, to allow employees to bring guns not only into the parking lot but also into the workplace itself. Are there ever circumstances in which doing so might be reasonable? Or would the presence of guns automatically violate the rights of other employees to be guaranteed a safe working environment?

5. What would a libertarian say about this issue? What considerations would a utilitarian have to take into account? What conclusion might he or she draw?

6. If you were on a company's board of directors, what policy would you recommend regarding handguns, rifles, or other weapons in employees' cars? In making your recommendation, what factors would you take into account? Would it make a difference how large the company was, the nature of its workforce, or where it was located? If you support banning firearms from the parking lot, what steps, if any, do you think the company should take to enforce that policy?

7. Explain whether (and why) you agree or disagree with the following argument: "If employees have a right to keep guns in the parking lot, then they also have a right to bring them into workplace. After all, we're only talking about licensed, responsible owners, and the same rationale applies: An employee might need a weapon for self-protection. What if a lunatic starts shooting up the company?"

CASE 8.5

Union Discrimination

THE NATIONAL RIGHT TO WORK LEGAL Defense Foundation is one of several anti-union organizations that have been active in recent years. The "right to work," in this context, means the alleged right of an individual to work without being obliged to join a union or pay union dues. To put it the other way around, it means that companies cannot sign contracts with unions agreeing to hire only workers who are willing to join the union or at least to pay the equivalent of union dues.

What follows is one of the Foundation's advertisements, titled "Job Discrimination . . . It Still Exists":[95]

Paul Robertson is not a member of a persecuted minority. But he has experienced blatant discrimination all the same because he has chosen not to join a union.

Paul Robertson is a working man, a skilled licensed electrician with more than twenty years experience. He found out the hard way how a big company and a big union can discriminate on the job.

Paul was hired by the Bechtel Power Corporation to work on their Jim Bridger Power Plant project in the Rock Springs, Wyoming, area. Only three months later, he was fired, supposedly because of a reduction in force.

But during the week preceding his discharge, Bechtel hired at least nineteen union electricians referred by the local union and retained at least sixty-five unlicensed electricians.

A determined Paul Robertson filed unfair labor practice charges against the company and the union.

An administrative law judge ruled and was upheld by the full National Labor Relations Board that the union and the employer had indeed discriminated. The judge ordered that Robertson and seven other electricians be given the back pay they would have earned if they had been treated fairly.

The NLRB later reversed part of its decision, but Paul Robertson did not give up. With the help of the National Right to Work Legal Defense Foundation, he appealed the Board's decision to the U.S. Court of Appeals, arguing that hiring hall favoritism is discriminatory and unlawful.

Paul Robertson was fortunate. He found experienced legal help—all important because the case dragged on for nearly four years in the courts and the union still refused to obey the NLRB's back-pay order.

The National Right to Work Legal Defense Foundation is helping everyone it can—currently in more than seventy-five cases involving academic and political freedom, protection from union violence, and other fundamental rights. But it would like to do even more.

If you'd like to help workers like Paul Robertson write to: The National Right to Work Legal Defense Foundation. . . .

DISCUSSION QUESTIONS

1. Assuming the Foundation's description of the case is accurate, was Paul Robertson treated unfairly? Was this a case of discrimination? If Robertson was an "at-will" employee, does he have any legitimate grounds for complaint?

2. Does it make a difference to your assessment of the case whether someone like Robertson knows, when he accepts a job, that he must join the union or that nonunion employees will be the first to be laid off?

3. If union employees negotiate a contract with management, part of which specifies that management will not hire nonunion employees, does this violate anyone's rights? Would a libertarian agree that the resulting union shop was perfectly acceptable?

4. Presumably Paul Robertson could have joined the union, but he chose not to. What principle, if any, do you think he was fighting for? Assess the union charge that people like Paul Robertson are "free riders" who want the benefits and wages that unionization has brought but try to avoid paying the dues that make those benefits and wages possible.

5. What do you see as the likely motivations of Bechtel Power and the union? How would they justify their conduct?

6. Why did the Foundation run this ad? Is the ad anti-union propaganda? Do you think the Foundation is sincerely interested in the rights of individual workers? Or is it simply interested in weakening unions vis-à-vis management?

7. Assess union shops from the moral point of view. What conflicting rights, interests, and ideals are at stake? What are the positive and negative consequences of permitting union shops?

CHAPTER 9

THE WORKPLACE (2): TODAY'S CHALLENGES

INTRODUCTION

IT WAS A ROUTINE BUSINESS DAY FOR EASTERN Airlines—until it received an anonymous tip that some of its baggage handlers at Miami International Airport were using drugs. Eastern quickly sprang into action, ordering security guards to round up the ten employees then at work in the airport's plane-loading area. The employees were marched between two rows of guards and into waiting vans—"like terrorists," a lawsuit later claimed—all in full view of other employees and passengers. After questioning the workers, suspicious supervisors put them on a bus, once again in front of onlookers, and took them to a hospital. There the employees were given an ultimatum: Either take a urine test or be fired on the spot.

The baggage handlers were union members, but they caved in and took the test. All ten of them tested negative (that is, free of drugs), but they weren't happy about what they'd been through. Not long afterward, they filed suit against the airline in federal court, seeking damages of $30,000 each on charges of invasion of privacy, defamation, and intentional infliction of emotional distress. Eastern has since gone out of business, but the case represents in dramatic form one of the major issues dividing employers and employees today: privacy. Companies are delving further into employees' personal lives than ever before, claiming the need to monitor their behavior and probe into their health and habits. Workers are resisting ever more adamantly, fighting back for the right to be left alone.

> COMPANIES ARE DELVING
> *further into employees'*
> *personal lives than*
> *ever before . . .*

In 1928, U.S. Supreme Court Justice Louis D. Brandeis described the right to privacy, or "the right to be let alone," as "the most comprehensive of rights and the right most valued by civilized men." He was referring to the Fourth Amendment's guarantee that citizens are protected against illegal searches and seizures by government. Today, many Americans are resisting invasions of their privacy not just by government agencies or pesky telemarketers but also by intrusive employers. And not without reason: One survey shows that American companies tend to be less respectful of employees' rights to privacy than their counterparts in Europe and Canada.[1]

It's not only ordinary employees, either, whose privacy companies sometimes fail to respect, as the world learned when the Hewlett-Packard boardroom exploded in controversy a few years ago. Concerned about leaks of confidential company information to the *Wall Street Journal* from someone on H-P's board of directors, board chairwoman Patricia Dunn had authorized the company's legal and security personnel to investigate. They did, and at a meeting of the board a few months later, the culprit was disclosed. Board member Jay Keyworth admitted to the group that he was the leaker but refused to resign. However, his friend and fellow board member Tom Perkins, a Silicon Valley venture capitalist, was so outraged at H-P's snooping into the phone records of board members that he resigned on the spot and stormed out of the meeting. End of story? Not quite. Perkins managed to get the ear of California's attorney general and other law-enforcement agencies, which launched an investigation into the legality of H-P's spy tactics—in particular, its "pretexting" or use of false pretenses to obtain phone records and other personal information. This eventually led to a congressional hearing, recriminations and denial of responsibility by various H-P executives, and, finally, criminal charges against Dunn and several underlings.²

Businesses and other organizations frequently believe, as Eastern Airlines and Hewlett-Packard evidently did, that they have a compelling need to know about the lives and conduct of their employees, whether on or off the job—a need that they believe justifies invading their privacy. Employees, however, tend to think otherwise, and more and more frequently these days they are responding by asserting a right to a personal sphere not subject to the needs, interests, or curiosity of their employers. "I don't think politicians and corporate executives realize how strongly Americans feel about it," says a San Francisco lawyer who specializes in employee lawsuits. "It's not a liberal or a conservative issue, and the fear of abuse doesn't emanate from personnel policies. It's coming out of the larger, impersonal notion that workers are fungible, expendable items."³

LEARNING OBJECTIVES

Chapter 8 examined personnel policies and procedures, trade unions, the state of civil liberties on the job, and the efforts of some successful companies to respect the rights, dignity, and moral integrity of their workers. This chapter also focuses on moral issues that emerge in the workplace. It looks in detail at one crucial civil liberty—the right to privacy—and at the ethical choices it poses inside the organization. The remainder of the chapter examines several other topics that are stirring up controversy in today's workplace. More specifically, this chapter explores the following:

1. The nature of privacy and the problems of organizational influence over private decisions
2. The moral issues raised by the use of polygraph, personality, and drug tests and by the monitoring of employees in the workplace
3. Working conditions—in particular, health and safety, styles of management, and provision of day-care facilities and maternity leave
4. Job satisfaction and dissatisfaction and the prospects for enhancing the quality of work life

ORGANIZATIONAL INFLUENCE IN PRIVATE LIVES

Privacy is widely acknowledged to be a fundamental right, yet corporate behavior and policies often threaten privacy, especially in the case of employees. One way this happens is through the release of personal information about employees. The data banks and personnel files of business and nonbusiness organizations contain an immense amount of private information, the disclosure of which can seriously violate employees' rights. Most firms guard their files closely and restrict the type of material that they can contain in the first place, but the potential for abuse is still great. Although a complicated set of laws and court rulings limits access to such information, a wide range of snoops still manage, legitimately or illegitimately, to get their hands on it.

As a related matter, more employees are successfully suing their former bosses for passing on damaging information to prospective employers. The courts have traditionally considered this sort of information exchange between employers to be "privileged," but companies can lose this protection by giving information to too many people or by making false reports. Through fear of defamation suits, in fact, many organizations now refuse to reveal anything about former employees except their dates of employment. Such reticence obviously makes it more difficult for companies to screen job applicants.

More significant are the threats to privacy that can arise on the job itself. For example, some bosses unhesitatingly rummage through the files of their workers, even when they are marked "private." Some companies routinely eavesdrop on their employees' phone calls, and a majority of them read their employees' e-mail and monitor their

How would you feel about being asked to supply a urine sample for drug testing by an employer?

use of the Internet.[4] Voice mail isn't safe, either, as Michael Huttcut, a manager of a McDonald's outlet in St. Louis, learned the hard way. He was having an affair with a coworker, and the romantic voice-mail messages he sent her were retrieved and played by his boss. When Huttcut complained, he was fired.[5] Other companies secretly quiz managers—or even call in private investigators—to gain knowledge about the personal habits and behavior of workers who call in sick.[6] Meanwhile, GPS technology lets companies track employees when they are in their company vehicles—often without their knowledge.[7]

Equally important is the way organizations attempt to influence behavior that ought properly to be left to the discretion of their employees—in particular, by trying to impose their own values on their workers. For example, Walmart fired Lauren Allen, who was married but separated from her husband, for dating a coworker, who was single. Walmart says that it "strongly believes in and supports the 'family unit'" and that the conduct of Allen and her coworker violated the company's rules.[8] Or consider the case of Virginia Rulon-Miller, a marketing manager in IBM's office products division. She made the mistake of falling in love. A week after receiving a 13.3 percent pay raise, she was called on the carpet for dating Matt Blum, a former IBM account manager who had gone to work for a competitor. She and Blum had begun dating when Blum was at IBM, and he still played on the IBM softball team. IBM told Rulon-Miller to give up Blum or be demoted. "I was so steeped in IBM culture," she says, "that I was going to break up with Matt." But the next day, before she had a chance to do anything, she was dismissed. Even though IBM's decision was based on written policy governing conflicts of interest, a California jury decided that Rulon-Miller's privacy had been invaded. It awarded her $300,000.

A year later, however, the Oregon Supreme Court upheld JCPenney's firing of a merchandising manager for dating another employee. He claimed that his right to privacy had been violated. Although it may seem harsh to fire an employee on the basis of personal lifestyle, the Oregon court said, private firms aren't barred from discriminating against workers for their choice of mates. And a federal district court permitted the firing of a New Mexico employee with an excellent work record because she was married to a worker at a competing supermarket.[9]

It's not only in affairs of the heart that companies sometimes intrude into the personal sphere of employees by imposing their values on them or telling them what to think or do in matters that bear little relation to their jobs. Some executives, for example, find themselves pressured to contribute cash to their company's political action committee.[10] And now that the Supreme Court's 2010 *Citizens United* decision has freed companies to use corporate money to endorse and campaign for political candidates, many of them are urging—some would say pressuring—their employees to vote for specific politicians.[11] It's hard to wear a pin or sport a bumper sticker or voice your support for a candidate against whom your company is campaigning.

THE IMPORTANCE OF PRIVACY

Both in the workplace and in general, our concern for privacy seems to have at least three dimensions to it. *First*, we want to control intimate or personal information about ourselves and not permit it to be freely available to everyone. We are concerned to limit the people who have certain kinds of knowledge about us, to control the means by which they can acquire it, and to restrict those to whom they may disclose it. *Second*, we wish to keep certain thoughts, feelings, and behavior free from the scrutiny, monitoring, or observation of strangers. We don't want our private selves to be on public display. *Third*, we value being able to make certain personal decisions autonomously. We seek to preserve and protect a sphere in which we can choose to think and act for ourselves, free from the illegitimate influence of our employers and others.

> Our concern for privacy has three aspects.

There is, however, no consensus among philosophers or lawyers about how precisely to define the concept of privacy, how far the right to privacy extends, or how to balance a concern for privacy against other moral considerations. All of us would agree, nonetheless, that we have a clear right to keep private certain areas of our lives and that we need to have our privacy respected if we are to function as complete, self-governing agents.

Even when a genuine privacy right is identified, the strength of that right depends on circumstances—in particular, on competing rights and interests. Privacy is not an absolute value. Corporations and other organizations often have legitimate interests that may conflict with the privacy concerns of employees. Determining when organizational infringement on a person's private sphere is morally justifiable is, of course, precisely the question at issue.

As a general rule, though, whenever an organization infringes on what would normally be considered the personal sphere of an individual, it bears the burden of establishing the legitimacy of that infringement. The fact that a firm thinks an action or policy is justifiable does not, of course, make it so. The firm must show both that it has some legitimate interest at stake and that the steps it is taking to protect that interest are reasonable and morally permissible. But what are the areas of legitimate organizational influence over the individual?

> The burden is on the organization to establish the legitimacy of encroaching on the personal sphere of the individual.

LEGITIMATE AND ILLEGITIMATE INFLUENCE

Employers are naturally and legitimately interested in anything that significantly influences employee work performance. What constitutes a significant influence on work performance, however, is often debatable.

Take, for example, the area of dress and grooming. A roofing company has a legitimate interest in the type and quality of shoes its workers wear because footwear affects safety and job performance. And perhaps specialty clothing stores such as Gap, Polo Ralph Lauren, and Abercrombie & Fitch have legitimate grounds for requiring their employees to dress in the store's latest styles. Enterprise Rent-A-Car also puts a high priority on employee grooming and appearance. It lays down thirty dress-code guidelines for female employees (no denim or skirts more than 2 inches above the knee) and twenty-six rules for male employees (no beards; dress shirts with coordinated ties). More debatable was the company's requiring employee Angela Garrett to remove the red tints from her hair because they weren't "appropriate" for her ethnic group (she's African American).[12] Likewise, it's questionable whether a genuine corporate interest was at stake when an airline ticket agent was fired for refusing to wear makeup or when American Airlines forbade a black employee from wearing her hair in corn rows because the style was thought to clash with the company's corporate image. Or consider the case of Debrahlee Lorenzana, an attractive thirty-three-year-old single mother. A Citibank branch fired her for wearing clothes—pencil skirts, turtlenecks, tailored jackets, and stiletto heels—that purportedly made her curvy figure "too distracting" to her male colleagues. When she pointed out that some female coworkers shopped where she shopped and wore the same styles, she was told that their unattractiveness made their sartorial choices irrelevant.[13]

A firm has a legitimate interest in employee conduct off the job only if it affects work performance.

The general proposition that a firm has a legitimate interest only in employee behavior that significantly influences work performance applies equally to **off-the-job conduct**. Bank of America probably ran afoul of this guideline when it fired Michael Thomasson, a legal secretary, for working as a gay stripper during his off-hours. After a coworker read a personal letter Thomasson had written on a company computer that mentioned his job as an exotic dancer, a group of bank employees, including several of Thomasson's supervisors, went to see him perform. Two weeks later he was dismissed—despite a record of positive job evaluations and a recent merit raise.[14]

Years ago, Henry Ford made his autoworkers' wages conditional on their good behavior outside the factory. He had 150 inspectors whose job was to keep tabs on his employees' hygiene and housekeeping habits. And Milton Hershey, another famous business leader, used to tour Hershey, Pennsylvania, the chocolate-manufacturing town, to make sure his workers were keeping up their lawns. He even hired private detectives to find out who was throwing trash in Hershey Park.[15] These days it's easy to say that Ford and Hershey crossed the line and were poking their noses into aspects of their employees' lives that had nothing to do with their jobs. In other cases, though, determining when off-the-job conduct bears on job performance can be difficult.

How would you decide the following case? In an off-the-job fight, a plant guard drew a gun on his antagonist. Although no one was injured, the guard's employer viewed the incident as grounds for dismissal. The employer reasoned that such an action indicated a lack of judgment by the guard. Do you think the employer had a right to fire the guard under those circumstances? The courts did. By contrast, consider the employee who sold a small amount of marijuana to an undercover agent, or the employee who made obscene phone calls to the teenage daughter of a client. Their employers fired them, but the employees were reinstated by an arbitrator or the court.

SUMMARY

Individuals have a right to privacy, in particular, a right to control certain information about themselves, to shelter aspects of their lives from public scrutiny, and to make personal decisions autonomously, free from illegitimate influence. Whenever an organization infringes on an individual's personal sphere, it must justify that infringement.

Then there's the amorphous area of company image and the question of whether it can be affected by off-the-job conduct. For example, the image a firm wishes to project might be hurt by the political activities of a corporate executive but probably not by what a low-level worker on an assembly line does. To be sure, companies and other organizations have a legitimate interest in protecting their good names, and the off-duty conduct of any employee could conceivably damage an organization's reputation. But in practice damage is often difficult to establish. For example, two IRS agents were suspended for mooning a group of women after leaving a bar. Would you agree with their suspension? An arbitrator didn't and revoked it. He couldn't see that their conduct damaged the IRS's reputation.[16]

Obviously we can't spell out exactly when off-duty conduct affects company image in some material way, any more than we can say precisely what constitutes a significant influence on job performance. But that doesn't prevent us from being able to judge that in many cases organizations step beyond legitimate boundaries and interfere with what should properly be personal decisions by their employees. That interference can take many forms, but two are worth looking at more closely.

Involvement in Civic Activities

To enhance their image in the community, businesses and other organizations have long prodded employees to donate to charitable causes during company-led fund-raising drives or encouraged them to participate in **civic activities** off the job—for example, by running for the local school board or joining community service organizations, such as Kiwanis, Lions, or Rotary. Moreover, the past decade has seen a boom in corporate-sponsored employee volunteer programs, with more and more firms encouraging employees to spend off-duty hours helping out at designated charities or donning a company T-shirt and pitching in on Saturdays at some company-run philanthropic project.[17]

There's no question that the trend toward corporate volunteer programs has been good for society. One in four adults does at least some volunteer work, and corporate programs have probably drawn many of them into doing so. But such programs can collide with accelerating job demands, forcing employees to spend valued off-duty time away from their families and fueling employee resentment and burnout. Moreover, the programs can raise moral questions, especially as the pressure to participate increases. Some employers have "unwritten rules" requiring volunteer work; other companies award employees points for approved volunteer work on their performance evaluations. Employees also have been downgraded, disciplined, or even fired for not contributing the "suggested" amount of money to the United Way or other charitable cause sponsored by the firm. The pressure can be real, too, when the boss solicits donations for his or her favorite charity or goes cubicle to cubicle with a sign-up sheet for Girl Scout cookies.[18]

By striving too hard for a do-gooder image, a company can thus be guilty of attempting to influence the personal choices and off-the-job behavior of employees in ways that constitute an invasion of privacy. By explicitly or implicitly requiring employees to associate themselves with a particular activity, group, or cause, firms are telling workers what to believe, what values to support, and what goals to promote outside work.

Wellness Programs

Sometimes organizations pressure employees in certain directions for "their own good." For example, a group of employers led by Ford, PepsiCo, and General Mills are campaigning to get their overweight employees to slim down.[19] And **wellness programs**, which push employees toward healthier lifestyles, are now a common feature of the corporate landscape. These paternalistic programs are aimed at helping employees live longer and improve their health and productivity. The programs teach them about nutrition, exercise, stress, and heart disease and encourage them to give up smoking, eat more healthfully, moderate their drinking, and work out in the company gym or join a company sports team after work.[20]

Wellness programs try to make fitness part of the corporate culture, and that goal seems innocent enough. But some companies are making employees pay more for their health care benefits if they are overweight, have high blood pressure, or don't exercise.[21] And employees have been fired for having a drink at home or for refusing to take a test to prove they're nonsmokers.[22] Penn State requires employees to pay a monthly surcharge of $100 if they do not fill out a detailed health risk assessment form.[23] Other organizations offer employees financial incentives for agreeing to complete health questionnaires, undergo comprehensive health assessments, or even work with a health coach. Whether it's an incentive or a surcharge, critics see it as a kind of "privacy tax." Those with good salaries may be able to afford to protect their privacy, but what about receptionists, file clerks, or other employees earning only a modest wage?[24]

Some companies are now intruding further into the personal sphere by bringing employees' families into wellness programs.[25] Others are trying to improve the mental health of their employees as well, seeking not only to combat depression, anxiety, and other psychological problems but also to promote positive thinking, coping under pressure, and "mental fitness" in an effort to increase creativity and productivity. Although this

---

Employee volunteer programs and other corporate-sponsored civic activities sometimes infringe on the right to privacy.

SUMMARY

A firm is legitimately interested in whatever significantly influences job performance, but some companies intrude where they shouldn't. Organizations may be invading privacy when they interfere with employees' off-the-job conduct or pressure them to contribute to charities, do volunteer work, or participate in wellness programs.

sounds enlightened and humane, it is often the companies themselves that are to blame for stressful work environments conducive to poor mental health. Moreover, many employees worry about their employers delving into their psychological and emotional lives. Can companies be trusted with the information they receive? Or will it find its way into annual appraisals or be held over employees' heads by manipulative managers? "I think employers are going to get deeper and deeper into the wellness business," says Professor Alan F. Westin of Columbia University. "This is going to throw up a series of profound ethical and legal dilemmas about how they should do it and what we don't want them to do."[26]

> SUMMARY
> Companies often gather highly personal information about employees. The critical issue here is informed consent, which implies deliberation and free choice. Deliberation requires that employees be provided all significant facts concerning the information-gathering procedure and understand its consequences. Free choice entails that the decision to participate must be voluntary and uncoerced.

TESTING AND MONITORING

It's no secret that firms frequently seek, store, and communicate information about employees, often highly personal information. The previous section examined privacy and organizational encroachment on employees' personal lives. This section focuses on two common methods of obtaining information about employees: monitoring them on the job and subjecting them to various tests—in particular, polygraph tests, personality tests, and drug tests. Before beginning this discussion, however, we need to look briefly at the concept of informed consent.

INFORMED CONSENT

Certainly no employee is ever compelled to take a lie-detector, personality, or genetic screening test in the sense that someone puts a loaded revolver to the person's head and says, "Take the test or else." But compulsion, like freedom, comes in degrees. Obviously if workers submit to an honesty exam or to a test for genetic disorders, then they agree to do so. But is their assent valid and legitimate? Does it constitute informed consent? That's the issue, and it is an altogether reasonable issue to raise because information collected on workers is often intimately personal and private and, when used carelessly, can injure them.

> The concept of informed consent implies deliberation and free choice.

Informed consent implies deliberation and free choice. Workers must understand what they are agreeing to, including its full ramifications, and must voluntarily choose it. Deliberation requires not only the availability of facts but also a full understanding of them. Workers must be allowed to deliberate on the basis of enough usable information, information that they can understand. But usable information is not of itself enough to guarantee informed consent. Free choice is also important—the *consent* part is as significant as the *informed* part of informed consent.

Everyone agrees that for consent to be legitimate, it must be voluntary. Workers must willingly agree to the privacy-invading procedure. They must also be in a position to act voluntarily. One big factor that affects the voluntariness of consent is the pressure, expressed and implied, exerted on employees to conform to organizational policy. Especially when the pressure to conform is reinforced with implicit threats of reprisal, it can effectively undercut the voluntariness of consent. That is obvious in the case of job applicants asked to undergo some invasion of their privacy. They can either submit or look for work elsewhere.

POLYGRAPH TESTS

When an individual is disturbed by a question, certain detectable physiological changes occur. The person's heart may begin to race, blood pressure may rise, and respiration may increase. The polygraph simultaneously records changes in these physiological processes and, thus, is often used in lie detection. But the use of **polygraph tests** rests on at least three assumptions that can be questioned.[27]

The *first* assumption is that lying triggers an involuntary, distinctive response that truth telling does not. But this is not necessarily the case. What the polygraph can do is record that the respondent was more disturbed by one question than by another, but it cannot determine why the person was disturbed. Perhaps the question made the person feel guilty or angry or frightened, but deception does not necessarily lurk behind the emotional response.

Second, it is assumed that polygraphs are extraordinarily accurate. Lynn March, president of the American Polygraph Association, says that "when administered correctly by qualified operators, the tests are accurate more than 90 percent of the time."[28] But David T. Lykken, a psychiatry professor, claims that this boast is not borne out by three scientifically credible studies of the accuracy of polygraphs used on actual criminal suspects. The accuracies obtained by qualified operators in these experiments were 63 percent, 39 percent, and 55 percent.[29] Whether the polygraph is accurate 90 percent of the time or less, the conclusion is the same: It cannot reveal with certainty whether a person is or is not telling the truth.

The *third* major assumption about polygraphs is that they cannot be beaten. Lykken, for one, suggests otherwise. The easiest way to beat the polygraph, the psychiatrist claims, is by augmenting your response to the control question by some form of covert self-stimulation, like biting your tongue. Not everybody believes this. Defenders of the polygraph contend that liars can't fool skilled operators of the machine. But even if the polygraph generally catches the guilty, it will also generate a disturbing number of **false positives**—that is, it will falsely identify as liars people who are telling the truth.

To see this, imagine that the polygraph is 95 percent accurate and suppose, for the sake of illustration, that at a large corporation with an in-house theft problem one out of every fifty employees is stealing from their employer. If the corporation has 1,000 employees, then 20 will be crooks and 980 will be honest. If every employee is tested, then the test, being only 95 percent accurate, will identify 19 of the 20 crooks; one will escape detection. But the test will identify as liars 5 percent of the company's 980 innocent employees; 49 people will be falsely accused. By firing all those who fail the polygraph, a company might succeed in weeding out the guilty, but it would also seriously harm many innocent employees.

In addition to these considerations, polygraphs infringe on privacy. As professor of politics Christopher Pyle says, they violate "the privacy of beliefs and associations, the freedom from unreasonable searches, the privilege against self-accusation, and the presumption of innocence."[30] That is not to say employers never have the right to abridge privacy or employees never have an obligation to reveal themselves. In important cases of in-house theft or corporate espionage, employers may be justified in using a polygraph as a last resort. But the threat to privacy remains.

The moral concerns embedded in the use of polygraphs suggest three points—in addition to the question of informed consent—to consider in evaluating their use in the workplace:

1. The information the organization seeks should be clearly and significantly related to the job. This caveat harks back to a determination of the legitimate areas of organizational influence over the individual.

2. Not only should the organization have job-related grounds for using the polygraph, but these must be compelling enough to justify violating the individual's privacy

> The use of polygraphs rests on three doubtful assumptions.

and psychic freedom. At the very least, the organization must have no viable alternative way of getting extremely important information or must have exhausted other, less intrusive means first.

3. Assuming the grounds for using the polygraph are sufficiently compelling, we must also be concerned about the sort of information being gathered, who will have access to it, and how it will be disposed of. Normally, not only the results but also the fact that a person is being tested at all should be kept confidential. And it is always important to treat that person respectfully.

> SUMMARY
> Polygraph tests can infringe employee privacy. Moreover, their accuracy and underlying assumptions are open to question, and they can generate false positives. Their use in employment situations is now legally restricted.

Responding to moral concerns about polygraphs as well as to their practical and statistical limitations, Congress passed the **Employee Polygraph Protection Act**. It prohibits most private employers from using lie detectors in the hiring process. Private security firms are exempted from this provision of the law, along with drug companies, contractors with certain government agencies, and selected others. The law permits the use of polygraphs in "ongoing investigations of economic loss or injury," but it provides a number of procedural safeguards. For instance, the employer must explain the test's purpose to the employee and the reason why he or she was selected to take it. The worker also has a right to consult with someone who will explain the workings and limitations of the machine. Ultimately, the worker retains the option not to submit to the test, and no one can be fired on the basis of a lie-detector test "without other supporting evidence."

Scientists, however, are experimenting with new techniques for detecting dishonesty, such as magnetic resonance imaging, "cognosensors," and electroencephalography (EEG), all of which look directly at brain activity to see who is lying and who is not.[31] Although these techniques are not yet foolproof, their proponents believe that they promise to prove far more accurate than the antiquated polygraph. Look for them soon at a workplace near you.

PERSONALITY TESTS

Companies often wish to determine whether prospective employees are emotionally mature, get along well with others, have a good work ethic, and, more generally, whether they would fit in with the organization, so they sometimes administer **personality tests**. One of the most popular of these tests, the Myers–Briggs Type Indicator, is used by eighty-nine of the *Fortune* 100 companies and taken by more than 2.5 million Americans every year.[32] Personality tests such as the Myers–Briggs can reveal highly personal information, and they often intrude into areas of our lives and thoughts that we normally consider private. Consent is usually less than fully voluntary because personality tests are generally part of a battery of tests that job applicants must take if they wish to be considered for a position.

> The supposition that individuals can be categorized based on a small number of personality traits is questionable.

Used properly, personality tests help screen applicants for jobs and current employees for particular assignments by indicating areas of adequacy and inadequacy. In theory, they simplify the complexities of business life by reducing the amount of decision making involved in determining whether an individual has the personal characteristics appropriate for a given position. But one key premise underlying such tests is questionable. That premise is that all individuals can usefully and validly be categorized on the basis of a relatively small number of personality characteristics. In fact, test designers typically believe that one's overall personality is shaped by only five factors and that these factors, which they seek to measure, account for "99 percent of the differences in human behavior."[33] However, the possession of a personality trait or characteristic is not an all-or-nothing thing, nor is it something that is permanently fixed. Most of us possess a variety of traits in various degrees, and social circumstances often influence the characteristics we display and the talents we develop. When organizations attempt to categorize employees in terms of their personalities, they simplify human nature and may miss their employees' true potential.

Personality tests also screen for organizational compatibility, sometimes functioning to eliminate prospective employees whose individuality or creativity may be exactly what the firm needs. Some companies, for example, seek employees who are extremely submissive to authority. Thus, when writer Barbara Ehrenreich submitted to a personality test for a job at Walmart, she was reprimanded for getting the "wrong" answer when she agreed only "strongly" with the proposition "All rules have to be followed to the letter at all times." The correct answer was "totally agree."[34] When used to secure complete conformity to organizational values, goals, and philosophy, personality tests heightened the danger that organizations by nature represent to individual freedom and moral autonomy.

Then, of course, there's the intrusive nature of the questions. Questions like "Does driving give you a sense of power?" "Do you like a lot of excitement in your life?" or "If you could, would you work as an entertainer in Las Vegas?" may seem innocuous, but what about a personality test that delves into your love life or that asks men, "Was there ever a time in your life when you liked to play with dolls?" One disgruntled test taker complains about "questions you wouldn't even answer for your own mother, if she asked you."[35] Worse, many of the tests asking these questions have little or no research to back them up or have not been validated for use in pre-employment situations. Even those who favor testing admit as much. John Kamp, an industrial psychologist, points out that even intelligent businesspeople can be swayed by a good marketing pitch from companies that peddle invalid or unreliable tests. "That's the unfortunate thing," he says. "A person with a slick pitch and no real research behind their tests can have a good business."[36]

SUMMARY

Personality tests help businesses screen candidates and match individuals to appropriate jobs. But their use rests on some questionable psychological premises, and they can invade privacy and reinforce conformity.

DRUG TESTING

Drug testing first became a live issue for some sports fans when the National Collegiate Athletic Association (NCAA) began banning college football players from postseason bowl competition based on the results of steroid testing. But political and legal battles over the drug testing of employees have raged for years. Numerous companies have warmly embraced testing. A study published in the *Journal of the American Medical Association* supports doing so. It showed that postal workers who tested positive for drug use in a pre-employment urine test were at least 50 percent more likely to be fired, injured, disciplined, or absent than those who tested negative.[37] Although many companies remain skeptical of the benefits of testing, 67 percent of large corporations now test either current employees or job applicants for illegal substances.[38]

In principle, testing employees to determine whether they are using illegal drugs raises the same questions that other tests raise: Is there informed consent? How reliable are the tests? Is testing really pertinent to the job in question? Are the interests of the firm significant enough to justify encroaching on the privacy of the individual? But rather than reiterate these issues, all of which are important and relevant, this section limits itself to four additional remarks:

1. The issue of drug testing by corporations and other organizations arises in the broader context of the drug-abuse problem in America today (which includes the abuse not just of illegal street drugs but of alcohol and prescription medicines as well).

To discuss this problem intelligently, one needs good information, reliable statistics, and sociological insight; yet these are difficult to come by. Newspapers, magazines, and television news shows often run sensationalistic stories on drugs, and politicians sometimes find it advantageous to portray themselves as battling courageously against a rising flood of drugs. The problems that alcohol and drug abuse can pose for businesses and other organizations are real and serious, but the use of illegal drugs, at least, appears to have dropped significantly among workers since the mid-1980s. However, media exaggeration and political posturing can create a false sense of crisis, leading people perhaps to advocate extreme or unnecessary measures.

2. Drugs differ, so one must carefully consider both what drugs one is testing for and why. Steroids, for instance, are a problem for the NCAA but not for IBM. And it is difficult to believe that Ford Meter Box was warranted in urine testing employees for nicotine in order to root out smokers.[39] To be defensible, drug testing must be pertinent to employee performance, and there must be a lot at stake. Testing airline pilots for alcohol consumption is one thing; testing the baggage handlers is something else. To go on a fishing trip in search of possible employee drug abuse when there is no evidence of a problem and no significant danger seems unreasonable.

3. Drug abuse by an individual is a serious problem, generally calling for medical and psychological assistance rather than punitive action. The moral assessment of any program of drug testing must rest in part on the potential consequences for those taking the test: Will they face immediate dismissal and potential criminal proceedings or therapy and a chance to retain their positions? To put the issue another way, when an organization initiates a testing program, does it approach this solely as a kind of police function? Or is it also responsive to the needs and problems of individual employees? Some business writers argue that voluntary, nonpunitive drug assistance programs are far more cost-effective for companies, in any case, than testing initiatives.[40]

4. Any drug-testing program, assuming it is warranted, must be careful to respect the dignity and rights of the persons to be tested. Some alternatives to body-fluid testing are less invasive of employee privacy. Due process must also be followed, including advance notification of testing as well as procedures for retesting and appealing test results. All possible steps should be taken to ensure individual privacy.

SUMMARY
Drug testing raises questions of test reliability and job relevance. Companies must also consider whether drug testing is really necessary and, if so, design such programs to respect the rights and dignity of employees as much as possible. They must also determine how to respond appropriately to individuals who fail the test.

MONITORING EMPLOYEES ON THE JOB

Many major employers routinely monitor the performance of their employees through the computers and telephones they use. They check the number of keystrokes that employees engaged in word processing enter during the day and record or listen in on calls handled by customer service agents. The Electronic Communications Privacy Act of 1986 restricts the government or unauthorized parties from eavesdropping on e-mail, fax transmissions, and cell phone conversations. The law applies to employers, but it allows exceptions when the consent of employees has been obtained, when the organization owns or maintains the system, or when there is a legitimate business purpose for the surveillance. Workers don't necessarily resent this monitoring, if it is in the open. "I don't think people mind having their work checked," says Morton Bahr, president of the Communications Workers of America. "It's the secretiveness of it" that bothers employees.[41]

According to the American Management Association, three-quarters of employers record employees' voice mail, e-mail, or phone calls; review their computer files; or even videotape them—often without their knowledge.⁴² In 2006, an Ohio firm took things a step further when it embedded RFID (radio frequency identification) chips in the arms of two employees to monitor them when they accessed secured areas—the first known case of a company's electronically tagging workers.⁴³ Tightening security and overseeing customer service are not the only reasons companies monitor their employees. Some companies, for example, check employees' computers to see whether they exceed the allotted time for lunch or work breaks; others listen in on phone conversations and examine e-mail messages to catch employees conducting personal business on company time.

"What are they going to think up to do to us next?" wonders one employee. "It's scary. I'll bet no one monitors the phones or e-mail of CEOs and other top executives."⁴⁴ Nancy Flynn, executive director of ePolicy Institute, agrees with that sentiment. "In a lot of organizations," she says, "the senior executives are immune from [electronic] monitoring."⁴⁵ If so, this raises a basic moral objection. As explained in Chapter 1 and again in Chapter 2's discussion of Kant, if we make a moral judgment, we must be willing to make the same judgment in any similar set of circumstances. These executives, however, are apparently willing to apply to others a policy that they are unwilling to see applied to themselves.

When in-house theft, sabotage, or other threatening conduct occurs, organizations frequently install monitoring devices—two-way mirrors, cameras, and electronic recorders—to apprehend the employees who are responsible. But monitoring suspected trouble spots or private acts can create moral problems. Consider the two male employees of Sheraton Boston Hotel who were secretly videotaped changing clothes in the locker room during a hunt for a drug dealer. They weren't suspects, just bystanders.⁴⁶

As with personality, polygraph, and drug tests, the **monitoring of employees** often gathers personal information without informed consent. Organizations frequently confuse notification of such practices with employee consent, but notification alone does not constitute agreement. When employee restrooms, dressing rooms, locker rooms, and other private places are bugged or video-taped, an obvious and serious threat to privacy exists—posted notices notwithstanding. It's true that in some cases surveillance devices may be the only way to apprehend the guilty. Nevertheless, they often can do more harm than good by violating the privacy of the vast majority of innocent employees. Obviously, even more serious moral questions arise when monitoring devices are used not exclusively for officially designated purposes but also for cajoling, harassing, or snooping on employees (sometimes with the goal of thwarting them from organizing unions⁴⁷).

> **SUMMARY**
> Monitoring employees may be necessary, but it can be abused and it can violate privacy.

> Notifying employees of workplace monitoring does not constitute consent.

WORKING CONDITIONS

In a broad sense, the conditions under which people work include personnel policies and procedures, as well as the extent to which an organization is committed to respecting the rights and privacy of its employees. This section, however, examines three other aspects of working conditions: health and safety on the job, styles of management, and the organization's maternity and day-care arrangements.

HEALTH AND SAFETY

The year is 2013: A fire at a propane plant in Florida triggers multiple explosions, injuring eight workers, some critically; a petrochemical plant southeast of Baton Rouge,

Louisiana, explodes, killing two workers and injuring 114; and an earth-shattering blast at a fertilizer plant in the town of West, Texas, kills 15 people, injures 160, and lays waste to the surrounding neighborhood. Among the 150 damaged or destroyed buildings are a middle school, a nursing home, a community hospital, and an apartment complex. Year 2010 wasn't a good year for safety, either. In the deadliest coal-mine incident in forty years, twenty-nine coalminers perished in a Massey Energy coal mine in West Virginia. And who will forget the explosion that year at the BP oil rig Deepwater Horizon off the coast of Louisiana, which left eleven workers dead and released millions of gallons of oil into the Gulf of Mexico?

These tragic episodes gained media coverage across the country, and some of them will remain seared in our memories for a long time. But most workplace deaths gather little or no publicity. For example, the national media ignored altogether the deaths of twenty-one-year-old Dennis Claypool and eighteen-year-old Mark DeMoss, who suffocated while working inside a tanker trailer at a trucking company outside Chicago. The two didn't know that the tanker had recently been cleaned with nitrogen, which removes oxygen from the air. A freak accident? Each year between eighty and one hundred workers die in such "confined space" incidents.[48]

The scope of occupational hazards remains awesome and generally unrecognized. In a given year about 5,000 workers are killed on the job.[49] Deaths are just part of the problem. Census Bureau statistics reveal that although the rate of industrial injury has been declining since 1960, the absolute number of workers disabled at work every year—approximately 5 million men and women—remains disturbingly high.[50] Researchers believe, however, that government statistics undercount workplace injuries and illnesses.[51] One expert estimates that a worker is hurt every 2.5 seconds or dies every eight minutes from workplace injuries or illnesses.[52]

Employers clearly have a moral obligation not to expose workers to needless risks or to negligently or recklessly endanger their lives or health. In the case of a drilling company that lowered a twenty-three-year-old worker to the bottom of a 33-foot-deep, 18-inch-wide hole, where he then suffocated, a Los Angeles county prosecutor put it this way: "Our opinion is you can't risk somebody's life to save a few bucks. That's the bottom line."[53] Issues of legal liability aside, however, employers are not morally responsible for all workplace accidents. Sometimes coworkers are negligent or act irresponsibly, and sometimes the victims themselves may have behaved stupidly or failed to exercise due care. Sometimes, as people often say, accidents "just happen." Moreover, nothing in life is free of risk, and we often judge the risk worth taking (for example, when we choose to drive a car). And in some circumstances or in certain occupations, an injured worker can reasonably be said to have voluntarily assumed the risk. But although there is some truth in all these points, they are somewhat misleading about the nature of accidents.

To begin with **assumption of risk**, the proposition that Dennis Claypool, Mark DeMoss, or the young Los Angeles man who died at the bottom of the shaft can be inferred to have freely and knowingly decided to gamble with their lives is dubious, to say the least. Voluntary assumption of risk presupposes informed consent. As we have seen, that would require the worker to have been fully informed of the danger and to have freely chosen to assume it, which is rarely true of workers who are just doing what the boss tells them to do. Informed consent entails that employees have a moral right to refuse work when it exposes them to imminent danger and that employers are wrong to reprimand or otherwise retaliate against them for doing so. The U.S. Supreme Court has acknowledged the **right to refuse dangerous work** to be a legal right, too.

> Voluntary assumption of risk presupposes informed consent. Employees have a right to refuse dangerous work.

In a crucial workplace decision, it ruled in favor of two employees of Whirlpool Corporation who had refused to follow their foreman's order to undertake activities they considered unsafe.[54] Of course, what constitutes an "imminent" danger may sometimes be open to debate, and workers should always behave reasonably and, when trying to avoid a perceived danger, take the least disruptive course of action open to them.

Employers, for their part, should inform workers of any life-threatening hazards, and, indeed, a number of states make that a legal requirement. Still, employees are often unaware of the dangers they face, many of which may be long-term, rather than imminent, hazards. Take the electronics industry, for example. It may look safe in comparison with other occupations, but behind its clean, high-tech image lurk health hazards for workers—in particular, the chemical toxins that are indispensable to the manufacture of computer chips. One workplace toxin causing concern recently is beryllium, a miracle metal—one-third the weight of aluminum yet six times stiffer than steel—which is used in a number of products these days, including computers, cell phones, and golf clubs. More toxic than plutonium, a few millionths of a gram of beryllium can trigger an immune system attack and fatally damage the lungs and other organs. Current legal standards suffice to keep workers handling the stuff from dying after a few days or weeks on the job, but they don't adequately protect them from developing chronic beryllium disease, a risk they may be unaware of.[55]

Putting aside assumption of risk and the right to know about and refuse hazardous work, we turn now to the causes of workplace accidents. As previously stated, it seems that accidents often result not from direct employer malfeasance but rather from employee blunders, coworker negligence, or just plain bad luck with nobody at fault. According to safety experts, though, this way of thinking is inaccurate. Industrial accidents don't just happen. They are caused—by inadequate worker training, sloppy procedures, lack of understanding of the job, improper tools and equipment, hazardous work environments, poor equipment maintenance, and overly tight scheduling.[56] And these are all matters that fall within the purview of the employer. For example, when a worker falls to his death from the tenth floor of a construction site because he wasn't wearing the required safety harness, the accident almost certainly has causes that go beyond poor judgment on his part.[57] Or consider the case of Michael Rodriguez. When some heavy machinery crushed his ankle, he was unable to leave his workplace and get to the hospital for several hours. That's because, until unfavorable publicity forced a policy change, Walmart would lock its employees in at night, and there was no one on duty with a key.[58]

> Accidents don't just happen. They result from poor job practices and workplace environments that fail to prioritize safety.

Workplace injuries, most experts believe, are related not to shortcomings in technology but rather to unsafe human behavior resulting from poor job practices, bad management, and a workplace environment that fails to put safety first. The key to a safer workplace, says risk-management consultant Beth Rogers, is not engineering but changing the company's "hidden culture"—the "unspoken rules that are adhered to"—to a culture that is proactively oriented toward safety.[59] As evidence for what Rogers is saying, consider two of the cases mentioned at the beginning of this section. With a long history of industrial mishaps, including a deadly refinery explosion in Texas five years earlier that killed fifteen people and injured 170, BP had a reputation within the industry for subordinating safety management to aggressive growth. It's not surprising, then, that managers ignored the safety concerns expressed by crew members before the Deepwater Horizon oil rig blew up.[60] Likewise, Massey Energy had a long record of safety violations and a history of playing cat-and-mouse with regulators. Its West Virginia mine was known to be a "ticking time bomb."[61]

OSHA

> **SUMMARY**
> Employers have a moral obligation not to expose workers to needless risk, and employees have a right to know about and refuse hazardous work. Although industrial accidents sometimes seem to result from employee recklessness or to "just happen," experts believe that they are caused by factors that are under the control of the company.

With the 1970 Occupational Safety and Health Act, the prime responsibility for regulating working conditions passed from the states to the federal government. The thrust of the act is "to ensure so far as possible every working man and woman in the nation safe and healthful working conditions," and it places a duty on employers to provide a workplace "free from recognized hazards that are causing or are likely to cause death or serious injury." In its early years, the **Occupational Safety and Health Administration (OSHA)**, created by the act, added to its own troubles by promulgating some rules that seemed trivial and nitpicking—for example, detailed guidelines regulating toilet seats and the belts to be worn by telephone line workers.[62] Fortunately, most of those rules have been repealed, but controversies have raged over how far OSHA should go in the cause of safety. The organization seeks to require only safeguards that are feasible. It has, for example, never attempted to entirely eliminate toxins in the workplace. But is "feasibility" to be understood in a broad economic and technological sense or must the gains in safety outweigh the costs that particular companies must bear? And how are those costs and gains to be measured? Sometimes, even when union and industry representatives have agreed on new safety measures, politicians have prevented OSHA from introducing them because of ideological opposition to regulation.[63]

With limited resources and only 2,000 inspectors to monitor 8 million workplaces,[64] OSHA has always faced a daunting task, and its performance has been spotty. For instance, the fertilizer plant mentioned earlier that exploded in West, Texas, had not been visited by OSHA for twenty-eight years.[65] Worse, the relationship between OSHA and the businesses and industries it regulates has often been too cozy. Consider the case of Stephen Golab, a fifty-nine-year-old immigrant from Poland who worked for a year stirring tanks of sodium cyanide at the Film Recovery Services plant in Elk Grove, Illinois. One day he became dizzy from the cyanide fumes, went into convulsions, and died. OSHA then inspected the plant and fined Film Recovery Services $4,855 for twenty safety violations. OSHA subsequently cut the fine in half. In contrast, the state attorney general for Cook County filed criminal charges. Three company officials were convicted of murder and fourteen counts of reckless conduct. The company itself was also found guilty of manslaughter and reckless conduct and fined $24,000.[66]

Since the Golab case, budget cuts have shrunk OSHA's staff further and inspections and citations have dropped. For example, an examination of 1,242 cases in which the agency itself concluded that workers had died because of their employer's "willful" safety violations revealed that in 93 percent of those cases OSHA declined to prosecute. At least seventy of those employers willfully violated safety laws again, resulting in more deaths. Yet even those repeat offenders were rarely prosecuted.[67] Why the leniency? "A simple lack of guts and political will," says John T. Phillips, a former regional OSHA administrator.[68] Congress, however, is at least partly responsible. It has pushed the agency from rule making and enforcement to helping businesses comply with federal requirements. As a result, critics call OSHA a "toothless tiger" that has moved from "beat cop to social worker."[69]

New Health Challenges

One problem that both OSHA and business need to address is the epidemic of occupational injury and illness known as **musculoskeletal disorders**. In offices and factories across the country, millions of workers suffer from aching backs, crippled fingers, sore wrists, and other problems caused or aggravated by their jobs. Every year, carpal tunnel syndrome, low back pain, sciatica, tendinitis, and other musculoskeletal disorders cause hundreds of thousands of workers to miss time on the job.

Numb fingers, swollen knuckles, and aching wrists from the constant repetition of awkward hand and arm movements may sound like minor complaints, but they are anything but trivial to the many employees who suffer from them. Ask Janie Jue of San Francisco. For seventeen years she keyed in up to 48,000 strokes a day on an automatic letter-sorting machine. Today, even picking up a book or a coffee pot sends bolts of pain tearing up her hand and arm. "I wish I could work," she says, "but it hurts from my elbow to my fingertips."[70] "For many years," remarks one expert, "it was just considered a cost of doing business. If you did certain jobs, you would end up with hands crippled at the end of your career. That's not acceptable in this country any more."[71]

No longer associated only with manufacturing, musculoskeletal disorders are also rampant among white-collar office workers, especially those who spend all day at a computer. The redesign of jobs, adjustable chairs, training in the proper use of computer terminals, and other preventive measures can often reduce the problem. In the meantime, it is not only the employees who are suffering. Musculoskeletal disorders decrease productivity and dampen morale, and having a skilled worker go out on long-term disability and vocational rehabilitation can cost a company a small fortune. Nevertheless, various employer groups and business lobbies continue to fight vigorously any step toward ergonomic regulation, even thwarting a thirteen-year effort by the National Safety Council to draft voluntary guidelines for preventing repetitive-motion injuries.[72]

An aspect of work life over which OSHA exercises little direct control is the shifts people work. Yet a team of scientists from Harvard and Stanford universities believes that the health and productivity of 25 million Americans whose work hours change regularly could be measurably improved if employers scheduled shift changes to conform with the body's natural and adjustable sleep cycles. This is particularly important given that sleep deprivation and fatigue are prime causes of industrial accidents and cost employers billions a year in absences, accidents, and diminished productivity.[73]

Related to fatigue is an aspect of work we have only recently begun to appreciate fully—the health implications of **job stress**. More than 30 percent of American workers say they are "always" or "often" under stress at work, and a majority of them report increased workloads that leave them "overtired and overwhelmed." One reason, of course, is the long hours many of them put in. In addition, four out of ten employees now work "mostly at nonstandard times," according to Harriet Prosser of the University of Maryland. They juggle rotating shifts and work evenings, nights, and weekends to meet the demands of global supply chains and customers in every time zone. Furthermore, technology leashes many employees to the job even when they're at home. As a result, says Donald I. Tepas, a professor of industrial psychology, "the distinction between work and nonwork time is getting fuzzier all the time."[74]

The relation between workplace stress and ill health is now well established. In fact, scientists have ascertained that stressful job conditions diminish mental health and damage physical functioning as much as smoking does.[75] Workers who report being stressed incur significantly higher health care costs than do other employees. Revamping working environments that produce stress and helping employees learn to cope with it are among the major health challenges facing American business now and in the years to come.

MANAGEMENT STYLES

How managers conduct themselves on the job—**management styles**—can do more to enhance or diminish the work environment than any other facet of employer–employee

....
SUMMARY
The scope of occupational hazards, including musculoskeletal disorders, shift work, fatigue, and stress, and the number of employees harmed by work-related injuries and illness are greater than many people think. OSHA's enforcement of existing regulations has too often been lax.
....

Nothing affects work environment more than the style and quality of management.

relations. Indeed, a poor relationship with their immediate supervisor is the most common reason people give for leaving a job; office politics comes second.[76] "Management creates the conditions in which most adults spend half their waking lives," writes Thomas A. Stewart, editor of *Harvard Business Review*. "Bad management makes lives miserable."[77] In survey after survey, employees rank honest communication, personal recognition, and respectful treatment as more important than good pay. Unfortunately, according to a Columbia University psychologist, millions of workers suffer from bosses who are abusive, dictatorial, devious, dishonest, manipulative, and inhumane.[78] "Managers from hell," says another expert, are "costing the United States an estimated $450 billion to $550 billion annually."[79]

This workplace reality runs contrary to the teachings of almost all management theorists. For example, in his classic work *The Human Side of Enterprise*, Douglas McGregor described two styles of management, which he called "Theory X" and "Theory Y." Theory X managers believe that workers dislike work and will do everything they can to avoid it.[80] These managers insist that the average person wishes to avoid responsibility, lacks ambition, and values security over everything else. Accordingly, they believe they must coerce and bully workers into conformity with organizational objectives. In contrast, McGregor advocated a Theory Y management style. Theory Y managers assume that employees basically like work and view it as something natural and potentially enjoyable. They believe that workers are motivated as much by pride and a desire for self-fulfillment as by money and job security and that workers don't dodge responsibility but accept it and even seek it out.

Since the publication of McGregor's book, other management writers have pursued this line of thought and described other management styles—including Theory Z, which touts Japanese-style respect for workers. More recently, some theorists have advocated a management style that eschews a masculine, hierarchical, aggressive, analytic, winner-take-all approach in favor of a more personal, empathetic, and collaborative style, thought to be characteristic of, and more congenial to, women.

This is not the place to discuss different theories of management, but clearly the management styles recommended by different writers, as well as the management styles actually adopted by different bosses, rest on implicit or explicit assumptions about human nature. However, no set of assumptions about human nature is absolutely correct or incorrect, nor is there one perfectly right way to manage. But that's precisely the point. Problems inevitably arise when managers routinize their leadership style, regardless of the needs, abilities, and predilections of their particular employees. When managers ignore individual differences, they risk creating a work atmosphere that's distressing to workers and less productive than it might be. Moreover, implicit assumptions about human nature can easily become self-reinforcing because people tend to behave as they are treated. Thus, managers who treat employees as if they were incapable of taking initiative or thinking for themselves will probably end up with employees who don't take initiative or think for themselves. Manager, therefore, must carefully examine their preconceptions when determining the most appropriate leadership style to adopt in their workplace. That is easier said than done for most managers. A recent survey shows that managers overestimate their skills and rarely display any self-doubt.[81] And those who have been successful can be the most rigid. "With the success they've achieved," says Michael Feiner of the Columbia Business School, "bosses can come to believe that their way is the right way, the best way—perhaps the only way."[82]

A different problem of management style, which also has moral overtones, stems from the bureaucratic character of many American corporations. The United States has more managers per employee than any other industrial nation,[83] and they make up a bigger share of the workforce than ever before.[84] Corporate bureaucracies often create an environment in which managers and other executives must pay excessive attention to hierarchy—often hoarding information and keeping subordinates in the dark—and in which they are tempted to put personal ambition ahead of other things and spend their energy trying to move up the company ladder. "Corporate infighting," "management power struggles," "maneuvering and politics and power grabbing," and "Machiavellian intrigues" are the phrases one business observer, H. Ross Perot, uses to describe the reality of corporate life.[85]

SUMMARY
Management style greatly affects the work environment. Managers who operate with rigid assumptions about human nature or who devote themselves to infighting and political maneuvering damage employees' interests.

DAY CARE AND MATERNITY LEAVE

One area often overlooked in discussions of working conditions is the provision of maternity/paternity leave and child-care services for workers with children. The need for both is steadily growing as more and more women enter the paid labor force. Women's participation in the labor force has nearly doubled since 1960; today they occupy more than half of all professional and management positions.[86] In 1960 only 18.6 percent of married women with children under the age of six were in the paid labor force; today 64.2 percent are.[87] Despite these statistics, the United States lags behind many industrialized nations in the provision of child care.[88] Those countries, unlike the United States, view child care as a national responsibility and publicly subsidize it. The situation is even more striking with respect to maternity leave. Only California and Washington require *paid* **maternity leave**, and today fewer U.S. companies (about 16 percent) offer it than in 1998.[89] By contrast, 160 countries around the world guarantee women paid maternity leave, and 139 countries require paid sick leave, with 117 of them ensuring at least one week.[90] The United States, however, guarantees only *unpaid* time off for pregnancy or for personal or family illness (and then only if you work for a company with more than fifty employees). Even so, corporate America has recently been campaigning to tighten the rules for unpaid medical absences.[91]

Given that women in our society continue to bear the primary responsibility for child rearing, their increasing participation in the paid workforce represents a growing demand for reasonable maternity-leave policies and affordable child-care services. Nor is that demand likely to diminish. Many families are unable to make satisfactory child-care arrangements, either because the services are unavailable or because the parents cannot

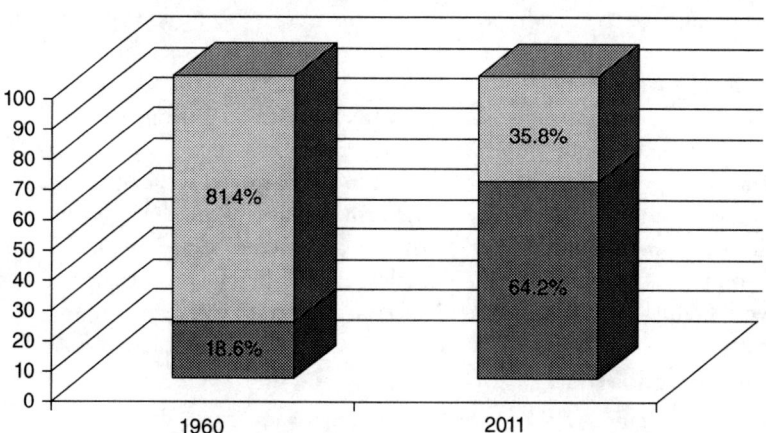

Percentage (in dark) of married women with children under age six in the paid labor force in 1960 and in 2011.

afford them. An estimated 5 million children are thus left alone without any supervision while their parents work. The need for child-care services is particularly acute among single-parent families, 91 percent of which are headed by women. Single mothers have a higher rate of participation in the labor force than do married mothers. Nevertheless, many of them are too poor to pay for satisfactory child-care services.

Business and Child Care

Some companies try hard to help with employee child care.[92] Campbell Soup Co., for example, offers on-site **day care**, spending over $200,000 annually to subsidize 50 percent of tuition costs at the child-care center for the children of employees at corporate headquarters. Procter & Gamble holds priority rights for 75 percent of the spaces in two off-site centers near its Cincinnati headquarters. It also provides a day-care resource and referral service for the entire community. IBM provides a free nationwide referral system for its employees and has helped develop child-care services where they have been deficient or lacking. Polaroid Corporation provides assistance with child-care costs for permanent employees earning less than $30,000. Because its employees worked at all hours, America West Airlines (now absorbed into US Airways) provided 24-hour child care with a sliding-scale subsidy to make it affordable. The Goldman Sachs Group, Time Warner, and Chase Manhattan Bank opened child-care centers for employees whose regular child-care arrangements are temporarily disrupted. Unfortunately, these encouraging examples contrast with an overall corporate record on child care that is, to put it mildly, not very impressive.

Employers are in a good position to assist in the provision of child-care services, and the need for it is there, given the paucity of government funding. However, only 4 to 6 percent of employers offer on-site child-care services,[93] primarily because initiating and maintaining such programs cost money. Yet viewed from a broader perspective, day-care arrangements set up by companies themselves or by several companies together in the same area can be socially cost-effective. With in-house day-care arrangements, parents need not make special trips to pick up and drop off their children. Because the parents are not far away, they can have more interaction with their children. Depending on the specific organization of work and the firm's flexibility, parents could share in the actual running of the child-care facility at assigned intervals during the course of their working day. Hewlett-Packard took an innovative step in this regard when, in conjunction with the local school district, it set up kindergarten and first-grade classes on company grounds for the children of employees. Some other companies now do the same thing.[94]

Assistance with child care and flexible, family-oriented policies can be cost-effective.

Some business writers argue that offering child care as a fringe benefit and dealing as flexibly as possible with employees' family needs can prove advantageous for most employers. Such policies can be cost-effective in the narrower sense by decreasing absenteeism, boosting morale and loyalty to the firm, enhancing productivity, and attracting new recruits. A growing body of empirical research demonstrates the bottom-line benefits for companies that promote their employees' well-being and engage their hearts and minds with family-friendly policies.[95] This is an important consideration.

Three Moral Concerns

Even more important are three underlying moral considerations.

Even more important are the underlying moral issues. *First*, women have a right to compete on an equal terrain with men. The legal requirement that large firms provide at least unpaid maternity leave and reinstatement respects that right. Whether companies should also provide paid maternity leave is more controversial, although one might argue that paid leave is necessary to give substance to that right. Or one might defend such a policy on the utilitarian ground that it would enhance total social welfare. As mentioned, many organizations find it in their interest to provide paid leave and flexible work arrangements so that they can attract better and more-talented employees, and some are working hard at luring stay-at-home moms back to work.[96] On the other hand, the trend toward tough performance standards and no-fault absence policies can penalize workers for missing work regardless of the reason. That happened to Tanya Frazier, office manager for a payroll company in Burbank, California. After receiving a call from her daughter's elementary school telling her to pick up her flu-stricken nine-year-old, she stayed home from work for a day—and was fired because of it. She claims she had missed work only a handful of days that year, but her boss says he was tired of her taking so much time off.[97] Even when employees aren't sacked, their performance appraisal, year-end bonus, or raise can be affected by their taking a legally protected, unpaid family leave.[98]

Second, from various ethical perspectives, the development of our potential capacities is a moral ideal—perhaps even a human right. For that reason, or from the point of view of promoting human well-being, many theorists would contend that women should not be forced to choose between childbearing and the successful pursuit of their careers. Nor should they be forced to reduce the quality of their commitment either to their children or to their careers. If employment circumstances force them to do so, and if those circumstances could reasonably be changed, then we have not lived up to the ideal of treating those women as persons whose goals are worthy of respect.

Third, although the past two or so decades have seen many criticisms of, and attempts to move beyond, the traditional male–female division of labor within the family, there can be little doubt that the world of work tends to reproduce those patterns. For instance, as mentioned in Chapter 8, men who leave work to help raise children often face enormous hurdles when returning to the job market. It seems clear that many fathers today feel hampered by work arrangements that pit meaningful career advancement against a fully developed family life.[99] Enhanced opportunities for part-time employment and job sharing, along with generous parental-leave arrangements and flexible, affordable, and accessible firm-sponsored child-care facilities—even efforts to facilitate workplace lactation by nursing mothers—can assist employees, both male and female, to achieve a more personally desirable balance between paid work and family relations.

The moral value here is not to promote any single vision of the good life but rather to permit individuals, couples, and families as much autonomy as possible, given other social goals. They should be able to define the good life for themselves and to seek the arrangement of work and personal relations that makes that life possible. Firm-affiliated child-care services and other institutional arrangements that accommodate parental needs clearly promote this moral goal.

> **SUMMARY**
> Day-care services and reasonable parental-leave policies also affect working conditions. Despite the genuine need for and the ethical importance of both day care and flexible work arrangements for parents, only a handful of companies strive seriously to provide them.

REDESIGNING WORK

Chapter 4 looked at alienation under capitalism and changing attitudes toward work in America. It remains true that many, perhaps even most, employees are at least somewhat dissatisfied with their jobs. Any investigation of the moral issues arising around the workplace and any discussion of the challenges facing business today must confront this basic problem and consider ways of improving the quality of work life.

> Business must confront the fact of widespread job dissatisfaction and consider ways of improving the quality of work life.

DISSATISFACTION ON THE JOB

In the early 1970s, the federal government conducted a major study of work in America, the basic findings of which remain relevant.[100] The *Work in America* report identified three chief sources of worker dissatisfaction. The first was industry's preoccupation with quantity, not quality; the rigidity of rules and regulations; and the fracturing of work into the smallest possible tasks, together with the monotonous repetition of those tasks. The second source of dissatisfaction was the lack of opportunities to be one's own boss. The third source of dissatisfaction was "bigness": More people today work for large corporations than ever before.

The *Work in America* survey reported similar sources of dissatisfaction in the managerial ranks. One out of three middle managers at that time was willing to join a union. Moreover, just as industrial workers voiced general complaints about work, so did middle managers. Some resented having so little influence in their organizations; others objected to the organization's goals, policies, and ways of operating. Still other managers complained about the tension, frustration, and infighting that intraorganizational competition can breed. Beyond these complaints, the *Work in America* survey reported that many managers felt like cogs in a machine, like parts that could and would be replaced when a better part came along.

Other studies over the years confirm that workers at all occupational levels express dissatisfaction with employer policies and practices and with the behavior of top management.[101] According to the Conference Board, a business policy organization, only half of American workers are satisfied with their jobs, down from 60 percent in 1995. Only 14 percent said they were "very satisfied," and one quarter admitted they were simply "showing up to collect a paycheck."[102] The results of a 2013 Gallup poll were similar. It found that 52 percent of American workers are "not engaged" with their work—essentially clock-watchers who can't wait to get home. An additional 18 percent were "actively disengaged," meaning that they tend to undermine their colleagues and employers and shirk their duties whenever possible.[103] Whatever the statistics, if industry is to improve productivity, enhance customer satisfaction, and be more competitive, it must seriously confront these attitudes and the sources of employee dissatisfaction. It must devise ways to make work more satisfying and to improve the quality of work life.

Factors Affecting Job Satisfaction

As early as the 1920s, researchers began to realize that workers would be more productive if management met those needs that money cannot buy. Managers at the Hawthorne factory of Western Electric Company were conducting experiments to determine the effect of the work environment on worker productivity. In the literature of work motivation, these studies have become known as the Hawthorne studies. What they discovered has been termed the **Hawthorne effect**.

Researchers at the Hawthorne plant chose a few employees to work in an experimental area, apart from the thousands of employees in the rest of the factory. Every effort was made to improve working conditions, from painting walls a cheerful color to making lights brighter. Worker productivity increased with each improvement. Then the experimenters decided to reverse the process. For example, lights were made dimmer. To everyone's surprise, productivity continued to increase.

Workers respond well to attention and recognition.

The conclusion the researchers drew was that workers were producing more because they were receiving attention. Instead of feeling that they were spokes in an organizational wheel, they felt important and recognized. The attention had the effect of heightening their sense of personal identity and feeling of control over their work environment. Recognition of this effect can help management increase worker motivation and job satisfaction and also increase the organization's productivity.

Subsequent research corroborates and deepens the Hawthorne results.[104] In studying the problem of poor worker motivation, the influential management theorist Frederick Herzberg discovered that the factors that promote **job satisfaction** differed from those producing job dissatisfaction. Herzberg found that although job dissatisfaction frequently arises from extrinsic problems (such as pay, supervision, working conditions, and leadership styles), resolving those extrinsic problems does not necessarily produce satisfied workers. The reason, Herzberg contends, is that worker satisfaction depends on such intrinsic factors as a sense of accomplishment, responsibility, recognition, self-development, and self-expression.[105] Recent surveys add support to Herzberg's findings. When employees at all occupational levels are asked to rank what is important to them, they list interesting work; sufficient help, support, and information to accomplish the job; enough authority to carry out the work; good pay; the opportunity to develop special skills; job security; and a chance to see the results of their work. Other research shows that what makes people content is being respected by members of groups they respect. In line with this, Roger Martin, dean of the school of management at the University of Toronto, argues that employees are happiest when they are respected members of a team they admire and when the team and company are respected by the outside world.[106]

Importance of Job Satisfaction

Numerous mental-health problems stem from a lack of job satisfaction—low self-esteem, anxiety, impaired interpersonal relations, and psychosomatic ailments such as ulcers and hypertension—especially in low-status, boring, unchallenging jobs that offer little autonomy. In fact, although having a job is better for one's mental health than being unemployed, being in a bad job is worse than having no job at all.[107] Furthermore, dreary, unchallenging jobs tend to inhibit intellectual growth and the pursuit of richer, more fulfilling activities outside work. Even worse, researchers have found that workers in boring, passive jobs are 33 to 35 percent more likely to die prematurely than workers in active jobs. Stressful work that offers little decision-making opportunity makes an untimely demise even more likely.[108] In contrast, job satisfaction is strongly linked to longevity.[109]

Because the design of work materially affects the total well-being of workers, work content and job satisfaction are paramount moral concerns. But if we also assume that a happier, more contented worker is generally a more productive one, then it follows that business has an economic reason as well as a moral obligation to devise ways, in concert with labor and perhaps even government, to improve the quality of work life.

> Job satisfaction is both a moral concern and an economic one.

IMPROVING WORK LIFE

This book isn't the place for determining precisely what measures firms should take to improve employees' work lives. For some firms it may mean less supervision and more autonomy for workers. For others it may mean offering opportunities to develop and refine skills. Still other firms might try to provide workers with greater participation in the conception, design, and execution of their work—that is, with greater responsibility and a deeper sense of achievement.

Granting workers new responsibilities and respect can benefit the entire organization. Randy Pennington, vice president of Performance Systems Corporation, tells of a friend who showed an ad for a new American car to a Japanese businessperson. The ad said that the car "set a new standard for quality because it was examined by 34 different quality inspectors." "Now, *this*," he said to his Japanese colleague, "is what we need to compete with you. Imagine: 34 quality inspectors!" The Japanese looked at the ad, smiled, and said, "You don't need 34 inspectors to get quality. You just need everyone who works on the car to be proud of the work. Then you'll need only one inspector."[110]

> **SUMMARY**
>
> Studies report extensive job dissatisfaction at all levels. Various factors influence satisfaction and dissatisfaction on the job. Redesigning the work process and increasing employee responsibility and participation can enhance the quality of work life, the well-being of workers, and even productivity.

Thawing the antagonistic worker–boss relations that characterize many plants isn't always easy. Some union members are wary of "being co-opted and looking like management flunkies."[111] Investigators believe that the success of workplace reform efforts depends on the ability of the organization to reinforce high levels of trust. To the extent that it does so, organizational performance can improve. But, warns William Cooke, professor at Wayne State University and author of a book on workplace reform, "if [workers] perceive management as doing this without due consideration for the welfare of employees . . . it will have the potential of destroying the efforts altogether."[112]

After Gerard Arpey took over as CEO of American Airlines, the company began the arduous but ambitious process of developing better and more stable working relations between managers and employees, something that had long eluded American Airlines. In an apparently successful effort to end adversarial relations with the unions, Arpey created new structures of consultancy across the company, captured in the slogans "Involve before Deciding. Discuss before Implementing. Share before Announcing." "We are trying to make our unions our business partners," Arpey says. "It is not about sitting around the campfire singing Kumbaya."[113]

These days, closer union–management relations also characterize many GM plants. For example, Mike Spitzley, manager of GM's 5,300-worker car-truck plant in Janesville, Wisconsin, says, "Most of the things we talk about, it's 'we.' It's not us versus them. We've pretty much realized that our goals are the same" as the union's. Mike O'Brien, president of the local chapter of the United Auto Workers, agrees. "There's something different going on," he says. "Years ago, it wasn't any of our business what went on in the business."[114] This is more true than ever, now that the union is deeply involved in resuscitating GM after its 2010 Chapter 11 bankruptcy restructuring.

At GM and American Airlines, the ideals of improved work atmosphere, employee participation, and job security appear to have meshed nicely with the goal of increased productivity. The same is true at BMW, which also gives its creative and motivated workforce a share of the profits—one reason the company receives 200,000 job applications annually.[115] Not only is productivity 5 to 10 percent greater in companies with profit sharing, but productivity is also consistently higher in enterprises with an organized program of worker participation.[116] This is in line with the views of experts who insist that worker-friendly companies outperform traditional command-and-control employers. They argue that new organizational structures and work practices that put a premium on collaboration and cooperation are fundamental to the nation's future economic success.[117]

> Worker participation can increase productivity. Worker-friendly companies tend to outperform traditional command-and-control employers.

A range of social and economic research supports that conclusion, but there is no watertight guarantee that worker participation and an improved quality of work life will always boost productivity. For example, although diversifying tasks may make work more satisfying, Japanese carmakers reduced the number of rejects on their assembly line not by diversifying but by standardizing the cars produced. And some years ago Volkswagen found that its productivity and quality were higher when production consisted solely of the standard Rabbit than when other models were introduced. Job-enlargement programs, by definition, add to the variety of tasks the worker is assigned; job-enrichment programs add some planning, designing, and scheduling to the operative worker's tasks. Both programs may slow output in some cases. Also, worker involvement in production management may not fit well, some argue, with the two other ingredients that managers and management consultants see as essential for manufacturing efficiency: a just-in-time approach to eliminating waste and rigorous statistical process control to improve quality.

Employee involvement, however, is essential to work elimination programs—programs that eliminate wasteful and unnecessary tasks, thus enhancing job satisfaction while making the organization leaner and more productive. This is particularly important as competition pressures manufacturers in the car industry and elsewhere to move to smaller, more flexible factories. Still, the possibility of a conflict between the obligation to make work more satisfying and the goal of increasing productivity will likely be at the heart of moral decisions in this area for years to come. To resolve them will require a cooperative effort by labor and management, rooted in the recognition that trade-offs are inevitable.

STUDY CORNER

KEY TERMS AND CONCEPTS

- assumption of risk
- civic activities
- day care
- drug testing
- Employee Polygraph Protection Act
- false positives
- Hawthorne effect
- informed consent
- job satisfaction
- job stress
- management styles
- maternity leave
- monitoring of employees
- musculoskeletal disorders
- Occupational Safety and Health Administration (OSHA)
- off-the-job conduct
- personality tests
- polygraph tests
- privacy
- right to refuse dangerous work
- wellness programs

POINTS TO REVIEW

- examples of business actions that encroach upon privacy (pp. 434–436)
- three dimensions of privacy (p. 437)
- difficulties of determining when companies have a legitimate interest in employee conduct, on and off the job (pp. 437–438)
- privacy issues raised by company-sponsored civic activities and wellness programs (pp. 438–440)
- what informed consent implies (p. 440)
- debatable assumptions behind polygraphs (p. 441)
- problem of false positives (p. 441)
- three points to consider in evaluating workplace use of polygraphs (pp. 441–442)
- one questionable assumption of personality tests (pp. 442–443)
- four points about drug testing (pp. 443–444)
- assumption of risk and the right to refuse hazardous work (pp. 446–447)
- what causes accidents (p. 447)
- the key to workplace safety (p. 447)
- OSHA's spotty record (p. 448)
- new health challenges in the workplace (pp. 448–449)
- management theories and human nature (p. 450)
- corporate record on child care (p. 452)
- three moral reasons to accommodate employees' parental and family needs (pp. 452–453)
- the Hawthorne experiment and the factors affecting job satisfaction (pp. 454–455)
- health effects of job dissatisfaction (p. 455)
- effect of participation and improved quality of work life on productivity (pp. 456–457)

FOR FURTHER REFLECTION

1. How important is privacy to you personally? Describe a situation, work-related or otherwise, in which you felt your privacy was threatened.
2. Describe your experiences with drug testing or personality testing. Have you or has anyone you know been subjected to job monitoring that seemed too intrusive?
3. Does business have a responsibility to provide employees with more satisfying work lives? Or to better accommodate their family needs?

CASE 9.1

Unprofessional Conduct?

TEACHING ELEMENTARY SCHOOL CHILDREN with intellectual disabilities requires skill, patience, and devotion, and those who undertake this task are among the unsung heroes of our society. Their difficult and challenging work rarely brings the prestige or financial rewards it deserves. Mrs. Pettit was one of those dedicated teachers. Licensed to teach in California, she had been working with mentally challenged children for over thirteen years when her career came to an abrupt end. Throughout that career, her competence was never questioned, and the evaluations of her school principal were always positive.

Teaching was not Pettit's only interest, however. She and her husband viewed with favor various "nonconventional sexual lifestyles," including "wife swapping." Because so-called sexual liberation was a hot topic at the time, the Pettits were invited to discuss their ideas on two local television shows. Although they wore disguises, at least one fellow teacher recognized them and discussed Mrs. Pettit's views with colleagues. A year later Pettit, then forty-eight years old, and her husband joined "The Swingers," a private club in Los Angeles that sponsored parties intended to promote diverse sexual activities among its members. An undercover police officer, Sergeant Berk, visited one of those parties at a private residence. Amid a welter of sexual activity, he observed Mrs. Pettit perform fellatio on three different men in a one-hour period.

Pettit was arrested and charged with oral copulation, which at the time contravened the California Penal Code (although now it does only if one of the parties is under eighteen). After a plea bargain was arranged, she pleaded guilty to the misdemeanor of outraging public decency and paid a fine. The school district renewed her teaching contract the next academic year, but two years later, disciplinary proceedings were initiated against her. The State Board of Education found no reason to complain about her services as a teacher, and it conceded that she was unlikely to repeat her sexual misconduct. But the Board revoked her elementary school life diploma—that is, her license to teach—on the ground that by engaging in immoral and unprofessional conduct at the party, she had demonstrated that she was unfit to teach.

Pettit fought the loss of her license all the way to the California Supreme Court, which upheld the decision of the Board of Education.[118] In an earlier case, the court had reversed the firing of a public school teacher for unspecified homosexual conduct, concluding that a teacher's actions could not constitute "immoral or unprofessional conduct" or "moral turpitude" unless there was clear evidence of unfitness to teach. But Pettit's case was different, the court hastened to explain.

The conduct in the earlier case had not been criminal, oral copulation had not been involved, and the conduct had been private. Further, in that case the Board had acted with insufficient evidence of unfitness to teach; by contrast, three school administrators had testified that in their opinion, Pettit's conduct proved her unfit to teach. These experts worried that she would inject her views of sexual morality into the classroom, and they doubted that she could act as a moral example to the children she taught. Yet teachers, the court reaffirmed, are supposed to serve as exemplars, and the Education Code makes it a statutory duty of teachers to "endeavor to impress upon the minds of the pupils the principles of morality . . . and to instruct them in manners and morals."

In a vigorous dissent, Justice Tobringer rejected the opinion of the majority, arguing that no evidence had established that Pettit was not fit to teach. The three experts didn't consider her record; they couldn't point to any past misconduct with students, nor did they suggest any reason to anticipate future problems. They simply assumed that the fact of her sexual acts at the "swingers" party itself demonstrated that she would be unable to set a proper example or to teach her pupils moral principles.

Such an attitude is unrealistic, Tobringer argued, when studies show that 75 to 80 percent of the women of Pettit's educational level and age range engage in oral copulation. The majority opinion "is blind to the reality of sexual behavior" and unrealistically assumes that "teachers in their private lives should exemplify Victorian principles of sexual morality." Pettit's actions were private and could not have affected her teaching ability. Had there not been clandestine surveillance of the party, the whole issue would never have arisen.

DISCUSSION QUESTIONS

1. In concerning itself with Pettit's off-the-job conduct, did the Board of Education violate her right to privacy? Or was its concern with her lifestyle legitimate and employment related?
2. Was Pettit's behavior "unprofessional"? Was it "immoral"? Did it show a "lack of fitness" to teach? Explain how you understand the terms in quotation marks.
3. Was the Board of Education justified in firing Pettit? Explain.
4. Was the court's verdict consistent with its earlier handling of the case of the homosexual teacher?
5. If teachers perform competently in the classroom, should they also be required to be moral exemplars in their private lives? Are employees in other occupations expected to provide a moral example—either on or off the job?
6. Which of the following, in your view, would show unprofessional conduct, immorality, or lack of fitness to teach: drunken driving, smoking marijuana, advocating the use of marijuana, forging a check, resisting arrest for disorderly conduct and assaulting a police officer, being discovered in a compromising position with a student, propositioning a student, cheating on income tax, calling attention to one's openly homosexual lifestyle?
7. Under what conditions do employers have a legitimate interest in their employees' off-the-job conduct?

CASE 9.2

Testing for Honesty

AT CHRISTMAS TIME, HOLIDAY SHOPPERS DROP all sorts of things into the Salvation Army's red kettles: diamond rings, lottery tickets, casino chips—even Viagra.[119] Most people, of course, put in coins and dollar bills. Some years ago, however, one of the Army's local branches found that money also seemed to be disappearing out of its kettles. Worried about theft by its kettle workers, Army officials sought the assistance of Dr. John Jones, director of research for London House Management Consultants.

London House is one of several companies that market honesty tests for prospective employees.[120] Employee theft is a serious problem for many companies. Honesty-test makers say the best way to deal with it is before workers are hired—by subjecting them to a pre-employment psychological test that will identify those prospective employees who are likely to steal.

James Walls, one of the founders of Stanton Corporation, which has offered written honesty tests for twenty-five years, says that dishonest job applicants are clever at hoodwinking potential employers in a job interview. "They have a way of conducting themselves that is probably superior to the low-risk person. They have learned what it takes to be accepted and how to overcome the normal interview strategy," he says. "The high-risk person will get hired unless there is a way to screen him." For this reason, Walls maintains, written, objective tests are needed to weed out the crooks.

Millions of written honesty tests are given annually, thanks to congressional restrictions on polygraph testing. In addition to being legal, honesty tests are also economical because they cost only a fraction of what polygraph tests cost. Furthermore, honesty tests are easily administered at the workplace and can be quickly evaluated by the test maker. The tests also are nondiscriminatory because the race, gender, or ethnicity of applicants has no significant impact on scores.

A typical test begins with some cautionary remarks. Test takers are told to be truthful because dishonesty can be detected, and they are warned that incomplete answers will be considered incorrect, as will any unanswered questions. Then applicants ordinarily sign a waiver permitting the results to be shown to their prospective employer and authorizing the testing agency to check out their answers. Sometimes, however, prospective employees are not told that they are being tested for honesty, only that they are being asked questions about their background. James Walls justifies this lack of candor by saying that within a few questions it is obvious that the test deals with attitudes toward honesty. "The test is very transparent, it's not subtle."

Some questions do indeed seem transparent—for example, "If you found $100 that was lost by a bank truck on the street yesterday, would you turn the money over to the bank, even though you knew for sure there was no reward?" But other questions are more controversial: "Have you ever had an argument with someone and later wished you had said something else?" If you were to answer no, you would be on your way to failing. Other questions that may face the test taker are "How strong is your conscience?" "How often do you feel guilty?" "Do you always tell the truth?" "Do you occasionally have thoughts you wouldn't want made public?" "Does everyone steal a little?" "Do you enjoy stories of successful crimes?" "Have you ever been so intrigued by the cleverness of a thief that you hoped the person would escape detection?" Or consider questions like "Is an employee who takes it easy at work cheating his employer?" or "Do you think a person should be fired by a company if it is found that he helped employees cheat the company out of overtime once in a while?" These ask you for your reaction to hypothetical dishonest situations. "If you are a particularly kind-hearted person who isn't sufficiently punitive, you fail," says Lewis Maltby, director of the workplace rights office at the American Civil Liberties Union. "Mother Teresa would never pass some of these tests."

A big part of some tests is a behavioral history of the applicant. Applicants are asked to reveal the nature, frequency, and quantity of specific drug use, if any. They also must indicate if they have ever engaged in drunk driving, illegal gambling, traffic violations, forgery, vandalism, and a host of other unseemly behaviors. They must also state their opinions about the social acceptability of drinking alcohol and using other drugs.

Some testing companies go further in this direction. Instead of honesty exams, they offer tests designed to draw a general psychological profile of the applicant, claiming that this sort of analysis can predict more accurately than either the polygraph or the typical honesty test how the person will perform on the job. Keith M. Halperin, a psychologist with Personnel Decision, Inc. (PDI), a company that offers such tests, complains that most paper-and-pencil honesty tests are simply written equivalents of the polygraph. They ask applicants whether they have stolen from their employers, how much they have taken, and other questions directly related to honesty. "But why," asks Halperin, "would an applicant who is dishonest enough to steal from an employer be honest enough to admit it on a written test?" It is more difficult for applicants to fake their responses to PDI's tests, Halperin contends.

Not everyone is persuaded. Phyllis Bassett, vice president of James Bassett Company of Cincinnati, believes tests developed by psychologists that do not ask directly about the applicant's past honesty are poor predictors of future trustworthiness. This may be because, as some psychologists report, "it is very difficult for dishonest people to fake honesty." One reason is that thieves tend to believe that "everybody does it" and that therefore it would be implausible for them to deny stealing. In general, those who market honesty exams boast of their validity and reliability, as established by field studies. They insist that the tests do make a difference, that they enable employers to ferret out potential troublemakers—as in the Salvation Army case.

Dr. Jones administered London House's PSI to eighty kettler applicants, which happened to be the number that the particular theft-ridden center needed. The PSIs were not scored, and the eighty applicants were hired with no screening. Throughout the fund-raising month between Thanksgiving and Christmas, the center kept a record of each kettler's daily receipts. After the Christmas season, the tests were scored and divided into "recommended" and "not recommended" for employment. After accounting for the peculiarities of each collection neighborhood, Jones discovered that those kettlers the PSI had not recommended turned in on the average $17 per day less than those the PSI had recommended. Based on this analysis, he estimated the center's loss to employee theft during the fund drive at $20,000.

The list of psychological-test enthusiasts is growing by leaps and bounds, but the tests have plenty of detractors. Many psychologists believe the tests often lack validity or reliability, and the American Psychological Association favors the establishment of federal standards for written honesty exams. But the chief critics of honesty and other psychological exams are the people who have to take them. They complain about having to reveal some of the most intimate details of their lives and opinions.

For example, until an employee filed suit, Rent-A-Center, a Texas corporation, asked both job applicants and employees being considered for promotion true–false questions like these: "I have never indulged in any unusual sex practices," "I am very strongly attracted by members of my own sex," "I go to church almost every week," and "I have difficulty in starting or holding my bowel movements." A manager who was fired for complaining about the test says, "It was ridiculous. The test asked if I loved tall women. How was I supposed to answer that? My wife is 5 feet 3 inches." A spokesman for Rent-A-Center argues that its questionnaire is not unusual and that many other firms use it.

Firms who use tests like Rent-A-Center's believe that no one's privacy is being invaded because employees and job applicants can always refuse to take the test. Critics disagree. "Given the unequal bargaining power," says former ACLU official Kathleen Bailey, "the ability to refuse to take a test is one of theory rather than choice—if one really wants the job."

DISCUSSION QUESTIONS

1. Describe how you'd feel if you had to take a psychological test or an honesty test either as an employee or as a precondition for employment. Under what conditions, if any, would you take such a test?

2. How useful or informative do you think such tests are? Is their use a reasonable business policy? Assuming that tests like those described are valid and reliable, are they fair? Explain.

3. Do you think tests like these invade privacy and, if so, that this invasion is justified? Explain why or why not.

4. What ideals, obligations, and effects must be considered in using psychological tests as pre-employment screens? In your view, which is the most important consideration?

5. If you were an employer, would you require either employees or job applicants to pass an honesty exam? Explain the moral principles that support your position.

6. What do you think a business's reaction would be if the government required its executive officers to submit to an honesty test as a precondition for the company's getting a government contract? If, in your opinion, the business would object, does it have any moral grounds for subjecting workers to comparable tests?

7. Utilitarians would not find anything inherently objectionable about psychological tests as long as the interests of all parties were taken into account and given equal consideration before such tests were made a pre-employment screen. Do you think this is generally the case?

8. Should there be a law prohibiting or regulating psychological tests as a pre-employment screen? Should a decision to use these tests be made jointly by management and labor, or is testing for employment an exclusive employer right?

CASE 9.3

She Snoops to Conquer

JEAN FANUCHI, MANAGER OF A MODERATELY large department store, was worried. Shrinkage in the costume jewelry department had continued to rise for the third consecutive month. In fact, this time it had nearly wiped out the department's net profit in sales. Worse, it couldn't be attributed to damage or improper handling of markdowns or even to shoplifting. The only other possibility was in-house theft.

Fanuchi ordered chief of security Matt Katwalski to instruct his security people to keep a special eye on jewelry department employees as they went about their business. She also instructed that packages, purses, and other containers employees carried with them be searched when workers left the store. When these measures failed to turn up any leads, Katwalski suggested they hire a couple of plainclothes officers to observe the store's guards. Fanuchi agreed. But still nothing turned up.

"We're going to have to install a hidden camera at the checkout station in the jewelry department," Katwalski informed the manager.

"I don't know," Fanuchi replied.

"Of course," said Katwalski, "it won't be cheap. But you don't want this problem spreading to other departments, do you?" Fanuchi didn't.

"One other thing," Katwalski said. "I think we should install some microphones in the restroom, stockroom, and employee lounge."

"You mean snoop on our own employees?" Fanuchi asked, surprised.

"We could pick up something that could crack this thing wide open," Katwalski explained.

"But what if our employees found out? How would they feel, being spied on? And then there's the public to consider. Who knows how they'd react? Why, they'd probably think that if we are spying on our own workers, we were surely spying on them. No, Matt," Fanuchi decided. "Frankly, this whole approach troubles me."

"Okay, Ms. Fanuchi, but if it was my store . . ."

Fanuchi cut in, "No."

"You're the boss," said Katwalski.

When the shrinkage continued, Fanuchi finally gave in. She ordered Katwalski to have the camera and microphones installed. Within ten days the camera had nabbed the culprit.

The microphones contributed nothing to the apprehension of the thief. But because of them Fanuchi and Katwalski learned that at least one store employee was selling marijuana and perhaps hard drugs, that one was planning to quit without notice, that three were getting food stamps fraudulently, and that one buyer was out to discredit Fanuchi. In solving their shrinkage problem, the pair had unwittingly raised another: What should they do with the information they had gathered while catching the thief?[121]

DISCUSSION QUESTIONS

1. If you were Jean Fanuchi, how would you feel about your decision to order the installation of the viewing and listening devices? What other options did she have? Did she overlook any moral considerations or possible consequences?

2. Do employees have a right not to be spied on? If you were an employee at Fanuchi's store, would you think your privacy had been wrongly invaded?

3. How would you assess Fanuchi's actions if you were the owner of the store? Whose interests are more important in this case—the employer's or the employees'?

4. Do you think Fanuchi acted immorally? Why or why not? Evaluate her action by appeal to ethical principles.

5. How should Fanuchi and Katwalski handle the information they've gathered about their employees? What ideals, obligations, or effects are relevant to your answer?

CASE 9.4

Protecting the Unborn at Work

THE UNOBTRUSIVE FACTORY SITS BEHIND A hill-side shopping center in the small college town of Bennington, Vermont. Inside, the men and women make lead automobile batteries for Sears, Goodyear, and other companies. However, until the 1990s, none of the women employed there was able to have children. The reason was simple. The company, Johnson Controls, Inc., refused to hire any who could.[122]

Why? Because tiny toxic particles of lead and lead oxide fill the air inside the plant. According to the company, the levels of lead are low enough for adults but too high for children and fetuses. Numerous scientific studies have shown that lead can damage the brain and central nervous system of a fetus. Moreover, lead lingers in the bloodstream, which means that fetuses can be affected by it even if a woman limits her exposure to lead once she learns she is pregnant. Because of this, Johnson Controls decided that it would exclude women at all fourteen of its factories from jobs that entail high exposure to lead—unless they could prove that they couldn't become pregnant. The company made no exceptions for celibate women or women who used contraceptives. The company's position was simple: "The issue is protecting the health of unborn children."

Johnson Controls's stance was in line with the national Centers for Disease Control's recommendation that women of childbearing age be excluded from jobs involving significant lead exposure. Because by law its standards must be "feasible," Occupational Safety and Health Administration (OSHA) regulations permit chemicals in the workplace that are known to cause harm both to fetuses and to some adult employees. But OSHA holds that employers have a general duty to reduce the hazards of the workplace as far as possible. On this basis, employers such as Olin Corporation, American Cyanamid, General Motors, Monsanto, Allied Chemical, Gulf Oil, and B. F. Goodrich also adopted policies excluding women from chemical plant jobs judged to be hazardous to their potential offspring.

Unfortunately, there are relatively few scientific studies of the effect of exposure to toxic manufacturing chemicals on workers' reproductive health. Only a small percentage of the workplace chemicals with a potential for damaging reproduction have been evaluated, and each year many new chemicals are introduced into factories. Although employers are obviously dealing with many unknowns, no one doubts that they have a moral and legal obligation to control and limit these risks as best they can. Lawsuits and even criminal sanctions have battered companies that have managed hazardous chemicals irresponsibly. Monsanto Chemical Company, for example, agreed to pay $1.5 million to six employees because exposure to a chemical additive used for rubber production allegedly gave them bladder cancer. Fetal protection policies aren't just dictated by management, though. "Women who become pregnant," the *New York Times* reports, "are beginning to demand the right to transfer out of jobs they believe to be hazardous, even when there is only sketchy scientific evidence of any hazard."

But many women were unhappy about the decision of Johnson Controls. They worried that fetal protection policies would be used to exclude women from more and more workplaces on the grounds that different chemical substances or certain tasks such as heavy lifting might be potential causes of miscarriage and fetal injury. In line with this, the United Automobile Workers, which represents many of the Johnson employees, sought to overturn the U.S. Court of Appeals decision that judged Johnson's policy to be "reasonably necessary to the industrial safety-based concern of protecting the unborn child from lead exposure." The union contends, to the contrary, that the policy discriminates against women, jeopardizing their hard-won gains in male-dominated industries.

Many women's advocates see the issue in slightly different terms. They believe policies like that of Johnson Controls challenge a woman's right not only to control her fetus but to control her unfertilized eggs as well. In addition, such policies infringe on privacy: By taking a job at Johnson, a woman was in effect telling the world that she was sterile. And there is also the fundamental question of who knows what is best for a woman.

After bearing two children, Cheryl Chalifoux had a doctor block her fallopian tubes so that she couldn't become pregnant again. Although career advancement wasn't the reason she made her decision, it did enable her to switch from a factory job paying $6.34 an hour to one at Johnson's Bennington plant paying $15 an hour. Still, she says that the policy was unfair and degrading. "It's your body," she complains. "They're implying they're doing it for your own good." Cheryl Cook, also a mother of two who had surgery for the same reason, joined Chalifoux in leaving the other company to work for Johnson Controls. She says, "I work right in the lead. I make the oxide. But you should choose for yourself. Myself, I wouldn't go in there if I could get pregnant. But they don't trust you."

Isabelle Katz Pizler, director of women's rights at the American Civil Liberties Union, agrees. "Since time immemorial," she says, "the excuse for keeping women in their place has been because of their role in producing the next generation. The attitude of Johnson Controls is: 'We know better than you. We can't allow women to make this decision. We have to make it for them.'" And the ACLU has argued in court that "since no activity is risk-free, deference to an employer's analysis of fetal risk could limit women's participation in nearly every area of economic life."

To this the company responded that it has a moral obligation to the parties that cannot participate in the woman's decisions—namely, the unfertilized ovum and the fetus. In addition, the company has an obligation to stockholders, who would bear the brunt of lawsuits brought by employees' children born with retardation, nervous system disorders, or other ailments that lead can cause.

Joseph A. Kinney, executive director of the National Safe Workplace Institute in Chicago, sides with Johnson Controls, but only because he believes that letting women assume the burden of their safety undermines OSHA's responsibility to mandate workplace safety rules. "The discrimination side of the issue needs to be resolved," Kinney says. "But the ideal thing is to regulate lead out of the workplace and any other toxin that poses fetal damage."

However, the U.S. Supreme Court ruled unanimously that the fetal protection policy at Johnson Controls violated the Civil Rights Act of 1964, which prohibits sex discrimination in employment.[123] Pointing to evidence that lead affects sperm and can thus harm the offspring of men exposed to it at the time of conception, the Court stated:

> Respondent does not seek to protect the unconceived children of all its employees. Despite evidence in the record about the debilitating effect of lead exposure on the male reproductive system, Johnson Controls is concerned only with the harms that may befall the unborn offspring of its female employees. . . . [The company's policy is] discriminatory because it requires only a female employee to produce proof that she is not capable of reproducing.

The Court was divided over whether fetal protection policies could ever be legally justified. Justice Harry A. Blackmun, writing for a majority of the Court, declared that they could not, that the Civil Rights Act prohibited all such policies:

> Decisions about the welfare of future children must be left to the parents who conceive, bear, support and raise them rather than to the employers who hire those parents. Women as capable of doing their jobs as their male counterparts may not be forced to choose between having a child and having a job.

Referring to the Pregnancy Discrimination Act of 1978, which amended the 1964 Civil Rights Act and prohibits employment discrimination on the basis of pregnancy or potential pregnancy, Blackmun added:

> Employment late in pregnancy often imposes risks on the unborn child, but Congress indicated that the employer may take into account only the woman's ability to get her job done.

A minority of the justices, however, were unwilling to go so far, and in a concurring opinion, Justice Byron R. White wrote that "common sense tells us that it is part of the normal operation of business concerns to avoid causing injury to third parties as well as to employees." But he added that, in his view, a fetal protection policy would not be defensible unless an employer also addressed other known occupational health risks.

Should pregnant police officers or military personnel be allowed to be in situations that endanger the life of their unborn child?

DISCUSSION QUESTIONS

1. Do you agree that Johnson Controls's fetal protection policy discriminated against women? Do pregnant women have a moral—not just a legal—right to work with lead?

2. Suppose exposure to lead did not affect sperm or the male reproductive system. Would Johnson's policy still have been discriminatory? Would it hamper women's efforts to win equality in the workplace?

3. Can there be a nondiscriminatory fetal protection policy? Is Justice White correct in arguing that companies have an obligation to avoid causing injury to fetuses just as they do to other "third parties"?

4. Suppose a company forbids any employee capable of reproducing from working with lead. Would such a policy wrongly interfere with employees' freedom of choice? Would it be an invasion of their privacy? Would it be fair to employees who are fertile but plan to have no children?

5. Evaluate fetal protection policies from the egoistic, utilitarian, and Kantian perspectives. What rights are involved? What are the likely benefits and harms of such policies?

6. If they are fully informed, do employees with a certain medical condition have a right to work at jobs that can be hazardous to the health of people in their condition? Or can company policy or OSHA regulations justifiably prevent them from doing so for their own good?

7. Would you agree with Joseph Kinney that the real issue is the need to remove toxins from the workplace? Is this a realistic goal?

CASE 9.5

Swedish Daddies

YEARS AGO, THE FAMOUS ECONOMIST PAUL Samuelson quipped that "women are just men with less money." He was referring to the financially dependent position of women at that time, when they were unlikely to be employed outside the home and, if they were, were likely to earn substantially less than men. That has now changed for the better. Although women have yet to achieve full equity at the highest levels of business, they constitute nearly half the U.S. workforce, and their pay is not so very far behind that of men. Moreover, with the decline of manufacturing and the growing importance of the service sector in today's economy, brain power matters more than brawn. Here women can compete as well as men, and they have proved their value to employers over and over again. In fact, they now outnumber men in professional and managerial positions. And with women continuing to graduate from college at a higher rate and in greater numbers than men, their future looks bright.[124]

But for many women there is one continuing source of frustration. They often feel forced to choose between motherhood and a high-powered career. Jobs that offer the hours and flexibility that suit women with family responsibilities tend to pay less, while the most financially rewarding jobs frequently require brutal hours and total commitment to the job. And the higher you go, the rougher it gets. Not only must those who want to fight their way to the top of the corporate world work long, grueling hours, but they are also often expected to gain experience working in different departments and divisions and even in different countries. That tends to rule out women with family commitments. As a result, women with children, especially single mothers, earn less on average than men do while childless women earn almost as much as men.

Over the years, some business writers have argued that we should simply accept this fact and that companies should distinguish between the career-primary woman and the career-and-family woman. Those in the first category put their careers first. They remain single or childless or, if they do have children, are satisfied to have others raise them. The automatic association of all women with babies is unfair to these women, argues Felice N. Schwartz, an organizer and advocate for working women. "The secret to dealing with such women," she writes, "is to recognize them early, accept them, and clear artificial barriers from their path to the top."

The majority of women, however, fall into the second category. They want to pursue genuine careers while participating actively in the rearing of their children. Most of them, Schwartz and others believe, are willing to trade some career growth and compensation for freedom from the constant pressure to work long hours and weekends. By forcing these women to choose between family and career, companies lose a valuable resource and a competitive advantage. Instead, firms must plan for and manage maternity, they must provide the flexibility to help career-and-family women be maximally productive, and they must take an active role in providing family support and in making high-quality, affordable child care available to all women. In other words, companies should provide women with the option of a comfortable but slower "mommy track."

Although distinguishing between career-primary women and career-and-family women seems reasonable and humane, there's rarely any mention of fathers or of shared parental responsibility for raising children. The mommy track idea also takes for granted the existing values, structures, and biases of a corporate world that is still male dominated. As authors Barbara Ehrenreich and Deidre English write, "Eventually it is the corporate culture itself that needs to slow down to a human pace . . . [and end] workloads that are incompatible with family life."

One country that is trying to push things in a new direction is Sweden. Whereas America stands almost alone in the world in not guaranteeing women paid maternity leave, Sweden provides sixteen months paid leave per child, with the costs shared between the employer and the government. However—and this is what is novel—at least two of these months are reserved for fathers. No father is forced to take baby leave, but the leave is nontransferable so it's "use it or lose it." And more and more men are using it. In fact, more than eight in ten Swedish fathers now take advantage of parental leave. And some Swedish politicians are arguing that more months—perhaps half of them—should be exclusively for fathers. Germany has now followed Sweden's lead. In 2007 it began guaranteeing fathers two months' paternity leave. No country, however, has gone further toward parental equity than Iceland. It reserves three months of parental leave for the father and three months for the mother and allows parents to share an additional three months.

In the meantime, the paternity-leave law is helping to redefine masculinity in Sweden. Take game warden Mikael Karlson. A former soldier who owns a snowmobile, two hunting dogs, and five guns, he's a man's man. Cradling his two-month-old baby girl in his arms, he says he cannot imagine not taking parental leave. "Everyone does it." Not only does his wife agree, but she says that he never looks more attractive to her than "when he is in the forest with his rifle over his shoulder and the baby on his back." Some men admit that they were unsure of themselves at first—the cooking, cleaning, and sleepless nights—but that they adjusted to it and even liked it. One Swedish father calls it a "life-changing experience."

"Many men no longer want to be identified just by their jobs," says Bengt Westerberg, who as deputy prime minister helped to bring the law about. "Many women now expect their husbands to take at least some time off with the children." "Now men can have it all—a successful career and being a responsible daddy," adds Birgitta Ohlsson, another government minister. "It's a new kind of manly. It's more wholesome." Some also think the paternity-leave law is the reason that the divorce rate in Sweden has declined in recent years.

There are, however, stories of companies' discouraging men from taking long baby leaves, and managers admit that parental leave can be disruptive. Still, by and large Swedish business has adapted, and many companies find that a family-friendly work environment helps them attract talented employees. "Graduates used to look for big paychecks," says one human resources manager. "Now they want work–life balance."

Many men in the United States would like a better balance between work life and family life, too. But even when paternity leave is an option, men are reluctant to take it. One reason is the attitude of their colleagues and employers, who tend to believe that, for men, work should come first. And, indeed, a recent study has found that fathers who are active caregivers are seen as distracted and less dedicated and that they are more likely than are so-called traditional fathers to be teased and insulted at work, accused of being "wimpy" or "henpecked" by their wives.[125]

DISCUSSION QUESTIONS

1. If you have, or plan to have, children, what sort of balance do you seek between career and family life? Do you believe that the mindset of corporate America is conducive to the type of work-and-family arrangement that would suit you?

2. Should the United States require companies to provide paid maternity leave? Should it assist them to do so? What about paternity leave?

3. Do companies already have a mommy track, whether they call it that or not? Is the idea a good one? Is it somehow discriminatory against women? Against men?

4. Should men be more actively involved in childrearing? If not, why not? If so, what steps, if any, should either business or society take to encourage this?

5. Should special organizational arrangements be made for workers who wish to combine career and child raising? If so, identify the steps that companies can take to accommodate parental needs more effectively.

6. Does a firm have an obligation to give employees the flexibility to work out the particular balance of career and family that is right for them? Or does this go beyond the social responsibilities of business?

7. Can paid maternity or paternity leave make sense from a business point of view, even if it is not subsidized by the government?

CHAPTER 10

MORAL CHOICES FACING EMPLOYEES

INTRODUCTION

WHEN HIS ELDEST DAUGHTER ASKED HIM, "WHY don't you just do what they want?" George Betancourt wasn't sure how he should answer. Betancourt was a senior engineer at Northeast Utilities, which operates five nuclear power plants in New England, and all he had done was to speak up and express his professional judgment. Now Northeast wanted him to shut up. First, Northeast's human resources officer had called him in. After complaining that Betancourt wasn't being a "team player," she described to him the company's termination policies. Three weeks later, Betancourt was informed he was being reassigned. "We'd like to help you, George," Eric DeBarba, vice-president of technical services, told him. "But you've got to start thinking company."[1]

George Galatis was the Northeast engineer on whose behalf Betancourt had spoken up. Galatis had discovered what he considered to be a glaring safety problem at Northeast's Millstone No. 1 plant. In an effort to save downtime (and hence money) during the refueling process, the plant's procedures routinely violated federal guidelines and pushed its spent-fuel pool well beyond its design capacity. For eighteen months, Galatis's supervisors denied the problem existed and refused to report it to the Nuclear Regulatory Commission (NRC). Northeast brought in a series of outside experts to prove Galatis wrong, but the consultants ended up agreeing with him. Within the company, Betancourt backed up Galatis's safety concerns. When Northeast finally began to acknowledge a possible problem, it didn't move fast enough to satisfy Galatis. Two years after he first raised his safety concerns, he finally took the case directly to the NRC, only to learn that it had known about the unsafe procedures for years. He also discovered evidence that suggested collusion between Northeast and NRC officials to subordinate safety to profitability.

As a result of going to the NRC, Galatis experienced "subtle forms of harassment, retaliation, and intimidation." He wasn't being paranoid. Two dozen Millstone No. 1 employees claimed they were fired or demoted for raising safety concerns. Some of his colleagues sided with the company, however, accusing Galatis of aiding anti-nuclear activists and trying to take away their livelihood. But Galatis didn't stop. He hired a lawyer who specializes in representing whistle-blowers and kept after the NRC. With the lawyer's help, the public spotlight was focused on Millstone No. 1. Local politicians began asking questions. Even though the NRC ignored Galatis, it ended up validating his concerns, and Millstone No. 1 was shut down. Citing chronic safety concerns, employee harassment, and a "historic emphasis on cost savings vs. performance," the NRC also put Northeast's other two Millstone plants on its high-scrutiny "watch list." And a new NRC head vowed to shake up the regulatory body itself.

> GALATIS HAD DISCOVERED what he considered to be a glaring safety problem at Northeast's Millstone No. 1 plant.

Galatis and Betancourt managed to hang on to their jobs, but their careers came to a standstill. "The two Georges had better watch their backs," says one engineer. "Up at Northeast, they've got long memories." A disillusioned Galatis says, "If I had it to do over again, I wouldn't."

For someone in the shoes of George Galatis or George Betancourt, two general issues come up. *First* is the question of where an employee's overall moral duty lies. For a professional engineer to go public with documented safety concerns may seem to be a more straightforward moral decision than that faced by an employee who suspects irregularities, unsafe procedures, or wrongdoing in an area unrelated to his or her own job. In that case, the employee may possibly have conflicting moral obligations. Furthermore, if an employee reports irregularities to the appropriate authority, the employee must then decide whether he or she is morally obligated to pursue the matter further. Again other moral considerations come into play.

Second, once they have decided that they ought to blow the whistle, employees must face the possible negative consequences. Galatis and Betancourt are skilled, mature, and respected professionals, with established records and good credentials; in terms of employment options, they may have had less to risk than do potential whistle-blowers who are just starting their careers or who have limited job options or heavy financial obligations. Nor is this simply a tug-of-war between moral duty and self-interest. Most moral theorists would agree that depending on the circumstances, certain personal sacrifices might be so great that a person cannot reasonably be morally obliged to make them.

LEARNING OBJECTIVES

These two themes—determining one's moral responsibility amid a welter of conflicting demands and paying the personal costs that can be incurred from living up to one's obligations—recur throughout this chapter. In particular, it looks at the following topics:

1. Employees' obligations to the firm, company loyalty, and the problem of conflicts of interest
2. Illegitimate use of one's official position for private gain, especially through insider trading or access to proprietary data
3. Domestic and foreign bribery and the factors to consider in determining the morality of giving and receiving gifts in a business context
4. The obligations employees have to third parties and the considerations they should weigh in cases of conflicting moral duties or divided loyalties
5. What whistle-blowing is and the factors relevant to evaluating its morality
6. The problem of how considerations of self-interest are to be weighed by an employee facing a tough moral choice

⁂

OBLIGATIONS TO THE FIRM

The employment contract governs the employer–employee relationship and provides the framework for understanding the respective obligations of employer and employee.

When you accept employment, you generally agree to perform certain tasks, usually during certain specified hours, in exchange for financial remuneration. Whether oral or written, implicit or explicit, a contract governs your employment relationship and provides the basic framework for understanding the reciprocal obligations between you and your employer. Your employment contract determines what you are supposed to do or accomplish for your employer, and it may cover other matters ranging from parking privileges to your dress and deportment while carrying out your responsibilities. The terms of your employment contract may be specific and detailed or vague and open-ended.

LOYALTY TO THE COMPANY

Because you are hired to work for your employer, you have an obligation, when acting on behalf of the organization, to promote your employer's interests. Insofar as you are acting as an agent of your employer, the traditional law of agency places you under a legal obligation to act loyally and in good faith and to carry out all lawful instructions. For example, Polo Ralph Lauren successfully sued a sales clerk for violating his duty of loyalty by letting a friend buy clothes with his employee discount and with merchandise credits made out to fictitious people. The employee argued that he was such a low-level employee that he had no duty of loyalty, but the court disagreed.[2] However, it would be morally mistaken to view employees simply as agents of their employers or to expect them to subordinate entirely their autonomy and private lives to the organization. Morality requires neither blind loyalty nor total submission to the organization.

Some writers deny that employees have any obligation of loyalty to the company, even a prima facie obligation, "because companies are not the kind of things that are properly objects of loyalty." Why not? Because a business firm functions to make money, the argument goes, self-interest is all that binds it together, whereas "loyalty depends on ties that demand self-sacrifice with no expectation of reward."[3] From this perspective, then, one can owe loyalty to family, friends, or country but not to a corporation; employees simply work to get paid and are misguided if they see themselves as owing loyalty to the company.

However, the notion of **company loyalty** is commonplace, and most people find it a coherent and legitimate concept. For the many employees who willingly make sacrifices for the organization above and beyond their job descriptions, loyalty is a real and important value. Indeed, it is not clear how well any business or organization could function without employee loyalty, and certainly most companies want more than minimal time and effort from their employees. Loyalty, though, is a two-way street, and most employees believe that it's up to the company to earn and retain their loyalty.

Arguably, some obligations of loyalty simply come with the job—for example, the obligation to warn the organization of danger, the obligation to act in a way that protects its legitimate interests, and the obligation to cooperate actively in the furtherance of legitimate corporate goals. To be sure, many businesses demand more than this in the name of loyalty. They may expect employees to defend the company if it is maligned, to mentor coworkers, to work overtime when the company needs it, to accept a transfer if necessary for the good of the organization, or to demonstrate their commitment to it in countless other ways. Being loyal in these ways may be important to an employee, even if it is not morally required. In addition, employees, like other individuals, can come to identify with the groups they are part of, accepting group goals and norms as their own. Some moral theorists believe not only that loyalty to the group can become an important value for the individual employee, but also that in the appropriate circumstances the process of group identification can create an additional obligation of loyalty that the employee otherwise would not have.[4]

> Although some writers deny that employees owe loyalty to the company, most people find company loyalty a coherent and legitimate concept.

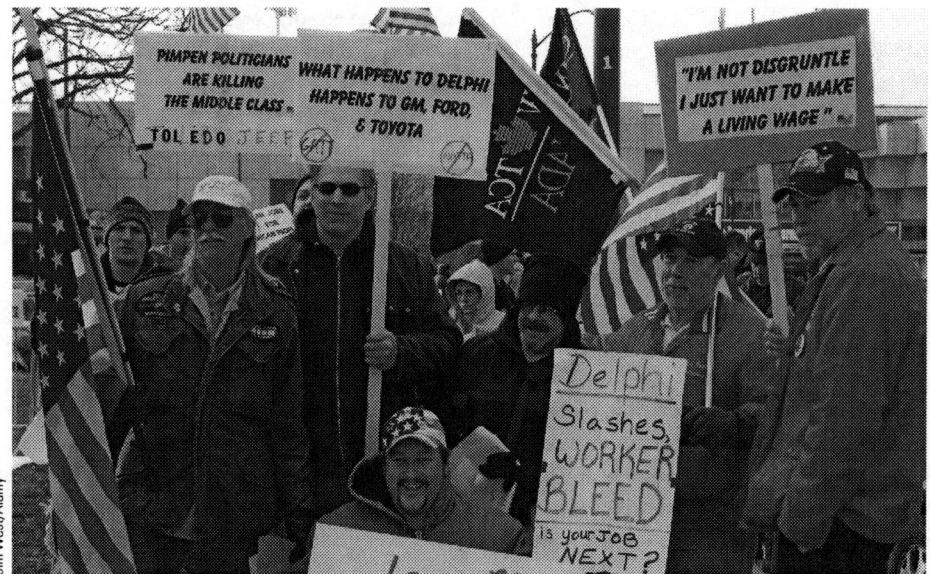

Are employees who publicly protest wages or working conditions being disloyal to their employer?

CONFLICTS OF INTEREST

Even the most loyal employees can find that their interests collide with those of the organization. You want to dress one way, but the organization requires you to dress another way; you'd prefer to show up for work at noon, but the company expects you to be present at 8 A.M.; you'd like to receive $75,000 for your services, but the organization pays you a fraction of that figure. The reward, autonomy, and self-fulfillment that workers seek aren't always compatible with the demands of the organization. Whatever the matter in question, the perspectives of employee and employer can differ.

Sometimes this clash of goals and desires can take the serious form of a conflict of interest. In an organization, a **conflict of interest** arises when employees at any level have special or private interests that are substantial enough to interfere with their job duties—that is, when their personal interests lead them, or might be anticipated to lead them, to make decisions or to act in ways that are detrimental to their employer's interests. That was certainly the case when Enron's chief financial officer, Andrew Fastow, represented the company in negotiations with several firms of which he was a managing partner (and as a result eventually earned millions of dollars from the deals).

As mentioned, the work contract is the primary source of an organization's right to expect employees to act on its behalf in a way that is unprejudiced by their personal interests. In general, if the contents of the work agreement are legal and if the employee freely consents to them, then he or she is under an obligation to fulfill the terms of the agreement. Implicit in any work contract is the assumption that employees will not sacrifice the interests of the organization for personal advantage. Of course, individuals may seek to benefit from being employed with a certain business or organization, but in discharging their contractual duties, employees should not subordinate the welfare of the organization to their own gain.

When an employee's private interests run counter to the interests of his or her employer in some significant way—or, to put the point differently, when those interests are likely to interfere with the employee's ability to exercise proper judgment on behalf of the organization—a conflict of interest exists. The danger, then, is that those interests will lead the employee to sacrifice the interests of his or her employer. For example, Bart Erdman, sales manager for Leisure Sports World, gives all his firm's promotional work to Impact Advertising because its chief officer is Erdman's brother-in-law. As a result, Leisure Sports World pays about 15 percent more in advertising costs than it would if its work went to another agency. Here, Erdman has allowed his decisions as an employee to be influenced by his personal interests, to the detriment of Leisure Sports World. Note that Erdman's interest is not financial; conflicts of interest can take various forms.

Suppose that Erdman does not throw all of his company's promotional work to his brother-in-law; rather, he gives the firm's business to his brother-in-law only when he sincerely believes that doing so is best for Leisure Sports World. Nevertheless, a conflict of interest can still be said to exist. Because of his brother-in-law, Erdman still has a private interest in his business dealings for Leisure Sports World that could possibly lead him to act against the interests of the company. In other words, there is a danger that Bart's judgment may not be as objective as it should be.

Conflicts of interest are morally worrisome not only when an employee acts to the detriment of the organization but also when the employee's private interests are significant enough that they could tempt the person to do so. Indeed, research shows that conflicts of interest can unconsciously distort the decisions of even very honest people.[5] That's why alarm bells went off when *Businessweek* disclosed that two members of the audit committee at Qwest Communications—already under fire for dubious accounting

---

SUMMARY

The employment contract creates various obligations to one's employer. In addition, employees often feel loyalty to the organization. Conflicts of interest arise when employees have a personal interest in a transaction substantial enough that it might be expected to affect their judgment or lead them to act against the interests of the organization.

Conflicts of interest are morally worrisome even if the employee doesn't act to the detriment of the employer.

practices—directed companies with million-dollar contracts with Qwest, thus raising questions about their ability to exercise independent judgment.[6] Even the appearance of impropriety can undermine trust and erode the confidence that others are entitled to have in the impartiality and objectivity of one's decisions.

By definition, to have a conflict of interest is to be in a morally risky situation; that is why employees should promptly extricate themselves from such conflicts or avoid them in the first place. But deciding when an employee's private interests are substantial enough for the situation to constitute a conflict of interest can be difficult. Equally difficult can be deciding exactly how the person should deal with a specific conflict. Sometimes people are encouraged simply to disclose the conflict to those relying on their judgment, thus preventing deception and allowing those relying on them to adjust their reliance accordingly. That is often good counsel, but it doesn't end the conflict of interest. Moreover, it's no panacea. Supposedly, if I tell you that I have a financial reason for skewing my advice to you, you'll take that into account and everything will be fine. Unfortunately, however, experimental evidence suggests that even when informed that the advice they're receiving may be biased, people fail to discount it as much as they should.[7] Moreover, those who disclose a conflict of interest often end up giving more biased advice than those who do not disclose.[8]

Finally, it is worth mentioning auditors. They face a different sort of conflict, namely, between their duty to report the truth and their running successful businesses. That's because they are hired and paid by the companies that they are supposed to audit. It's one of the reasons credit-rating agencies were so generous, to put it mildly, in their grading of many financial products in the run-up to the subprime mortgage crisis. A large Harvard study has now confirmed what one might have guessed: When auditors are paid by a third-party, they report more accurately.[9]

Financial Investments

Conflicts of interest may exist when employees have financial investments in suppliers, customers, or distributors with whom their organizations do business. During the dot-com boom, executives at high-tech firms often owned stock in other young companies in the same or closely related fields. Those tangled financial relationships sometimes produced conflicts of interest. For example, eight executives at EMC were heavily invested in the start-up StorageNetworks. They recommended it to their clients, and those referrals quickly grew to 40 percent of the younger company's business. But as StorageNetworks got larger and as EMC expanded its own services division, the two companies found themselves competing, leading some at EMC to complain that the other firm was poaching its employees and interfering with its customer relationships. Today, EMC says the impact on business was negligible. But a former board member maintains that the eight executives were recommending StorageNetworks when they should have been pushing EMC equipment: "No question, it had an impact on their day-to-day decisions. It was a tremendous financial incentive."[10]

How much of a financial investment does it take to create a conflict of interest? There's no simple answer. Certainly it is acceptable to own stock in large publicly held corporations, such as Coca-Cola or Hewlett-Packard, that are listed on the stock exchange and whose stock price is unlikely to be influenced by your company's buying their products or not. Sometimes companies limit the percentage of outstanding stock their employees may own in a potential supplier, customer, distributor, or competitor (usually up to 10 percent). But in the EMC case, the eight executives owned shares of StorageNetworks before the company went public, and with the latter's stock rocketing

SUMMARY
When employees have financial investments in suppliers, customers, or distributors with whom their organization does business, conflicts of interest can arise. Company policy usually determines the permissible limits of such financial interests.

from 50 cents a share to over $90, adhering to the 10-percent rule wouldn't have prevented the problem. Frequently companies require key officials to disclose all outside interests that could cloud their judgment or adversely affect their ability to promote the organization's interests. That's important, but as previously mentioned, full disclosure alone doesn't make the conflict disappear; further steps should probably still be taken. Organizations need a detailed policy, customized to reflect their needs and interests, that spells out the limits of permissible outside financial investments and what employees should do when they have possible conflicts of interest. Because such a policy can affect the financial well-being of those who fall under it, however, it should be open to negotiation just as employee compensation is.

ABUSE OF OFFICIAL POSITION

Using one's official position for personal gain is likely to violate one's obligations to the organization.

The use of one's official position for personal gain always raises moral concerns and questions because of the likelihood that one is violating one's obligations to the firm or organization. Examples of **abuse of official position** range from misusing expense accounts to billing the company for unnecessary travel and from using subordinates for work outside the firm to exploiting a position of trust within an organization to enhance one's own financial leverage and holdings. Executives who use corporate funds for private purposes like health club memberships, extravagant parties, vacation travel, or remodeling their homes are guilty of abusing their official position, as were Bernard J. Ebbers of WorldCom, John Legere of Global Crossing, and L. Dennis Kozlowski of Tyco International, who used their high positions to borrow huge amounts of money at below-market rates—in Ebbers's case over $400 million—from the companies they worked for.[11]

INSIDER TRADING

Insider trading is the buying or selling of stocks on the basis of nonpublic information that is likely to affect their price.

One common way of abusing one's official position is through **insider trading**: the buying or selling of stocks (or other financial securities) by business "insiders" on the basis of information that has not yet been made public and is likely to affect the price of the stock.[12] For example, as soon as he learned that the Food and Drug Administration (FDA) was not going to approve his company's highly touted cancer drug Erbitux, Dr. Sam Waksal, CEO of ImClone Systems at the time, knew its stock would plummet. Before the FDA's decision was made public, Waksal quickly but quietly sold his stock in the company and told his father and one of his daughters to do so as well. He is also alleged to have passed the word on to his friend Martha Stewart, who dumped her ImClone stock the day before the FDA announced its decision. One doesn't have to profit personally to cross the line, however. For example, the wife of Genentech's president and chief executive officer was charged with insider trading for providing confidential information to her brother. Before the biotechnology firm was partly acquired by another company, she told her brother that "some good things were about to happen" to the company and suggested that he buy a few thousand dollars' worth of stock, even if he had to borrow the funds. She also advised him to keep the purchase secret and make it in the name of a "trustworthy" friend.

Inside traders ordinarily defend their actions by claiming that they don't injure anyone. It's true that trading by insiders on the basis of nonpublic information seldom directly harms anyone. But moral concerns arise from indirect injury, as well as from direct.

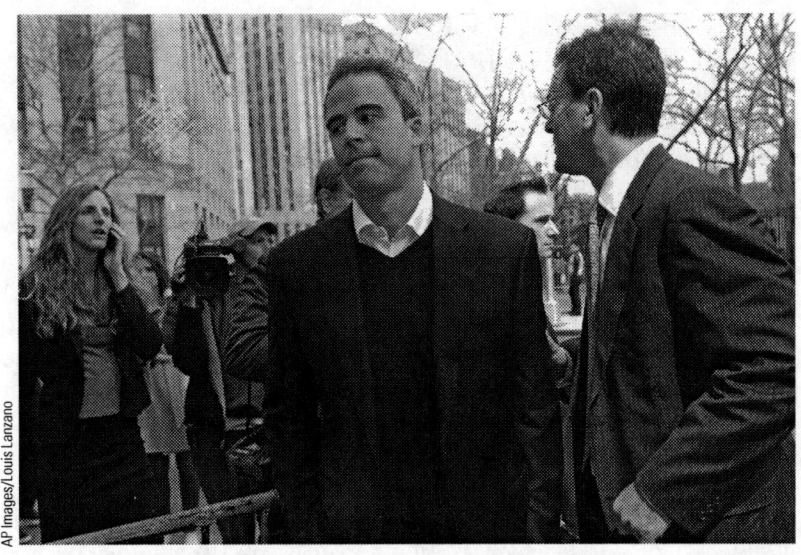

In December 2013, a jury found Michael Steinberg, a trader at SAC Capital Advisors, guilty of insider trading. Some consider insider trading a victimless crime. Do you agree?

As one author puts it, "What causes injury or loss to outsiders is not what the insiders knew or did; rather it is what [the outsiders] themselves did not know. It is their own lack of knowledge which exposes them to risk of loss or denies them an opportunity to make a profit."[13] Case in point: the famous Texas Gulf Sulphur stock scandal.

When test drilling by Texas Gulf indicated a rich deposit of ore near Timmins, Ontario, some officials at Texas Gulf attempted to play down the potential worth of the Timmins property in a press release by describing it as only a prospect. But four days later a second press release termed the Timmins property a major discovery. In the interim, inside investors made a handsome personal profit through stock purchases. At the same time, stockholders who unloaded stock after the first press release or who sold the stock short, anticipating its price would fall, lost money.

The Securities and Exchange Commission (SEC), which is charged with policing the stock market, subsequently charged that a group of insiders—including Texas Gulf directors, officers, and employees—had violated the disclosure section of the Securities Exchange Act of 1934 by purchasing stock in the company while withholding information about the rich ore strike the company had made. The courts upheld the charge, finding that the first press release was "misleading to the reasonable investor using due care."[14] As a result, the courts not only ordered the insiders to pay into a special court-administered account all the money they had made but also directed them to repay profits made by outsiders whom they had tipped off. The courts then used this account to compensate people who had lost money by selling their Texas Gulf Sulphur stock on the basis of the first press release.

Insiders and "Misappropriation"

Insider dealings raise intriguing questions. When can employees buy and sell securities in their own companies? How much information must they disclose to stockholders about the firm's plans and prospects? When must this information be disclosed? There's also the question: Who is considered an insider? Corporate executives, directors, officers, and other key employees are certainly insiders. But what about outsiders whom a company temporarily employs, such as accountants, lawyers, and contractors? Or what about those who just happen upon inside information?

In its effort to police the marketplace, the SEC has interpreted "insider" in a broad sense to mean anyone who buys or sells stock based on nonpublic information—whether or not the person is a corporate officer or otherwise linked to the company whose stock is being bought or sold. However, in 1980 the U.S. Supreme Court challenged the SEC's broad conception of insider trading in the case of Vincent Chiarella, a financial printer who traded on information he culled from documents passing through his shop. The Court ruled that Chiarella was not an insider with fiduciary responsibilities and thus had not violated the Securities Exchange Act. The Court reinforced its decision three years later when it reversed the conviction of securities analyst Raymond Dirks, who advised several of his clients to dump their shares in a company that he was about to blow the whistle on for fraud. In so ruling, the Court held that there is nothing improper about an outsider's using information, as long as the information is not obtained from an insider who breaches a legal duty to the corporation's shareholders for personal gain or to show favor to friends.

Since then the SEC has developed a new tactic, arguing that people who trade on confidential information but who are not, strictly speaking, company insiders are guilty of insider trading if they have "misappropriated" sensitive information. Although some appellate courts had rejected the SEC's approach, in 1997 the Supreme Court endorsed the misappropriation theory of insider trading in ***U.S. v. O'Hagan***, thus upholding one of the SEC's main legal weapons against insider trading. In this case, James O'Hagan, a lawyer, had reaped a $4.3 million profit after learning that a company represented by his law firm was planning a hostile takeover of another company. O'Hagan had not worked on the case himself, but he had—the Court ruled—misappropriated confidential information belonging to his firm and its client. Writing for the majority, Justice Ruth Bader Ginsburg stressed that the Court's decision reflected the "animating purpose" of the Securities Exchange Act, namely, "to insure honest securities markets and thereby promote investor confidence."

Conflicting Perspectives on Insider Trading

Arthur Levitt, Jr., chairman of the Securities and Exchange Commission at the time, applauds the Court's *O'Hagan* decision, stating that it "reaffirms the SEC's effort to make the stock market fair to all people, whether you're a Wall Street veteran or a Main Street newcomer."[15] Law professor Henry Manne, however, sees nothing inherently wrong with insider trading and thinks the SEC should stay totally out of the insider-trading field. "The use of insider information should be governed by private contractual relationships," he believes, such as those between a corporation and its personnel or among the partners and associates of a law firm.[16]

At the core of this disagreement are two opposed perspectives on what makes the market work. Levitt and like-minded analysts contend that the marketplace can work only if it is perceived as being honest and offering equal investment opportunity. Insider trading, they argue, makes that impossible. Those who think like Manne believe that permitting insiders to trade is good for the market because it accelerates the flow of positive or negative information about the stock to other shareholders and investors. As a result, this information is more quickly reflected in the stock's price, which is healthy for the market. They also believe that permitting insider trading can benefit a company by providing employees an incentive to invent new products, put together deals, or otherwise create new information that will increase the value of a company's stock.

Contrary to the view expressed by Manne, however, it's difficult to believe that insider trading does much to promote genuine market efficiency. That's because insiders

Some business theorists dispute the need to outlaw insider trading.

hoard information, profiting on the lag between when they start buying or selling and when the rest of the market learns what the insiders already know. In addition, insiders can benefit from negative, not just positive, information about the company they work for; this creates a dangerous incentive for them to act in ways that hurt it. Even if insider trading does promote market efficiency in some cases, this fact would have to be weighed against its moral drawbacks.

Insider trading makes some ordinary investors worse off than they would have been if they had had the same information. This strikes many people as unfair. True, it's not always unfair for one party to a transaction to know more than another, but insider traders often do seem to be taking unfair advantage of outsiders. Moreover, as Justice Ginsberg and Arthur Levitt suggest, widespread perception that "the game is rigged" would discourage ordinary investors from buying stocks. Even more important, when executives engage in insider trading, they are putting their own interests ahead of their shareholders, thus violating the fiduciary responsibility that is central to business management. All employees, but especially company insiders, have a duty to act in the interests of the firm and its shareholders, but many ways of profiting from insider information do not benefit the company at all—indeed, they may damage its interests.[17]

The information that employees garner within the company is not always the kind that affects stock prices. Sometimes the information concerns highly sensitive data related to company research, technology, product development, and so on. How employees treat such secret or classified data can also raise important moral issues.

PROPRIETARY DATA

Companies guard information that can affect their competitive standing with all the zealousness of a bulldog guarding a ham bone. This is especially true of high-tech firms. A typical example is Lexar Media, which sued Toshiba for abusing its business relation with Lexar and passing the latter's confidential flash-memory technology to SanDisk, one of its competitors.[18] But even in the low-tech world, spats over **proprietary data** break out all the time. Procter & Gamble, for example, once sued three rival food chains for allegedly using the patented baking technique in its Duncan Hines brand of chocolate-chip cookies to make "infringing cookies." P&G further claimed that these companies had spied at a sales presentation and at cookie plants. One of the defendants, Frito-Lay, admitted to sending a worker to photograph the outside of a Duncan Hines bakery. But it denied telling the man's college-age son to walk into the plant and ask for some unbaked cookie dough—which the enterprising youth did, and got.[19]

Trade Secrets

When novel information is patented or copyrighted, it is legally protected but not secret. Others may have access to the information, but they are forbidden to use it (without permission) for the life of the patent or copyright. When a company patents a process, as Kleenex, for example, did many years ago with pop-up tissues, the company has a monopoly on that process. Until the patent expires, no other firm may compete in the production of pop-up facial tissues. Although on the face of it this rule violates the ideal of a free market and would appear to slow the spread of new processes and technology, patents and copyrights are generally defended on the ground that without them technological innovation would be hampered. Individuals and companies would not be willing to invest in the development of a new process if other firms could immediately exploit any new invention without having invested in developing it.

....
SUMMARY
Insider trading is the buying or selling of stocks on the basis of nonpublic information likely to affect stock prices. Insider trading seems unfair; it can injure other investors and undermine public confidence in the stock market. In practice, determining what counts as insider trading is not always easy, but it typically involves misappropriating sensitive information. Although some writers defend insider trading as performing a necessary and desirable economic function, executives who do it are putting their own interests before those of the company and its shareholders.
....

Although patent law is complicated and patents are not easy to acquire, what it means for something to be patented is well defined legally. By contrast, the concept of a trade secret is broad and imprecise. The standard legal definition says that a **trade secret** is "any formula, pattern, device, or compilation of information which is used in one's business and which gives him an opportunity to obtain an advantage over competitors who do not know or use it."[20] Virtually any information that is not generally known (or whose utility is not recognized) is eligible for classification as a trade secret, as long as such information is valuable to its possessor and is treated confidentially. Most states have laws against the theft of **trade secrets**, and the **Economic Espionage Act** of 1996 makes it a federal crime. By contrast with patents and copyrights, one does not have to declare or register something as a trade secret for it to be protected. Trade secrets, however, do not enjoy the same protection as patented information. The formula for Coca-Cola, for instance, is secret, as is the recipe for KFC's "finger-lickin' good" chicken, but neither is patented. No competitor has yet succeeded in figuring them out by "reverse engineering," but if your company managed to do so, then it would be entitled to use this information itself.

Almost any information that is not generally known can be classified as a trade secret if it is valuable to its possessor and treated confidentially.

There are at least three arguments for legally protecting trade secrets: (1) Trade secrets are the intellectual property of the company, (2) the theft of trade secrets is unfair competition, and (3) employees who disclose trade secrets violate the confidentiality owed to their employers.[21] In individual cases, what constitutes intellectual property, unfair competition, or a violation of confidentiality is often controversial. But clearly one of the biggest challenges facing an organization can be to prevent its trade secrets and proprietary data from being misused by employees who leave the company.

Three arguments for legally protecting trade secrets.

Employees Who Join a Competitor

Employees who leave the company are often privy to confidential or proprietary information, which their new employer can sometimes take unfair advantage of. For example, Starwood Hotels and Resorts charged that when some of its executives left to take high-profile jobs at Hilton Hotels, they brought with them documents that helped Hilton create a new luxury-hotel brand.[22] Or take Thomas' English Muffins. It sued to stop a former employee from going to work for rival Hostess. He was one of only seven executives who knew the secret, the company said, to producing the muffins' distinctive "nooks and crannies" and their ability to toast up crunchy on the outside and soft on the inside.[23] And Mattel, maker of the famous Barbie doll, sued MGA Entertainment for having gotten the idea for its popular Bratz doll line from a designer it had hired away from Mattel and who had originally conceived the idea while working there.[24] The problem posed by employees who quit to work for a competitor is especially troublesome for high-tech firms because their employees are so prone to job-hopping (at one point, the job tenure of an executive in the software industry was estimated to be a scant twenty-two months)[25] and because of the difficulty of separating trade secrets from the technical know-how, experience, and skill that are part of the employee's own intellect and talents.

A classic case involved Donald Wohlgemuth, who worked in the spacesuit department of B.F. Goodrich in Akron, Ohio.[26] Eventually Wohlgemuth became general manager of the spacesuit division and learned Goodrich's highly classified spacesuit technology for the Apollo flights. Shortly thereafter, Wohlgemuth, desiring a higher salary, joined Goodrich's competitor, International Latex Corporation in Dover, Delaware, as manager of engineering for the industrial area that included making spacesuits in competition with Goodrich. Goodrich protested by seeking a court order restraining

Wohlgemuth from working for Latex or for any other company in the space field. The Court of Appeals of Ohio denied Goodrich's request for an injunction, respecting Wohlgemuth's right to choose his employer, but it did provide an injunction restraining Wohlgemuth from revealing Goodrich's trade secrets.

Cases like Wohlgemuth's pit a firm's right to protect its secrets against an employee's right to seek employment wherever he or she chooses. As a result, the moral dilemmas that arise in proprietary data cases are not easily resolved. For one thing, the trade secrets that companies seek to protect have often become an integral part of the departing employee's total job skills and capabilities. These may, for instance, manifest themselves simply in a subconscious or intuitive sense of what will or will not work in the laboratory. Wohlgemuth's total intellectual capacity included the information, experience, and technical skills acquired at his former workplace. Goodrich might be justified in claiming much of Wohlgemuth's intellectual capacity as its corporate property, but it is difficult to see how he could divest himself of it.

Sometimes companies require employees to sign contracts restricting their ability to get a job with, or start, a competing company within a certain geographical radius or for a certain time. Because they can conflict with freedom of employment, not all such "noncompete" contracts are legally valid, however. Moreover, some believe that such contracts decrease employee motivation, discourage innovation, and reduce economic efficiency.[27] Even without them, however, companies sometimes sue departing employees as Essex Temporary Services did when Frank Cumbo and ten colleagues left the organization to start a competing business. Essex filed a second suit against six other employees who quit a few months later to join the new firm of Lerner, Cumbo, and Associates.[28]

The underlying issue of fairness isn't, of course, just a legal question. Frank Cumbo claims that he didn't take any information from Essex that couldn't be found in a phone book. That's relevant to assessing the morality of his conduct, but one would have to know all the details to determine if he wrongly took advantage of information, connections, or business know-how that he had acquired at Essex. In the Goodrich case, it appears that Donald Wohlgemuth didn't take this moral question very seriously. When asked whether he had acted ethically in leaving Goodrich for a competitor, he replied, "Loyalty and ethics have their price, and International Latex has paid the price."[29]

> Proprietary data cases sometimes pit the firm's right to protect its secrets against an employee's right to seek employment wherever he or she chooses.

• • •

BRIBES AND KICKBACKS

In a professional or organizational context, to **bribe** someone is to pay the person to violate his or her official duties; that is, to perform an action that is inconsistent with the person's work contract or job responsibilities or with the nature of the work the person has been hired to do. Although usually financial, the payment can be anything that is of value to the recipient. Offering a bribe is wrong because it is an inducement to act dishonestly, to disregard one's duties, or to betray a trust—for example, tendering cash to a building inspector to ignore a code violation. For the same reasons, it is wrong to accept a bribe. This is true even if one happens to end up not doing what one was bribed to do.[30]

Thus, employees working in a facilities management department of a Ford plant in Germany acted dishonestly and violated their duties to the company when they participated in bribery by accepting "material benefits" from suppliers in exchange for preferential treatment and for drafting fraudulent invoices.[31] Or take the case of

> **SUMMARY**
> Proprietary data are an organization's classified or secret information. Problems arise as employees with access to sensitive information and trade secrets quit and take jobs with competitors. Proprietary data issues pose a conflict between two legitimate rights: the right of employers to keep certain information secret and the right of individuals to work where they choose.

Norman Rothberg, an accountant working at ZZZZ Best Carpet Cleaning Company in the Los Angeles area. When he learned that ZZZZ Best had falsified accounts on insurance restoration jobs, he passed on the information to the accounting firm of Ernst & Whinney, which was overseeing ZZZZ Best's planned multimillion-dollar acquisition of another carpet-cleaning chain. When an investigation began, Rothberg accepted $17,000 from ZZZZ Best officials to back off from his initial reports.[32] Rothberg's conduct was wrong because he received money in exchange for violating his responsibilities as an accountant. By contrast, a server who accepts a gratuity for providing good service to a customer in a restaurant is not accepting a bribe, for she is not violating her duties. However, the situation would be different if she took money in exchange for not charging the customer for the drinks he ordered. Bribery can, of course, be less blatant than in the Rothberg case—for example, a contractor who charges a company executive only a nominal fee for building her a home patio on the tacit understanding that the executive will see that her company accepts the contractor's bid for an important project.

Bribery sometimes takes the form of a **kickback**, which is a percentage payment to a person able to influence or control a source of income. Thus, Alicia Rocha, sales representative for Sisyphus Books, offers a textbook-selection committee member in a large school district a percentage of the handsome commission she stands to make if a Sisyphus civics text is adopted. The money the committee member receives for the preferred consideration is a kickback. A flagrant case of kickbacks involved American executives of the Honda Motor Company. For years they pocketed millions in bribes and kickbacks from local car dealers; in return, the dealers received permission to open lucrative dealerships and had no trouble obtaining models that were in scarce supply and could be sold at a large profit.[33] More recently, Allergan was alleged to have paid kickbacks to doctors for prescribing the wrinkle-smoothing drug Botox for unapproved medical uses.[34]

THE FOREIGN CORRUPT PRACTICES ACT

In 1977 the FCPA made it illegal for American companies to engage in bribery overseas.

Bribery is generally illegal in the United States, but U.S. companies have a history of paying off foreign officials for business favors. Such acts were declared illegal in the **Foreign Corrupt Practices Act (FCPA)** of 1977, which was passed in the wake of the discovery that nearly 400 U.S. companies, including Exxon, Gulf Oil, and United Brands, had made such payments. Egregious within this sordid pattern of international bribery were Lockheed Aircraft Corporation's secret payoffs to foreign politicians to get aircraft contracts. Lest one understate the effects of such bribery, it is worth noting that revelations of Lockheed bribes in Japan caused a government crisis there and that in Holland Prince Bernhard was forced to resign his government duties after admitting that he took a $1 million payoff from Lockheed.

The FCPA provides stiff fines and prison sentences for corporate officials engaging in bribery overseas and requires corporations to establish strict accounting and auditing controls to guard against the creation of slush funds from which bribes can be paid. The FCPA does not, however, prohibit **grease payments** to the employees of foreign governments who have primarily clerical or ministerial responsibilities. These payments are sometimes necessary to ensure that the recipients carry out their normal job duties. On the other hand, the FCPA makes no distinction between bribery and extortion. A company is extorted by a foreign official if, for instance, the official threatens to violate the company's rights, perhaps by closing down a plant on some legal pretext, unless the official is paid off.

One company caught violating the FCPA was Ashland Oil. Under its then-CEO Orin Atkins, Ashland had agreed to pay an entity controlled by an Omani government official approximately $29 million for a majority interest in Midlands Chrome, Inc.—a price far higher than it was worth—for the purpose of obtaining crude oil at a highly favorable price. When Atkins proposed the acquisition of Midlands Chrome to his board of directors, he said that although the acquisition was a high-risk project, it "had the potential for being more than offset by a potential crude oil contract." Midlands Chrome did not in fact prove particularly profitable, but the Omani government awarded Ashland a contract for 20,000 barrels a day for one year at a $3-per-barrel discount from the regular selling price—a discount worth $21.9 million.[35] More recently, Johnson & Johnson has admitted that its subsidiaries bribed doctors and hospital administrators in Greece, Poland, and Romania to order the company's surgical products, and Walmart acknowledged that its Mexican subsidiary paid government officials to gain the necessary permits for expanding its operations there. In 2014 Alcoa paid $384 million to settle allegations of bribery in Bahrain, and bribery charges involving bags of cash, jewelry, and tours of the Grand Canyon for foreign officials cost Hewlett-Packard $108 million in fines. Around the same time Ralph Lauren and Archer Daniels Midland were fined for bribes paid by subsidiaries, respectively, in Argentina and in Germany and Ukraine. In those two cases, the companies discovered the misconduct themselves and reported it to authorities.[36]

THE CASE AGAINST OVERSEAS BRIBERY

The FCPA has been weakened by amendments that expand the exemption for grease payments and offer corporations more defenses against prosecution. In 1998, however, the law was extended to include bribery by foreign firms on American territory, and, thanks to the Federal Sentencing Guidelines, penalties are now stiffer than those originally specified by the FCPA. Moreover, recently the Justice Department has been going after overseas bribery more vigorously than before—in 2013, for instance, it brought eight enforcement actions, compared to a total of nine between 1978 and 2001.[37] Critics of the FCPA disapprove of this. They insist that the law puts American corporations at a competitive disadvantage in relation to foreign firms whose governments permit them to bribe. For example, in response to a Senate probe into corrupt activities by oil companies in Africa, an oil executive complained that if his company chose to take the moral high road, "Someone [else] will come [in]. The French will, the Russians will, Petronas [of Malaysia] will."[38] Alexandra Wrage of Trace International, a business ethics group based in Washington, D.C., is sympathetic. "The lack of a level playing field is an enormous competitive advantage for non-U.S. companies," she says. "U.S. companies feel like they are in the cross-hairs, which is a good thing for anti-bribery enforcement, but it comes at a pretty high cost."[39]

Such reasoning, however, can be a way of rationalizing conduct that is morally indefensible. For one thing, competition is often not a factor at all. For example, when United Brands paid a Honduran official a $1.25 million bribe, it was to gain a reduction in the country's business export tax, not to win a contract that might have gone to a foreign competitor. Moreover, when, before passage of the FCPA, U.S. firms did use bribery to beat out competitors, their competitors were usually other U.S. companies.[40] Furthermore, studies show that the FCPA has been at most a minor disincentive to export expansion. Even in nations where the FCPA is alleged to have hurt American business, there has been no statistically discernible effect on U.S. market share. In fact, since passage of the FCPA, U.S. trade with bribe-prone countries has outpaced U.S. trade with other countries.[41]

....

SUMMARY

A bribe is payment in some form for an act that runs counter to the work contract or the nature of the work one has been hired to perform. The Foreign Corrupt Practices Act prohibits corporations from engaging in bribery overseas. Critics charge that the FCPA puts American firms at a disadvantage and imposes U.S. standards on foreign countries. However, bribery can injure individuals, competitors, and political institutions. It also hurts economic growth and damages the free-market system.

....

Thirty-seven countries, including all the world's industrialized nations, have now passed domestic legislation implementing the **OECD** (Organization for Economic Co-operation and Development) **Anti-Bribery Convention**, a formal treaty that outlaws bribing public officials in foreign business transactions and sets up review and monitoring mechanisms. As a result, these days many nations are going after overseas bribery as zealously as the United States does. A Munich court, for example, fined Siemens AG, the German giant, nearly $300 million for trying to win contracts by bribing officials in Nigeria, Russia, and Libya.[42] The OECD Convention has been reinforced by separate European anti-corruption conventions, various industry-specific agreements, and by the efforts of the United Nations, World Bank, and International Monetary Fund to combat corruption. Even China is getting more aggressive about enforcing its anti-bribery laws.[43]

These developments make it doubtful that the FCPA puts American business at a competitive disadvantage. Furthermore, companies like Reebok, Google, and Novo Nordisk have prospered in emerging markets without getting their hands dirty, and the Swedish company IKEA has done well in Russia despite having to fight hard against corruption (for example, by threatening to halt its expansion there, firing managers who pay bribes, and even buying its own generators to thwart officials attempting to extort it by holding up its access to electricity).[44] But even if the FCPA does handicap U.S. firms and cause them to lose exports, that fact would have to be carefully weighed against the ample documentary evidence of the serious harm done to individuals, companies, and governments as a result of systematic bribery overseas.

> The argument that the FCPA wrongly imposes U.S. standards on foreign countries is weak.

A frequently heard argument against the FCPA is that the law imposes U.S. standards on foreign countries and that bribery and payoffs are common business practices in other nations. But that argument is too glib, especially when it comes from those who don't really have a working knowledge of another culture. In some other nations, to be sure, bribery does seem more widespread than it is here, but that doesn't imply that bribery is considered morally acceptable even in those nations. (Drug dealing is not morally acceptable here, even though it is, unfortunately, widespread.) If other countries really did consider bribery and related practices to be morally acceptable, then presumably the people engaging in them would not mind having this fact publicized. But it is difficult to find a real-life example of foreign officials willing to let the public know they accept bribes.

Certainly the FCPA reflects our own moral standards, but those standards are not simply matters of taste (like clothing styles) or completely arbitrary (like our decision to drive on the right whereas the British drive on the left). Good, objective arguments can be given against bribery and related corrupt practices because they are intended to induce people inside a business or other organization to make a decision that would not be justifiable according to normal business or other criteria. For example, by encouraging on nonmarket grounds the purchase of inferior goods or the payment of an exorbitant price, bribery can clearly injure a variety of legitimate interests—from stockholders to consumers, from taxpayers to other businesses. It subverts market competition by giving advantage in a way that is not directly or indirectly product related.

There is nothing "relative" about the damage that such corruption can do to a society. Studies show that the more corrupt a nation is, the less investment there is and the slower its economic growth.[45] For example, corruption is a major reason that Russia has attracted only half the foreign investment that India has and less than one-fifth of what's been invested in China and Brazil.[46] If we were to permit U.S. companies to engage in bribery overseas, we would be encouraging in other countries practices that we consider too harmful to tolerate at home. Moreover, even an occasional corporate bribe overseas can foster bribery and kickbacks at home and lead employees to subordinate the interest of the organization to their own private gain. Corruption is difficult to cordon off; once a company engages in it, corruption can easily spread throughout the organization.

The multiple impacts of bribery can be succinctly drawn out in one final case, which involved Bethlehem Steel Corporation, once the nation's second-largest steel company. Bethlehem was convicted of bribery and other corrupt practices for paying ship owners' representatives, including officers of the Colombian Navy, to steer ships needing repairs to Bethlehem's eight shipyards. Thus, competitive bidding for the contracts was effectively eliminated, various members of the Colombian Navy were corrupted, and the Colombian government presumably ended up paying more for the repair work than it had to. Beyond that, Bethlehem generated the money for the payoffs by padding bills and skimming profits from legitimate shipyard repair work. Thus, unsuspecting clients of Bethlehem were made to pay the bill for Bethlehem's bribery.

> Permitting U.S. companies to engage in foreign bribery would be encouraging something in other countries that we consider too harmful to tolerate at home.

• • •
GIFTS AND ENTERTAINMENT

Business gifts and entertainment of clients and business associates are familiar parts of the business world. Normally, giving someone a small gift or taking the person out for a nice meal is a gesture of good will or friendship and can help cement a relationship between two people. Unlike a bribe, it involves no quid pro quo or expectation that the recipient will do something specific in return. But gifts do tend to create a sense of gratitude in the recipient, who may feel obligated to reciprocate in some way. For this reason, in a business context gifts can raise conflict-of-interest problems and even border on bribery. Knowing where to draw the line here is not always easy. But one thing is clear: Those who cross that line, wittingly or not, can end up in big trouble. Ask the former General Services Administration (GSA) official who pleaded guilty to a criminal charge of accepting free lunches from a subsidiary of BellSouth Corporation, which was seeking a telephone contract with the GSA.

The federal government provides its procurement officers with two days of lectures and case-study discussions on the ethics of government contracting. Procurement officers, for example, are taught that they may accept an invitation to speak before a trade association consisting of the contractors they buy from, but they must decline the $50 honorarium, whatever the topic of their talk. They also must refuse a ticket for their transportation to the meeting, although they may be permitted to accept lunch as a guest seated at the head of the table, if this is compatible with the policy of their particular agency.

For people in the business world, the rules are not so cut-and-dried, and some of them manage to ignore altogether the conflict-of-interest issues that gifts create. Consider Colin Dalzell, an executive at MCI Systemhouse. Just before it went public, the e-biz software maker Commerce One offered Dalzell, who had done business with it, a chance to buy its shares. He did, and in one day made a profit of $40,000, which he used to buy a 1965 Cobra racing-car kit. Dalzell says that he had a long, established relationship with Commerce One and that the payment wasn't enough to influence his future dealings with it.[47] But most companies and most businesspeople view behavior like his as morally problematic, to say the least.

Determining the morality of giving and receiving gifts in a business situation can be challenging. But there are several factors a conscientious businessperson should take into account:

1. **What is the value of the gift?** Is the gift of nominal value or is it substantial enough to influence a business decision? Undoubtedly, definitions of "nominal" and "substantial" are open to interpretation and are often influenced by situational and cultural variables. Nevertheless, many organizations consider a gift worth less than $25 and given infrequently—perhaps once a year—only nominal but view anything larger or more frequent as problematic. Although this standard won't fit all cases, it does indicate that accepting even a rather inexpensive present might be deemed inappropriate. And, indeed, it's been shown that even small gifts can sometimes be surprisingly influential.[48]

2. **What is the purpose of the gift?** Dick Zolezzi, a department store manager, accepts small gifts such as USB flash drives from an electronics firm. He insists that the transactions are harmless and that he doesn't intend to give the firm any preferential treatment in store advertising displays. As long as the gifts are not intended or received as bribes, remain nominal, and are given only occasionally, there doesn't appear to be a problem. But it would be important to ascertain the electronics firm's intention in giving the gifts. Is it to influence how Zolezzi lays out displays? Does Zolezzi himself expect them as palm-greasing before he'll ensure that the firm receives equal promotional treatment? If so, extortion may be involved. Relevant to the question of purpose is whether a gift has some business purpose or reflects a customary business practice. For example, appointment books, calendars, or pens and pencils with the donor's logo imprinted on them serve to advertise a firm. Golf clubs or the use of a holiday home in Hawaii rarely serves this purpose.

3. **What are the circumstances under which the gift was given or received?** A gift given during the holiday season, for a store opening, or to signal other special events is circumstantially different from one unattached to any special event. Whether the gift was given openly or secretly should also be considered. An open gift, say, with the donor's name embossed on it, raises fewer questions than a gift known only to the donor and the recipient.

4. **What is the position or decision-making authority of the person receiving the gift?** Is the person in a position to affect materially a business decision on behalf of the gift giver? In other words, could the recipient's opinion, influence, or decision result in preferential treatment for the donor? Another important point is whether the recipient has made it clear to the donor that the gift won't influence his or her action one way or the other.

5. **What is the accepted business practice in the industry?** Is this the customary way of conducting this kind of business? Monetary gifts and tips are standard practice in numerous service industries. Their purpose is not only to reward good service but to ensure it again. But it's not customary to tip the head of the produce department in a supermarket so that the person will put aside the best tomatoes for you. When gratuities or the giving of certain kinds of gifts are an integral, publicly acknowledged aspect of customary business practice, they are far less likely to pose moral questions.

6. **What is the company's policy?** Many firms explicitly limit or even forbid altogether the giving or receiving of gifts. Walmart, for example, doesn't permit employees to accept anything from companies doing business with it, not even a cup of coffee, and Kmart requires not only its managers but also its vendors, suppliers, and real-estate associates to sign a no-gifts policy.[49] When such a policy exists, the giving or receiving of a gift is almost certainly wrong.

7. **What is the law?** Certain federal, state, or local government employees may be legally forbidden from receiving gifts from firms with which they do business. Sometimes the law also regulates gift-giving in specific industries. For example, the Securities and Exchange Commission fined Fidelity Investments, the mutual fund company, because some of its traders had accepted gifts from brokers seeking to do business with it.[50] And several title insurance companies violated Washington state law by lavishing pro-basketball tickets and other goodies on bankers, builders, and representatives of real-estate companies as a way of drumming up referrals.[51] When gift transactions violate the law, they are clearly unacceptable.

> **SUMMARY**
> The following considerations are relevant in determining the moral acceptability of gift giving and receiving: the value of the gift, its purpose, the circumstances under which it is given, the position of the person receiving the gift, accepted business practice, company policy, and what the law says.

Related to gift giving is the practice of entertaining. Some companies distinguish entertainment from gifts as follows: If you can eat it or drink it on the spot, it's entertainment. In general, entertainment should be interpreted more sympathetically than gifts because it usually occurs within the context of doing business in a social situation. Still, the morality of entertainment should be evaluated along the same lines as gifts—that is, with respect to value, purpose, circumstances, position of the recipient, accepted business practice, company policy, and the law. In each case the ultimate moral judgment hinges largely on whether an objective party could reasonably suspect that the gift or entertainment might influence the recipient's judgment or lead him or her to act other than in the best interest of the firm.

> The same seven considerations are also relevant to the moral evaluation of business entertainment.

CONFLICTING OBLIGATIONS

Consider the following situations:

> An employee knows that a coworker occasionally sips whiskey on the job. Should she inform the boss?

> A dishwasher observes that the restaurant's chef typically reheats three- or four-day-old food and serves it as fresh. When he informs the manager, he is told to forget it. What should the dishwasher do?

> A consulting engineer discovers a defect in a structure that is about to be sold. If the owner will not disclose the defect to the potential purchaser, should the engineer do so?

> A clerical worker learns that the personnel department has authorized hirings that violate the firm's anti-nepotism rules and neglect its affirmative action commitments. What should she do about it?

> On a regular basis, a secretary is asked by her boss to lie to his wife about his whereabouts. "If my wife telephones," he instructs her, "tell her that I'm calling on a client." In fact, as the secretary well knows, the boss is having an affair with another woman. What should the secretary do?

Such cases are not unusual, but they are different from the ones previously considered in this chapter because they involve workers caught in the crossfire of competing ethical concerns and moral responsibilities. Should the employee ensure the welfare of the organization by reporting the fellow worker who drinks, or should she be loyal to her coworker and say nothing? Should the dishwasher go public with what he knows, or should he simply forget the matter? Should the secretary carry out her boss's instructions, or should she tell his wife the truth? In each case the employee may experience conflicting obligations, diverging ideals, and divided loyalties.

Many of the difficult moral decisions that employees sometimes face involve such conflicts. How are they to be resolved? According to the procedure recommended in Chapter 2, our moral decisions should take into account our specific obligations, the effects or consequences of the different actions open to us, and any important ideals that our actions would support or undermine. To begin with consequences, remember that even staunch nonconsequentialists acknowledge that the likely results of our actions are relevant to their moral assessment and that we have some duty to promote human well-being. In general, the fuller our understanding of the possible results of the different actions we might take in the specific situation before us—that is, the better we understand the exact ramifications of the alternatives—the more likely we are to make a sound moral decision. Reflecting on the effects of these different courses of action can help us understand what ideals are at stake and determine the exact strength of the more specific obligations we have.

> Recall from Chapter 2 that our moral decisions should take into account the relevant obligations, ideals, and effects.

The impact of our actions on significant moral ideals must always be considered. Any serious moral decision should take into account the various ideals advanced or respected, ignored or hindered, by the alternative courses of conduct open to us. In addition, our moral choices are often strongly influenced by the personal weight we place on the different values at stake in a specific situation. Sometimes those values can point in different directions, as when our simultaneous commitment to professional excellence, personal integrity, and loyalty to friends pulls us in different ways.

Finally, any responsible moral decision must, of course, take into account the more specific obligations we have—in particular, those obligations that are a function of the particular relationships, roles, or circumstances we happen to be in. This chapter has already discussed the obligations employees have to the organization based on a freely negotiated work contract, and it is easy to see that employees have moral obligations arising from the business, professional, or organizational roles they have assumed. For example, teachers have an obligation to grade fairly, bartenders to refrain from over-serving intoxicated customers, engineers to guarantee the safety of their projects, and accountants to certify that financial statements present data fairly and according to generally accepted accounting principles. Because of his or her role responsibilities, an auditor who suspects some irregularity has an obligation to get to the bottom of the matter, an obligation that is probably lacking when an ordinary employee has a hunch that something is not in order in another department.

SUMMARY

Balancing our obligations to employer or organization, to friends and coworkers, and to third parties outside the organization can create conflicts and divided loyalties. In resolving such moral conflicts, we must identify the relevant obligations, effects, and ideals and decide where the emphasis among them should lie.

Thus, employees have certain general duties to their employers, and because of the specific business, professional, or organizational responsibilities they have assumed, they may have other more precise role-based obligations. In addition, employees are human beings with moral responsibilities to friends, family, and coworkers—to those flesh-and-blood people with whom their lives are intertwined, both inside and outside the workplace. These ongoing relationships are the source of important moral obligations.

The workers at the Fukushima Daiichi nuclear power plant took an enormous risk by staying at the plant to try to prevent a nuclear meltdown after a devastating earthquake and tsunami hit Japan in March 2011. In making this decision, what moral considerations do you think influenced them?

What about the obligations of employees to other parties or to society in general? In particular, what obligations do employees have to people with whom they have no relationship and for whom they have no specific professional, organizational, or other role responsibility? Here, different moral theories may steer us in slightly different directions, but simply as a matter of ordinary commonsense morality it is clear that employees—like everyone else—have certain elementary duties to other people. Of particular significance are the obligations to avoid injuring others and to be truthful and fair.

When faced with a moral decision, then, employees should follow the two-step procedure set forth in Chapter 2: identifying the relevant obligations, effects, and ideals, and then trying to decide where the emphasis should lie among these considerations. There is nothing mechanical about this process, but when we weigh moral decisions, two simple things can help keep our deliberations free from the various rationalizations to which we are all prone. *First*, we can ask ourselves whether we would be willing to read an account of our actions in the newspaper. Is the course of action we are considering one that we would be willing to defend publicly? *Second*, discussing a moral dilemma or ethical problem with a friend can often help us avoid bias and gain a better perspective. People by themselves, and especially when emotionally involved in a situation, sometimes focus unduly on one or two points, ignoring other relevant factors. Input from others can keep us from overlooking pertinent considerations, thus helping us make a better, more objective moral judgment.

As the preceding discussion mentioned, employees sometimes learn about the illegal or immoral actions of a supervisor or firm. When an employee tries to correct the situation within institutional channels and is thwarted, a central moral question emerges: Should the employee go public with the information? Should a worker who is ordered to do something illegal or immoral, or who knows of the illegal or immoral behavior of a supervisor or organization, inform the public?

> Two simple things can help keep our moral decisions free from rationalization.

WHISTLE-BLOWING

Morris H. Baslow, a middle-aged biologist and father of three, won't forget the day he dropped an envelope in the mail to Thomas B. Yost, an administrative law judge with the Environmental Protection Agency (EPA). Later that day, Baslow was fired from his job with Lawler, Matusky & Skelly, an engineering consulting firm hired by Consolidated Edison of New York to help it blunt EPA demands. The EPA was insisting that the power company's generating plants on the Hudson River had to have cooling towers to protect fish from the excessively warm water that it was discharging into the river.

Baslow claimed that the documents he sent showed that Con Ed and Lawler, Matusky & Skelly had knowingly submitted to the EPA invalid and misleading data, giving the false impression that the long-term effects of the utility's effluent on fish were negligible. On the basis of his own research, Baslow believed that the fish could be significantly harmed by the warm-water discharge. He said that for two years he tried to get his employers to listen, but they wouldn't.

Shortly after being fired, Baslow sent seventy-one company documents supporting his allegation to the EPA, the federal Energy Regulatory Commission, and the Justice Department. In the month following those disclosures, Baslow's employers accused him of stealing the documents and sued him for defamation. Baslow countersued, citing the Clean Water Act, which protects consultants from reprisals for reporting findings prejudicial to their employers and clients.

A year later, Lawler, Matusky & Skelly dropped all legal action against Baslow and gave him a cash settlement, reportedly of around $100,000. In return, Baslow wrote to the EPA and other government agencies, withdrawing his charges of wrongdoing and perjury but not recanting his own scientific conclusions. Asked why he finally accepted the cash payment, the unemployed Baslow said, "I've had to bear the brunt of this financially by myself. . . . I just wish somebody had listened to me six months ago."[52]

Other whistle-blowers express similar sentiments, even when they have been proved right. Microbiologist David Franklin blew the whistle on Warner-Lambert for promoting its epilepsy drug Neurontin for off-label uses such as migraines, hiccups, and bipolar disorder. Among other things, the company paid doctors to listen to pitches for uses of Neurontin that lacked FDA approval and even treated them to luxury trips to Hawaii and to the Olympics. (Although doctors are free to prescribe drugs for uses not on their FDA-approved label, the agency forbids companies from promoting their drugs for off-label uses.) After a lengthy legal battle, Franklin was completely vindicated when Warner-Lambert pled guilty and agreed to pay more than $430 million to settle the Justice Department's claims against it. As part of the settlement, Franklin even received a multimillion-dollar reward under the False Claims Act, originally passed in 1863 to crack down on Civil War profiteering. Still, says Franklin, "This has been the most disruptive thing I can imagine can take place in anyone's life."[53]

Or talk to David Graham, an FDA researcher, who endured rebukes and harassment from superiors for first investigating and then exposing the risk of heart attack that the painkiller Vioxx poses. "I can guarantee you, there are other whistle-blowers at the FDA," says Graham. "Fear has them by the throat. And they struggle with their conscience and they struggle with the wrong they see, and they are paralyzed by their fear. They are looking to see—can that Graham fellow get away with committing the truth?

> **SUMMARY**
>
> Employees have duties to their employers, and they may also have other obligations based on the business or professional roles and responsibilities they have assumed. In addition, they have the same elementary moral obligations that all human beings have—including the obligation not to injure others and to be truthful and fair.

It remains to be seen whether I can." He adds, "Please understand, I am not a hero, and I'm not endowed with extraordinary courage."[54] For his part, David Franklin offers the following advice to potential whistle-blowers: "People who are in the position I was need to think about their own futures and how they feel about themselves and what their kids look up to and why they got into this business in the first place," he says. "That's where the endurance of the thing comes into play."[55]

The Baslow, Franklin, and Graham cases illustrate the ethical issues and personal risks facing employees who blow the whistle on what they perceive as organizational misconduct. We now address three more specific questions: What exactly is whistle-blowing? What motivates whistle-blowers to do what they do? When is one morally justified in blowing the whistle?

THE DEFINITION OF WHISTLE-BLOWING

Whistle-blowing refers to an employee informing the public about the illegal or immoral behavior of an employer or an organization. One expert defines whistle-blowing more fully as

> A practice in which employees who know that their company is engaged in activities that (a) cause unnecessary harm, (b) are in violation of human rights, (c) are illegal, (d) run counter to the defined purpose of the institution, or (e) are otherwise immoral inform the public or some governmental agency of those activities.[56]

Another business ethicist spells out the concept in a somewhat different way:

> Whistle-blowing is the voluntary release of nonpublic information, as a moral protest, by a member or former member of an organization outside the normal channels of communication to an appropriate audience about illegal and/or immoral conduct in the organization or conduct in the organization that is opposed in some significant way to the public interest.[57]

These definitions, although not identical, clearly limit the scope of what constitutes whistle-blowing. Whistle-blowing is something that can be done only by a (past or present) member of an organization. An investigative reporter, for example, who exposes corporate malfeasance is not a whistle-blower. Nor is an employee who spreads gossip about in-house gaffes and indiscretions, thus abusing confidentiality and acting disloyally to colleagues and to the organization. By contrast, whistle-blowing involves exposing activities that are harmful, immoral, or contrary to the public interest or to the legitimate goals and purposes of the organization. It does not encompass sabotage or taking retaliatory action against the employer or firm, but it does require going outside normal channels, typically, to the media or some external agency. (Most writers on the subject, however, hold that there can also be internal whistle-blowing, which is the disclosure of inappropriate conduct to someone inside the organization, especially when doing so is contrary to standard procedure or outside the normal chain of command.)

> **SUMMARY**
> Whistle-blowing refers to an employee's informing the public about the illegal or immoral behavior of an employer or organization. Whistle-blowers frequently act out of a sense of professional responsibility.

WHAT MOTIVATES WHISTLE-BLOWERS?

Professor of philosophy Norman Bowie correctly points out that today's discussion of whistle-blowing parallels the discussion of **civil disobedience** in the 1960s.[58] Just as civil disobedients of that time felt their duty to obey the law was overridden by other moral obligations, so the whistle-blower believes that the public interest morally outweighs loyalty to colleagues and his or her duties to the organization. Coleen Rowley, for example,

> Whistle-blowers believe that the public interest can be more important than loyalty to the organization.

was a veteran FBI agent with twenty-one years of experience who had never worked anywhere else—indeed, she had wanted to be an agent ever since she was in fifth grade. When she decided to go public with evidence that her bosses had failed to follow up on information that might have thwarted the terrorist attacks of September 11, 2001, and were now misleading the public about what the FBI had known, her desire to do what was right took precedence over her lifelong love of the Bureau. Although whistle-blowers such as Rowley are often stigmatized as "disloyal," many of them see themselves as acting in the best interests of the organization.

What motivates whistle-blowers? Often, it's simply a sense of professional responsibility. Take F. Barron Stone, for example. He warned his bosses at Duke Power that they were overcharging ratepayers in the Carolinas. When they wouldn't listen, he told state regulators. That triggered an investigation, which led to Duke Power's agreeing to change its accounting procedures and reimburse customers. "I was just doing my job" is all Stone says.[59] Or consider Cynthia Cooper. An internal auditor at WorldCom, she got wind that some of the company's divisions were engaged in crooked accounting practices. She raised the matter with the firm's external auditor, Arthur Andersen, but it assured her there was no problem. When she didn't drop the issue, WorldCom's chief financial officer, Scott Sullivan, told her that everything was fine and she should back off. Troubled and suspicious about what was going on, Cooper ignored Sullivan's order. She and her team began doing what the external auditor was supposed to do. For weeks and weeks they pored over company books, working late at night to avoid detection by management, before eventually exposing the accounting scams Sullivan and others were involved in. "I'm not a hero," she told friends and colleagues. "I'm just doing my job."[60]

In the case of Noreen Harrington, the motivation was a little different. A veteran of the mutual fund industry, she resigned from Stern Asset Management because her in-house complaints about improper transactions were disregarded. But she had no intention of telling authorities. Then a year later, her older sister asked her for advice about her 401(k). She had lost a lot of money and wasn't sure that she would be able to retire. "All of a sudden, I thought about this from a different vantage point," Harrington explains. "I saw one face—my sister's face—and then I saw the faces of everyone whose only asset was a 401(k). At that point I felt the need to try to make the regulators look into [these] abuses." That's when she called the office of Eliot Spitzer, then the New York State attorney general, who was on a crusade to clean up the mutual fund industry.[61]

WHEN IS WHISTLE-BLOWING JUSTIFIED?

Although the motivations of whistle-blowers such as F. Barron Stone, Cynthia Cooper, and Noreen Harrington are honorable and praiseworthy, whistle-blowing itself is a morally problematic action, as Professor Sissela Bok reminds us.[62] The whistle can be blown in error or malice, privacy invaded, confidentiality violated, and trust undermined. Not least, publicly accusing others of wrongdoing can be very destructive and brings with it an obligation to be fair to the persons accused. In addition, internal prying and mutual suspicion make it difficult for any organization to function. And, finally, one must bear in mind that whistle-blowers are only human beings, not saints, and they sometimes have their own self-serving agenda.[63]

In developing his analogy with civil disobedience, Professor Bowie proposes several conditions that must be met for an act of whistle-blowing to be morally justified. These conditions may not be the last word on this controversial subject, but they do provide a good starting point for further debate over the morality of whistle-blowing. According to Bowie, whistle-blowing is morally justified if and only if

1. **It is done from an appropriate moral motive.** For an act of whistle-blowing to be justified, it must be motivated by a desire to expose unnecessary harm, illegal or immoral actions, or conduct counter to the public good or the defined purpose of the organization. Desire for attention or profit or the exercise of one's general tendency toward stirring up trouble is not a justification for whistle-blowing.

    Although, as Chapter 2 explained, the question of motive is an important one in Kantian ethics, not all moral theorists would agree with Bowie's first condition. Might not an employee be justified in blowing the whistle on serious wrongdoing by the employer, even if the employee's real motivation was the desire for revenge? Granted that the motivation was ignoble, the action itself might nonetheless have been the morally right one. An action can still be morally justified, say some theorists, even when it is done for the wrong reason. Still, many people were troubled to learn that the whistle-blowing paralegal who provided anti-tobacco lawyers with crucial documents about a tobacco company's secret studies on the health dangers of cigarettes was paid more than $100,000 by the lawyers.[64]

2. **The whistle-blower, except in special circumstances, has exhausted all internal channels for dissent before going public.** The duty of loyalty to the firm obligates workers to seek an internal remedy before informing the public of a misdeed. This is an important consideration. In some cases, however, the attempt to exhaust internal channels may result in dangerous delays or expose the would-be whistle-blower to retaliation. When the personal risks are great, some writers recommend going outside official channels and blowing the whistle anonymously.[65]

3. **The whistle-blower has compelling evidence that wrongful actions have been ordered or have occurred.** Spelling out what constitutes "compelling evidence" is difficult, but employees can ask themselves whether the evidence is strong enough that any reasonable person in possession of it would be convinced that an illegal or immoral activity has happened or is likely to happen. Although this may not be an unambiguous guideline, the standard of what a reasonable person would believe is commonly invoked in other cases, such as deceptive advertising and negligence lawsuits.

4. **The whistle-blower has acted after careful analysis of the danger: How serious is the moral violation? How immediate is the problem? Can the whistle-blower point to specific misconduct?** These criteria focus on the nature of the wrongdoing. Owing loyalty to employers, employees should blow the whistle only for grave legal or moral matters. The greater the harm or the more serious the wrongdoing, the more likely is the whistle-blowing to be justified. Additionally, employees should consider the time factor. The greater the time before the violation is to occur, the more likely it is that the firm's own internal mechanisms will prevent it, whereas the more imminent a violation, the more justified is the whistle-blowing. Finally, the whistle-blower must be specific. General allegations, such as that a company is "not operating in the best interests of the public" or is "systematically sabotaging the competition," won't do. Concrete examples are needed that can pass the other justificatory tests.

SUMMARY
An act of whistle-blowing can be presumed to be morally justified if it is done from a moral motive; if the whistle-blower has, if possible, exhausted internal channels before going public; if the whistle-blower has compelling evidence; if the whistle-blower has carefully analyzed the dangers; and if the whistle-blowing has some chance of success.

5. **The whistle-blowing has some likelihood of success.** This criterion recognizes that the probability of remedying an immoral or illegal action is an important consideration. Sometimes the chances are good; other times they're slim. Probably most cases fall somewhere between these extremes. In general, given the potential harmful effects, whistle-blowing that stands no chance of success is less justified than that with some prospect of succeeding. Even so, sometimes merely drawing attention to an objectionable practice, although it may fail to improve the specific situation (perhaps because the events disclosed happened in the past), encourages government and society to be more watchful of certain behavior.

The phrase "morally justified" can be ambiguous, and the preceding discussion does not explicitly distinguish between situations in which whistle-blowing is morally permissible and situations in which it is also morally required (in the sense that one would act wrongly if one failed to blow the whistle). Factors 3, 4, and 5 are particularly relevant to determining this. Speaking generally, though, if the harm in question is great enough and if an employee is well positioned to prevent it by blowing the whistle on the organization, then he or she may well be morally obligated—not just morally justified or morally permitted—to do so.

SELF-INTEREST AND MORAL OBLIGATION

For many employees, protecting themselves or safeguarding their jobs is the primary factor in deciding whether to put third-party interests above those of the firm. Concern with **self-interest** in cases that pit loyalty to the company against other obligations is altogether understandable and even warranted. After all, workers who subordinate the organization's interests to an outside party's expose themselves to charges of disloyalty, disciplinary action, freezes in job status, forced relocations, and even dismissal. Furthermore, even when an employee successfully blows the whistle, he or she can be blacklisted in an industry. Given the potential harm to self and family that employees risk in honoring obligations to third parties, it is perfectly legitimate to inquire about the weight that considerations of self-interest should be given in resolving cases of conflicting obligations.

Sadly, there is no clear, unequivocal answer to this question. Moral theorists and society as a whole do distinguish between **prudential reasons** and moral reasons. "Prudential" (from the word *prudence*) refers here to considerations of self-interest; "moral" refers here to considerations of the interests of others and the demands of morality. Chapter 1 explained that it is possible for prudential and moral considerations to pull us in different directions. One way of looking at their relationship is this: If prudential concerns outweigh moral ones, then employees may do what is in their own best interest. If moral reasons override prudential ones, then workers should honor their obligations to others.

Some theorists believe that prudential concerns sometimes outweigh moral ones.

Consider the case of a cashier at a truck stop who is asked to write up phony meal receipts so truckers can get a larger expense reimbursement from their employers than they really deserve. The cashier doesn't think this is right, so she complains to the manager. The manager explains that the restaurant is largely dependent on trucker business and that this is a good way to ensure it. The cashier is ordered to do the truckers' bidding and thus to act dishonestly and in a way that is unfair and harmful to the trucking companies. Given these moral considerations, the cashier ought to refuse, and perhaps she should even report the conduct to the trucking companies.

But let's suppose that the cashier happens to be a single mother with only a high school education. She lacks occupational skills and stands little chance of getting another job in an economy that is depressed—for months she was unemployed before landing her present position. With no other means of support, the consequences of job loss for her would be serious indeed. Now, given this scenario and given that the wrongdoing at issue is relatively minor, prudential concerns would probably take legitimate precedence over moral ones. In other words, the cashier would be justified in "going along," at least on a temporary basis.

Some moral theorists would agree with this conclusion but analyze the case somewhat differently. They think it is incorrect to say that in some circumstances we may permit prudential considerations to outweigh moral considerations. There is no neutral perspective outside both morality and self-interest from which one can make such a judgment. Furthermore, they would say that, by definition, nothing can outweigh the demands of morality.

Does that mean the cashier should refuse to do what her manager wants and, thus, lose her job? Not necessarily. Morality does not, these theorists contend, require us to make large sacrifices to right small wrongs. Writing up inaccurate receipts does violate some basic moral principles, and the cashier has some moral obligation not to go along with it. But morality does not, all things considered, require her—under the present circumstances—to take a course of action that would spell job loss. She should, however, take less drastic steps to end the practice (like continuing to talk to her boss and the truckers about it) and perhaps eventually find other work. Thus, according to this way of thinking, the cashier is not sacrificing morality to self-interest in "going along" for a while. The idea is that morality does not impose obligations on us without regard to their cost; it does not, under the present circumstances, demand an immediate resignation by the cashier.

> Other theorists say that nothing can outweigh morality but that morality itself does not require us to make large sacrifices to right small wrongs.

Whichever way one looks at it, the question of balancing our moral obligations to others and our own self-interest is particularly relevant to whistle-blowing. On the one hand, in situations in which whistle-blowing threatens one's livelihood and career, prudential concerns may properly be taken into account in deciding what one should do, all things considered. This doesn't mean that if the worker blows the whistle despite compelling prudential reasons not to, he or she is not moral. On the contrary, such an action could be highly moral. (As Chapter 2 explained, ethical theorists term such actions *supererogatory*, meaning that they are, so to speak, above and beyond the call of duty.) On the other hand, when the moral concerns are great (for example, when the lives of others are at stake), elementary morality and personal integrity can require people to make substantial sacrifices.

Two further points are pertinent here. *First*, an evaluation of prudential reasons obviously is colored by one's temperament and perceptions of self-interest. Each of us has a tendency to magnify potential threats to our livelihood or career. Exaggerating the costs to ourselves of acting otherwise makes it easier to rationalize away the damage we are doing to others. In the business world, for instance, people talk about the survival of the firm as if it were literally a matter of life and death. Going out of business is the worst thing that can happen to a firm, but the people who make it up will live on and get other jobs. Keeping the company alive (let alone competitive or profitable) cannot justify seriously injuring innocent people.

> Exaggerating the costs to ourselves allows us to rationalize away the damage we are doing to others.

Not only do we tend to exaggerate the importance of self-interested considerations, but also most of us have been socialized to heed authority. As a result, we are disinclined to question the orders of someone above us, especially when the authority is an employer or supervisor with power to influence our lives for better or worse. It's easy for us to assume that any boat rocking will be very harmful, even self-destructive.

It follows, then, that each of us has an obligation to perform a kind of character or personality audit. Do we follow authority blindly? Do we suffer from moral tunnel vision on the job? Do we mindlessly do what is demanded of us, oblivious to the impact of our cooperation and actions on outside parties? Have we given enough attention to our possible roles as accomplices in the immoral undoing of other individuals, businesses, and social institutions? Do we have a balanced view of our own interests versus those of others? Do we have substantial evidence for believing that our livelihoods are really threatened, or is that belief based more on an exaggeration of the facts? Have we been imaginative in trying to balance prudential and moral concerns? Have we sought to find some middle ground, or have we set up a false "self–other" dilemma in which our own interests and those of others are erroneously viewed as incompatible? These are just some of the questions that a personal inventory should include if we are to combat the all-too-human tendency to stack the deck in favor of prudential reasons whenever they are pitted against moral ones.

A *second* point about the relationship between prudential and moral considerations concerns our collective interest in protecting the welfare of society by encouraging people to act in non-self-interested ways. As we have seen, in some cases considerations of self-interest may mean that one does not have an overriding obligation to blow the whistle. When that is the case, how can society be protected from wrongdoing? Is its welfare to be left to those few heroic souls willing to perform supererogatory actions? And even when employees have a clear duty to blow the whistle, the personal risk involved may, human nature being what it is, keep them from doing the right thing. Who protects society then? The only realistic and reasonable approach, it seems, is to restructure our legal, business, and social institutions so that acting in a morally responsible way no longer brings the severe penalty that it often does. Whether people do what they know to be right—whether they act in a way that respects others and protects their important interests—is not simply a matter of their conscience and the strength of their moral convictions. It is also a function of the environment in which they must act and the incentives and disincentives they face.

PROTECTING THOSE WHO DO THE RIGHT THING

Although a hodgepodge of legal precedents and state and federal legislation already afforded some assistance to employees who blow the whistle, the **Sarbanes-Oxley Act** of 2002 marked an important advance. The act provides sweeping new legal protection for employees who report possible securities fraud, making it unlawful for companies to "discharge, demote, suspend, threaten, harass, or in any other manner discriminate against" them. Fired workers can sue, and they are guaranteed the right to a jury trial instead of having to endure months or years of administrative hearings. In addition, the Labor Department can order companies to rehire terminated whistleblowers with no court hearings whatsoever. Moreover, executives who retaliate against employees who report possible violations of *any* federal law now face imprisonment for up to ten years.

Unfortunately, Sarbanes-Oxley came too late to help Christine Casey. After a few years working at Mattel, Casey was assigned by the toymaker to develop a system to allocate production among its factories. But she soon discovered that Mattel's official sales forecasts were so high that managers routinely ignored the numbers. "It was a joke around the office," she says. Managers kept two sets of figures and would telephone around to find out what they should really tell their factories to produce. Casey went to a company director with a proposal to fix the numbers and help the company forecast profits more accurately. She then began experiencing hostility from company executives, received her first negative performance review, and was shunted off to a tiny cubicle, stripped of most of her work responsibilities. When Mattel's chief financial officer ignored her concerns, and its human resources department turned a blind eye to her mistreatment, she telephoned the SEC. Although Mattel later had to pay $122 million to shareholders who sued it for deliberately inflating its sales forecasts, Casey lost her wrongful-termination suit against the company for having harassed her into resigning. She has little chance of getting a job like the one she lost because big companies routinely check job applicants' litigation history.[66]

It is not enough, however, merely to change the law. Corporate attitudes need to change as well. In America, *The Economist* magazine writes, "it is almost always thought cheaper to fire whistle-blowers than to listen to them, despite years of legislation designed to achieve the opposite."[67] Lehman Brothers is a good illustration. A few days after vice-president Matthew Lee sent a letter to top management pointing out serious irregularities in the company's books, in particular, their completely unrealistic appraisals of assets, he was pulled out of a meeting and fired on the spot. Two months later Lehman Brothers was forced to file bankruptcy (the largest in U.S. history) and was quickly liquidated. Examples such as this make Kris Kolesnik, director of the National Whistleblower Center, pessimistic. "No matter how many protections whistleblower laws have created over the years," he says, "the system always seems to defeat them."[68]

In the long run, however, organizations benefit more from encouraging employees to come forward with their ethical concerns than they do from ignoring possible wrongdoing and retaliating against those who raise awkward queries. Openness and a receptive attitude toward moral questioning by employees give the organization a chance to take corrective action. This can save it money (by rooting out embezzlement, say, or forestalling litigation) or at least—as recent scandals make clear—help it to head off worse trouble when the problems bothering employees eventually leak out to the public. This is especially true on Wall Street now that financial reform legislation passed in 2010 gives potential whistle-blowers a strong incentive for providing information to the SEC: between 10 and 30 percent of any fines or penalties over $1 million.

To discharge their moral responsibilities and safeguard their own interests, companies need to develop explicit, proactive whistle-blowing policies. At a minimum, these policies should state that employees aware of possible wrongdoing have a responsibility to disclose that information; specific individuals or groups outside the chain of command should be designated to hear those concerns; employees who in good faith disclose perceived wrongdoing should be protected from adverse employment consequences; and there should be a fair and impartial investigative process. Some large companies also hire outside vendors to set up software systems, websites, or toll-free call centers for employees to alert them anonymously to ethical problems.[69] Then, of course, there must be follow-through. In these ways, management can create organizational procedures and a corporate culture that make it less likely that employees will be forced to blow the whistle externally.

SUMMARY
Prudential considerations based on self-interest can conflict with moral considerations, which take into account the interests of others. Some sacrifices of self-interest would be so great that moral considerations must give way to prudential ones. But employees must avoid the temptation to exaggerate prudential concerns, thereby rationalizing away any individual moral responsibility to third parties. Legislation and changes in corporate culture can reduce the personal sacrifices that whistle-blowers must make.

Companies need to develop explicit, proactive whistle-blower policies.

STUDY CORNER

KEY TERMS AND CONCEPTS

abuse of official position	Foreign Corrupt Practices Act (FCPA)	prudential reasons
bribe		Sarbanes-Oxley Act
business gifts and entertainment	grease payments	self-interest
civil disobedience	insider trading	trade secret
company loyalty	kickback	*U.S. v. O'Hagan*
conflict of interest	OECD Anti-Bribery Convention	whistle-blowing
Economic Espionage Act	proprietary data	

POINTS TO REVIEW

- two issues facing someone like George Galatis or George Betancourt (pp. 493–494)
- importance of the work contract (p. 494)
- why some writers reject the idea of company loyalty (p. 495)
- why conflicts of interest are a moral problem (p. 496)
- why disclosing a conflict of interest doesn't necessarily solve the problem (p. 497)
- financial investments as possible conflicts of interest (p. 497)
- examples of abuse of official position (p. 498)
- significance of the Chiarella and Dirks cases (p. 500)
- the Supreme Court's position on insider trading in *U.S. v. O'Hagan* (p. 500)
- arguments for and against insider trading (pp. 500–501)
- differences between a patented idea or process and a trade secret (pp. 501–502)
- three arguments for legally protecting trade secrets (p. 502)
- issues raised by the Wohlgemuth/Goodrich case (pp. 502–503)

- FCPA's handling of grease payments and extortion (p. 504)
- pros and cons of the FCPA (pp. 505–507)
- seven factors relevant to determining the morality of business gifts and entertainment (pp. 508–509)
- procedure recommended in Chapter 2 for making moral decisions (pp. 510–511)
- two ways of trying to keep your moral decisions free from rationalization (p. 511)
- the analogy between civil disobedience and whistle-blowing (pp. 513–514)
- why whistle-blowing can be morally problematic (p. 514)
- five factors to consider when morally evaluating whistle-blowing (pp. 515–516)
- self-interest and the demands of morality (pp. 516–518)
- how to reduce the personal sacrifices that whistle-blowers must often make (pp. 518–519)

FOR FURTHER REFLECTION

1. What does the concept of company loyalty mean to you? Does it still make sense today?
2. Have you ever experienced a conflict of interest or been tempted to do something that you thought went against your job responsibilities? Describe an employment- or business-related situation where your self-interest diverged from what you believed to be morally right.
3. When, if ever, is an employee justified in blowing the whistle? What do you see as the most important factors that he or she needs to consider in deciding whether to blow the whistle?

CASE 10.1

Changing Jobs and Changing Loyalties

CYNTHIA MARTINEZ WAS THRILLED WHEN SHE first received the job offer from David Newhoff at Crytex Systems. She had long admired Crytex, both as an industry leader and as an ideal employer, and the position the company was offering her was perfect. "It's just what I've always wanted," she told her husband, Tom, as they uncorked a bottle of champagne. But as she and Tom talked, he raised a few questions that began to trouble her.

"What about the big project you're working on at Altrue right now? It'll take three months to see that through," Tom reminded her. "The company has a lot riding on it, and you've always said that you're the driving force behind the project. If you bolt, Altrue is going to be in a real jam."

Cynthia explained that she had mentioned the project to David Newhoff. "He said he could understand that I'd like to see it through, but Crytex needs someone right now. He gave me a couple of days to think it over, but it's my big chance."

Tom looked at her thoughtfully and responded, "But Newhoff doesn't quite get it. It's not just that you'd like to see it through. It's that you'd be letting your whole project team down. They probably couldn't do it without you, at least not the way it needs to be done. Besides, Cyn, remember what you said about that guy who quit the Altrue branch in Baltimore."

"That was different," Cynthia responded. "He took an existing account with him when he went to another firm. It was like ripping Altrue off. I'm not going to rip them off, but I don't figure I owe them anything extra. It's just business. You know perfectly well that if Altrue could save some money by laying me off, the company wouldn't hesitate."

"I think you're rationalizing," Tom said. "You've done well at Altrue, and the company has always treated you fairly. Anyway, the issue is what's right for you to do, not what the company would or wouldn't do. Crytex is Altrue's big competitor. It's like you're switching sides. Besides, it's not just a matter of loyalty to the company, but to the people you work with. I know we could use the extra money, and it would be a great step for you, but still . . ."

They continued to mull things over together, but the champagne no longer tasted quite as good. Fortunately, she and Tom never really argued about things they didn't see eye to eye on, and Tom wasn't the kind of guy who would try to tell her what she should or shouldn't do. But their conversation had started her wondering whether she really should accept that Crytex job she wanted so much.

DISCUSSION QUESTIONS

1. What should Cynthia do? What ideals, obligations, and effects should she take into account when making her decision?
2. Would it be unprofessional of Cynthia to drop everything and move to Crytex? Would it show a lack of integrity? Could moving abruptly to Crytex have negative career consequences for her?
3. Is it morally wrong, morally permissible, or morally required for Cynthia to take the new job? Examine Cynthia's choice from a utilitarian point of view. How would Kant and Ross look at her situation?
4. What does loyalty to the company mean, and how important is it, morally? Under what circumstances, if any, do employees owe loyalty to their employers? When, if ever, do they owe loyalty to their coworkers?

CASE 10.2

Conflicting Perspectives on Conflicts of Interest

IN 2009, RICHARD PARSONS, FORMERLY CHAIR of Time Warner, became head of the board of directors of Citibank, that enormous but troubled financial organization. One of Citi's clients is Providence Equity Partners, a large private equity firm that has significant holdings in MGM, Univision, and other companies. Always on the lookout for new investments, Providence Equity Partners, like other private equity firms, often needs financing to undertake those investments. Providing such financing is just what Citibank does for a living.

Within a year of his arrival, however, Parsons, while remaining chairman of the board at Citibank, became a senior advisor to Providence. He gets paid for this and will presumably also receive bonuses if Providence does well, as is the normal practice. Parsons will thus be chair of a company that is potentially a huge lender to Providence at the same time that he is working for Providence. (Although it ultimately fell through, Citi was once involved with Providence in a $51.5 million acquisitions deal.) Because Parsons has a clear-cut fiduciary duty to Citibank's shareholders and must put their interests ahead of his or anyone else's, his financial stake in Providence looks like a paradigm of a conflict of interest—not to mention the fact that Citibank, with all its problems, probably needs the full-time attention of the chairman of its board. "Is he so good at rescuing megabanks," ask business writer Ben Stein, "that he can do that and another major job at the same time?"

Citibank, however, sees no problem. A spokesperson says that the bank would not allow "even the appearance" of a conflict of interest and that its board of directors has approved what Parsons has done as long as he recuses himself from taking part in any decisions about Providence. One naturally wonders not only why Citibank would permit this situation to arise in the first place but also how effective its proposed handling of it will be. Sometimes Providence needs financing, and Citibank often lends money to firms like it for just that purpose. Parsons says he will not take part in those decisions. But are disclosure and recusal enough? Even if Parsons is not in the room, how could a manager at Citibank go against a deal involving his boss? Furthermore, easier terms for Providence mean less money for Citibank's shareholders, but will Citibank executives really negotiate the best deal for Citi when they know it hurts Providence—and therefore Parsons?

Here, the question is how best to avoid, or deal with, a conflict of interest. In other cases, however, it is less certain whether there's a conflict of interest at all and, if so, what exactly the conflict is. Take the example of Joe Noel and KeyOn Communications, a small broadband provider that serves about 15,000 rural customers in eleven states. After getting hammered during the financial meltdown, its stock climbed in 2009 from 4 cents to $2.10—an increase of more than 5,000 percent. Investors bid up the company's stock on the hope that it would get a slice of the billions that the federal government was planning to dole out to expand Internet service around the country. "We certainly weren't worth [just] 4 cents," says CEO Jonathan Snyder. "We have a real business with real customers and real product, and a business that can generate real cash flow."

In truth, however, the company isn't generating much, if any, cash, and it's doubtful it will ever deliver on the high hopes of investors. In fact, the bullish run on its stock was largely fueled by one man, Joe Noel, an analyst for Emerging Growth Research. In a typical online report, he writes, "You're going to see this company awarded a lot of money," a refrain that he was repeating well into 2010. What he doesn't tell investors is that before he began covering KeyOn Communications, the company awarded him 75,000 shares. However, "if people ask," he says, "I'm very up front about [my financial stake]." CEO Snyder defends Noel, saying his analysis of the company has been "pretty evenhanded." He adds that if Noel is "not properly disclosing, I don't think he's doing it maliciously."

As it turns out, the competition among Internet providers for government support was keen, and in March 2010 all of KeyOn's applications were turned down, causing the price of its stock to fall back to $0.95. But even though independent experts had said all along that the odds were against KeyOn's getting any broadband money at all, as recently as February of that year Joe Noel was touting the stock as vigorously as ever, writing, "As we have said many times over the past 6 months— We believe KeyOn will get a significant award," and pointing to the fact that a number of people had invested in the company based on that belief. This is why Michael W. Mayhew of Integrity Research Associates says that it's a red flag when analysts have the kind of financial involvement that Joe Noel did. "The paid-for-research-industry," he says, "has a stink to it, of being biased, of maybe even being a scam."[70]

Whether there is a stink or not, is this an example of a conflict of interest?

DISCUSSION QUESTIONS

1. Based on the definition given earlier in the chapter, does Richard Parsons have a conflict of interest? If so, explain what it is. If not, explain why not.
2. If Citibank's board permits Parsons to work for Providence Equity Partners, does this mean that he has honored his fiduciary responsibilities to Citibank's shareholders? If you were a stockholder in Citibank, what would you think? Why do you think Citibank permitted Parsons to accept the position with Providence in the first place?
3. Are disclosure and recusal sufficient to deal with the situation? Are there any other steps that Citibank might take?
4. Joe Noel clearly had a financial interest in KeyOn's doing well. But did he have a conflict of interest? If so, what exactly was the conflict? If not, was there anything morally objectionable about his conduct?
5. Should people who discuss or recommend specific stocks online, on television, or in print disclose their own investments in those companies? Is it sufficient for them to do so only "if people ask"?

CASE 10.3

Inside Traders or Astute Observers?

IN 2009, FEDERAL AUTHORITIES BROKE UP THE biggest insider-trading ring ever. Originally focused on the Galleon Group hedge fund, the investigation soon unraveled a complicated network of nearly two dozen traders, analysts, and lawyers at several different companies who were engaged in a criminal conspiracy to buy insider information, usually about pending corporate acquisitions. Using throw-away cellphones to avoid detection, they had netted $20 million in illegal profits. Allegedly at the center of it all was ringmaster Zvi Goffer of the Schottenfeld Group and later Galleon, nicknamed "Octopussy" because his arms reached out to so many sources of information. Among those caught up in the federal dragnet was a senior vice-president at IBM, Robert Moffat, who had been induced by his lover into divulging confidential information, which she then passed on to the head of Galleon Group.

Since that case, the Securities and Exchange Commission (SEC) has been pushing hard against securities fraud in general and insider trading in particular, using informants, wiretaps, and sophisticated software tools to make a number of prominent arrests. "Illegal insider trading is rampant and may even be on the rise," says Preet Bharara, the U.S. attorney in Manhattan. A main target of recent investigations has been the so-called "expert network firms" that arose in response to an SEC rule in 2000 that banned companies from selectively divulging significant information, such as upcoming earnings reports, to favored analysts. These firms purport to offer "independent investment research" but routinely deliver inside information on revenue numbers and sales forecasts. In Bharara's view, however, it's not just about the prosecuting the big fish on Wall Street: "The people cheating the system include bad actors not only at Wall Street firms, but also at Main Street companies." However, some think the SEC is now pushing too hard and too far.

Take the case of Gary Griffiths and Cliff Steffes, who worked in a rail yard owned by Florida East Coast Railways in Jacksonville, Florida. The SEC charged them with making more than $1 million by trading on inside information, specifically, on the information that their company was going to be sold. How did they do it? After all, one of them is a mechanical engineer, the other a trainman—not your usual corporate insiders. The answer is simply that they were observant. According to the SEC, the two noticed that "there were an unusual number of daytime tours" of the rail yard with "people dressed in business attire." Although they were not told anything, officially or unofficially, Griffiths and Steffes had a hunch that something was up. Along with members of their families, they bet that a deal was in the works by buying tens of thousands of call options on the company's stocks. That gave them the right to buy the stock at its current price at some future date. (Purchasers of call options make money if the stock increases in value because they can then buy it at its earlier, lower price. If the stock decreases in value, then the buyers simply don't exercise the options; they're out only whatever they paid for the options.) In this case, when Fortress Investment Group acquired Florida East Coast Railways, the value of the latter's stock shot up, and Griffiths, Steffes, and their families were able to cash in big-time.

Critics of the SEC say that it is going beyond making sure that insiders are not abusing their positions or violating their fiduciary duties. Joel M. Cohen, a partner at the law firm of Gibson, Dunn & Crutcher, has written that the SEC is moving from "deterring and punishing those who abuse special relationships at the expense of shareholders into a murkier area . . . [of] policing general financial unfairness." Other business observers agree with him that the SEC shouldn't focus on trying to make the markets "feel" fair to everyone.

For its part, the SEC contends that Gary Griffiths and Cliff Steffes were more than just observant. After the tours began, they had heard "rail yard employees . . . expressing concerns that [it] was being sold, and that their jobs could be affected by the sale." It also claims that Griffiths was asked to make a list of all the locomotives, freight cars, trailers, and containers owned by the company, along with their current value, something he had never been asked to do before. "Is all of that material information?" asks *New York Times* business columnist Andrew Ross Sorkin. "Clearly, it is nonpublic. But without being told directly that a deal was in the works, did the men actually have inside information? What would have happened if there had been no deal? Or if the company was later sold for a price below its prevailing stock market value?" And as Joel Cohen points out, in most cases, "if you overhear something and divine from the conversation that Party A is about to buy Party B, and you buy Party B, that's fine. You can do that."

On the other hand, both Griffiths and Steffes had signed the company's code of conduct, which states that employees cannot trade on or disseminate material nonpublic information. So maybe they breached a fiduciary duty after all. Or maybe they were just alert employees, who happened to be good guessers and—until the SEC showed up, anyway—very lucky.[71]

Update

After the SEC charged Griffiths, Steffes, and four members of Steffes's family with insider trading, Griffiths and one of Steffes's relatives signed agreements with the SEC to avoid prosecution. Although neither admitted guilt, they agreed to pay fines of $120,000 and $240,000, respectively. The other defendants went to trial in 2014 but were acquitted by a jury.

DISCUSSION QUESTIONS

1. Did Griffiths and Steffes violate any legal or moral duties toward their employer? Did they act unfairly in some way?
2. Were they "insiders"? If so, explain why. If not, does that imply that they cannot be guilty of insider trading or that what they did was morally permissible?

3. Should the law prohibit employees acting as Griffiths and Steffes did? Explain why or why not. If actions like theirs are tolerated, will it diminish people's faith in the fairness of the stock market? Would permitting it set a bad precedent in other cases?

4. Putting legal technicalities aside, did Griffiths and Steffes act unethically? Explain the facts and moral principles that support your answer.

5. In your view, is insider trading a serious moral problem? Explain why or why not. Should we legalize insider trading, as some argue, and simply let different companies decide how they want to deal with the issue?

6. Suppose Griffiths and Steffes were not employees of Florida East Coast Railways, but merely lived across the street and guessed what was going on. Could they still be guilty of insider trading?

7. Assuming that insider trading should remain outlawed, does prosecuting Griffiths and Steffes represent a wise use of the SEC's resources, or should it ignore cases like this?

CASE 10.4

The Housing Allowance

WILSON MUTAMBARA GREW UP IN THE SLUMS outside Stanley, capital of the sub-Saharan African country of Rambia.[72] Through talent, hard work, and luck he made it through secondary school and won a scholarship to study in the United States. He eventually received an MBA and went to work for NewCom, a cellular telephone service. After three years in the company's Atlanta office, Wilson was given an opportunity to return to Rambia, where NewCom was setting up a local cellular service. Eager to be home, Wilson Mutambara couldn't say yes fast enough.

NewCom provides its employees in Rambia with a monthly allowance of up to $2,000 for rent, utilities, and servants. By Western standards, most of the housing in Stanley is poor quality, and many of its neighborhoods are unsafe. By providing the allowance, NewCom's intention is to see that its employees live in areas that are safe and convenient and that they live in a style that is appropriate to the company's image.

To claim their housing allowance, NewCom's employees in Rambia are supposed to turn in receipts, and every month Wilson Mutambara turned in an itemized statement for $2,000 from his landlord. Nobody at NewCom thought it was unusual that Wilson never entertained his coworkers at home. After all, he worked long hours and traveled frequently on business. However, after Wilson had been in Rambia for about fifteen months, one of his coworkers, Dale Garman, was chatting with a Rambian customer, who referred in passing to Wilson as a person living in Old Town. Garman knew Old Town was one of the slums outside Stanley, but he kept his surprise to himself and decided not to mention this information to anyone else until he could independently confirm it. This wasn't difficult for him to do. Wilson was indeed living in Old Town in the home of some relatives. The house itself couldn't have rented for more than $300, even if Wilson had the whole place to himself, which he clearly didn't. Dale reported what he had learned to Wilson's supervisor, Barbara Weston.

When Weston confronted him about the matter, Wilson admitted that the place did rent for a "little less" than $2,000, but he vigorously defended his action this way: "Every other NewCom employee in Rambia receives $2,000 a month. If I live economically, why should I be penalized? I should receive the same as everyone else." In response, Weston pointed out that NewCom wanted to guarantee that its employees had safe, high-quality housing that was in keeping with the image that the company wanted to project. Wilson's housing arrangements were "unseemly," she said, and not in keeping with his professional standing. Moreover, they reflected poorly on the company. To this, Wilson Mutambara retorted: "I'm not just a NewCom employee; I'm also a Rambian. It's not unsafe for me to live in this neighborhood, and it's insulting to be told that the area I grew up in is 'unseemly' or inappropriate for a company employee."

Barbara Weston pointed out that the monthly receipts he submitted had been falsified. "Yes," he admitted, "but that's common practice in Rambia. Nobody thinks twice about it." However, she pressed the point, arguing that he had a duty to NewCom, which he had violated. As the discussion continued, Mutambara became less confident and more and more distraught. Finally, on the verge of tears, he pleaded, "Barbara, you just don't understand what's expected of me as a Rambian or the pressure I'm under. I save every penny I have to pay school fees for eight nieces and nephews. I owe it to my family to try to give those children the same chance I had. My relatives would never understand my living in a big house instead of helping them. I'm just doing what I have to do."

DISCUSSION QUESTIONS

1. Did Wilson Mutambara act wrongly? Explain why or why not. Assess each of the arguments he gives in his own defense. What other courses of action were open to him? What would you have done in his place?

2. Was Dale Garman right to confirm the information he had received and to report the matter? Was it morally required of him to do so?

3. What should Barbara Weston and NewCom do? Should Wilson be ordered to move out of Old Town and into more appropriate housing? Should he be terminated for having falsified his housing receipts? If not, should he be punished in some other way?

4. Is NewCom unfairly imposing its own ethnocentric values on Wilson Mutambara? Is the company's housing policy fair and reasonable? Is it culturally biased?

CASE 10.5

Ethically Dubious Conduct

BRENDA FRANKLIN HAS WORKED AT ALLIED Tech for nearly eight years. It's a large company, but she likes it and enjoys the friendly work environment. When she tacked her list onto the bulletin board outside her office, she didn't intend to make things less friendly. In fact, she didn't expect her list to attract much attention at all.

It had all started the week before when she joined a group of coworkers for their weekly lunch get-together, where they always talked about all sorts of things. This time they had gotten into a long political discussion, with several people at the table going on at great length about dishonesty, conflicts of interest, and shady dealings among politicians and corporate leaders. "If this country is going to get on the right track, we need people whose integrity is above reproach," Harry Benton had said to nods of approval around the table, followed by a further round of complaints about corruption and corner-cutting by the powerful.

Brenda hadn't said much at the time, but she thought she sniffed a whiff of hypocrisy. Later that night, after pondering the group's discussion, she typed up her list of "Ethically Dubious Employee Conduct." The next day she posted it outside her door.

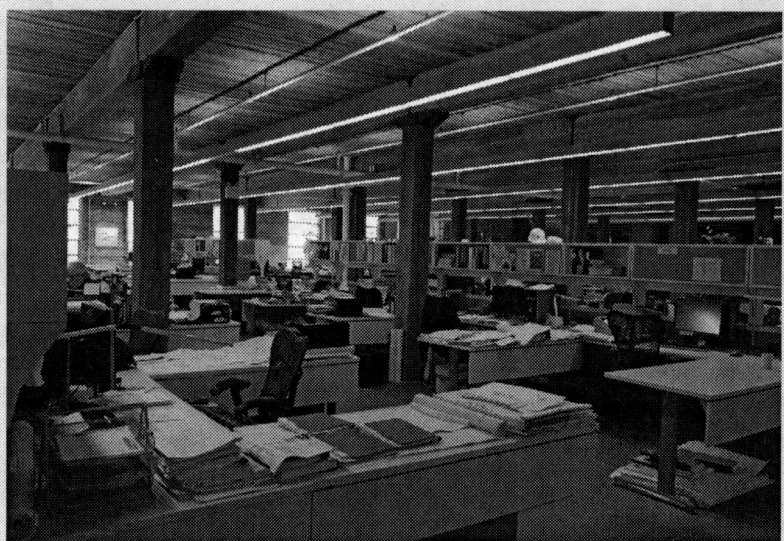

Are open-plan work premises likely to prevent employee theft?

Harry Benton was the first one to stick his head in the office. "My, my, aren't we smug?" was all he said before he disappeared. Later that morning, her friend Karen dropped by. "You don't really think it's immoral to take a pad of paper home, do you?" she asked. Brenda said no, but she didn't think one could just take it for granted that it was okay to take company property. She and Karen chatted more about the list. On and off that week, almost everyone she spoke with alluded to the list or commented on some of its items. They didn't object to her posting it, although they seemed to think it was a little strange. One day outside the building, however, an employee she knew only by sight asked Brenda sarcastically whether she was planning on turning people in for "moral violations." Brenda ignored him.

Now she was anticipating her group's weekly lunch. She had little doubt about what the topic of discussion would be, as she again glanced over her list:

Ethically Dubious Employee Conduct

1. Taking office supplies home for your personal use.
2. Using the telephone for personal, long-distance phone calls.
3. Making personal copies on the office machine.
4. Charging the postage on your personal mail to the company.
5. Making nonbusiness trips in a company car.
6. On a company business trip: staying in the most expensive hotel, taking taxis when you could walk, including wine as food on your expense tab, taking your spouse along at company expense.
7. Using your office computer to shop online, trade stocks, view pornography, or e-mail friends on company time.
8. Calling in sick when you need personal time.
9. Taking half the afternoon off when you're supposedly on business outside the office.
10. Directing company business to vendors who are friends or relatives.
11. Providing preferential service to corporate customers who have taken you out to lunch.

DISCUSSION QUESTIONS

1. Review each item on Brenda's list and assess the conduct in question. Do you find it morally acceptable, morally unacceptable, or somewhere in between? Explain.
2. Examine Brenda's list from both the utilitarian and the Kantian perspectives. What arguments can be given for and against the conduct on her list? Is the rightness or wrongness of some items a matter of degree? Can an

action (such as taking a pad of paper) be both trivial and wrong?

3. Someone might argue that some of the things listed as ethically dubious are really employee entitlements. Assess this contention.

4. How would you respond to the argument that if the company doesn't do anything to stop the conduct on Brenda's list, then it has only itself to blame? What about the argument that none of the things on the list is wrong unless the company has an explicit rule against it?

5. What obligations do employees have to their employers? Do companies have moral rights that employees can violate? What moral difference, if any, is there between taking something that belongs to an individual and taking something that belongs to a company?

6. What, if anything, can we learn about an employee's character based on whether he or she does or does not do the things on Brenda's list? Would you admire someone who scrupulously avoids doing any of these ethically dubious things, or would you think the person is a prig?

7. What should Brenda do when she finds a fellow employee engaging in what she considers ethically dubious conduct?

CHAPTER 11

JOB DISCRIMINATION

INTRODUCTION

THE UNIVERSITY OF TEXAS BEGAN ITS 2014 SEASON with a new head football coach, Charlie Strong. Nothing unusual about a university hiring a new coach, one might think, but many took it as a "sign of progress and fairness" because Strong is African American and Texas is a powerhouse team. It's "like when Tyrone Willingham was hired at Notre Dame, even bigger," says Floyd Keith, a consultant for the NCAA, "because this is a program that can win a national championship."[1]

When Notre Dame hired Willingham back in 2002, he was its first black coach in any sport; moreover, signing him made Notre Dame the only top-notch football team in the nation with a black coach. At the time only five coaches in the NCAA's top football division were black. Today, the situation is a little better. Fourteen of the 120 schools in the NCAA's Football Bowl Subdivision now have black or non-white head coaches. However, only 17 of the other 463 college football programs in the country do. Altogether that means that even though nearly half of the country's college football players are black, fewer than 6 percent of their coaches are.[2]

What explains this imbalance? Experts suggest several answers. At many universities, football is the biggest moneymaking sport, and search committees may fear that boosters and alumni will donate less if the team has a black coach. Another reason is that black men are often passed over for decision-making positions early in their athletic careers. Relatively few blacks play quarterback, for instance, and black assistant coaches may be relegated to recruiting or smoothing out race relations rather than calling plays. In addition, young black athletes may pursue careers in which they have seen their role models succeed—going on to the pros, in particular, instead of becoming a coach.

Finally, most commentators agree that the old-boys' network among athletic directors and coaches is part of the problem. "I don't see the problem as being the same as it was thirty or forty years ago, when people said they didn't want a 'Negro' around," says Allen L. Sach, director of sports management at the University of New Haven. "It's more systemic than it is overt." Athletic directors, naturally enough, tend to look to people they know to fill coaching positions, and only 4 percent of the former are ethnic minorities, according to the Center for the Study of Sport in Society at Northeastern University. "Athletic directors, to the extent that they're white, generally have contacts who are also white, and they use those contacts as they engage in searches at the informal level," says sociologist Jay Oakley of the University of Colorado at Colorado Springs.

> MOST COMMENTATORS agree that the old-boys' network among athletic directors and coaches is part of the problem.

In the case of Willingham, it's no secret that he wasn't Notre Dame's first choice. It had initially hired George O'Leary, who resigned five days later when it became known that he had lied on his résumé about his academic and athletic background. In discussing the appointment, Notre Dame athletic director Kevin White explained that he had been charmed by O'Leary's Irish-American background and his rah-rah style. O'Leary was like "something out of central casting," White said. In other words, the flamboyant O'Leary matched White's stereotype about what a Notre Dame coach should be. Sports columnist Mark Purdy writes that White's remark "basically confirms that athletic directors—at Notre Dame and too many other places—really do look for middle-aged white guys as the top choices for the top jobs. And that's depressing." It's to Notre Dame's credit, however, that after the O'Leary debacle, it took a second look at Willingham.

Unfortunately, the story doesn't end happily there. Three years later, Notre Dame fired Willingham. Football recruitment was solid, the team's morale was strong—it was on its way to a postseason bowl—and its academic performance had never been better. But that season, the squad had posted only a 6–5 record, and Notre Dame desperately wanted its team to rejoin the elite of college football. A case of job discrimination? It's difficult to say, but at the time some sportswriters and other observers thought so—including the university's outgoing president, Father Edward A. Malloy, who said the decision to fire Willingham was an embarrassment to the university. That's because Willingham's overall record was a respectable 21–15, and Notre Dame, which claims to adhere to higher values than other schools, had never before dismissed a coach after only three years into a five-year contract. In fact, Willingham's record was better than the three-year marks of his two predecessors, who both had kept their jobs.

As it turned out, three years later Willingham's successor, Charlie Weis, had a 22–15 record—almost identical to Willingham's—but Notre Dame retained him for another two years, during which he posted a 13–12 record. On the other hand, after leaving Notre Dame, Willingham spent four years coaching the University of Washington, where he had a poor 6–29 record. Looking back, sportswriter Jon Wilner says, "I don't think Willingham was treated differently because he was black. I think he was treated differently by Notre Dame because he was different, and being black was not an insignificant part of that difference." As Wilner sees it, Willingham wasn't a Notre Dame guy. He had no ties to South Bend, and his reserved personality "wasn't the type to make boosters and trustees feel comfortable and important—to make them feel like the head coach was one of them." By contrast, "Weiss is one of them. He's a white guy who went to Notre Dame."

Most people oppose racial or sexual bias and reject job discrimination as immoral. But, as the paucity of minority coaches reveals, explicit prejudice and overt discrimination are only part of the problem. Even open-minded people may operate on implicit assumptions that work to the disadvantage of women and minorities, and many who believe themselves to be unprejudiced harbor unconscious racist or sexist attitudes.

No one is more cognizant of the complexities of people's attitudes toward race, their conscious and unconscious assumptions about it, and the many-sided reality of race in American society than is President Barack Obama. "Understanding this reality," he has said,

> requires a reminder of how we arrived at this point. As William Faulkner once wrote, "The past isn't dead and buried. In fact, it isn't even past." We . . . need to remind ourselves that so many of the disparities that exist in the African-American community today can be directly traced to inequalities passed on from an earlier generation that suffered under the brutal legacy of slavery and Jim Crow.
>
> Segregated schools were, and are, inferior schools; we still haven't fixed them, fifty years after *Brown v. Board of*

North Carolina State University research shows the disparity between the percentage of black players and that of black coaches at the Football Bowl Subdivision (FBS) level of college football.

Education, and the inferior education they provided, then and now, helps explain the pervasive achievement gap between today's black and white students.

Legalized discrimination—where blacks were prevented, often through violence, from owning property, or loans were not granted to African-American business owners, or black homeowners could not access FHA mortgages, or blacks were excluded from unions, or the police force, or fire departments—meant that black families could not amass any meaningful wealth to bequeath to future generations. That history helps explain the wealth and income gap between black and white, and the concentrated pockets of poverty that persist in so many of today's urban and rural communities.

A lack of economic opportunity among black men, and the shame and frustration that came from not being able to provide for one's family, contributed to the erosion of black families. . . . And the lack of basic services in so many urban black neighborhoods . . . helped create a cycle of violence, blight, and neglect that continue to haunt us.

. . . What's remarkable is not how many failed in the face of discrimination, but rather how many men and women overcame the odds. . . . But for all those who scratched and clawed their way to get a piece of the American Dream, there were many who didn't make it—those who were ultimately defeated, in one way or another, by discrimination. That legacy of defeat was passed on to future generations—those young men . . . who we see standing on street corners or languishing in our prisons, without hope or prospects for the future.[3]

LEARNING OBJECTIVES

We must bear this history in mind as we explore the issue of job discrimination. In particular, this chapter examines the following topics:

1. The meaning of job discrimination and its different forms
2. Statistical and attitudinal evidence of discrimination
3. The historical and legal context of affirmative action
4. Moral arguments for and against affirmative action
5. The doctrine of comparable worth and the controversy over it
6. The problem of sexual harassment in employment—what it is, what forms it takes, what the law says about it, and why it's wrong

THE MEANING OF JOB DISCRIMINATION

To discriminate in employment is to make an adverse decision regarding an employee or a job applicant based on his or her membership in a certain group.[4] More specifically, **job discrimination** occurs when (1) an employment decision in some way harms or disadvantages an employee or a job applicant; (2) the decision is based on the person's membership in a certain group rather than on individual merit; and (3) the decision rests on prejudice, false stereotypes, or the assumption that the group in question is in some way inferior and thus does not deserve equal treatment. Because historically most discrimination in the American workplace has been aimed at women and at minorities such as African Americans and Hispanics, the following discussion focuses on those groups.

Job discrimination takes different forms.

Job discrimination can take different forms. It can be individual or institutional, and it can be either intentional or unwitting. Individuals, for instance, sometimes intentionally discriminate out of personal prejudice or on the basis of stereotypes. For example, an executive at Rent-A-Center, the nation's largest rent-to-own furniture and home appliance company, purposely disregarded job applications from women because he believed that they "should be home taking care of their husbands and children."[5]

Individuals also may discriminate because they unthinkingly or unconsciously accept traditional practices or stereotypes. For example, suppose that the merit-pay recommendations of a Walmart manager are influenced by his implicit assumption that male employees are career oriented and have families to support, whereas female employees are there just to make a little extra money.[6] If the manager is unaware that this bias affects his decisions, his actions would fall into this category. Unconscious bias explains the fact that when researchers change a male name to a female name or a white-sounding name (say, Emily Walsh or Greg Baker) to a black-sounding name (say, Lakisha Washington or Jamal Jones) on otherwise identical (but fictional) résumés, they receive fewer call-backs—even though hiring managers opine that qualified female or minority candidates have a leg up because recruiters are seeking diversity.[7]

Institutions discriminate. Sometimes they do so explicitly and intentionally—for example, employment agencies that screen out African Americans, Latinos, older workers, and others at the request of their corporate clients,[8] or the Shoney's restaurants that color-coded job applications to separate blacks from whites and that directed blacks, if hired, into kitchen jobs so that they would not be seen from the dining room.[9] Sometimes the routine operating procedures of a company reflect stereotypes and prejudiced practices that the company is not fully aware of. That seems to have been the case at Abercrombie & Fitch, which paid $50 million to settle a class-action job-discrimination lawsuit. The suit charged that in trying to cultivate its distinctive retail image, the company put minorities in less visible jobs and hired a disproportionately white sales force. The same is alleged to have been true at Wet Seal.[10] Or, to take another example, for years the FBI routinely transferred Hispanic agents around the country on temporary, low-level assignments where a knowledge of Spanish was needed; the agents functioned as little more than assistants to non-Hispanic colleagues. Hispanic agents dubbed this the "taco circuit" and claimed that it adversely affected their opportunities for promotion. A federal court agreed with them that the practice was indeed discriminatory.[11]

In addition, institutional practices that appear neutral and nondiscriminatory may harm members of groups that have been discriminated against in the past. When membership in an all-white craft union, for instance, requires nomination by those who are already members, racial exclusion is likely to result even if the motivation of those who do the nominating is purely nepotistic and results from no racially motivated ill will or stereotyping. Similarly, when USAir had a special backdoor hiring channel for pilots recommended by employees or friends of the company, only white pilots were ever hired this way.[12] Although the policy may look racially neutral, its outcome was biased. Institutional procedures like these may not involve job discrimination in the narrow sense, but they clearly work to the disadvantage of women and minority groups, denying them full equality of opportunity.

From a variety of moral perspectives there are compelling arguments against job discrimination on racial or sexual grounds. Since discrimination involves false assumptions about the inferiority of a certain group and harms individual members of that group, utilitarians would reject it because of its ill effects on total human welfare. Kantians would clearly repudiate it as failing to respect people as ends in themselves. Universalizing the maxim underlying discriminatory practices is practically impossible. No people who now discriminate would be willing to accept such treatment themselves. Discrimination on grounds of sex or race also violates people's basic moral rights and mocks the ideal of human moral equality. Furthermore, such discrimination is unjust. To use Rawls's theory as an illustration, parties in the original position would clearly choose for themselves the principle of equal opportunity.

There are no respectable arguments in favor of racial and sexual discrimination. Whatever racist or sexist attitudes people might actually have, no one today is prepared to defend job discrimination publicly, any more than someone would publicly defend slavery or advocate repealing the Nineteenth Amendment (which gave women the right to vote). This attitude toward job discrimination is reflected in legal and political efforts to develop programs to root it out and to ameliorate the results of past discrimination.

There are strong moral arguments against job discrimination on racial or sexual grounds.

Before looking at those programs, however, and at the relevant legal history, we need to examine the relative positions of whites and minorities and of males and females in the American workplace to see what they reveal about ongoing discrimination.

EVIDENCE OF DISCRIMINATION

> **SUMMARY**
> Discrimination in employment occurs when decisions adversely affect employees or job applicants because they are members of a group that is an object of prejudice or false stereotypes or is viewed as inferior and not deserving of equal treatment. Discrimination can be individual or institutional, intentional or unintentional. From various moral perspectives, there are strong arguments against job discrimination.

When investigators sent equally qualified young white and black men—all of them articulate and conventionally dressed—to apply for entry-level jobs in Chicago and Washington, D.C., the results clearly showed racial discrimination against young African-American men.[13] Subsequent studies have confirmed that result.[14] In fact, one of them found that white applicants were more successful than black applicants even when they had criminal records and the otherwise-identical blacks did not.[15] Similarly, Hispanics and African Americans are more likely to be turned down for home mortgages or to pay higher interest rates than are whites at the same income level.[16] The same is true for auto loans.[17]

Job discrimination certainly exists, but determining how widespread it is isn't easy. However, when statistics indicate that women and minorities play an unequal role in the work world and when endemic attitudes, practices, and policies are biased in ways that seem to account for the skewed statistics, then there is good reason to believe that job discrimination is a pervasive problem.

STATISTICAL EVIDENCE

Racial minorities bear the brunt of poverty in our nation. Whereas one in eight white Americans lives in poverty, one out of every four African Americans and Hispanics is poor. Today, a black child has one chance in three of being born into poverty.[18] Furthermore, life expectancy for blacks is lower than it is for whites, and blacks are twice as likely to die from disease, accident, and homicide.[19]

The median wealth of white households today is more than fourteen times that of Hispanic or African-American households—$110,500 versus $7,683 for Hispanics and $6,314 for African Americans.[20] In line with this, the rate of home ownership is 50 percent greater for white households than for black or Hispanic households.[21] At the same time, the median income of African-American families is only 62 percent, and that of Hispanic families only 73 percent, the median income of white households.[22] Unemployment also hits racial minorities hard; compared with whites, they are nearly twice as likely to be out of work.[23]

About 40 percent of working African Americans hold white-collar jobs, up from 11 percent in 1960. But black workers with an advanced degree earn 25 percent less than whites with the same education.[24] Moreover, black and other minority workers still tend to be clustered in low-paying, low-prestige, dead-end work. United States government statistics reveal clearly the extent to which the most desirable occupations (in professional and technical jobs, management, and administration) are dominated by whites; blacks, Hispanics, and other ethnic minorities are relegated to less desirable jobs (in manual labor, service industries, and farm work). African Americans, for instance, make up 11 percent of the workforce, but they constitute one-fifth to one-third of the nation's barbers, bus and taxi drivers, garbage collectors, and security guards. In contrast, only 3 percent of reporters and news analysts, 3.9 percent of psychologists, 0.3 percent of dentists, 2.1 percent of architects, and 6.4 percent of managers are black.[25]

Along with racial inequalities in rates of employment and in family income and wealth, these occupational disparities between blacks and whites take on even greater importance because of the role that social networking and help from family and friends play in landing a good job. "Such favoritism has a strong racial component," says Nancy DiTomaso, a professor at Rutgers Business School. "It's a powerful, hidden force driving [racial] inequality in the United States."[26]

Women, too, are clustered in poorer-paying jobs—the so-called **pink-collar occupations**. They tend to work as librarians, nurses, elementary school teachers, salesclerks, secretaries, bank tellers, and waitresses—jobs that generally pay less than traditionally male occupations such as electrician, plumber, auto mechanic, shipping clerk, and truck driver. In the real world of work, the top-paying occupations have been, and to a large extent continue to be, almost exclusively male preserves. For example, 95 percent of dental hygienists, but only 25.5 percent of dentists, are women.[27]

In recent years, the across-the-board wage gap between men and women has shrunk slightly, but only slightly. In 1992 women who worked full-time made 75 percent of what men earned; they now make 77 percent.[28] Today, 45 percent of young women (ages twenty-five to thirty-four) have graduated from college whereas only 36 percent of young men have done so, but young men still earn significantly more.[29] Perhaps this is not so surprising, given that, in general, full-time female workers with a bachelor's degree take home only three-quarters of what their male counterparts make—the same now as in 1992.[30]

Even when women do the same work as men, they make less money. In fact, according to a General Accounting Office report, since 1995 the pay difference between full-time female managers and their male counterparts has increased in seven of the ten industries that collectively employ 71 percent of all female workers.[31] For example, in entertainment and recreation, female managers now earn only 62 cents for each dollar earned by males; in finance, insurance, and real estate, it's 68 cents; in retail trade, 65 cents. In education and in hospital and medical services, women managers have done better. Their earnings have increased to 91 and 85 percent, respectively, of what men make.

In recent decades both women and minorities have made considerable inroads into white-collar and professional ranks, but few have made it to the very top of their professions—as a glance at the companies that make up the *Fortune* 500 confirms. At these companies, women account for only 8 percent of those who have reached the level of executive vice-president or higher, and they constitute only 5 percent of those who rank among their company's top five earners.[32] The situation for blacks is no better, a fact that is powerfully illuminated by one simple statistic: Until Franklin Raines became CEO of Fannie Mae in 1999, no African American had ever been in charge of a *Fortune* 500 company. And it was only in 2009, when Ursula Burns took the helm at Xerox, that an African-American woman became a *Fortune* 500 CEO.

ATTITUDINAL EVIDENCE

Although some would disagree, statistics alone do not conclusively establish discrimination because one can always argue that other things account for the disparities in income and position between men and women and between whites and other races. The U.S. Supreme Court, in fact, has stated that "no matter how stark the numerical disparity of the employer's work force," statistical evidence by itself does not prove discrimination.[33] But when widespread attitudes and institutional practices and policies are taken into account, they point to discrimination as a significant cause of the statistical disparities.

SUMMARY
Studies reveal the persistence of discrimination in American life, and statistical evidence shows wide economic disparities between whites and racial minorities. It also shows significant occupational and income differences between white males, on the one hand, and women and minorities, on the other.

Few women and minorities can be found at the very top of the business world.

Statistics by themselves don't prove discrimination. One must also consider widespread attitudes and institutional practices.

Take the case of Bari-Ellen Roberts. She left an $80,000-a-year job at Chase Manhattan Bank to join Texaco's finance department after a white friend, whose husband worked for the company, assured her that "Texaco's changing" and that the company was "looking for blacks." Her new job was closer to home and held the promise of overseas assignments, but her friend was mistaken about Texaco's having changed. Soon after she arrived, Roberts found herself subjected to demeaning racial comments from colleagues and superiors (for example, one referred to her as a "little colored girl"). They couldn't understand why Roberts found such remarks offensive. A report on diversity that she and some other black employees were asked to prepare was summarily dismissed with the comment "the next thing you know we'll have Black Panthers running down the halls." And a supervisor downgraded her performance record because he thought she was "uppity."[34]

Fed up with a "plague of racial insults" and "egregious acts of bigotry," she and several other black employees filed a discrimination suit citing "the poisonous racial atmosphere" at Texaco. Texaco settled the suit for $141 million in retroactive raises after the news media got hold of a tape recording of an executive strategy session at Texaco. In the meeting, one official referred to black employees as "black jelly beans," saying, "This diversity thing, you know how all the black jelly beans stick together," to which another responded, "That's funny. All the black jelly beans seem to be stuck at the bottom of the bag." One of Roberts's supervisors said, "I can't punch her [Roberts] in the face, so I play mind games with her." The executives were also heard agreeing to shred incriminating personnel records.

Consider some other well-known instances of job discrimination. In a precedent-setting case, Elizabeth Hishon sued King & Spalding, a big Atlanta law firm, contending that the firm's sexism prevented her from attaining partner status, causing her to be terminated as a result. (The case was eventually settled out of court.) A few years later, Nancy O'Mara Ezold became the first woman to win a sex-discrimination case against a law firm in a partnership decision. Shortly after that, another legal precedent was set when Price Waterhouse, the accounting firm, was ordered to give a partnership and back pay to Ann Hopkins, against whom it had discriminated. And in 2002 the Equal Employment Opportunity Commission filed its first sex-discrimination lawsuit against a major Wall Street firm, alleging that Morgan Stanley fired Allison Schieffelin, one of its top bond dealers, for complaining about pay discrimination.

Of particular interest here are the discriminatory attitudes and policies revealed by these cases. In the Ezold case, the judge found that the prominent Philadelphia law firm for which she had worked had applied tougher standards to women seeking partnerships than to men. Ezold said, "It wasn't just that similarly situated men were treated better than me, which is the double-standard idea. Another thing that came out of the trial was that in the year preceding the partnership decision, [the firm] assigned me to less complex cases and to fewer partners than it did men, so that I was denied the exposure that was critical to the partnership decision."[35]

In Ann Hopkins's case, sex stereotyping was at the root of the discrimination. Though she was considered an outstanding worker, Price Waterhouse denied her the position because she was allegedly an abrasive and overbearing manager. Coworkers referred to her as "macho," advised her to go to charm school, and intimated that she was overcompensating for being a woman. One partner in the firm even told her that she should "walk more femininely, talk more femininely, dress more femininely, wear makeup, have her hair styled, and wear jewelry." Hopkins argued, and the court agreed, that comments like these revealed underlying sexism at the firm and that her strident manner and occasional cursing would have been overlooked if she had been a man.[36]

The same issue came up in the case of Schieffelin, who was viewed by her firm as insubordinate, verbally abusive, and "physically threatening."

As for the Hishon decision, the case is noteworthy because the defendants expressed no specific complaints about Hishon's work. They apparently denied her a partnership based on a general feeling that "she just didn't fit in." In the words of another woman who had been an associate at King & Spalding, "If you can't discuss the Virginia–North Carolina basketball game, you're an outcast."[37] Her pithy comment speaks volumes about how deep-seated attitudes operate against women and minorities in the workplace.

Women entering male turf, or minority workers of either sex going into a predominantly white work environment, can find themselves uncomfortably being measured by a white male value system. At large companies, for instance, 42 percent of female executives and 34 percent of male minority executives report feeling constrained by the white male model, consciously and continually editing themselves to look, sound, and act like their white male counterparts.[38] Here's how Florence Blair, a twenty-five-year-old African American, described working as a civil engineer at Corning Glass Works:

> As a minority woman, you are just so different from everyone else you encounter.... I went through a long period of isolation.... When I came here, I didn't have a lot in common with the white males I was working with. I didn't play golf, I didn't drink beer, I didn't hunt. All these things I had no frame of reference to.
>
> You need to do your job on a certain technical level, but a lot of things you do on the job come down to socializing and how well you mesh with people. Sometimes I look at my role as making people feel comfortable with me.
>
> Sometimes it's disheartening. You think why do I have to spend all of my time and energy making them feel comfortable with me when they're not reciprocating?[39]

Surveys support the evidence of these cases. Over the years, they have indicated that sex stereotyping and sexist assumptions are widespread in business. Male managers frequently assume that women place family demands above work considerations, that they lack the necessary drive to succeed in business, that they take negative feedback personally rather than professionally, and that they are too emotional to be good managers. Even worse, researchers have found that women internalize many of the stereotypes that men have of them as less-effective leaders despite the well-established fact that there is little difference between the leadership styles of successful male and female bosses.[40] Perhaps it is not surprising, then, that psychological experiments show that, even when they state that it doesn't matter to them, both men and women tend to prefer male bosses.[41]

When it comes to race, the stereotypes can be even more damaging. Many whites, even very well-educated ones, still accept the canard that blacks are less intelligent than whites. Psychologists at a number of universities have also documented that most whites harbor hidden racial biases that they are unaware of and do not consciously agree with.[42]

Myths, stereotypes, false preconceptions, and biased attitudes victimize both women and minorities in the world of work, leading to decisions that disadvantage them in all aspects of their careers. This is especially true when companies give managers too much discretion in hiring, task assignment, promotion, and pay. In such circumstances, writes sociology professor William T. Bielby, all people unknowingly revert to stereotypes in making decisions: "The tendency to invoke gender stereotypes in making judgments about people is rapid and automatic. As a result, people are unaware of how stereotypes affect their perceptions and behavior," including "individuals whose personal beliefs are

Women and minorities often find themselves measured by a white male value system.

SUMMARY
Evidence of biased attitudes and sexist or racist assumptions also points to significant job discrimination in the workplace. As they try to fit into a work world dominated by white men, women and minorities can be disadvantaged by stereotypes, false preconceptions, and prejudiced attitudes.

relatively free of prejudice."[43] Commenting on racial stereotypes, business consultant Edward W. Jones, Jr., writes:

> All people possess stereotypes, which act like shorthand to avoid mental overload.... Most of the time stereotypes are mere shadow images rooted in one's history and deep in the subconscious. But they are very powerful. For example, in controlled experiments the mere insertion of the word *black* into a sentence has resulted in people changing their responses to a statement.
>
> One reason for the power of stereotypes is their circularity. People seek to confirm their expectations and resist contradictory evidence, so we cling to beliefs and stereotypes that become self-fulfilling. If, for example, a white administrator makes a mistake, his boss is likely to tell him, "That's OK. Everybody's entitled to one goof." If, however, a black counterpart commits the same error, the boss thinks, "I knew he couldn't do it. The guy is incompetent." The stereotype reinforces itself.[44]

Taken together with the statistics, the attitudes, assumptions, and practices reviewed here provide powerful evidence of ongoing discrimination against women and minorities in the American workplace. Recognizing the existence of such discrimination and believing for a variety of reasons that it is wrong, we have as a nation passed laws to provide equality of opportunity to women and minorities. Such laws expressly forbid discrimination in recruitment, screening, promotion, compensation, and firing. But anti-discrimination laws do not address the present-day effects of past discrimination. To remedy the effects of past discrimination and counteract visceral racism and sexism, some companies and institutions have adopted stronger and more controversial affirmative action measures.

> Laws guaranteeing equality of opportunity are one response to the problem of discrimination. Another, more controversial response is affirmative action.

AFFIRMATIVE ACTION: THE LEGAL CONTEXT

In 1954, the U.S. Supreme Court decided in the case of **Brown v. Board of Education** that racially segregated schooling is unconstitutional. In doing so, the Court conclusively rejected the older doctrine that "separate but equal" facilities are legally permissible. Not only were segregated facilities in the South unequal, the Court found, but also the very idea of separation of the races, based as it was on a belief in black racial inferiority, inherently led to unequal treatment. That decision helped launch the civil rights movement in this country. One fruit of that movement was a series of federal laws and orders that attempt to safeguard the right of each person to equal treatment in employment.

The changes began in 1961, when President John F. Kennedy signed Executive Order 10925, which decreed that federal contractors should "take affirmative action to ensure that applicants are employed without regard to their race, creed, color, or national origin." In 1963, the Equal Pay Act was passed by Congress. Aimed especially at wage discrimination against women, it guaranteed the right to equal pay for equal work. That was followed by the **Civil Rights Act of 1964** (later amended by the Equal Employment Opportunity Act of 1972). Applying to all employers, both public and private, with fifteen or more employees, it prohibits all forms of discrimination based on race, color, sex, religion, or national origin. Title VII, the most important section of the act, prohibits discrimination in employment. It says:

> It shall be an unlawful employment practice for an employer (1) to fail or refuse to hire or to discharge any individual, or otherwise discriminate against any individual

with respect to his compensation, terms, conditions, or privileges of employment, because of such individual's race, color, religion, sex, or national origin; or (2) to limit, segregate, or classify his employees or applicants for employment in any way that would deprive or tend to deprive any individual of employment opportunities or otherwise adversely affect his status as an employee, because of such individual's race, color, religion, sex, or national origin.

Employers may violate Title VII not only if they treat an individual differently because of sex, race, religion, color, or national origin (**disparate treatment**) but also if they have a rule or practice that, although not discriminatory on its face, excludes or adversely affects too many people of a particular sex, race, or other protected category (**disparate impact**). Disparate impact, however, does not automatically establish discrimination. In particular, if the employer can show that the practice in question was a legitimate, job-related business necessity, then it does not break the law. Avoiding job discrimination, though, can sometimes pose tricky dilemmas. Fearing a lawsuit, the City of New Haven threw out the results of an exam it had developed for determining which firefighters to promote to lieutenant or captain because of its disparate impact: No blacks scored high enough to win promotion. However, the whites who had done well on the exam sued the city. In 2009, the Supreme Court sided with them, ruling that discarding the test discriminated against them on grounds of race—it was a form of disparate treatment.[45]

Congress has gone beyond the 1964 Civil Rights Act to outlaw other forms of job discrimination as well. Of particular importance are the Age Discrimination in Employment Act (1967, amended in 1978) and the Americans with Disabilities Act (1990), which extends to people with disabilities the same rights to equal employment opportunities that the Civil Rights Act of 1964 guarantees to women and minorities. In addition, several acts and executive orders regulate government contractors and subcontractors and require equal opportunities for veterans. All of these acts are enforced through the **Equal Employment Opportunity Commission (EEOC)**.

> **SUMMARY**
> The Civil Rights Act of 1964 forbids discrimination in employment on the basis of race, color, sex, religion, or national origin. Employment practices that involve disparate treatment or disparate impact can violate the law. Subsequent legislation also forbids discrimination based on age or disability.

AFFIRMATIVE ACTION PROGRAMS

By the late 1960s and early 1970s, companies contracting with the federal government (first in construction and then generally) were required to develop **affirmative action programs**, designed to correct imbalances in employment that exist directly as a result of past discrimination. These programs reflected the courts' recognition that job discrimination can exist even in the absence of conscious intent to discriminate.[46] Affirmative action riders were added, with various degrees of specificity, to a large number of federal programs. Many state and local bodies adopted comparable requirements.

What do affirmative action programs involve? According to EEOC guidelines, large companies and other organizations should issue a written equal employment policy and appoint an official to publicize their commitment to affirmative action and to direct and implement their program. They are expected to survey current female and minority employment by department and job classification. Whenever underrepresentation of these groups is evident, companies are to develop goals and timetables to improve in each area of underrepresentation. They should then develop specific programs to achieve these goals, establish an internal audit system to monitor them, and evaluate progress in each aspect of the program. Finally, companies are encouraged to develop supportive in-house and community programs to combat discrimination.

We saw earlier that Texaco was forced to pay its black employees $141 million, the largest race-discrimination settlement in history, because the company had discriminated against qualified African Americans by refusing to promote them or pay them comparable salaries. In 2010 a jury found Novartis guilty of discriminating against female sales employees in pay and promotions, requiring it to pay $3.3 million in compensatory and $250 million in punitive damages. Lawsuits have also exposed discriminatory pay practices at many other companies, including Mitsubishi, Home Depot, Merrill Lynch, American Express, Walmart, and Boeing. Other firms are guilty of ignoring the spirit of equal employment opportunity even if they don't violate the letter of the law. For example, some companies forbid their employees from speaking Spanish among themselves even when their jobs do not require English proficiency or dealing with the public; others have made no effort to expand employment opportunities for women or minorities.

> Most large corporations find that diversity benefits the bottom line.

Yet today most large corporations not only accept the necessity of affirmative action but also find that the bottom line benefits when they make themselves more diverse. Affirmative action expands the pool of talent available to corporations. It also allows them to reach out to a demographically wider customer base—between now and 2020 most new customers will be minorities—and makes them better able to compete both in the global marketplace and in an increasingly multicultural environment at home.[47] United Parcel Service, for example, credits its commitment to diversity for its high customer-satisfaction ratings, and Nicole Barde, a network manager at Intel Corporation, says, "We view diversity as one of our major competitive advantages. It allows us to understand global markets and the needs of our customers."[48] As Christine A. Edwards, chief legal officer at Bank One, puts it, "Diversity is good business."[49]

Empirical evidence supports the proposition that organizations made up of different types of people are more productive than homogeneous organizations.[50] It also shows that companies with a high percentage of women in leadership positions are more efficient and profitable than their rivals.[51] However, despite the strong business case for diversity,[52] genuine equality of opportunity has yet to be achieved in the corporate world. According to a National Urban League survey, only 32 percent of employees believe that their firms do a decent job of hiring and promoting people other than white males. Company executives tend to agree with them; only 47 percent of them think their diversity efforts are working.[53]

> **SUMMARY**
> Affirmative action programs aim to correct racial imbalances existing as a result of past discrimination. Today, many companies believe that they benefit from affirmative action by becoming more diverse. Critics charge, however, that in practice affirmative action has often meant preferential treatment of women and minorities and even reverse discrimination against white men.

Those sentiments notwithstanding, many Americans oppose affirmative action, and political opposition to it, especially to government affirmative action programs, has grown greater than ever. Critics of affirmative action charge that, in practice, it means illegal quotas, preferential treatment of African Americans and women, and even reverse discrimination against white men. In the 1960s and early 1970s, federal courts dismissed legal challenges to affirmative action, and in 1972 Congress gave it increased legislative validity by passing the Equal Employment Opportunity Act. Eventually, however, the Supreme Court had to address the question. Although its decisions determine the law of the land with regard to affirmative action, the Court's rulings have not always been as simple and straightforward as one might wish.

THE SUPREME COURT'S POSITION

The U.S. Supreme Court's first major ruling on affirmative action was in 1978, in the case of ***Bakke v. Regents of the University of California***. Allan Bakke, a white man, applied for admission to the medical school at the University of California at Davis. At the time almost all its medical students were white. To help remedy this situation, Davis's affirmative action program set aside for minority students 16 out of its 100 entrance places.

If qualified minority students could not be found, those places were not to be filled. In addition to the special admissions process, minority students were free to compete through the regular admissions process for the unrestricted 84 positions. When Bakke was refused admission, he sued the University of California, contending that he had been discriminated against because he would have won admission if those 16 places had not been withdrawn from open competition and reserved for minority students. Bakke's grades, placement-test scores, and so on, were higher than those of several minority students who were admitted. The university did not deny this but defended its program as legally permissible and socially necessary affirmative action.

Bakke won his case, although it was a close, 5-to-4 decision. In announcing the judgment of the Court, Justice Lewis F. Powell's opinion rejected explicit racial criteria setting rigid quotas and excluding non-preferred groups from competition. At the same time, Powell held that the selection process can take race and ethnic origin into account as one factor and pointed to Harvard's admission program as a model. In such a program, "race or ethnic background may be deemed a 'plus' in a particular applicant's file, yet it does not insulate the individual from comparison with all other candidates for the available seats."

A year later, in *United Steelworkers of America v. Weber*, the Supreme Court took up the issue again. At Kaiser Aluminum's Gramercy, Louisiana, plant, only 5 out of 273 skilled craft workers were black, although the local workforce was 39 percent black. Kaiser therefore entered into an agreement with the United Steelworkers to train employees from its workforce for these craft positions on the basis of seniority, except that 50 percent of the positions would be reserved for African Americans until their percentage in these jobs approximated the percentage of African Americans in the local workforce. The program was challenged in court, and the case eventually reached the Supreme Court, which upheld Kaiser's affirmative action program. In delivering the court's opinion, Justice William Brennan made clear that legal prohibition of racial discrimination does not prevent "private, voluntary, race-conscious affirmative action plans." Kaiser's program, he wrote, "does not unnecessarily trammel the interest of the white employees. . . . Moreover, the plan is a temporary measure . . . simply to eliminate a manifest racial imbalance."

A few years later, though, the Supreme Court upheld seniority over affirmative action in *Memphis Firefighters v. Stotts*. When financial difficulties forced the city to lay off firefighters, it respected the customary practice of "last hired, first to be let go," even though that undermined its recent efforts to increase the number of black firefighters. After reviewing the case, the Supreme Court ruled that seniority systems are racially neutral and that the city may not lay off white workers to save the jobs of black workers with less seniority. However, the court reaffirmed the principle of affirmative action in 1987, this time in a case concerning women. In *Johnson v. Transportation Agency*, it held that considerations of sex were permissible as one factor in promoting Diane Joyce, a female county employee, to the position of road dispatcher over an equally qualified male employee, Paul Johnson. In summing up the Court's position, Justice Brennan stated that the promotion of Joyce "was made pursuant to an affirmative action plan that represents a moderate, flexible, case-by-case approach to effecting a gradual improvement in the representation of minorities and women in the Agency's work force."

Since then, however, the Court has grown more antagonistic to affirmative action programs. For example, in *City of Richmond v. Croson*, the Court invalidated a Richmond, Virginia, law that channeled 30 percent of public-works funds to minority-owned construction companies (see Case 11.1). In *Adarand Constructors v. Pena*, the Supreme Court examined a federal program that provided financial incentives for contractors to

> **SUMMARY**
>
> Although the legal situation is complex, in a series of rulings over the years a majority of the Court has upheld the general principle of affirmative action, as long as such programs are moderate and flexible. Race can legitimately be taken into account in employment-related decisions, but only as one among several factors. Affirmative action programs that rely on rigid and unreasonable quotas or that impose excessive hardship on present employees are illegal.

hire "socially or economically disadvantaged" subcontractors. In her majority opinion in the 5-to-4 decision, Justice Sandra Day O'Connor affirmed the principle that "federal racial classification, like those of a State, must serve a compelling government interest, and must be narrowly tailored to further that interest." Accordingly, all government action based on race should be subjected to "the strictest judicial scrutiny" to ensure that no individual's right to equal protection has been violated. The Court then sent the case back to a lower court for rehearing.

In addition to O'Connor's majority opinion, however, five other justices wrote opinions in the *Adarand* case, and these reveal a range of perspectives on affirmative action. For instance, Justice David Souter criticized the Court for departing from past practice, reminding his colleagues that it is well established "that constitutional authority to remedy past discrimination is not limited to the power to forbid its continuation, but extends to eliminating those effects that would otherwise persist and skew the operation of public systems even in the absence of current intent to practice any discrimination."

In his dissenting opinion, Justice John Paul Stevens also defended the general principle of affirmative action:

> There is no moral or constitutional equivalence between a policy that is designed to perpetuate a caste system and one that seeks to eradicate racial subordination. . . .
>
> A decision by representatives of the majority to discriminate against the members of a minority race is fundamentally different from those same representatives' decision to impose incidental costs on the majority of their constituents in order to provide a benefit to a disadvantaged minority. Indeed, as I have previously argued, the former is virtually always repugnant to the principles of a free and democratic society, whereas the latter is, in some circumstances, entirely consistent with the ideal of equality.

However, Justice Clarence Thomas explicitly challenged Stevens's position. In an opinion concurring with the majority's judgment, he asserted that

> there is a "moral and constitutional equivalence" between laws designed to subjugate a race and those that distribute benefits on the basis of race in order to foster some current notion of equality. Government cannot make us equal; it can only recognize, respect, and protect us as equal before the law. . . .
>
> In my mind, government-sponsored racial discrimination based on benign prejudice is just as noxious as discrimination inspired by malicious prejudice. In each instance, it is racial discrimination, plain and simple.

The upshot of recent judicial developments relative to affirmative action is not clear, tangled up as the rulings are in details, legal technicalities, and split opinions. The legal future is difficult to predict. Clearly, the Court is more attuned than ever to what it perceives to be excesses in the cause of affirmative action. Nevertheless, when in 2003 the Supreme Court revisited affirmative action in higher education for the first time in twenty-five years, it reaffirmed the principles it had enunciated in *Bakke*.

> The Supreme Court has reaffirmed the legality of affirmative action if such programs are moderate and flexible.

In *Grutter v. Bollinger* the Court upheld, by a 5-to-4 majority, the affirmative action program at the University of Michigan's law school. Citing testimony from various business and military leaders, who urged that diversity is essential to the country's economy and security, the Court ruled that the state has a "compelling interest" in promoting educational diversity and that the law school's method of doing so was "narrowly tailored" to meet that interest. Under the law school's "highly individualized" and "holistic" approach, minority race is a "plus factor" in evaluating potential students, but it's also possible for a white student likely to make a particularly interesting contribution to the law school's academic climate to beat out a minority student with better grades and test scores. But in *Gratz v. Bollinger*, a companion case, a different majority of justices ruled, 6 to 3, that Michigan's undergraduate affirmative action program was unconstitutionally rigid and mechanistic because it gave members of underrepresented groups an automatic 20-point bonus on the 150-point scale used to rank applicants.

Whether the Supreme Court will reverse itself in the future and outlaw moderate and flexible affirmative action programs is uncertain. However, the Court is clearly impatient. In her majority opinion in *Grutter*, Justice O'Connor stated that "race-conscious admissions policies must be limited in time" and that the Court "expect[s] that 25 years from now, the use of racial preferences will no longer be necessary." That's a hope undoubtedly shared by those on both sides of the debate over affirmative action.

• • •

AFFIRMATIVE ACTION: THE MORAL ISSUES

Understanding the Supreme Court's evolving position on affirmative action is important, because the Court sets the legal context in which business operates and lets employers know what they are and are not legally permitted to do. But legal decisions by themselves do not exhaust the relevant moral issues. Employers—as well as women, minorities, and white men—want to know whether affirmative action programs are morally right. Indeed, it is a safe bet that the Supreme Court's own decisions are influenced not only by technical legal issues but also by how the justices answer this moral question.

Before evaluating arguments for and against affirmative action, one needs to know what is being debated. *Affirmative action* here means programs taking the race or sex of employees or job candidates into account as part of an effort to correct imbalances in employment that exist as a result of past discrimination, either in the company itself or in the larger society. To keep the discussion relevant, it is limited to affirmative action programs that might realistically be expected to be upheld by the Supreme Court. Excluded are programs that establish rigid, permanent quotas or that hire and promote unqualified persons. Included are programs that hire or promote a woman or an African American who might not otherwise, according to established but reasonable criteria, be the best-qualified candidate.

A word about terminology: Critics of affirmative action often label it "reverse discrimination," but this term is misleading. According to the definition offered earlier, job discrimination involves prejudice, inaccurate stereotypes, or the assumption that a certain group is inferior and deserves unequal treatment. No such forces are at work in the affirmative action cases already discussed. Those who designed the programs that worked to the disadvantage of white men like Allan Bakke and Paul Johnson did not do so because they were biased against white men and believed them inferior and deserving of less respect than other human beings. Those who designed the programs in question were themselves white men.

ARGUMENTS FOR AFFIRMATIVE ACTION

1. **Compensatory justice demands affirmative action programs.**

    POINT: "As groups, women and minorities have historically been discriminated against, often viciously. As individuals and as a nation, we can't ignore the sins of our fathers and mothers. In fact, we have an obligation to do something to help repair the wrongs of the past. Affirmative action in employment is one sound way to do this."

COUNTERPOINT: "People today can't be expected to atone for the sins of the past. We're not responsible for them, and in any case, we wouldn't be compensating those who rightly deserve it. Young African Americans and women coming for their first job have never suffered employment discrimination. Their parents and grandparents may deserve compensation, but why should today's candidates receive any special consideration? No one should discriminate against them, of course, but they should have to compete openly and on their merits, just like everybody else."

2. **Affirmative action is necessary to permit fairer competition.**

   POINT: "Even if young blacks and young women today have not themselves suffered job discrimination, blacks in particular have suffered all the disadvantages of growing up in families that have been affected by discrimination. In our racist society, they have suffered from inferior schools and poor environment. In addition, as victims of society's prejudiced attitudes, young blacks and young women have been hampered by a lack of self-confidence and self-respect. Taking race and sex into account makes job competition fairer by keeping white men from having a competitive edge that they don't really deserve."

   COUNTERPOINT: "Your point is better when applied to blacks than to women, it seems to me, but I'm still not persuaded. You overlook the fact that there are a lot of disadvantaged whites out there, too. Is an employer going to have to investigate everyone's life history to see who had to overcome the most obstacles? I think an employer has a right to seek the best-qualified candidate without trying to make life fair for everybody. And isn't the best-qualified person entitled to get the job or the promotion?"

3. **Affirmative action is necessary to break the cycle that keeps minorities and women locked into low-paying, low-prestige jobs.**

   POINT: "You advocate neutral, nondiscriminatory employment practices, as if we could just ignore our whole history of racial and sexual discrimination. Statistics show that African Americans in particular have been trapped in a socioeconomically subordinate position. If we want to break that pattern and eventually heal the racial rifts in our country, we've got to adopt vigorous affirmative action programs that push more African Americans into middle-class jobs. Even assuming racism were dead in our society, with mere nondiscrimination alone it would take a hundred years or more for blacks to equalize their position."

   COUNTERPOINT: "You ignore the fact that affirmative action has its costs, too. You talk about healing the racial rifts in our country, but affirmative action programs make everybody more racially conscious. They also cause resentment and frustration among white men. Many African Americans and women also resent being advanced on grounds other than merit. Finally, if you hire and promote people faster and farther than they merit, you're only asking for problems."

ARGUMENTS AGAINST AFFIRMATIVE ACTION

1. **Affirmative action injures white men and infringes their rights.**

   POINT: "Even moderate affirmative action programs injure the white men who are made to bear their brunt. Other people design the programs, but it is Allan Bakke, Paul Johnson, and others like them, who find their career opportunities hampered. Moreover, such programs violate the right of white men to be treated as individuals and to have racial or sexual considerations not affect employment decisions."

> **SUMMARY**
> The moral issues surrounding affirmative action are controversial. Its defenders argue that compensatory justice demands affirmative action programs, that affirmative action is needed to permit fairer competition, and that affirmative action is necessary to break the cycle that keeps minorities and women locked into poor-paying, low-prestige jobs.

COUNTERPOINT: "I'm not sure that Bakke and Johnson have the rights you are talking about. Racial and sexual considerations are often relevant to employment decisions. Jobs and medical school slots are scarce resources, and society may distribute these in a way that furthers its legitimate ends—like breaking the cycle of poverty for minorities. I admit that with affirmative action programs white men do not have as many advantages as they did before, and I'm against extreme programs that disregard their interests altogether. But their interests have to be balanced against society's interest in promoting these programs."

2. **Affirmative action itself violates the principle of equality.**

    POINT: "Affirmative action programs are intended to enhance racial and sexual equality, but you can't do that by treating people unequally. If equality is the goal, it must be the means, too. With affirmative action programs, you use racial and sexual considerations—but that is the very thing that has caused so much harm in the past and that affirmative action itself is hoping to get rid of."

    COUNTERPOINT: "I admit that it is distasteful to have to take racial and sexual considerations into account when dealing with individuals in employment situations. I wish we didn't have to. But the unfortunate reality is that in the real world racial and sexual factors go a long way toward determining what life prospects an individual has. We can't wish that reality away by pretending the world is color blind when it is not. Formal, color-blind equality has to be encroached upon now if we are ever to achieve real, meaningful racial and sexual equality."

3. **Nondiscrimination will achieve our social goals; stronger affirmative action is unnecessary.**

    POINT: "The 1964 Civil Rights Act unequivocally outlaws job discrimination, and numerous employees and job candidates have won discrimination cases before the EEOC or in court. We need to insist on rigorous enforcement of the law. Also, employers should continue to recruit in a way that attracts minority applicants and to make sure that their screening and review practices do not involve any implicit racist or sexist assumptions. And they should monitor their internal procedures and the behavior of their white male employees to root out any discriminatory behavior. Stronger affirmative action measures, in particular taking race or sex into account in employment matters, are unnecessary. They only bring undesirable results."

    COUNTERPOINT: "Without affirmative action, progress often stops. The percentage of minorities and women employed by those subject to federal affirmative action requirements has risen much higher than it has elsewhere. Take the example of Alabama. In the late 1960s, a federal court found that only twenty-seven out of the state's 3,000 clerical and managerial employees were African American. Federal Judge Frank Johnson ordered extensive recruiting of blacks, as well as the hiring of the few specifically identified blacks who could prove they were victims of discrimination. Nothing happened. Another suit was filed, this time just against the state police, and this time a 50 percent hiring quota was imposed, until blacks reached 25 percent of the force. As a result, Alabama's state police quickly became the most thoroughly integrated state police force in the country."[54]

The debate over affirmative action is not the only controversy connected with job discrimination. Two other issues, both primarily concerning women, have been the topic of recent moral, legal, and political discussion: the issue of comparable worth and the problem of sexual harassment on the job.

> **SUMMARY**
> Critics of affirmative action argue that affirmative action injures white men and infringes their rights, that affirmative action itself violates the principle of equality, and that nondiscrimination (without affirmative action) will suffice to achieve our social goals.

The newest U.S. Supreme Court Justice, Elena Kagan, was sworn into office in August 2010. These days, American presidents seem to be under political pressure to ensure that minorities and women are represented on the Supreme Court. Is this desire for diversity a kind of affirmative action?

SUMMARY

Comparable worth is the idea that women and men should be paid on the same scale for doing different jobs if they involve equivalent skill, effort, and responsibility. Advocates of comparable worth say that women have been shunted into low-paying jobs, that they suffer from a discriminatory labor market, and that justice requires that they receive equal pay for doing jobs of equal worth.

Proponents of comparable worth believe that women have been directed into certain occupations and held back by a biased wage system.

COMPARABLE WORTH

Louise Peterson was a licensed practical nurse at Western State Hospital in Tacoma, Washington. For supervising the daily care of sixty men convicted of sex crimes, she was paid $192 a month less than the hospital's groundskeepers and $700 a month less than men doing work similar to hers at Washington state prisons. Convinced of the inequity of the state's pay scale, Peterson filed a suit claiming that she and other women were being discriminated against because men of similar skills and training and with similar responsibilities were being paid significantly more. A federal judge found Washington guilty of sex discrimination and ordered the state to reimburse its female employees a whopping $838 million in back pay.

Although an appellate court later overturned that ruling, the state of Washington began a program intended to raise the pay for government jobs typically considered "women's work." Even though the program had flaws,[55] it helped raise to national prominence the doctrine of comparable worth and signaled a dramatic escalation in women's fight for equal employment rights.

In essence, the doctrine of **comparable worth** holds that women and men should be paid on the same scale not only for doing the same or equivalent jobs but also for doing different jobs involving equal skill, effort, and responsibility. Advocates of comparable worth point to the substantial statistical evidence demonstrating that women are in more low-paying jobs than men. They also note the consistent relationship between the percentage of women in an occupation and the salary of that occupation: The more women dominate an occupation, the less it pays.[56] Comparable-worth advocates contend that women have been shunted into a small number of pink-collar occupations and that a biased and discriminatory wage system has kept their pay below that of men in occupations involving a comparable degree of skill, education, responsibility, and so on. For example, studies have shown that legal secretaries and instrument-repair technicians hold jobs with the same relative value for a company in terms of accountability, know-how, and problem-solving skill; yet legal secretaries, who are almost all women, earn an average of $9,432 less than instrument-repair technicians, who generally are men.[57]

As comparable-worth advocates see it, justice demands that women receive equal pay for doing work of comparable value. Jobs should be objectively evaluated in terms of the education, skills, and experience required and in terms of responsibilities, working conditions, and other relevant factors. Equivalent jobs should receive equivalent salaries, even if discriminatory job markets would otherwise put them on different pay scales. Some comparable-worth advocates further argue that when women have not received equivalent pay for jobs of comparable worth, justice requires that employers pay them reparation damages for the money they have lost. That would be expensive. But whether pay adjustments are retroactive or not, all comparable-worth programs envision adjusting the salary schedules of women upward rather than the pay of men downward.

Opponents of comparable worth insist that women, desiring flexible schedules and less taxing jobs, have freely chosen lower-paying occupations and thus are not entitled to any readjustment in pay scales. Phyllis Schlafly, for one, calls comparable worth "basically a conspiracy theory of jobs. . . . It asserts that, first, a massive societal male conspiracy has segregated or ghetto-ized women into particular occupations by excluding them from others; and then, second, devalued the women's job by paying them lower wages than other occupations held primarily by men." She adds: "For two decades, at least, women have been free to go into any occupation. . . . But most women continue to choose traditional, rather than non-traditional, jobs. This is their own free choice. Nobody makes them do it."[58]

> Opponents insist that women have freely chosen lower-paying occupations.

Others who are sympathetic to the concept of comparable worth worry about its implementation. How are different jobs to be evaluated and compared, they wonder. "How do you determine the intrinsic value of one job and then compare it to another?" asks Linda Chavez, former staff director of the Commission on Civil Rights. She points out that "for 200 years, this has been done by the free marketplace. It's as good an alternative as those being suggested by comparable-worth advocates. I'm not sure the legislative bodies or courts can do any better."[59] Job evaluation studies, however, are common in the public sector, and many private companies also utilize them to determine the skill, effort, responsibility, and working conditions that characterize different job categories and, hence, the wages appropriate to them. However, even if reasonably objective judgments of comparability are possible, opponents worry about the price tag: Revising salaries could cost a medium-size company millions of dollars in increased pay and benefits.

Advocates of comparable worth respond to those criticisms by pointing to statistical evidence demonstrating gender-linked pay inequities, as well as to the reality of visceral sexism in the workplace and to the thousands of cases every year involving workplace discrimination against women. They reject the idea that women end up in jobs that pay less than comparable jobs held by men because of their free choice. Rather, discrimination distorts the operation of the labor market and needs to be corrected. Moreover, proponents of comparable worth reject the argument that implementing comparable worth would be prohibitively expensive. They point to Minnesota, which phased in a comparable-worth program over several years so that the state incurred an expense of only about 1 percent a year. But the core of their argument remains an appeal to fairness and equity, which, they insist, should not be sacrificed on the altar of economics.

The comparable-worth issue continues to engender controversy because, as one commentator puts it, "The issue pits against each other two cherished American values: the

> **SUMMARY**
> Opponents of comparable worth claim that women have freely chosen their occupations and are not entitled to compensation. They contend that only the market can and should determine the value of different jobs and that revising pay scales would be expensive.

ethics of nondiscrimination versus the free enterprise system."[60] The federal courts have not explicitly accepted the doctrine of comparable worth, even when they've rendered legal decisions that seem to support it. One form of job discrimination against women that the courts agree about, however, is sexual harassment.

* * *

SEXUAL HARASSMENT

Sexual harassment—we hear about it all the time. Recently, for example, Hewlett-Packard CEO Mark Hurd resigned because of it, NFL quarterback Brett Favre was fined for obstructing an investigation into it, and comedian David Letterman confessed to a pattern of conduct—namely, routinely bedding the women who work for him—that at least borders on it. But sexual harassment is not merely a matter of a few rich and powerful guys misbehaving. It is a form of sexual discrimination that violates Title VII of the Civil Rights Act, and nearly 12,000 complaints of it are filed annually with the EEOC or state and local authorities.[61] No large American corporation has escaped the issue. Indeed, charges of sexual harassment have cost some of them a small fortune. In the late 1990s, for instance, Ford paid $7.75 million and Mitsubishi $34 million to settle class-action sexual-harassment lawsuits against them. According to the Supreme Court, men as well as women can be victims of sexual harassment.[62] The focus here is on women, however, because they are the ones who suffer most from it. One survey found that 21 percent of women report having been harassed at work and that 54 percent of them believe that supervisors are likely to retaliate if a subordinate rejects their romantic overtures.[63]

Critics may find it odd that sexual harassment is viewed by the courts as a kind of sex discrimination. If an infatuated supervisor harasses only the female employee who is the object of his desire, is his misconduct really best understood as discrimination against women? He does not bother women in general, only this particular individual. In viewing sexual harassment as a violation of the 1964 Civil Rights Act, however, the courts are rightly acknowledging that such behavior, and the larger social patterns that reinforce it, rest on male attitudes and assumptions that work against women.

Accepting this viewpoint still leaves puzzles, however. Assume that the infatuated supervisor is a woman and the employee a man. Are we to interpret this situation as sex discrimination, considering that it does not take place against a social backdrop of exploitation and discrimination against men? Or imagine a bisexual employer who sexually harasses both male and female employees. Because he discriminates against neither sex, is there no sexual harassment?

> Legally, sexual harassment is a form of discrimination. But that may not be the worst aspect of it, morally speaking.

These conceptual puzzles have to do with the law's interpretation of sexual harassment as a kind of sex discrimination. Practically speaking, this interpretation has benefited women and brought them better and fairer treatment on the job, but it clearly has its limits. Legally speaking, the most important aspect of sexual harassment may be that it represents discrimination, but it is doubtful that discrimination is morally the worst aspect of sexual harassment. Morally, there is much more to be said about the wrongness of sexual harassment.*

---

*By analogy, compare the fact that often the only grounds on which the federal government can put a murderer on trial is on the charge of having violated the civil rights of his or her victim. The charge of violating the victim's civil rights doesn't get to the heart of the murderer's wrongdoing, even if it is the only legally relevant issue.

THE DEFINITION OF SEXUAL HARASSMENT

What exactly is sexual harassment? According to the Equal Employment Opportunity Commission, **sexual harassment** is "unwelcome sexual advances, requests for sexual favors, and other verbal or physical conduct of a sexual nature." Catherine A. MacKinnon, author of *Sexual Harassment of Working Women*, describes sexual harassment as "sexual attention imposed on someone who is not in a position to refuse it." Alan K. Campbell, former director of the Federal Office of Personnel Management, defines it as "deliberate or repeated unsolicited verbal comments, gestures, or physical contact of a sexual nature which are unwelcome."[64] Here is a more complete legal definition that reflects the way most courts understand sexual harassment:

> Unwelcome sexual advances, requests for sexual favors, and other verbal or physical conduct of a sexual nature constitute sexual harassment when (1) submission to such conduct is made either explicitly or implicitly a term or condition of an individual's employment, (2) submission to or rejection of such conduct by an individual is used as the basis for employment decisions affecting such individual, or (3) such conduct has the purpose or effect of substantially interfering with an individual's work performance or creating an intimidating, hostile, or offensive working environment.

Sexual harassment divides into two types: "quid pro quo" and "hostile work environment." The phrase *quid pro quo* refers to giving something in return for something else. **Quid-pro-quo harassment** occurs when a supervisor makes an employee's employment opportunities conditional on the employee's entering into a sexual relationship with, or granting sexual favors to, the supervisor. Sexual threats are an example—in their crudest form, "You'd better agree to sleep with me if you want to keep your job." The immorality of such threats seems clear. In threatening harm, they are coercive and violate the rights of the person being threatened, certainly depriving her or him of equal treatment on the job. Obviously such threats can be seriously damaging, psychologically and otherwise, and hence are morally wrong.

Sexual offers are another species of quid-pro-quo sexual harassment: "If you sleep with me, I'm sure I can help you advance more quickly in the firm." Often such offers harbor an implied threat, and, unlike with genuine offers, the employee may risk something by turning them down. Larry May and John Hughes have argued that such offers by a male employer to a female employee put her in a worse position than she was in before and are therefore coercive. Even sexual offers with no hint of retaliation, they contend, change the female employee's working environment in an undesirable way.[65] In the case of both threats and offers, the supervisor is attempting to exploit the power imbalance between him and the employee.

The second kind of sexual harassment—**hostile-work-environment harassment**—is broader, but it may be more important because it is so pervasive. This form of sexual harassment is behavior of a sexual nature that is distressing to women and interferes with their ability to perform on the job, even when the behavior is not an attempt to pressure the woman for sexual favors. Sexual innuendos; sexually explicit e-mails; leering at or ogling a woman; sexist remarks about women's bodies, clothing, or sexual activities; the posting of pictures of nude women; raunchy office banter; and unnecessary touching, patting, or other physical conduct can all constitute sexual harassment. Such behavior is humiliating and degrading to its victim. It interferes with her peace of mind and undermines her work performance.

Legally, a woman is not required to prove that she was psychologically damaged or unable to work in order to establish sexual harassment. On the other hand, an isolated or occasional sexist remark or innuendo does not constitute harassment. To qualify as

> There are two types of sexual harassment.

> **SUMMARY**
> Sexual harassment is widespread. It includes unwelcome sexual advances and other conduct of a sexual nature when either (1) employment decisions are based on submission to it (quid pro quo) or (2) such conduct substantially interferes with an individual's work performance (hostile work environment). Sexual harassment is a kind of discrimination and is illegal.

harassment, the objectionable behavior must be persistent. The same holds for racial slurs and epithets. An ethnic joke by itself does not constitute discriminatory harassment, but a concerted pattern of "excessive and opprobrious" racially derogatory remarks and related abuse does violate the law.[66]

Human beings are sexual creatures, and when men and women work together, there may be sexual undertones to their interactions. Women as well as men can appreciate, with the right persons and at the appropriate times, sexual references, sex-related humor, and physical contact with members of the opposite sex. Flirting, too, is often appreciated by both parties. It is not necessary that a serious and professional work environment be entirely free from sexuality, nor is this an achievable goal.

When, then, is behavior objectionable or offensive enough to constitute harassment? What one person views as innocent fun or a friendly overture may be seen as objectionable or demeaning by someone else. Comments that one woman appreciates or enjoys may be distressing to another. Who can decide what is right? In the case of sexual harassment, who determines what is objectionable or offensive?

> In sexual harassment cases, the courts look to what a reasonable person would find offensive. But what matters morally is to respect each person's choices and wishes.

To answer that question, the courts ask what the hypothetical "reasonable person" would find offensive if the person were a woman in that situation. What matters morally, however, is to respect each person's choices and wishes. Even if the other women in the office like it when the boss gives them a little hug, it would still be wrong to hug the one woman who is made uncomfortable. If the behavior is unwanted—that is, if the woman doesn't like it—then persisting in it is wrong. The fact that objectionable behavior must be persistent and repeated to be sexual harassment allows for the possibility that people can honestly misread coworkers' signals or misjudge their likely response to a sexual innuendo, a joke, or a friendly pat. That may be excusable; what is not excusable is persisting in the behavior once you know it is unwelcome.

Some lower courts have extended the concept of sexual harassment to include **sexual favoritism**, upholding the claims of women to have been discriminated against because the boss was sleeping not with them but with one or more other employees. That seems to stretch the concept of sexual harassment almost to the breaking point, because the rights of the complaining employee have not been violated. Her employment opportunities have not been made contingent on her acquiescing to her employer's sexual wishes. However, the women who entered into sexual relations with their supervisor may have benefited from doing so, possibly at the expense of the employee who had no such relationship with the boss. Moreover, such conduct by a supervisor can create a sexually charged work environment that interferes with the ability of other employees to do their job. It also reinforces beliefs that demean women and perpetuate discrimination against them because, in the words of one judge, "a message is conveyed that managers view women as sexual playthings."[67]

DEALING WITH SEXUAL HARASSMENT

> SUMMARY
> Employees encountering sexually harassing behavior from coworkers should make it clear that the behavior is unwanted. If it persists, harassed employees should document the behavior and report it to the appropriate person or office in the organization. In the case of sexual threats or offers from supervisors, they should do this immediately. If internal channels are ineffective, employees should seek legal advice.

Neither the wrongness nor the illegality of sexual harassment requires that the harassing conduct be by the employee's supervisor. This is particularly relevant in hostile-work-environment cases, in which the harassment a woman endures may come from coworkers. Furthermore, companies can be held legally liable for harassing behavior by their employees even if they are unaware of it, especially in cases of quid-pro-quo harassment by supervisors. In hostile-work-environment cases, companies can escape liability if they can show that (1) they took reasonable steps to prevent and promptly correct sexually harassing behavior and (2) the employee unreasonably failed to take advantage of the preventive or corrective procedures established by the company. This fact gives companies an incentive to be proactive, and many have responded by developing comprehensive programs to educate employees about, and to protect them from, sexual harassment. Legal issues aside, companies clearly have a moral obligation to provide a work environment in which employees are free from sexual harassment. They need to be alert to the possibility of sexual harassment, take reasonable steps to prevent it, and deal with it swiftly and fairly should it occur.

Practically speaking, what should a female employee do if she encounters sexual harassment? *First,* she must make it clear that the behavior is unwanted. That may be more difficult to do than it sounds, because most of us like to please others and do not want to be thought to be prudes or to lack a sense of humor. The employee may wish to be tactful and even pleasant in rejecting behavior she finds inappropriate, especially if she thinks the offending party is well intentioned. But in any case, she has to make her feelings known clearly and unequivocally. *Second,* if the behavior persists, she should try to document it by keeping a record of what has occurred, who was involved, and when it happened. If others have witnessed some of the incidents, then that will help her document her case.

Third, the employee should complain to the appropriate supervisor, sticking to the facts and presenting her allegations as objectively as possible. She should do this immediately in the case of sexual threats or offers by supervisors. In the case of inappropriate behavior by coworkers, she should generally wait to see if it persists despite her having told the offending party that she objects. If complaining to her immediate supervisor does not bring quick action, then she must try whatever other channel is available to her in the organization—the grievance committee, for example, or the chief executive's office.

Fourth, if internal complaints do not bring results, then the employee should seriously consider seeing a lawyer and learning in detail what legal options are available. Many women try to ignore sexual harassment, but the evidence suggests that in most cases it continues or grows worse. When sexual threats or offers are involved, a significant number of victims are subject to unwarranted reprimands, increased workloads, or other reprisals. The employee must remember, too, that she has both a moral and a legal right to work in an environment free from sexual harassment.

What you should do if you encounter sexual harassment.

STUDY CORNER

KEY TERMS AND CONCEPTS

- affirmative action programs
- *Bakke v. Regents of the University of California*
- *Brown v. Board of Education*
- Civil Rights Act of 1964
- comparable worth
- Equal Employment Opportunity Commission (EEOC)
- disparate impact
- disparate treatment
- hostile-work-environment harassment
- job discrimination
- pink-collar occupations
- quid-pro-quo harassment
- sexual favoritism
- sexual harassment

POINTS TO REVIEW

- what the case of Notre Dame and Willingham illustrates (pp. 558–559)
- three defining features of job discrimination (p. 560)
- four different forms of job discrimination (pp. 560–561)
- moral arguments against job discrimination (p. 561)
- statistical evidence of inequality (pp. 562–563)
- attitudes that victimize women like Ezold, Hopkins, and Hishon (pp. 564–565)
- how stereotypes can lead to discrimination (pp. 565–566)
- what was decided in *Brown v. Board of Education* (p. 566)
- what the Civil Rights Act says about discrimination (pp. 566–567)
- the difference between disparate treatment and disparate impact (p. 567)
- EEOC guidelines for affirmative action programs (p. 567)
- why many companies believe in affirmative action (p. 568)
- where the Supreme Court stands on affirmative action (pp. 568–571)
- what's misleading about calling affirmative action "reverse discrimination" (p. 571)
- three arguments for affirmative action (pp. 571–572)
- three arguments against affirmative action (pp. 572–573)
- what the doctrine of comparable worth requires employers to do (p. 574)
- arguments for and against comparable worth (pp. 574–575)
- what's puzzling about viewing sexual harassment as sex discrimination (p. 576)
- two types of sexual harassment (p. 577)
- who decides what is sexual harassment (p. 578)
- sexual favoritism as a possible form of sexual harassment (p. 578)
- how companies can escape legal liability for hostile-work-environment claims (p. 579)
- four things to do when you encounter sexual harassment (p. 579)

FOR FURTHER REFLECTION

1. In your view, how pervasive is job discrimination these days? Have you or anyone you've known experienced some form of it?
2. Do you think affirmative action programs are misguided, or are they justifiable and socially beneficial? Which side of the comparable-worth issue are you on?
3. What explains sexual harassment?

CASE 11.1

Minority Set-Asides

RICHMOND, VIRGINIA, THE FORMER CAPITAL of the Confederacy, is not the sort of place one would normally associate with controversial efforts at affirmative action. But aware of its legacy of racial discrimination and wanting to do something about it, the Richmond City Council adopted what it called the Minority Business Utilization Plan—a plan that eventually brought it before the U.S. Supreme Court.

The plan, which the council adopted by a 5-to-2 vote after a public hearing, required contractors to whom the city awarded construction contracts to subcontract at least 30 percent of the dollar amount of their contracts to minority business enterprises (MBEs). A business was defined as an MBE if minority group members controlled at least 51 percent of it, and a minority-owned business from anywhere in the United States could qualify as an MBE subcontractor. (The 30 percent set-aside did not apply to construction contracts awarded to minority contractors in the first place.)

Proponents of the set-aside provision relied on a study that indicated that whereas the general population of Richmond was 50 percent African American, only 0.67 percent of the city's construction contracts had been awarded to minority businesses. Council member Marsh, a proponent of the ordinance, made the following statement:

> I have been practicing law in this community since 1961, and I am familiar with the practices in the construction industry in this area, in the state, and around the nation. And I can say without equivocation, that the general conduct of the construction industry . . . is one in which race discrimination and exclusion on the basis of race is widespread.

Opponents questioned both the wisdom and the legality of the ordinance. They argued that the disparity between minorities in the population of Richmond and the low number of contracts awarded to MBEs did not prove racial discrimination in the construction industry. They also questioned whether there were enough MBEs in the Richmond area to satisfy the 30-percent requirement.

The city's plan was in effect for five years. During that time, it was challenged in the courts. A federal district court upheld the set-aside ordinance, stating that the city council's "findings [were] sufficient to ensure that, in adopting the Plan, it was remedying the present effects of past discrimination in the construction industry." However, the case was appealed to the Supreme Court, which ruled in *City of Richmond v. Croson* that the Richmond plan was in violation of the equal protection clause of the Fourteenth Amendment.[68] In delivering the opinion of the majority of the Court, Justice Sandra Day O'Connor argued that Richmond had not supported its plan with sufficient evidence of past discrimination in the city's construction industry:

> A generalized assertion that there has been past discrimination in an entire industry provides no guidance for a legislative body to determine the precise scope of the injury it seeks to remedy. It "has no logical stopping point." . . . "Relief" for such an ill-defined wrong could extend until the percentage of public contracts awarded to MBEs in Richmond mirrored the percentage of minorities in the population as a whole.

> [The City of Richmond] argues that it is attempting to remedy various forms of past discrimination that are alleged to be responsible for the small number of minority businesses in the local contracting industry. . . . While there is no doubt that the sorry history of both private and public discrimination in this country has contributed to a lack of opportunities for black entrepreneurs, this observation, standing alone, cannot justify a rigid quota in the awarding of public contracts in Richmond, Virginia. Like the claim that discrimination in primary and secondary schooling justifies a rigid racial preference in medical school admissions, an amorphous claim that

there has been past discrimination cannot justify the use of an unyielding racial quota.

It is sheer speculation how many minority firms there would be in Richmond absent past societal discrimination, just as it was sheer speculation how many minority medical students would have been admitted to the medical school at Davis absent past discrimination in educational opportunities. Defining these sorts of injuries as "identified discrimination" would give local governments license to create a patchwork of racial preferences based on statistical generalizations about any particular field of endeavor.

These defects are readily apparent in this case. The 30% quota cannot in any realistic sense be tied to any injury suffered by anyone. . . .

In sum, none of the evidence presented by the city points to any identified discrimination in the Richmond construction industry. We, therefore, hold that the city has failed to demonstrate a compelling interest in apportioning public contracting opportunities on the basis of race. To accept Richmond's claim that past societal discrimination alone can serve as the basis for rigid racial preference would be to open the door to competing claims for "remedial relief" for every disadvantaged group. The dream of a Nation of equal citizens in a society where race is irrelevant to personal opportunity and achievement would be lost in a mosaic of shifting preferences based on inherently unmeasurable claims of past wrongs. . . . We think such a result would be contrary to both the letter and spirit of a constitutional provision whose central command is equality.

But the Court's decision was not unanimous, and Justice Thurgood Marshall was joined by Justices William Brennan and Harry Blackmun in dissenting vigorously to the opinion of the majority. Justice Marshall wrote:

The essence of the majority's position is that Richmond has failed to . . . prove that past discrimination has impeded minorities from joining or participating fully in Richmond's construction contracting industry. I find deep irony in second-guessing Richmond's judgment on this point. As much as any municipality in the United States, Richmond knows what racial discrimination is; a century of decisions by this and other federal courts has richly documented the city's disgraceful history of public and private racial discrimination. In any event, the Richmond City Council has supported its determination that minorities have been wrongly excluded from local construction contracting. Its proof includes statistics showing that minority-owned businesses have received virtually no city contracting dollars; . . . testimony by municipal officials that discrimination has been widespread in the local construction industry; and . . . federal studies . . . which showed that pervasive discrimination in the Nation's tight-knit construction industry had operated to exclude minorities from public contracting. These are precisely the types of statistical and testimonial evidence which, until today, this Court has credited in cases approving of race-conscious measures designed to remedy past discrimination.

DISCUSSION QUESTIONS

1. What was the Richmond City Council trying to accomplish with its Minority Business Utilization Plan? If you had been a member of the council, would you have voted for the plan?

2. What are the pros and cons of a minority set-aside plan like Richmond's? Will it have good consequences? Does it infringe on anyone's rights? What conflicting moral principles, ideals, and values are at stake?

3. Do you believe that there was sufficient evidence of racial discrimination to justify the city's plan? Who is right about this—Justice O'Connor or Justice Marshall?

4. Justice O'Connor and the majority of the Court seem to believe that there must be some specific, identifiable individuals who have been discriminated against before race-conscious measures can be adopted to remedy past discrimination. Do you agree that affirmative action measures must meet this standard?

5. In light of the fact that no federal statute specifically bars racial discrimination in private domestic commercial transactions between two business firms, and given the evidence that racism is an obstacle to African-American business success,[69] what obligation, if any, does state, local, or federal government have to assist minority-owned companies?

6. What measures could Richmond have taken that would have increased opportunities for minority business but would not have involved racial quotas? Would such measures be as effective as the original plan?

CASE 11.2

Hoop Dreams

IN BASKETBALL, TALENT PLUS HARD WORK EQUALS success. That's an equation that holds true for women as well as men, and in recent years, dedicated female athletes have raised women's basketball to new heights and won the allegiance of many new fans.[70]

But what about their coaches? Do any obstacles stand between them and their dreams? Marianne Stanley didn't think so when she began coaching women's basketball for the University of Southern California, where she earned $64,000 a year—a fair sum, one might think, but less than half that of her counterpart, George Raveling, who coached the men's team. True, Raveling had been coaching for thirty-one years, had been an assistant on the U.S. Olympic team, and was twice named coach of the year. But Stanley was no slouch. She had been a head coach for sixteen years and won three national championships. In her last two years at USC, she had win–loss records of 23–8 and 22–7, which compared favorably with Raveling's 19–10 and 24–6.

So when her initial four-year contract expired, Marianne Stanley sought pay parity with Raveling. Stanley knew that Raveling was also earning tens of thousands of dollars in perks, but she was willing to overlook that and settle for an equal base salary of $135,000. Instead, USC offered Stanley a three-year contract starting at $88,000 and increasing to $100,000. When she rejected that offer, USC countered with a one-year contract for $96,000. Stanley declined the offer and left USC, her hoop dreams diminished, although she later began coaching at UC Berkeley, where her salary was equivalent to that of the men's coach.

For his part, George Raveling didn't mind Stanley's making as much money as he did. But he understood why USC paid him more. He was, after all, a hot property, and if USC was going to prevent his being lured away by some other university trying to boost its basketball program, then it had to pay him a high salary. By contrast, Marianne Stanley didn't have any other job offers.

Too bad, one might say, but that's how the market works in a capitalist society. But what if the market itself is discriminatory? Defenders of comparable worth argue that it is and that coaches like Stanley can't negotiate for comparable salaries because women's basketball isn't valued as highly as men's. And it's college administrators, they argue, who are to blame for that. As one feminist puts it:

> The women didn't get the advertising and marketing dollars. They didn't get the PR. Then when fans weren't showing up, the TV stations weren't carrying the games and other universities weren't fighting over the best coaches, administrators told the women that, because they and their sport didn't draw as much attention as men, they shouldn't be paid as much.

In response, defenders of USC deny that it or any other university is responsible for the fact that men's sports are big revenue earners and women's are not. The higher pay for those who coach men simply reflects that social and cultural reality, which is something college administrators have no control over. If someone like Marianne Stanley wants to enter the big leagues, then she should coach men.

Still, many find it distressing that even though 40 percent of American athletic participants are female, their sports get less respect and less attention—to be specific, less than 5 percent of all media coverage and only 1.62 percent of sporting airtime on big networks.[71] Shouldn't universities try to combat this, at least by paying equivalent salaries to the coaches of male and female teams?

Update

Sadly, sometimes even those who have fought against discrimination can discriminate against others. Just a few years after Marianne Stanley assumed her head coaching position at UC Berkeley, one of the assistant coaches, Sharrona Alexander, filed suit against the university, alleging that Stanley told her to get an abortion or lose her job. Stanley denied the abortion allegation, but admitted that she did ask Alexander to resign because of her pregnancy. Either way, a champion of women's rights was guilty of trampling on someone else's hoop dreams. Ironically, Stanley herself played college basketball when she was pregnant (returning to practice eleven days after her daughter was born) and went on, single and with a toddler, to coach Old Dominion University to three national championships. Moreover, some sports commentators believe that, far from being a handicap, motherhood can give a coach an edge in recruiting because the parents of prospective recruits prefer their daughters to be coached by women who, when they say that they treat their teams as family, know what they are talking about. In addition, Arizona State coach Charli Turner Thorne says, because "you're taking young ladies at a very formative time, you have to play the parent role." She adds, "There's absolutely no doubt [motherhood] makes me a better coach."

DISCUSSION QUESTIONS

1. The doctrine of comparable worth holds that men and women should be paid the same wage for doing jobs of equal skill, effort, and responsibility. Were Marianne Stanley and George Raveling doing work of comparable value?

2. Was Stanley treated unfairly or in some way discriminated against? Should USC have offered to pay her more?

3. Why do sports played by men tend to be more popular and generate more revenue than sports played by women? Are female athletes—and their coaches—disadvantaged? Are they discriminated against? If so, who is responsible for this discrimination, and do colleges and universities have an obligation to do something about it?

4. Should universities like USC base their coaching salaries entirely on market considerations? Or should they pay the coaches of men's and women's sports comparable salaries based on experience, skill, and performance?

5. Respond to the argument that because men are free to coach women's teams and women to coach men's teams, there is nothing discriminatory in the fact that one job pays more than the other.

6. Was Sharrona Alexander's pregnancy likely to have adversely affected her coaching performance? If so, was Marianne Stanley wrong to ask her to resign? How should Stanley have handled the situation?

CASE 11.3

Raising the Ante

HAVING SPEARHEADED THE WOMEN'S CAUSE ON behalf of equal pay for jobs of equal value, Phyllis Warren was elated when the board decided to readjust salaries. Its decision meant Phyllis and the other women employed by the manufacturing firm would receive pay equivalent to men doing work of comparable worth. But in a larger sense it constituted an admission of guilt by the board, acknowledgment of a history blemished by implicit sexual discrimination.

In the euphoria that followed the board's decision, neither Phyllis nor any of the other activists thought much about the implied admission of female exploitation. But some weeks later, Herm Leggett, a sales dispatcher, half-jokingly suggested to Phyllis over lunch that she shouldn't stop with equal pay now. Phyllis asked Herm what he meant.

"Back pay," Herm said without hesitation. "If they're readjusting salaries for women," he explained, "they obviously know that salaries are out of line and have been for some time." Then he asked her pointedly, "How long you been here, Phyl?" Eleven years, she told him. "If those statistics you folks were passing around last month are accurate," Herm said, "then I'd say you've been losing about $2,000 a year, or $22,000 over eleven years." Then he added with a laugh, "Not counting interest, of course."

"Why not?" Phyllis thought. Why shouldn't she and other women who'd suffered past inequities be reimbursed?

That night Phyllis called a few of the other women and suggested that they press the board for back pay. Some said they were satisfied and didn't think they should force the issue. Others thought the firm had been fair in readjusting the salary schedule, and they were willing to let bygones be bygones. Still others thought that any further efforts might, in fact, roll back the board's favorable decision. Yet a nucleus agreed that workers who had been unfairly treated in the past ought to receive compensation. They decided, however, that because their ranks were divided, they shouldn't wage as intense an in-house campaign as previously but instead take the issue directly to the board, while it might still be inhaling deeply the fresh air of social responsibility.

The following Wednesday, Phyllis and four other women presented their case to the board, intentionally giving the impression that they enjoyed as much support from other workers as they had the last time they appeared before it. Although this wasn't true, Phyllis suggested it as an effective strategic ploy.

Phyllis's presentation had hardly ended when board members began making their feelings known. One called her proposal "industrial blackmail." "No sooner do we try to right an injustice," he said testily, "than you take our good faith and threaten to beat us over the head with it unless we comply with your request."

Another member just as vigorously argued that the current board couldn't be held accountable for the actions, policies, and decisions of previous boards. "Sure," he said, "we're empowered to alter policies as we see fit and as conditions change to chart new directions. And we've done that. But to expect us to bear the full financial liability of decisions we never made is totally unrealistic—and unfair."

Still another member wondered where it would all end. "If we agree," he asked, "will you then suggest we should track down all those women who ever worked for us and provide them compensation?" Phyllis said no, but the board should readjust retirement benefits for those affected.

At this point the board asked Phyllis if she had any idea what her proposal would cost the firm. "Whatever it is, it's a small price to pay for righting wrong," she said firmly.

"But is it a small price to pay for severely damaging our profit picture?" one of the members asked. Then he added, "I needn't remind you that our profit outlook directly affects what we can offer our current employees in terms of salary and fringe benefits. It directly affects our ability to revise our salary schedule." Finally, he asked Phyllis whether she'd accept the board's reducing everyone's current compensation to meet what Phyllis termed the board's "obligation to the past."

Despite its decided opposition to Phyllis's proposal, the board agreed to consider it and render a decision at its next meeting. As a final broadside, Phyllis hinted that, if the board didn't comply with the committee's request, the committee was prepared to pursue legal action.

DISCUSSION QUESTIONS

1. If you were a board member, how would you vote? Why?
2. What moral principles are involved in this case?
3. Do you think Phyllis Warren was unfair in taking advantage of the board's implied admission of salary discrimination on the basis of sex? Why or why not?
4. Do you think Phyllis was wrong in giving the board the impression that her proposal enjoyed broad support? Why or why not?
5. If the board rejects the committee's request, do you think the committee ought to sue? Give reasons.

CASE 11.4

Consenting to Sexual Harassment

IN THE CASE OF *VINSON V. TAYLOR*, HEARD BEFORE the federal district court for the District of Columbia, Mechelle Vinson alleged that Sidney Taylor, her supervisor at Capital City Federal Savings and Loan, had sexually harassed her.[72] But the facts of the case were contested.

In court Vinson testified that about a year after she began working at the bank, Taylor asked her to have sexual relations with him. She claimed that Taylor said she "owed" him because he had obtained the job for her. Although she turned down Taylor at first, she eventually became involved with him. She and Taylor engaged in sexual relations, she said, both during and after business hours, in the remaining three years she worked at the bank. The encounters included intercourse in a bank vault and in a storage area in the bank basement. Vinson also testified that Taylor often actually "assaulted or raped" her. She contended that she was forced to submit to Taylor or jeopardize her employment.

Taylor, for his part, denied the allegations. He testified that he had never had sex with Vinson. On the contrary, he alleged that Vinson had made advances toward him and that he had declined them. He contended that Vinson had brought the charges against him to "get even" because of a work-related dispute.

In its ruling on the case, the court held that if Vinson and Taylor had engaged in a sexual relationship, that relationship was voluntary on the part of Vinson and was not employment related. The court also held that Capital City Federal Savings and Loan did not have "notice" of the alleged harassment and was therefore not liable. Although Taylor was Vinson's supervisor, the court reasoned that notice to him was not notice to the bank.

Vinson appealed the case, and the Court of Appeals held that the district court had erred in three ways. First, the district court had overlooked the fact that there are two possible kinds of sexual harassment. Writing for the majority, Chief Judge Spottswood Robinson distinguished cases in which the victim's continued employment or promotion is conditioned on giving in to sexual demands and those cases in which the victim must tolerate a "substantially discriminatory work environment." The lower court had failed to consider whether Vinson's case involved harassment of the second kind.

Second, the higher court also overruled the district court's finding that because Vinson voluntarily engaged in a sexual relationship with Taylor, she was not a victim of sexual harassment. Voluntariness on Vinson's part had "no bearing," the judge wrote, on "whether Taylor made Vinson's toleration of sexual harassment a condition of her employment." Third, the Court of Appeals held that any discriminatory activity by a supervisor is attributable to the employer, regardless of whether the employer had specific notice.

In his dissent to the decision by the Court of Appeals, Judge Robert Bork rejected the majority's claim that "voluntariness" did not automatically rule out harassment. He argued that this position would have the result of depriving the accused person of any defense, because he could no longer establish that the supposed victim was really "a willing participant." Judge Bork contended further that an employer should not be held vicariously liable for a supervisor's acts that it didn't know about.

Eventually the case arrived at the U.S. Supreme Court, which upheld the majority verdict of the Court of Appeals, stating that:

> [T]he fact that sex-related conduct was "voluntary," in the sense that the complainant was not forced to participate against her will, is not a defense to a sexual harassment suit brought under Title VII. The gravamen

In the movie *North Country*, Charlize Theron plays a character who has no choice but to take on a miner's job in order to survive as the mother of two. Confronted with unrelenting verbal and physical abuse at the hands of her male coworkers, she fights back and ultimately wins a sexual harassment lawsuit.

of any sexual harassment claim is that the alleged sexual advances were "unwelcome.". . . The correct inquiry is whether respondent by her conduct indicated that the alleged sexual advances were unwelcome, not whether her actual participation in sexual intercourse was voluntary.

The Court, however, rejected the Court of Appeals's position that employers are strictly liable for the acts of their supervisors, regardless of the particular circumstances.[73]

DISCUSSION QUESTIONS

1. According to her own testimony, Vinson acquiesced to Taylor's sexual demands. In this sense her behavior was "voluntary." Does the voluntariness of her behavior mean that she had "consented" to Taylor's advances? Does it mean that they were "welcome"? Do you agree that Vinson's acquiescence shows there was no sexual harassment? Which court was right about this? Defend your position.

2. In your opinion, under what circumstances would acquiescence be a defense to charges of sexual harassment? When would it not be a defense? Can you formulate a general rule for deciding such cases?

3. Assuming the truth of Vinson's version of the case, do you think her employer, Capital City Federal Savings and Loan, should be held liable for sexual harassment it was not aware of? Should the employer have been aware of it? Does the fact that Taylor was a supervisor make a difference? In general, when should an employer be liable for harassment?

4. What steps do you think Vinson should have taken when Taylor first pressed her for sex? Should she be blamed for having given in to him? Assuming that there was sexual harassment despite her acquiescence, does her going along with Taylor make her partly responsible or mitigate Taylor's wrongdoing?

5. In court, Vinson's allegations were countered by Taylor's version of the facts. Will there always be a "your word against mine" problem in sexual harassment cases? What could Vinson have done to strengthen her case?

CASE 11.5

Facial Discrimination

SCENE: A CONFERENCE ROOM OF A BRANCH OFFICE of Allied Products, Inc., where Tom, Frank, and Alice have been interviewing college students for summer internships.

Tom: Did you see that last candidate? Jeez, was he sorry looking.

Frank: Too ugly to work here, that's for sure. And those thick glasses didn't help. Still, he wasn't as ugly as that young woman you hired last summer. What was her name . . . Allison? Boy, she was enormous! And remember that hair of hers? It wasn't surprising we had to let her go.

Alice: Come on, Frank. Don't be so hung up on looks. That last guy seemed to know his stuff, and he certainly was enthusiastic about working for Allied.

Frank: Hey, don't get me wrong, Alice. I know you don't have to be beautiful to work for Allied—after all, look at Tom here. Still, with a face like that guy's, you got to wonder.

Tom: Wisecracks aside, Alice, Frank's got a point. Studies show that it's natural for people to discriminate on the basis of looks. I've read that even babies will look at a pretty face longer than an ugly face.

Alice: I know that. Studies also show that people attribute positive characteristics to people they find attractive and that they treat unattractive people worse than other people in lots of ways. For example, strangers are less likely to do small favors for unattractive people than they are for attractive people, and even parents and teachers have lower expectations for ugly, fat, or odd-looking children. Attractive people also earn more money than average-looking people. So what this really boils down to is implicit discrimination.

Tom: That's what I'm saying. It's natural. Besides, it's not illegal to discriminate on the basis of appearance.

Frank: That's right. You wouldn't want us to hire somebody with green hair and rings in his nose and put him out at the front desk, would you? This is a business, not a freak show.

Alice: Hey, slow down, guys. First, it may be natural and it may even be legal to favor good-looking people, but that doesn't make it right. And second, I'm not talking about grooming or dress. It's your choice to dye your hair and decorate your face, and if you don't fit in because of that, that's your fault. But the guy we talked to today didn't choose to be ugly, so why hold it against him?

Frank: I suppose next you'll be telling us that we should have kept Allison on last summer just because she was fat.

Alice: No, I'm not saying you have to give preferential treatment to overweight people. But I think that nobody in the office cut her any slack. If she'd been normal size, things would have worked out okay, but people took one look at her and prejudged her to be a loser. You know, Frank, some courts have held that discrimination against the obese violates the Americans with Disabilities Act.

Tom: That's only if it's a medical condition.

Frank: Yeah, Allison's only problem was that she liked to eat.

Alice: You don't know that. You don't know anything about her.

Frank: I suppose her hair was a medical condition, too.

Tom: Okay, you two, take it easy. Seriously, though, Alice, a number of our interns have to interact with the public, and people can be put off by having to deal with ugly people, fat people, or even very short people. So why aren't an employee's looks a job-relevant issue?

Alice: No, I think that as long as the person is clean and well groomed, then the public shouldn't be put off by having to deal with someone who is unattractive or unusual looking. It's unreasonable.

Tom: That's what you say. But what if the public is "unreasonable"? What if they prefer companies with attractive or at least normal-looking employees?

Alice: It's still irrelevant. It's the same as if a company had customers who didn't like dealing with blacks. That's no reason for it not to hire blacks.

Tom: Yeah, I can see that.

Frank: Okay, but what about this ugly guy? Do we have to offer him an internship?

DISCUSSION QUESTIONS

1. How frequently are people discriminated against on the basis of their looks? Is it a serious problem in job situations? What about the fact that students give higher instructional rankings to attractive professors?[74]

2. Assess the argument that there is nothing wrong with "facial discrimination"—that it simply reflects the fact that human beings are naturally attracted to, or repelled by, other human beings on the basis of their physical characteristics.

3. Under what circumstances is physical attractiveness a job-related employment criterion? Is it relevant to being a salesperson, a flight attendant, or a receptionist?

4. What arguments can be given for and against a law preventing job discrimination on the basis of immutable aspects of one's appearance?

5. Assess the argument that because fat, ugly, or strange-looking people have it tougher throughout their lives than do attractive people, we should give them preferential treatment whenever we can—for example, in job situations—to make up for the disadvantages they've suffered and to help level the playing field.

6. Are businesses morally obligated to try to prevent or reduce appearance discrimination in the workplace? What steps can they take?

INDEX

A

ABA. *See* American Bar Association (ABA)
Abacus-2007 AC1, 183
Abbott Laboratories, 241
Abercrombie & Fitch, 437, 561
ABN Amro, 183
abortion, 12
abuse, of official position, 498–503
ACLU. *See* American Civil Liberties Union (ACLU)
act utilitarianism, 61, 77
ADA. *See* Americans with Disabilities Act (ADA)
A7D Affair, The (case), 35–37
Adams, Henry C., 424–425
Adelphia Communications, 171
administrative regulations, defined, 6–8
Adventures of Huckleberry Finn, The (Twain), 15
advertising. *See also* specific types
    associative, 314
    and consumer needs, 292–294
    deception in, 283–292
    free speech and media, 295
    manipulative, 314
    market economics, 294–295
    subliminal, 288
Advest Group, 393
Aetna Life and Casualty, 384
AFDC. *See* Aid to Families with Dependent Children (AFDC)
affirmative action, 25, 567–568, 571–574
Affluent Society, The (Galbraith), 199, 293, 315, 316, 317
Affordable Care Act, 234, 235
AFL. *See* American Federation of Labor (AFL)
AFL-CIO, 401, 404
AIC Securities, 394
AID. *See* U.S. Agency for International Development (AID)
AIDS in the Workplace (case), 409–410
Aid to Families with Dependent Children (AFDC), 133
AIG. *See* American International Group (AIG)
Airborne, 286
Alabama Supreme Court, 276
Alcoa, 505

Alderson Federal Prison Camp, 109
Alexander, Sharrona, 583
Alexandra Wrage of Trace International, 505
alienation, and exploitation, 166–167
Allen, Lauren, 436
Alliance for Bangladesh Worker Safety, 175
all-terrain vehicles (ATVs), 273
AMA. *See* American Medical Association (AMA)
Amazon, 237
ambiguity, as deceptive advertising, 284–285
American Airlines, 280, 437, 456
American Bar Association (ABA), 414
American Civil Liberties Union (ACLU), 464
American Dream, 172
American Electric Power, 342
American Express, 568
American Federation of Labor (AFL), 400–401
American Home Products, 285
American International Group (AIG), 150, 226
American Management Association, 19, 444
American manufacturing, decline of, 168–171
American Medical Association (AMA), 177, 298
American Polygraph Association, 441
American Psychological Association, 461
Americans with Disabilities Act (ADA), 387, 567
America West Airlines, 452
amoral business, myths of, 39–40
Analyzing Insider Trading (reading), 533–540
Anarchy, State, and Utopia (Nozick), 114
Angell, Marcia, 230, 231
animals, treatment of, 352–354
    and factory farming, 353–354
Anshen, Melvin, 212, 213
anti-bribery convention, 506
AOL Time Warner, 202
Apple, 152, 237, 238, 280
Apply Yourself, Inc., 83
Aquafina, 282
Aquinas, 536
Araskog, Rand, 398
Arendt, Hannah, 48, 429
arguments
    defined, 23
    invalid, 23
    moral, 24
    revising and modifying, 27

    sound, 24
    unsound, 24
    valid, 23
Aristech Chemical Corporation, 347
Aristotle, 18, 108, 481, 484
Arming, Scott, 236, 237
Armour-Dial company, 287
Arons, Charles, 389
Arpey, Gerard, 456
Arrow, Kenneth J., 223, 347
Arthur Andersen, 1
Asch, Solomon, 20
Ashland Oil, 505
Associated Press, 181
associative advertising, 314
assumption of risk, 446
Atkins, 282
Atkins, Orin, 505
AT&T, 163, 202
attitudinal evidence, 563–566
ATVs. *See* all-terrain vehicles (ATVs)
Auschwitz, 47
authorization, 406
automobile safety, 270–271
autonomy, 319–320

B

Baby Boon: How Family-Friendly America Cheats the Childless, 483
Bacon, Francis, 390
Bacon, Kevin, 54
Badaracco, Joseph L., Jr., 19
Bahr, Morton, 444
Baier, Annette, 350
Bailey, Kathleen, 461
Bakke, Allan, 568–569
Balke, Carol, 391, 392
Balmford, Andrew, 339
Bangladesh Accord for Fire and Building Safety, 175
Bank of America, 203, 236, 379, 380, 438
Barbie, 278, 502
Barde, Nicole, 568
Barry, Bruce, 384
basic structure, theory of justice, 126–127
Bassett, Phyllis, 460
Baton Rouge, 445
Battling over Bottled Water (case), 131–132

631

Baum, Gregory, 431
Baxter, William F., 351
Bayer, 285
Baytown Company, 235–236
Beam, Jim, 478
Bean, L. L., 276
Bear Stearns, 150
Bechtel, 204
BellSouth Corporation, 507
Bender, Thomas, 426
Benenson, Lisa, 481
Bennett, William, 426
Bentham, Jeremy, 60–61, 352
Benton, Harry, 526–527
Berle, Adolf, 215, 239
Berman Bioethics Institute, 231
Bernstein, Paul, 173
Best Lock Corporation, 388
Betancourt, George, 493
Bethlehem Steel Corporation, 507
Better Bagels, 409
B.F. Goodrich, 35
BFOQ. *See* Bona Fide Occupational Qualifications (BFOQ)
Bharara, Preet, 208, 524
Bible, 11
Bielby, William T., 565
Big Mac, 354
"Big One, The," 283
Binko, Christine, 304
Biotechnology Industry Organization, 231
birth control, 97
Black, Sandra E., 425
Black & Decker, 279
Blackmun, Harry A., 464, 536, 582
Blackstone, William T., 338
Blair, Florence, 565
Blanchflower, David G., 425
Bloch, Byron, 87
Blood for Sale (case), 88–89
Bloomberg Businessweek, 365
Blough, Roger, 210
Blum, Matt, 436
BMW, 267, 276
Boazman, Wright, 302, 303
Body Trim, 287
Boeing, 568
Boisjoly, Roger, 551, 553–554, 556–557
Bok, Sissela, 514
Bolton, Derrick, 83
Bona Fide Occupational Qualifications (BFOQ), 386
Bon Marché, 174
Bork, Robert, 426, 586
Bowery Bank, 285
Bowie, Norman, 431–432, 433, 513, 514–515

Boyd, Tom, 236
Boy Scouts, 235, 236, 237
Boyte, Harry, 427
Brady Center to Prevent Gun Violence, 414
Brake Breakers, Inc., 41–44
Brandeis, Louis D., 434
Brandt, Richard, 14, 78, 113
Bratz Dolls, 502
Breast Implants (case), 297–299
Brecht, Bertolt, 161
Brenkert, George, 33, 468, 472, 475–476
Brennan, William, 569
Bretton Woods, 187, 189
bribes, and kickbacks, 503–507
Bristol-Myers Squibb, 220, 290
Brittain, John A., 144
broader view of corporate responsibility, 211–213
Brown, Harrison, 200
Buber, Martin, 7
Buddhist Economics (reading), 197–201
Building America, 427
Burbank, 453
Burger King, 279
Burkett, Elinor, 483
Burton, Edwin T., 208
Bush, George W., 151, 171
business
  attitudes toward environment, 335–337
  and child care, 452
  and corporate welfare programs, 163–165
  defined, 4
  and ecology, 334–337
  egoism, 66
  social responsibility of, 247–248
Business and Environmental Ethics (reading), 372–378
business-can't-handle-it argument, 219–220
business ethics
  defined, 3
  and organizational ethics, 3–4
  three Cs of, 40
Business Ethics: On Getting to the Heart of the Matter (reading), 252–257
business gifts, and entertainment, 505–507
businesspeople, defined, 4
business responsibility, 275–283.
  See also corporate responsibility; social responsibility
  and labeling and packaging, 281–283
  and manipulative pricing, 277–278
  for meaningful work, 432–433
  and price fixing, 278–279
  and price gouging, 279–281
  and pricing, 276–281

  and product quality, 275–276
  and product safety, 271–275
Businessweek, 83–84, 496
Butler, Nicholas Murray, 204
Butner Federal Correctional Institution I, 109
bystander apathy, 22

C

Cadillac Escalade Hybrid, 361
California Avocado Commission, 288
California Wine Institute, 288
Calvin Klein, 288
Camenisch, Paul, 220, 221, 252
Campbell, Alan K., 577
Campbell Soup Co., 452
Campos, Oswaldo, 358
cannibalism, ethical relativism and, 12
Capital City Federal Savings, 586
capitalism
  arguments for, 157–160
  challenges to, 168–173
  criticisms of, 160–167
  defined, 151, 156–157
  financial, 153
  globalized, 154
  historical background of, 152–154
  human nature and, 161–162
  industrial, 153
  inheritance and, 144–147
  key features of, 154–157
  mercantile, 153
  nature of, 150–151
  and oligopolies, 162–163
  operational criticisms of, 160
  state welfare, 154
  theoretical criticisms of, 160
Capitalism and Freedom, 210
card check, 403
Carnegie, Andrew, 153
Carolina Panthers, 184
Carr, Albert, 13, 44
Carson, Thomas L., 306
Cartus, Joseph, 274
cascade effect, 34
Cascadian Farm, 282
Casco Industries, 389
case(s)
  A7D Affair, The, 35–37
  AIDS in the Workplace, 409–410
  Battling over Bottled Water, 131–132
  Blood for Sale, 88–89
  Breast Implants, 297–299
  Casino Gambling on Wall Street, 182–184
  Catastrophe in Bangaldesh, 174–176
  Changing Jobs and Changing Loyalties, 521

Charity to Scouts?, 235–237
Closing the Deal, 302–303
Conflicting Perspectives on Conflicts of Interest, 522–523
Consenting to Sexual Harassment, 586–587
Corporate Taxation, 237–238
Corporations and Religious Faith, 234–235
Drug Dilemmas, 230–232
Eminent Domain, 129–131
Ethically Dubious Conduct, 526–528
Facial Discrimination, 588–589
Fight over the Redwoods, The, 361–364
Fordasaurus, The, 360–361
Ford Pinto, The, 85–87
Free Speech or False advertising?, 232–233
Hacking into Harvard, 83–85
Have Gun, Will Travel . . . to Work, 413–415
Hazardous Homes in Herculaneum, 356–357
Hoop Dreams, 583–584
Hot Coffee at McDonald's, 299–300
Housing Allowance, 525–526
Inside Traders or Astute Observers?, 523–525
Just Drop off the Key, Lee, 33–35
Licensing and Laissez Faire, 176–178
Made in the U.S.A, 30–32
Minority Set-Asides, 581–582
A New Work Ethic?, 181–182
One Nation Under Walmart, 179–181
Palm Oil and Its Problems, 364–366
Paying College Athletes, 184–185
Poverty and Pollution, 358–359
Poverty in America, 133–135
Protecting the Unborn at Work, 463–465
Raising the Ante, 584–585
Rise and Fall of Four Loko, The, 304–305
She Snoops to Conquer, 462
Sniffing Glue Could Snuff Profits, 300–301
Speaking Out about Malt, 412–413
Swedish Daddies, 466–467
Testing for Honesty, 459–461
Union Discrimination, 415–416
Unprofessional Conduct?, 456–457
Web Porn at Work, 411
Yahoo in China, 228–229
Casey, Christine, 518
Casino Gambling on Wall Street (case), 182–184
Cassidy, John, 238
Catastrophe in Bangaldesh (case), 174–176

categorical imperative, 67–69
  humanity as an end, 69
  universal acceptability, 68–69
Caterpillar, 152, 238
caveat emptor, 265, 290, 306
Caverject, 285
CDO. *See* collateralized debt obligation (CDO)
Ceballos, Richard, 383
Center for Corporate Governance, 393
Center for the Health Professions, 177
Cephalon, 278
Cescau, Patrick, 337
Chalifoux, Cheryl, 464
Challenge of Man's Future, The (Brown), 200
challenges, to moral argument patterns of, 25
Chamberlain, Wilt, 116–117
Champion International, 225
Changing Jobs and Changing Loyalties (case), 521
Chant, Robert, 174
character building, 386
Charity to Scouts? (case), 235–237
Chase Manhattan Bank, 452, 564
Chavez, Linda, 575
Chemerinsky, Erwin, 233
Chemical Bank, 225
Cherney, Darryl, 362
Chevron, 203, 217, 291, 342
Chiarella, Vincent, 500
Chicken McNuggets, 290
child care, and business, 452
childhood obesity, 292
Chilean miners, 91
Christian tradition, 10–12
Chrysler, 151, 204, 270
Churchill, Winston, 431
Cicero, 4, 536
CID structures. *See* corporate internal decision (CID) structures
CIO. *See* Congress of Industrial Organizations (CIO)
Circuit City, 278
Cisco, 228
Citibank, 437, 522
Citigroup, 183, 203, 209, 219
Citizens United v. Federal Election Commission, 206, 234
City of Richmond v. Croson, 569, 581
civic activities, 438–439
civil disobedience, 513–514
civil liberties, workplace, 380–385
Civil Rights Act, 189, 190, 234, 382, 464, 566–567, 573
civil society, unions as, 426–427
Clairol, 290
Clark, Kim B., 83

Claypool, Dennis, 446
Clean Air Act, 333, 344
Clean Air Act Amendments of 1990, 333, 346
Clean Water Act, 209, 332, 342, 512
Clendenin, John, 236
Clinton, Bill, 218
Closing the Deal (case), 302–303
Coalition on Resistoleros, 301
Coase, Ronald, 188
Coca-Cola, 179, 216, 279, 280, 287, 292, 497, 502
codes
  corporate moral, 223–224
  ethical, and economic efficiency, 222–223
  of ethics, professional, 8–9
Colgate-Palmolive, 286
collateralized debt obligation (CDO), 182–183
collective bargaining, 403, 404–405
Colonial Pipeline of Atlanta, 209
Coltrane, Scott, 389
Columbus Mitchell Restaurants, 282
Commerce One, 507
common law, 6–8
Communications Workers of America, 408, 444
Communist Manifesto (Engels), 166
companies, as feature of capitalism, 154–155
company loyalty, 494–495
Comparable worth, 574–576
comparative advantage, 170
competition, as feature of capitalism, 155–156
competitive markets, and unions, 425–426
complicity theory, 554–556
Computer Associates, 171
concealment of facts, 285–286
conclusion, defined, 23
Con Ed, 512
Conestoga Wood Specialties, 234
conflicting obligations, 509–511
Conflicting Perspectives on Conflicts of Interest (case), 522–523
conflicts of interest, 496–498
conformity, 20–21
Congress, and Enron, 2
Congress of Industrial Organizations (CIO), 401
conscience
  defined, 14
  limits of, 15–16
Consenting to Sexual Harassment (case), 586–587
consequentialist theories, defined, 56
considered moral beliefs, defined, 28

constitutional law, defined, 6–8
consumer choice, 267–268
consumer needs, 292–294
Consumer Product Safety Commission (CPSC), 266, 269, 270, 271, 274
Consumer Reports, 283
consumer sovereignty, 293
Contemporary Business News, 228
contractual model, job relevance and, 475
Cook, Cheryl, 464
Cooke, William, 456
Coomaraswamy, Ananda, 198
Cooper, Cynthia, 514
Cooper, George, 143
Coors Brewing Company, 282, 285
Copernicus, 28
corporate campaign, 407
corporate culture, 224–226
"corporate decision," 207
corporate internal decision (CID) structures, 207
Corporate Library, 215
corporate moral agency, 206–209
corporate moral codes, 223–224
corporate punishment, 208
corporate responsibility. *See also* business responsibility; social responsibility
    broader view of, 211–213
    and business-can't-handle-it argument, 219–220
    and invisible-hand argument, 216–317
    and let-government-do-it argument, 217–219
    narrow view of, 210–211
    rival views of, 209–215
    stockholders and corporation, 214–215
Corporate Taxation (case), 237–238
corporate welfare programs, and business, 163–165
corporations
    defined, 155, 203
    hollow, 169
    institutionalizing ethics within, 221–226
    and stockholders, 214–215
Corporations and Religious Faith (case), 234–235
Corvino, John, 601
Cosmopolitan, 180
cost-benefit analysis, 85, 338
Costco, 278
Cotto, Gonzalo, 380, 381, 382
counterexample, defined, 23
Covance, 231
Covenant House, 301
CPSC. *See* Consumer Product Safety Commission (CPSC)

Craig's List, 283
Credo, The, 226
Crestar Bank, 408
Crick, Francis, 189
Crimson, The, 84
Crytex, 521
Cumbo, Frank, 503
Cypress Semiconductor, 248, 250

D

Dahl, Robert A., 257
Daisy Manufacturing, 269
Dalkon Shield, 30, 48
Daly, Herman E., 186
Dalzell, Colin, 507
Dannon, 288
Dan River experiment, 65
Davis, Keith, 212, 213, 220
Davis, Michael, 551
day care, and maternity leave, 451–452
"d-contraxol," 287
DeBarba, Eric, 493
Debate on the Social Responsibility of Business, A (reading), 244–252
decision making, moral, 79–82
declining marginal utility of money, 113
Deepwater Horizon, 331, 446, 447
defense, patterns of, 25
Defense of Programs of Preferential Treatment (reading), 589–593
defensible moral judgments, 25
deforestation, 325, 328
De George, Richard T., 258
de Jouvenel, Bertrand, 200
Dell Computer, 202
Del Monte, 179
Delta Air Lines, 291, 381, 383, 384
Democracy Forum, 228
DeMoss, Mark, 446
deontological theories, 56. *See also* nonconsequentialist theories
dependence effect, 293, 317
"dermo-smoothing complex," 287
DesJardins, Joseph, 428, 468, 475–476
destructive obedience, psychology of, 48–49
Dial, 287
Diet Coke, 290
difference principle, 124
diffusion of responsibility, 208
Dilbert, 166
direct strikes, 406
Dirks, Raymond, 500
discharge, and discipline, 393–396
discrimination
    defined, 602

    evidence of, 562–566
    unions, 415–416
    wrongful, 386–387
dismissing employees, 394–396
disparate impact, 567
disparate treatment, 567
dissatisfaction, job, 454–455
distributive justice, 109
divine command theory, 11
Doe Run Company, 356–357
Domaine Chardonnay (wine product), 282
Dominick's, 277
Domino's, 387
Donahue (talk show), 226
Donaldson, Thomas, 207, 256
Donaldson, William, 225
Dow Chemical, 298, 347, 384
Dow Corning, 297
DowElanco, 30
Dow Jones Industrial Average, 150
downsizing, arguments against, 194–195
Drexel Burnham Lambert, 362
Drug Dilemmas (case), 230–232
drug testing, 443–444
    limitations on, 471
Drug Testing in Employment (reading), 468–473
drug use, 469
    illegality contention, 471–472
    job performance, 469–470
    job-relevant information, 469
    to prevent harm, 470–471
duBrowa, Corey, 238
due care, 265
due process, 394, 417, 420–421
Duke Power Company, 390
Duncan Hines, 501
Dunn, Patricia, 434–435
DuPont, 381
Duska, Ronald, 468
Dynegy, 171

E

E. & J. Gallo, 412
Eastern Airlines, 434–435
East India Company, 204
eBay, 279, 283
Ebbers, Bernard J., 498
ecological economics, 339
ecology
    and business, 334–337
    defined, 334
Economic and Philosophic Manuscripts (Marx), 166
economic costs, 267

INDEX

economic distribution, and utilitarianism, 112–114
economic efficiency and ethical codes, 222–223
Economic Espionage Act, 502
Economic integration, 186
economics
    ecological, 339
    market, 294–295
Economist, The, 365, 519
ecosystems, 334–335
educational requirements, 388
Edwards, Christine A., 568
Edwards, Richard, 403
EEOC. *See* Equal Employment Opportunity Commission (EEOC)
efficiency argument, 534–535
egoism/egoists
    business, 66
    defined, 56, 57
    impersonal, 57
    misconceptions with, 57
    personal, 57
    problems with, 58–60
    psychological, 58
Ehrenreich, Barbara, 443, 466
Ehrlich, Paul, 335
Einstein, Albert, 127
El Corte Inglés, 174
Electronic Communications Privacy Act of 1986, 444
Elegido, Juan M., 528
Eli Lilly, 220
Elizabeth, Queen, I, 204
Ellwood, David T., 427
Elson, Charles, 393
eminent domain, 65
Eminent Domain (case), 129–131
employee consent, voluntariness, 472
Employee Polygraph Protection Act, 442
Employment at Will and Due Process (reading), 417–422
employment history, gap in, 389
Endangered Species Act, 363
Energy Choice, 287
Energy Regulatory Commission, 512
Engels, Friedrich, 167
English, Deidre, 466
Enron, 171, 215, 496
    and Congress, 2
    scandal involving, 1–2
    stock price of, 2
Enterprise Rent-A-Car, 204, 437
entertainment, and business gifts, 505–507
entitlement theory, 115
environment
    business attitudes toward, 335–337
    and future generations, 349–351
    protection, ethics of, 337–343
    regulatory approach, 343–344
Environmental Defense Fund, The, 374
environmental goals, 343–347
    incentives, 344–345
    and pollution permits, 345–347
    regulations, 343–344
Environmental Protection Agency (EPA), 30, 333, 512
environmental protection ethics, 337–343
    pollution control costs, 338–340
EPA. *See* Environmental Protection Agency (EPA)
ePolicy Institute, 445
Equal Employment Opportunity Commission (EEOC), 386, 564, 566, 567, 577
equality of income, and utilitarianism, 113–114
Equal Pay Act, 564
Erdman, Bart, 496
Ernst & Whinney, 504
Essex Temporary Services, 503
Ethical Dilemmas for Multinational Enterprise (reading), 258–261
Ethically Dubious Conduct (case), 526–528
ethical relativism, 10, 12–14
ethical tradition, 49–50
ethics
    codes and economic efficiency, 222–223
    defined, 3
    of environmental protection, 337–343
    institutionalizing within corporations, 221–226
    of Kant, 66–72
    and market, 93–94
    professional code of, 8–9
    sales of, 306–313
    teleological, 429
    utilitarian, 534
    virtue, 321
    vs. morals, 3–4
    as a way of thinking, 44–45
    work, 172
Ethics of Corporate Downsizing, The (reading), 190–197
Ethics of Sales, The (reading), 306–313
ethos, 45
etiquette
    defined, 5
    and morality, 5–6
Ewing, A. C., 64
Ewing, David W., 381, 383
exaggeration, 286–287
exploitation, and alienation, 166–167
Export Enhancement Program, 164
Export-Import Bank, 164
express warranties, 276
externality/externalities, 213, 337. *See also* spillover
ExxonMobil, 164, 202, 203, 207, 504
Ezold, Nancy O'Mara, 564

F

Face Lift, 287
Facial Discrimination (case), 588–589
factory farming, 353–354
factual claims, evaluating, 25
Faden, Ruth, 231
Fadiman, Jeff, 541
Fagothey, Austin, 406
Fair Labor Association, 233
Fair Labor Standards Act, 397
fairness, *vs.* justice, 108
False Claims Act, 512
false positives, 441
Families and Work Institute, 327
Fannie Mae, 150, 171, 225, 563
Fanuchi, Jean, 462
farming, factory, 353–354
Fastow, Andrew, 496
Favre, Brett, 576
FCPA. *See* Foreign Corrupt Practices Act (FCPA)
FDA. *See* Food and Drug Administration (FDA)
Federal Trade Commission (FTC), 284, 289–290
FedEx, 237
Feiner, Michael, 450
Feinstein, Dianne, 363
Feldbaum, Carl B., 231
Femina, 287
FHM, 180
Fidelity Investments, 509
fiduciary duties, 191–192
    argument, 538
fiduciary responsibility, 214
Fifth Amendment, 206
Figg, Derek, 33
Fight over the Redwoods, The (case), 361–364
financial capitalism, 153
financial investments, 497–498
Financial Times, 228
Fine, Glenn, 427
"Firestone's policy," 154
firing, 394
firms, obligations, 494–498
First Amendment, 206, 233, 295
Fisher, Don, 363

636 INDEX

Fisher, Doris, 363
Flint Sit-Down Strike, 379
Flynn, Nancy, 445
Foley, Daniel, 383
Food and Drug Administration (FDA), 30, 269
Ford, Bill, 360, 361
Ford, Henry, 438
Ford, Henry, II, 270
Fordasaurus, The (case), 360–361
Ford Foundation, 45
Ford Motor Company, 85, 152, 202, 237, 267, 360–361, 439, 503, 591
Ford Pinto, The (case), 85–87
Foreign Corrupt Practices (reading), 541–550
Foreign Corrupt Practices Act (FCPA), 504–505, 541
Foreign Military Financing Program, 164
Fortune, 144, 180, 226, 384, 442, 473, 563, 601
Four Loko, 304–305
Fourteenth Amendment, 206, 420
Fourth Amendment, 206
Framers, Ed, 236
Francis, Karen, 291
"Frankenfood," 281
Franklin, David, 512–513
Fraser, Douglas, 487
fraud argument, 537–538
Frazier, Tanya, 453
Freddie Mac, 150
Frederick, Robert, 375
free exchange, markets and, 118–119
free market, 117
free-rider problem, 337
free speech and media, 295
Free Speech or False advertising? (case), 232–233
French, Peter, 207
Friedel, Walter, 269
Friedman, Milton, 144, 177–178, 193, 210, 211, 214, 240, 244, 248, 251, 340, 424
FTC. *See* Federal Trade Commission (FTC)
FTC v. Standard Education, 289, 290
Fugger, Hans, 152–153
Fugger, Jacob, 153
future generations, and environment, 349–351

G

Galatis, George, 493–494
Galbraith, John Kenneth, 199, 217–218, 222, 293, 315, 317, 319, 320
Galleon Group, 523
Gap, 330, 437
Garamendi, John, 363
Garman, Dale, 525

Garrett, Angela, 437
Gates, Bill, 141, 229
GDP. *See* gross domestic product (GDP)
GE. *See* General Electric (GE)
General Dynamics, 395
General Electric (GE), 155, 202, 212, 225, 237, 287, 384
General Mills, 220, 225, 282, 286, 439
General Motors, 87, 151, 162, 202, 283, 360, 407, 421, 456, 463
General Services Administration (GSA), 507
genetically modified (GM) food, 281
Genge, William H., 316
Genovese, Kitty, 22
Geoghegan, Thomas, 422, 427
Gerber, 132, 282
Gering, Erik F., 183
Gibson, Joel, 524
Gill, Robert, 274
Gini, Al, 431
Ginsburg, Ruth Bader, 500
Glamour, 180
Glen Canyon Dam, 342
Global Crossing, 171
global environmental fairness, 347–349
globalization, 154
    consequences of, 187–189
    defined, 186
    risks of, 188–189
Globalization and Its Discontents (reading), 186–190
globalized capitalism, 154
global warming, 325, 327
GM (genetically modified) food, 281
Gobbell, Lynne, 380
God, 10–12
Goffer, Zvi, 523
Goizueta, Roberto C., 216
Golab, Stephen, 448
"Golden Rule," 10, 49, 91, 309
Goldman Sachs, 183, 225, 452
Goldwater, Barry, 423
Gompers, Samuel, 401
Gonsalves, Milton A., 406
Goodlatte, Ron, 423
Goodpaster, Kenneth E., 207
Good Samaritan laws, 8, 66
good will, and Kant's ethics, 66–67
Google, 228–229, 238
Gore, Ira, 276
Goskin, Lawrence O., 231
"The Gospel of Joy," 10–11
Gould, Jay, 153
Gourson, John, 34
government safety regulation, product safety, 266–268

consumer choice, 267–268
economic costs, 267
legal paternalism, 268
Graham, David, 512–513
grease payments, 504
Great Depression, 133, 401
Green, Ronald M., 96
Greenberg, Maurice Hank, 226
Greenman v. Yuba Power Products, 266
Greenpeace, 365
Gretzinger, Ralph, 36
Griffiths, Gary, 524
Griggs v. Duke Power Company, 389
Grimshaw, Richard, 86
gross domestic product (GDP), 162, 188
Grotius, 536
groupthink, 21
GSA. *See* General Services Administration (GSA)
Gulf Oil, 504
gullible-consumer standard, 289

H

Habitat Protection Plan, 363
hacking, 83
Hacking into Harvard (case), 83–85
Halperin, Keith M., 460
Halverson, Steve, 414
Hamilton, Alexander, 205
Hamlet (Shakespeare), 60
Hand, Learned, 238, 290
Hardin, Garrett, 336
Hare, R. M., 90, 318, 320
Harmon, Sidney, 384
Harmon International Industries, 384
Harrington, Noreen, 514
Harris, Bruce, 301
Harvard Business Review, 3, 4, 44, 318, 381, 382, 450, 541
Hasbro, 278
Haslett, D. W., 143
Have Gun, Will Travel . . . to Work (case), 413–415
Hawthorne effect, 454
Hayek, Friedrich, 317, 423, 425
Hazardous Homes in Herculaneum (case), 356–357
H.B. Fuller Company, 300
health, and safety, 445–447
hedge funds, 54–56
"hedonic calculus," 60
hedonism, 57
    paradox of, 17
Heilbroner, Robert, 155
Heisman trophy, 184
Held, Virginia, 321

Hershey, Milton, 438
Herzberg, Frederick, 455
Heublein, 277
Hewlett, Sylvia Ann, 481
Hewlett, William, 384
Hewlett-Packard, 217, 384, 434–435, 452, 497, 505, 576
Hilton Hotels, 502
hiring, 385–391
Hishon, Elizabeth, 564–565
Hitler, Adolf, 47
Hobby Lobby Stores, 234
Hoffman, W. Michael, 372
Holley, David, 306
Holley's Theory, 307
hollow corporations, 169
Holocaust, 48
Home Depot, 130, 215, 269, 403, 568
Honda Motor Company, 330, 504
Hoop Dreams (case), 583–584
Hoopes, John E., 180
Hooters, 386
Hopkins, Ann, 564
Hopkins, Mariann, 297
horizontal price fixing, 278
hostile-work-environment harassment, 577–578
Hot Coffee at McDonald's (case), 299–300
Housing Allowance, The (case), 525–526
Hubbard, Abigail, 172
Hughes, John, 577
Human Condition, The, 429–431
human fulfillment model, 429–431
human nature, and capitalism, 161–162
human rights, 75
Human Rights Charter (1948), 75–76
Human Side of Enterprise, The, 450
Hurd, Mark, 576
Hurricane Katrina, 180, 279
Hurwitz, Charles, 362, 363
Huttcut, Michael, 436
hypothetical imperatives, 68

I

Iacocca, Lee, 85, 270
IBM, 196, 202, 436, 444, 452
Icahn, Carl, 240
Ice Mountain, 132
ideals, defined, 81
IKB Deutsche Industriebank, 183
IKEA, 506
ImClone Systems, 498
imperatives
  categorical, 67–69
  hypothetical, 68
impersonal egoists, 57

implied warranties, 276
inbreeding, 392
incentives, as environmental goal, 344–345
Income Distribution (reading), 135–142
income equality, and utilitarianism, 113–114
Inconclusive Ethical Case against Manipulative Advertising, The (reading), 314–324
industrial capitalism, 153
Industrial Revolution, 153
inequality, as criticism of capitalism, 160–161
infanticide, ethical relativism and, 12
"infectious greed," 171
informed consent, 440
inheritance
  and capitalism, 144–147
  proposal for abolishing, 147–148
Inquiry into the Nature and Causes of the Wealth of Nations, An (Smith), 65, 155, 158, 404
Insider, The, 263
insiders, and misappropriation, 499–500
insider trading, 498–501
  arguments against, 535–536
  arguments for, 534–535
  conflicting perspectives, 500–501
Inside Traders or Astute Observers? (case), 523–525
Institute for International Economics, 163
Integrity Research Associates, 523
Intel Corporation, 568
"intellectual property," 186
Interactive Data Corporation, 383
"internationalization," 186
International Labor Organization, 175
International Latex Corporation, 502
International Monetary Fund, 187
interviewing, 390–391
invalid argument, defined, 23
invisible-hand argument, 216–217
invisible hand concept, 158
Ipana, 290
iPhone, 280
Irish famine, 119
Isbister, John, 135
"Is Business Bluffing Ethical?", 13
Is Inheritance Justified? (reading), 143–149
It's Good Business (reading), 38–45

J

J. P. Stevens & Co., 407
Jacoby, Jacob, 288
Jakes-Johnson, Philip, 130
James Bassett Company, 460
Jazzercise, 388

JCPenney, 274–275, 436
Jefferson, Thomas, 189
Jenkins, Ralph, 412–413
Jensen, Michael, 215, 240
Jesus of Nazareth, 10
Jewish tradition, 10–12
job description, 386
job discrimination, defined, 560–562
Job Discrimination and Gay Rights (reading), 601–607
job dissatisfaction, 454–455
job nature, 397
job performance, and drug use, 469–470
job relevance, and contractual model, 475
jobs, outsourcing, 169–170
Jobs, Steve, 280
job satisfaction, 455
job screening, 386
job security, 398
job specification, 386, 387
job stress, 449
Johnson, D. Gale, 138
Johnson, Frank, 573
Johnson, Paul, 569
Johnson, Samuel, 275
Johnson, Tomasz, 365
Johnson Controls, Inc, 463
Johnson & Johnson, 179, 225, 226, 285, 505
Johnson Wax, 275, 384
Jones, Edward W., Jr., 566
Jones, John, 459
Jordan, Michael, 139, 140
Joss, Robert, 83
Journal of the American Medical Association, 230, 443
JP Morgan Chase, 150, 379, 398
Jue, Janie, 449
just cause, 394, 406
Just Drop off the Key, Lee (case), 33–35
justice
  distributive, 109
  nature of, 107–110
  Nozick's theory of, 114–116
  Rawl's theory of (*See* Rawl's theory of justice)
  vs. fairness, 108

K

Kagan, Elena, 574
Kaiser Aluminum's Gramercy, 569
Kallman, Rhonda, 305
Kant, Immanuel, 45, 49, 90, 320, 322, 445
  ethics of, 66–72
  organizational context of, 70
Kantianism, 92–93

638 INDEX

Kant's ethics
   and categorical imperative, 67–69
   critical inquiries of, 70–72
   and good Will, 66–67
   and organizational context, 70
Kari, Nanci, 427
Karlson, Mikael, 467
Kasky, Marc, 232–233
Katwalski, Matt, 462
Katz, Saul, 55
Kay, John, 212
Kellogg's, 292
Kelo, Susette, 129, 130
Kennedy, Anthony M., 206, 383
Kennedy, John F., 566, 602
Kessler, David A., 297
Ketchum Communications, 316
Key, Wilson Bryan, 288
Keynes, John Maynard, 189
KeyOn Communications, 522
Keyworth, Jay, 434
KFC, 502
kickbacks, and bribes, 503–507
King, Martin Luther, Jr., 7, 9
King & Spalding, 564–565
Kleenex, 501
Kmart, 278
Knight, Philip, 232
Knights of Labor, 400
knowledge, without responsibility, 50–52
knowledge conditions, 50
Kodak, 276
Koellmann, Benjamin, 33, 34
Kohn, Alfie, 165
Kolesnik, Kris, 519
Koling, Barry, 408
Konopka, Kristin, 388
Kostek, Paul, 162
Koufax, Sandy, 54
Kozlowski, L. Dennis, 139, 498
Kraft, 285
Kraft Cheez Whiz, 290
Kroger, 277
Kumarappa, J. C., 198
Kupfer, Joseph, 474
Kyoto protocol, 341, 346

L

labeling and packaging, 281–283
Laborem Exercens, 431
labor unions, 400–408, 422–428
Ladd, David K., 132
laissez faire, 155, 168, 210, 222
Lange, Louis G., 230, 231
language, and job, 387
Lanman, Cecilia, 363

LaPierre, Wayne, 414
Larsen, Ralph, 226
Lasch, Christopher, 321
Lauren, Ralph, 505
"law and economics" movement, 240
Lawler, Matusky & Skelly, 512
laws.
   morality and, 6–8, 95–96
   types of, 6
   and U.S. Constitution, 6–8
Laws (Plato), 136
Lawson, Searle, 35
Lay, Kenneth, 1
layoff, 394
Leach, Richard, 230
Lee, Matthew, 519
Lee, Susan, 236
legal liability, of manufacturers, 265–266
legal paternalism, 268
legal right, 74
Legere, John, 498
Leggett, Herm, 584
Lehman Brothers, 150, 519
Leisure Sports World, 496
Leone, Dan, 381
let-government-do-it argument, 217–219
Letter from Birmingham Jail, 7
Letterman, David, 576
Levering, Robert, 384
Levin, Michael, 602
Levin, Sol, 88
Levine, Peter, 422
Levi Strauss & Co., 236
Levitt, Arthur, Jr., 500, 501
Levitt, Theodore, 210, 220, 293, 318
Lexar Media, 501
liberal model, of work, 431–432
Libertarian Critique of Labor Unions, The, 422–428
libertarianism
   defined, 114
   and liberty, 117–118
liberty
   defined, 114
   libertarian view of, 117–118
Licensing and Laissez Faire (case), 176–178
Liebeck, Stella, 299
lifestyle, job, 388
Light Classics desserts, 284
Li Keqiang, 229
limited liability company, 203–205
Lincoln Electric and Russell Corporation, 384
Lindblom, Charles E., 424
Lindley, Craig, 411
Line, Russell, 36, 37
Linowitz, Sol M., 210

Lipitor, 280
Lippke, Richard L., 319, 320, 473
Little Traverse Bay Bands of Odawa Indians, 132
Liu Xiabo, 228
Liverpool Corporation, 204
living wage, 399–400
Loblaw, 174
Locke, John, 115, 157, 203
Lockean rights, 115
Lockheed Aircraft Corporation, 504
Lockheed Martin, 204
Lockyer, Bill, 233
Lodge, George Cabot, 373
Logan Chemical Company, 381
Lombard, Carla, 409–410
London Development Corporation, 129
London House, 459–460
L'Oréal, 287
Lorenzana, Debrahlee, 437
Loyal Employee (reading), 528–533
loyalty
   to company, 494–495
   employee, 529
LTV Aerospace Corporation, 35
Luban, David, 46
Lukes, Steven, 319
Lutz, Bob, 361
Lykken, David T., 441
Lynch, Lisa M., 425

M

MacIntire, Louis, 381, 382
Mackey, John, 244, 247, 248, 249
MacKinnon, Catherine A., 577
MacPherson, Donald, 265
MacPherson v. Buick Motor Car, 265
Made in the U.S.A (case), 30–32
Madoff, Bernard, 54, 109
mafia, 13
Magnani, Peter, 236
Maitland, Ian, 192
Majdanek, 47
Malkovich, John, 54
Maltby, Lewis, 381, 460
management styles, 449–451
manipulative advertising. *See also* advertising
   defined, 314
   effects of, 315–316
manipulative pricing, 277–278
Manne, Henry, 500, 534, 539
Manne, Robert, 363
manufacturers, legal liability of, 265–266
Marathon Asset Management, 363
Marcus, Bernie, 403

INDEX

marginal utility of money, declining, 113
market economics, 294–295
markets
    and ethics, 93–94
    and free exchange, 118–119
Marlboro Intense, 262
Marlboro Man, 262
Mars, 204
Marshall, John, 155, 205
Martin, Lynn, 236
Martin, Roger, 455
Martino, Barbara A., 291
Marx, Karl, 47, 162, 166–167, 249, 251, 430
Mason, Paul, 363
Massey Energy Company, 342, 446, 447
Matas, Arthur, 89
maternity leave, and day care, 451–452
Mattel, 278, 502, 518–519
Matthews, John B., 207
Maxim, 180
maxim, defined, 67–68
maximin rule, 123
Maxxam, Inc., 362
May, Larry, 577
Mayhew, Michael W., 523
McCain-Feingold Act, 206
McCall, John J., 486
McClellan, Maxine, 131
McCormick, Cyrus, 153
McDonald's, 204, 279, 283, 292, 354, 398, 436
McDonough, William J., 106
McGee, Robert W., 533
McGregor, Douglas, 450
MCI Systemhouse, 507
McKenna, Rob, 304
McLaughlin, Gayle, 130
MCWC. *See* Michigan Citizens for Water Conservation (MCWC)
Mead Corporation, 389
Meaning and Value of Work, The (reading), 428–434
Means, Gardiner, 215, 239
means of production, 156
Meckling, William, 240
media and free speech, 295
Medicaid, 179
Medical Economics, 176
Mendel, Gregor, 189
Mendocino Redwood Company, 363
Mentor Corporation, 298
mercantile capitalism, 153
Mercedes-Benz, 178, 268
Mercer, Peter, 304
merchantability, 276
Merrill Lynch, 568

Miami International Airport, 434
Michigan Citizens for Water Conservation (MCWC), 132
Microsoft, 155, 163, 228, 238
Middle Way, The, 199
Midland, Archer Daniels, 505
Midlands Chrome, 505
Milgram, Stanley, 48
Milken, Michael, 362
Mill, John Stuart, 60–61, 108, 110–114, 161
Miller Brewing Company, 132, 282
Mills, Claudia, 480
Minority Business Utilization Plan, 581
Minority Set-Asides (case), 581–582
Minow, Nell, 215, 393
misappropriation, and insiders, 499–500
Mitsubishi, 568, 576
MNCs. *See* multinational corporations (MNCs)
Mobil Chemical Company, 383
monitoring
    of employees, 445
    and testing, 440–445
Monsanto Chemical Company, 463
Montgomery Ward, 278
Moore, Ann, 291, 538
moral arguments, defined, 24
moral codes
    corporate, 223–224
    optimal, 78
moral decision making, 79–82
moral equality, of workers and shareholders, 191–193
morality
    in the broad sense, 18
    and etiquette, 5–6
    and law, 6–8, 95–96
    in the narrow sense, 17
    and personal values, 17–19
    and religion, 10–12
    and self interest, 16–17
moral judgments
    defensible, 25
    requirements for, 27–28
Moral Man and Immoral Society, 47
moral obligation, 452–453, 515
    self-interest and, 516–519
Moral Responsibility in the Age of Bureaucracy (reading), 46–53
moral rights, 108
    defined, 74
    and nonconsequentialist theories, 74–76
moral standards
    challenging, 25–26
    defending, 26
    defined, 4–5
    source of, 9–10

morals *vs.* ethics, 3–4
Moral Thinking: Its Levels, Method, and Point (Hare), 90
moral thinking, levels of, 91–93
moral vegetarians, 354
moral worth, 67
Morell, David, 356
Morgan Stanley, 564
Morton-Thiokol, 551, 553
Moseley, Shannon, 87
Moskowitz, Milton, 384
Mosteller, Rachel, 381, 382
Mother Teresa, 66
Motorola, 394
Mr. Potato Head, 278
MSN Spaces, 228
Multi-Developers, Inc., 388
multinational corporations (MNCs), 258–261
"Muppets," 225
musculoskeletal disorders, 448–449
Mutambara, Wilson, 525–526
Myers–Briggs Type Indicator, 442
MySpace.com, 381

N

Nabisco, 286
Nader, Ralph, 248, 251
NAFTA. *See* North American Free Trade Agreement (NAFTA)
narrow view of corporate responsibility, 210
Nash, Laura, 209
National Campaign Against Toxic Hazards, 357
National Collegiate Athletic Association (NCAA), 443–444
National Geographic, 358
National Highway Traffic Safety Administration (NHTSA), 85, 270, 271
National Industrial Conference Board, 210
National Labor Relations Act, 401, 403
National Labor Relations Board (NLRB), 185
National Parenting Association, 481
National Priorities List Sites, 357
National Rifle Association (NRA), 413
National Right to Work Legal Defense Foundation, 415–416
National Safety Council, 449
National Survey of the Changing Workforce, 327
National Textile, 392
National Whistleblower Center, 519
National Workrights Institute, 381
naturalistic ethic, 351
Natural Resources Defense Council, 275
natural right to property, 157
nature, job, 397
nature, value of, 351–352

Nazareth, Jesus of, 10
Nazis, 7
NCAA. *See* National Collegiate Athletic Association (NCAA)
Neath, Gavin, 365
negative rights, 75
Nelson, Steve, 83
nepotism, 393
Nestlé, 132, 365
Neurontin, 512
NewCom, 525
New England Journal of Medicine, 230, 298
Newhoff, David, 521
New Industrial State, The (Galbraith), 293
Newport, 288
Newton, Cam, 184
New Work Ethic?, A (case), 181–182
New York Stock Exchange, 42
New York Times, 139, 217, 240, 247, 463, 481, 524
Nexium, 280
NFL, 184, 185
NHTSA. *See* National Highway Traffic Safety Administration (NHTSA)
Niebuhr, Reinhold, 47
Nike, 179, 232, 233
1984 (Orwell), 473
1948 Human Rights Charter, 75–76
Nixon, Richard, 271
NLRB. *See* National Labor Relations Board (NLRB)
Noble Eightfold Path, 197
Noel, Joe, 522–523
nonconsequentialist theories, 56. *See also* deontological theories
 critical inquiries of, 77
 and moral rights, 74–76
 in organizational context, 76
 and prima facie obligations, 72–73
 and supererogatory actions, 73–74
normative theories, defined, 56
Norris-LaGuardia Act, 401
North American Free Trade Agreement (NAFTA), 32
North Country, 587
Nozick, Robert, 114
 and Chamberlain, 116–117
 and theory of justice, 114–116
NRA. *See* National Rifle Association (NRA)
Nuclear Regulatory Commission, 493
NutraSweet, 290
Nuvigil, 278

O

Obama, Barack, 379, 403, 559
Obama, Michelle, 180
Oberhelman, Douglas, 398

obligations
 conflicting, 509–511
 defined, 80
 firms, 494–498
O'Brien, Mike, 456
Occupational Safety and Health Act (OSHA), 448
Occupational Safety and Health Administration (OSHA), 65, 448, 463
O'Connell, Ed, 129
O'Connor, John, 357
O'Connor, Sandra Day, 129, 570, 571
OECD. *See* Organization for Economic Co-operation and Development (OECD)
off-the-job conduct, 437–438
O'Hagan, James, 500, 538
oligopolies, 162
Olson, Jim, 132
O'Neil, Ed, 177
One Nation Under Walmart (case), 179–181
One Philosopher's Approach to Business Ethics (reading), 90–96
open-shop laws, 401
operational criticisms, of capitalism, 160
optimal moral code, 78–79
ordinances, 6
organization, defined, 4. *See also* corporations
organizational context
 nonconsequentialist theories in, 76
 utilitarianism in, 62–63
organizational ethics, business and, 3–4
organizational influence, private lives, 435–440
organizational norms, 19–20
Organization for Economic Co-operation and Development (OECD), 506
Organization of Man, The, 46
original position, and Rawl's theory of justice, 121–122
Orlando, John, 190
O'Rouke, Dara, 175
O'Rourke, Brendan, 132
OSHA. *See* Occupational Safety and Health Act (OSHA); Occupational Safety and Health Administration (OSHA)
Oswald, Andrew J., 425
outsource, defined, 169
Overseas Private Investment Corporation, 164
Overspent American, The, 328
Overworked American, The, 484
Oxford English Dictionary, 306

P

Pacific Lumber Company, 361–363
packaging and labeling, 281–283

Palm Oil and Its Problems (case), 364–366
Panasonic, 278
paradox of hedonism, 17
Parisi, Anthony J., 203, 207
Parsons, Richard, 522
Participation in Employment (reading), 486–492
Pate, Jackie, 291
Patterson, John, 395
Paulson, John, 183
Paying College Athletes (case), 184–185
pedophilia, ethical relativism and, 12
Pennington, Randy, 455
Pepsi, 279
PepsiCo, 202, 218, 439
Perelman, Ronald, 240
Performance Systems Corporation, 455
Perkins, Tom, 434
Perot, H. Ross, 451
Perrier, 132, 285
personal egoists, 57
personality tests, 442–443
personal values, and morality, 17–19
Petersen, Douglas, 209
Peterson, Louise, 574
Pfizer, 129
Philadelphia Cream Cheese, 285
Philadelphia Eagles, 381
Phillips, John T., 448
Phillips, Michael J., 314
philosophical theory, 49–50
physical appearance, 388
Pickens, T. Boone, 240
pink collar occupations, 563
Pirko, Tom, 283
Pizler, Katz, 464
Place of Nonhumans in Environmental Issues, The (reading), 366–371
Plank Road Brewery, 282
Plasma International, 88
Plato, 107, 135
Plexiglas, 286
Plutarch, 429
Podgursky, Michael, 403
poker game, 13
Polaroid, 276, 452
pollution control costs, 338–340
pollution permits, 345–347
Polo, 437
polygamy, ethical relativism and, 12
polygraph tests, 440–442
Ponzi, Charles, 55
Pope John Paul II, 430
population growth, in America, 341
Portnick, Jennifer, 388
position elimination, 394
positive rights, 75

Posner, Richard A., 425
potato blight, 119
Pothier, 536
Poverty and Pollution (case), 358–359
Poverty in America (case), 133–135
Powell, Lewis F., 569
preemptive duties, 51
Pregnancy Discrimination Act of 1978, 464
premises, defined, 23
Preston, Ivan L., 287, 290
Preven, 180
Preventing Employment Lawsuits, 598
price fixing, 278–279
price gouging, 279–281
pricing, 276–281. *See also* specific types
    manipulative, 277–278
    mechanisms, as environmental goal, 345–347
    price fixing, 278–279
    price gouging, 279–281
prima facie obligations, 72–73
Primark, 174
primary boycott, 407
primary goods
    defined, 432
    social, 122
Prince, Charles, 209
Principles of Political Economy (Mill), 112
privacy, 435
    importance, 437
    right to, 468–469
    value of, 474
    work and autonomy, 473–479
privately held company, 204
private property, as feature of capitalism, 156–157
Procter & Gamble, 155, 202, 215, 220, 282, 283, 287, 365, 384, 452, 501
production, means of, 156
product liability, strict, 266
product quality, 275–276
product safety, 264–275
    automobile safety, 270–271
    business responsibilities, 271–275
    consumer choice, 267–268
    economic costs, 267
    government safety regulation, 266–268
    legal liability of manufacturers, 265–266
    legal paternalism, 268
    regulation effect, 268–271
    self-regulation, 270
    strict product liability, 266
professional code of ethics, 8–9
profit maximization, 210–211
profit motive, as feature of capitalism, 155
promotions, 391–393
Propecia, 286
property rights, 119, 120, 191
proprietary data, 501–503
Prosser, Harriet, 449
Protecting the Unborn at Work (case), 463–465
Providence Equity Partners, 522
Provigil, 278
prudential reasons, 516
psychological appeal, 287–289
psychological egoism, 58
psychology of destructive obedience, 48–49
Public Broadcast Corporation, 374
publicly held company, 204
Pufendorf, 536
puffery, 287
Putnam, Robert, 426
Pyle, Christopher, 441

Q

quantity surcharges, 283
quid-pro-quo harassment, 577, 579
Qwest Communications, 171, 496–497

R

Rabinowitz, Andrew, 363
race *vs.* sexual orientation, 603
Rachels, James, 320
Radin, Tara J., 417
Raines, Franklin, 563
Raising the Ante (case), 584–585
Ralph Lauren, 437, 494, 505
Ramirez, Jorge, 274
Rana, Sohel, 174
Rana Plaza, 174–175
Rapid Shave, 286
Raveling, George, 583
Rawls, John, 157, 195, 350
    theory of justice, 120–128
Rawl's theory of justice, 120–128
    benefits and burdens, 127–128
    choosing principles, 122–123
    fairness and basic structure, 126–127
    fundamental principles, 123–126
    original position, 121–122
    principles of, 123–126
    veil of ignorance, 122
RC 2 Corporation, 226
readings
    Analyzing Insider Trading, 533–540
    Buddhist Economics, 197–201
    Business and Environmental Ethics, 372–378
    Business Ethics: On Getting to the Heart of the Matter, 252–257
    Debate on the Social Responsibility of Business, A, 244–252
    Defense of Programs of Preferential Treatment, 589–593
    Drug Testing in Employment, 468–473
    Employment at Will and Due Process, 417–422
    Ethical Dilemmas for Multinational Enterprise, 258–261
    Ethics of Corporate Downsizing, The, 190–197
    Ethics of Sales, The, 306–313
    Foreign Corrupt Practices, 541–550
    Globalization and Its Discontents, 186–190
    Income Distribution, 135–142
    Inconclusive Ethical Case against Manipulative Advertising, The, 314–324
    Is Inheritance Justified?, 143–149
    It's Good Business, 38–45
    Job Discrimination and Gay Rights, 601–607
    Loyal Employee, 528–533
    Meaning and Value of Work, The, 428–434
    Moral Responsibility in the Age of Bureaucracy, 46–53
    One Philosopher's Approach to Business Ethics, 90–96
    Participation in Employment, 486–492
    Place of Nonhumans in Environmental Issues, The, 366–371
    Rethinking Sexual Harassment, 594–600
    Some Paradoxes of Whistleblowing, 551–557
    Toxic Side Effects of Shareholder Primacy, The, 239–244
    When Is "Everybody's Doing It" a Moral Justification?, 96–104
    Why Do We Consume So Much?, 324–330
    Work, Privacy, and Autonomy, 473–479
    Workplace Wars, 480–485
Reagan, Ronald, 105, 402, 421
reasonable-consumer standard, 289
Redbook, 180
Red Dog beer, 282
Rees, Dan, 175
Regan, Tom, 28, 353
Regenerist, 287
regulatory approach, environmental, 343–344
Reich, Robert, 193, 218, 219, 222, 229
Reihart, Michael, 31, 304
Reiter, Roland, 233
relativism, and business, 13–14. *See also* ethical relativism
religion, and morality, 10–12

Religious Freedom Restoration Act (RFRA), 234, 235
Rent-A-Center, 560
replacement jobs, 169–170
Reporters Without Borders, 228
Republic Windows and Doors, 379, 380
resistance, source of, 490–492
responsibility. *See also* specific types
    diffusion of, 21–22
    without knowledge, 50–52
Rethinking Sexual Harassment (reading), 594–600
Reuther, Walter, 423
Revlon, 179, 318
Revson, Charles, 318
Reye's Syndrome, 274
Reynolds, Morgan O., 423
RFRA. *See* Religious Freedom Restoration Act (RFRA)
Ricardo, David, 170
Richmond City Council, 581
Riesman, David, 46
Right Livelihood, 197–201
rights-based approach, 534
right to a livable environment, 338
right to refuse dangerous work, 446
right-to-work states, 401, 405
Rio-Tinto Alcan, 217
Rise and Fall of Four Loko, The (case), 304–305
Rite Aid, 171
Ritz-Carlton, 130
Rivera, Jorge, 408
Rivera, Lauren, 391
"robber barons," 153
Roberts, Bari-Ellen, 564
Robertson, Paul, 415
Robinson, Spottswood, 586
Rocha, Alicia, 504
Rockefeller, John D., 153
Rocky Mountain News, 481
"Rocky Mountain spring water," 285
Rodgers, T. J., 244, 248, 250, 251
Rodriguez, Manuel, 391
Rodriguez, Michael, 391, 447
Rogers, Beth, 447
Rogers Commission, 551, 553–554, 556
Roland, Wall, 390
Roman Catholicism, 10–11
Roosevelt, Franklin D., 400
Roosevelt, Teddy, 218
Root, Lawrence, 132
Rorty, Richard, 426
Roseberg, David, 34
Ross, Andrew, 524

Ross, W. D., 72, 77, 79
Rothberg, Norman, 504
Roundtable on Sustainable Palm Oil (RSPO), 364, 365
Rowley, Coleen, 513–514
Rowman, Bob, 398
Royal Dutch Shell, 202
RSPO. *See* Roundtable on Sustainable Palm Oil (RSPO)
Ruggiero, Renato, 187
Ruggiero, V. R., 80
rule utilitarianism, 61, 78
Rulevich, Robert, 393
Rulon-Miller, Virginia, 436
Russian Clinical Trials, 231

S

SAC Capital, 208
Sach, Allen L., 556
safety
    automobile, 270–271
    and health, 445–447
    product (*See* product safety)
Safeway, 204, 277
sales, ethics of, 306–313
Sam Adams, 305
Sam's Club, 278
Samsung, 279
Samuelson, Paul, 466
Sandel, Michael J., 346
Sapienza, Paola, 34
Sara Lee, 220, 284
Sarbanes-Oxley Act, 518
Scanlon, T. M., 421
Schick, Wayne, 282
Schieffelin, Allison, 564
Schlafly, Phyllis, 575
Schmalensee, Richard L., 83
Schmidt, Richard, 363
Schor, Juliet B., 324, 484
Schultz, Vicki, 594
Schumacher, E. F., 197, 256
Schumann, Thomas, 389
Schumer, Charles E., 304
Schumpeter, Joseph, 189
Schwartz, Adina, 432, 477
Schwartz, Felice N., 466
Scott, Lee, 403
screening, 386–389
Sears, 225
Sebastiani Vineyards, 282
SEC. *See* Securities and Exchange Commission (SEC)
Second Amendment, 414–415
secondary boycott, 407

Second Chance Body Armor, 272
Second Harvest Food Bank, 248
Securities and Exchange Commission (SEC), 215, 225, 240, 499, 500, 509, 523, 537, 541
Securities Exchange Act of 1934, 499
Segal, Jerome, 484
self-actualization, 57
self-interest
    and moral obligation, 516–519
    and moral principles, 16–17
self-regulation, 270
Semel, Terry S., 229
Sen, Amartya, 119
seniority, 391–392
Serious Materials, 379
Service Employees International Union, 407
Seventh Amendment, 206
sexual conduct, prohibiting, 598–599
sexual favoritism, 578–579
sexual harassment, 576–579
Sexual Harassment of Working Women, 577
sexual orientation, *vs.* sex, 603
Shapiro, Carl, 54
shareholder primacy, 239–240
shareholders, 191
    moral equality of workers and, 191–193
Sheehy, James, 181–182
Sherman Antitrust Act, 278–279, 401
She Snoops to Conquer (case), 462
Shi Tao, 228
short-term focus, 171
"short-term friction," 169
Siebel, Brian, 414
Siemens AG, 506
Sierra Club, 344
Sigler, Andrew C., 225
Sikkema, Ken, 132
Silverman, William, 164
Simon, Paul, 33
Simon, Yves, 429
Simonetti, Ellen, 381
Sinar Mas, 365
Singer, Peter, 88, 352, 366, 368
Sink, Robert, 35
Sismondi, Jean, 189
Sisyphus Books, 504
situational interview, 391
Sixteenth Amendment, 105
60 Minutes (talk show), 226, 373
Skocpol, Theda, 484
slavery, ethical relativism and, 12
Slimspadiet, 287
Sloan, Alfred, 271
Sloan, Allan, 238

Slywotsky, Adrian, 171
Smetana, Al, 411
Smirnoff, 277
Smith, Adam, 65, 117, 151, 155–156, 161, 165, 203, 205, 210, 246, 404, 549
   and invisible hand concept, 158–160
Smith, Christopher H., 228
Smith, Kathleen Logan, 357
Sniffing Glue Could Snuff Profits (case), 300–301
Snoeyenbos, Milton, 224
Snyder, Wallace S., 291
social entity model, 212
socialism, and worker control, 152
social responsibility, 211. *See also* business responsibility; corporate responsibility
   of business, 247–248
soil erosion, 328
Solomon, Robert C., 38
Solow, Robert M., 347
Some Paradoxes of Whistleblowing (reading), 551–557
Sony, 279
Soros, George, 161
sound arguments, 24
Souter, David, 570
Speaking Out about Malt (case), 412–413
species extinction, 327
Spheres of Justice (Walzer), 110
Spielberg, Steven, 54
spillover, 337. *See also* externality/externalities
Spitzley, Mike, 456
Sports Illustrated for Kids, 291
Sprint, 283, 290
St. Joseph Aspirin for Children, 273
stakeholder model, 212
Standard Oil, 163, 212
Stanley, Marianne, 583–584
Stanley, Paul, 414
Stanton Corporation, 459
Starbucks, 238, 330
Starch Away, 287
Starwood Hotels and Resorts, 502
state of nature, 115
state welfare capitalism, 154
statutes, defined, 6
stealing, ethical relativism and, 12
Steffes, Cliff, 524
Stein, Ben, 522
Steinbeck, John, 336
Stern Asset Management, 514
Stevens, John Paul, 206, 570
Stewart, Martha, 109
Stewart, Thomas A., 450

stockholders, 202
   and corporation, 214–215
Stone, Christopher, 222, 223, 377
Stone, F. Barron, 514
Stone, John, 380
StorageNetworks, 497
Stout, Lynn A., 239
strict product liability, 266
Strudler, Alan, 46
subliminal advertising, 288
Sullivan, Scott, 514
Summers, Clyde, 382
Sunrise Land Developers, 302
supererogatory actions, 73–74
Surace, Kevin, 379
Swedish Daddies (case), 466–467
sympathetic strikes, 401, 406–407

T

Taft-Hartley Act, 401, 407
TANF. *See* Temporary Assistance to Needy Families (TANF)
Target, 180
TARP. *See* Troubled Assets Relief Program (TARP)
tax breaks, 483
Taylor, Frederick Winslow, 381, 596
Taylor, Sidney, 586
Teamsters, 407
teleological ethics, 429
Temporary Assistance to Needy Families (TANF), 134
Tennessee Iron & Steel, 209
Tepas, Donald I., 449
Terkel, Studs, 167, 428
termination, 394
testing, 389–390
   and monitoring, 440–445
Testing for Honesty (case), 459–461
Testor Corporation, 301
test reliability, 389
test validity, 389
Texas Gulf Sulphur, 499, 537, 538
Textile Workers Union, 407
Theis, Frank, 48
theoretical criticisms, of capitalism, 160
Theory of Justice (Rawls), 120, 128
Theory of Moral Sentiments, The (Smith), 246
Theron, Charlize, 587
Thomas, Clarence, 570
Thomas' English Muffins, 502
Thomasson, Michael, 438
Tiananmen Square, 228
Tide Pods, 283
Time Warner, 202, 330, 452, 522

Titmuss, Richard, 88
Toshiba, 501
Toxic Side Effects of Shareholder Primacy, The (reading), 239–244
Toyota Motor Corporation, 169, 267
trade secrets, 501–502
tragedy of commons, 336
"transfer pricing," 238
Treblinka, 47
Tribe, Lawrence, 233, 377
Trident chewing gum, 287
Troubled Assets Relief Program (TARP), 151, 165
Tsutomu Ohshima, 169
Turner, Charli, 584
Turner, Jim, 391–392
Turner Broadcasting System, 388
Tushnet, Mark, 414
Twain, Mark, 15
Tyco International, 139, 171, 498
Tylenol, 285, 290
Tylenol crisis, 226

U

Ulrich, Judy, 86
UltraLipoLean, 287
Uniform Commercial Code of 1968, 307
Unilever, 337, 365
Union Discrimination (case), 415–416
union ideals, 404–405
union movement, history of, 400–401
unions
   as civil society, 426–427
   and competitive markets, 425–426
   in defense of rights, 424–425
   discrimination, 415–416
   against individual rights, 423–424
union tactics, 406–408
United Auto Workers, 402, 407, 456, 463, 487
United Brands, 504
United Electrical, Radio and Machine Workers of America, 379
United Farm Workers, 407
United Financial Group, 362
United Nations' 1948 Human Rights Charter, 75–76
United States Steel, 209
universal acceptability, 68–69
Unocal, 164
Unprofessional Conduct? (case), 456–457
unsound arguments, 24
Up in the Air, 395
Ursula Burns, 563
U.S. Agency for International Development (AID), 31

U.S. Agriculture Department's Market Access Program, 164
U.S. Constitution, laws and, 6–8
U.S. Consumer Product Safety Commission, 30
U.S. Court of Appeals, 234
U.S. Department of Agriculture, 134
U.S. Department of Interior, 339, 340
U.S. Food and Drug Administration, 220
U.S. Forest Service, 164
U.S. Trade Deficit, 170–171
US Airways, 452, 561
Useem, Jeffrey, 180
utilitarianism, 60–66, 193–194, 317–319
   act, 61, 77
   critical inquiries of, 63–66
   defined, 56, 60
   and economic distribution, 112–114
   and greater equality of income, 113–114
   organizational context of, 62–63
   rule, 61, 78
   six points about, 61–62
   and worker participation, 112–113

V

Valiant Networks, 396
valid argument, defined, 23
Valliant, Caroline, 430
Valliant, George, 430
Vanderbilt, Cornelius, 153
Vandivier, Kermit, 35, 36
veil of ignorance, 122
Velasquez, Manuel, 207
Verizon, 155
vertical price fixing, 278
Viagra, 285
Vinson, Michelle, 586
Vinson & Elkins, 1
Vioxx, 269, 512
virtue ethics, 321
Volkswagen, 402–403, 456
Volvo, 286

W

wages, 396–400
   community, 397
   company's affordability of, 398
   laws and legislations, 397
   prevailing, 397
   rate discrimination, 398

Wagner Act of 1935, 382, 401, 402, 407
Waide, John, 314
Waksal, Sam, 498
Walls, James, 459, 460
Wall Street, 131, 202, 362
Wall Street Journal, 217, 226, 267, 283, 434
Walmart, 162, 168, 179–180, 202, 399, 402, 403, 404, 436, 443, 447, 505, 509, 561, 568
Walzer, Michael, 110
Warner-Lambert, 512
Warner Music Group, 202
warranties, 275
   express, 276
   implied, 276
Warren, John, 35
Warren, Phyllis, 584
Warshow, Robert, 39
Washington Gas Company, 407
Washington Mutual Bank, 150
Wasserman, David, 46
Wasserstrom, Richard, 589
water shortages, 328
Watkins, Sherron, 1
Watson, James, 189
Wealth of Nations, The (Smith), 65, 155, 158, 246
weasel words, 284
Webb, Allen P., 19
Web Porn at Work (case), 411
Webster's Dictionary, 306
Weight Watchers, 285
Weis, Charlie, 559
wellness programs, 439–440
Wells Fargo Bank, 236
Werhane, Patricia H., 256, 417
West Coast sports, 391
Western Electric Company, 454
Westin, Alan F., 440
Weyerhaeuser, 413
When Is "Everybody's Doing It" a Moral Justification? (reading), 96–104
Whirlpool Corporation, 447
whistle-blowing, 512–516
   justification of, 514–516
Whitacre, Mark, 279
White, Byron R., 464
Whitewater Brewing Company, 412
Whole Foods Market, 245, 248, 251, 354

Why Do We Consume So Much? (reading), 324–330
Whyte, William H., 46
wife swapping, 458
Wigand, Jeffrey, 263
Williams-Sonoma, 277
Willingham, Tyrone, 558, 559
Winn-Dixie, 180
Winstrol, 30
Wise, Richard, 171
Wohlgemuth, Donald, 502–503
Wolff, Edward N., 136
Women's Wear Daily, 30
Wood, Alan, 231
Woods, Tiger, 315
work
   ethics, 172
   liberal model of, 431–432
   organization of, 477–479
   privacy, and autonomy, 473–479
   redesigning, 453–457
Work, Privacy, and Autonomy (reading), 473–479
worker control socialism, 152
worker participation, 112–113
Working (Terkel), 428
working conditions, 445–453
Working Mother, 481
workplace, and civil liberties, 380–385
Workplace Wars (reading), 480–485
World Bank, 187, 359, 365, 404
WorldCom, 171, 498, 514
World Trade Organization, 163, 187
wrongful discrimination, 386–387

X

Xerox Corporation, 171, 210, 225, 563

Y

Yahoo in China (case), 228–229
Yang, Jerry, 228
Yellowstone Park, 334
YouTube, 365

Z

Zhuy, Christina, 392
Zolezzi, Dick, 508
Zoloft, 280
ZZZZ Best Carpet Cleaning Company, 504